1996-1997
EDITION

WASHINGTON FISHING

The Complete Guide to More Than 1,000 Fishing Spots on Streams, Rivers, Lakes, and the Coast

BY TERRY RUDNICK

Foghorn Press
BOOKS BUILDING COMMUNITY

ISBN 0-935701-95-8

9 780935 701951

W0010532

To order individual books, please call Foghorn Press:
1-800-FOGHORN (364-4676) or (415) 241-9550.

Foghorn Press titles are distributed to the book trade by Publishers Group West, Emeryville, California. To contact your local sales representative, call 1-800-788-3123.

Library of Congress ISSN Data:
March 1996
Washington Fishing
The Complete Guide to More than 1,000 Fishing
Spots on Streams, Rivers, Lakes, and the Coast
1996-1997 Edition
ISSN 1086-783X

The Color of Commitment

Foghorn Press has always been committed to printing on recycled paper, but up to now, we hadn't taken the final plunge to use 100-percent recycled paper because we were unconvinced of its quality. And until now, those concerns were valid. But the good news is that quality recycled paper is now available. We are thrilled to announce that Foghorn Press books are printed with Soya-based inks on 100-percent recycled paper, which has a 50-percent post-consumer waste content. The only way you'd know we made this change is by looking at the hue of the paper—a small price to pay for environmental integrity. You may even like the color better. We do. And we know the earth does, too.

Printed in the United States of America

To the memory of Betty Rudnick, the best mom any young angler could hope to have. I miss you.

PREFACE

When Judith Pynn, Acquisitions Editor for Foghorn Press, called me in January of 1994 to ask if I was interested in writing a complete guide to fishing in Washington, I was surprised, flattered, and, to tell the truth, not too sure about the idea. I was very impressed by the detail in Foghorn's *California Fishing*, written by fellow outdoor writer and good friend Tom Stienstra, but wasn't sure that I wanted to take on a project of that magnitude. What's more, Northwest fishery managers at that time were warning that the prospects for a coastal salmon season were dim and that other areas of the state would also see severe salmon-fishing restrictions. With morale at an all-time low among Washington anglers, was this really a good time to be thinking about a fishing guide?

Then it occurred to me that perhaps this was the perfect time to be thinking about a guide to Washington fishing. A coastal salmon closure might cause some people to sit at home and complain, but it would prompt the majority to go looking for new places to fish and other species to catch. Washington anglers, I decided, needed a book that would tell them everything they had to know. I think *Washington Fishing* does that.

Like *California Fishing* and *Alaska Fishing*, this is a complete guide to fishing in the Evergreen State. It contains information on more than 1,000 lakes, reservoirs, streams, rivers, and saltwater fishing areas, including precise driving directions and contacts to call for every body of water. No other Washington fishing guide has ever provided that much information. It has taken six months of nearly constant writing to get it all into book form, and I've been doing the "research" virtually all of my life.

If you have read any of the previous complete guides from Foghorn Press, including Tom Stienstra's *Pacific Northwest Camping* or *Pacific Northwest Hiking* by Ron C. Judd and Dan A. Nelson, you may notice that something is missing from *Washington Fishing*. Unlike the other authors, I have declined to give the lakes, reservoirs, rivers, creeks, and marine fishing areas of Washington a numerical rating. I feel that rating these places from 1 to 10 might cause too many anglers to visit the waters with a high rating and put undue fishing pressure on those spots.

Some of Washington's best fishing holes are so great because they get light fishing pressure, and sending crowds of anglers to their shores might turn them into not-so-good fishing holes. Some waters that I might give a low rating, on the other hand, could provide excellent fishing on any given day, so why dissuade anglers from fishing them? Another reason I opted to abandon the rating system is that my idea of a "10" might differ greatly from everyone else's. You might hate the things I love about a particular lake or stream, so why incorporate a value system that doesn't work for everyone?

With that, I encourage you to sit down and spend a little time with *Washington Fishing*. I think you'll discover some things you didn't know about the vast angling opportunities available to us here in the Evergreen State, and I hope you take advantage of as many of those opportunities as time allows.

As for me, spending the past six months writing this book has been one of the greatest adventures of my life, but it has left no time to do anything else. I'm off to re-visit some of the places that inspired me to keep going during the past half-year. I'll see you there.

—Terry Rudnick

CONTENTS

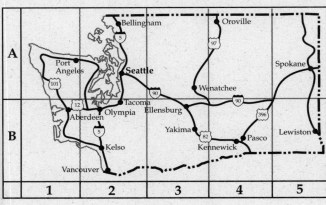

How to Use This Book

1

If you know the name of the lake, creek, reservoir, river, or coastal area you want to fish or the corresponding geographical area (a town or national park, for example), turn to the index beginning on page 492 to locate it.

2

If you want to fish in a particular part of the state, turn to the Washington state map on page 5, which is divided into 10 map sections. Locate the area you're interested in and turn to the corresponding section of the book. To make locating each destination easier, every fishing spot is numbered on the map or maps within each section.

3

If you're interested in a particular type of fish and/or want to find out which areas offer the best angling opportunities for that species, turn to the Washington Sport Fish section beginning on page 7 or consult the index on page 492.

WASHINGTON SPORT FISH

INTRODUCTION

Evergreen State anglers have no shortage of options when it comes to finding a place to fish, not to mention plenty of choices about what to catch—or, at least, what to try to catch. Some of Washington's lakes, reservoirs, rivers, creeks, and marine waters offer only a few species, while others provide a wide range of possibilities. Deciding what to fish for and how to fish for it can be a tough decision. To help make the job a little easier, this section of the book is dedicated to describing the state's many and varied sport species. Use this species-by-species rundown as a reference when reading about specific waters in other parts of the book. If you see a reference to a particular species mentioned under a fishing spot, turn to this section to find out more about it.

The San Juan Islands offer a wide variety of bottomfish opportunities as well as year-round salmon fishing.

Since a few fish species are more popular or command more interest from anglers than the others, I've first listed what I consider the top 10 sport fish Washington has to offer. For each of these species, I've also suggested several waters where you're most likely to find them. Fish that made the top 10 are those that are the most exciting and challenging, the most popular with a majority of anglers, and the most widely available, or those that simply happen to fit my personal prejudices about what a fish should be. You may disagree, and that's perfectly okay with me. I'm not trying to sell you on any of my favorites.

If you don't find the fish you're looking for in the top 10, don't fear; it's probably described farther back in the "Honorable Mention" section, which is broken down into freshwater, saltwater, and anadromous (sea-run) categories.

1
CHINOOK:
OUTSMARTING THE KING

There can be only one king, and here in the Pacific Northwest, the title belongs to the chinook salmon. When it comes to size, strength, speed, streamlined beauty, and table quality, the crown goes to the adult chinook every time.

The success of most Washington saltwater fishing trips is measured by the number of kings in the fish box. But, despite its immense popularity, the king's secrets are known and understood by relatively few. It seems that most Washington anglers are content to settle for less, so they limit out on seven-pound coho or dredge up a couple of sweet-eating bottomfish and call it a day, hoping that maybe their luck will change next time and they'll get a shot at a king.

But, to loosely paraphrase Tina Turner, what's luck got to do with it? If you want to catch kings, you fish for kings, and there are really only a few simple rules to remember. Fish the right way, at the right time, in the right places, and you'll catch them consistently.

Fishing Chinooks in Salt Water

Serious saltwater king salmon anglers have a saying that sums up the best time of day to fish: "If you can see the bait, it's too late." In other words, don't plan to pull away from the docks at daybreak; be fishing at daybreak. The hottest chinook bite of the day usually occurs at first light, and in July or early August that means sometime between 4 and 4:30 A.M.

If you do sleep in until 5 A.M. and miss the day's best fishing, don't lose hope. Usually there will be a period of feeding activity on the tide change, especially a flood tide. When a tide bite comes on, though, fish hard while it lasts, since it might be only 10 minutes long. A day in king country often ends the way it starts, with an evening bite during the last few minutes of daylight.

Unlike most other Pacific salmon species, the chinook tends to be a creature of the bottom, found within a few feet of the sand and rocks and sometimes with its nose right down in the dirt. Successful king anglers keep their baits and lures within a foot or two of the bottom, always aware of the depth and yo-yoing their offerings along the bottom contours to stay down in the strike zone.

Fishing bottom doesn't necessarily mean fishing extremely deep. Many of the Northwest's top king spots are in 125 feet of water or less. The key is to find certain kinds of structure that draw bait fish, which in turn draw hungry kings.

"Break lines," for example, are places where a flat or gently sloping bottom suddenly breaks off into much deeper water. Kings often patrol the edge of a break line in search of bait fish and sometimes use such lines as migration routes. A trolling path or tidal drift that carries you along such break lines will often put you right in the thick of things.

Plateaus are flat or gently sloping table tops where the water is shallower than surrounding areas. Bait fish such as herring or candlefish sometimes congregate on these plateaus, and the kings come looking for them.

Bait fish also collect in the current breaks formed by points of land, creating a natural attraction for hungry kings. The "edges" where fast and slow water meet on the downstream side of these points are often best.

Sometimes the best king "structure" of all, though, is the shoreline itself. Mature chinooks headed for fresh water are like wolves on the prowl, often patrolling coves, small bays, and kelp beds in search of the oil-rich bait fish that will sustain them through the rigors of spawning. "Pocket fishing" for these near-shore kings provides some of salmon fishing's most spectacular action.

Mooching—the salmon-fishing version of stillfishing—with herring bait is one of three angling techniques that take chinooks, and is perhaps the most deadly of the three when done right. Most serious king anglers like their whole or plug-cut herring to make wide, slow "barrel rolls" as they go through the water, but some like a faster, tighter roll more commonly associated with coho fishing.

Fresh herring make the best bait, and it's often possible to catch a day's supply in the area you're fishing. Strings of small, beaded herring jigs are available at most tackle shops, and when you locate schools of herring it doesn't take long to jig enough for the day's fishing. Besides being fresh and firm, locally caught bait happens to be what local kings are used to eating, so you're "matching the hatch" and not offering some odd-sized bait that the fish aren't used to seeing. Using the right-sized bait for the occasion often makes an important difference.

Many king anglers match their hook size to the size of their bait, using something as small as a size 1 or 1/0 with three-inch baits and going as large as 4/0 or 5/0 with a seven-inch herring. With small baits, some anglers abandon the tandem-hook rigs altogether and thread a single hook twice through the front end of the bait, at the top, then push it into the body cavity, back out the side, and seat it into the side of the bait, just in front of the tail.

Proper sinker size is a key to successful mooching for kings. The mooching sinker has to be heavy enough to take the bait down to within a few inches of the bottom and keep it working there, but not so heavy that it hangs straight down and holds the bait motionless. Most king anglers want a 45- to 60-degree line angle with the water's surface. You may get by with a two- or three-ounce sinker if you're fishing light line (10- or 12-pound mono) during a slack tide with no wind, but as line diameter, current, and wind increase, so will the size of the sinker you'll need to keep the bait down.

Unlike cohos, which often hit a bait with the finesse of a demolition driver, chinooks take it slowly and deliberately, so don't get overanxious. Pay out line when you feel those first two or three tap-tap-taps, then, as the fish moves steadily down or away with the bait, drop the rod tip until the line tightens and make sure there's steady pressure before hitting them.

The chinook salmon has it all—size, power, stamina, and beauty—making it a favorite of Washington anglers.

There was a time when trolling for big kings meant dragging a bait or lure around behind a sinker weighing up to several pounds, fished on a rod that was better suited to playing pool than to fishing. Fortunately, downriggers have changed all that, and it's now possible to get down to where the kings are while still enjoying the thrill of catching them on light tackle.

A troller willing to "work" his downriggers can follow the contours of those break lines and rocky points within a few inches of the bottom, keeping a bait or lure right down where it belongs. Some anglers fish whole or plug-cut herring (just like those used for mooching) behind their downrigger balls, while others prefer spoons, wobbling plugs, large streamer flies, or plastic squid (often referred to as "hoochies"). Flies and hoochies have little action of their own, so they're usually trolled behind a flasher, a metal or plastic attractor that rotates in a wide arc that gives the trailing lure an erratic, darting action.

Vertical jigging is the Northwest's newest king-fishing technique, growing steadily more popular the past 10 years or so. At least two dozen different jig styles, all of them simulating or approximating the size, shape, color, and wiggle of an injured herring, anchovy, or candlefish, will take kings consistently when fished by a good jigger.

The standard technique is to free-spool the lure to the bottom, then jig it up and down in two- to six-foot sweeps of the rod, dropping the rod tip quickly on the downward stroke to allow the lure to flatten out into a horizontal position. A horizontal jig is a jig that's most active—wiggling, spinning, wobbling, and darting from side to side as it falls through the water.

Salmon strikes on a jig are subtle, often nothing more than a slight slackening of the line as the fall of the jig is interrupted, so the jigger has to stay on his toes and react to anything that doesn't feel quite right. Keeping those hooks needle-sharp is more important in jigging than in any other kind of salmon fishing, to give the lure that extra split second of "hang time" in a salmon's jaw between the strike and the instant the jigger reacts and gets the hook set in earnest.

As with other king-fishing methods, it's important to keep the jig working near the bottom, but don't use any heavier jig than you need to reach the desired depth. If you're reaching bottom just fine with a four-ounce jig, try going to a three-ouncer and see if you can still hit bottom okay. A smaller, lighter jig is a more active jig, and an active jig is more likely to catch the eye of a prowling king.

What about rods, reels, and lines for king fishing? Most veterans prefer a seven-and-a-half to nine-foot rod with a sensitive tip, lots of backbone at the lower end, and a long butt for leverage. Such a rod will wear down even the most stubborn 50-pounder if you give it enough time to do its damage. A good jigging rod is lighter and stiffer than the rod preferred for mooching or trolling. The reels are revolving-spool jobs, usually levelwinds with enough capacity for at least 150 to 200 yards of line. Jiggers and moochers generally go with smaller, lighter, faster reels than those used by trollers. The monofilament main line ranges from eight- to 40-pound test, with 15- to 25-pound monofilament favored by the majority of anglers.

Fishing Chinooks in Fresh Water

The king's popularity among anglers doesn't diminish much when it moves from salt water into the freshwater stream where it will eventually spawn and die (or be killed and spawned in a salmon hatchery facility). Freshwater fishing opportunities for chinook, in fact, are as far-ranging and abundant as the saltwater possibilities. If you're willing to do a little traveling throughout western Washington, you may be able to hook hefty chinook salmon in various rivers from as early as March to as late as November.

Some of the standard rules of king fishing in the marine environment also apply to freshwater fishing. The action is usually best during the first half-hour and last half-hour of the day, you want your bait or lure hugging the rocky bottom most of the time, and you have to be patient enough to "feed 'em line" for a few seconds before attempting to set the hook into their tough jaw.

Chinooks that return to their home streams several months before spawning provide the most popular freshwater fishery. Arriving as early as March or April, they've earned the appropriate name "spring chinook" or just plain "springers," and they can best be described as pure piscatorial energy.

I can't say with any degree of honesty that I remember the first spring chinook I ever caught, but I can certainly remember one of the toughest, even though I would kind of like to forget it.

The episode took place on Washington's Cowlitz River several years ago. I was fishing with guide Joe Bergh, who at the time was one of the only guides in Washington who had mastered the art of back-bouncing, a technique he brought to the Cowlitz from his home in western Oregon. I had even gone out and bought a new rod and reel to fish that way, but rather than getting the reel Joe had suggested, I had skimped a little and bought a cheaper model. That turned out to be a big mistake on my part, one the soon-to-be-hooked springer from hell would exploit to its advantage.

The bite started almost immediately, with Joe sticking the first salmon and handing the rod off to a third member of our party. He landed the 12-pounder after a short fight, and we moved back up to the head end of the pool and started back-bouncing our way downstream once again. My four-ounce sinker hit bottom almost straight beneath the boat, bounced once, and the rod tip lunged downward as a fish only 10 feet away inhaled my bait and headed back toward the Pacific.

Seconds later the fish was 50 yards away and gaining speed, my el-cheapo reel was still in free-spool, and my right thumb was beginning to smell like overdone meat loaf.

At that point my brain finally kicked into gear and I reached for the lever that would engage the reel spool (being an el-cheapo, it didn't engage with a turn of the handle). I must have let my thumb slip from the spool just a split-second early, though, and a loop of slack line billowed from the reel and found its way into that narrow crevice between the end of the spool and the reel's sideplate.

At that point, things really got ugly. The unstoppable force soon met the immovable object, and the force won. The bottom end of my reel's levelwind arm popped from its track and bent grotesquely under the strain of the line, and the 25-pound monofilament screeched painfully before popping with a report that sounded like a .30-30 carbine. The whole thing was over as quickly as it had started.

I was so stunned that I couldn't say anything, but Joe Bergh, master of understatement, summed it up nicely with, "That was a mean fish." Then he turned the boat back upstream to start another drift.

Many spring chinook react similarly when they feel a hook penetrate their jaw, and that's part of the thrill of this fishery. The good news is that the fish don't always beat you up the way that crazy Cowlitz River springer pounded on me several years ago.

How long they stay in the food-rich Pacific Ocean determines how large those salmon will be when they return to fresh water. Fish that come back after only three years at sea are the "little guys" of the spring chinook world, if you can call a fish of 10 to 12 pounds a small one. Four-year returnees will weigh in at 14 to 20 pounds, while five-year-olds are the trophies that may run to 30 pounds and larger.

Whatever its size, a spring chinook will almost always "fight bigger" than it really is.

"These fish enter a river with enough energy reserves to get them through until the late-summer or fall, and they use their abundant energy to fight back when they feel a hook," says Buzz Ramsey, promotions director for Oregon-based tackle manufacturer Luhr Jensen & Sons and a long-time springer enthusiast.

Blazing runs, rolling jumps, and deep-fighting, slug-it-out tactics are all part of the spring chinook's repertoire when its at the business end of a fishing line.

Springers tend to move right along on their upstream journey, spending less time holding in resting water and more time chugging upstream than, say, steelhead or fall runs of salmon. The fact that you're often fishing for "moving" fish may dictate certain angling techniques for these fish.

Spinners account for a good number of moving chinook. Spinner anglers don't cast and retrieve for their fish; they use a two- to six-ounce sinker on a dropper leader to hold the lure in place, and the keys are to fish the right "slots" and to match the blade size to the amount of current.

"Back-trolling" wobbling plugs also takes springers, and will often work on both moving fish and those holding deeper, slower water. Large Kwikfish and Flatfish are the plugs most commonly used, and they work best when adorned with a sardine wrap—a fillet of fresh sardine lashed to the underside of the plug with several dozen wraps of thread.

"Back-bouncing" may sound like some kind of Swedish massage technique, but it's another method of taking river chinook, and it works better on holding fish than on movers. As its name implies, back-bouncing is a matter of backing your boat downstream, bouncing a sinker-and-bait rig through fishy-looking water ahead of you. Lifting, dropping, and paying out line as needed, the back-bouncer keeps his sinker slipping along the rocky bottom, always alert for a change in rhythm that could mean he has a customer.

Baits for back-bouncing include large clusters of salmon roe, live ghost shrimp, roe/shrimp combinations, plug-cut herring, and fresh prawns, which are usually dyed pink, purple, or deep-red. Picking a "best bait" may depend on personal preference or local trends, but there are certainly times when one of the aforementioned works better than the others. Veteran springer anglers carry a variety and know the secrets of rigging and fishing them.

Not all spring chinook salmon are caught by boat anglers. Bank fishing with shrimp, roe, herring, prawns, wobbling plugs, and spinners also accounts for good numbers of these fish every season. As with boat fishing, though, the key is often not so much what bait or lure you have tied to the end of your line, but exactly where you place it in the river. You can fish the right lure in the wrong place all your life without ever getting a strike, so do your fishing where other anglers are catching fish, and watch closely to learn the springers' travel routes and resting spots in any given stream.

Summer and fall runs of chinook also enter many Washington rivers, and the techniques already discussed will work just as well in September as in April. Patience, however, may become more important to the angler as spring turns to summer and summer turns to fall. Fish that arrive in the rivers later—and thereby closer to spawning time—are often less eager and less cooperative when it comes to taking a bait or lure. Stick with them, however, and you can eventually coax them into hitting.

And when they decide to respond, hang on!

Where to Go for Chinook Salmon

Ilwaco, Willapa Bay, Westport, Neah Bay, Sekiu, Port Angeles, San Juan Islands, Point No Point, Lake Chelan, Hanford Reach of the Columbia, Cowlitz River, North Fork Lewis River.

2
STEELHEAD:
WELL WORTH A LITTLE HARDSHIP

Snow was falling horizontally, thanks to a 20-mile-per-hour wind, and the man on the radio had just announced that high temperatures for the Puget Sound area weren't expected to top 25 degrees that day. But it was Saturday, so fishing partner Dave Borden and I were on the road just after daylight, heading for one of our favorite winter steelhead spots on the Puyallup River. Confident in the fact that we were the only ones stupid enough to go fishing in that kind of weather, we weren't in any particular hurry.

When we arrived at our usual parking spot, though, another pickup was already there, a pickup that neither of us had ever seen along the river before.

"Must be somebody who got a new steelhead rod for Christmas," I chuckled. "He won't be here long."

But there were two sets of boot tracks in the snow as we made our way down the winding trail that led to the river, and by the amount of snow that had already fallen on them, they had been made some time before we arrived.

Still, we were confident in our knowledge of the river and in our ability to catch steelhead from it, so we plodded on toward a long stretch of river that had always treated us generously in the past.

Our first little "secret" spot behind a submerged boulder on the far side of the river had already been worked over, as evidenced by all the tracks at river's edge, so we didn't spend much time there. Things were even worse at our next stop. Near the lower end of a slow-moving pocket that had produced steelhead for us in the past, we found a big patch of crimson in the muddy snow. Our worst fears were being realized; the guys ahead of us seemed to know what they were doing.

Now hoping to catch up with our adversaries and pass them before they reached the best steelhead hole on this entire stretch of river, we quit fishing all the "maybe" spots and took off down-river at a fast walk.

Too late! As we rounded a bend and peered through the blowing snow toward the piscatorial promised land, we could easily make out two vertical forms on the otherwise horizontal landscape. They were fishing "our" spot, alright, and to make matters even worse, one of them was playing a fish. By the time we strolled up to make a little light conversation with the two strangers, they were beaching their third steelhead of the morning, a sleek, chrome-bright specimen of perhaps 12 pounds.

The fact that two out-of-towners had rolled in and caught three steelhead from one of our favorite haunts was bad enough, but then they had the nerve to rub our noses in it.

"You guys shouldn't have slept in so late this morning," the first one offered. And then the second one really made our day.

"You can't let a little bad weather keep you off the river," he advised.

Rather than saying what we really thought of their free advice, Dave and I trudged on down the river to find places that hadn't yet been fished.

Winter steelhead anglers have what normal people might consider a rather unusual way of looking at things. Members of the steelheading fraternity actually spend lots of money just for the privilege of getting up long before daylight, braving icy roads, wading around a partially frozen river in leaky boots, and getting skunked more often than not.

Most winters, about half of Washington's steelhead anglers go through the season without catching a single steelhead, and even when you figure in the experts who catch lots of fish, the average isn't much over half a steelhead per licensed angler, for the entire season. I know a guy who started fishing for them in the 1950s and tried for 13 years before actually catching one.

There's obviously something about the steelhead that keeps these anglers going, helping them to put up with the miserable weather and the endless weeks of fruitless casting. The sea-run rainbow trout that we call a steelhead is a thing of beauty and an angling trophy without equal, at least to those who pursue it, and if a winter of fishing provides a single opportunity to hook just one, most steelheaders would consider it a winter well-spent.

A typical winter steelhead weighs five to 10 pounds, and any fish over 20 pounds is considered a trophy. They occasionally grow as large as 30 pounds or more, and the state-record winter steelie for Washington is a 32-pound, 12-ouncer that was caught from the East Fork of the Lewis River back in 1980.

Whatever their size, you can depend on them to show amazing strength and stamina when they're at the end of a line, making long, powerful runs and high, twisting leaps from the time they feel the sting of a hook until they're finally landed—or escape to fight again.

For their size and power, though, steelhead often take a bait or lure with unbelievable subtlety. One of the most difficult things for a beginning angler to learn is how to detect the steelhead's soft strike, to somehow distinguish it from the rhythmic bouncing of the sinker along the rocky river bottom.

But before worrying about whether or not you'll feel the strike, you first have to locate the fish and put the right bait or lure in front of their noses, neither of which is particularly easy, especially for the novice steelheader.

Winter steelhead moving through a river toward upstream spawning grounds or hatcheries seldom make the entire trip in one prolonged sprint. They stop to rest along the way, and it's these resting or "holding" spots where most savvy steelheaders concentrate their efforts. Veteran anglers call it "reading the water," and if you never learn how to do it you'll never catch many steelhead.

Most of the places that steelhead choose to stop and rest along their upstream journey have two things in common. They provide the fish adequate cover, so that the fish feel safe and at least somewhat hidden, and they provide a break from the fastest and heaviest currents. Put another way, holding water is a place where steelhead can hide and rest at the same time. Any place offering that combination of qualities is probably worth fishing for steelhead.

Examples of good holding water might include a slow, deep run immediately downstream from a major rapids or stretch of heavy current. Mid-stream logs, stumps, or boulders that break the flow of the current are also attractive to migrating steelhead, as are undercut banks and the converging currents where a small stream or side-channel meets the main river.

Other kinds of potential holding water may not be so obvious to the angler who sees the river only from the "outside." A raging Northwest river may gouge out deep-water channels and small pockets in the river bottom that can't be seen from above, or there may be mid-sized rocks on the bottom that break the current of a deep-water run without showing any signs on the stream's surface. These are spots where knowledgeable, veteran steelhead anglers catch fish while less-experienced steelheaders whip the water to a froth in frustration. It takes a trained hand, sensitive steelhead rod, and thorough knowledge of the river to "feel" these changes in the bottom that can spell the difference between catching a two-fish limit and just another day on the stream.

If you really want to learn how to catch winter steelhead, study those who are catching fish, and pay special attention not only to how they do things, but exactly where they place their casts.

Winter steelhead anglers employ several different fishing techniques, but the most common is referred to as drift-fishing. As the name implies, it's a matter of casting across the river or slightly upstream and allowing the bait or lure to drift downstream with the current. The key to successful drift-fishing is using the right sinker for the job. You want to keep it near bottom without constantly hanging in the rocks and snags, and you have to adjust sinker size to the depth and speed of the water.

Too large and heavy a sinker will result in constant hang-ups and lost tackle, while too light a sinker won't keep your bait or lure down where it belongs, within a few inches of the river bottom. If you fish all day without bouncing bottom, you have almost no chance of hooking a steelhead.

Winter drift-anglers have plenty of choices when it comes to what goes on the end of their lines. A cluster of fresh salmon or steelhead roe is a long-time favorite, and most steelheaders use a special loop-knot on their hooks to hold the clusters in place. A live ghost shrimp is another good steelhead bait, and you can dig your own along a muddy beach or buy them from some area bait and tackle shops.

As for artificial lures, steelhead will hit metallic-finish spinners and wobbling spoons, leadhead jigs fished below a float, deep-diving plugs, or any of the wide range of steelhead "bobbers"—brightly colored little pieces of wood, plastic, or foam that come in all sizes and shades.

If you're wondering what rod to use for steelhead, make it an eight-and-a-half or nine-footer with a sensitive tip and a long butt handle. Graphite provides the kind of sensitivity that most steelheaders prefer. A spinning or bait-casting reel with enough capacity to hold at least 125 yards of premium-grade monofilament line in the 10- to 17-pound range rounds out the list of basic tackle requirements.

While drift-fishing is the most popular technique for winter steelhead, there are other methods of catching this most challenging of Northwest game fish.

Plunking might be described as the lazy man's steelheading technique in that, rather than going to the fish as the drift-angler does, the plunker sits on the bank and waits for the fish to come to him. Plunkers use much the same baits and lures that drift-anglers use, but instead of letting them move through the water with the current, plunkers anchor the offerings in deep water with a heavy sinker. The key to plunking success is to place that sinker and bait in exactly the right spot, so that a passing steelhead virtually runs into it.

A technique called back-trolling, or plugging, was developed by boaters and has since become a favorite of some bank anglers as well. The idea is to work a diving plug downstream through the river, with tension from upstream, so that it dives to the bottom, wiggling and wobbling enticingly as it's worked through potential holding water.

Leadhead jigs were mentioned earlier, but they deserve special attention since an entire steelheading technique has developed around them over the past decade or so. While leadheads would no doubt catch steelhead if they were simply bounced along the river bottom in conventional jigging style, most steelheaders use them suspended beneath a float, or bobber. The float helps to impart action on the jig as it bounced along on the water's surface, tipping the jig up and down as it moves along. The key to fishing a jig beneath a float lies in adjusting the distance between the float and the jig, so that the lure works along just off the bottom. Too long a line between the two allows the jig to drag and hang on the rocks, but if the distance is too short, the jig will be too high in the water column to attract much interest from the bottom-hugging fish.

Timing can make a big difference in whether you catch winter steelhead or not. Fish move upstream throughout the winter, but a day of heavy rain that causes river levels to rise may draw a large number of fish into the river all at once. That's why the best time to go steelheading is right after the rains stop and a river begins to recede. Some streams rise and fall faster than others, with smaller rivers and creeks usually responding to weather changes more quickly than larger rivers. Getting to know how fast your favorite steelhead river drops after a minor flood, and being there when it happens, can greatly improve your steelhead catch.

There's another timing factor that can play a big part in your success or lack thereof. Steelhead tend to return to some rivers earlier in the season, some later, and you should learn to fish a few of each kind to help extend your winter steelheading opportunities. Catch statistics compiled by the Washington Department of Fish and Wildlife, which are available to the public, can be very valuable in helping you determine which months might be most productive on a particular steelhead river.

You should also know that many—in fact, most—Washington winter steelhead streams are stocked with hatchery steelhead to help supplement runs of wild fish that are not as large as they used to be. Hatchery steelhead tend to "come home" earlier in the winter than their wild counterparts, so streams with large hatchery plants may be best in December and January, while wild-run rivers and creeks often provide their best fishing during February, March, or even April.

Shirtsleeve Steelheading

Now that you've read a little about winter steelheading, let's find out how much you know with a one-question quiz: To catch a steelhead, you should stand for weeks, knee-deep in a raging river, raw winds slapping your face and ice water dripping down your neck, hoping against hope that your frozen fingers will detect the subtle strike if it happens to be your month to find a cooperative fish. True or false?

Yes, it's a trick question, because the answer is both true and false.

It's true if you happen to be talking about winter-run steelhead, that coveted prize of the world's most masochistic anglers. But steelheading and freezing to death need not be synonymous. Summer-run steelhead are found in many Washington rivers, providing a kinder, gentler fishery for those who like the idea of catching a big, bad, ocean-run rainbow trout, but aren't crazing about snow and sub-freezing temperatures.

The only real difference between summer-run steelhead and their winter-run counterparts is timing. Although wild runs of both strains spawn sometime between mid-winter and late-spring, summer-run steelies are in a bigger hurry to come home from the Pacific. While winter steelhead may return in February, ready to spawn within days or weeks of the time they hit freshwater, summer fish come back months earlier, perhaps May or June, then stay in the river through the fall and early winter before spawning.

The sleek and shiny steelhead is one of Washington's most highly prized angling trophies.

Water temperatures are, of course, much warmer in June and July than in December and January, and that often makes a big difference in the way summer-run steelhead take a lure and how they fight when they feel the sting of a hook. Summer steelies are, well, a lot more active and energetic, willing to chase down a bait or lure and slam it with all the subtlety of a runaway bus, then tearing up the river's surface with twisting leaps and blazing runs that might leave a beginning steelheader wondering what he's gotten himself into.

The same baits, lures, and techniques that work for winter steelhead are effective in summer, and it's even safe to say that you have a broader range of options this time of year. Anyone who has fished for winter steelhead or cast spoons and spinners to river trout should have little trouble getting into the swing of summer steelhead fishing. Basically, winter steelheaders may have to tone down their tackle to adjust for lower, clearer river conditions of summer. Trout anglers, on the other hand, should gear up a little so their tackle will have the strength to handle fish in the five to 15-pound class. Generally acceptable summer steelhead tackle includes seven-and-a-half- to eight-and-a-half-foot spin or casting rods, medium capacity spin or levelwind reels, and monofilament lines of six- to 10-pound test.

The drift-fishing strategy employed by winter steelheaders also works well for summer steelies. Drift-fishing is simply a matter of casting upstream, allowing the bait or lure to settle to the bottom, then letting the current carry it along until, eventually, it passes within range of a cooperative steelhead.

As for terminal tackle, keep in mind that drift-fishing with bait or small, brightly colored steelhead bobbers is the most popular method of taking these fish, winter or summer. A good selection for summer steelheading would include hooks in the size one to four range; an assortment of sinkers that might include various sizes of split shot or three-sixteenth-inch lead wire; small McMahon swivels; spools of four-, six-, or eight-pound monofilament leader; two or three dozen steelhead bobbers (the Corky, Okie Drifter, and Birdy Drifter are three favorites); and perhaps a couple of spools of nylon yarn in hot, fluorescent colors.

Many veteran steelheaders wouldn't be caught without a supply of bait. Top summer-run baits include whole ghost shrimp, small clusters of salmon or steelhead roe, nightcrawlers, crawfish tails, and grasshoppers. Some anglers use bait and lures together, combining a small tuft of yarn with a roe cluster or sliding a steelhead bobber down the line so that it rides atop a shrimp-baited hook.

Another effective technique is working a weighted spinner or wobbling spoon through the current, just off bottom. Summer steelies tend to wallop these lures, so be sure to have a tight grip on that rod and reel. An assortment of spoons and spinners in chrome, copper, brass, and a few hot colors should get you through a day of summer steelheading. If you're fishing right—just above the rocky bottom—you'll lose a few lures, so take extras.

Diving plugs also tend to draw a jolting response from active summer steelies. Worked from upstream, so that the current pulls them down toward bottom in the fishy-looking pools and drifts, plugs such as the Luhr Jensen Hot Shot and

Storm Wiggle Wart work well for both boat and bank anglers. These diving plugs account for a large share of the summer steelhead catch on the Columbia, lower Snake, and other large Washington rivers. Since much of this fishing is in the still waters of big-river reservoirs, the technique is really nothing more than trolling with the various plugs. One interesting twist on the Columbia/Snake is that much of the fishing occurs in the dead of night.

And, if you want a real challenge, try fly-fishing for summer steelhead. The warmer, clearer waters of summer make for good fly-fishing conditions, and that first steelie on a fly is an event not soon forgotten.

Upstream-bound summer steelhead stop to rest in spots along the river that offer adequate cover, a break from the current, and plenty of dissolved oxygen in the water. Shallow flats of slow water seldom produce fish. Many Washington steelhead streams continue to drop and clear throughout the summer, and as this happens, good "holding water" may become more and more limited. A pool with plenty to offer in June may offer little in the way of protection or oxygen by August, after river levels have dropped considerably.

Keep in mind also that summer steelhead tend to avoid bright, direct sunlight, so fish open water early and late in the day and shaded areas when the sun is high.

Thanks to hatchery plants from state fish and wildlife agencies, there are runs of summer steelhead in many Washington streams now that didn't exist two or three decades ago, increasing the opportunities for you to go out and match wits with this spectacular game fish.

Like its wintertime counterpart, however, summer steelheading doesn't come with any guarantees of success. If anything, the clear waters of summer make the warm-weather version of steelheading an even greater challenge than winter steelheading. The big, sea-run rainbow of the Northwest is a wary, street-wise sort of fish that isn't easily fooled or out-smarted, and its strength and stamina are enough to test the skills of any angler. Every time you land one you've accomplished something that the vast majority of anglers never accomplish.

Where to Go for Steelhead

Cowlitz River, Skykomish River, Bogachiel River, East Fork Lewis River, Snoqualmie River, Hoh River, Skagit River, Quinault River, Lower Columbia River, Kalama River, Snake River, Drano Lake.

3
Coho:
Expect the Unexpected

The morning salmon bite had failed to materialize, so after more than two hours of unsuccessful trolling, it was time to pursue other options. A day earlier, father-in-law Bob Howard, wife Sandy, and yours truly had discovered a rocky ledge that produced good catches of various deep-water rockfish and two or three hefty lingcod, so we decided to give up on coho and try for bottomfish.

Tidal conditions weren't yet right for effective bottom-bouncing, so we took our time getting to the rockfish spot, had a cup of coffee when we got there, and took the extra minutes to check equipment and re-tie knots that had taken some abuse during the previous day's bottomfishing exercise.

As we set up for our first drift and prepared to drop our lines overboard, Sandy noticed some activity on the water's surface, maybe 50 yards away. Within a half-minute there were dozens of fish boiling on top of the water, so Sandy and I quickly reeled in our heavy jigs and exchanged our deep-water jigging rods for light-action spinning outfits. Hers was equipped with a chrome-and-blue, one-ounce Deadly Dick jigging spoon, mine a chrome Krocodile of about the same size. Black rockfish often begin feeding near the surface on short notice, so we usually keep the spinning rigs within easy reach for just such an opportunity.

The two shiny lures hit the water a few yards apart, several feet from the outer edge of the obvious feeding frenzy. The strikes came instantly. My rockfish was a small one, and I was releasing it at the side of the boat when I realized that Sandy's fish was still giving her a good run for her money. As I was about to comment on the stubbornness of her hard-fighting rockfish, the reason for its power quickly became apparent. Two feet of streamlined silver came twisting out of the water only 30 feet from the boat, with Sandy's lure dangling from the corner of its mouth. Her black rockfish was a coho salmon.

Thinking the whole thing was a lucky coincidence, we netted the fish and took several minutes for photographs before turning our attention back to fishing. The rockfish were still feeding nearby, so we resumed casting. Again the lures touched down a few feet from the frenzy, again there were simultaneous strikes, and again one of the two fish was a coho. This time I was the lucky one, and by the time I had landed my spunky six-pounder, Sandy had retrieved and unhooked her rockfish, stashed it safely in the fish box, cast again, and was happily playing what turned out to be a third salmon.

I would like to say we limited on coho that morning, but the final tally was three in the boat and one lost. Still, since all three came as bonus prizes with a catch of rockfish, we weren't about to complain.

The whole episode served as yet another example of the fact that when it comes to coho salmon, you never know what might happen next. If you fish for coho—or even if you fish for something else when there are coho around—expect the unexpected.

The coho is a fish for all Washingtonians, one that can be as susceptible to the efforts of the first-time charter boat customer as it is to the skills and equipment of the 30-year veteran of the saltchuck. From the southern Oregon coast to the Bering Sea, the coho, or silver, has long been the bread-and-butter fish of the salmon fishery, caught by the hundreds of thousands every summer, at least until recently.

Its wide distribution and availability, however, doesn't make it a pushover, and for every story about a coho limit, there's a story about someone being totally baffled by the fish's unpredictable nature or blistered by its wild, hook-shaking antics. While there are no guarantees for coho-fishing success, there are some things you can do to catch them more consistently. Coho large enough to be worth catching—two-and-a-half-year-old fish that have spent a year in salt water—show up along the Northwest coast as three- to five-pounders in June. By the end of July, coastal anglers are catching six- to eight-pounders, and by the end of August, the first "hook-nose" adults start to show. These are the prizes of the coho fishery, and their numbers build as they approach fresh water throughout September. That's when anglers are most likely to catch coho of 10 to 15 pounds.

Migrations into Washington's "inside" waters may vary by as much as several weeks during unusual water conditions, but the sport catch records show that you can almost assure good coho catches if you spend time on the water from the last week of August to the third week in September. That's when the largest number of fish are moving in from the Pacific, and it's a time when the average size of those fish goes up almost daily. The farther north you are in the coho's range, the earlier in this four-week time period you can expect to find peak fishing.

Tide rips are the best place to look for coho. These places where marine currents collide are marked by long, meandering lines of swirling water and floating debris, and they provide a smorgasbord for the coho. Krill—the planktonic crustaceans and larvae that make up the bulk of a young coho's diet—are abundant in tide rips, and even adult salmon will gorge on these suspended little snacks. All those tiny tidbits also attract candlefish, herring, and other baitfish, more major draws for hungry coho. Fish a tide rip thoroughly, because conditions may be different from one side of a rip to the other. All the fish-attracting bait may be on one side, and you might troll along the other side for hours without capitalizing on the bonanza only a few yards away.

Feeding birds are another sign that hungry silvers may be nearby. The Bonapart gull is called a "coho bird" by many salmon anglers, and for good reason. Often misidentified as a tern, this small gull with the distinctive black head feeds primarily on krill, and when you see several of them dancing and dipping along the surface, it means they've found food. Since krill is also coho food, well, you get the picture. Herring gulls, murres, and other fish-eating birds may also be an indication that there are coho below.

When tide rips and birds aren't present, or when there aren't coho below these obvious signs, it certainly doesn't mean all is lost. At times like this, savvy silver anglers start paying close attention to their depthsounders to locate the coho or the baitfish that may attract them.

And there are many times when it isn't important to find bait at all. During the height of the inshore migrations in late summer and early fall, thick concentrations of adult coho may be found in places where krill and baitfish are nonexistent. It's not that they aren't feeding, but just that following certain marine routes is much more important to them than actively searching for food.

Coho salmon sometimes are so cooperative that anglers score limit catches in a matter of minutes.

Find where they're traveling and you'll find action. Coho headed for Hood Canal and Puget Sound, for example, will often follow narrow pathways through the 12-mile-wide Strait of Juan de Fuca, and when you get on one of these ribbons of silver, you may be in for some of the hottest fishing you've ever had. These coho freeways are often well out in open water, with no obvious reason for their existence.

Coho are most often caught well up in the water column, usually within 50 feet of the surface and often within 20 feet. But, like the baitfish on which they feed, coho are very light-sensitive, and they usually drop deeper as the sun gets higher. On clear, sunny days, near-surface coho action is hottest from sunrise to about 9 or 10 A.M., then it drops off quickly and stays slow until shortly before sunset. On cloudy days, though, you may find fish within 20 or 30 feet of the top all day.

When they "quit biting" around mid-morning, it's usually because anglers continue fishing for them at the depth they started, while the coho have dropped into deeper water, beyond where people are fishing. A depthsounder will tell you this, if you pay attention to it and react to what it shows you.

When silvers are in their usual near-surface haunts, most people troll for them, and it doesn't require any special technique or fancy equipment. A simple spin sinker-and-herring rig will do it, but you can use a diving plane in place of the sinker or add a "herring dodger" attractor ahead of the bait. If you don't want to use bait at all, troll a plastic squid or a large streamer known locally as a coho fly 16 or 18 inches behind another type of attractor called a flasher. A flasher revolves and jerks the squid or fly from side to side, giving it a darting action.

Coho will sometimes feed right on top, and you can catch them by trolling with little or no weight. That's when the coho fly really becomes a killer. When you see surface swirls, a sure sign of top-feeding coho, remove your sinker, tie on a fly, and troll it fast, about seven knots, so that it creates a steady wake without breaking the surface. Serious fly rodders even catch near-surface coho by casting to them with streamer flies fished on floating or sink-tip fly lines. This technique works both on adult fish returning from the Pacific and immature coho that you might find in estuaries and inshore waterways throughout the summer. Such a fly fishery has gained popularity in recent years among anglers around Puget Sound, where so-called resident silvers may provide excellent shallow-water fishing throughout the spring, summer, and early fall.

Trolling is the preferred coho-fishing method, but mooching accounts for thousands of coho every year. Just ask anyone who spends much time fishing from a charter boat at Westport and he or she will testify to the effectiveness of mooching for silvers. A coho angler mooching within 40 or 50 feet of the surface with 10- to 14-pound mono can fish effectively with a two- or two-and-a-half-ounce sinker, while the troller using the same line might prefer a three- or four-ounce sinker.

Silvers that are in a biting mood won't hesitate to chase down a fast-moving bait or lure, and lots of them are caught at trolling speeds of three to five knots.

But don't troll at a steady speed. Changes in lure speed are what really prompt silvers to strike. You'll improve your coho catch greatly if you do a lot of turning, zig-zagging, and throttling up and down.

The speed at which a herring is spinning is just as important as how fast it's moving through the water. Serious coho anglers plug-cut their herring at a sharp angle, so that the bait spins in tight, quick circles. Salmon anglers using the standard tandem-hook rig can enhance the bait's spinning action by impaling the herring only on the top hook and allowing the bottom hook to hang free.

As adult coho near and enter the estuary, they move into range of shore-bound anglers, and that's when Northwest docks, piers, bridges, and beaches become crowded with coho anglers, most of them casting wobbling spoons or such metal jigs as the Buzz Bomb. Although they have usually stopped feeding actively by the time they reach the estuaries, mature coho remain aggressive, and they'll attack an artificial lure fiercely.

Coho are more likely than any other Pacific salmon species to hook themselves on the strike. While a Chinook may make pass after pass, tapping a bait softly, sucking it in and spitting it out perhaps a half-dozen times before inhaling it for keeps, the coho usually isn't so subtle. The typical response of a salmon angler who has just been blasted by a streaking silver goes something like: "Jeeze, woah, damn!" and it's over.

And they fight about the same way they strike, with reckless abandon and no particular battle plan. They'll race 50 yards one way, turn-tail, and charge off 50 yards in the opposite direction, capping the second run with two or three wild, somersaulting leaps, and then the whole sequence may be repeated all over again. Losing a fish for every one you manage to put in the boat is a typical average.

Needle-sharp hooks are a must for the coho angler who wants to put more than an occasional fish in the box. Because of the fish's quick, often surprising strike, you need every advantage you can get, and a hook that will pierce a patch of flesh on incidental contact may hang there just long enough for you to do the rest with an upward sweep of the rod.

Let's face it, the silver salmon's antics will make you look silly often enough even if you keep your hooks sharp and do everything else right. Luckily, there are so many of these hard-hitting, sweet-eating streaks of silver out there that you can be pretty sure of getting another chance.

The coho fishery doesn't end when the runs reach fresh water. In rivers where adequate numbers of fish are available, coho provide excellent stream-fishing opportunities. Since these adult coho getting ready to spawn are no longer actively feeding, though, the angling techniques change from those used in salt water.

Artificial lures account for many of the silvers caught from Washington rivers, with spoons, spinners, and diving plugs heading the list of coho-catchers. There's something about the wiggle and flash of these lures that triggers aggressive strikes from fish that have long since stopped taking food. They might still be instinctively attempting to eat, or perhaps the response is a territorial one against what might look like a competing aquatic creature. It might even be a combination of these two or maybe something totally unrelated that we haven't even considered. Whatever the reason, river coho that ignore a big cluster of fresh roe or some other delectable bait may slam into a flashy plug or spinner with reckless abandon.

While river chinook often stop to rest in the deepest, slowest pools, coho show a preference for the shallower flats where current flow is moderate. Fish for them in the same kinds of spots where you might find winter steelhead and chances are you'll find action. Such places as current "edges," the mouths of tributary streams and side channels, around boulders and other current obstructions, and the flat water immediately above and below whitewater riffles are all good places to toss a spinner or back-troll a plug for river coho.

The tight regulations and season closures that have affected Northwest salmon fishing in recent years have taken a toll on the places and times anglers can pursue and catch coho salmon, so you have to be on your toes to take advantage of the opportunities that do exist. The unpredictable coho is still available, if you know where and when to look. And remember, there will be times, often when you least expect it, that the coho will find you.

Where to Go for Coho Salmon

Ilwaco, Willapa Bay, Westport, Neah Bay, Sekiu, Port Angeles, Snohomish River system, Puyallup River.

4
Pacific Halibut:
Heavyweight Champ
of the Northwest

Talk about the biggest, baddest, roughest, toughest denizen of the deep you can hope to find in the marine waters of the Northwest and you can be talking about only one fish, the Pacific halibut. It's a fish that grows to 200, 300, even 400 pounds or more, and it may battle with an angler for several hours before being boated or breaking loose to gain its freedom.

What's more, unlike some fish species that were much more abundant 20, 50, or 100 years ago than they are now, Pacific halibut populations boomed a few years back and have more or less held their own since, providing anglers with more chance than ever of doing battle with this monster of the deep. Halibut fishing appears to be here to stay, and that's great news for saltwater anglers from southern Oregon to central Alaska.

Fishery managers offer several explanations for the halibut explosion that began in the early 1980s, but much of the credit apparently goes to the Fishery Conservation and Management Act of 1976, which gave the United States a 200-mile fishing boundary. The 200-mile limit has cut down substantially on the number of Pacific halibut caught by foreign trawlers. Strict prohibitions against the foreign harvest of halibut have provided better escapement and reproduction and more fish available to U.S. anglers.

Washington anglers, though, don't spend much time contemplating the reasons for this halibut come-back. They just know what they like, and they like a fish that grows bigger than a human, fights like a bulldog, and is about as good on the dinner table as any fish that swims. That's why halibut is ranked near the top of my list of top sport fish. If it was more widely available and the halibut season was longer, it would be even closer to the top of that list.

The halibut starts life looking pretty much like any other species of saltwater fish, with one eye on each side of its head and pigmentation giving it color over its entire body. But as the fish grows, some strange things happen, the sort of things you might expect to see in a Stephen King movie. The left eye moves over to join the other one on the right side of the head, while the body grows flatter and one side turns completely white. By this time it's pretty obvious that this fish is destined for a life on the ocean bottom, and there's little doubt about which side is up.

After those first few weeks, the halibut spends the rest of its life on or near the bottom, and that's where you have to fish if you hope to catch them consistently. Luckily, halibut prefer a fairly smooth bottom of sand, gravel, and cobble-sized rocks, so dragging your baits and lures around down where they live isn't as costly or as frustrating as it might be with such rock-loving bottomfish species as the lingcod.

When searching out halibut, look for underwater plateaus and gently sloping drop-offs rather than the hard, rough structure you might fish for lings. Finding these underwater humps and sidehills is more important than fishing any particular water depth. Depending on the area you fish, you may find halibut as deep as 700 feet or as shallow as 15 feet. Some of the most productive halibut spots along the Washington coast are in 300 to 500 feet of water, but the protected waters of the Strait of Juan de Fuca boast a few halibut humps that are only 100 feet beneath the surface.

Halibut can be caught on both bait and artificial lures, and you'll find about an equal number of successful anglers using each. Whole herring are perhaps the most popular Northwest halibut baits, and the bigger the herring, the better. These fish aren't particularly dainty when it comes to taking a meal, and they can inhale a foot-long herring with absolutely no trouble.

While herring are readily available from Northwest bait shops, marinas, even grocery stores, they do have one major shortcoming as a halibut bait: they're not all that tough and durable. That's why some halibut anglers prefer other kinds of bait, such as whole squid, pieces of octopus, live greenling or tomcod, even whole rock crab. All of these stay on a hook better than herring, but they are also harder to find and often impossible to buy.

Whatever bait you choose for halibut, you'll probably want to fish it on a wire spreader rig. This L-shaped piece of heavy wire, often homemade from a coat hanger or length of stainless steel, has a swivel at each end and one at the bend. The bait is attached with a short, stout leader to one arm of the spreader, a sinker to the other, while the main line is tied to the middle swivel. Many halibut anglers use a cheap, brass snap-swivel to attach the sinker, so that it tears away on a hang-up and the rest of the rig can be retrieved. A good spreader is balanced, so that the arm to which the bait is attached stays horizontal as the rig is dropped through the water. If it tips up too much, the bait will swing up and wrap around the line, a problem which the spreader is supposed to eliminate. To achieve a "balanced" spreader, be sure the arm that's connected to the sinker is about half the length of the arm connected to the bait.

There's no such thing as a "right" sinker weight for use with a spreader. A six-ouncer may take your bait to the bottom in shallow water with little or no current, but deep-water halibut fishing on a windy day or when the tide is running hard may dictate the use of sinkers as heavy as 24, 32, even 48 ounces or more. Halibut fishing under those conditions tends to be more work than fun.

Since many of the top Northwest halibut spots are in deep water, fishing with bait poses certain problems. The spiny dogfish is one of those problems. Often found in the same places as halibut, this pesky nuisance isn't the least bit shy about attacking anything that smells like an easy meal, and many a bait-fishing halibut angler has spent the better part of a day fooling with dogfish instead of fishing productively for halibut.

Another problem with using bait—especially herring—in deep water is that you have some hard decisions to make if you miss a strike. A missed strike often means a lost bait, but not always, so when you reel back on the rod to set the hook into a halibut and the halibut isn't there, what do you do? Murphy's Law dictates that if you spend the next 20 minutes cranking your spreader bar and heavy sinker to the surface, your bait will be just fine and you will have just wasted a lot of valuable fishing time and energy for nothing. If, on the other hand, you decide to take your chances and leave your rig down there, you'll probably discover upon finally retrieving your line that you've been fishing with bare hooks ever since the missed strike.

Using artificial lures will help solve both of these problems, and they're also highly effective halibut-getters to boot. Halibut will happily take homemade pipe jigs, manufactured metal jigs, leadheads with plastic grubs or pork rind attached—almost any artificial offering that's heavy enough to reach bottom in the area you happen to be fishing. Dogfish, on the other hand, pretty much ignore these phony imitations of free-swimming protein.

What's more, when you miss a halibut strike with an artificial, you simply keep jigging. There's no need to reel the lure up through 450 feet of water to check your bait, because there wasn't any bait to begin with.

As with the sinkers you tie to your wire spreaders, there's no magic-sized metal jig or leadhead that works for halibut. The right size is the one that will reach bottom, but don't overdo it. If you can reach bottom with a 10-ounce lure, don't wear your arm out jigging a 20-ouncer. Use a lure that's just heavy enough to get down to where the fish are, and no heavier.

Charters are available in many of Washington's most productive halibut-fishing areas, and fishing with a pro is certainly recommended to anyone thinking about trying halibut fishing for the first time. Not only do these folks know where the halibut are and how to catch them, but they also know how to deal with a barn-door fish once it's coaxed to the surface, not always an easy task when the fish in question weighs in at 75 pounds or more. They aren't all that big, of course, but if they are you have to know what to do.

Tackle is included on most halibut charter trips, but serious halibut anglers have their own rods and reels. Typically, the rod is a stiff-action five-and-a-half- to seven-footer, usually with a roller tip and often a roller stripper guide, both of which are a very good idea if you use braided Dacron line, as many halibut anglers do.

Braided line has little or no stretch, which can be especially advantageous when you're trying to set the hook into a halibut in several hundred feet of water. Braided Dacron, which is about the same diameter as monofilament of equal breaking strength, offers a real advantage, but the new "super" braids, made of space-age materials such as Spectra, seem to have been made with halibut fishing in mind. Not only are they low-stretch lines, but their extremely small diameter makes it possible to fish lighter jigs and lighter sinkers in deeper water, which makes a day of deep-water halibut fishing all that much easier.

With these smaller-diameter lines, you can also get by using lighter rods and smaller reels.

As mentioned earlier, there are a few places in Washington where halibut may be found in less than 150 feet of water, and in these places you can get by using standard salmon tackle or even the rods and reels you might use for some freshwater species. Since the "average" halibut caught from our waters is a fish of 15 to 40 pounds, you don't necessarily have to use back-breaking rods, reels, and lines to land them. The heavy tackle often used in deep-water halibut fishing is meant to handle the needed terminal tackle, not the fish you might hook.

The battle with a halibut isn't over when you get the fish to the surface. In fact, depending on the size of the fish, your problems may just be starting when that big, brown form materializes a few feet below the boat. These are strong fish that can inflict damage on you and your boat if you aren't careful about landing them. Even smaller fish should be dispatched quickly and handled carefully. Rap them several times sharply between the eyes, then cut a couple of gill arches to bleed them as quickly as possible (which takes some wind out of their sails and makes for better eating later). Halibut can also be controlled by looping a rope around their tail and (carefully) through the gills and mouth, then pulling the rope tight and drawing the halibut into a "U."

More and more halibut anglers are using harpoons to deal with larger halibut at boatside, and it's a technique worth considering by anyone who fishes seriously for these big, strong fish. The harpoon has a detachable head, and that pointed head has a line attached to it. When the harpoon is plunged through the middle of the halibut, the head pivots 90 degrees against the pressure of the line, so that it opens up on the far side of the fish and won't pull back through the hole. The halibut is now tethered on the harpoon line, and the opposite end of the line is tied

The average Washington halibut weighs 15 to 40 pounds, but this giant took two people to hold it up for the camera.

to a large buoy, which goes overboard when the halibut is harpooned. A minute or two of fighting the buoy usually saps the last of the halibut's strength, and you can control and dispatch it. It's not quite as easy as it sounds, but you get the idea.

Many anglers shoot and/or sever the gill arches of big halibut (over 100 pounds) before attempting to boat them, or better yet, kill them outside the boat, lash them securely alongside, and never bring them aboard.

Smaller halibut may be gaffed and brought aboard, depending on the size of your boat and the size of your fish box. Remember, though, that even a little 15-pounder can get downright nasty if left to flop around the deck out of control. Get 'em clubbed, cut, and controlled quickly or they'll make a mess and perhaps do some damage.

It's important to give these big, strong fish the respect they deserve.

Where to Go for Halibut

Neah Bay, La Push, Twin Rivers, Freshwater Bay, Port Angeles, Hein Bank.

5
RAINBOW TROUT: OLD RELIABLE

The first fish I ever caught was a rainbow trout. How about you? Ask any 10 Washington anglers about their earliest angling efforts and chances are eight or nine of them will describe some experience involving the ever-present rainbow. A survey of this state's anglers a few years ago showed that 80 percent of them fished for rainbows on a regular basis. It's stocked in and caught from more lakes and streams around here than any other fish, and its adaptability has made it a favorite not only here in its historic range in the Pacific Northwest, but throughout much of the world.

Native populations of rainbow trout in many parts of Washington were long ago depleted by eager trout enthusiasts, so much of the angling action they provide now is the result of stocking efforts by the state's Department of Fish and Wildlife. Millions of rainbows are stocked each year to keep the trout fisheries alive in several hundred Northwest lakes, reservoirs, rivers, and creeks.

Judging by the wide variety of baits and lures used by successful anglers, one might think that the rainbow is some kind of omnivorous scavenger, but in its natural setting it feeds primarily on plankton and small aquatic and terrestrial insects. Yes, given the opportunity it might gladly gulp a white marshmallow, a small ball of cheese, a plump nightcrawler, a kernel of corn, a salmon egg, a wad of bread dough, a flashy spinner, a wobbling spoon, a plastic bass plug, a leadhead jig, an artificial fly, or any of dozens of other baits and lures an angler might throw its way, but these are only treats in the rainbow's varied diet. I once saw a kid catch a rainbow of nearly four pounds on a half-inch-thick piece of wiener that he bit off the end of a hot dog he was chomping on while he fished.

Rainbows are so widely available in Washington that it's possible to fish for—and catch—them 365 days a year. Where and when you fish, of course, may determine the angling technique that's most likely to pay off.

In early spring, when the region's lakes and reservoirs are still cold, many anglers stillfish for their rainbows. On a sunny day, when the trout may be drawn to the warmer water near the surface, try suspending a garden worm, a salmon egg or two, a couple kernels of yellow corn, or some combination of these three baits beneath a small bobber. Attach the bobber four to seven feet up the line and fish the rig with little or no additional weight. Even "dumb" hatchery trout may be light, deliberate biters when the water is still cool and their metabolism is low, so you have to offer them a small meal and be on your toes for subtle strikes.

When even the surface temperatures are low, you may have to reverse your strategy and fish a bait on or near bottom. Lethargic, cold-water rainbows may

Rainbow trout are abundant throughout the entire Northwest, providing year-round angling action for everyone from the die-hard bait angler to the purist fly-caster.

lie near bottom and take little or no food, but may bite if you make them an offer they can't refuse. That means floating a bait just off bottom rather than suspending it from the surface. Small marshmallows are a good bait for this kind of fishing because of their buoyancy, and some anglers will combine that little 'mallow with a salmon egg, kernel of corn, piece of worm, or small piece of cheese. Manufactured floating baits, such as Berkley's Power Nuggets, work the same way. To make doubly sure that a slow-moving rainbow takes your bait and doesn't get suspicious, use some kind of hollow slip-sinker to anchor it. By running your line through this slip-sinker and either keeping the bail open on your spinning reel or peeling two or three feet of line off your casting reel to provide slack, you decrease the chances of a fish feeling line tension and dropping the bait.

Slow-trolling may also pay off for early season rainbows. A trout that refuses to chase down a fast-moving lure may be tempted by one that's just barely drifting by, but not all trolling lures are designed for this kind of slow-motion fishing. The blades of many spinners simply won't revolve at slow speed, and heavier wobbling spoons will just hang there and do nothing. Paper-thin spoons, flasher-and-worm combinations, even wet fly or streamer patterns pulled behind the boat, may be your best options for this cool-water trolling.

As the water warms and the trout become more active, anglers in search of rainbows have more options available to them. The usual trolled goodies provide consistent catches, and energetic 'bows willingly gobble a wide range of natural—and not-so-natural—baits.

When spring turns to summer and the water temperature continues to climb beyond the rainbow's comfort level, it may be time to go deep once again. Find a spot well out of reach of the sun's blistering effects where water temperatures remain low and that's where you're likely to find the rainbow. If you know the whereabouts of cool-water springs or tributary streams, they're good places to fish during the warm months. Where legal, night fishing may be the ticket to success, or you may have to get on the water at sunrise and give up hope by 7 or 8 A.M.

Rainbows come to life again in the fall, as water temperatures drop and the fish go on a feeding spree that will help them put on a little fat for the upcoming winter. Many fly rodders think this is the best time of year to apply their techniques, especially during the first few hours and last few hours of the day, or whenever some kind of aquatic or terrestrial insect hatch takes place to spark trout activity.

If you think you have to give up on the rainbow trout during winter, guess again. Plenty of Washington lakes are open to year-round fishing, and patient anglers can do as well on the cooperative rainbow in January as they can in May. Many of the popular ice-fishing lakes of eastern Washington provide excellent rainbow trout fishing. Again, the key is to fish small baits, usually near the bottom. Be alert for light strikes. When fishing artificials in open water during the winter, keep them small and keep them moving slowly. Although fair-weather anglers may not believe it, winter is a good time to fish wet flies and nymph imitations with that fly rod.

As for stream fishing, spring starts out with most Northwest rivers and creeks on the cool side, so you may have to work hard to coax rainbows into hitting. Since the streams may also be high and off-color from spring snow-melt, it's often a good time to fish worms and other natural baits that can be rolled slowly along the bottom.

As the streams warm in early summer, anglers enjoy some of their best fishing of the year for rainbows. This is also the time of year when hatchery plants are made in some rivers and creeks, greatly increasing angler success on many waters. The full range of baits, lures, and flies works during this time of year.

Fishing gets tougher as stream levels drop and the water gets warmer and clearer. Mid-summer to mid-fall is a challenging time for trout anglers in many parts of the state, but those who are knowledgeable and patient manage to find productive fishing. The first rains of fall often spark a flurry of good stream trout fishing, which frequently holds up until the season closes for winter or the weather and water conditions simply become too brutal for most anglers.

For those who may not know, the "average" Northwest rainbow trout is a fish of perhaps eight to 11 inches that weighs between half a pound and one pound. Rainbows of 15 to 20 inches, though, are caught throughout the year, and larger fish are certainly within the realm of possibility.

When talking about trophy-class trout, a rainbow subspecies called the Beardslee trout deserves some special mention. It's found only one place in the world: the clear, cold waters of the Olympic Peninsula's Crescent Lake.

This unique trout grows to impressive size, often topping 10 pounds, and is usually caught by anglers who deep-troll large spoons or plugs.

If you haven't yet gotten to know the rainbow trout, you haven't savored the true essence of freshwater fishing in the Northwest, so do it at your earliest convenience. Whenever and wherever you happen to read this, there are probably rainbows biting nearby.

Where to Go for Rainbow Trout

Jameson Lake, Spectacle Lake, West Medical Lake, Silver Lake (Spokane County), Fishtrap Lake, Wenas Lake, Lake Scanewa, Mineral Lake, Silver Lake (Whatcom County).

6
LARGEMOUTH BASS: AMERICA'S FISH

Jay Wilcox had a pretty good reputation for knowing his way around eastern Washington's best bass fishing, so when he invited me to join him for a half-day trip to one of his favorite spots north of Spokane, I jumped at the chance. Early the next morning I found myself in the back of his high-powered bass boat, casting spinnerbaits around the edge of a big slough off the Pend Oreille River.

Nosing the bow of the big boat to within a few feet of a high bank, Wilcox pitched a black, plastic salamander toward the wide mouth of a dilapidated culvert. The little lizard imitation sank only about a foot before the line twitched sharply and Wilcox reared back on his light casting rod to set the hook. Within a minute he was displaying a hefty largemouth bass and a broad smile for my camera.

A second cast with a second plastic salamander drew a second bass strike for Wilcox. At perhaps four pounds, it was a little larger than the first, so another short photo session was in order.

"You give it a try," he said as I put my camera back in its case. "Just cast over there by that culvert."

He failed to tell me about the tangle of wire and rebar that lay hidden off to the left of the culvert, and my spinnerbait didn't travel a foot before becoming hopelessly ensnarled in the mess.

"We'd better just leave it there," my mentor suggested. "The water's only about two feet deep there, so we can get it later. Let's stay back and cast to the culvert a little more before getting too close." So I gave a sharp tug and snapped the line.

As I rummaged through a tackle box in search of anything resembling a plastic salamander, Wilcox made another cast to the culvert, and within seconds was involved in another tug-of-war with a scrappy largemouth, this one even larger than the first two. By now I was too intent on re-tying my tackle to even bother dragging the camera out of its case.

My fishing companion was playing bass number four by the time I was ready to give it another try. My first cast hit the water right above the culvert entrance, and as it sank into the darkness I felt a tap on the line, then another, and I set the hook. Somebody has to catch the smallest one, and it was apparently my day. The two-pounder provided several seconds of excitement before being coaxed away from the culvert and to the side of the boat.

"Want me to take your picture?" Wilcox asked. I didn't even look up as I unhooked what would normally have been a respectable bass.

Jay hooked and lost a big bass on his fifth cast, then coaxed a largemouth of perhaps five pounds to the boat three or four casts later. It was 15 minutes of the hottest bass fishing I've ever seen, as one of us enjoyed a week's worth of good largemouth fishing in maybe 10 casts.

The largemouth bass is perhaps America's most popular game fish, one that millions of anglers spend billions of hours fishing for each year. That popularity extends to Washington, where the largemouth isn't native but was introduced more than 100 years ago. After a slow start in this part of the world where salmon and trout have long been the main attractions, bass fishing is now a big deal in Washington.

It's easy to understand why largemouth bass fish-

Largemouth bass aren't native to Washington, but they have a large and dedicated following among freshwater anglers throughout the state.

ing has a lot of followers. Ol' bucketmouth is just plain fun to fish for and even more fun to catch. It's a fish that will, when it's in the mood, smash into almost any lure that comes within five feet of it and nearly tear a fishing rod from the hands of an unsuspecting angler. But when it's not in the mood, it can be the most finicky, cagey, frustrating, and challenging fish that swims. The fun lies in never knowing for sure which personality you're going to encounter on a given day next to a given stump, or with a given bass.

While the Northwest growing season for largemouths is shorter than in some parts of the country that produce lots of lunkers, anglers here do find their share of bragging-size bass. A day's catch of bass in the half-pound to two-pound range may also include a three or four-pounder, and there are enough six-pound bass in Washington lakes, ponds, and reservoirs to make catching one a real possibility. Now and then someone makes news by catching one over eight pounds. Washington's record bass, caught from Banks Lake, weighed just over 11¹/₂ pounds.

The largemouth's adaptability is demonstrated by the kinds of places you may find it in Northwest lakes. Often caught from weedy, brushy tangles of vegetation, under lily pads, or around stumps and submerged trees or thick stands of cattails, it's also comfortable beneath overhanging trees or under man-made docks and floats. If none of these bass hiding spots are available, the largemouth can eke out a living around rocky points or submerged boulders.

The kind of habitat you find them in may dictate what lures and fishing techniques you use. Most bass anglers use casting rods and levelwind reels filled with 12- to 20-pound monofilament, but heavier or lighter tackle will get you by. While casting tackle is still prevalent, more and more spinning rods are showing up every season in the boats of serious bass anglers.

Bass anglers use a wide range of artificial lures for largemouth bass. Spinnerbaits look like safety pins that have been bent open, with a weighted, skirted hook on one end, a spinner blade or two on the other, and the line attached to an eye in the middle. Depending on their size and design, spinnerbaits may work well at fast, moderate, or slow speeds. Because the hook points inward and is lined up directly behind the wire arm that runs to the spinner blade, this lure is relatively snagless, so it can be fished in thick weeds or brush without constantly hanging up.

Bass anglers also use a wide variety of plugs, or "hard baits," as they're often called. Some, known as crankbaits, may have large metal or plastic lips in front to catch water and make them dive as they're retrieved. Other plugs, with smaller lips on the front or none at all, are designed to be fished nearer the surface, either with a steady retrieve or in short jerks and jumps that draw the attention of any nearby bass.

Plastic lures such as the black salamanders mentioned at the start of this story are also highly effective for largemouths. They come in many shapes and sizes, from one-inch grubs to 10-inch worm imitations. Fake frogs, lively lizards, creepy crawdads, and phony fish are all made of soft plastic these days, and you can buy them in any color you might imagine. Some, like Berkley's Power Baits, are impregnated with special scents and flavors that seem to convince bass they're eating the real thing. Plastics are often fished with a large, single hook and sliding sinker, but may also be used with leadhead jigs or totally unweighted.

Some of the most exciting largemouth bass fishing of all occurs when the fish are taken on surface lures, because the angler not only feels the fight, but gets to see the start of it, as a hungry bass boils to the top and pounces on the lure. Various plugs, poppers, and "buzz-baits" are used for this kind of fishing. All are designed to wiggle, dart, sputter, pop, gurgle, splash, or do all of the above to create a surface disturbance that might attract bass. This top-water bass action is most likely to occur early and late in the day.

Bass anglers spend much of their time fishing the shallows, casting as close as they can to fallen trees, brush piles, stumps, lily pads, coves, and pockets in the banks, rocky points, docks, pilings, and other likely looking bass haunts. These are the places where bass lie in wait for unsuspecting creatures to wander by within striking range. Bass aren't made for long pursuits, so they hide and wait, striking quickly when food—or a lure—is within range.

The types of hiding spots mentioned above protect bass from their predators and hide them from their prey, and they usually hug it tightly. When fishing these spots, it's often necessary to cast accurately, laying your lure right up against the stumps, brush, and weeds without hitting them and snagging the lure.

The largemouth bass in most Washington lakes don't spend all of their time in the shallows along the shoreline. When the shallows get too warm or too cold, or when the mid-day sun makes it impossible for bass to find suitable cover in the shallows, they may seek out the comfort and safety of deeper water. Even when they move into what looks from the surface like wide-open water, though, they seek out drop-offs, submerged boulders and rock piles, underwater creek channels, sunken trees and stumps, springs, ledges, and humps that provide a break in what may be an otherwise smooth bottom. All of these variations in the bottom are known as "structure," and structure fishing can be every bit as exciting and productive as fishing the shoreline cover. Many of these open-water fishing spots are too far from the shore to be fished by bank anglers, and serious structure anglers use contour maps and depthsounders to locate them.

Veteran bass anglers put a lot of thought, a lot of effort, and a lot of money into the pursuit of their favorite fish, but the largemouth can be caught and enjoyed just as well by the more budget-minded and casual angler. Chances are there's a lake or pond within easy driving range of your home that has plenty of largemouth bass.

And if you happen to locate a culvert that opens up into shallow water at the edge of that lake or pond, try casting black, plastic salamanders toward it. You never know!

Where to Go for Largemouth Bass

Lacamas Lake, Silver Lake (Cowlitz County), Tanwax Lake, Lake Sawyer, Lake Terrell, Potholes Reservoir, Eloika Lake.

7
SMALLMOUTH: WASHINGTON'S "OTHER" BASS

"Lay one over there next to that submerged boulder," advised fishing partner and bass-fishing mentor Jeff Boyer. Since he catches more bass in a typical month than I've caught in my entire life, it seemed logical to follow his advice. I let rip with the crawfish-colored crankbait at the end of my line and was pleasantly surprised to see it splash down within a couple of feet of where I wanted it to, just beyond one side of an automobile-sized rock whose top lay just beneath the surface of the water about 75 feet from the boat.

A few cranks on the reel handle sent the billed lure plunging for the bottom, and as I began pulling it steadily toward the boat my mind wandered back to the big island a few hundred feet away, where Jeff and I had spent close to an hour earlier that morning hooking one husky largemouth after another on surface lures. Even though we had fished the spot thoroughly and the action there had long since died a natural death, a half-hour of futile casting over a large field of submerged boulders was having a negative effect on my enthusiasm, and I was thinking that maybe we could get one more of those surface-feeding largemouths to hit if we put an end to this current foolishness and went back to where we at least knew there were some bass to be found.

I was jolted back to the present tense by one of the most violent strikes I had ever experienced, and came so close to losing my grip on the rod and reel that I'm a little embarrassed to admit it. A second or two after the tiny crankbait was assaulted in mid-wiggle, it came flying out of the water, firmly attached to the lower lip of an obviously very angry fish. Exactly what species of fish, I wasn't really sure, but Jeff identified it almost immediately as a smallmouth bass, and I was far too busy to even think about challenging his identification.

The first jump was an exciting thing to witness, but a second was even more impressive, and yet a third took the fish higher and farther than before. It's actually an injustice to call them mere jumps, since each was more like a twisting, shaking somersault. The bass seemed to manage a complete "360" both vertically and horizontally on every leap, splashing down on a different portion of its anatomy every time it re-entered the water.

And when it wasn't jumping it was racing through the water with amazing speed and strength. It was so strong and so fast, in fact, that at one point in the battle I turned to Jeff and said, "Are you sure this is a bass?"

His only response was a sly grin and the comment, "Welcome to the world of smallmouth fishing."

My prize finally tired, and when I coaxed it alongside the boat and hoisted it out of the water I was once again in for a surprise. The bass that had given me such a run for my money and fought with such amazing strength and ferocity was only about a $2^{1}/_{2}$-pounder. I was so impressed that the only thing I could say for the next half-hour was "What a tough fish," over and over and over.

I was hooked. For the rest of that day I had little trouble concentrating on fishing for smallmouths, and it was several hours later, over a late-afternoon hamburger, before I thought back to the early-morning surface action on large-mouths that at the time seemed so impressive. One round with a smallmouth was enough to spoil me on largemouth fishing. My first encounter with a smallmouth bass was probably similar to that of thousands of other western anglers. This is a fish that will impress and inspire you from the moment you first set a hook into its jaw. Many anglers say it's a good thing the smallmouth doesn't grow as large as a largemouth, because if it did, you might never land one with a rod and reel.

While the popularity of bass fishing in general has grown in Washington just as it has throughout the rest of the country over the past 15 or 20 years, the largemouth has received most of the attention while the smallmouth has lived in relative obscurity. The largemouth grows to greater size, is much more abundant, and therefore gets most of the hype and a bulk of the fishing pressure.

But an ever-growing group of western anglers is climbing aboard the smallmouth bandwagon, and the fish's popularity will no doubt continue to grow— for good reason. The smallmouth is, above all else, a fighter. Decades ago, bass expert Dr. James A. Henshall wrote that the smallmouth black bass is "inch for inch and pound for pound, the gamest fish that swims," and that sentiment has been repeated, both verbally and in print, thousands of times since. It fights with astonishing strength, and even a pan-size smallmouth will "jerk your string" until you hoot and holler. When shear muscle doesn't work, it may turn on the speed in its attempt to gain its freedom, or it may go airborne any number of times to throw the hook. As often as not it will use its strength, speed, and jumping ability, perhaps all at the same time. Quite simply, when it's hooked, a smallmouth will give all it has until the battle ends—one way or another.

While generally smaller than the largemouth, the bronzeback grows to unusually impressive proportions in this part of the country. The smallmouth records for most western states top six pounds, several are over seven pounds, and a couple—California and Washington—boast state-record smallmouths of more than $8^{1}/_{2}$ pounds. The top smallmouth for California is a whopping nine-pound, one-ouncer from Clair Engle Lake, while Washington's eight-pound, 12-ouncer came from the Hanford Reach section of the Columbia.

By comparison, the all-tackle world's record, as recognized by both the International Game Fish Association and the National Fresh Water Fishing Hall of Fame, is an 11-pound, 15-ounce monster from Kentucky's Dale Hollow Reservoir.

It should come as no big surprise that western waters produce healthy small-mouth bass. The bronzeback likes cooler water than its largemouth cousin, does well in moving water, and flourishes in lakes and streams with rock and/or gravel bottoms. Sound familiar? The fact is that Washington rivers and reservoirs are in many cases ideal habitat for smallmouths, and when stocked in

The smallmouth bass is a tough fighter and grows to impressive size, qualities that endear it to thousands of Washington anglers.

the right spots, they've grown fast and reproduced well.

By now you probably already know that neither the smallmouth nor the largemouth bass is native to the western United States, and we won't spend a lot of time detailing exactly when and how they arrived at their various destinations out here, but most smallmouth transplants to this part of the country occurred between about 1875 and 1925. The ancestors of most smallies caught here arrived in metal milk cans after journeys of several days from "back east," and the fact that any made it this far alive is a tribute to the fish's toughness.

Anyone interested, by the way, in the story of just how bass, shad, catfish, and other exotic fish species came to the western states might want to find a copy of a fascinating book entitled "The Coming of the Pond Fishes." It details how many of those first transplants were made, when, and by whom, and it's fun reading. The author is Ben Hur Lampman, whose name alone should be enough to inspire at least some reader interest.

When some Northwesterners, anglers, and fishery managers talk honestly about smallmouth and largemouth bass, walleyes, channel catfish, and other "imports" from various parts of the country, many will confess that they think these fish are nothing but bad news for the region's native salmon, trout, and steelhead populations. But at least one Washington fish biologist can cite cases where the smallmouth bass seems to get along just fine with native salmonids, and there's even some evidence that perhaps the introduction of smallmouths can be beneficial to salmonid populations. Doug Fletcher of the Washington Department of Fish and Wildlife made that disclosure to fellow fish managers in literature he presented at the first-ever International Smallmouth Bass Symposium a few years back.

In trying to determine what, if any, impact smallmouths had on Northwest trout and salmon populations, Fletcher studied 10 case histories of introduced smallmouths. None of those cases showed a clear indication of reduced salmonid survival after the bass entered a habitat, and in five there were indications of increased survival rates of salmonids after smallmouths became established.

Although Washington produces its share of trophy-class smallmouths, a large majority of the smallies caught are in the half-pound to one-pound range, and in many places there are large numbers of even-smaller fish. These "little guys," however, seem every bit as aggressive as larger fish, and they'll usually pounce on virtually anything happening by that looks the least bit like a potential meal.

While providing a great deal of fun for the angler who takes them on ultralight tackle, large numbers of little smallmouths are often a tip-off to go looking elsewhere for large fish. Six-inch and 16-inch smallmouths aren't often found in the same places at the same time.

You may find smallmouth bass in and around a wide range of cover and structure, but areas with lots of rocks and hard bottoms are usually the best places to start looking. Slide areas with jumbles of broken rock provide excellent places for smallmouths to forage for one of their favorite foods, crayfish. Likewise, boulders of all sizes offer both food and cover for smallmouths. And don't overlook gravel or even sand flats where bass often hunt for sculpins and other small fish. Rocky points of any kind are almost sure to hold bronzebacks at one time or another.

Woody structure may not always hold smallmouths, but it's usually worth investigating. Some of Washington's lakes and reservoirs have submerged forests or at least stump fields beneath their surfaces, and such wood may provide excellent cover and forage for smallies.

Smallmouth bass are susceptible to a wide range of lures and fishing techniques, depending at least in part on what kind of structure you find them in, what they're feeding on, water and weather conditions, and your own preferences in bass fishing.

In relatively open water where the rocks aren't too grabby and the water isn't too shallow, crankbaits can be deadly on smallmouths. Many bass anglers prefer smaller offerings than those they might use for largemouths, but scaling down for smallmouths isn't always necessary or even advantageous. What does often seem to help is offering them something in a crawdad finish, since these little crustaceans do make up a good part of the smallmouth's diet. It's also beneficial most of the time to throw a crankbait that will wiggle and wobble along close to the bottom, so you'll have to carry a variety that includes shallow, medium, and deep-running lures.

While some anglers stick with crankbaits for most of their smallmouth fishing, others use the plugs only to locate fish, then settle in to fish via more subtle methods. "Subtle" means "plastics" to a large number of smallmouth anglers. Such offerings as a two- or three-inch grub fished on a one-sixteenth-ounce or one-eighth-ounce leadhead can be deadly when fished carefully around a sub-merged boulder pile or along the face of a rock slide. Likewise, a small plastic crawdad, fished Texas-style through a jumble of broken rock or over a cobble bottom, can be lethal. And today's smaller, livelier plastic worms, so popular in finesse fishing for largemouths, also work quite well for smallmouths, as do the hollow, tube-type plastic baits.

When smallmouths are acting finicky or simply feeding on minnows and other small fish, you may want to try "ultra-finesse" or "mini-jigging" for them. This is another technique I learned from bassing guru Jeff Boyer several years ago, on a morning when standard methods were providing only modest results. Many western waters that hold smallmouths are also home to steelhead and one or more Pacific salmon species, and Boyer long ago reasoned that imitating a little salmon or steelhead fry might be an effective way to coax a hungry smallmouth. The lure that best represents an inch-long salmonid fry is an inch-long, plastic mini-jig, the kind of lure long popular with crappie anglers and West Coast shad anglers. Pick a color such as white, gray, light green, or even blue, fish it on light line, and you're well on your way to fooling smallmouths that might have a taste for tiny salmon and steelhead.

When you can find smallmouths near the surface, get ready for some of the most exciting freshwater fishing you can hope to find anywhere. As you might expect, these bronze beauties that fight so hard and so long when hooked in deeper water can really put on a show when they're near the top. A two-and-a-half- or three-inch minnow-type lure, twitched slowly along the surface, will often draw explosive strikes when smallies are feeding shallow, and they'll tear up the water when you stick a hook in their lip.

All the techniques and lures mentioned so far will take smallmouths from both lakes and moving water, but river smallmouths seem especially responsive to yet another type of lure, and that's the spinner. Pitch one alongside a mid-stream rock, let it sink a second or two, then reel just fast enough to get the blade turning in the current and you're likely to entice a strong strike from any smallmouth that may be on the lookout for a quick meal. Spinner fishing allows the angler to cover a lot of good water quickly and effectively, and on our large Washington rivers, that can pay off. Experiment with various spinner sizes and colors, but be sure that your arsenal includes at least a few lures with fur or feather tails. For whatever reason, smallies seem to prefer these over spinners with bare hooks.

Rods, reels, and lines that work for bass and trout fishing will also do the job on most smallmouth waters. A good outfit for casting crankbaits or throwing surface plugs might be a medium-action casting rod, about five feet long, with a small-capacity levelwind spooled with about eight-pound monofilament.

If you aren't any good with a baitcaster, a six-foot spinning rod with a fairly stiff action will do the job, but you may have a little more trouble with line twist unless you add an in-line swivel.

A spinning rod and reel will also work fine for fishing leadheads or pitching spinners, and I'd suggest something in graphite, about six-and-a-half-feet long, with a medium-light action. A cork handle on the rod will help in detecting strikes when you're using plastics. Equip the rod with a good spinning reel that has a smooth drag, and spool up with a fairly abrasion-resistant monofilament. You might carry two reels, or at least two spools, one with four-pound line for fishing those little mini-jigs and small leadheads, and one with six-pound mono for most other situations.

Fly anglers needn't feel left out when it comes to taking a crack at the small-mouth. A wide range of streamers and bucktails, fished either on a floating line or a sink-tip, will take them, and when they're near the top they'll gulp many of the same poppers and hair flies that work for surface-feeding largemouths. If you've never experienced true angling excitement, hook a smallmouth on the surface. It's wild.

Where to Go for Smallmouth Bass

Lake Sammamish, Banks Lake, Lake Roosevelt, Okanogan River, Palmer Lake, Sprague Lake, Snake River.

8
STURGEON: THE NORTHWEST'S HOTTEST "NEW" FISHERY?

There's more than a little irony in the fact that sturgeon fishing is one of what you might call the newest, hottest sport fisheries in the Pacific Northwest. Sturgeon have been here all along—millions of years, in fact—but their popularity among anglers has soared since the mid-1980s.

The decline of salmon fishing in many areas, and the desire of anglers to find something else to fill the void, has no doubt played a part in the growth of the sturgeon's popularity, but there's more to it than that. Sturgeon fishing actually has a heck of a lot going for it.

Take, for example, the size of the fish itself. White sturgeon, the more common of the two species a Washington angler is likely to hook, grows to monstrous proportions. Fish measuring six feet long and weighing 100 pounds are fairly common, and there's always the possibility of hooking a really big one, something in the seven-, eight-, even nine-foot class. Fishing just downstream of McNary Dam a couple of years ago, I thought I was pretty hot when I managed to subdue and release an eight-and-a-half footer that would have tipped the scales at well over 300 pounds. Before that day was over, however, other members of our group released sturgeon measuring nine-and-a-half, 10, and 13^1/$_2$ feet, reducing my catch to runt-of-the-litter status. If you like the possibility of hooking a freshwater fish that's even bigger than you are, sturgeon fishing is your best bet, and the fish's huge size alone qualifies it for any list of Washington's 10 top sport fish, as far as I'm concerned.

Although the sturgeon is a bottom-feeder that spends most of its time searching the rocks, sand, and mud for an easy meal, it can be a surprisingly spectacular fighter. When hooked, many of these piscatorial vacuum cleaners will take to the air, coming straight out of the water like a Polaris missile, twisting to one side and crashing back into the river with a resounding splash.

Not every hooked sturgeon will do one of these tarpon-on-steroids impersonations, but it happens often enough to keep it interesting, and it's most likely to happen with a larger fish of six feet or more. On a rainy May morning in 1993, while fishing with Columbia River guide Herb Fenwick, I had the good fortune of watching a white sturgeon over eight feet long jump more than a half-dozen times before it was brought to the boat, unhooked, and released to fight again. Three of those jumps brought the big fish almost completely out of the water, and one of those was so close to the boat that we all got wet from the huge splash.

Another time, fishing immediately below Hells Canyon on the Snake River, several of us took turns playing a sturgeon of maybe eight feet. I wanted photos of jumping sturgeon, but as luck would have it, the only time the fish jumped was when I was manning the rod. Needless to say, some members of the group got their jumping-sturgeon shots, but I didn't.

Besides being big and tough, the sturgeon is one of the Northwest's best-eating fish, which certainly hasn't hurt its popularity. Cleaned properly, it's a gourmet's delight, whether you bake, barbecue, broil, or smoke it, and a legal-sized sturgeon provides plenty of fresh fish to go around.

Speaking of legal size, there has long been what anglers call a slot limit in effect on sturgeon here in the Evergreen State. That means it's okay to keep fish between 42 inches and 66 inches long, but those under 42 and over 66 have to be released (except for the upper Columbia River, where the minimum size is 48 rather than 42 inches). Fish under the minimum size are considered babies, while those over 66 inches tend to be mature adults needed for spawning.

The Columbia River is the Northwest's top sturgeon producer. Where, when, and how you fish the big river is likely to determine whether you'll catch a lot of sub-legal fish, fewer fish but most of them keepers, or even fewer fish but many of them whoppers over the 66-inch maximum legal size.

"It's really a cyclical thing," says guide Herb Fenwick, who spends several months of the year targeting the big bottomfish. "There are, for example, lots of keepers in the lower river from February through April, when the smelt are in the river and smelt are the preferred bait."

When the smelt disappear in the late-spring, however, smaller sturgeon tend to move into the Columbia estuary, where they forage on shrimp, anchovies, and other sources of food. About that same time, though, the vast Columbia River shad runs begin, and that's prime time for hook-and-release fishing on lunker-sized sturgeon of six feet and larger.

I fished with Fenwick during one of those June lunker-fests a few years ago and enjoyed a morning on the river I won't soon forget. Starting about 6:15 in the morning, we hooked five fish in the seven- to eight-foot range, losing one after a short fight and releasing the other four after lengthy battles—and we were done fishing at noon. Whole shad were used for bait, so we didn't have any problems with "little guys" getting in the way.

Sometimes, though, especially when you're looking to catch a legal-size keeper or two, it's best to fish small baits for these hefty fish. Former sturgeon guide Gary Waxbaum of Umatilla, Oregon, once demonstrated that point to me in graphic detail. As we rigged our sturgeon rods for a morning of fishing below McNary Dam, Waxbaum handed me one of his favorite sturgeon rigs, encouraging me to tie it to the end of my line. At first I thought he might be kidding, but his expression was one of absolute seriousness. The rig consisted of a large, brightly colored steelhead bobber on the line above a big single hook, and on the hook was threaded a small strip of belly meat from a salmon he had caught earlier in the summer. The triangular salmon strip was only about two inches long, and the entire bobber-and-bait combination was well under three inches.

Sturgeon fishing has grown dramatically in popularity throughout the Columbia River and other Northwest river systems.

"With their fantastic ability to sniff out a meal, sturgeon don't have any problem finding something this small, and I think the bright color of the bobber helps them see it as well," Waxbaum explained. "And, because the whole thing is so small, they can take it right in and you hook them almost every time."

Later that morning, as we released our fourth sturgeon of the morning on four bites, I was convinced.

While monster-sized sturgeon make for great photos, carrying around a wallet-sized snapshot of a lunker sturgeon to show your fishing buddies can get you into trouble in the Pacific Northwest these days. Not only is it illegal to possess a Columbia River sturgeon over six feet long, but it's also illegal to drag one of the oversized bottom-dwellers into the boat, shoot a few pictures to document the feat, and release the fish. Enforcement personnel with Washington's Department of Fish and Wildlife have publicly announced on more than one occasion that they will show little leniency in dealing with anglers who make big sturgeon say "cheese" before letting the fish go. Dragging oversize sturgeon onto the beach or into a boat for a short photo session can result in serious injury or even death to the fish, and that's what fisheries officials want to avoid. Sturgeon have no skeletal structure, and when removed from the water, all the fish's weight lies on its internal organs. Since the regulation calling for the release of all big sturgeon is aimed at protecting the large, mature fish needed for spawning, it's necessary that the big ones be released alive and uninjured. Boating or beaching a seven or eight-footer weighing several hundred pounds could well mean the loss of millions of eggs needed to produce future generations, according to Fish and Wildlife biologists. The older a sturgeon gets, the greater its reproductive potential.

While we've talked only about the sturgeon fishery on the Columbia and Snake rivers, other big Northwest river systems also have fishable numbers of these prehistoric lunkers. The Chehalis River comes immediately to mind and is probably the best sturgeon fishery outside the Columbia system.

Sturgeon also show up from time to time in other Northwest waterways, sometimes causing great surprise among local residents who at first think they may have a sea monster on their hands. Such a situation arose a few years ago in Seattle, when an 11-foot creature floated up from the depths of Lake Washington, shocking a few boaters and sending young swimmers scurrying for the beach. The monster, of course, was eventually identified as a white sturgeon, one that weighed an estimated 600 pounds and may have lived in the lake for upwards of 100 years.

As if to prove the big fish can live almost anywhere, fish and wildlife officials treating eastern Washington's Sprague Lake with rotenone to eliminate carp several years ago were surprised to see not one but two big sturgeon come floating to the surface a few hours after the chemical was applied. Since there's no direct link between the lake and any body of water with a known sturgeon population, biologists theorized that the fish were "transplanted" by humans, probably anglers who had been fishing the Columbia River, two hours away via Interstate 90.

And there are lots more sturgeon legends circulating through the Northwest. I could tell you the one about the guy who hitched his plow horse to a big sturgeon in hopes of yarding it onto the banks of the Columbia, but instead the monster fish dragged the horse into the river, never to be seen again. But if I tell you that one, you might not want to go sturgeon fishing, so forget I even mentioned it.

Where to Go for Sturgeon

Columbia River mouth, Columbia River below Bonneville Dam, Columbia River below McNary Dam, Snake River, lower Chehalis River.

9
YELLOW PERCH: ANYTIME IS PERCH TIME

The yellow perch is often overlooked, even scorned, by anglers in search of more glamorous game fish species, seldom getting the respect it deserves. This Rodney Dangerfield of fresh water, however, is a fish for all seasons, and unlike some of those fair-weather species, you can catch a bucketful of perch virtually any month of the year here in Washington. It's so abundant and caught in such great numbers by such a broad range of anglers with a broad range of angling skills that it rates among Washington's 10 top sport fish.

The perch's abundance, in fact, is one of the things some anglers don't like about it. It's a highly adaptive and highly productive fish, and when conditions are right, it reproduces too fast for its own good and for the good of the lake or reservoir it inhabits. The result is a lake full of stunted perch that are too small to interest anglers and too numerous to allow any other fish species to compete. Even patient anglers fishing such a lake give up in frustration after catching 150 perch in two hours, not a one of them longer than five inches.

Show me a lake where the perch population is in balance with its food source and with the populations of other species, however, and I'll show you some fast fishing for perch that are big enough to provide worthwhile angling action and some of the best fish fillets you'll find anywhere.

One thing the successful perch angler soon learns is that perch of a certain size tend to hang out with others of the same size, so if you find a school of six-inchers it's a good idea to move on until you find larger ones. Most anglers prefer fish of at least eight inches, and 10-inchers are more like it. Many of Washington's lakes boast populations of perch in the 12-inch class, and there are 15- and 16-inchers out there to be caught.

Locating small perch is often easy, but finding the larger ones that are more worthy of your angling efforts can be a little more difficult. Oftentimes the key to finding bigger ones lies in fishing deeper water. The little guys spend much of their time feeding in shallow water, and if you fish weed beds and shallow flats of four- to 10-feet deep, the little guys are all you'll catch. Big perch are often found in 20 feet of water or more, and sometimes much deeper than that. I've caught them at depths of 40 feet while I was fishing bait on the lake bottom for rainbow trout, and my experiences certainly aren't unique.

The major exception to this big-perch/deep water pattern is in the spring, when adult yellow perch move into the shallows to spawn. Fishing around shoreline weed patches or shallow-water docks and floats can pay big dividends then, and when perch are concentrated to spawn, it's possible to fill a five-gallon bucket with hefty fish from water as shallow as five to 10 feet.

But whether the perch are shallow or deep, certain time-proven baits, lures, and techniques always seem to coax them into biting. A plain old garden worm is probably America's all-time top perch-getter, one that's readily available from back yards and bait shops wherever perch are found. If there's any problem with using worms, it's that the juicy morsel often is quickly devoured by a hungry perch, resulting in deeply hooked fish. That's fine if all the biters are big enough to keep and fillet, but not so fine if they happen to be running a skinny five-and-a-half inches apiece. Small perch (or any fish) hooked somewhere south of

Yellow perch aren't large or glamorous, but they are abundant and cooperative, and excellent table fare.

the tonsils get to be a messy hassle for an angler and are likely to be killed and wasted. Using large hooks, such as size four or six bait holders, reduces the problem, as does increasing the size of the worm on that hook, but it doesn't eliminate it completely.

That's why many perch anglers prefer to use artificial lures or bait/lure combinations. The fakes simply aren't as likely to be swallowed, so most of the perch are hooked in the lip, jaw, or roof of the mouth, making it much easier to unhook all fish and release the smaller ones unharmed.

If there's one all-round top artificial lure for yellow perch, it has to be the leadhead jig, adorned with either a plastic skirt, plastic curl-tail grub of some kind, or marabou feathers. One-sixteenth-ounce leadheads usually will do the job for shallow-water fishing on calm days, while one-eighth ouncers and sometimes three-sixteenth ouncers are better for deeper water and fishing on windy days when it's harder to get a lure down to where the fish are. As for colors, a red-and-white combination is perhaps the all-time favorite among veteran perch enthusiasts, but yellow, chartreuse, black, and combinations of the three can also be effective. Adding a small piece of worm to the hook of any leadhead jig tends to enhance its popularity with yellow perch, but isn't an absolute necessity.

When the perch are particularly deep, that's a good time to try vertical jigging for them with any of several styles of metal jig. Crippled Herring, Hopkins No=EQL, and other so-called jigging spoons in weights of one-sixth to one-half ounce can be deadly on big perch in deep water. Again, adding a little "meat" to the hook in the form of a small piece of garden worm or strip of perch meat doesn't hurt your odds of drawing strikes. The various scents now available also seem to help.

Vertical jigging with the aforementioned jigs and other small, flashy lures, by the way, is a popular method for taking perch through the ice. Wintertime ice fishing for perch is a popular pastime from December through February during a cold winter in eastern Washington. As in the summer, you're better off fishing near bottom if you want to catch the bigger perch, and if you don't find them in the first hole you chop or drill in the ice, move on to another one. Instead of a worm on the hooks, wintertime perch anglers often use a small strip of perch meat or the eye of a previously caught perch on the hook of their favorite jigging lure. Those are the most readily available baits, since worms are hard to find in the frozen ground of winter.

Like their big cousin the walleye, yellow perch are not spectacular fighters, so using ultralight rods, reels, and line allows you to get the most from every hooked fish. A four-foot rod weighing only a few ounces and a tiny reel spooled with two- to four-pound monofilament is what many would consider the perfect perch outfit.

Because of their cooperative nature, wide availability, and willingness to take something as basic as a worm on a hook, perch are perfect "starter" fish for youngsters or anyone else new to the sport of fishing. Kids like action, and they don't care if the fish they're catching are six inches or 16 inches long, and finding a school of perch fits the bill perfectly. Keep that in mind when the fat rainbows aren't cooperating and that six-year-old has eaten the last candy bar. Perch will keep things interesting and help convert that little one into a young angler.

Where to Go for Yellow Perch

Lake Washington, Lake Sawyer, Silver Lake (Pierce County), Potholes Reservoir, Lind Coulee Wasteway, Soda Lake, Scooteney Reservoir.

10
Lingcod:
Beauty and the Beast
Rolled into One

The smirks on their faces should have tipped us off before they said a word.

"What is that?" chided one of three anglers already cleaning their morning's catch when we arrived at the dockside fish-cleaning table.

"It's a lingcod," two or three of us answered in unison as one member of our party flopped his whopping 58½-pounder onto the table, splattering water, slime, and blood on everyone within about 15 feet.

"Well, it's the ugliest damned thing I've ever seen," one of the three continued, wiping some of the mess from the front of his shirt. His two buddies cackled like a couple of hyenas when he added, "I wouldn't even drag anything that ugly into my boat."

One look at his pals might have led us to challenge that statement, but instead we assured him that, although the lingcod may not be pretty, it's mighty good on the table.

"But not as good as these," he insisted, looking admiringly at the half-dozen two or three-pound pink salmon he and his partners were whittling into meal-sized morsels.

Rather than keeping the argument alive, we set about filleting our catch of assorted bottomfish as the three salmon anglers across the table finished cleaning and packaging the salmon of which they were obviously quite proud.

After two monstrous fillets were sliced from the ribs of our lunker ling, we decided to open the carcass to see what was causing the obvious bulge in its belly. To our amazement, out spilled a slightly digested, seven-pound chinook salmon!

The three oversized mouths on the other side of the cleaning table dropped open, and six eyes bulged like those of a deep-water rockfish bobbing to the surface. They didn't say a word, but loaded their fish into a cooler as quickly as possible and headed up the dock toward their cabin.

But they weren't yet out of earshot when someone in our party got in the final word:

"Yeah, lingcod are ugly, but they eat bigger fish than some people around here catch!"

It's true that some folks might consider the lingcod a homely cuss, but whoever coined the phrase, "Beauty is in the eye of the beholder," may have been a lingcod angler. This fish has a huge head, gaping mouth full of long, pointed teeth, wing-like pectoral fins, and a mottled gray-brown paint job that can't hold a candle to the chrome-sided beauty of a salmon.

But—like your parents always said when they were trying to coerce you into going out with the skinny, freckle-faced kid of the opposite sex who lived down the street—looks aren't everything. While the lingcod might have a kisser that would stop a clock, it has plenty to offer anglers. Even though it's not as plentiful as it used to be, the big, tough, nasty lingcod has to rank in the top 10 among Washington's sport fish.

For one thing, lingcod grow to impressive size. Fish of 40 pounds and over are fairly common, especially in the northern half of their range that extends from Baja California to the Bering Sea, and fish of 50 pounds or better are caught regularly enough to keep things interesting. Now and then they even top 60 pounds, and the current International Game Fish Association all-tackle world's record is a 64-pounder from the Elfin Cove area of Southeast Alaska. Lingcod exceeding 70, even 80 pounds have been reported by anglers, but not documented by the IGFA or state fish and game record-keepers.

As for fighting ability, a hooked lingcod won't make any blazing, 100-yard runs or come twisting out of the water in a series of spectacular leaps, but it will give you a run for your money. Typically, an angler who sets the hooks into a big ling will have little trouble pumping it those first few yards, but just when he thinks he has the battle won, his prize will turn tail, streak for the bottom with amazing speed, and duck into some jumble of broken rocks or deep-sea cavern, where it quickly saws off the line and is free.

The pugnacious lingcod can also be incredibly aggressive and easy to entice. When it decides it's hungry, it will pounce on virtually anything even remotely resembling a free meal, including a wide range of baits and lures. More than one ling has been known to inhale a multi-hook pipe jig or other metallic phony, fight for a minute or two, come unhooked, and immediately grab the lure again. Any fish that willing to cooperate has to be a favorite of anglers.

And there's something else about the lingcod that endears it to anglers and non-anglers alike. It happens to be one of the best-eating fish that ever graced a dinner plate. Whether you sprinkle it with a few drops of lemon juice or plunge it into a pool of tartar sauce, a forkful of lingcod fillet is a fish-eater's delight.

But, as you might expect with any big, hard-fighting, sweet-eating fish, lots of other anglers are as interested in catching lingcod as you might be, and some of them are pretty good at it. There are a few tricks to catching big lingcod, and if you master them you'll improve your chances of boating these trophy bottomfish.

Timing can be everything to the lingcod angler, and we're talking here both about what time of year and what time of day you fish for them.

Lingcod spawn in winter, with the larger females moving up out of the depths to deposit their eggs in the relatively shallow waters of submerged rock piles and rocky pinnacles. The large egg masses are then fertilized by male lings, which hang around to protect them until they hatch. Although the females don't help out with the egg-guarding chores, they don't seem to be in any big hurry to get back to their deep-water haunts, often staying and feeding in the shallower spawning areas for weeks, even months.

The fact that both males and females are to be found somewhat congregated well into spring should be a valuable tip for lingcod anglers and would-be lingcod anglers. It's a whole lot easier to catch lings when they're fairly well concentrated, and it's certainly easier to fish for them in 75 to 150 feet of water than in 250, 300, 400 feet of water or more.

Catching the shallow-water lingcod of late-winter and early spring requires lighter sinkers and lighter lures, which means you can fish lighter lines, rods, and reels and enjoy their fighting ability that much more. There's also less of a problem with line stretch when you're trying to set the hooks into those toothy lingcod jaws and when you need to feel your way over the rocky bottom with your bait or lure. Quite simply, it's much easier and a great deal more effective to fish for lingcod when they're shallow, as most of them are in the spring.

While springtime fishing for lingcod is some of the year's best, it's important here to point out that not all lingcod areas are open to fishing in early spring. Seasonal closures extend into April or May in some places—primarily to protect nest-guarding males and the eggs they're watching over—so be sure to study the fishing regulations before planning that spring ling fling.

The other timing factor involved in lingcod fishing concerns the daily tidal change. Even in shallow water it may be difficult to fish effectively when the tide is snorting along at several knots, so smart lingcod anglers concentrate most of their efforts during high and low slack or on days of moderate tidal flow. That's when you can best hold directly above those rocky pinnacles and fish them with a minimum of hang-ups and lost lures. Also, lingcod often bite best during minimum tidal flow.

In order to catch these shallow-water lingcod, of course, you have to find them, and the two most important pieces of equipment in that search is a good chart of the fishing area and a depthsounder. The rocky spires and steep-sided cliffs where lings are most likely to be hanging out will show on a chart as lots of contour lines in close proximity.

Of course, spotting those rocky underwater hillsides that hold lings is easy on a chart, not so easy out on open water. You have to know how to read your compass, line up landmarks, and chart a course accurately to locate them, even though sometimes other boats in the area may make the job much easier. Once you get in the general area, though, you have to watch your depthsounder and concentrate your efforts on the rocky humps and drop-offs where lings are most likely to be.

There's more than one way to catch a trophy ling, and you often have the choice of fishing either artificials or bait. Metal jigs, both the real-looking, store-bought "slab" types and the not-so-perfect pipe jigs you can make at home, are effective lingcod-getters. Like most other big fish, the lingcod's diet consists mostly of smaller fish, and these hunks of metal in various shapes and sizes often look enough like the real thing to coax a lingcod into striking. They're available in weights from under an ounce to over two pounds. Leadheads also account for a lot of Washington lingcod. Most anglers adorn them with large, plastic, curl-tail bodies, but a strip of pork rind is just as effective and usually holds up better to those jagged lingcod teeth. Black, brown, blue, and purple tend to work better than the hot or light colors. Deep-water jigging may require 20- to 32-ounce leadheads, but light-line anglers fishing shallow water in calm tides may get by using jigs as light as a couple of ounces.

There are times when lingcod aren't all that interested in artificials, and that's when you have to go to the real thing to bring them to the dinner table. Dead bait, such as whole herring, will often do the job, but if you really want to get them interested, you may have to offer them something that's still alive and kicking. It could be a large herring, if they're available, or maybe you'll have to first catch a few greenling, rockfish, shiner perch, or other small fish for bait, and then start fishing lingcod. Of all these smaller fish that will do the job as lingcod bait, the greenling is perhaps best. Averaging about 12 inches long, it's just bite-sized for a husky ling, and it doesn't have all the sharp spines you'll find on rockfish and some other species, so it's easy to handle and easy for a lingcod to swallow. What's more, greenling are easy to find and catch from shallow-water kelp patches and rock piles, and they're hardy enough to stay alive several hours in an aerated live-well or five-gallon pail of water.

Most anglers fish live bait on a wire spreader, snapping on cannon-ball weights of various sizes to take it to the bottom and using a short, stout leader between the bait and the horizontal arm of the spreader. Some people prefer wire leaders, but 40- to 60-pound monofilament usually works just fine.

Hook size for live-bait lingcod fishing should be at least 6/0, and 8/0 to 10/0 hooks are usually even better. With small baits, such as herring or shiner perch, you can get by with one hook, simply hooking the baitfish through both lips or

A big lingcod is a handful, maybe even a handful for two anglers.

near the middle of the back. A two-hook rig works better with big baits, such as foot-long greenling or rockfish. Tie the hooks in tandem, at least a foot apart, and run the first one through both lips of the baitfish. The second hook goes under the skin, an inch or two in front of the tail. Lingcod may take a baitfish head-first, tail-first, or cross-ways, and with the two-hook rig you always have at least one point at the right end of the bait. Keep your lingcod hooks razor-sharp to get maximum penetration into those hard, toothy jaws.

You want to keep the baitfish swimming just off bottom, which isn't always easy when you're trying to work those jagged rock piles that lingcod seem to love. Watching your depthsounder at all times helps, but you'll also have to drop and retrieve line constantly to follow those rugged bottom contours. Don't simply let the sinker drag bottom all the time; if you do you'll be hung up constantly, either from the sinker lodging in the rocks or because the baitfish will find a little hiding spot and dodge into it.

When jigging artificials, of course, you'll want to set the hooks as soon as you feel anything a bit unusual, but not with live bait. While lings sometimes simply gulp the bait and hook themselves, you'll usually want to give them a couple of seconds to take it down before hitting them. Some anglers don't use the rod to set hooks at all, but simply point the rod toward the water and reel as fast as they can for several seconds. Lingcod often hang onto a bait whether they're hooked or not, and they'll clamp down even harder if they feel it pulling away. This fast-reeling strategy also gets the lingcod away from the bottom faster, giving them less chance to turn back into the rocks and lodge in some crevice from which you'll never remove them.

When playing and trying to boat a bait-hooked lingcod, always remember that it may not be hooked but is simply holding on to the baitfish. Pump the fish up to the surface as smoothly as possible, and be ready with a net or gaff when it gets to the top. They'll often let go right at the surface, so stick 'em or scoop 'em an instant before they break water, if possible.

If the lingcod is bound for the dining table, smack it once across the eyes with your fish club and quickly slice through a couple of gill arches to bleed it. The table quality of those fillets will be much better that way.

But don't assume for a minute that the only good lingcod is a dead lingcod. All trophy-sized lings are females, and these are also the brood fish that will provide the fisheries in years and decades to come. These fish are tough and have no swim bladder, which means they can be fought, boated, photographed, and released with few ill effects, so if you find good fishing for big lingcod, release a few for next time.

Selection of rods, reels, and line for lingcod depends a lot on how much fun you want to have with each fish and the kind of fishing you're most likely to do. You may want to go with a fairly stout boat rod, low-geared reel, and 50-pound monofilament or braided dacron if you plan to fish a lot of live bait/spreader rigs in deeper water. If, on the other hand, you want to really have a good time, maybe set an IGFA line-class record, and fish shallow water, try something like your favorite freshwater flipping rod and a levelwind reel loaded with 10- to 20-pound mono. Such tackle handles small to medium-weight jigs quite well in water of 75 to 150 feet deep. When fishing lingcod on such light line, however, always remember to use a heavy two- or three-foot shock leader between your line and your bait or lure. Running light monofilament directly to the hook is a bad idea, because it simply won't hold up to the rocky bottom and those dagger-like teeth.

Armed with this basic information, you're ready to go lingcod fishing. But remember, I warned you that they're ugly, so if you have nightmares after catching your first one, don't blame me.

Where to Go for Lingcod

Westport, La Push, Neah Bay, Port Angeles Rock Pile, Middle Bank (east end of the Strait of Juan de Fuca), beneath the Tacoma Narrows Bridge.

HONORABLE MENTION

FRESHWATER

Cutthroat Trout

Sea-run, resident, and the unique Crescent Lake cutthroat all are available to western Washington anglers, while east-siders can fish for native cutts or transplanted Lahontan cutthroat. All are cooperative biters that will take a wide range of baits, artificial lures, and flies.

Brown Trout

Although not native to Washington, browns are being stocked in more and more lakes to provide added angling opportunities through the summer and fall. Most of the baits and lures that take rainbows will also fool brown trout.

Brook Trout

A char rather than an actual trout, the brookie is abundant in many north-central and far-eastern Washington lakes and streams. Where you find one you'll often find lots of them, although catching one larger than 10 inches may be difficult. Small spoons, spinners, and artificial flies will fool all but the wisest brook trout.

Lake Trout

Another char, this big transplant is most commonly called a Mackinaw by western anglers. It grows to more than 30 pounds and is found in a handful of central and eastern Washington lakes, where it can be caught on large spoons and minnow-imitating plugs.

Bull Trout/Dolly Varden

Populations of these two closely related chars have been drastically reduced by habitat loss and over-fishing, so most Washington waters are closed to the taking of either. Check the fishing pamphlet closely, both for exceptions to this closure regulation and for illustrations so that you'll know one if you should catch it.

Kokanee

This landlocked sockeye salmon is a favorite of anglers and fish gourmets alike. Also known as a "silver trout," it's found in many Washington lakes, and can be caught by trolling, stillfishing, or jigging. Averaging 10 to 12 inches, it's so abundant in some lakes that special bonus limits may be in effect.

Mountain Whitefish

Found in rivers throughout the state, this silvery, foot-long fish is most readily available during the winter, when large numbers of them congregate for spawning. They have tiny mouths, so use maggots and other little tidbits on very small hooks to catch them.

Lake Whitefish

This inhabitant of larger Columbia Basin lakes and reservoirs grows to three or four pounds and may be found in large schools. Catch them through the ice in winter or up in the shallows when they move in during the spring to spawn. Try small wobbling spoons for them.

Walleyes

This Midwestern transplant was illegally stocked in the Columbia River system in the 1960s, and now it's a favorite of anglers from the Canadian border to Portland. Walleyes grow to impressive size and provide outstanding table fare. They're best caught on leadhead jigs bounced along the bottom or on trolled minnow-imitating plugs or spinner-and-nightcrawler combinations.

Crappies

These dark-spotted panfish are fond of submerged limbs, stumps, and other woody cover, and where you find one you'll probably find a school. Try a small, plastic-skirted leadhead jig suspended beneath a bobber for best results.

Bluegill Sunfish

Sometimes growing to 10 inches or more, this husky panfish in becoming increasingly popular among Washington anglers. The best bluegill lakes are east of the Cascades, and late spring usually provides the best bluegill fishing. Cast a BeetleSpin around open-water cover or work a small bait into little coves and openings in thick brush to catch them.

Pumpkinseed Sunfish

Considered a nuisance by most anglers, this little panfish is a great "first fish" for kids and fishing novices. It will take almost any small bait or lure you might throw its way.

Rock Bass

This red-eyed panfish is found only in a few south Puget Sound area lakes, where it will take small wobbling plugs, spoons, spinnerbaits, and artificial flies. It typically grows to about 10 inches.

Tiger Muskies

A cross between a northern pike and a muskellunge, this big predator may grow to 30 pounds or larger, and it was first stocked in southwest Washington's Mayfield Lake to provide a trophy fishery and reduce the lake's squawfish population. It was successful on both counts, and has subsequently been planted in Spokane County's Newman Lake. Large plugs and bucktail spinners, fished around weed beds and stumps, will draw vicious tiger musky strikes.

Brown Bullhead Catfish

The state's most abundant member of the catfish family, the brown bullhead is found in lakes and ponds throughout Washington. Fishing at night with worms, nightcrawlers, or various stinkbait concoctions works best for them.

Channel Catfish

They grow to a very impressive size in some of eastern Washington's bigger Columbia River tributaries, and channel cats are now being stocked in more and more Washington lakes as well. Hard fighters that are also excellent on the dinner table, channel catfish can be caught on nightcrawlers, chicken livers, various stinkbaits, and strips of flesh cut from the sides of smaller fish.

Burbot

The so-called freshwater ling is found in deeper lakes and reservoirs of central and eastern Washington, where it's especially popular with wintertime ice anglers. Nightcrawlers, smelt, and other large baits, fished on or near the bottom, work best for them.

Northern Squawfish

Although long considered a pest, the squawfish's popularity has grown dramatically since it became the target of a Columbia River bounty program early in this decade. It hits small spoons, spinners, jigs, and wobbling plugs hard, then gives up and lets you reel it right in.

SALTWATER

Rockfish

Available in shallow-, mid-, and deep-water models, there's a rockfish for virtually every saltwater fishing situation here in Washington. The black rockfish, often found in shallow water and even right on the surface, is perhaps most well known and provides the bread-and-butter action for coastal "bottomfish" anglers. Other shallow-water species include the blue, yellowtail, copper, and brown rockfish. Mid-depth and deep-water species available to Washington anglers include the China, widow, quillback, canary, tiger, bocaccio, and yelloweye rockfish, the last two of which sometimes top 20 pounds. Many rockfish species are slow-growing and susceptible to over-fishing. Herring, anchovies, leadhead, and metal jigs are among the baits and lures that will take all varieties of rockfish.

Flounder and Sole

The starry flounder, which sometimes tops 10 pounds, is one of the biggest, best, and most popular of Washington's marine flatfish, but the possibilities also include arrowtooth flounder, Dover sole petrale sole, English sole, rock sole, sand sole, Pacific sanddab, speckled sanddab, and several others. All but the arrowtooth flounder provide excellent eating. Generally found over sand, gravel, or even mud bottoms, they're easy to fish for and easy to fool with a variety of natural baits and artificial lures. Estuaries and shallow bays often provide excellent flatfish action

Albacore Tuna

This highly migratory fish provides lots of angling excitement when it passes within reach of the Washington charter fleet. Strong, stubborn, and fast, it's a fantastic sport fish, and its flesh is among the best of all marine fish. Charters troll large jigs along the surface to locate a school of albacore, then live anchovies are cast over the side to provide some of the Northwest's hottest angling action.

Saltwater Perch

The redtail surfperch is the most commonly caught prize in the ocean breakers of the Washington coast, while the pile perch and striped seaperch are more likely to turn up around pilings, piers, and jetties in the calmer waters of coastal estuaries, the Strait of Juan de Fuca, and Puget Sound. Shrimp, blood worms, sand crabs, pieces of clams and mussels, and other small baits work well for all of them, especially at the front end of an incoming tide. All three are tough fighters and provide prime, white-meated fillets.

Cabezon

It looks like something from a kid's worst nightmare, but this biggest Northwest member of the sculpin family is a prized bottomfish. Although cabezon feeds primarily on crabs and other crustaceans, it can be caught on herring, anchovies, metal jigs, and lead-and-plastic grub combinations. It grows to 20 pounds and is a tough fighter.

Greenling

Sometimes called sea trout, kelp greenling, white-spotted greenling. and rock greenling are fun to catch, easy to handle, and very good to eat. The kelp variety is most abundant and most often caught in Washington, both by boat and shore anglers. Both natural baits and artificial lures will draw greenling strikes.

Pacific Cod

Often called true cod because it's a bona fide member of the codfish family (unlike lingcod and "rock cod," which aren't really cod at all), this bottomfish sometimes grows to 15 pounds and is prized for its thick, firm, white fillets. Found both in the ocean and in our "inside" marine waters, cod can be caught on herring baits and on a wide variety of metal jigs and other artificials. The walleyed pollock and tomcod are smaller members of the same family that also provide decent sport and great fish 'n chips for Washington anglers.

ANADROMOUS
(SEA-RUN)

Chum Salmon

Also called a dog salmon, the chum is no dog when it comes to fighting ability. In fact, this second-largest of the five Pacific salmon species is perhaps the toughest and strongest fighter of the bunch. It's also the last to return from the ocean each fall, usually coming back to Washington rivers and creeks in November, December, and January. Whether fishing them in salt or freshwater, think "small" and think "green" and you'll probably do alright.

Pink Salmon

This smallest of the five Pacific salmon returns to Washington streams only on odd-numbered years, but it often returns in very good numbers. Trolling small herring baits or brightly colored spoons works well for pinks—also known as humpies—in saltwater, and the same pink or orange spoons will also do the job in freshwater.

Sockeye Salmon

Although sockeye may be the most highly prized of all Pacific salmon when it comes to table quality, Washington anglers catch very few of them. Sockeye fisheries in Lake Washington and Lake Wenatchee are on-again, off-again affairs, mostly off-again in recent years. There are summertime sockeyes to catch in the Strait of Juan de Fuca every year, but the competition from commercial nets is fierce, and as yet no one has developed an effective means of catching those fish on sporting tackle.

American Shad

This biggest member of the herring family was brought to the West Coast last century, but it still doesn't get the respect and angling interest it deserves. The best shad fishing around here is in the Columbia, especially the stretch immediately below Bonneville Dam during the month of June, where record shad runs have been the rule in recent years. Try small, plastic-skirted leadheads or simply slide two colored beads onto your line above a bare hook and you'll catch shad.

WASHINGTON FISHING SPOTS

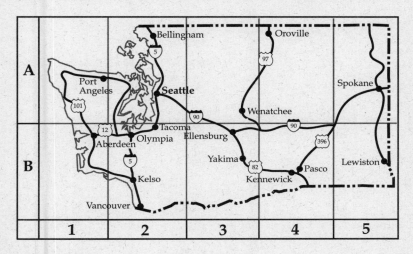

1. Neah Bay/Cape Flattery, 2. Sekiu River, 3. Hoko River, 4. Sekiu/Clallam Bay, 5. Northwest Coast, 6. Elk Lake, 7. Pysht River, 8. Pillar Point, 9. East and West Twin Rivers, 10. Lyre River, 11. Salt Creek, 12. Freshwater Bay, 13. Port Angeles Saltwater, 14. Ozette Lake, 15. Lake Pleasant, 16. Beaver Lake, 17. Lake Crescent, 18. Lake Sutherland, 19. Elwha River (including Lake Aldwell and Lake Mills), 20. Dickey River, 21. Quillayute River, 22. Sol Duc River, 23. Calawah River, 24. Bogachiel River, 25. Seven Lakes Basin, 26. Goodman Creek, 27. Hoh River, 28. Kalaloch Surf, 29. Clearwater River, 30. Queets River, 31. Salmon River, 32. Lake Quinault, 33. Quinault River, 34. Lake Wynoochee.

1. Dakota Creek, 2. Lake Terrell, 3. Nooksack River, 4. Wiser Lake, 5. Fazon Lake, 6. Silver Lake, 7. Tennant Lake, 8. Toad Lake, 9. Squalicum Lake, 10. Lake Whatcom, 11. Lake Padden, 12. Northern San Juan Islands, 13. Cascade Lake, 14. Mountain Lake, 15. Lake Samish, 16. Cain Lake, 17. Egg Lake, 18. Sportsman's Lake, 19. Killebrew Lake, 20. Samish River, 21. Grandy Lake, 22. Southern San Juan Islands, 23. Hummel Lake, 24. Heart Lake, 25. Whistle Lake, 26. Lake Erie, 27. Campbell Lake, 28. Pass Lake, 29. Cranberry Lake, 30. Lower Skagit River, 31. Clear Lake, 32. Beaver Lake, 33. Big Lake, 34. Lake Ten, 35. Lake Sixteen, 36. Lake McMurray, 37. Ketchum Lake, 38. Lake Cavanaugh, 39. Banks of the Eastern Strait of Juan de Fuca, 40. Sunday Lake, 41. Pilchuck Creek, 42. Bryant Lake, 43. Stillaguamish River, 44. Lake Armstrong, 45. Ebey (Little) Lake, 46. Riley Lake, 47. Twin Lakes, 48. Dungeness Spit, 49. Port Townsend and Admiralty Inlet, 50. Martha Lake, 51. Lake Ki, 52. Lake Howard, 53. Lake Goodwin, 54. Shoecraft Lake, 55. Crabapple Lake, 56. Lake Cassidy, 57. Canyon Creek, 58. Morse Creek, 59. Siebert Creek, 60. McDonald Creek, 61. Dungeness River, 62. Anderson Lake, 63. Goss Lake, 64. Lone Lake, 65. Lake Stevens, 66. Bosworth Lake, 67. Gibbs Lake, 68. Peterson Lake, 69. Lake Leland, 70. Crocker Lake, 71. Tarboo Lake, 72. Tarboo Creek, 73. Sandy Shore Lake, 74. Ludlow Lake, 75. Teal Lake, 76. Buck Lake, 77. Deer Lake, 78. Lake Serene, 79. Stickney Lake, 80. Silver Lake, 81. Martha Lake, 82. Snohomish River, 83. Blackman's Lake, 84. Flowing Lake, 85. Panther Lake, 86. Storm Lake, 87. Lake Roesiger, 88. Chain Lake, 89. Wagner (Wagner's) Lake, 90. Woods Creek, 91. Cochran Lake, 92. Skykomish River, 93. Little Quilcene River, 94. Quilcene River, 95. Devil's Lake, 96. Lake Ballinger,

97. Devil's Lake, 98. Echo Lake, 99. Fontal Lake, 100. Lake Hannan, 101. Lake Margaret, 102. Lake Joy, 103. Lake Constance, 104. Dosewallips River, 105. Duckabush River, 106. Upper Hood Canal, 107. Haller Lake, 108. Green Lake, 109. Cottage Lake, 110. Tolt River, 111. Langlois Lake, 112. Lena Lakes, 113. Armstrong Lake, 114. Hamma Hamma River, 115. Wildcat Lake, 116. Kitsap Lake, 117. Lake Washington, 118. Phantom Lake, 119. Lake Sammamish, 120. Pine Lake, 121. Beaver Lake, 122. Snoqualmie River, 123. Raging River, 124. Lake Alice, 125. Tokul Creek, 126. Mildred Lakes, 127. Elk and Jefferson Lakes, 128. Lake Cushman, 129. Price (Price's) Lake, 130. Melbourne Lake, 131. Kokanee Lake, 132. Skokomish River, 133. Lower Hood Canal, 134. Wood and Wildberry Lakes, 135. Dewatto-Area Lakes, 136. Dewatto River, 137. Maggie Lake, 138. Tahuya River, 139. Howell Lake, 140. Haven Lake, 141. Lake Wooten, 142. Twin Lakes, 143. Panther Lake, 144. Mission Lake, 145. Tiger Lake, 146. Union River, 147. Long Lake, 148. Angle Lake, 149. Green River, 150. Panther Lake, 151. Lake Wilderness, 152. Shady Lake, 153. Lake Desire, 154. Otter (Spring) Lake, 155. Shadow Lake, 156. Lake Meridian, 157. Walsh Lake, 158. Benson Lake, 159. Mason Lake, 160. Prickett (Trails End) Lake, 161. Devereaux Lake, 162. Coulter Creek, 163. Wye Lake, 164. Carney Lake, 165. Horseshoe Lake, 166. Crescent Lake, 167. Central Puget Sound, 168. Lake Fenwick, 169. Steel (or Steele) Lake, 170. Star Lake, 171. Lake Dolloff, 172. North Lake, 173. Lake Morton, 174. Lake Sawyer, 175. Ravensdale Lake, 176. Lake Twelve, 177. Retreat Lake.

1. Tomyhoi Lake, 2. Twin Lakes, 3. Galena Chain Lakes, 4. Ross Lake, 5. Hidden Lakes Chain, 6. Black Lake, 7. Baker River, 8. Baker Lake, 9. Thornton Lakes, 10. Diablo Lake, 11. Gorge Lake, 12. Watson Lakes, 13. Lake Shannon, 14. Upper Skagit River, 15. Granite Creek, 16. Lake Ann, 17. Rainy Lake, 18. Trapper Lake, 19. Cutthroat Lake, 20. Early Winters Creek, 21. Chewack (Chewuch) River, 22. Buck Lake, 23. Pearrygin Lake, 24. Davis Lake, 25. Patterson Lake, 26. Twin Lakes, 27. Twisp River, 28. Black Pine Lake, 29. Stehekin River, 30. Sauk River, 31. Suiattle River, 32. Lake Chelan-Sawtooth Wilderness Lakes, 33. Domke Lake, 34. Glacier Peak Lakes, 35. White Chuck River, 36. Heather Lake, 37. Lake Twentytwo (or Twenty-Two, or even 22), 38. Boardman Lake, Upper Boardman (Island) Lake, and Lake Evan, 39. Goat Lake, 40. Spada Lake (Sultan Reservoir), 41. Lake Chelan, 42. Antilon Lake, 43. Dry Lake, 44. Wapato Lake, 45. Roses Lake, 46. White River, 47. Fish Lake, 48. Chiwawa River, 49. Lake Wenatchee, 50. Nason Creek, 51. Entiat River, 52. Eagle Creek, 53. Chumstick Creek, 54. Icicle Creek (Icicle River), 55. Columbia River, 56. Wenatchee River, 57. Alpine Lakes Wilderness, 58. Upper Cle Elum River, 59. Cooper Lake, 60. Rattlesnake Lake, 61. Keechelus Lake.

1. Osoyoos Lake, 2. Sidley and Molson Lakes, 3. Similkameen River, 4. Chopaka Lake, 5. Palmer Lake, 6. Blue Lake, 7. Wannacut Lake, 8. Muskrat Lake, 9. Spectacle Lake, 10. Whitestone Lake, 11. Lost Lake, 12. Beth, Beaver, and Little Beaver Lakes, 13. Bonaparte Lake, 14. Curlew Lake, 15. Aeneas Lake, 16. Blue Lake (Sinlahekin Valley), 17. Fish Lake, 18. Long, Round, and Ell Lakes, 19. Ferry Lake, 20. Swan Lake, 21. Crawfish Lake, 22. Conconully Lake, 23. Conconully Reservoir, 24. Salmon Creek, 25. Cougar Lake, 26. Campbell Lake, 27. Lime Belt Lakes, 28. Brown Lake, 29. Green Lakes, 30. Duck Lake, 31. Leader Lake, 32. Omak Lake, 33. Cook and Little Goose Lakes, 34. Okanogan River, 35. Rat Lake, 36. Big Goose Lake, 37. Methow River, 38. Alta Lake, 39. Columbia River (Lake Pateros and Rufus Woods Lake), 40. Foster Creek, 41. Buffalo Lake, 42. Rebecca Lake, 43. McGinnis Lake, 44. Lower Lake Roosevelt, 45. San Poil River, 46. Banks Lake, 47. Grimes Lake, 48. Jameson Lake, 49. Dry Falls Lake, 50. Deep Lake, 51. Perch Lake, 52. Vic Meyers (Rainbow) Lake, 53. Park Lake, 54. Blue Lake, 55. Alkali Lake, 56. Lake Lenore, 57. Billy Clapp Lake, 58. Middle Crab Creek, 59. Lake Creek Chain.

1. Summit Lake, 2. Big Sheep Creek, 3. Cedar Lake, 4. Pierre Lake, 5. Deep Lake, 6. Sullivan Lake, 7. Davis Lake, 8. Williams Lake, 9. Kettle River, 10. Little Pend Oreille Chain of Lakes, 11. Trout Lake, 12. Ellen Lake, 13. Colville River, 14. Little Twin Lakes, 15. Black Lake, 16. Rocky Lake, 17. Hatch Lake, 18. Starvation Lake, 19. McDowell Lake, 20. Bayley Lake, 21. Upper Lake Roosevelt, 22. Browns Lake, 23. Skookum Lakes, 24. Bead Lake, 25. Marshall Lake, 26. Pend Oreille River, 27. Davis Lake, 28. Waitts Lake, 29. Borgeau Lake, 30. North Twin Lake, 31. South Twin Lake, 32. Jumpoff Joe Lake, 33. Deer Lake, 34. Loon Lake, 35. Sacheen Lake, 36. Diamond Lake, 37. Horseshoe Lake, 38. Fan Lake, 39. Eloika Lake, 40. Mudgett Lake, 41. Bear Lake, 42. Little Spokane River, 43. Long Lake,

44. Newman Lake, 45. Spokane River, 46. Liberty Lake, 47. West Medical Lake, 48. Medical Lake, 49. Silver Lake, 50. Clear Lake, 51. Fish Lake, 52. Hog Canyon Lake, 53. Chapman Lake, 54. Badger Lake, 55. Fishtrap Lake, 56. Amber Lake, 57. Williams Lake, 58. Downs Lake, 59. Sprague Lake, 60. Fourth of July Lake.

Map B1 (36 listings) .... page 338

1. Moclips River, 2. Copalis River, 3. North Beach Surf, 4. Humptulips River, 5. Failor Lake, 6. Chenois Creek, 7. Hoquiam River, 8. Wishkah River, 9. Lake Aberdeen, 10. Wynoochee River, 11. Satsop River, 12. Cloquallum Creek, 13. Lower Chehalis River, 14. Duck Lake, 15. Grays Harbor North Jetty and Point Brown, 16. South Grays Harbor Streams, 17. Johns River, 18. Westport Inshore, 19. Westport Offshore, 20. Elk River, 21. South Beach Surf, 22. North River, 23. Smith Creek, 24. Willapa River, 25. Willapa Bay, 26. Palix River, 27. Nemah River, 28. Long Beach Peninsula Surf, 29. Long Beach Peninsula Lakes, 30. Bear River, 31. Naselle River, 32. Ilwaco Offshore, 33. Columbia River Estuary, 34. Grays River, 35. Skamokawa Creek, 36. Elochoman River.

Map B2 (97 listings) .... page 366

1. Lake Nahwatzel, 2. Lost Lake, 3. Island Lake, 4. Lake Isabella, 5. Spencer Lake, 6. Phillips Lake, 7. Bay Lake, 8. South Puget Sound, 9. Steilacoom Lake, 10. American Lake, 11. Puyallup River, 12. Lake Killarney, 13. Lake Geneva, 14. Five Mile Lake, 15. Trout Lake, 16. White River, 17. Lake Tapps, 18. Fish Lake, 19. Deep Lake, 20. Bass Lake, 21. Walker Lake, 22. Spanaway Lake, 23. Carbon River, 24. Kennedy Creek, 25. Summit Lake, 26. Nisqually River, 27. Chambers Lake, 28. Hicks Lake, 29. Long Lake, 30. Lake St. Clair, 31. Pattison (Patterson) Lake, 32. Ward Lake, 33. Munn Lake, 34. Deschutes River, 35. Black Lake, 36. Capitol Lake, 37. Kapowsin Lake, 38. Whitman Lake, 39. Tanwax Lake, 40. Clear Lake, 41. Ohop Lake, 42. Coplay Lake/Clearwater Wilderness Lakes, 43. Carbon Glacier Lakes, 44. Mowich Lake, 45. Rapjohn Lake, 46. Silver Lake, 47. Harts Lake, 48. Offut Lake, 49. Deep Lake, 50. McIntosh Lake, 51. Black River, 52. Upper Chehalis River, 53. Skookumchuck River, 54. Lawrence Lake, 55. Clear Lake, 56. Mashel River, 57. Alder Lake, 58. Mineral Lake, 59. Skate Creek, 60. Newaukum River, 61. Tilton River, 62. Mayfield Lake, 63. Riffe Lake, 64. Swofford Pond, 65. Lake Scanewa, 66. Cispus River, 67. Yellowjacket Ponds, 68. Olequa Creek, 69. Lacamas Creek, 70. Cowlitz River, 71. Green River, 72. Toutle River, 73. Silver Lake, 74. Upper Green River Lakes, 75. Coldwater Lake, 76. Castle Lake, 77. Abernathy Creek, 78. Germany Creek, 79. Mill Creek, 80. Coweeman River, 81. Kress Lake, 82. Kalama River, 83. Lower Columbia River, 84. Merrill Lake, 85. Swift Creek Reservoir, 86. Yale Lake (Reservoir), 87. Lake Merwin, 88. North Fork Lewis River, 89. Horseshoe Lake, 90. East Fork Lewis River, 91. Battle Ground Lake, 92. Vancouver Lake, 93. Lacamas Lake, 94. Washougal River, 95. Hamilton Creek, 96. Rock Creek, 97. Wind River.

Map B3 (40 listings) .... page 432

1. Kachess Lake, 2. Lake Cle Elum, 3. Lower Cle Elum River, 4. Lake Easton, 5. Teanaway River, 6. Greenwater River, 7. Upper White River, 8. Echo and Lost Lakes, 9. Manastash Lake, 10. Taneum Creek, 11. American River, 12. Bumping River, 13. Dewey Lake, 14. Swamp and Cougar Lakes, 15. Bumping Lake (Reservoir), 16. Rattlesnake Creek, 17. Wenas Lake, 18. Upper Yakima River, 19. Oak Creek, 20. Tieton River, 21. William O. Douglas Wilderness Lakes, 22. Dog Lake, 23. Leech Lake, 24. Packwood Lake, 25. Clear Lake, 26. Rimrock Lake (Reservoir), 27. Naches River, 28. Cowiche Creek, 29. Rotary Lake, 30. Ahtanum Creek, 31. I-82 Ponds (Freeway Ponds), 32. Walupt Lake, 33. Horseshoe, Takhlakh, Council, Olallie, and Chain of Lakes, 34. Klickitat River, 35. White Salmon River, 36. Little White Salmon River/Drano Lake, 37. Northwestern Lake (Reservoir), 38. Rowland Lake(s), 39. Columbia River, 40. Horsethief Lake.

Map B4 (20 listings) .... page 462

1. Rocky Ford Creek, 2. Moses Lake, 3. Quincy Wildlife Area Lakes, 4. George and Martha Lakes, 5. Winchester Wasteway, 6. Caliche Lakes, 7. Potholes Reservoir, 8. Lind Coulee Wasteway, 9. Potholes Area Seep Lakes, 10. Lenice, Nunnally, and Merry Lakes, 11. Lower Crab Creek, 12. Scooteney Reservoir, 13. Columbia River, 14. Emma Lake, 15. Dalton Lake, 16. Lower Snake River, 17. Lower Yakima River, 18. Giffen Lake, 19. Touchet River, 20. Walla Walla River.

Map B5 (10 listings) .... page 482

1. Rock Lake, 2. Union Flat Creek, 3. Palouse River, 4. Deadman Creek, 5. Upper Snake River, 6. Tucannon River, 7. Pataha Creek, 8. Tucannon River Lakes, 9. Asotin Creek, 10. Grande Ronde River.

MAP A1

WASHINGTON MAP .... see page 5
Adjoining Maps
NORTH .... no map
EAST (map A2) .... see page 100
SOUTH (map B2) .... see page 366
WEST .... no map

34 Listings
PAGES 70-99

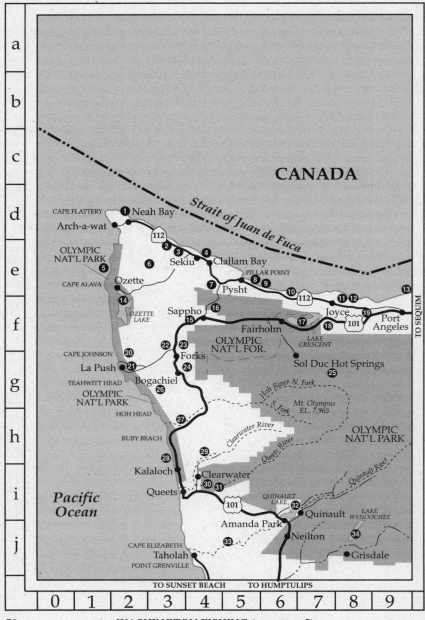

CAPE FLATTERY

1 Neah Bay

Arch-a-wat

OLYMPIC NAT'L PARK

5

6

Ozette

CAPE ALAVA

14

OZETTE LAKE

112

2 **3**

Sekiu

4 Clallam Bay

7 Pysht

PILLAR POINT

8 **9**

10

112

11 **12**

Joyce

13

19

Port Angeles

TO SEQUIM

CANADA

Strait of Juan de Fuca

Sappho

15 **16**

17

18

Fairholm

OLYMPIC NAT'L FOR.

LAKE CRESCENT

101

CAPE JOHNSON

20

22 **23**

Forks

24

21

La Push

Bogachiel

26

TEAHWITT HEAD

OLYMPIC NAT'L PARK

HOH HEAD

27

RUBY BEACH

28

Kalaloch

29

Queets

30 **31**

Clearwater

Hoh River N. Fork

S. Fork

Mt. Olympus EL. 7,965

Clearwater River

Queets River

OLYMPIC NAT'L PARK

Sol Duc Hot Springs

25

Quinault River

Pacific Ocean

101

QUINAULT LAKE

32

Quinault

LAKE WYNOOCHEE

Amanda Park

33

Neilton

34

Grisdale

CAPE ELIZABETH

Taholah

POINT GRENVILLE

TO SUNSET BEACH   TO HUMPTULIPS

0 1 2 3 4 5 6 7 8 9

a b c d e f g h i j

Map Section A1 features:

1. Neah Bay/Cape Flattery
2. Sekiu River
3. Hoko River
4. Sekiu/Clallam Bay
5. Northwest Coast
6. Elk Lake
7. Pysht River
8. Pillar Point
9. East and West Twin Rivers
10. Lyre River
11. Salt Creek
12. Freshwater Bay
13. Port Angeles Saltwater
14. Ozette Lake
15. Lake Pleasant
16. Beaver Lake
17. Lake Crescent
18. Lake Sutherland
19. Elwha River (including Lake Aldwell and Lake Mills)
20. Dickey River
21. Quillayute River
22. Sol Duc River
23. Calawah River
24. Bogachiel River
25. Seven Lakes Basin
26. Goodman Creek
27. Hoh River
28. Kalaloch Surf
29. Clearwater River
30. Queets River
31. Salmon River
32. Lake Quinault
33. Quinault River
34. Lake Wynoochee

1. NEAH BAY/CAPE FLATTERY

Reference: **At Neah Bay, northwest tip of the Olympic Peninsula; map A1, grid d2.**

How to get there: Follow U.S. 101 north from Hoquiam or west from Port Angeles to the town of Sappho and turn north on State Route 113, which meets State Route 112 about 11 miles north of Sappho and continues on as State Route 112 about 26 miles to Neah Bay. The road narrows and becomes windy just past Sekiu.

Facilities: Neah Bay has cabins, motels, RV parks, and fishing resorts, none of them fancy. Charters and boat rentals are available from spring to fall. A grocery/dry goods store carries everything from rubber boots to peanut butter. Tackle and car and boat fuel also are available in Neah Bay.

Contact: Big Salmon Fishing Resort, (360) 654-2374; Far West Resort, (360) 654-2270; Westwind Resort, (360) 654-2751. For nautical charts of the Neah Bay area, contact Captain's Nautical Supply, (206) 283-7242.

Species available: Chinook, coho and pink salmon; Pacific halibut; lingcod; a wide variety of rockfish species.

Fishing Neah Bay: No one comes to Neah Bay by accident, since it's not on the way to anywhere else. Most of the people who brave the narrow, winding, 14-mile stretch of State Route 112 from Sekiu to Neah Bay do so for one reason: to go fishing.

In recent years, with salmon-fishing restrictions greatly affecting Neah Bay, bottomfish have become a huge draw, and this place where the Strait of Juan de Fuca meets the mighty Pacific Ocean offers some of the best bottomfishing to be found anywhere.

Lingcod season on Washington's "inside waters" (Strait of Juan de Fuca, Puget Sound, San Juan Islands, and Hood Canal) opens in mid-spring, and that's the traditional start of the "season" for many Neah Bay regulars. The rocky coastline, scattered islands, and numerous submerged reefs and rock piles provide almost limitless lingcod-fishing opportunities, not only in the Strait, but "around the corner" on the Pacific Ocean side of Cape Flattery.

Duncan Rock, a small island several miles northwest of Neah Bay, is a popular ling fishing spot, but a close look at a nautical chart reveals dozens of other possibilities. NOAA's Cape Flattery charts #18485 and #18460, by the way, are the ones you want if you plan to fish this area. Use them to locate the steep, rocky drop-offs that lings like. Pin-point those locations with your depthsounder and you'll be in the right neighborhood for Neah Bay lings.

Besides lingcod, near-shore fishing around Neah Bay in the spring and early summer also provides some excellent rockfish action. Black rockfish are the most abundant and most popular. Although commonly lumped in with all the other marine bottomfish, the black is more likely to be found suspended well up in the water column, sometimes right on top. Take along a trout or bass rod to fish for them.

If you're not sure where to look for black rockfish around Neah Bay, near-shore kelp beds are always good starting points. Black rockfish often show a preference for small, light-colored lures, so take along an assortment of leadheads in the quarter-ounce to two-ounce range and plenty of two- to four-inch plastic grubs, worms, and tube skirts in white, clear, smoke, light-blue, and other light colors. A selection of metal jigs, such as Darts, Crippled Herring, and Hopkins No=EQLs weighing from half an ounce to three ounces, will also come in handy for black rockfish.

Although less abundant than blacks, the Neah Bay area also has blue, yellowtail, copper, brown, and China rockfish, all of which may be caught on light tackle from relatively shallow water. Quillback, canary, bocaccio, yelloweye, and other deep-water rockfish species are also abundant around offshore reefs and underwater ledges. Most of these fish will come from water of 150 feet or deeper.

To many Northwest anglers, Neah Bay's most famous feature is Swiftsure Bank. It's actually more than 20 miles to the north by boat, but this huge reef at the edge of the Pacific Ocean is one of the best places to go in the Neah Bay area for halibut. It's a pretty safe bet that the big reef has given up more halibut to Washington anglers over the past five years than any other spot in the state. The Swiftsure sport fishery started on a full scale in 1984 and, although the average size of the fish has dropped since then and the seasons have been shortened, the fishing has remained consistent. Most of the halibut are in the 15- to 30-pound range, but you never know when you're going to get a chance to do battle with a fish of barn-door proportions.

Due to the rather complicated sport halibut seasons of recent years, the best advice I can give to would-be Swiftsure halibut anglers is to plan on fishing in May or early June. Be sure to check on season dates for this year before planning a trip.

The many charters operating out of Neah Bay offer the safest, most comfortable way to enjoy Swiftsure halibut action. Contact local resorts and charter offices directly for details on this year's halibut season or to book a trip.

Swiftsure isn't the only place where Neah Bay anglers might encounter a hefty halibut. Several areas right around Cape Flattery provide decent halibut fishing, and a number of flatties over 100 pounds have been caught by small-boat anglers within a few minutes' run of port.

Good salmon fishing used to be a sure thing around Neah Bay during the summer and early fall, but there are no longer any sure things where Northwest coastal salmon seasons are concerned. When regulations allow, July is a good month for big chinooks throughout the Neah Bay area. Drift-mooching and motor-mooching with plug-cut herring accounts for many of the fish, but jigging is also effective.

The area south of Tatoosh Island, just off Cape Flattery several miles west of the Neah Bay harbor, is traditionally a good chinook producer. But if you visit when salmon season is open, don't be afraid to ask around when you get there, and be willing to move to where the action is if you don't find good fishing at your primary location. The hot bite may be at any one of a half-dozen locations within a 30-minute run of Neah Bay.

Late-summer coho (silver) salmon fishing at Neah Bay is legendary. Trolling a plastic squid or streamer fly behind a flasher or pulling a plug-cut herring within 30 feet of the surface is the standard way to catch these five- to 20-pound acrobats.

---

2. SEKIU RIVER

Reference: **Flows into Strait of Juan de Fuca west of Sekiu; see map A1, grid e3.**

How to get there: Drive west out of Sekiu on State Route 112. After passing the Hoko-Ozette Road, about two miles west of town, continue for about 2.5 miles to where the highway crosses the Sekiu River. A logging road turning left just before the bridge provides access to the river.

Facilities: Food, fuel, and lodging are available in the Sekiu-Clallam Bay area.

Contact: Washington Department of Fish and Wildlife, Montesano Office, (360) 249-4628; Olson's Resort, (360) 963-2311; Coho Resort, (360) 963-2333.

Species available: Winter steelhead, sea-run cutthroat trout.

Fishing the Sekiu River: The stocking of about 12,000 winter steelhead smolts a year keeps this fishery going through the winter, but it's local anglers who do most of the catching. Let's face it: the Sekiu is a long way from Washington's population centers, and for the three dozen or so steelhead it produces each season, it's hardly worth the drive. Short bursts of fishing action occur throughout the winter, once the Mokan tribal fishery ends in December.

Cutthroat fishing, on the other hand, can be well worth the trip if you like to do battle with sea-run cutts of 14 to 16 inches. Freshets during the months of October and November offer the best chances of cutthroating success.

3. HOKO RIVER

Reference: **Enters Strait of Juan de Fuca just west of Sekiu; see map A1, grid e3.**

How to get there: Take State Route 112 about two miles west past Sekiu and turn south (left) on Hoko-Ozette Road, which parallels much of the river.

Facilities: Food, gas, and lodging are available in Clallam Bay and Sekiu.

Contact: Washington Department of Fish and Wildlife, Montesano Office, (360) 249-4628; Olson's Resort, (360) 963-2311; Coho Resort, (360) 963-2333.

Species available: Winter steelhead, resident and sea-run cutthroat trout.

Fishing the Hoko River: December and January are usually the top months to fish this small river for steelhead, especially in its lower reaches from the upper Hoko bridge downstream to the river mouth. Runs of adult fish from hatchery plants totalling about 25,000 smolts a year peak during these months.

On the upper Hoko, which is open to fly-fishing only, anglers take steelhead throughout the winter, but the month of March can be particularly productive as well. Those fly-fishing regulations apply throughout the summer and winter, so this is a spot to consider if you like to toss feathers and feel like getting away from the worm-dunking folks.

Sea-run cutthroat fishing is best throughout the river in October, but there are sea-runs to be found in the river from August to December.

4. SEKIU/CLALLAM BAY

Reference: **At Sekiu, on the north side of the Olympic Peninsula; map A1, grid e4.**

How to get there: Drive west from Port Angeles on U.S. 101 and either exit to the right onto State Route 112 about four miles from town and continue west, or stay on 101 for about 43 miles to the town of Sappho and turn north on State Route 113. Where State Routes 112 and 113 meet, about 11 miles north of Sappho, continue northwest for about 15 miles to Clallam Bay and then to nearby Sekiu.

Facilities: Food, lodging, boat rentals, launch ramps, moorage, bait, tackle, and other needs all are available in Sekiu and Clallam Bay.

Contact: Washington Department of Fish and Wildlife, Montesano Office, (360) 249-4628; Olson's Resort, (360) 963-2311; Coho Resort, (360) 963-2333. For nautical charts of the Sekiu/Clallam Bay area, contact Captain's Nautical Supply, (206) 283-7242.

Species available: Chinook, coho, and pink salmon; halibut; lingcod; various rockfish.

Fishing Sekiu/Clallam Bay: Salmon fishing restrictions have even come to Sekiu in recent years, which is really too bad, because this is one of those places where even the small-boat angler could almost always get out and find a place to catch kings and/or silvers. I'll never forget my first trip to this gem of Northwest salmon-fishing spots where, on a July evening in the early 1970s, I had the good fortune of catching my first-ever chinook from the Strait of Juan de Fuca. It was one of those third-time's-the-charm events, as the thick-bodied slab of chrome hit the line of one of my companions, stole the bait, hit a second partner's with the same result, then grabbed my herring-baited hooks and connected solidly. The tails of the two stolen herring still poked out of the 22-pounder's throat as we admired it on the deck of the boat after a 15-minute battle.

Chinooks inhabit the waters in and around Clallam Bay throughout the year, and the area has a lost history of providing good catches of five- to 20-pound blackmouth (immature chinooks) during the late winter and early spring. Waters immediately west of Clallam Bay, commonly referred to as The Caves, were for decades considered among the state's top areas for mature chinook (king) salmon during the summer months. Some of those fish topped 40 pounds. In September, the waters farther offshore from Sekiu have long been considered to be among the Northwest's top spots for adult cohos. These big "hook-nose" silvers sometimes weigh in at 15 pounds or more. Both the summertime chinook fishery and fall fishery for silvers have been severely hampered by closures and angling restrictions the past few years.

But bottomfishing remains pretty good here, and with crowds generally smaller than in the past, you may have considerable elbow room to fish for lingcod and rockfish. You'll find black rockfish in shallow water over submerged rock piles and around kelp beds, and yelloweye, canary, China, quillback, and other rockfish species over submerged rocks in deeper areas. A special slot limit is in effect on lingcod throughout the Strait of Juan de Fuca, but Sekiu offers several rocky areas where you can find keeper lings in the 26- to 40-inch range.

Halibut fishing has gotten very popular throughout this area in recent years, and during the spring-summer season you can usually find someone who knows where the big flatties are biting. Often it's near the mouth of the Hoko River, but other nearby flats may also be worth prospecting. Ask around when you arrive and head for the action.

5. NORTHWEST COAST

Reference: **From Cape Flattery south to La Push, west side of Olympic Peninsula; map A1, grid e2.**

How to get there: Take U.S. 101 to La Push Road, about two miles north of Forks, and turn west. Follow La Push Road for approximately 14 miles to La Push. Or follow U.S. 101 north from Hoquiam or west from Port Angeles to the town of Sappho, turn north on State Route 113, which meets State Route 112 about 11 miles north of Sappho and becomes State Route 112. Drive west on State Route 112 about 26 miles to Neah Bay.

Facilities: Neah Bay has cabins, motels, RV parks, and fishing resorts. Charters and boat rentals are available from spring to fall. A grocery/dry goods store carries everything from rubber boots to peanut butter. La Push has a small boat ramp and little else, but all amenities are available in Forks.

Contact: Big Salmon Fishing Resort, (360) 654-2374; Far West Resort, (360) 654-2270; Westwind Resort, (360) 654-2751; Olympic Sporting Goods,

(360) 374-6330. For nautical charts of the Northwest Coast, contact Captain's Nautical Supply, (206) 283-7242.

Species available: Lingcod, rockfish, halibut, chinook and coho salmon.

Fishing the Northwest Coast: Many of the anglers who fish this hard-to-reach corner of the Pacific Northwest come "around the corner" from Neah Bay to work their way down the coast to some of the state's traditional salmon and bottomfish hot spots. Others come out of La Push or even run north from the Westport area to fish these fish-filled waters. Places such as (from north to south) Skagway, Greenbank, Mukkaw Bay, Spike Rock, Father and Son, and the Rock Pile have at various times provided phenomenal fishing for both salmon and bottomfish.

Restrictions on both salmon and halibut have made things tough for anglers here in recent years, but when seasons are open and the Pacific is calm enough to allow small boats to come and go as they please, this stretch of the Washington coast can be an angler's paradise. Likewise, charters from both Neah Bay and Westport sometimes run to this area to capitalize on the good fishing possibilities.

When salmon seasons are open here, big chinook are often found right in close to the shoreline, where they may corner herring and other baitfish in the shallow water. Early mornings and tide changes often provide the best action, but a hot bite may turn on with little notice and end just as quickly as it begins. The Skagway area is a favorite among Neah Bay anglers for just this kind of fast-action king fishing.

This part of the coast is dotted with underwater humps, hills, and plateaus that act as a magnate for Pacific halibut. Umatilla Reef, west of La Push, is one of the biggest and best-known of these halibut spots, and there are dozens of others that are smaller and more difficult to locate but every bit as productive. Some of these humps, which receive light fishing pressure during those short periods when the halibut season is open, are home to barn-door fish averaging 50 pounds or more.

Rockfish and lingcod seasons are more dependable, and there are hundreds of places to catch them between Cape Flattery and La Push. Near-surface black, blue, and yellowtail rockfish are plentiful for light-tackle anglers, or you can drop a live greenling or other small bottomfish to the bottom over a rocky hump or steep ledge and find lingcod that sometimes top 50 pounds. This is perhaps Washington's last great stronghold of excellent lingcod fishing. As with salmon fishing, the great bottomfish action is within reach of private-boat anglers when the weather cooperates. But don't forget that this is the wide-open Pacific, and if the ocean is rough, save your adventure for another day when Ma Nature is in a more cooperative mood.

Nautical charts #18485, #18460, and #18480 are extremely valuable to anyone thinking about fishing this wide-open corner of the Pacific Northwest.

6. ELK LAKE

Reference: **Northeast of Ozette; map A1, grid e2.**

How to get there: Take the Hoko-Ozette Road south off State Route 112 about two miles west of Sekiu and drive about 15 miles to the 7000 Line. The 7000 Line is gated, so you must either walk or ride a bicycle or a horse about five miles to the west side of the lake.

Facilities: No facilities are available at the lake. As a local reminded me, "You have to go back to Sekiu or Clallam Bay for a soda pop." The nearest food, gas, lodging, and tackle are available in Sekiu and Clallam Bay.

Contact: Olympic Sporting Goods, (360) 374-6330.

Species available: Cutthroat trout.

Fishing Elk Lake: The advice from most folks is "Don't bother," but if you really have the urge to work hard for your trout, this is the only real lake between the Hoko-Ozette Road and Neah Bay. The cutthroats are pan-sized, and if you catch a 14-incher, you've got yourself a trophy. Fish 'em with wet flies or small streamers, your favorite wobbling spoons and weighted spinners, or the time-proven cutthroat getter, a garden worm below a bobber. Give yourself plenty of time to get to and from the lake if you're going for the day.

7. PYSHT RIVER

Reference: **Enters Strait of Juan de Fuca at Pysht, east of Clallam Bay; map A1, grid e4.**

How to get there: Take U.S. 101 to Sappho and turn north on State Route 113, which crosses the river half a mile south of the State Route 112 intersection. Turn left on the gravel road just south of the bridge to follow the river upstream. To follow the river downstream, turn east (right) on State Route 112.

Facilities: Silver King Resort, near the mouth of the river at Pillar Point, has tent sites and RV hookups, but it's a good idea to call ahead. Clallam Bay, about 10 miles to the north, has food, gas, lodging, tackle, and RV sites.

Contact: Washington Department of Fish and Wildlife, Montesano Office, (360) 249-4628; (360) Silver King Resort, (360) 963-2800.

Species available: Winter steelhead, sea-run cutthroat trout.

Fishing the Pysht River: Okay, before you can fish it, you have to know how to say it. The "y" is pronounced like a short "i," so it's "Pisht," not "P-eye-sht." To help you remember, just say to yourself: "I fysht the Pysht." (But you might not want to say it when there are lots of people around.) Anyway, the Pysht is a little river that depends on annual steelhead plants of 10,000 to 20,000 fish for its livelihood. During a typical winter, anglers catch 100 to 200 fish. Since they're hatchery steelies, most of them come back in December or January. In skimming the steelhead catch figures compiled by Washington's Department of Fish and Wildlife, I noticed something a little unusual and at least moderately unnerving about the steelhead fishery here. Those records show that anglers catch a fair number of steelhead from the Pysht in March, which would be cool, except for the fact the river always closes to fishing at the end of February. Hmmmm.

8. PILLAR POINT

Reference: **At Pysht, east of Clallam Bay, on Strait of Juan de Fuca; map A1, grid e5.**

How to get there: Drive west out of Port Angeles on U.S. 101 and either turn right (north) on State Route 112 about four miles from town and follow it 30 miles to the "Silver King Resort" sign, or stay on U.S. 101 about 43 miles to the town of Sappho, turn north (right) on State Route 113, follow it 11 miles to the intersection of State Route 112, turn east (right), and drive about seven miles to the "Silver King" sign.

Facilities: Silver King Resort has tent and RV sites, a boat ramp and moorage, fuel, bait, tackle, and some groceries.

Contact: Silver King Resort, (360) 963-2800. For nautical charts of the Pillar Point area, contact Captain's Nautical Supply, (206) 283-7242.

Species available: Chinook, coho, and pink salmon; Pacific halibut; lingcod; rockfish.

Fishing Pillar Point (and the Strait of Juan de Fuca east to the mouth of the East Twin River): This section of the Strait of Juan de Fuca was once one of the Northwest's premier summer and fall fishing spots for coho salmon, but the coho-fishing restrictions of recent times have closed that fishery completely in recent years. The chinook season has closed down during the summer in recent years as well, which means lost opportunity to fish a spot known over the years for producing some of Washington's biggest kings. As if this wasn't bad enough, many anglers have taken these closures to mean a complete salmon-fishing closure at Pillar Point, but such is not the case. In fact, the winter and spring chinook fishing here is as good as it ever was, and sometimes that means damned good. Although you have to keep an eye on the weather—which can turn ugly and downright dangerous for small-boat anglers in a hurry—good blackmouth fishing can be found at Pillar Point from the time it opens in late-fall until the time it closes in June. March, April, and May are often excellent times to fish the Pillar Point area, and both moochers and trollers share in the fun.

Although considered by some to be rather poor consolation for the loss of coho and chinooks, there is a productive pink salmon fishery here during odd-numbered years. The pinks—or humpies—show up in the area from several days to a couple of weeks before they start providing action for Puget Sound-area anglers, usually sometime around early August. More and more anglers are taking advantage of this opportunity, but there's still plenty of room for more when the pink salmon arrive.

During the spring, the Pillar Point area can be a good base of operations for halibut anglers. Seven or eight miles to the east is the gently sloping beach at the mouth of the Twin Rivers, perhaps the most productive spring halibut spot between Neah Bay and Port Angeles. The halibut season here usually lasts for a couple of months from May to July, but it changes from year to year and may be closed certain days of the week, so bone up on the seasons and regulations before planning your trip.

As far as lingcod and other bottomfish are concerned, there are several steep-rocky drop-offs and submerged rock piles to investigate. You'll need a depthsounder and a good chart to find and fish them effectively, so pick up a copy of NOAA's nautical chart #18460 before heading out.

9. EAST AND WEST TWIN RIVERS

Reference: **Flow into Strait of Juan de Fuca west of Joyce; see map A1, grid e6.**

How to get there: From Port Angeles, drive west on U.S. 101 for about four miles and turn right on State Route 112. Drive about 11 miles west to Joyce and continue another 13 miles to bridges that cross both rivers, less than half a mile apart. A gravel road to the south (left) just west of the East Twin and another about 1.5 miles west of the West Twin run upstream to provide access.

Facilities: There's nothing in the immediate area except an undeveloped camping spot on the water side of the highway about six miles to the west. The nearest RV park and campground is at Lyre River Park, about eight miles to the east. Food, gas, lodging, and tackle are available in Port Angeles.

Contact: Washington Department of Fish and Wildlife, Montesano Office, (360) 249-4628; Lyre River Park, (360) 928-3436.

Species available: Sea-run cutthroat trout, a few winter and summer steelhead.

Fishing the East and West Twin Rivers: Anglers catch 10 to 20 winter steelhead and about half that number of summer-runs from these two side-by-side rivers during a typical year, so they're hardly worth driving to if you lust in your heart for a steelhead. Most, if not all, of the steelhead caught here are taken by locals who can drop what they're doing and fish these little streams when conditions are right.

The same could be said for sea-run cutthroats, except that the numbers are several times as many cutts in the first place, so your chances of hooking a fish or two are greater overall. The rewards, of course, are smaller with a 14-inch cutthroat than with a 10-pound steelhead, so you decide whether they're worth the trip. Neither steelhead nor cutthroat smolts are planted, so any fish you hook will be a wild beauty.

10. LYRE RIVER

Reference: **Enters Strait of Juan de Fuca west of Joyce; map A1, grid e6.**

How to get there: Take State Route 112 off U.S. 101 about three miles west of Port Angeles and follow it west about 15 miles to the river.

Facilities: A campground/RV park near the mouth of the river has a small grocery store, showers, and a laundry facility. All other amenities are available in Port Angeles.

Contact: Lyre River Park, (360) 928-3436; Elwha Resort and Cafe, (360) 457-7011.

Species available: Winter and summer steelhead, sea-run cutthroat trout.

Fishing the Lyre River: This may not be the world's shortest river, but it has to rank right up there near the top of the list. The entire Lyre River, from its headwaters in crystal-clear Lake Crescent to its confluence with the Strait of

Juan Fuca, is a grand total of five miles long. And the distance that steelhead can travel up the river is even shorter, thanks to an impassable falls about three miles from the river mouth.

For its size, though, the Lyre is a productive steelhead stream, especially in winter. Liberal doses of hatchery smolts provide anglers with the chance to catch about 300 winter steelies here every year, most of them landed during December and January. The best fishing is right after a soaking rain, and I mean right after. The river drops and clears into fishing condition almost immediately after the rain stops.

The summer steelhead fishery here is no big deal, with the annual smolt plants providing maybe 30 to 40 fish during an average summer season. Low, clear water makes for tough fishing until the fall rains stir things up a little.

11. SALT CREEK

Reference: **Enters Strait of Juan de Fuca at Crescent Bay, northeast of Joyce; map A1, grid e8.**
How to get there: Take State Route 112 off U.S. 101 about three miles west of Port Angeles and drive west for approximately seven miles to Camp Hayden Road. Turn north (right) to follow Salt Creek downstream.
Facilities: Grocery stores are in nearby Joyce, and all other amenities can be found in Port Angeles.
Contact: Elwha Resort and Cafe, (360) 457-7011.
Species available: Winter steelhead, resident and sea-run cutthroat trout.
Fishing Salt Creek: Although not stocked with hatchery smolts, this tea-colored stream has a self-sustaining wild steelhead run that's healthy enough to provide sport for a few local anglers. They catch about 20 fish from the river during a good season, and only about 10 during a poor year. You probably won't catch any, but feel free to try. Steelheading is allowed only from the mouth of the creek up to the highway bridge.

The 14-inch minimum size limit pretty much eliminates any chance that you might catch a legal resident cutthroat from the creek, but you might find a 14-incher among the sea-run cutts that move in with the first good rains of fall. The section of creek above the highway closes at the end of October and doesn't reopen until June, so be sure to confine your cutthroating to the lower reaches after that.

12. FRESHWATER BAY

Reference: **Strait of Juan de Fuca, between Port Angeles and Joyce; map A1, grid e8.**
How to get there: Drive west from Port Angeles on U.S. 101 about three miles and turn right onto State Route 112, which continues west. After driving just under five miles on State Route 112, turn north (right) onto Freshwater Bay Road and continue 3.5 miles to the bay.
Facilities: Freshwater Bay has a concrete boat ramp, lots of parking, and a couple of rest rooms, but the ramp is high and dry during low tide. The nearest food, gas, lodging, and tackle are in and around Port Angeles.

Contact: Thunderbird Boathouse, (360) 457-4274; Swain's (360) 452-2357. For nautical charts of the Freshwater Bay area, contact Captain's Nautical Supply, (206) 283-7242.

Species available: Chinook, coho, and pink salmon; halibut; lingcod; rockfish; greenling.

Fishing Freshwater Bay (and the Strait of Juan de Fuca west to the Lyre River mouth): This is one of my favorite saltwater fishing spots in the entire Pacific Northwest. But before we talk about the fishing, we should talk a little more about the boat ramp and the people who use it. First, if you arrive at the boat ramp and there are only a few boat trailers in the lot, the fishing is probably slow. That doesn't mean you won't catch fish, but you can expect to work for them. Conversely, if the lot is packed when you get there, fishing is hot, or, at least it was yesterday. As for the ramp itself, it's not a great place to launch big boats. If the tide is out you'll have to back down the ramp and perhaps several hundred feet out into the shallow bay. Even when you get to the water, it will only be inches deep, and after backing into it 50 feet more, it will still only be inches deep. It's best to leave this ramp to the smaller, lighter craft or plan your trip so that you're going in and out on the high tide, which makes for a long day.

Salmon, especially chinooks, are caught in the Freshwater Bay area throughout much of the year, or at least during any time of the year when salmon season is open. Things are changing in that regard from year to year, so be sure you know what's open and what's not before hitting the water. Summertime chinook and coho fishing has been closed here recently. The prime time to fish for chinooks, of course, is during July and August, and Freshwater Bay has a long history of treating anglers well during this two-month period. Most of the action takes place to the west, from Observatory Point (at the western end of the bay) to the mouth of Salt Creek and Crescent Bay, a distance of about three miles. A few anglers troll this stretch, but most drift-mooch plug-cut herring or fish metal jigs such as the Crippled Herring, Point Wilson Dart, or Metzler Mooch-A-Jig. At times the kings might be right up against the kelp, but be willing to experiment and keep an eye on where other anglers are hooking fish.

Jigging and mooching may also take coho here (regulations permitting), but trolling can sometimes be the most effective way of locating and catching these unpredictable fish. Some are caught along with the chinooks near shore, but most of the time you'll have to move out toward the center of the Strait of Juan de Fuca to locate incoming silvers.

Some of Washington's biggest halibut have been hooked between Freshwater Bay and the mouth of the Lyre River, so serious bottomfishing might be in order if you visit the area in spring or summer. The same metal jigs used for chinook salmon will take halibut, or fish a whole herring on a wire spreader with a big cannon-ball sinker.

This section of the Strait also has a few underwater rock piles and pinnacles that might produce a lingcod or two. If you can't locate such structure, try for lings right up against the kelp beds and steep rock bluffs at high tide. Lingcod will sometimes move into these areas with the tide, where you can fool them with a whole herring or, better yet, a small, live greenling. You'll have little trouble catching the "bait" in and around the many kelp beds that line the beach along this entire stretch. These same kelp beds may produce copper, brown, or even black rockfish.

13. PORT ANGELES SALTWATER

Reference: **Strait of Juan de Fuca from Angeles Point to Dungeness Spit; map A1, grid e9.**

How to get there: Take U.S. 101 to Port Angeles and continue straight through to the west end of town rather than turning south on U.S. 101 at the end of the "main drag." Drive right along the water for one mile to the public boat ramp or continue another mile to Ediz Hook.

Facilities: A large public boat ramp is located at the west end of town and two more can be found out on Ediz Hook, the long spit of land that protects the harbor. Lodging, restaurants, and all other amenities are available in Port Angeles.

Contact: Thunderbird Boathouse, (360) 457-4274; Swain's, (360) 452-2357. For nautical charts of the Port Angeles Saltwater area, contact Captain's Nautical Supply, (206) 283-7242.

Species available: Chinook, coho, and pink salmon; Pacific halibut; lingcod rockfish and other bottomfish.

Fishing Port Angeles Salwater: Long a favorite of anglers looking for summertime chinook and coho salmon, Port Angeles no longer offers the wide-open salmon fishery it once had. Coho and chinook season has, in fact, been closed here during the summer recently. But winter and spring fishing remains a good option for resident chinooks, or blackmouth, as they are commonly called. A series of underwater plateaus just outside Ediz Hook, referred to locally as "The Humps," are good places to start looking for these five- to 15-pound salmon, but at times the fishing is better to the east, around the Green Point area. Mooching with whole or plug herring accounts for a lot of fish, but this is the birthplace of jigging for salmon in Washington, and such metal jigs as the Mooch-A-Jig, Crippled Herring, and Deep Stinger can be very productive for Port Angeles chinooks.

During odd-numbered years, the waters around Port Angeles are productive for pink salmon that surge through the Strait of Juan de Fuca on their way toward the rivers of Puget Sound. They seem to funnel down into fairly tight schools as they approach the eastern end of the Strait, and it isn't unusual for Port Angeles anglers to locate a school of fish and catch a limit in an hour or less.

Green Point, mentioned earlier, can provide very good fishing for springtime halibut. Big fish are rare, but one 20-pounder is enough to provide plenty of good eating for the whole family and a fairly good cross section of your neighbors as well. Nearby reefs and rock piles, most notably Coyote Bank to the north, also provide fair to good halibut-fishing opportunities when the season is open.

A favorite place to fish for lingcod and deep-water rockfish is referred to simply as the Rock Pile, and it's located several miles offshore to the north of town. Nautical chart #18465, which covers the eastern end of the Strait of Juan de Fuca and Admiralty Inlet, will help you locate it and also provide insights into other worthwhile fishing spots throughout the area.

14. OZETTE LAKE

Reference: **South of Ozette, west side of Olympic Peninsula; see map A1, grid f2.**

How to get there: Drive west out of Sekiu on State Route 112 and turn south (left) on Hoko-Ozette Road. Drive about 16 miles and turn left on Swan Bay Road to reach the east side of the lake or continue for another four miles to Ozette, at the north end of the lake.

Facilities: Swan Bay has a boat ramp and small park, and a couple of more boat ramps are located near the north end of the lake. A few camp sites are scattered around the lake, most notably at the end of·Erickson Bay, at the northwest corner of the lake. The nearest gas, food, lodging, and tackle are in Sekiu and Clallam Bay.

Contact: Olympic National Park, (360) 452-4501; Olympic Sporting Goods, (360) 374-6330.

Species available: Rainbow and cutthroat trout, kokanee, yellow perch.

Fishing Ozette Lake: You might expect a lake this large located this far out in what some might consider the middle of nowhere to offer excellent fishing, but you'd be wrong. The fishing is fair to good at times, but rarely excellent. Part of the problem might be that few serious anglers take the time to thoroughly investigate the lake's potential and unravel its secrets.

Ozette Lake is impressively large, and because of its location so far off the beaten path, it's a place where you can still find angling solitude. Trolling for kokanee might produce some nice fish for the table, and fall cutthroating could pay off with a trophy-class trout, but Ozette doesn't treat everyone to an easy limit, so don't come here for fast action.

A word of warning: The combination of Ozette Lake's large size, shallow water, and proximity to the open Pacific makes this a bad place to be when the wind starts to pick up. Since most folks who fish here do so in canoes, car-toppers, and other small craft, the five-foot waves that form on Ozette's surface can be deadly. If you boat the lake, be careful and always keep an eye on the weather.

15. LAKE PLEASANT

Reference: **West of Sappho; map A1, grid f4.**

How to get there: Take U.S. 101 north from Forks or west from Port Angeles to Beaver, which is at the west end of the lake. About 1.5 miles east of Beaver, turn north on Lake Pleasant Road, which runs along part of the lake's east side.

Facilities: A boat ramp is located at the west end of the lake. Lake Pleasant Grocery has the minimum daily requirements. Other amenities are available in Forks.

Contact: Lake Pleasant Grocery, (360) 327-3211.

Species available: Cutthroat trout and kokanee.

Fishing Lake Pleasant: Lake Pleasant has a somewhat unusual regulation that would really hack you off if you were fishing for kokanee and caught a monster, that kokanee of a lifetime that would make you an angling legend in your own time. You see, besides an eight-inch minimum size limit, Lake Pleasant has a 20-inch maximum size limit on kokanee, so if you catch a really big one, you have to throw it back. Now, most of the serious kokanee anglers I know are in it for the meat; they love that firm, red flesh of a mature kokanee better than any other fish that swims. Even though they're law-abiding folks, they might have a really hard time releasing a 20-inch kokanee. I guess they should find a place other than Lake Pleasant to con-centrate their kokanee-fishing efforts. Knowing the reason for the regula-tion, though, might make it a little easier to swallow. The lake has a small population of sockeye salmon passing through it every year, and it's impos-sible to tell an ocean-run sockeye from the resident version of the same fish, which we call the kokanee. To protect the larger sockeye while allowing the smaller kokanee to be caught, the Department of Fish and Wildlife simply imposed a 20-inch maximum size limit. The chances of catching a resident kokanee of 20 inches or more are extremely rare, so any larger fish you might land is almost certainly a protected sockeye. Does that help?

Kokanee fishing can be fairly good here, and so can the cutthroat fishing. Trolling is the favorite method of fishing for both. You can get away with fishing fairly shallow in the spring, but as the water warms in summer, you may have to go the leaded-line or downrigger route to stay in the strike zone.

16. BEAVER LAKE

Reference: **North of Highway 101 at Sappho; map A1, grid f4.**
How to get there: Take U.S. 101 to Sappho and turn north on State Route 113. Drive about four miles to the lake, which is alongside the road on the right.
Facilities: Groceries and gas are available in Sappho, but you'll have to go north about 22 miles to Clallam Bay for lodging or camping.
Contact: Lake Pleasant Grocery, (360) 327-3211.
Species available: Cutthroat trout.
Fishing Beaver Lake: Although open year-round and within casting distance of the road, this 40-acre Clallam County lake is fished only by a few local anglers. Most of the people who see it are on their way to or from Neah Bay, Sekiu, and other havens of big-fish opportunity, so Beaver Lake gets little fishing pressure from "tourists." The cutthroat here are small but coopera-tive, and will hit a worm dangling beneath a bobber, a Super Duper, Mepps spinner, Rooster Tail, or most any small, flashy offering you might toss their way. Although I've never seen anyone doing it, Beaver Lake would be a good place to go prospecting with a float tube.

17. LAKE CRESCENT

Reference: **Midway between Port Angeles and Sappho; map A1, grid f7.**
How to get there: Take U.S. 101 north from Forks or west from Port Angeles and you can't miss it. Lake Crescent is that deep, clear lake that's right outside your car window for about 12 miles.

Facilities: Log Cabin Resort is on the north end of the lake and has rental cabins, a fishing dock, a store, and boat rentals. You can reach it by taking East Beach Road at the east end of the lake. Fairholm Resort is at the west end, just off the highway, and offers similar facilities. In the middle, right along the highway, is Crescent Lake Lodge. Gas is available along U.S. 101 between the lake and Port Angeles.

Contact: Log Cabin Resort, (360) 928-3325; Elwha Resort and Cafe, (360) 457-7011; National Park Service, (360) 452-4501.

Species available: Beardslee rainbow trout, Lake Crescent cutthroat trout, kokanee.

Fishing Lake Crescent: It's rare to find a body of water that boasts a unique species of game fish all its own, so the fact that Lake Crescent has two such species is indeed unusual. This 5,000-acre gem near the north end of the Olympic Peninsula is the only place in the world where you can find the Beardslee rainbow and the Lake Crescent cutthroat trout. Both are native to the lake and sustain themselves without any supplemental help in the form of hatchery plants or artificial propagation, and both grow to impressive size. The record Beardslee trout was a 16-pound, five-ounce fish, while the Crescent cutthroat record weighed in at 12 pounds. Fish that size need a big meal, and both species feed heavily on the lake's abundant kokanee.

To catch them, troll large plugs and spoons, using downriggers to take your lures into the 90- to 120-foot range where the fish are most commonly found. As in any trophy fishery, though, don't expect to catch fish every time out; you'll get skunked more often than you'll find success. Although it doesn't happen often, every once in a while someone casting from shore around one of the many creek mouths manages to hook a big Beardslee or cutthroat.

As for the kokanee, they're small but abundant in this cool, clear lake. Trolling accounts for most of them, and when the sun is high on the water, you may have to go nearly as deep for kokanee as you do for the big trout.

18. LAKE SUTHERLAND

Reference: **East of Lake Crescent; map A1, grid f7.**

How to get there: Take U.S. 101 west from Port Angeles and drive about 12 miles to the lake, which is on the south (left) side of the highway.

Facilities: Lake Sutherland has a Department of Fish and Wildlife boat ramp and access area with rest rooms. Small stores and gas stations can be found along U.S. 101, and all amenities are available in Port Angeles.

Contact: Elwha Resort and Cafe, (360) 457-7011.

Species available: Cutthroat and rainbow trout, kokanee.

Fishing Lake Sutherland: It doesn't produce as many trophy-class cutthroats as it used to, but Sutherland is still a place where you can expect to find brightly marked cutts along with the hatchery rainbows stocked here for the catching. Anglers occasionally catch a cutthroat to 20 inches, but eight- to 12-inchers are much more common. Although the lake is open to year-round fishing, most of the 3,000 or so legal-sized rainbows are stocked in March to provide early spring fishing action.

As the trout fishing tapers off in the summer, kokanee fishing improves, and during some years this 370-acre lake provides excellent kokanee catches. Trolling with Wedding Ring spinners or stillfishing with white corn or maggots are good ways to catch them. The lake doesn't have any kind of special bonus limit on kokanee, but it is one of those places where chumming with creamed corn and other "attractants" is legal. The practice, long popular with lake anglers, is illegal on most Washington lakes, but allowed on some of those where kokanee fishing is a big draw.

---

19. ELWHA RIVER
(including Lake Aldwell and Lake Mills)

Reference: **Flows into Strait of Juan de Fuca west of Port Angeles; map A1, grid f8.**

How to get there: Take U.S. 101 west from Port Angeles for about four miles and go right on State Route 112, then right on Elwha River Road after 2.5 miles to reach portions of the lower river. Stay on U.S. 101 for about eight miles from Port Angeles and turn south (left) on Olympic Hot Springs Road to reach upper portions of the river, Lake Aldwell, and Lake Mills.

Facilities: A public access area and boat ramp are located on Lake Aldwell. Elwha Resort and Cafe is right off U.S. 101 and has cabins, RV spaces, tent sites, and other amenities. There are U.S. Forest Service campgrounds on Lake Aldwell, and complete amenities are available in Port Angeles.

Contact: Elwha Resort and Cafe, (360) 457-7011.

Species available: Winter and summer steelhead; coho and chinook salmon; rainbow, cutthroat, and brook trout.

Fishing the Elwha River: Of all the dams built across Northwest rivers and creeks during the past century, few have generated more emotion in recent years than Elwha and Glines Canyon dams, built on the Elwha in 1912 and 1920, respectively, on a little river that at the time was so far back in the sticks that nobody really noticed. It seems that lately everyone has noticed, and "Free the Elwha" has become the battle cry of a broad cross section of folks who would love to see both dams—which were built without any fish-passage facilities or compensation for the fish losses they caused—removed from the river.

Before the dams were built, the Elwha was one of only three rivers used by all eight species of Northwest anadromous fish: chinook, coho, chum, sockeye, and pink salmon; steelhead; sea-run cutthroat trout; and sea-run Dolly Varden. Most impressive of these were the chinooks, since Elwha chinooks sometimes grew to 70, 80, 90, perhaps even 100 pounds. You won't find all eight species here now, at least not in numbers large enough to support a fishery. That race of giant king salmon is gone forever, replaced by hatchery chinooks that are lucky to reach 25 pounds. Likewise, the wild coho and steelhead have also been replaced by hatchery runs, while some species simply don't exist in the river anymore at all.

Still, the Elwha provides some good fishing. Anglers catch several hundred winter steelhead here every season, along with a few dozen summer-run fish. The Lower Elwha Indian Tribe gets first crack at these hatchery steelhead and catches a like number in their gillnets before anglers get a crack at the fish. The same goes for coho salmon, which provide some on-again, off-again fishing when conditions are right in October. That's the only month salmon fishing is permitted here, and anglers are allowed to keep only cohos.

Of the two reservoirs, Lake Aldwell has the most to offer anglers. Selective fishery regulations requiring anglers to use only artificial lures and flies with barbless hooks have been in effect here for several years, and the 12-inch minimum size limit ensures that any trout you decide to take home will be well worth keeping. There are a few cutthroat and brook trout in the lake, but wild rainbows provide most of the fishing opportunity. Fishing is best during the summer and fall, after the chilly water has had some time to warm. Time it right during this period and you might get in on some good evening fly-fishing. The special regulations in effect on Lake Aldwell also apply to the stretch of river between the two reservoirs, and it's a place where both spin-casters and fly-rodders find fair-to-good action on wild rainbows.

Lake Mills may or may not be worth your fishing time, but when you get above the reservoir and back into the free-flowing river, decent trout fishing is once again available. Trails along the river provide most of the access to this upper stretch of the Elwha, which is well within the boundaries of Olympic National Park.

---

20. DICKEY RIVER

Reference: **Northeast of La Push; map A1, grid g2.**
How to get there: Turn west off U.S. 101 onto La Push Road about 1.5 miles north of Forks and turn right on Mora Road to reach the mouth of the river. To fish upper portions of the river, bear right off La Push Road onto Quillayute Road, following it about four miles to Mina Smith Road; turn right and follow it to the river, on the left.
Facilities: Food, gas, lodging, and tackle are available in Forks.
Contact: Olympic Sporting Goods, (360) 374-6330.
Species available: Winter steelhead, sea-run cutthroat trout, chinook and coho salmon.
Fishing the Dickey River: This little river, which runs into the Quillayute about a mile from the Pacific Ocean, is fair for winter steelhead and salmon, and good for sea-run cutthroat in the fall. Although it seldom gives up more than 100 steelhead a season, anglers who fish it in March and April manage to take a fish or two for their efforts. Salmon-fishing regulations have gotten increasingly restrictive, so check the fishing pamphlet carefully before committing to the long drive out to the edge of the state. A good fall rain may bring lots of native cutthroats in from the estuary and provide hot trouting for a day or two.

21. QUILLAYUTE RIVER

Reference: **Enters Pacific Ocean at La Push, west side of Olympic Peninsula; map A1, grid g2.**

How to get there: Take U.S. 101 to the town of Forks and turn west on La Push Road about two miles north of town. Drive eight miles and turn right on Mora Road, which parallels the north side of the Quillayute River.

Facilities: A boat ramp and considerable access to the river can be found at Lyendecker Park, where the Bogachiel and Sol Duc rivers converge to form the Quillayute. Mora Park, farther downstream near the river mouth, also provides access and a rough boat take-out spot. Also nearby is Three Rivers Resort, which offers cabins, RV and tent sites, hot showers, a small store with groceries and tackle, laundry facilities, and a guide service. Food, gas, lodging, tackle, and fishing guides are available in Forks.

Contact: Olympic Sporting Goods, (360) 374-6330; Three Rivers Resort, (360) 374-5300.

Species available: Winter and summer steelhead; coho, chum, spring, and fall chinook salmon; sea-run cutthroat trout.

Fishing the Quillayute River: Though officially only six miles long, the Quillayute is one of the Northwest's busiest salmon and steelhead rivers. That's because every anadromous fish bound for the Bogachiel, Sol Duc, and Calawah rivers has to pass through the Quillayute to get to their respective destinations. Now, if you're one of those calculating types, you're already thinking that stationing yourself somewhere along the Quillayute will put you in perfect position to ambush tens of thousands of salmon and steelhead that will be funneled right past you as they swim upstream. Unfortunately, most of those fish passing by your ambush point will be going like hell, meaning you won't catch many of them. So much for your logical solution to a sticky problem. It's true that fish headed for the productive Quillayute tributaries must pass through the lower end of the system to get wherever they're going, but it's "holding" fish that provide most of the action for freshwater salmon and steelhead anglers, not moving fish, so the Quillayute isn't the hot spot that it might appear to be at first glance.

But the river is still worth fishing. Anglers here pick off their share of winter steelhead beginning in November and continue catching fish right on through April, not in huge numbers but at a better clip than on lots of other streams. Likewise, it's not a red-hot place for summer-run steelhead, but you can catch 'em here if you work at it.

Spring chinook bound for the upstream tributaries are also picked off on the Quillayute, although not in particularly large numbers. The springer fishing may be better when the Sol Duc is low and clear, as it often is in the spring. Under those conditions, the salmon may lie in the Quillayute, waiting for a little rain to raise river levels, presenting anglers a good opportunity to pick them off. Although there's the possibility of hooking a fall chinook the size of a compact car, anglers here catch relatively few of them. Most years, in fact, anglers catch more chum salmon than fall chinook from the Quillayute.

The traditional highlight for fall salmon anglers on the Quillayute has been the annual coho run, but recently the river has been closed to the taking of coho, so don't count on that possibility.

22. SOL DUC RIVER

Reference: **North and west of Forks, flowing into Quillayute River; map A1, grid f3.**

How to get there: Drive west from Port Angeles or north from Hoquiam on U.S. 101, which parallels much of the river and crosses it just north of the town of Forks. Whitcomb Dimmel Road, Clark Road, Sol Duc Valley Road, and others to the east and south of U.S. 101 provide access to the upper river. La Push Road and Quillayute Road will take you to the lower river.

Facilities: Three Rivers Resort has cabins, RV and tent sites, a grocery store with tackle and fishing licenses, a restaurant that serves lunch and dinner, hot showers, a laundry, and a guide service. Other guides, motels, bed and breakfasts, groceries, gas, restaurants, and more services are available in Forks.

Contact: Three Rivers Resort, (360) 374-5300; Olympic Sporting Goods, (360) 374-6330; Forks Chamber of Commerce, (360) 374-2531.

Species available: Winter and summer steelhead; spring and fall chinook, coho, chum, and sockeye salmon; sea-run cutthroat trout.

Fishing the Sol Duc River: While looking over a salmon-catch report from the Washington Department of Fish and Wildlife one day, I made a discovery about the Sol Duc that I had never picked up on while fishing the river or talking to those who fish it a lot more often than I do. While most people come to this famous Olympic Peninsula river to fish for steelhead and coho and chinook salmon, the Sol Duc provides anglers with the possibility of catching all five species of Pacific salmon, plus winter and summer steelhead and sea-run cutthroat trout. It's not that you're likely to hook all eight in a single trip or even a single year, but there's that possibility, which makes the Sol Duc a Northwest rarity.

But, as I said before, most people come here to fish for steelhead and coho and chinook salmon, and that's where the odds are on the Sol Duc. Winter steelheading is the best bet of all, since anglers catch 1,200 to 1,500 of them here each winter. A slow starter, the river isn't too hot in December, but the months of January through April offer excellent possibilities. January and February offer lots of hatchery fish, but by March the late runs of big Sol Duc natives are on the scene, and you stand a reasonable chance of hooking one in the high-teens or even 20 pounds at any time during the month. Big fish remain a possibility through April. Summer-run steelhead aren't stocked here, but the Sol Duc does produce a few dozen per month, beginning in June.

This is the best spring chinook river in the Quillayute system, but low, clear water is more the rule than the exception during the height of the springer runs from April to June. A period of rainy weather during this time may spur some hot chinook fishing, especially if it produces enough water to raise and color the river. Without such conditions, you have to work hard, fish early, and fish late to catch Sol Duc springers. Although difficult to cast and fish with, especially from the bank, herring baits account for a high percentage of the spring chinooks caught here. The normal low water at this time of year not only makes the fish difficult for bank anglers to catch, but makes life miserable for boaters, too, as they bang, clang, and drag their craft through the riffles and rocky stretches of river.

The fall salmon fishery on the river has traditionally been dominated by some good coho fishing that begins as early as August and holds up well into November. Before planning an assault on Sol Duc silvers, though, check the angling regulations, since coho closures have come into play here in recent years.

23. CALAWAH RIVER

Reference: **Flows into the Bogachiel River west of Forks; map A1, grid f4.**
How to get there: Take U.S. 101 north from Aberdeen or west from Port Angeles to Forks and turn east on Forest Road 29 about 1.5 miles north of town to reach the upper Calawah River.
Facilities: Three Rivers Resort has cabins, RV and tent sites, a grocery store with tackle and fishing licenses, a restaurant that serves lunch and dinner, hot showers, a laundry, and a guide service. Klahanie Campground is located about six miles upriver from the highway. Food, gas, lodging, and tackle are available in Forks.
Contact: Olympic Sporting Goods, (360) 374-6330; Three Rivers Resort, (360) 374-5300.
Species available: Winter and summer steelhead, coho salmon.
Fishing the Calawah River: The Calawah isn't a big river, but when it comes to steelhead fishing, it's a reliable one. Thanks to liberal releases of both winter and summer steelie smolts, the Calawah gives up steelhead every month of the year except May. "Why no steelhead in May?" you might ask. "Because it's closed that month," I might answer.

The salmon fishing isn't as productive and certainly doesn't last as long as the steelheading. Coho closures have pretty well knocked the river's main salmon fishery right in the head.

For those of you who like to do your river fishing from a drift boat, don't just throw your boat in the Calawah without doing a little research first. It has a couple of spots that could eat you alive even if you know what you're doing. Check it out first.

24. BOGACHIEL RIVER

Reference: **Follows Clallam-Jefferson county line to join the Sol Duc River west of Forks; map A1, grids g4.**
How to get there: Take U.S. 101 north from Hoquiam or west from Port Angeles and drive to Forks. Turn west at the south end of town to reach Bogachiel Road, which goes to the Bogachiel Rearing Ponds. Turn west off U.S. 101 onto La Push Road about two miles north of town to reach the lower end of the river. To reach upper portions of the river, drive east off U.S. 101 on South Bogachiel Road or turn off the highway at Bogachiel State Park, which is well-marked.

Facilities: Bogachiel State Park has a few tent and RV sites, plus rest rooms, showers, and a boat ramp. Several other boat ramps (some of them not too fancy) are located both upstream and downstream from the highway. Forks has motels, restaurants, grocery stores, gas stations, some rough-and-tumble bars and taverns, and several river-guide businesses.

Contact: Olympic Sporting Goods, (360) 374-6330; Bogachiel State Park, (360) 374-6356.

Species available: Winter steelhead, chinook salmon, sea-run cutthroat trout.

Fishing the Bogachiel River: Although there is an open salmon season on this major tributary to the Quillayute River, winter steelheading is the main reason virtually everyone comes to the "Bogey." As many as 50,000 winter steelhead smolts are released from the Bogachiel Rearing Ponds every year, and when adult fish from those plants return to the river, things really get busy. The most productive months are December and January, and the most productive—and crowded—part of the river during this time is the four-mile stretch from the boat launch at the rearing ponds to the boat launch at the Wilson Access, just off La Push Road. Every weekend during December and January, and especially during the year-end holiday period, there's a steady parade of drift boats through this part of the river. And most of them have fish to show for their efforts. Bank anglers also catch their share of hatchery-bound steelhead along this portion of the river. The best access and most productive fishing is from the rearing ponds downstream to the mouth of the Calawah River, but you won't be the only one who knows about it, so don't bother looking for solitude.

Unlike some Northwest rivers that are heavily stocked with hatchery steelhead, the Bogachiel also provides good fishing later in the winter season, and it stays open through April to accommodate anglers and their late-winter fishery. March and April can be nearly as productive as December and January on the Bogachiel, and the average size of the fish is considerably larger. This is the time of year when the Bogey gives up most of its 15- to 25-pound trophy steelhead. It's also the time to concentrate more effort on the upper sections of the river, above the rearing ponds. Boat ramps and bank-fishing spots upstream from U.S. 101 bridge, including the state park and South Bogachiel Road, get a lot more use in March and April.

25. SEVEN LAKES BASIN

Reference: **Southeast of Sol Duc Hot Springs, near Clallam-Jefferson county line; map A1, grid g7.**

How to get there: Drive west from Port Angeles on U.S. 101 for about eight miles to Olympic Hot Springs Road and turn south (left). Continue driving to Boulder Creek Campground at the end of the road and hike several miles to the lakes. Or take U.S. 101 about 25 miles west from Port Angeles to the west end of Lake Crescent and turn south (left) on Sol Duc Hot Springs Road. Follow the road to the end and hike from two to 12 miles to the various lakes, all of which are on the south side of the trail.

Facilities: Sol Duc Hot Springs Resort has everything from tent sites and RV hookups to cabins with kitchens, a small store, and a restaurant. Just as important to bone-weary hikers and anglers are the tiled hot pools, which may be used for a daily fee even if you aren't staying at the resort. Hot pools are also an attraction if you hike in from Olympic Hot Springs Road. The Olympic Hot Springs aren't fancy, but they're free. All other necessities are available in Port Angeles.

Contact: Sol Duc Hot Springs Resort, (360) 327-3583; Elwha Resort and Cafe, (360) 457-7011.

Species available: Cutthroat and brook trout.

Fishing the Seven Lakes Basin (and other nearby lakes): Although only about 1,000 to 1,500 feet above sea level and not really what most anglers would consider high-country lakes, these small lakes in a forest setting certainly offer the opportunity to get out and stretch your legs before you give your casting arm a workout. About 15 of the lakes are named, and they range in size from about an acre and a half to more than 30 acres, so you should be able to find one that suits you. Sol Duc Lake, about five miles from Sol Duc Hot Springs, is the largest of the bunch.

While most of the lakes require an overnight stay if you want time to fish them more than a few minutes, a few are within reach of day-hikers. Mink Lake is within an hour of Sol Duc Hot Springs by trail, and you could probably make it in to Hidden Lake with enough time to fish and get back. As you might expect, though, the fishing isn't as good in the easily accessible lakes as it is in those that are farther from the roads and farther off the main trails. But even the best of these lakes are only worth fishing if you like to hike and get away from the crowds. If you think a little sweat and a few blisters will ensure hot trout fishing, guess again. Go elsewhere if catching fish is your only priority.

You might do alright, though, if you spend the first and last hours of daylight casting small spinners or bobber-and-fly combinations around the edges of any of these lakes.

---

26. GOODMAN CREEK

Reference: **Flows into Pacific Ocean south of La Push; map A1, grid g3.**

How to get there: Take U.S. 101 north from Hoquiam about 95 miles and turn west (left) just north of the Hoh River bridge on Lower Hoh Road (also known as Oil City Road). Drive five miles and turn north (right) on 3000 Road and follow it to the creek.

Facilities: No facilities are located nearby, but food, gas, lodging, and tackle are available in Forks.

Contact: Olympic Sporting Goods, (360) 374-6330.

Species available: Winter steelhead, sea-run cutthroat trout.

Fishing Goodman Creek: Once a pretty well-kept secret among a few tight-lipped locals, Goodman Creek has become fairly well-known in steelheading circles over the past decade or so. The creek produces only a few dozen steelhead each winter, but it's a place for the small-stream enthusiast to get away from at least most other folks. There's a fair amount of brush and other obstacles in and around it, so a hooked steelhead certainly doesn't always mean a landed steelhead. Although Goodman Creek is now stocked with hatchery smolts, the catch hasn't improved all that much over the time when it was an all-wild steelhead fishery.

27. HOH RIVER

Reference: **Flows into Pacific Ocean north of Kalaloch; map A1, grid h3.**
How to get there: Take U.S. 101 north from Hoquiam or west from Port Angeles. The highway parallels the south side of the river downstream from the Hoh River bridge, where several gravel roads lead to the north, toward the river, or turn west on Lower Hoh Road just north of the bridge to drive down the north side of the river. To reach the upper Hoh, turn east on Upper Hoh Road about two miles north of the bridge.
Facilities: A store and campground are located on the south side of the river just south of the bridge, with another store and campground on the upper river. Both campgrounds have cabins for rent. Motels and other amenities are available in Forks. Several Department of Natural Resources campgrounds are scattered along the river, including Cottonwood Campground on the lower Hoh, and Willoughby, Morgan's Crossing, Spruce Creek, Huelsdonk, and Hoh Rain Forest Campgrounds on the upper river.
Contact: Westward Hoh Resort, (360) 374-6657; Olympic Sporting Goods, (360) 374-6330.
Species available: Winter and summer steelhead, chinook and coho salmon, sea-run cutthroat trout.
Fishing the Hoh River: Liberal plants of more than 100,000 winter steelhead smolts and a self-sustaining run of summer steelhead combine to make the Hoh one of the better coastal steelhead rivers, despite a rather intensive tribal net fishery near the mouth of the river. Anglers typically catch between 1,000 and 2,500 winter-run steelies here annually. March is typically a top month to fish the Hoh, but it may also provide excellent catches from December to April. The river produces its share of bragging-sized fish in the 15- to 20-pound range. The catch of summer steelhead is much smaller, usually 300 to 500 fish, but that's not bad at all when you consider the fact that the Hoh is dirty from glacial runoff on and off throughout much of June, July, and August. That higher, dirtier water, in fact, is part of the reason why the Hoh is one of the area's best summer steelheading spots, since most of the rivers to the north and south are low, clear, and hard to fish during much of the summer.

Salmon fishing can be very good here, especially for chinooks. There are some big spring-run fish in the river when it opens to salmon fishing in May, and it's possible to catch chinook salmon here from that point until September or even early October. While adult chinooks—some of them topping 40 pounds—are the star attraction for salmon anglers, the river sometimes hosts large runs of jack (immature) chinooks, and these one- to eight-pound fish are loads of fun to catch. Like their adult counterparts, they'll inhale a large cluster of salmon roe, a fresh ghost shrimp, or a combination of these two popular baits.

Although many of the big-fish anglers in search of salmon and steelhead ignore it, another summertime high point on the Hoh is the sea-run cutthroat fishery. Sea-runs start trickling into the river in July, and by August the fishing can be quite good. These 10- to 18-inch anadromous trout continue to provide fishing opportunity until November. Like cutthroat trout any-where, they'll take a juicy nightcrawler rolled slowly along the bottom. The Hoh has a number of small log jams, submerged stumps, and overhanging trees in the water to attract sea-run cutthroats. Fish these woody spots and you'll find trout.

Several good bank-fishing spots are available on both sides of the lower Hoh and off the road along the north side of the upper river. There are also a half-dozen decent spots to launch a drift boat, and that's the way many anglers choose to fish this large stream. Several local fishing guides also work the Hoh, most of them out of Forks.

28. KALALOCH SURF

Reference: **Northern Washington coast between Queets and Hoh rivers; map A1, grid h3.**

How to get there: Drive north from Hoquiam for about 65 miles on U.S. 101, cross the Queets River, and start watching for the beach access signs.

Facilities: Kalaloch Lodge has cabins, guest rooms, and a restaurant. Kalaloch Campground has RV and tent sites and rest rooms with showers. The near-est gas, groceries, and tackle are to the north, at the Hoh River.

Contact: Kalaloch Lodge, (360) 962-2271.

Species available: Redtail surfperch, cutthroat trout, sole, flounder.

Fishing the Kalaloch Surf (and the Pacific Ocean surf north to Ruby Beach and south to the mouth of the Queets River): This northern stretch of beach doesn't get as much fishing pressure as other parts of Washington's Pacific Coast throughout much of the year, and the perch fishing can be very good. Standard baits that work elsewhere—pieces of razor clam neck, ghost shrimp, limpets, and pieces of blood worm—will do the job. If the perch aren't bit-ing too well and you want to experiment a little, try fishing around the mouth of Kalaloch Creek or Cedar Creek and see if you can find a sea-run cutthroat trout or maybe a school of starry flounder.

29. CLEARWATER RIVER

Reference: **Flows into Queets River, east of Queets, west side of Olympic Peninsula; map A1, grid h4.**

How to get there: Take U.S. 101 north from Hoquiam about 62 miles and turn north (right) on Clearwater Road, which roughly parallels the river for more than a dozen miles.

Facilities: A rough boat launch is located on the upper river and another is at the confluence of the Clearwater and the Queets, but don't look for much in the way of amenities in this neck of the woods. Food and lodging are avail-able at Kalaloch, 10 miles north on U.S. 101, and all other facilities can be found in Amanda Park, 25 miles south on U.S. 101.

Contact: Clearwater Ranger Station, (360) 962-2283 (daytime hours only).
Species available: Winter steelhead, coho and chinook salmon.
Fishing the Clearwater River: The Clearwater provides fair steelheading all
winter, but if you want to make the most of your trip to this Queets River
tributary that lives up to its name, plan your visit for March. That's when
the bulk of the Clearwater's wild adult steelhead return from the Pacific (it's
not stocked with hatchery smolts). The river gives up maybe 150 winter-
runs during a poor season and as many as 300 during a good year. Those
numbers are pretty puny when compared to some of the bigger, more well-
known rivers along this side of the Olympic Peninsula, but it takes only one
mint-bright, 15-pounder to make for a good day of March steelheading.

As for salmon, the Clearwater has 'em but, like winter steelhead, the
numbers aren't enough to make many folks drop what they're doing and
race to the river. There are a few chinooks to be found, but Clearwater is
mostly an October and November coho fishery with spoons and spinners.

30. QUEETS RIVER

Reference: **Enters Pacific Ocean at Queets, near Jefferson-Grays Harbor
county line; map A1, grid i4.**
How to get there: Take U.S. 101 north from Hoquiam about 60 miles and turn
north (right) on Queets River Road, at the Grays Harbor-Jefferson county
line. Follow the road, which roughly parallels the river, upstream as far as
14 miles.
Facilities: Queets River Campground is at the end of Queets River Road and
has tent spaces with no hookups of any kind. The nearest food and lodging
are in Kalaloch, with all amenities available to the south in Amanda Park.
Contact: Clearwater Ranger Station, (360) 962-2283 (daytime hours only).
Species available: Winter and summer steelhead, chinook and coho salmon,
sea-run cutthroat trout.
Fishing the Queets River: Winter steelheading is the biggest draw at the Queets
River, especially since large numbers of hatchery steelhead smolts started
being planted in the Salmon River (see page 96) back in the 1980s. That's
why most of the winter fishing pressure, both boat and bank, is concentrated
from the mouth of the Salmon downstream. The most popular drift boat trip
is from a large gravel bar about a mile above the Salmon down to the
Clearwater Road bridge, a drift of just over five miles. Three other commonly used boat-launching spots are located above Mud Creek, above
Matheny Creek, and at Queets River Campground at the end of Queets River
Road. These upstream drifts may not produce as many fish, but the chances
of hooking a large, wild steelhead are just as good, and you're not as likely
to see other anglers. There's also some beautiful fishing water and equally
beautiful scenery to be enjoyed. The Queets produces 400 to 1,000 winter
steelhead a year, with January and February providing the biggest numbers.
If you're willing to fish longer and harder for one crack at a big fish, try it in
March or April.

31. SALMON RIVER

Reference: **Flows into Queets River east of Queets; map A1, grid i4.**

How to get there: Drive north from Hoquiam about 60 miles on U.S. 101, turn north (right) on Queets River Road and drive about 1.5 miles to the bridge over the Salmon River.

Facilities: The nearest facilities are in Queets, and they're limited. Amanda Park, several miles to the south, has food, gas, and lodging.

Contact: Clearwater Ranger Station, (360) 962-2283 (daytime hours only).

Species available: Winter steelhead.

Fishing the Salmon River: Generous plants of winter steelhead smolts in recent years have done wonders for the popularity of this little Queets River tributary. As with many other small streams, timing is everything. But if you hit it right, just after a good rain, you can get into some hot small-stream steelheading. If you have just one shot at it, go in January.

---

32. LAKE QUINAULT

Reference: **At Amanda Park; map A1, grid i6.**

How to get there: Take U.S. 101 north from Hoquiam about 38 miles and turn east (right) on South Shore Road before you cross the river at Amanda Park or right on North Shore Road about three miles past Amanda Park.

Facilities: Lodges and campgrounds are located on the south side of the lake and a walk-in campground is on the north side. Food, gas, and tackle are available in nearby Amanda Park.

Contact: Quinault Tribal Office, (360) 276-8211; Quinault Rain Forest Information Center, (360) 288-2644.

Species available: Dolly Varden, cutthroat trout, kokanee.

Fishing Lake Quinault: Grays Harbor County's biggest lake is also one of its most lightly fished, probably because of its location nearly 40 miles north of Hoquiam. It receives a fair amount of fishing pressure during the height of the summertime vacation season, most from anglers who aren't quite sure how to go about fishing it. But you may have it all to yourself during some of the best fishing times of spring and fall.

Quinault is one of the few Northwest lakes where it's legal to catch and keep Dolly Varden char, and several times a year the lake gives up a Dolly in the four- to eight-pound class. Forget the bobber-and-worm rig or whimpy little spoons and spinners if you want big Dollies. Offer them something better suited to their aggressive nature and hearty appetite, such as a large, minnow-imitating wobbling plug or two- to three-inch spoon.

The smaller lures will work okay on the lake's cutthroats, some of which run 17 or 18 inches. If your favorite trolling lure fails to entice them, try a Dick Nite or Canadian Wonder spoon in a nickel/brass finish.

Kokanee fishing can be good here in spring and summer, but many anglers miss out by trolling all over the lake instead of locating schools of fish and working them over. The kokanee may be 60 to 80 feet down, and they simply won't come up to take a lure that goes wobbling by a few feet under the surface. Use a depthsounder to locate the fish and then get down to them by stillfishing or working your trolling lures off a downrigger. A small, cerise Dick Nite is most deadly, but don't tell anyone you heard it here.

Lake Quinault is on the Quinault Indian Reservation, so you need a tribal permit to fish it. The permits, which cost $15 last time I checked, are available at stores and resorts throughout the area.

33. QUINAULT RIVER

Reference: **Flows into Pacific Ocean at Taholah; map A1, grid j5.**

How to get there: To get to the upper Quinault, drive north from Hoquiam on U.S. 101 about 36 miles and turn east (right) on South Shore Road before crossing the river at Amanda Park. Drive along the south side of Lake Quinault to the river.

Facilities: Quinault Indian fishing guides are available out of Taholah, but there isn't much in the way of facilities on the lower river. Amanda Park has food, gas, and other necessities, and there are a couple of major lodges and several camp sites on Lake Quinault.

Contact: Quinault Tribal Office, (360) 276-8211; Quinault Ranger Station, (360) 288-2444.

Species available: Winter steelhead, coho salmon.

Fishing the Quinault River: This is a river with three distinct personalities, depending on what part of it you happen to visit. Unfortunately for anglers who may be looking for simplicity in life, the river also has three different management schemes in effect, each with its own governing body and its own different set of rules and regulations. For the newcomer, the whole thing may be difficult to sort out, or even to understand. To avoid long explanations, let's just say that you're fishing tribal waters on the lower Quinault from Lake Quinault downstream to the Pacific, state waters from the east end of the lake upstream for about 10 miles, and national park waters the rest of the way up to the river's source.

A substantial majority of the winter steelhead caught from this productive river are taken from the lower section, which is entirely within the Quinault Indian Reservation. The Quinaults release as many as half a million hatchery steelhead smolts a year into the lower river, then harvest 5,000 to 15,000 adult steelhead as they return to the river each winter. Anglers can also get in on the action, but they have to hire and fish with a tribal guide in order to get at any of the lower Quinault. The peak of the hatchery returns are in December and January, so those are the months to fish here if you're looking for quantity. But late-winter is better if you want a crack at some of the huge wild steelhead for which the river is still famous. Steelhead of 20 to 25 pounds are caught here every year, and even larger ones are landed now and then.

Those large numbers of hatchery fish never get to the upper Quinault, but anglers still manage to catch a few dozen wild steelhead here each season. Your best shot is in March, but remember that you may fish the upper Quinault's crystal-clear waters for days without a strike, even at that time of year.

Above the park boundary, the river is closed during winter steelhead season, opening only for summer season from late-April to the end of October. Anglers catch a few respectable trout from this stretch of the Quinault every year.

There is a small sport salmon fishery on the Quinault, with most fish caught from the lower river. Again, remember that you can't fish here without an Indian guide. Coho provide most of this fall salmon action, and October is usually the best month.

34. LAKE WYNOOCHEE

Reference: **Olympic National Forest, north of Grisdale; map A1, grid j8.**

How to get there: Take State Route 8 and U.S. 12 west from Olympia about 38 miles, turning north (right) on Wynoochee Road about a mile west of Montesano. Drive way the hell and gone up the road, and about the time you think you're about to fall off the end of the earth, you'll come to the lake, on the left. It's nearly 40 miles from U.S. 12 to Wynoochee Dam.

Facilities: Coho Campground and a boat ramp are located near the dam at the southwest corner of the lake, and two primitive campgrounds (Chetwoot and Tenas) can be reached only by boat or by foot. Fees of $7 to $10 are charged at Coho Campground, but there's no fee for using the primitive campgrounds. There are no stores, gas stations, or lodging facilities near the lake, so bring everything you may need. The nearest food, gas, and tackle are available in Montesano.

Contact: Balcombe's Reel and Rod Service, (360) 249-6282; Olympic National Forest Headquarters, (360) 956-2400.

Species available: Cutthroat trout.

Fishing Lake Wynoochee: Bring your small boat or even a float tube to this impoundment on the upper Wynoochee River to fish it more effectively. Lake Wynoochee is a big reservoir with lots of possibilities. Fishing isn't great, but there are some nice cutthroat trout that will take spoons, spinners, or small wobbling plugs such as Flatfish, Kwikfish, or Hot Shots. If you decide to fish the lake, wait until at least June 1, since it doesn't open until that date, and then stays open through October. Not only does it have a late opener like area streams, but it also has a stream-type catch limit of only two trout per day.

Winter steelheaders find lots of action on the Hoh River, which is among the best steelie rivers on the coast. Fish weighing in at 20 pounds are a definite possibility.

MAP A2

WASHINGTON MAP .... see page 5

Adjoining Maps

NORTH .... no map
EAST (map A3) .... see page 212
SOUTH (map B2) .... see page 366
WEST (map A1) .... see page 70

177 Listings
PAGES 100-211

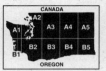

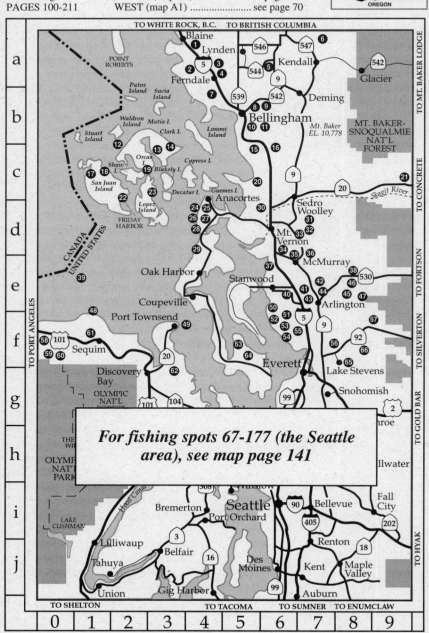

For fishing spots 67-177 (the Seattle area), see map page 141

Map Section A2 features:

1. Dakota Creek
2. Lake Terrell
3. Nooksack River
4. Wiser Lake
5. Fazon Lake
6. Silver Lake
7. Tennant Lake
8. Toad Lake
9. Squalicum Lake
10. Lake Whatcom
11. Lake Padden
12. Northern San Juan Islands
13. Cascade Lake
14. Mountain Lake
15. Lake Samish
16. Cain Lake
17. Egg Lake
18. Sportsman's Lake
19. Killebrew Lake
20. Samish River
21. Grandy Lake
22. Southern San Juan Islands
23. Hummel Lake
24. Heart Lake
25. Whistle Lake
26. Lake Erie
27. Campbell Lake
28. Pass Lake
29. Cranberry Lake
30. Lower Skagit River
31. Clear Lake
32. Beaver Lake
33. Big Lake
34. Lake Ten
35. Lake Sixteen
36. Lake McMurray
37. Ketchum Lake
38. Lake Cavanaugh
39. Banks of the Eastern Strait of Juan de Fuca
40. Sunday Lake
41. Pilchuck Creek
42. Bryant Lake
43. Stillaguamish River
44. Lake Armstrong
45. Ebey (Little) Lake
46. Riley Lake
47. Twin Lakes
48. Dungeness Spit
49. Port Townsend and Admiralty Inlet
50. Martha Lake
51. Lake Ki
52. Lake Howard
53. Lake Goodwin
54. Shoecraft Lake
55. Crabapple Lake
56. Lake Cassidy
57. Canyon Creek
58. Morse Creek
59. Siebert Creek
60. McDonald Creek
61. Dungeness River
62. Anderson Lake
63. Goss Lake
64. Lone Lake
65. Lake Stevens
66. Bosworth Lake
67. Gibbs Lake
68. Peterson Lake
69. Lake Leland
70. Crocker Lake
71. Tarboo Lake
72. Tarboo Creek
73. Sandy Shore Lake
74. Ludlow Lake
75. Teal Lake
76. Buck Lake
77. Deer Lake
78. Lake Serene
79. Stickney Lake
80. Silver Lake
81. Martha Lake
82. Snohomish River
83. Blackman's Lake
84. Flowing Lake
85. Panther Lake
86. Storm Lake
87. Lake Roesiger
88. Chain Lake

89. Wagner (Wagner's) Lake
90. Woods Creek
91. Cochran Lake
92. Skykomish River
93. Little Quilcene River
94. Quilcene River
95. Devil's Lake
96. Lake Ballinger
97. Devil's Lake
98. Echo Lake
99. Fontal Lake
100. Lake Hannan
101. Lake Margaret
102. Lake Joy
103. Lake Constance
104. Dosewallips River
105. Duckabush River
106. Upper Hood Canal
107. Haller Lake
108. Green Lake
109. Cottage Lake
110. Tolt River
111. Langlois Lake
112. Lena Lakes
113. Armstrong Lake
114. Hamma Hamma River
115. Wildcat Lake
116. Kitsap Lake
117. Lake Washington
118. Phantom Lake
119. Lake Sammamish
120. Pine Lake
121. Beaver Lake
122. Snoqualmie River
123. Raging River
124. Lake Alice
125. Tokul Creek
126. Mildred Lakes
127. Elk and Jefferson Lakes
128. Lake Cushman
129. Price (Price's) Lake
130. Melbourne Lake
131. Kokanee Lake
132. Skokomish River
133. Lower Hood Canal
134. Wood and Wildberry
     Lakes
135. Dewatto-Area Lakes
136. Dewatto River
137. Maggie Lake
138. Tahuya River
139. Howell Lake
140. Haven Lake
141. Lake Wooten
142. Twin Lakes
143. Panther Lake
144. Mission Lake
145. Tiger Lake
146. Union River
147. Long Lake
148. Angle Lake
149. Green River
150. Panther Lake
151. Lake Wilderness
152. Shady Lake
153. Lake Desire
154. Otter (Spring) Lake
155. Shadow Lake
156. Lake Meridian
157. Walsh Lake
158. Benson Lake
159. Mason Lake
160. Prickett (Trails End) Lake
161. Devereaux Lake
162. Coulter Creek
163. Wye Lake
164. Carney Lake
165. Horseshoe Lake
166. Crescent Lake
167. Central Puget Sound
168. Lake Fenwick
169. Steel (or Steele) Lake
170. Star Lake
171. Lake Dolloff
172. North Lake
173. Lake Morton
174. Lake Sawyer
175. Ravensdale Lake
176. Lake Twelve
177. Retreat Lake

1. DAKOTA CREEK

Reference: **Flows into Drayton Harbor, southeast of Blaine; see map A2, grid a4.**

How to get there: Take Interstate 5 about 1.5 miles south of Blaine and cross over the mouth of Dakota Creek. After passing over it on I-5, continue a half-mile and exit to the east (right) on Sweet Road, go one mile east, and turn south (right) on Harvey Road. Drive about a half-mile to Hoier Road and turn left; go another half mile and turn right to the creek or continue on to Giles Road, which crosses the creek.

Facilities: All amenities are available in Blaine.

Contact: Wolten's Coast to Coast, (360) 332-4077 (ask for Jerry).

Species available: Cutthroat trout, coho salmon.

Fishing Dakota Creek: Summertime anglers catch a few resident cutthroat at Dakota Creek, and a fall run of sea-run cutthroat also provides some angling action, but the salmon fishery generates the most interest among anglers. As with many small salmon streams, timing is everything, which explains why "tourist" anglers don't account for many of the salmon.

2. LAKE TERRELL

Reference: **West of Ferndale; map A2, grid a3.**

How to get there: Take Interstate 5 to the Ferndale exit and turn west to town. Mountain View Road is the main drag out of town to the west. Follow it for four miles to Lake Terrell Road. Turn right and drive about three-quarters of a mile to the lake.

Facilities: A Department of Fish and Wildlife access area with a boat ramp and public fishing dock is located on the lake. Ferndale has restaurants, motels, gas, tackle, and other necessities.

Contact: Lake Terrell Wildlife Area, (360) 384-4723.

Species available: Largemouth bass, yellow perch, brown bullhead catfish, a few cutthroat trout.

Fishing Lake Terrell: Large, shallow Lake Terrell is ideally suited to warm-water fish, and that's exactly what you'll find here in the greatest abundance. Largemouth bass head the list, and spring and summer bass fishing is excellent, with anglers starting to catch good-sized bass as early as March. The lake has a slot limit to protect fish between 12 and 15 inches long.

This 440-acre lake offers some of western Washington's best perch fishing as well, with enough small fish to keep the kids busy and enough large ones to provide a first-rate fish-fry. Only about 10 feet deep, Terrell warms fast in the spring and can provide good catfish action as early as April. The brown bullheads continue to bite through spring and summer. If you don't have a boat, try fishing for perch and catfish from the public dock.

3. NOOKSACK RIVER

Reference: **Flows into Bellingham Bay, northwest of Bellingham; map A2, grid a5.**

How to get there: To reach the South Fork Nooksack, exit Interstate 5 onto State Route 20 at Burlington and drive six miles east to Sedro Woolley, where you turn north on State Route 9 and drive 14 miles to the river. To reach the North Fork and Middle Fork Nooksack, continue north on State Route 9 to Deming and turn east (right) onto State Route 542. Drive three miles and turn south (right) onto Mosquito Lake Road to reach the Middle Fork, but stay on State Route 542 to reach several good stretches of the North Fork.

Some popular fishing areas on the main Nooksack are within easy driving range of State Route 9 west of Deming. To reach them, follow the above directions to Deming, but turn west (left) on State Route 9 and continue to Everson, where you turn west (left) on Timon Road to Lynden, then continue downstream toward Ferndale. Along the way, about a dozen roads extend to or near the river. Reach the south side of the main river between Ferndale and Everson by driving east out of Ferndale on Paradise Road and turning north on Northwest Drive. Again, several intersecting roads reach the river.

Facilities: Ferndale Campground, about 1.5 miles north of the town of Ferndale, just off Interstate 5, has tent and RV sites and other camping facilities. Scottish Lodge Motel and several bed and breakfasts are also available in Ferndale. Dutch Village Inn, Windmill Inn Motel, and Hidden Village RV Park are among the possibilities in Lynden. Food, gas, restaurants, and tackle are available in Ferndale, Lynden, and the smaller towns along the river.

Contact: Wolten's Coast to Coast, (360) 332-4077 (ask for Jerry); Ferndale Campground, (360) 384-2622.

Species available: Chinook, coho, and chum salmon; winter steelhead; sea-run cutthroat trout.

Fishing the Nooksack River: This vast river system, stretching from northern Skagit County nearly to the Canadian border and from Bellingham Bay to the North Cascades, is a shadow of the once-productive steelhead and salmon river it was a decade or two ago. As recently as 1985 anglers caught more than 1,800 winter-run steelhead from the main Nooksack, but by 1994 the catch had dropped to a dismal 44 fish. The North Fork and South Fork Nooksack contributed only a couple of dozen more winter steelies to that total. For a river system stocked with 50,000 to 80,000 hatchery steelhead smolts every year, those are mighty poor numbers. The bottom line is that whether you choose to plunk the slower waters downstream of Emerson or drift-fish the main stem from Emerson up to and including the North and South forks, steelheading on the Nooksack is a tough proposition. Don't bother.

The same may go for sea-run cutthroat, which once provided excellent angling action. Local anglers do catch a cutthroat here and there throughout the river from September through November, but the harvest-trout fishery certainly isn't worth a long trip from anywhere.

Salmon fishing is a better bet, especially on the main stem of the Nooksack. Boat and bank anglers catch several hundred hatchery coho from the river during September and October each year, a catch that's often comprised of about half adult fish and half one- to two-pound jacks. November and December provide some fairly good chum salmon fishing.

4. WISER LAKE

Reference: **Southwest of Lynden, Whatcom County; map A2, grid a5.**

How to get there: Take Interstate 5 to Ferndale and exit to the east at the golf course onto Axton Road. Drive about four miles to State Route 539, turn north (left), and follow it four miles to the lake.

Facilities: A boat ramp is located at the public access area. Hidden Village RV Park is just south of the lake and has both tent and RV spaces, a laundry, a dump station, and other facilities.

Contact: Hidden Village RV Park, (360) 398-1041; Priced Less Sporting Goods, (360) 855-0895.

Species available: Largemouth bass, yellow perch, brown bullhead catfish, some cutthroat trout.

Fishing Wiser Lake: This popular bass and panfish lake has been known to give up its share of respectable bass. It has a bass slot limit, explained thoroughly in the regulations pamphlet. Perch and catfish (brown bullhead) fishing are also dependable, but you'll have to work hard to catch a trout. The lake has a year-round season and produces fish from late winter to late fall.

5. FAZON LAKE

Reference: **South of Everson, Whatcom County; map A2, grid a6.**

How to get there: Take State Route 542 northeast from Bellingham about four miles to Everson-Goshen Road, turn north (left) and drive four miles to Hemmi Road. Turn right on Hemmi, go one-quarter mile, and turn left to the lake.

Facilities: Fazon Lake has an access area, boat ramp, and rest rooms. Food, gas, and lodging are available in Bellingham.

Contact: Priced Less Sporting Goods, (360) 855-0895.

Species available: Rainbow trout, largemouth bass, channel catfish, bluegills.

Fishing Fazon Lake: The planting of channel catfish here a few years ago added an interesting twist for Fazon Lake anglers. A put-and-take trout fishery is already provided by the annual stocking of about 4,000 hatchery rainbows, and bass do well enough to draw anglers from some distance away. The bluegill fishing is pretty good in the spring and summer. And now channel cats. Anglers are just now figuring out how to catch them, mostly on night crawlers. If you get the hang of it, don't get carried away, since a special, two-fish catfish limit is in effect. That's more than enough for a good catfish dinner, and gives you a good reason to come back to Fazon again.

6. SILVER LAKE

Reference: **North of Maple Falls, Whatcom County; map A2, grid a8.**

How to get there: Take Interstate 5 to Bellingham and turn east on State Route 542, following it about 32 miles to Maple Falls. Turn north (left) on Silver Lake Road and drive about four miles to the lake.

Facilities: A public access area and boat ramp are located on the lake, and a county park provides beach access. The nearest food and gas are in Deming, 15 miles to the south. The nearest motels are way back in Bellingham.

Contact: Silver Lake Park, (360) 599-2776.

Species available: Rainbow, cutthroat, and some brook trout.

Fishing Silver Lake: Of the many Silver Lakes in the Evergreen State, this is the one that's farthest away from everything. Locate it on a map and you might decide that it's too far away for you to bother fishing it, but don't be too hasty. This 175-acre lake near the British Columbia border in northern Whatcom County is a jewel of a trout lake, perhaps one of western Washington's best.

It gets a lot of help, in the form of generous hatchery plants that may top 16,000 legal-sized rainbows prior to the season opener in late-April. As if that wasn't enough, Silver Lake has a self-sustaining population of cutthroat trout, too, and some of those cutts grow to respectable size. If you need more reason to make the long drive to Silver, add brook trout to the menu. They aren't big and they aren't abundant, but they're usually eager, cooperative, and found within casting distance of the bank. Put Silver Lake on your must-do list for spring fishing.

7. TENNANT LAKE

Reference: **Southeast of Ferndale; map A2, grid a4.**

How to get there: Take Interstate 5 to Ferndale and drive south from town on Vista Drive. The lake is directly west of the intersection of Vista Drive and Smith Road.

Facilities: The lake has no facilities, but food, gas, lodging, and supplies are available in and around Ferndale.

Contact: Priced Less Sporting Goods, (360) 855-0895.

Species available: Largemouth bass.

Fishing Tennant Lake: Year-round fishing and fair bass action are the main draws at this 43-acre lake. Since there isn't a developed boat ramp, some anglers fish it in float tubes or small rafts and car-top boats.

8. TOAD LAKE

Reference: **Northeast of Bellingham; map A2, grid b5.**

How to get there: Take Interstate 5 to Bellingham and then take State Route 542 northeast. Just over two miles off the freeway State Route 542 crosses over Squalicum Creek, then passes under some power lines. Take the next right, Toad Lake Road, and then bear left off it to the lake.

Facilities: A public access area with a boat ramp and rest rooms is located on the lake. All other amenities can be found in Bellingham.

Contact: Priced Less Sporting Goods, (360) 855-0895.

Species available: Rainbow trout, kokanee.

Fishing Toad Lake: At less than 30 acres, this lake near the north flank of Squalicum Mountain certainly isn't one of Whatcom County's biggest lakes, but when it comes to trout fishing, it's one of the best. Liberal plants of legal-sized rainbows, to the tune of 5,000 fish, are stocked here before the season opens in April, and the early season catch average is often one of the best in the northern Puget Sound region. As the rainbows begin to disappear, kokanee of eight to 10 inches start to show in the catch.

9. SQUALICUM LAKE

Reference: **Northeast of Bellingham; map A2, grid b5.**

How to get there: Take Interstate 5 to Bellingham and follow State Route 542 northeast out of town. About six miles from Bellingham, you'll come to the end of a two-mile straight-away. As the highway turns left, take the gravel road to the right. If you miss it and go straight, you'll quickly come to Squalicum Lake Road, but it doesn't really go to Squalicum Lake. Go figure.

Facilities: The lake has a public access area and boat ramp, and everything else you'll need is available in Bellingham.

Contact: Priced Less Sporting Goods, (360) 855-0895.

Species available: Cutthroat trout.

Fishing Squalicum Lake: You can fish this 30-acre Whatcom County lake year-round, but you can't fish it with your favorite spinning rod. That's because it's a fly-fishing-only lake. Cutthroat trout provide the action, and some of them grow to impressive dimensions. Spring and fall are the best times to fish the lake, but if you're suffering a severe case of wintertime cabin fever, feel free.

10. LAKE WHATCOM

Reference: **Southeast of Bellingham; map A2, grid b6.**

How to get there: Take Interstate 5 to Bellingham and then take Exit 254 onto Iowa Street. Drive east on Iowa Street about half a mile to Yew Street and turn north (left). Turn east (right) on Alabama Street and drive about a mile to Electric Avenue. Turn south (right) and go a block to the Bloedel Donavan access area and boat ramp.

Facilities: There's a boat ramp at the city park near the north end of the lake and another at the public access area at the south end. All amenities are available in Bellingham.

Contact: Priced Less Sporting Goods, (360) 855-0895.

Species available: Kokanee, cutthroat trout, smallmouth and largemouth bass, yellow perch.

Fishing Lake Whatcom: Smallmouth bass fishing has really taken off in this big, deep lake on the outskirts of Bellingham. It has lots of smallies over two pounds and now and then gives up a smallmouth over five pounds. Although these scrappy fish are found throughout the lake, the best smallmouth fishing often occurs at the north end, from about Geneva Point northward. Crankbaits, a wide variety of plastic grubs and tubes, and even spinnerbaits account for good smallmouth catches. The lake also provides fair fishing for largemouth bass, some of which top the five-pound mark.

Kokanee also draw lots of anglers to Whatcom, and it's easy to understand why. Annual kokanee plants here typically total several million, and the lake has long been used as a source of kokanee fry for other lakes throughout Washington. Trolling with Wedding Ring or Jeweled Bead spinners, Needlefish, or small Dick Nite spoons behind a string of gang trolls is effective, but stillfishing with white corn and other small baits also takes kokanee, which come on strong in late-May and provide good fishing all summer. Those stillfishing benefit from the fact that chumming is allowed here.

Kokanee anglers sometimes hook and land one of the lake's hefty cutthroat trout, some of which top 24 inches. A special regulation allowing anglers to keep only one trout over 14 inches is in effect to protect these trophy cutthroats.

Perch fishing has dropped off somewhat in recent years, but the lake still offers some large ones. Most are caught along the north shore and south end of the lake on worms and nightcrawlers.

---

11. LAKE PADDEN

Reference: **South of Bellingham; map A2, grid b5.**

How to get there: Take the North Samish Way exit off Interstate 5 at Bellingham and follow the road 2.5 miles to the north end of Lake Padden.

Facilities: The lake has a good boat ramp, and a city park provides lots of shoreline access. Food, gas, lodging, tackle, and other facilities are available in Bellingham.

Contact: Priced Less Sporting Goods, (360) 855-0895.

Species available: Rainbow and cutthroat trout, kokanee.

Fishing Lake Padden: Anglers pack a lot of fishing activity into a mere six months of open season on this 150-acre lake at the south end of Bellingham. Lake Padden is the mother lode of rainbow trout just before the season opens, when the Department of Fish and Wildlife dumps something like 17,000 hatchery trout into the confines of the lake. I won't say that only a bozo can keep from catching rainbows once those hungry hatchery clones hit the water, but I might think it to myself. Anyway, the rainbow fishing is good all spring, and the fish run a hefty 11-inch average and weigh about a half-pound apiece.

By June the attention of anglers turns to kokanee fishing, which can be pretty good. Most of the kokanee are smaller than the average rainbow, and fishing for them can be a little more complicated, but if you locate a school of these fine-eating fish and stay with it, you'll do okay. Cutthroats also begin to come alive in June, and anglers catch a few of them throughout the summer and well into fall.

Part of the joy in fishing Lake Padden is that gas-powered motors aren't allowed, so things are a lot more peaceful and quiet than at many of the Northwest's top trout lakes.

12. NORTHERN SAN JUAN ISLANDS

Reference: **Marine waters immediately surrounding Orcas, Stuart, Waldron, Patos, Sucia, Lummi, and the smaller islands comprising the northern half of the San Juan Island group; map A2, grid c2.**

How to get there: Take the ferry from Anacortes to Orcas Island or launch at Anacortes and run west, across Rosario Strait. From the south, run north across the Strait of Juan de Fuca from Sequim or Port Angeles.

Facilities: Marine state parks, motels, resorts, and good restaurants are available on and around Orcas Island. Among the boat ramp possibilities are those at Deer Point, Cascade Bay, West Beach, and Deer Harbor, all on Orcas Island. Moorage options include Doe Island State Park, Rosario, West Sound, West Beach, and Deer Harbor, all on Orcas Island, as well as Jones Island, Stuart Island, Patos Island, Sucia Island, Matia Island, and Clark Island state parks.

Contact: Ace in the Hole Tackle Company, (360) 293-1125; Fish Tales Charters, (360) 293-5766; Washington State Parks and Recreation Commission, (360) 902-8500.

Species available: Chinook, coho, and pink salmon; lingcod; various rockfish and other bottomfish species.

Fishing the northern San Juan Islands: As recently as the mid-1980s, it was still accurate to call the northern San Juans a last frontier of saltwater fishing in the Northwest, but the area was "discovered" in a big way during the 1990s. Getting to the islands by ferry has become more of a waiting game, especially during the summer and on weekends, and much of the area's once-great bottomfishing has been heavily exploited.

Still, this is an interesting and sometimes-productive area to fish. It's one of the few spots where Washington anglers can still find places to fish for salmon throughout the year, and such places are indeed rare. In fact, the chinook fishing can be downright good if you time your trip right. Winter and spring blackmouth fishing can be especially productive along the west side of Waldron Island, the west side of Orcas Island, and the Point Lawrence area on the east side of Orcas Island. Pink salmon fishing during odd-numbered years can be good on the north and east sides of Orcas Island, especially for trollers using flasher-and-squid or flasher-and-spoon combinations.

The slow-growing lingcod and rockfish populations have taken a heavy pounding, but there are still lots of submerged reefs and rock piles that might produce a hefty ling or a good catch of quillback rockfish. Some of the same places also offer a chance at a big, colorful yelloweye rockfish, one of the truly impressive bottomfish species of the Northwest. Open-water reefs north of Waldron Island and around the far-northern islands (Patos, Sucia, and Matia) offer the best bottomfishing, but you might also find a big ling along the edges of the larger islands as well. The rocky shoreline along the west side of Orcas, for example, still gives up a worthwhile lingcod now and then.

To learn more about boating and fishing the northern San Juans, buy a couple of good nautical charts before visiting the area. NOAA nautical chart #18421 provides an overview, but you may also want to get a copy of charts #18430, #18432, #18433, and #18434.

13. CASCADE LAKE

Reference: **Just east of Eastsound on Orcas Island; map A2, grid c3.**

How to get there: Take the ferry from Anacortes to Orcas Island and drive north the town of to Eastsound. From there drive southeast on Orcas-Olga Road about four miles to the lake, which is on the left.

Facilities: Moran State Park offers bank fishing and a boat ramp, as well as a limited number of tent sites. All other amenities are available in Eastsound, including some interesting shops and restaurants.

Contact: Moran State Park, (360) 376-2326.

Species available: Rainbow and cutthroat trout, kokanee.

Fishing Cascade Lake: The combination of hatchery plants and some self-sustaining populations make fishing a worthwhile proposition in this shallow Orcas Island lake. The Department of Fish and Wildlife stocks rainbows here to provide steady fishing action all spring, but there are also cutthroats in the lake to help prolong the fun and excitement into June. By that time, kokanee are on the bite, giving anglers something to do throughout much of the summer. Things get pretty busy around Cascade Lake in the summer, so if you're thinking about catching fish in July and August, plan on hitting the water early or staying well into the evening.

14. MOUNTAIN LAKE

Reference: **Eastern Orcas Island; map A2, grid c3.**

How to get there: Take the ferry from Anacortes to Orcas Island and drive north on Orcas-Olga Road through Eastsound, continuing southeast on Orcas-Olga Road. Drive past Cascade Lake for two miles to Mountain Lake.

Facilities: Moran State Park provides public access and a boat ramp, as well as a few tent sites for campers. Other amenities are available in Eastsound.

Contact: Moran State Park, (360) 376-2326.

Species available: Kokanee, cutthroat and brook trout.

Fishing Mountain Lake: At nearly 200 acres, this is the biggest lake in the San Juans. At more than 100 feet deep, it's also the deepest and coolest, and it provides good fishing opportunity throughout the summer. The lake has a year-round fishing season, but fishing sometimes gets off to a slow start, due at least in part to the lake's cool temperatures. Once it gets going, though, it offers good kokanee fishing. All the usual trolling and stillfishing techniques work for these 10- to 12-inch salmon. If you want trout, try trolling or casting small spoons or spinners around the shallows at the edge of the lake. Fly fishing on a summer evening also pays off here for brookies and cutts, which average about eight inches.

15. LAKE SAMISH

Reference: **Southeast of Bellingham; map A2, grid c5.**

How to get there: Take Interstate 5 to approximately six miles south of Bellingham, where the freeway parallels the east side of the lake for about two miles. Exit 242 takes you to the lake's south end; exit 246 leads to the north end.

Facilities: A public access area and boat ramp are located on the east side of the lake. Food, gas, and tackle are readily available in Bellingham, and there are plenty of accommodations nearby, including bed and breakfasts and motels.

Contact: Priced Less Sporting Goods, (360) 855-0895.

Species available: Cutthroat trout, kokanee, largemouth bass, crappies.

Fishing Lake Samish: This 815-acre lake within easy view of freeway drivers is really two distinctly different lakes connected by a narrow neck of shallow water. The "main lake," except for its large size and the relatively deep hole near its center, is a lot like hundreds of other western Washington lowland lakes, with a gently sloping bottom that provides shallow water for good bass and crappie fishing. Farther out, where the water drops off to 50, 60, even 70 feet or more in a couple of places, kokanee anglers do pretty well in June and July. This section of the lake also has some big cutthroats, which bite best in the fall.

The west end of the lake has a totally different personality. The bottom drops off quickly from the 10-foot shoals where the bridge crosses the narrow channel, and the middle of this "upper lake" has spots nearly 150 feet deep. This deep water stays cool throughout the lake's year-round season, which makes it a worthwhile possibility for kokanee and cutthroats even during the warm days of mid-summer. Lake Samish has some restrictive regulations on cutthroat fishing, so be sure to check the fishing pamphlet for details before you hit it big and find yourself with more trout than you're supposed to have.

16. CAIN LAKE

Reference: **South of Lake Whatcom, on Whatcom-Skagit county line; map A2, grid c6.**

How to get there: Drive about 11 miles north from Burlington on Interstate 5 and take the Alger exit, driving east about a mile to Alger. From Alger, take Cain Lake Road out of town to the west and follow it 3.5 miles to the lake.

Facilities: Cain Lake has a public access area with a boat ramp and toilets. Bellingham, about 10 miles to the northeast, offers the nearest amenities, including lodging and a choice of restaurants.

Contact: Priced Less Sporting Goods, (360) 855-0895.

Species available: Rainbow trout, largemouth bass, yellow perch.

Fishing Cain Lake: Planted rainbows provide good trout fishing at Cain Lake for the first several weeks of the season and again in the fall. Trolling with various lake trolls and worms is the standard plan of attack, but smaller lures and sportier tackle also are effective. Largemouths begin to go on the bite in May, and bass fishing is good throughout the summer. If you like catching and eating perch, Cain has some big ones.

17. EGG LAKE

Reference: **Immediately west of Sportsman's Lake, northwest of Friday Harbor, San Juan Island; map A2, grid c2.**

How to get there: Take the Anacortes ferry to Friday Harbor (San Juan Island), turn right at the top of the hill, and drive northwest on Roche Harbor Road.

About half a mile past Sportsman's Lake, turn left on Egg Lake Road and follow it for about half a mile to the lake.

Facilities: A Department of Fish and Wildlife access area and a boat ramp are located on the west side of the lake. Other amenities can be found in Friday Harbor and Roche Harbor.

Contact: Ace in the Hole Tackle Company, (360) 293-1125.

Species available: Rainbow trout, largemouth bass.

Fishing Egg Lake: The rainbows are planted during the spring, the bass are self-sustaining, and both provide good fishing in this tiny San Juan Island lake. Although covering only seven acres, Egg Lake is a big hit, mainly because it's the island's only consistent trout fishery. There isn't much carry-over from the 1,000 or so hatchery trout stocked here each year, so your chances of catching a big rainbow are fairly slim. The bass fishing turns on early, often by April, and remains fairly good until fall. The lake is open year-round, but if you fish it from October to March, you can expect to have it pretty much to yourself.

---

18. SPORTSMAN'S LAKE

Reference: **Northwest of Friday Harbor, San Juan Island; map A2, grid c2.**

How to get there: Take the Anacortes ferry to Friday Harbor (San Juan Island), turn right at the top of the hill, and drive northwest on Roche Harbor Road. The lake is on the left side of the road, about five miles from Friday Harbor.

Facilities: Sportsman's Lake has a boat ramp and access area, and all other amenities are available in Friday Harbor and Roche Harbor. Prices, however, are on the high side.

Contact: Ace in the Hole Tackle Company, (360) 293-1125.

Species available: Largemouth bass, a few cutthroat trout.

Fishing Sportsman's Lake: This is the best bass-fishing lake in the San Juans, and some anglers think it's one of the best in western Washington. The 65-acre lake is only about 10 feet deep at its deepest point, has lots of brushy cover and weeds around its edges, and grows some pretty impressive largemouths.

Sportsman's Lake is open to year-round fishing, but May to September offer the best fishing for bass. The only problem is that during the warm months the lake is nearly choked with weeds. You'll still catch fish, but use something that's as weedless as possible or you'll lose a lot of tackle. Most Sportsman's Lake regulars gear up for all the vegetation, using 17- to 25-pound line to help turn hooked bass away from the thick tangles.

You might be disappointed if you fish the lake for trout, but persistent casting with a small wobbling spoon or trolling with a Kwikfish or Flatfish might eventually turn up a decent-sized cutthroat. Do your trout fishing in the spring, before the weeds get too thick.

19. KILLEBREW LAKE

Reference: **South end of Orcas Island; map A2, grid c2.**

How to get there: Take the ferry from Anacortes to Orcas Island, turn right as you exit the ferry ramp, and drive east on White Beach Road about 2.5 miles to the lake, which is on the left, immediately west of the Dolphin Bay Road intersection.

Facilities: Orcas has food, fuel, lodging, and other amenities.

Contact: Ace in the Hole Tackle Company, (360) 293-1125.

Species available: Largemouth bass, yellow perch.

Fishing Killebrew Lake: Either fish this small lake from the bank or wade in with your float tube to explore it more thoroughly. At only 13 acres, Killebrew Lake is usually overlooked and only lightly fished. The bass aren't big, but they're fairly abundant. It's a good place to fish a bobber-and-worm for yellow perch.

20. SAMISH RIVER

Reference: **Flows into Samish Bay, west of Sedro Woolley, Skagit County; map A2, grid c6.**

How to get there: To reach the lower Samish River, exit Interstate 5 to the west just north of Burlington and follow State Route 11 about 2.5 miles to Allen West Road. Turn west (left) and drive 1.5 miles to Thomas Road, then turn north (right) and drive half a mile to the river. To fish the upper river, take the Bow Hill Road exit off Interstate 5 and drive east toward the Samish Salmon Hatchery, following Prairie Road up the river. Prairie Road first hits the river three miles east of Interstate 5.

Facilities: A KOA campground is located on the river, about a mile south of the salmon hatchery on Old U.S. 99. The nearest food, gas, lodging, and tackle are in Burlington and Mount Vernon.

Contact: Burlington KOA, (360) 724-5511. Priced Less Sporting Goods, (360) 855-0895.

Species available: Winter steelhead; chinook, coho, and a few chum salmon; sea-run and resident cutthroat trout.

Fishing the Samish River: Although it doesn't get a lot of publicity, fall salmon fishing can be worth a trip to the Samish. Both adult and jack chinooks begin to show in August and provide good fishing through September and into early October. Coho fishing can range from fair to good in October— fair when there aren't many 12- to 18-inch jack cohos in the river and good when the jacks show up. By November the focus of the salmon fishery turns from the last of the jack cohos to the small run of chums that provide only marginal fishing action. Salmon fishing is open only on the lower river, from the mouth to Interstate 5.

Steelheading is a possibility throughout the river. Be sure to check the regulations pamphlet, though, because wild-steelhead-release rules are usually in effect throughout the season. The best steelhead catches here are usually recorded in January, with December and February a toss-up for second-best fishing months.

21. GRANDY LAKE

Reference: **Northeast of Hamilton, Skagit County; map A2, grid c9.**

How to get there: Drive 16 miles east on State Route 20 from Sedro Woolley and turn north on Baker Lake Road about five miles east of Hamilton. Follow Baker Lake Road four miles to Grandy Lake.

Facilities: The lake has a rough boat ramp where small boats may be launched. A private campground is located at the intersection of State Route 20 and Baker Lake Road, about four miles from Grandy Lake. The nearest food, gas, tackle, and lodging are in Hamilton.

Contact: Creekside Camping, (360) 826-3566.

Species available: Cutthroat trout.

Fishing Grandy Lake: Trolling and casting small wobbling spoons or fishing a bobber-and-worm combination will produce trout here for patient anglers. Grandy isn't a big lake, so it's possible to fish it comfortably from a float tube or canoe. May and September are good months to fish the lake, and if I were to visit in September, I'd take along a light-weight fly rod and a selection of small streamer patterns.

22. SOUTHERN SAN JUAN ISLANDS

Reference: **Marine waters immediately surrounding San Juan, Lopez, Shaw, Decatur, Blakely, Cypress, and the smaller islands that comprise the southern half of the San Juan Island group; map A2, grid c2.**

How to get there: Take the ferry from Anacortes to Lopez Island, Shaw Island, or San Juan Island or launch at Anacortes and run west, across Rosario Strait. From the south, run north across the Strait of Juan de Fuca from Sequim or Port Angeles.

Facilities: Boat ramps and/or moorage facilities are located at the north end of Blakely Island; at Spencer Spit, Fisherman Bay, and Odlin County Park on Lopez Island; at Indian Cove and Blind Bay on Shaw Island; and at Friday Harbor, Roche Harbor, and Smuggler's Cove on San Juan Island. Food, gas, lodging, and other amenities are available in Roche Harbor and Friday Harbor.

Contact: Ace in the Hole Tackle Company, (360) 293-1125; Fish Tales Charters, (360) 293-5766.

Species available: Chinook, coho, pink, and sockeye salmon; halibut; lingcod; various rockfish; greenling.

Fishing the southern San Juan Islands: The southern San Juans offer more salmon-fishing opportunities than the northern islands, thanks in part to their proximity to the Strait of Juan de Fuca and the many productive banks near the east end of the strait. Anglers out of Friday and Roche harbors and Shaw and Lopez islands can easily run south to fish Middle, Hein, Salmon, and Eastern banks, often finding good blackmouth, halibut, and lingcod fishing for their efforts. These areas are especially good for salmon in late-winter and spring. May is often the time to fish them for lingcod and halibut.

During odd-numbered years, the Strait is also a good place to fish for pink salmon, which pour through these waters by the hundreds of thousands. August and early September mark the peak of the pink salmon runs, and fishing at that time may be simply a matter of trolling a small herring or flasher-and-hoochie rig near the surface for an hour and going home with your limit. Although tens of thousands of sockeye salmon also pass through the Strait and through some of the major waterways within the islands, anglers catch very few of them. One of these years some inventive salmon angler is going to unlock the key to catching saltwater sockeyes consistently, and then look out!

Closer to the islands, the west side and south end of San Juan Island is a productive salmon-fishing spot in its own right, especially in the summer when adult kings are passing through the area. Such places as Lime Kiln Point, Pile Point, Eagle Point, and Cattle Point give up some husky fish in July and August, and if you time your trip so that you're around during a series of evening flood tides, try jigging or mooching around tiny Goose Island, just inside San Juan Channel from Cattle Point. Winter blackmouth fishing can also be good within the protected waters of the islands. Several points and bays on either side of San Juan Channel are among the favorite spots for this cold-weather salmon fishing.

As for bottomfish, if you don't want to run to Middle Bank or Hein Bank for halibut and/or lingcod, you might find a decent ling or two along the west side of San Juan Island. There are several rocky reefs and steep drop-offs to fish, and all of them have something worthwhile living on, in, or around them. Look closely at NOAA nautical chart #18421 or one of the other San Juan charts and you'll quickly spot other rocky humps that might be worth investigating.

Kelp greenling are readily available along all rocky shorelines and kelp beds, in 10 to 50 feet of water. They'll hit small metal jigs or herring strips.

23. HUMMEL LAKE

Reference: **East of Fisherman Bay, near north end of Lopez Island; map A2, grid c3.**

How to get there: Take the ferry from Anacortes to Lopez Island and drive south from the ferry dock on Ferry Road about two miles to the "T," where you should go left. From there it's about two miles to the lake, which is on the left.

Facilities: The lake has a public access area and boat ramp, and there are tent sites at Spencer Spit State Park, about three miles away. You'll have to boat or ferry to Orcas or Friday Harbor for other necessities.

Contact: Spencer Spit State Park, (360) 468-2551.

Species available: Rainbow trout, largemouth bass, bluegills.

Fishing Hummel Lake: Although open to year-round fishing, Hummel is most productive during the spring and summer. Legal-sized hatchery rainbows provide much of the angling action in May, but by June the bass and blue-gills start providing good fishing. Besides its small size—only 35 acres—Hummel Lake is only about 10 feet deep, which explains why it warms quickly and quits producing trout during summer.

24. HEART LAKE

Reference: **Southwest of Anacortes, map A2, grid d4.**

How to get there: Take Interstate 5 to Burlington, turn west on State Route 20, and drive 18 miles to Anacortes. Drive west through town to 11th Avenue and turn south (left). Follow 11th Avenue to Heart Lake Road, which continues south to the lake, on the right.

Facilities: A boat ramp is located at the public access area, and Anacortes has all the needed amenities.

Contact: Ace in the Hole Tackle, (360) 293-1125.

Species available: Rainbow trout.

Fishing Heart Lake: Fishing is good at Heart Lake for the first several weeks after the April opener, but by summer the action drops off. The hatchery rainbows planted here tend to run a little larger than those stocked in other western Washington lakes, so a May fishing trip to Heart could provide a limit of 10- to 11-inchers. Trolling with small versions of the Dick Nite, McMahon, Triple Teazer, and other small spoons is effective here. Stillfishing is also productive, especially if you use Berkley Power Bait in pink or any of the other hot colors.

25. WHISTLE LAKE

Reference: **South of Anacortes, map A2, grid d4.**

How to get there: Take Interstate 5 to Burlington, turn west on State Route 20 and drive to Anacortes. Turn south (left) as soon as you get into Anacortes and follow the only road that continues south. The lake is about a 1.5 miles out of town.

Facilities: A small access area is located at the north end of the lake. Food, gas, and lodging are available in nearby Anacortes.

Contact: Ace in the Hole Tackle, (360) 293-1125.

Species available: Cutthroat trout, largemouth bass, yellow perch.

Fishing Whistle Lake: You can't drive to the shores of this 30-acre lake south of Anacortes, which is part of its charm. You can, however, carry in a small boat or float tube to help you explore this mixed-species fishery. Cast or troll a small Super Duper or dark-colored Rooster Tail spinner around the edges of the lake for cutthroats, or fish a bobber-and-worm rig to catch both trout and perch. The lake also has a fairly good largemouth bass population, yet another good reason to fish it from a boat, canoe, or float tube. Whistle Lake has a year-round season but produces best from late-spring to fall.

26. LAKE ERIE

Reference: **Southwest of Anacortes, Fidalgo Island; map A2, grid d4.**

How to get there: Take State Route 20 west from Interstate 5 and drive about 13 miles to Dean's Corner. Turn south (left) and drive two miles to Campbell Lake Road. Turn right, drive about 1.5 miles to Rosario Road, and turn left to the lake.

Facilities: The public access area is at the west end of the lake and has a boat ramp and rest rooms. Other amenities are available in Anacortes.

Contact: Ace in the Hole Tackle, (360) 293-1125.

Species available: Rainbow trout.

Fishing Lake Erie: This is one of Skagit County's top trout lakes, especially the first month or so following the late-April season opener. Stocked with legal-sized hatchery rainbows, Lake Erie also offers the very real possibility of larger fish in the 12-inch range. Trolling and stillfishing are both productive here, and you might try fly-casting around the edges of the lake late in the day.

27. CAMPBELL LAKE

Reference: **South of Anacortes, Fidalgo Island; map A2, grid d4.**

How to get there: Take Interstate 5 to Burlington and turn west on State Route 20, driving about 13 miles to Dean's Corner (just past the golf course on the left). Turn south (left) and drive about two miles to the lake. Campbell Lake Road turns west (right) as you approach the north end of the lake.

Facilities: The lake has a public access area with a boat ramp and toilets. Food, gas, lodging, and tackle are available in Anacortes, about four miles to the north.

Contact: Ace in the Hole Tackle, (360) 293-1125.

Species available: Largemouth bass, yellow perch, brown bullhead catfish, rainbow and cutthroat trout.

Fishing Campbell Lake: Sort of a northern version of Cowlitz County's Silver Lake (see page 414), Campbell has a little something for everyone. It's especially popular with bass anglers, who come here to prospect for largemouths that sometimes top seven pounds. This 400-acre Skagit County lake ranks right up there with the best of western Washington's bass producers. It's no slouch when it comes to perch fishing, either, providing some of the county's biggest and best catches of these delectable panfish. Night-fishing during the spring and summer produces good caches of brown bullhead catfish. The lake also offers rainbow and cutthroat trout, although there are certainly better trout-fishing lakes nearby (such as Heart, Erie, and Pass lakes).

28. PASS LAKE

Reference: **Southwest corner of Fidalgo Island, just north of Deception Pass; map A2, grid d4.**

How to get there: Take Interstate 5 to Burlington and turn west on State Route 20, following it about 18 miles toward Deception Pass State Park. The lake is on the north (right) side of the highway, just north of the park.

Facilities: The lake has a public access area with a boat ramp and rest rooms. Nearby Deception Pass State Park has about 60 tent sites that are first-come, first-served. The nearest food, gas, lodging, and tackle are in Anacortes and Oak Harbor.

Contact: Deception Pass State Park, (360) 675-2417; Ace in the Hole Tackle, (360) 293-1125.

Species available: Rainbow, brown, and cutthroat trout; Atlantic salmon.

Fishing Pass Lake: To steal a line from Henry Ford, you can fish Pass Lake any way you want, as long as it's with a fly rod. This pretty 100-acre lake is open year-round to fly-fishing only and produces some beautiful trout. It's also one of western Washington's most popular and productive fly-fishing lakes. Most anglers catch and release their fish, but it's legal to keep one per day, provided it's at least 18 inches long. Some of the rainbows taken here look like mature steelhead, weighing in at five pounds or more. Planting Atlantic salmon in Washington was an experiment that failed in most lakes, but there are some of these large-spotted transplants in Pass Lake, adding to the attractive variety. Gas-powered motors aren't allowed here, and the lake is popular with float-tubers.

29. CRANBERRY LAKE

Reference: **Near northwest tip of Whidbey Island; map A2, grid d4.**

How to get there: Take Interstate 5 to Burlington and turn west on State Route 20, following it west, then south about 20 miles to Deception Pass State Park. Cross the Deception Pass bridge, drive about half a mile, and turn west (right) to the lake.

Facilities: Deception Pass State Park maintains a boat ramp on the north end of the lake and a fishing pier on the east side. The state park has about 60 tent sites, which are available on a first-come, first-served basis. The nearest gas, food, lodging, and tackle are in Anacortes and Oak Harbor.

Contact: Deception Pass State Park, (360) 675-2417.

Species available: Rainbow and some brown trout, largemouth bass, yellow perch, brown bullhead catfish.

Fishing Cranberry Lake: Most anglers come here to fish for hatchery rainbows, but patient types willing to work a little harder for bigger fish also like Cranberry Lake. Carry-over rainbows to 16 or 18 inches keep people coming back for more, and the possibility of catching a brown trout also adds incentive. Fish around the weedy spots near the shallow south end of the lake and there's a good chance of being rewarded with a couple of decent largemouth bass. Fish a bobber-and-worm rig during the day for perch or at night for brown bullheads.

30. LOWER SKAGIT RIVER

Reference: **From Skagit Bay northeast to Concrete; map A2, grid d6.**

How to get there: Take Interstate 5 to Exit 221 and drive west through Conway on Fir Island Road. Turn north (right) on Dike Road or Mann Road to fish the South Fork Skagit or continue west on Fir Island Road to Moore Road and turn north (right) to fish the North Fork. Exit Interstate 5 at Mount Vernon and drive west on Penn Road or State Route 536 to reach the main stem Skagit from the forks upstream to the Interstate 5 bridge. To reach the river upstream of Interstate 5, drive east on State Route 20 from Burlington and turn south (right) onto various roads in and around Sedro Woolley, Lyman, Hamilton, Birdsview, and Concrete.

Facilities: Many boat ramps are located along this stretch of river, including those at Conway (South Fork Skagit), off Moore Road (North Fork Skagit), Edgewater Park (Mount Vernon), Burlington, Sedro Woolley, Lyman Road (between Lyman and Hamilton), Hamilton, and Birdsview. Riverbend RV

Park near Mount Vernon, Riverfront RV Park at Sedro Woolley, and Creekside Camping near Concrete all have tent and RV sites. Mount Vernon, Sedro Woolley, and Concrete all offer motel and bed and breakfast accommodations. Food, gas, and other amenities are also available in all three towns.

Contact: Priced Less Sporting Goods, (360) 855-0895; Sedro Woolley Chamber of Commerce, (360) 855-1841; Creekside Camping, (360) 826-3566.

Species available: Winter and summer steelhead, sea-run cutthroat trout, Dolly Varden, pink and chum salmon.

Fishing the lower Skagit River: Once home to western Washington's most glorious run of summer chinook salmon and the state's top winter steelhead producer, the lower Skagit has gone downhill considerably since the mid-seventies. Still, there's enough angling variety available to make a trip to the Skagit worthwhile if your timing is good.

That famed summer chinook fishery is no longer an option, since anglers may now take only pink and chum salmon from the Skagit; at least that's what the regulations have dictated lately. Pink salmon only show here during odd-numbered years, but when they do they can provide fast action for about five weeks from the middle of August to late-September. Trolling or casting small wobbling spoons and diving plugs in such hot colors as pink, orange, and red are most likely to work on Skagit River pinks, most of which run two to four pounds. Some anglers intercept the pink salmon run when it enters the lower river and work their way upstream with the fish, enjoying hot fishing action several days in a row. Chum salmon enter the Skagit in good numbers every year, providing some hot fishing from about the middle of October through December. November is usually the best month for chums, and anything green or chartreuse is the best lure for these tough fighters.

Despite hatchery plants totaling in the hundreds of thousands, anglers seldom catch as many as 3,000 winter steelhead a year from the Skagit these days. That's not too impressive when compared to the good old days of the sixties, when this big river sometimes gave up as many as 34,000 winter steelies a year and consistently produced sport catches of more than 20,000 steelhead each winter. Still, as they say, on any given day.... The best "given days" often occur in January, February, and March, and during that period fair numbers of fish are caught by plunkers on the lower river, drift-anglers from Sedro Woolley upstream, and boat anglers throughout this entire stretch of the Skagit.

If you want to learn how to fish this long, wide river with lots of secrets, by the way, it's a good idea to hire a guide, at least for the first day. Several fishing guides work out of Mount Vernon, Sedro Woolley, and the smaller towns upriver, and they know more about the Skagit than you could hope to learn on your own over several weeks of experimenting and exploring.

Sea-run cutthroat fishing can be fairly good at times during September and October, especially downstream of Sedro Woolley, and the lower Skagit remains one of few places in Washington where it's still legal to keep a Dolly Varden or two as part of your daily bag limit. Any Dolly you keep, however, must be at least 20 inches long.

31. CLEAR LAKE

Reference: **South of Sedro Woolley; map A2, grid d7.**

How to get there: Exit Interstate 5 just north of Mount Vernon on College Way, which becomes State Route 538, and drive four miles east to State Route 9. Turn north (left) and drive just over three miles to the lake.

Facilities: The lake has a public access area with a boat ramp, as well as a county park that offers some beach-fishing access. The nearest food, gas, lodging, and tackle are in Burlington.

Contact: Lake McMurray Store, (360) 445-3565.

Species available: Rainbow and cutthroat trout, largemouth bass, yellow perch; brown bullhead catfish.

Fishing Clear Lake: Open year-round, Clear Lake offers at least some angling opportunity during all but the dead of winter. Rainbow and cutthroat trout fishing are fair in the spring and fall, and if you work at it, you might find some rainbows through the summer in the 40-foot depths near the southwest corner of the lake. June and July provide some good largemouth bass fishing, especially along the weedy southern shoreline. You can find cooperative yellow perch here almost year-round. If you're into night fishing, Clear Lake offers a pretty good shot at one- to two-pound brown bullheads from about mid-May through September.

32. BEAVER LAKE

Reference: **South of Sedro Woolley; map A2, grid d7.**

How to get there: Take Interstate 5 to just north of Mount Vernon and turn east on College Way (State Route 538). Drive four miles to State Route 9, turn north (left), and drive to Walker Valley Road. Turn right and drive about 1.5 miles to the lake.

Facilities: The Department of Fish and Wildlife maintains a public access area with a boat ramp and toilets on the lake's west side. The nearest stores and facilities are in Mount Vernon and Sedro Woolley.

Contact: Lake McMurray Store, (360) 445-3565.

Species available: Cutthroat trout, largemouth bass, yellow perch, brown bullhead catfish.

Fishing Beaver Lake: Many of the locals refer to this 73-acre lake as Mud Lake, which, although it may have some rather unsavory connotations, at least helps to distinguish it from the dozen or more other Beaver Lakes in Washington. This Beaver (or Mud) Lake contains a fair population of pan-sized cutthroat trout that provide some angling action in the spring and fall. Don't bother looking for a deep spot to try for trout, because you won't find one. The "depths" of Beaver Lake extend to only about 10 feet, and much of it is only five- to seven-feet deep. During the summer, the lake offers good perch fishing and a fair chance for largemouth bass and brown bullheads.

33. BIG LAKE

Reference: **Southeast of Mount Vernon; map A2, grid d7.**

How to get there: Take Interstate 5 to Conway and turn east on State Route 534, following it six miles to State Route 9. Go north on State Route 9 to the lake, or exit Interstate 5 just north of Mount Vernon on College Way (State Route 538), drive four miles, and turn south (right) on State Route 9 to the lake.

Facilities: A state access area and boat ramp are located on the lake. There's also a well-equipped resort on the west side of the lake that offers RV and tent sites, a boat ramp, boat rentals, a store with tackle, and snacks. The resort is open only from spring to early fall. There's a grocery store with tackle and fishing licenses near the north end of the lake.

Contact: Big Lake Resort, (360) 422-5755; Big Lake Grocery, (360) 422-5253.

Species available: Largemouth bass, yellow perch, crappies, brown bullhead catfish, a few cutthroat trout.

Fishing Big Lake: Although open year-round, Big Lake is at its best in spring, summer, and early fall. This large (545 acres), shallow lake warms quickly in the spring, and when it does, the bass, perch, catfish, and crappie fishing really turn on. Well-known for its excellent bass fishing, it's also a great panfish lake, with both perch and crappies growing to worthwhile size. The brown bullheads also get bigger than average here, and they draw lots of anglers to the lake every evening throughout the summer.

Evening and early morning, in fact, are the best times to fish the lake during the warmer months, since it becomes infested with water-skiers and other speed demons during the day. Night-fishing is a productive bass-fishing method here throughout the summer. A typical Big Lake bigmouth is a fish of one to two pounds.

Although not often considered a trout lake, Big Lake does produce a few large cutthroats, most of which make their way here through Lake Creek, which flows into the south end of Big Lake from Lake McMurray.

34. LAKE TEN

Reference: **Southeast of Mount Vernon, Skagit County; map A2, grid d6.**

How to get there: Take Interstate 5 to just north of Mount Vernon and turn east on College Way, which becomes State Route 538. Turn south (right) on State Route 9 and right again on Big Lake Boulevard. Drive one mile to the second right, turn onto the gravel road, and drive another two miles to the end of the gravel road. A hiking trail of about one mile leads to the lake from there.

Facilities: No facilities are available at the lake. The nearest food, gas, lodging, and tackle are in Mount Vernon.

Contact: Lake McMurray Store, (360) 445-3565.

Species available: Rainbow, cutthroat, and brook trout.

Fishing Lake Ten: If the crowds on Clear, Big, McMurray, and some of the larger lakes nearby get to you, try this little hike-in lake midway between the interstate and Big Lake. The short walk and lack of facilities keep most people away, and this pretty, little (16 acres) lake in a hilly, forested setting offers decent fishing at times. A rough trail around the shoreline makes it possible to fish the entire lake in a few hours. Take a float tube along if you really want to get at all the productive spots. A bobber-and-worm or well-cast Super Duper or Rooster Tail will catch all three trout species available here.

35. LAKE SIXTEEN

Reference: **East of Conway, Skagit County; map A2, grid e6.**

How to get there: Take the Conway (State Route 534) exit off Interstate 5 and drive east on State Route 534 about two miles to Lake Sixteen Road. Turn north (left) and drive less than a mile to the lake.

Facilities: The west side of the lake has a Department of Fish and Wildlife access area, a boat ramp, and toilets.

Contact: Lake McMurray Store, (360) 445-3565.

Species available: Rainbow and cutthroat trout.

Fishing Lake Sixteen: Generous plants of legal-sized rainbows help provide about a month of good fishing here after the lake opens in late-April. Summertime fishing is slow, but anglers do manage to catch a few fair-sized cutthroats in June and July. There's usually another short flurry of angling activity on this 40-acre lake in the fall, with both rainbows and cutthroats showing in the catch at that time.

36. LAKE McMURRAY

Reference: **Southeast of Conway, Skagit County; map A2, grid e7.**

How to get there: Drive to Conway on Interstate 5 and exit east on State Route 534, which meets State Route 9 on the west side of the lake, about six miles off Interstate 5.

Facilities: The southeast corner of the lake has an access area and a boat ramp. Parking space is limited, and the place is a mob scene the first few weekends of the season. On the west side of the lake is Lake McMurray Store, which carries tackle, licenses, food, and beverages.

Contact: Lake McMurray Store, (360) 445-3565.

Species available: Rainbow trout, largemouth and some smallmouth bass, black crappies, yellow perch.

Fishing Lake McMurray: This is one of Skagit County's most popular trout lakes, as evidenced by the 15,000 or so legal-sized rainbows stocked here before opening day in late April every year. With spots over 50 feet deep, Lake McMurray stays cool enough to provide fairly good trout fishing well into the summer. The trout catch occasionally includes rainbows to five pounds, and anglers also catch a few trophy-sized cutthroats.

As trout-fishing interest begins to wane, various warm-water species draw increased attention. The lake is famous for its big perch, and crappie fishing can also be good throughout the summer. Although a Department of Fish and Wildlife survey here earlier in the decade failed to turn up any bass, the locals will tell you (often in a whisper) that there are both largemouth and smallmouth bass in the lake, and they sometimes grow to hefty proportions. The 1995 season produced at least one largemouth of eight pounds, so McMurray is capable of growing some dandies.

37. KETCHUM LAKE

Reference: **North of Stanwood; map A2, grid e6.**

How to get there: Exit Interstate 5 onto State Route 532 about three miles north of the Stillaguamish River bridge and head west toward Stanwood about five miles to Prestliens Road. Turn north (right) and drive three miles to Ketchum Lake Road, then turn east (right) to the lake.

Facilities: A boat ramp and access area are located near the south end of the lake. Other amenities are available in Stanwood.

Contact: Stanwood Coast to Coast, (360) 629-3433.

Species available: Rainbow trout, largemouth bass, bluegills, brown bullheads.

Fishing Ketchum Lake: Trout fishing is pretty much a put-and-take proposition in this Snohomish County lake of just under 20 acres. The Department of Fish and Wildlife stocks about 2,000 legal-sized rainbows here each spring, and most of them disappear in fairly short order. Ketchum Lake produces some surprisingly big largemouth bass now and then, and night-fishing for 10- to 12-inch brown bullhead catfish is productive in the spring and summer. This is also a good place to take small kids out for an afternoon of bluegill and pumpkinseed sunfish action; all you need is a can of worms and a bobber. The fish are ready and waiting. All you have to do is get out and ketchum. Sorry, I just had to say it.

38. LAKE CAVANAUGH

Reference: **Northwest of Oso, just north of Skagit-Snohomish county line; map A2, grid e8.**

How to get there: Drive northeast from Arlington on State Route 530 and turn north (left) at Oso on Lake Cavanaugh Road or take the College Way (State Route 538) exit off Interstate 5 near Mount Vernon and drive east to State Route 9. Turn south, drive past Big Lake, and turn east (left) on Lake Cavanaugh Road, following it about 10 miles to the lake.

Facilities: A public access area and boat ramp are located near the east end of the lake, and limited facilities are available in Oso, about four miles away.

Contact: Lake McMurray Store, (360) 445-3565.

Species available: Rainbow, cutthroat, and brook trout; kokanee.

Fishing Lake Cavanaugh: This big, cool lake is open to year-round fishing, but the angling action often gets off to a slow start. You'll catch some rainbows and brookies in May, but June and July are often better. The kokanee and cutthroat don't often come to life before July, and August is often the best month to fish for both. If you're persistent enough to put in the time and effort, you might catch some large cutthroats here. The worst part of fishing Cavanaugh is that the water-skiers and jet skiers come to life about the same time the trout do, which means you may run into lots of competition for space on the water unless you fish early or late in the day. Avoid fishing on the weekends if you can.

39. BANKS OF THE EASTERN STRAIT OF JUAN DE FUCA

Reference: **At the east end of the Strait of Juan de Fuca, north of Sequim, south of Victoria and the San Juan Islands; map A2, grid e1.**

How to get there: Launch at Port Angeles, Sequim, or Port Townsend and run north. Run southwest from Anacortes or south from San Juan Island.

Facilities: Public boat ramps are available in Port Angeles, Sequim, Port Townsend, the west side of Whidbey Island, Anacortes, and the San Juans. These areas also have motels, restaurants, fuel, tackle, and other facilities as well.

Contact: Ace in the Hole Tackle Company, (360) 293-1125; Fish Tales Charters, (360) 293-5766.

Species available: Chinook salmon, Pacific halibut, lingcod, various rockfish and other bottomfish species.

Fishing the Banks of the eastern Strait of Juan de Fuca: The first time I ever took my own boat to Hein Bank, one of the two most well-known banks at the east end of the Strait of Juan de Fuca (along with the Middle Bank), the fishing was beyond slow. It was, in fact, as though my fishing partner and I were exploring some sort of biological desert. We gave it about seven hours of our lives and then returned to Sequim, where we soon discovered that other anglers fishing Hein Bank that day absolutely hammered both chinook salmon and Pacific halibut. It was strange, though, because we hadn't seen any of those other boats that were pulling into the ramp with full fish boxes. By now you might already know where this story is going, but it took us a while to discover that we had followed the wrong course and ended up spending the day not on Hein Bank, but on Eastern Bank, several miles away. Get off course just a little around the east end of the Strait of Juan de Fuca and it could happen to you.

The positive side of all this is that these eastern banks offer several possibilities for the visiting saltwater angler, and if one of the banks happens to be less than generous, a little prospecting on the others may well turn up some hot fishing.

The largest of these underwater plateaus is Middle Bank, which is well-known for its late-winter chinook, springtime lingcod, and spring/summer halibut fishing that can sometimes be quite good. February usually produces some of the best salmon fishing, and the resident blackmouth that come off Middle Bank run on the hefty side. Ten- to 15-pounders are common, which is a whole lot larger than the average blackmouth being caught from Washington waters that time of year. Tidal conditions make it tough for mooching and jigging, but for downrigger anglers it's "foolproof," according to Larry Carpenter, owner of Master Marine in Mount Vernon and one of the area's top salmon anglers.

Although it has been hit hard by lingcod anglers over the past decade or so, Middle Bank still is one of the better places to look for a husky spring ling, especially around the shallow, rocky northwest corner of the bank. Halibut are found farther south, over the sand and gravel bottoms that predominate the bank's central and southern portions. For those who have never been there, Middle Bank lies south of Pile Point, on the south side of San Juan Island, and pretty much due east of Victoria, British Columbia. A small portion of the bank extends across the United States and Canadian border.

Hein Bank, which juts up to within a few feet of the surface about three miles southeast of Middle Bank, has long been a favorite of springtime blackmouth anglers and also has a pretty good reputation as a halibut producer. Halibut catches used to be higher when the season was open in March, but there are enough of them around in April and May to provide a fair chance of hooking one. Both the salmon and halibut come here to feast on candlefish, which congregate on the bank by the millions. For that reason, jigging with a Deep Stinger, Point Wilson Candlefish Dart, or some other metal jig in a candlefish design can be very effective. Mooching with whole or plug-cut herring also works here, though, so if you're not a jigging enthusiast, you can still catch fish off Hein Bank. If you arrive early in the morning and don't catch fish—especially salmon—right off the bat, there's no need to panic. Tide changes usually prompt the best fishing action, so stick with it until the bite comes on. Calm weather is a must for fishing this spot in the middle of the Strait of Juan de Fuca, many miles from the nearest shore. Hein Bank is marked, by the way, with a navigation buoy near its north end.

A little farther to the southeast is Eastern Bank, a large plateau that has a bit of a reputation for providing on-again, off-again salmon and halibut action. When it's good, it can be very good, but when it's bad, forget it. Take it from someone who's been there when it's bad.

East and a little south of Eastern Bank lies Partridge Bank. Located not far off Whidbey Island, a short distance northwest of Partridge Point, this bank is marked with a bell buoy near its south end. A "sometimes" salmon spot, its rocky areas are also known to give up rockfish and lingcod.

Salmon Bank, aptly named for the blackmouth and summer chinook fishing it sometimes provides, is really an extension of the southeast tip of San Juan Island. Marked with a buoy, it's easy to spot when you come out of San Juan Channel and round Cattle Point.

Although not as well-known among anglers as some of the others, McArthur Bank can be a productive spot for lingcod and rockfish. Long and narrow, it runs north and south between the south end of Lopez Island and the northwest corner of the shoal that extends around Smith Island.

The most southeastern of the banks is Dallas Bank, which lies on the north side of Protection Island, a few miles west of Port Townsend. While overshadowed by Mid Channel Bank (see page 124) and other local salmon spots, it sometimes provides good fishing for winter blackmouth. Rockfish, lingcod, and an occasional halibut are other possibilities here.

---

40. SUNDAY LAKE

Reference: **East of Stanwood, map A2, grid e6.**

How to get there: Take Interstate 5 to State Route 532 and drive west to 28th Avenue NW. Turn south (left) and drive less than a mile to the lake.

Facilities: The lake has an undeveloped access area with a rough boat ramp that's suited only to smaller boats. If you're looking for a nice place to stay within five minutes of the lake, try Sunday Lake Bed and Breakfast, 2100 Sunday Lake Road, (360) 629-4356. The nearest food, gas, lodging, and tackle are in Stanwood.

Contact: John's Sporting Goods, (206) 259-3056.

Species available: Largemouth bass, crappies, yellow perch.

Fishing Sunday Lake: So you're looking for a good place to go test that new float tube or the 10-foot plywood boat you just bought at a garage sale for only $50 more than you would have paid for a new one? Sunday Lake is just that sort of place. At only 37 acres, it's small enough to investigate thoroughly in a day, and its limited boat-launching facilities keep most of the big, hot-rod bass boats away. The fact that the lake isn't stocked with trout also helps keep the crowds small. Take along your favorite bass rod or ultralight panfish outfit and you'll have a good time, especially from May to July and again in September.

---

41. PILCHUCK CREEK

Reference: **Flows into the Stillaguamish River near Sylvana; see map A2, grid e7.**

How to get there: To reach the lower section of the creek, exit Interstate 5 onto State Route 530 and drive west, through Sylvana, to Norman Road, which parallels about two miles of Pilchuck Creek. Some of the middle portion of the creek is accessible by taking the State Route 532 exit off Interstate 5 and driving east toward State Route 9. This road crosses the creek midway between Interstate 5 and State Route 9, two miles from the interstate. To reach upper portions of Pilchuck Creek, take State Route 9 north from Arlington and turn east (right) on Grandstrom Road, which parallels the west side of the creek for several miles.

Facilities: Small grocery stores and a few gas stations are in the vicinity of the creek, but little else. The nearest food, gas, tackle, and lodging are in Arlington.

Contact: John's Sporting Goods, (360) 259-3056.

Species available: Winter and summer steelhead, resident and sea-run cutthroat trout.

Fishing Pilchuck Creek: Steelheading is a tough proposition on this little Stillaguamish River tributary. I wouldn't call it a lost cause, but if there's such a thing as one step above the lost cause category, Pilchuck Creek might fit the definition. Despite hatchery plants of winter-run steelies totaling 5,000 to 10,000 fish annually, the creek gives up no more than two dozen fish a year to anglers. January is the top month, but even then it's lousy. Summer steelhead are even harder to catch than winter-runs, and anglers do it only a few times a year. Selective fishery regulations requiring artificial lures with barbless hooks during the summer season don't help matters, but there just aren't that many steelhead available in the first place.

Cutthroat fishing is better, especially when the sea-run cutts move in with the fall rains. Those artificials-only regulations remain in effect, though, during the prime cutthroat-fishing time, so the fishing isn't as good as it might be if it were okay to use nightcrawlers.

42. BRYANT LAKE

Reference: **Northwest of Arlington, Snohomish County; map A2, grid e7.**

How to get there: Take the State Route 530 exit off Interstate 5 and drive four miles east to Arlington and the junction with State Route 9. Turn north on State Route 9, drive three miles, and watch for the wide turn-out on the right side of the road. There's no sign, but if you reach the intersection of 268th Street NE, you've gone about a third of a mile past it. A half-mile trail leads from the highway to the lake.

Facilities: No facilities are available at the lake, but food, gas, and tackle can be found in Arlington.

Contact: Lake McMurray Store, (360) 445-3565; Hook, Line, and Sinker, (360) 435-0885.

Species available: Largemouth bass, crappies, cutthroat trout.

Fishing Bryant Lake: You can fish much of 20-acre Bryant Lake from the bank, but a float tube might be very helpful. The lake is open year-round, but June, July, and September are the best fishing months. Some of the cutthroats are fairly large (over 11 inches), and June bassing can be good for one- to two-pound fish. Arrive at daybreak or stay until dusk and try surface plugs for bass.

---

43. STILLAGUAMISH RIVER

Reference: **Flows into Port Susan west of Arlington, Snohomish County; map A2, grid e7.**

How to get there: Take Interstate 5 to State Route 530 and turn west toward the lower river or east toward Arlington to reach upstream stretches of the river. State Route 530 parallels the North Fork Stillaguamish. To reach the South Fork, drive east on State Route 530 out of Arlington, turn south (right) on Arlington Heights Road, and south (right) again on Jordan Road.

Facilities: Food, gas, tackle, fishing licenses, and one motel (Arlington Motor Inn) are available in Arlington.

Contact: Hook, Line, and Sinker, (360) 435-0885.

Species available: Winter and summer steelhead, chum and pink salmon, sea-run cutthroat trout, Dolly Varden.

Fishing the Stillaguamish River: Can you say "Stillaguamish"? Lots of visitors from other parts of the country can't, but that doesn't keep them from coming here to try their luck on one of western Washington's most famous steelhead streams. The "Stilly" has long been a favorite of both winter and summer steelheaders, and it also offers fair salmon and trout fishing.

The North Fork Stillaguamish is especially famous, having been among the favorites of Zane Grey and his fly-fishing cronies several decades ago. It's still open only to fly-fishing during the summer months, and feather-tossers may catch as many as 500 fish during a good season. July usually produces the best summer-run catches, but you can find summer steelies here throughout the summer and fall. January and February are the top months for winter steelheading on the North Fork Stilly.

The South Fork Stillaguamish also provides both winter and summer steelheading, but on a smaller scale than the North Fork. A year that sees anglers catch 150 summer steelies and 200 winter-runs is a good one on the South Fork.

Sea-run cutthroat fishing used to be a big draw during the fall, but the harvest trout aren't as abundant as they once were. There are, however, some flurries of activity from August to November that provide good cutthroat action.

Only the main river, downstream from Arlington, is open to salmon fishing, and then only for pinks (odd-numbered years) and chums. There are also chinooks and cohos in the river, but they've been off-limits to anglers lately. Pink salmon runs peak in early September, and what there is of a chum run happens during November.

The Stilly, by the way, is another stream where anglers may keep a Dolly Varden if they catch one, provided the fish is at least 20 inches long. Hey, it could happen.

44. LAKE ARMSTRONG

Reference: **North of Arlington; map A2, grid e7.**

How to get there: Take Interstate 5 to State Route 530 and drive east to Arlington. Head north out of town on State Route 9 and turn east (right) on Armstrong Road. Drive about half a mile to the first left and follow the gravel road to the lake.

Facilities: A public access area and boat ramp are located on the lake. Food, gas, lodging, and tackle are available in Arlington.

Contact: Hook, Line, and Sinker, (360) 435-0885; Lake McMurray Store, (360) 445-3565.

Species available: Rainbow and cutthroat trout.

Fishing Lake Armstrong: Most of the rainbows are legal-sized fish planted in the spring, but there is some carry-over and therefore some chance of finding a two-pound rainbow here. The rainbows bite best in April and May, with cutthroat adding a little excitement in May and continuing into the summer. Fall fishing is fair for cutts and a few rainbows. At 30 acres, Armstrong can be fished effectively in a float tube or canoe.

45. EBEY (LITTLE) LAKE

Reference: **Northeast of Arlington; map A2, grid e8.**

How to get there: Exit Interstate 5 onto State Route 530 and drive east through Arlington. Just past Trafton, turn south (right) onto Jim Creek Road and drive just over four miles to the gravel road on the left, which is known locally as Ebey Hill Road. Stay on the main gravel road for about two miles to the new gate, where you have to park and hike the remaining two miles to the short trail that leads to the left off the road. From the start of the trail, it's about 300 yards to the water's edge.

Facilities: The lake has no facilities. The nearest food, gas, lodging, and tackle are in Arlington.

Contact: Hook, Line, and Sinker, (360) 435-0885.
Species available: Rainbow and cutthroat trout.
Fishing Ebey Lake: The newly gated road up Ebey Hill has turned a 300-yard hike into a two-mile hike, but it will probably make the already-good trout fishing even better. Fly-fishing-only regulations have been in effect here for years, and Ebey has long been a favorite among the fly-rod set. The limit is one fish per day, and it must be at least 18 inches long. Although there are certainly a few "legal" 18- to 22-inch rainbows and cutts to be found here, most anglers are content to hook and release several 10- to 16-inchers for their day's efforts.

Part of the fun of fishing Ebey is that feeling that you're in some other part of the world, like maybe Florida's Everglades. Stumps and snags poke their bony heads through the lake's surface around much of the shoreline, adding an eerie sense of mystery to the place.

Although open all year, the lake offers its best fishing from May to September or early October.

46. RILEY LAKE

Reference: **South of Oso, northern Snohomish County; map A2, grid e9.**
How to get there: Take Interstate 5 to State Route 530 and drive east through Arlington. About four miles east of town, turn right to Trafton and stay on the main road, which winds southward and becomes 242nd Street NE. Lake Riley Road splits off to the left about six miles from the highway and leads to the lake.
Facilities: The lake has a public access area with a boat ramp and toilets. The nearest food, gas, tackle, and lodging are in Arlington and Granite Falls.
Contact: Hook, Line, and Sinker, (360) 435-0885.
Species available: Rainbow and cutthroat trout.
Fishing Riley Lake: Spring plants of about 3,000 rainbows a year supplement a self-sustaining population of pan-sized cutthroats in this 30-acre lake near Arlington. Those hatchery fish keep things hopping through May, when the cutthroat action picks up. Trolling with all the usual small spoons and spinners or gang-troll-and-worm combinations will work here during spring and early summer. In the fall, casting or trolling a fly becomes effective, especially during the evening hours.

47. TWIN LAKES

Reference: **North of Granite Falls, Snohomish County; map A2, grid e9.**
How to get there: Drive east from Arlington on State Route 530 and turn south (right) at Trafton on 242nd Street NE (known locally as Jim Creek Road). Follow it about 10 miles east to Jim Creek Naval Radio Station Reservation and the gated access road leading to the lakes.
Facilities: Boat rentals are available at the lakes, but there are few other facilities for civilians. Food, gas, tackle, and lodging are available in both Arlington and Granite Falls.
Contact: Jim Creek Reservation recreation office, (800) 734-1123.

Species available: Rainbow and cutthroat trout.

Fishing Twin Lakes: This paragraph may be moot if the Navy has followed through on its plan to close Twin Lakes to the public. Such a closure appeared likely as this book went to press, but, since public access has been allowed in the past and was still allowed during the 1995 season, I have included them. Regulations in recent years have included check-in and check-out for all anglers, a $2 daily permit requirement, and a $6 daily boat-rental fee (you can't use your own boat). The lakes have been stocked by the Washington Department of Fish and Wildlife and by the Navy, but one must assume that WDF&W will discontinue stocking the lake if public access is no longer allowed. Be sure to call the recreation office at (800) 734-1123 before heading to Twin Lakes.

48. DUNGENESS SPIT

Reference: **Strait of Juan de Fuca, north of Sequim; map A2, grid f2.**

How to get there: By land, take U.S. 101 to Sequim, turn north (right) on Sequim-Dungeness Way, and follow it about 11 miles to the water and public boat ramp. By boat, launch in Sequim Bay and run north about 10 miles to the end of the spit, or launch at Port Angeles and run about 15 miles east.

Facilities: A boat ramp is located on Dungeness Bay, about three miles from the tip of the spit. Food, gas, lodging, and tackle are available in Sequim.

Contact: Thunderbird Boathouse, (360) 457-4274; Sequim Bay State Park, (360) 683-4235.

Species available: Chinook, coho, and pink salmon; halibut; lingcod; rockfish and several species of smaller bottomfish.

Fishing Dungeness Spit: Salmon and bottomfish action at Dungeness Spit has a reputation for being hot one day and cold the next, so most of the fishing pressure is from local anglers who can afford to check it out on a regular basis and go back to doing something else if it happens to be one of those "cold" days. Restrictive salmon-fishing regulations have cut into this fishery much the same as in other areas along the Strait of Juan de Fuca, but when the season is open, chinook fishing can be worthwhile just inside the tip of the spit and on the outside near the bend—known locally as the "Knuckle." Jigging can be especially productive in both spots.

Anglers looking for lingcod and rockfish might want to run about two miles northeast from the tip of the spit to fish the rocky humps lying offshore. Yelloweye, canary, and quillback rockfish are fairly abundant here. There are also several less dramatic humps just to the east of the spit, and these underwater plateaus sometimes produce good catches of halibut.

49. PORT TOWNSEND AND ADMIRALTY INLET

Reference: **West side of Whidbey Island; map A2, grid f3.**

How to get there: Take U.S. 101 to Discovery Bay and turn north on State Route 20, following it 13 miles to Port Townsend, where several boat ramps are available. Or, from the east, launch at any of several ramps on the west side of Whidbey Island to reach the area.

Facilities: On the Port Townsend side of the inlet, boat ramps are located at Fort Worden State Park, Point Hudson, Fort Flagler and Mystery Bay state parks, Oak Bay county ramp, and Mats Mats Bay. Whidbey Island ramps include those at Dave Mackie County Park, Bush Point, Fort Casey State Park, and the Hastie Lake ramp. Fort Worden and Fort Flagler state parks have RV hookups. Fort Casey, Fort Ebey, and Fort Worden state parks all have tent sites. Port Townsend is a popular tourist town with all amenities and more than enough little shops for you to spend all of your money in a single day.

Contact: The Fish In Hole, (360) 385-6829; Fort Worden State Park, (360) 385-4730; Ford Flagler State Park, (360) 385-1259; Fort Ebey State Park, (360) 678-4636. For nautical charts of this area, contact Captain's Nautical Supply, (206) 283-7242

Species available: Chinook, coho, and pink salmon; lingcod; halibut; various rockfish.

Fishing Port Townsend and Admiralty Inlet: Resident chinook salmon provide good winter and spring fishing in several spots here, but the most popular and most productive place is certainly the underwater hump known as Mid Channel Bank. This submerged plateau is also good for summertime kings, but recent closures have taken a large bite out of that fishery. A few anglers troll here for their chinooks, but mooching plug-cut herring and jigging are the two top fishing methods. The Point Wilson Dart jig, developed right here in Port Townsend, is a favorite salmon-getter. Many of the adult salmon returning to Puget Sound rivers in the summer and fall are funneled through the narrow inlet, and they once provided good angling action. Closures on coho and chinook fishing, though, have made things tough. The best recent summer fishing has been for pink salmon that pass through by the tens of thousands in August.

Several spots offer productive bottomfishing. Some halibut and a few lings are caught from the west end of Mid Channel Bank during their respective spring seasons. The rocky humps and kelp beds just west of the Point Wilson Lighthouse can be worth fishing for small rockfish and an occasional lingcod. Partridge Bank, located to the north a short distance offshore from Partridge Point on Whidbey Island, can be a good bet for spring and summer rockfish and springtime lingcod fishing.

---

50. MARTHA LAKE

Reference: **Northwest of Marysville, near Warm Beach; map A2, grid e6.**

How to get there: Take the Smokey Point exit off Interstate 5 north of Marysville, drive west about seven miles on State Route 531. Bear right to Lakewood Road, which runs along the south side of the lake.

Facilities: The lake has a public access area and boat ramp, as well as a resort where anyone hardly ever answers the phone. The nearest food, gas, and lodging are at Smokey Point, and the closest tackle is in Marysville.

Contact: Martha Lake Resort, (360) 652-8412; Lake Goodwin Resort, (360) 652-8169 (just in case).

Species available: Rainbow and cutthroat trout.

Fishing Martha Lake: It's one thing for a state to have several Clear, Blue, or Silver lakes, but this is one of three Martha lakes within a few miles of each other. (The lake near Alderwood Manor in southwestern Snohomish County is described on page 148; the other, just north of Lake Cassidy, isn't fishable.) Although this Martha Lake is open to year-round fishing, the rainbows bite best in the spring. That's no doubt because most of them are stocked here in the spring, and anglers eagerly awaiting their arrival are on hand to take advantage of the situation. This popular 58-acre lake gets about 6,000 legal-sized rainbows every April, and they provide fast action through May. The cutthroats usually come to life about the time the rainbow fishery tapers off, with fishing for cutts at its best in the fall.

51. LAKE KI

Reference: **Northwest of Marysville; map A2, grid f6.**

How to get there: Take Interstate 5 to Smokey Point and turn west on State Route 531, which runs right alongside the north end of the lake.

Facilities: Wenberg State Park is at nearby Lake Goodwin, as are Lake Goodwin Resort and Cedar Grove Resort (see page 133). Lake Ki has a public access area with boat ramp and toilets. Smokey Point and Marysville offer food, gas, lodging, and tackle.

Contact: Lake Goodwin Resort, (360) 652-8169; Wenberg State Park, (360) 652-7417.

Species available: Rainbow trout, largemouth bass, yellow perch.

Fishing Lake Ki: It's easy to understand why this is one of western Snohomish County's most popular fishing lakes. A major highway runs right by it to provide easy access. But more importantly, though less than 100 acres in size, Lake Ki is stocked with as many as 6,000 legal-sized rainbow trout just before the late-April opener every spring. Those planters, some of which weigh in at nearly three-quarters of a pound, provide lots of bent rods and plenty of smiles through May and into early June. Whether you like to troll Ford Fenders and worms or soak Power Bait on the bottom, your technique will probably prove effective if you fish Lake Ki during the first several weeks of the season.

The trout fishing tails off during the summer and makes a little comeback in the fall, but during the time trouting is slow, bass fishing can be very productive. Like many other Snohomish County lakes, this one has a slot limit protecting bass between 12 and 15 inches long. Most anglers release their bass, but if you decide to keep a couple for the table, double-check the fishing pamphlet for details on this special regulation.

52. LAKE HOWARD

Reference: **Northwest of Marysville; map A2, grid f6.**

How to get there: Take Interstate 5 to Smokey Point and turn west on State Route 531. Drive to Lakewood Road, bear right, then turn south (left) on 65th Avenue NW, which goes about a quarter of a mile to the lake.

Facilities: The lake has a public access area and boat ramp, neither of which is too fancy. The nearest amenities are in Smokey Point and Marysville.

Contact: Lake Goodwin Resort, (360) 652-8169.

Species available: Rainbow and cutthroat trout, largemouth bass.

Fishing Lake Howard: This is another little lake that's well-suited to the adventurous angler who wants to get away in a float tube, canoe, or small inflatable and just cast or troll around for the morning. Although Lake Howard does offer a few fairly large cutthroats, they may or may not interrupt your solitude. The lake has a pretty large population of bass, but I don't know of anyone who has ever caught a large one. At least you won't have a lot of water-skiers or big bass boats washing you up into the shoreline weeds.

Lake Howard is open year-round, with April, May, June, and September best for bass. April, May, September, and October are the best trout months.

---

53. LAKE GOODWIN

Reference: **Northwest of Marysville; map A2, grid f6.**

How to get there: Take the Smokey Point exit off Interstate 5 and drive west five miles on State Route 531, then turn south (left) on Lake Goodwin Road to reach the east side of the lake. State Route 531 becomes Lakewood Road at that point, and if you drive past Lake Goodwin Road on Lakewood, you soon come to the north end of the lake. To reach the west side of Lake Goodwin, continue on to 52nd Avenue and turn south (left).

Facilities: Wenberg State Park is on the east side of the lake and has a boat ramp ($3 launch fee), rest rooms, showers, and tent and RV spaces. Lake Goodwin Resort, at the north end of the lake, also has tent and RV sites, as well as a small store with tackle and licenses, propane gas, laundry facilities, and an RV dump station. Cedar Grove Resort, on the west side of the lake, has tent and RV spaces and an RV dump station.

Contact: Wenberg State Park, (360) 652-7417; Lake Goodwin Resort, (360) 652-8169; Cedar Grove Resort, (360) 652-7083.

Species available: Rainbow and cutthroat trout, largemouth and smallmouth bass, crappies, yellow perch.

Fishing Lake Goodwin: This is one of those western Washington lakes with a year-round season that actually offers pretty good fishing the whole time. Most of the rainbows—about 5,000 of them—are planted in the spring, but you can usually find one or two in a cooperative mood even in the fall or winter. Trout can get lost in the depths of this big lake (nearly 550 acres) and not be found by anglers for some time, so you have a decent chance of finding a carry-over rainbow of 16 inches or better here. The cutthroats are also available throughout much of the year, and some of them grow to impressive size, too.

As for warm-water fish, the one-two combination of largemouth and smallmouth bass makes this a popular lake with spring and summer bass anglers, who catch a few largemouths over five pounds and an occasional smallmouth of three pounds or more. Perch fishing is good throughout the year, with fall often best for big ones.

54. SHOECRAFT LAKE

Reference: **Northwest of Marysville; map A2, grid f6.**

How to get there: Exit Interstate 5 at Smokey Point and drive west on State Route 531, which becomes Lakewood Road near the north end of Lake Goodwin. Turn south (left) on 52nd Avenue NW and follow it about 1.5 miles to the lake.

Facilities: Shoecraft Lake has a public access area, a boat ramp, and pit toilets near its southwest corner. Cedar Grove Resort is a mile away on the west side of Lake Goodwin. Lake Goodwin Resort and Wenberg State Park are both within two miles, on Lake Goodwin.

Contact: Cedar Grove Resort (360) 652-7083; Lake Goodwin Resort, (360) 652-8169; Wenberg State Park, (360) 652-7417.

Species available: Rainbow trout, largemouth and smallmouth bass, crappies, yellow perch, brown bullhead catfish.

Fishing Shoecraft Lake: Although stocked with legal-sized hatchery rainbows every spring, this 135-acre lake with a year-round fishing season is better known for its warm-water fish than for its trout. It offers both largemouth and smallmouth bass, which isn't all that common among western Washington lakes. Spring is good for both, with largemouths continuing to bite through the summer.

The perch, catfish, and crappie fishing can be excellent during the spring and summer, too.

55. CRABAPPLE LAKE

Reference: **Northwest of Marysville; map A2, grid f6.**

How to get there: Exit Interstate 5 at Smokey Point and drive west on State Route 531. Turn south (left) on Lake Goodwin Road and go left at the "Y" after passing the state park entrance. Continue about one-third of a mile to the lake, which is on the left.

Facilities: The lake has a rough boat launch and limited access area. Wenberg State Park, half a mile away, has tent and RV spaces, showers, and other facilities. Lake Goodwin Resort, two miles away, has tent and RV sites, showers, and a store that sells tackle, licenses, and some groceries.

Contact: Wenberg State Park, (360) 652-7417; Lake Goodwin Resort, (360) 652-8169.

Species available: Rainbow trout, pumpkinseed sunfish.

Fishing Crabapple Lake: This 35-acre lake half a mile east of Lake Goodwin may be fun to explore in your canoe, car-topper, or float tube, but don't expect too much in the way of fast fishing. Feel free to thin the sunfish population as much as you want, even if it means casting to them with a bobber and half a worm. The strategy might pay off with a trout or two, but the odds are against it.

56. LAKE CASSIDY

Reference: **East of Marysville; map A2, grid f8.**

How to get there: Take Interstate 5 to Everett and turn east on U.S. 2, then north on State Route 204. Turn north again on State Route 9 and drive just over three miles to the sign pointing right to Lake Cassidy.

Facilities: The Department of Fish and Wildlife has a public access area and boat ramp on the west side of the lake, and all other facilities are available in nearby Lake Stevens and Marysville.

Contact: John's Sporting Goods, (206) 259-3056.

Species available: Rainbow trout, largemouth bass, crappies, yellow perch, brown bullhead catfish.

Fishing Lake Cassidy: This 125-acre lake is open to year-round fishing and is popular with both trout and bass anglers. Most of the trout action takes place in April and May, after the Department of Fish and Wildlife has made its annual deposit of about 5,000 legal-sized rainbows. Many of those planters are gone by June, and the trout fishing gets tough after that. Bass fishing, however, takes off in late-May or early June, depending on whether there's ample warm weather to raise water temperatures and spur the largemouths to thoughts of love—or whatever it is bass feel at spawning time. The lake produces some good catches of largemouths that time of year, and decent bass catches continue through the summer. Summertime perch and crappie fishing is also productive, and night fishing produces some good catches of 10- to 14-inch brown bullheads from June through August.

---

57. CANYON CREEK

Reference: **Flows into South Fork Stillaguamish River near Granite Falls; map A2, grid f8.**

How to get there: Drive east from Lake Stevens on State Route 92 for about eight miles to the town of Granite Falls. Take the Mountain Loop Highway north from town and, after crossing the South Fork Stillaguamish at Granite Falls, take any of several roads to the left to reach the lower portion of the creek. To reach upper Canyon Creek, stay on the Mountain Loop Highway for about 6.5 miles to Forest Road 41, turn left, and follow the road upstream about six miles.

Facilities: Mountain View Inn is located on the Mountain View Highway, north of Granite Falls, less than a mile from the creek. Food and gas can be found in the town of Granite Falls.

Contact: Hook, Line, and Sinker, (360) 435-0885; Mountain View Inn, (360) 691-6668.

Species available: Winter and summer steelhead, resident cutthroat trout.

Fishing Canyon Creek: Like so many other Northwest streams that have given way to development and devastating logging practices, Canyon Creek isn't the steelhead producer it used to be. Fish it in July or August and you might find a summer steelhead or two, but the fishing isn't hot. Winter steelheading has been a little better than summer-run fishing lately, but not by much.

A 100-fish winter season is a good one here, and that catch is spread out through December, January, and February. Each winter rain brings thick, dirty water through the creek, making for tough fishing.

58. MORSE CREEK

Reference: **Enters Strait of Juan de Fuca just east of Port Angeles; map A2, grid f0.**

How to get there: Drive west from Sequim on U.S. 101. The highway crosses over the creek a mile west of Deer Park Road, and a gravel road just west of the bridge parallels the creek upstream from the highway.

Facilities: A KOA campground is located about three miles east of the creek on the south side of U.S. 101. Food, gas, lodging, and tackle can be found in and around Port Angeles.

Contact: Swain's, (360) 452-2357; Port Angeles KOA, (360) 457-5916.

Species available: Winter steelhead, sea-run and resident cutthroat trout.

Fishing Morse Creek: This little stream that crosses under Highway 101 just east of Port Angeles may be worth investigating from December through February if you're in the mood for some steelhead fishing and other northern Olympic Peninsula streams are out of shape from too much rain. The Department of Fish and Wildlife plants about 15,000 steelhead smolts here every year, enough to provide at least the possibility of hooking a fish or two for your efforts. Although an occasional summer steelie is taken from the creek, or at least marked as such on the steelhead report cards returned to the WDF&W, this isn't a place you'd want to spend a lot of time fishing specifically for summer-runs.

Resident cutthroat provide some action after Morse Creek opens in early June, and by September a fair number of sea-run cutts are usually available. Sea-run fishing may hold up until steelhead enter the river in December.

59. SIEBERT CREEK

Reference: **Flows into Strait of Juan de Fuca at Green Point, east of Port Angeles; map A2, grid f0.**

How to get there: Drive west from Sequim or east from Port Angeles on U.S. 101 and turn north on Lewis Road, about midway between the two towns, to reach the lower portion of the creek, or turn south on Blue Mountain Road to get to the upper reaches of the creek. Gravel roads to the west (right) at about 3.5 and 4.5 miles provide creek access.

Facilities: Port Angeles KOA is about a mile west of the creek, on the south side of the highway. All other amenities are available in Sequim and Port Angeles.

Contact: Port Angeles KOA, (360) 457-5916; Swain's, (360) 452-2357.

Species available: Resident and sea-run cutthroat trout.

Fishing Siebert Creek: Summertime fishing at Siebert Creek is pretty much a matter of catch-and-release, since few of the creek's resident trout grow to the legal minimum size of 14 inches. Things improve a little in September and October, when a few sea-run cutthroats make their way in from the Strait of Juan de Fuca.

60. McDONALD CREEK

Reference: **Flows into Strait of Juan de Fuca west of Dungeness; map A2, grid f1.**

How to get there: Drive west from Sequim or east from Port Angeles on U.S. 101. Turn south about 5.5 miles west of Sequim on Sherburn Road to fish the upper creek or north on Barr Road to get to the lower section.

Facilities: Port Angeles KOA is about three miles to the west of the creek. All other facilities are available in Sequim, about six miles east.

Contact: Swain's, (360) 452-2357; Port Angeles KOA, (360) 457-5916.

Species available: Resident and sea-run cutthroat trout.

Fishing McDonald Creek: Summertime fishing for resident cutthroat provides mostly catch-and-release action, but persistent anglers manage to hook an occasional trout over the minimum legal size of 14 inches. Some sea-run cutthroats entering in the fall make it a little easier to catch something for the table.

61. DUNGENESS RIVER

Reference: **Enters Strait of Juan de Fuca north of Sequim; map A2, grid f1.**

How to get there: Take U.S. 101 to Sequim and turn north on Sequim Avenue-Dungeness Way, which crosses the river near its mouth. Roads to the left near the river mouth provide access upstream. To reach the upper portion of the Dungeness, drive west from Sequim about 1.5 miles and turn south (left) on River Road.

Facilities: Rainbow's End RV Park is about 1.5 miles west of the river. Sequim Bay State Park, about six miles east, has about two dozen RV sites. Food, gas, tackle, and lodging are available in Sequim and Port Angeles.

Contact: Rainbow's End RV Park, (360) 683-3863; Sequim Bay State Park, (360) 683-4235; Swain's (360) 452-2357.

Species available: Winter and summer steelhead, sea-run cutthroat trout.

Fishing the Dungeness River: Although it contains four species of Pacific salmon, the Dungeness is now open only to fishing for steelhead and trout. Efforts to protect spawning salmon are so serious, in fact, that even the summer steelhead fishery closes at the end of June to protect one of the Northwest's earliest pink salmon runs, which enters the Dungeness in early July. That leaves only the month of June for summer steelhead anglers to try their luck, and they manage to catch two or three dozen steelhead during that time. The winter steelhead season is longer and more productive, with anglers catching as many as 200 fish from November through February. Hatchery steelhead comprise most of the catch, and if you do beach a wild-run fish, you have to release it.

62. ANDERSON LAKE

Reference: **Northwest of Chimacum on the Quimper Peninsula; map A2, grid f3.**

How to get there: Take U.S. 101 to the south end of Discovery Bay, turn east on State Route 20, and drive about four miles to Anderson Lake Road, where you turn east (right). Follow Anderson Lake Road about 1.5 miles to the lake, which is on the left.

Facilities: Anderson Lake State Park is a day-use park with no camping facilities, but it has rest rooms and a boat ramps that's suitable for car-toppers and small trailer boats. The nearest food, gas, lodging, and tackle are available in Discovery Bay and Port Townsend.

Contact: Anderson Lake State Park, (360) 385-4730.

Species available: Rainbow trout.

Fishing Anderson Lake: This 70-acre lake ranks right up there with the best trout lakes in Washington. It's one of few western Washington lakes that's planted with fingerling trout rather than legal-sized fish, and by opening day of the following year, these little guys have grown to a respectable 12 inches. A fairly large percentage of those 12-inchers aren't caught and carry-over a second winter, which is why Anderson produces above-average numbers of two to three-pound rainbows every season.

Some rather unusual regulations help get those first-year fish through their first season. The lake opens in late-April with typical trout-fishing regulations, meaning it's okay to use bait and okay to use barbed hooks. But on September 1, selective fishery regulations go into effect, so bait and barbed hooks are out. This allows anglers to catch and release all those eager little fingerlings without ripping their entrails out, which means more trout survive until the season closes at the end of October.

---

63. GOSS LAKE

Reference: Whidbey Island, northeast of Freeland, map A2, grid f5.

How to get there: Take the ferry from Mukilteo to Clinton and drive northwest on State Route 525 about 10 miles to Freeland. Turn north (right) on East Harbor Road and east (right) on Goss Lake Road. Goss Lake is about 1.5 miles away, on the right.

Facilities: A public access area and boat ramp are located on the east side of the lake. Clinton has food, gas, lodging, and tackle.

Contact: John's Sporting Goods, (206) 259-3056; Ted's Sports Center, (206) 743-9505.

Species available: Rainbow and cutthroat trout.

Fishing Goss Lake: The Department of Fish and Wildlife stocks about 5,000 legal-sized rainbows here just before the opener every spring, but the lake also has a pretty good population of cutthroats to provide angling variety. Unlike nearby Lone Lake (see page 139), Goss is fairly deep, with some holes near the west side reaching down 60 feet or more, which means the trout fishing holds up fairly well during the summer.

Trolling is good in spring and fall, but you may have to anchor up and try stillfishing near the middle of the lake or along the west side from June through August.

64. LONE LAKE

Reference: **Whidbey Island, east of Freeland; map A2, grid f5.**

How to get there: Take the ferry from Mukilteo to Clinton and then take State Route 525 about seven miles northwest to Bayview Road, where you should turn north (right). Drive just under two miles to Andreason Road, turn west (left), and drive half a mile to Lone Lake Road which leads south to the lake's access area.

Facilities: The lake has a Washington Department of Fish and Wildlife access area, a boat ramp, and rest rooms at its north end. The nearest amenities are in Clinton.

Contact: John's Sporting Goods, (206) 259-3056; Ted's Sports Center, (206) 743-9505.

Species available: Rainbow trout.

Fishing Lone Lake: Open year-round, this 90-acre Whidbey Island lake is a fair bet for spring and fall trout fishing. It's stocked with legal-sized rainbows in the spring, but the catch in April and May includes a pretty good mix of carry-overs that may run as large as 18 inches and weigh more than two pounds. The lake's maximum depth is only about 15 feet, shallow even by western Washington standards, which explains why summertime fishing is a pretty tough proposition.

---

65. LAKE STEVENS

Reference: **At the town of Lake Stevens, east of Everett: map A2, grid f8.**

How to get there: Take Interstate 5 to Everett and turn east on U.S. 2. Turn north on State Route 204 and follow it about three miles to the lake.

Facilities: The Department of Fish and Wildlife maintains an access area with a good boat ramp on the east side of the lake, and there's also a county park on the west side with a launch ramp and fishing dock. Food, gas, lodging, and all other amenities are plentiful throughout the area.

Contact: John's Sporting Goods, (206) 259-3056.

Species available: Rainbow and cutthroat trout, kokanee, largemouth and smallmouth bass, crappies, yellow perch.

Fishing Lake Stevens: Even though it covers more than 1,000 acres and offers some kind of fishing action 12 months out of the year, Lake Stevens doesn't get the publicity or recognition it deserves. Like many year-round lakes, it plays second fiddle to the area's many prime April-to-October trout lakes. It's really a gold mine of fishing opportunity that most anglers overlook.

Summertime kokanee fishing can be especially good, whether you prefer to catch these little landlocked sockeye salmon with trolling gear or stillfishing rigs. If you stillfish, this is one of relatively few Washington lakes where it's still legal to chum with creamed corn or other baits to attract kokanee to your hooks.

Don't be too surprised if your kokanee-fishing efforts draw the attention of an occasional rainbow or cutthroat trout. If you want to fish specifically for trout—and the lake has some big ones—try the time-proven lake trolls with worms or troll a Triple Teazer, Dick Nite, Flatfish, or Kwikfish behind a quarter-ounce trolling sinker that will help take the lure down a few feet beneath the surface. Some of the best trout action occurs from March through May and September to mid-November.

Lake Stevens does have a fairly good reputation for its largemouth bass fishing, and it usually comes through with a few fish in the six- to eight-pound range every summer. Although most serious bass anglers release their catch, it's okay to keep one bass a day, provided it's at least 18 inches long. Smallmouth bass are also available in fairly good numbers, and that alone should make this lake more popular with western Washington anglers.

Perch fishing is a decent bet throughout the year, with the lake giving up its share of perch in the foot-long range. Crappie fishing is best in the spring and fall.

66. BOSWORTH LAKE

Reference: **South of Granite Falls, Snohomish County; map A2, grid f8.**
How to get there: Take Interstate 5 to Everett and exit east on U.S. 2, then turn north on State Route 204 and cross State Route 9 to Lake Stevens. Drive northwest from Lake Stevens toward Granite Falls on State Route 92. Turn south on Ray Gray Road just west of Granite Falls and south again on Robe-Menzel Road, following it two miles to Utley Road. Turn right and drive about a mile to the lake, which is on the right.
Facilities: A Department of Fish and Wildlife access area on the lake has a boat ramp and toilets. Food, gas, and lodging can be found in Granite Falls.
Contact: John's Sporting Goods, (206) 259-3056.
Species available: Rainbow and cutthroat trout, largemouth bass.
Fishing Bosworth Lake: Don't fish 95-acre Bosworth Lake the first couple weeks of the season unless you like lots of company. This is one of the most popular of Snohomish County's several dozen productive trout lakes, thanks to heavy plants of hatchery rainbows. Most of those planters are standard-issue eight-inchers, but the Department of Fish and Wildlife includes enough half-pounders to keep it interesting. Cutthroats are scarce, but you might find one here and there as you catch rainbows in the spring and early summer. Fall fishing is best for cutts, but because they aren't as abundant as rainbows, few anglers target them. A growing bass population in the lake has added some variety to what has traditionally been considered a trout-only fishery, so summer sees somewhat of a change in emphasis from trout to bass fishing.

67. GIBBS LAKE

Reference: **Southeast of Discovery Bay, Jefferson County; map A2 inset, grid g3.**
How to get there: Drive to Quilcene on U.S. 101, turn onto Chimacum Road, and head northeast. Turn west (left) onto Eaglemont Road about two miles after crossing State Route 104. Drive about a quarter of a mile and turn north (right) on West Valley Road. Continue about 1.5 miles to Gibbs Lake Road and turn west (left). Gibbs Lake Road runs right alongside the lake.

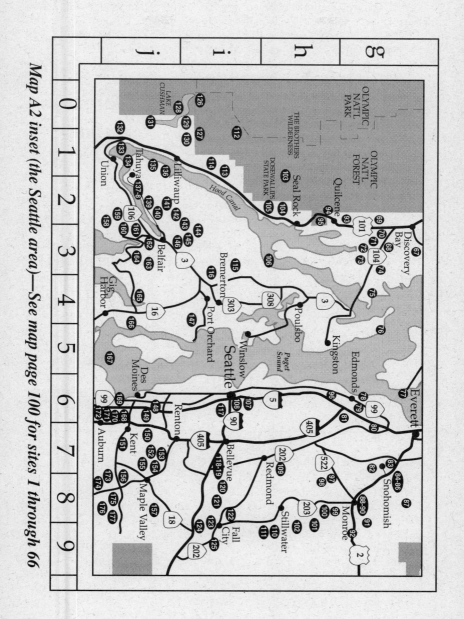

Map A2 inset (the Seattle area)—See map page 100 for sites 1 through 66

Facilities: The lake has no access area or other facilities. Food, gas, lodging, and tackle are available in Discovery Bay and Quilcene.

Contact: The Fish In Hole, (360) 385-7031; Maple Grove Motel, (360) 765-3410; Quilcene Hotel, (360) 765-3447.

Species available: Cutthroat trout, brown bullhead catfish.

Fishing Gibbs Lake: This is another lake that's better suited to getting away from the rat race than it is to catching lots of fish. You'll probably have it to yourself except for the occasional passing car, and you might even catch a decent trout. Night fishing with nightcrawlers will produce a few 10- to 14-inch catfish.

One word of caution, especially if you decide to fish on a Friday or Saturday evening: Gibbs is somewhat of a party spot for the local kids. If the boom boxes get too loud, the noise could scare the fish. The noise may also make you want to strangle someone, so leave before the urge gets too strong.

68. PETERSON LAKE

Reference: **South of Discovery Bay, Jefferson County; see map A2 inset, grid g3.**

How to get there: Take U.S. 101 to State Route 20 at the south end of Discovery Bay and turn east toward Port Townsend. Turn south (right) on Eaglemont Road and south (right) again on Peterson Road. Drive two miles and take a hard right onto the unsigned gravel road leading to the lake.

Facilities: The lake has no facilities at all, but food, gas, lodging, and tackle are available in Quilcene and Discovery Bay.

Contact: The Fish In Hole, (360) 385-7031; Maple Grove Motel, (360) 765-3410; Quilcene Hotel, (360) 765-3447.

Species available: Cutthroat trout, yellow perch, a few largemouth bass.

Fishing Peterson Lake: The fishing at Peterson Lake is nothing to get excited about, but you can escape the crowds and maybe spend a relaxing few hours in your float tube or small boat. Most of the fish are small, so take light tackle.

69. LAKE LELAND

Reference: **North of Quilcene, Jefferson County; map A2 inset, grid g3.**

How to get there: Drive north on U.S. 101 from Quilcene and turn left on Lake Leland Road. If you miss the first sign, just continue on and you'll get a second chance at Lake Leland Road about a mile farther up the road. From the east, take State Route 104 west from the Hood Canal Floating Bridge and turn south onto U.S. 101, then drive about 3½ miles to Lake Leland Road, which is on the right.

Facilities: A Department of Fish and Wildlife access area with a boat ramp and toilets is located at the lake. The nearest food, gas, and tackle are in Discovery Bay and Quilcene, and the closest lodging is in Quilcene.

Contact: The Fish In Hole, (360) 385-7031; Maple Grove Motel, (360) 765-3410; Quilcene Hotel, (360) 765-3447.

Species available: Rainbow trout, largemouth bass, black bullhead catfish, bluegills.

Fishing Lake Leland: This 100-acre lake just off U.S. 101 is heavily seeded with hatchery rainbow trout and provides good trout fishing throughout much of its year-round season. The hottest fishing is from April to June, but fall fishing can also be productive and offers a lot more solitude. Try all your favorite trolling and stillfishing techniques during the spring and casting or trolling dry flies early in the fall.

Leland also grows some good-sized largemouth bass, which provide solid fishing opportunities throughout the summer. Spinnerbaits and other weedless or semi-weedless lures should be included in your arsenal, because there's a lot of wood, brush, and weedy cover to fish.

Bluegill fishing is only fair, but mid-summer nights provide very good catfish action for anglers casting bobber-and-nightcrawler rigs around the edge of the lake.

70. CROCKER LAKE

Reference: **South of Discovery Bay, Jefferson County; see map A2 inset, grid g3.**

How to get there: Driving north on U.S. 101 from Quilcene, you'll see the lake on the right about three miles north of Lake Leland. From the east, take State Route 104 west from the Hood Canal Floating Bridge and turn south onto U.S. 101, then drive about a mile to the lake, which is on the left.

Facilities: The lake has a public access area and boat ramp, and there are limited facilities available to the north in Discovery Bay. To the south, there is one hotel and one motel in Quilcene, as well as food, gas, and other supplies.

Contact: The Fish In Hole, (360) 385-7031; Maple Grove Motel, (360) 765-3410; Quilcene Hotel, (360) 765-3447.

Species available: Rainbow trout, largemouth bass, black bullhead catfish.

Fishing Crocker Lake: Springtime plants of about 4,000 rainbow trout draw fair numbers of local anglers to Crocker, but the bass fishing here is generally overlooked. If you don't mind dragging that bass boat a few miles in the opposite direction from where you usually go, bring your favorite plastic offerings and top-water baits to Crocker some July evening and prepare to have some fun. If and when you tire of casting for bass, rig a bobber-and-nightcrawler combination and catch yourself a few one- to two-pound catfish.

71. TARBOO LAKE

Reference: **Northeast of Quilcene, Jefferson County; map A2 inset, grid g3.**

How to get there: Take U.S. 101 to Quilcene and turn off the highway to the right at the sign pointing to Chimacum. Follow the county road north to Tarboo Lake Road and turn west (left), then drive just under four miles to the lake.

Facilities: The only facilities at the lake are a public access area and boat ramp, but Quilcene has a hotel, a motel, groceries, tackle, and gas.

Contact: The Fish In Hole, (360) 385-7031; Maple Grove Motel, (360) 765-3410; Quilcene Hotel, (360) 765-3447.

Species available: Rainbow and cutthroat trout.

Fishing Tarboo Lake: Although only 24 acres in size, Tarboo gets a generous supply of hatchery rainbows every spring, so it provides good fishing for several weeks after the late-April opener. Rainbow carry-over is also quite good, so the chances of hooking a large trout of 14 inches or better are pretty good. While fishing for those planters, don't be too surprised if you hook a 12-inch cutthroat or two. Try trolling a small Flatfish or Kwikfish, and if that doesn't work, a slowly trolled Carey Special fly might do the trick.

72. TARBOO CREEK

Reference: **Flows into Tarboo Bay northeast of Quilcene, Jefferson County; map A2 inset, grid g3.**

How to get there: Take U.S. 101 to Quilcene and turn off the highway onto Chimacum Road toward Chimacum. Turn east (right) on Dabob Road, drive about two miles to the creek, and turn either upstream or down on roads that parallel the stream.

Facilities: The nearest food, gas, tackle, and lodging are in Quilcene.

Contact: The Fish In Hole, (360) 385-7031; Maple Grove Motel, (360) 765-3410; Quilcene Hotel, (360) 765-3447.

Species available: Resident and sea-run cutthroat trout.

Fishing Tarboo Creek: Nearby road access along much of Tarboo Creek's length makes it difficult to find a legal-sized resident trout here after about the first three days of the season. Fall, however, provides some fair to good fishing for sea-run cutts to about 16 inches. Fish right after a short period of high water any time during the month of October and you'll probably do alright.

73. SANDY SHORE LAKE

Reference: **Southwest of Port Ludlow, Jefferson County; map A2 inset, grid g3.**

How to get there: Take State Route 104 west from the Hood Canal Bridge or east from Discovery Bay and turn south onto Sandy Shore Road, following it about two miles to the lake.

Facilities: There are no facilities at the lake. The nearest food, gas, tackle, and lodging are in Quilcene and Port Ludlow. An RV park is also located in Port Ludlow.

Contact: The Fish In Hole, (360) 385-7031; Port Ludlow RV Park, (360) 437-9110; Port Ludlow Resort, (800) 732-1239.

Species available: Rainbow trout, largemouth bass.

Fishing Sandy Shore Lake: The rainbows planted in Sandy Shore Lake average about nine inches and provide pretty good fishing through April and May. By June, early morning and evening fishing are best, and by July this is pretty much a bass lake. There are some respectable largemouths here, but you'll likely catch several eight- to 10-inchers for every worthwhile bass.

74. LUDLOW LAKE

Reference: **West of Port Ludlow, Jefferson County; map A2 inset, grid g3.**

How to get there: Take State Route 104 west from the Hood Canal Bridge or east from Discovery Bay and turn north onto Sandy Shore Road. About a quarter of a mile off the highway, Sandy Shore Road makes a sharp left turn, with a gravel road turning to the right. Take that gravel road and drive about 100 yards to the short trail (also about 100 yards) leading toward the lake.

Facilities: The lake has no facilities. The nearest food, gas, tackle, and lodging can be found in Quilcene and Port Ludlow. There's also an RV park in Port Ludlow.

Contact: The Fish In Hole (360) 385-7031; Port Ludlow RV Park, (360) 437-9110; Port Ludlow Resort, (800) 732-1239.

Species available: Rainbow trout, largemouth bass.

Fishing Ludlow Lake: The season here runs year-round, but the best fishing occurs immediately after the Department of Fish and Wildlife makes its annual March or April plant of about 500 legal-sized rainbows. The action usually lasts about a month.

Although Ludlow Lake covers only about 15 acres, it offers decent bass fishing all summer, especially for anglers who carry in small boats, canoes, or float tubes.

---

75. TEAL LAKE

Reference: **South of Port Ludlow, Jefferson County; map A2 inset, grid g4.**

How to get there: Take State Route 104 to about three miles west of the Hood Canal Floating Bridge's west end and turn north on Teal Lake Road. Drive two miles to the lake, which is on the west side of the road.

Facilities: The lake has no public access area as such, but bank access is allowed, and it's okay to launch small boats along the shore. The nearest food, lodging, and other amenities are in Port Ludlow.

Contact: The Fish In Hole, (360) 385-7031; Port Ludlow RV Park, (360) 437-9110; Port Ludlow Resort, (800) 732-1239.

Species available: Rainbow trout.

Fishing Teal Lake: Though nothing spectacular, this 15-acre lake by the side of the road is stocked with legal-sized rainbows every spring and provides fair angling opportunities from April to June, plus a little surge of activity again in the fall. Teal Lake is somewhat out of the way if you don't happen to live around the east end of Jefferson County, but it could be worth a visit some Saturday in May when you don't have anything else to do. The mood here is laid back, as it should be with fishing.

---

76. BUCK LAKE

Reference: **North end of Kitsap Peninsula; map A2 inset, grid g5.**

How to get there: Take State Route 104 west from Kingston and turn north (right) on Hansville Road, or take Bond Road north from Poulsbo to Hansville Road and go left. Drive north on Hansville Road just over seven miles. Immediately past the signs pointing right to Point No Point, turn left on Buck Lake Road, which leads half a mile to the lake.

Facilities: A small county park on the lake provides bank access and a boat ramp. Food, gas, and tackle are available in Hansville. Lodging and other amenities can be found in Poulsbo.

Contact: Poulsbo Sports Center, (360) 779-5290.

Species available: Rainbow, brook, and a few cutthroat trout; largemouth bass.

Fishing Buck Lake: Except for the county park and two or three houses set back from the water, Buck Lake looks pretty much as it must have 50 years ago. There aren't any docks, piers, bulkheads, or closely cropped lawns, and a few hours here may give you the feeling that you're well off the beaten path. The brush, trees, and weeds surrounding most of the lake offer lots of shallow-water trout cover that seem to call out for you to cast an artificial fly in their direction.

At just over 20 acres, Buck Lake is as inviting to the float-tuber or canoe enthusiast as it is the guy with a 16-foot trailer boat. Although most anglers come here to fish for planted rainbows and an occasional brookie or cutthroat, the bass population continues to grow, and abundant shoreline cover makes this an exceptional place to try for largemouths.

77. DEER LAKE

Reference: **West of Clinton, near southeast corner of Whidbey Island; map A2 inset, grid g6.**

How to get there: Take the Washington State Ferry from Mukilteo to Clinton, drive up the hill several blocks, and turn left on Holst Road, following it southwesterly from town. The lake is on the right, just over a mile from Clinton.

Facilities: A Department of Fish and Wildlife access area and boat ramp are located at the northeast corner of the lake. Food, gas, and several bed and breakfasts are available in Clinton.

Contact: John's Sporting Goods, (206) 259-3056; Ted's Sports Center, (206) 743-9505.

Species available: Rainbow and cutthroat trout, brown bullhead catfish.

Fishing Deer Lake: Heavily stocked with hatchery rainbows, this 80-acre Whidbey Island lake is a steady producer early in the season. A regular who said he had fished Deer for over 30 years once told me that if you can't catch a limit of trout here on opening day you should give up fishing completely. I don't think I'd make that recommendation to anyone, but the liberal spring trout plants certainly do offer anglers a great chance of success. The Department of Fish and Wildlife dumped more than 7,500 legal-sized rainbows into the lake before the 1995 opener, for example, and that's a pretty typical plant for Deer Lake. But perhaps the best thing about Deer is that it's quite deep, so many of those spring planters scatter to the depths after the early season onslaught, where they continue to provide good trout-fishing opportunities throughout much of the summer and again in the fall.

Bottom line: This is a trout lake worth visiting virtually any time during its April-through-October season. If you stay into the night, try a bobber-and-worm rig for pan-sized catfish. And yes, you're right, it's not the only Deer Lake in Washington. My unofficial count lists it as one of seven lakes by the same name, but it's the only one on Whidbey Island, if that helps.

78. LAKE SERENE

Reference: **Southwest of Everett, map A2 inset, grid g6.**

How to get there: Drive north from Lynnwood on State Route 99 to Shelby Road and turn west (left). Drive three-quarters of a mile to 43rd Avenue, turn north (right), and drive three blocks to the lake.

Facilities: A public access area with a boat ramp and toilets is located at the west end of the lake. Food, gas, lodging, and other amenities are available to the south in Lynnwood.

Contact: Ted's Sports Center, (206) 743-9505.

Species available: Rainbow trout.

Fishing Lake Serene: This 42-acre lake close to the King-Snohomish County population centers doesn't always live up to its name, especially after the April plants of hatchery trout. Those plants are usually quite generous—something in the neighborhood of 3,500 fish—so the trout fishing holds up fairly well despite the lake's popularity.

The warm weather of summer, however, tends to knock things in the head pretty well, thanks to the fact that the lake is quite shallow throughout. If there's anything resembling a deep spot where you might try for summer-time rainbows, it would be the area of 25-foot-deep water near the east end of the lake. Worms, marshmallows, Berkley Power Bait, salmon eggs, and all the usual spoons and spinners seem to work here when the bite is on.

79. STICKNEY LAKE

Reference: **Southwest of Everett; map A2 inset, grid g6.**

How to get there: Take State Route 99 north from Lynnwood or south from Everett, turn east on North Manor Way, drive half a mile to Admiralty Way, turn south (right), and drive about 100 yards to the lake.

Facilities: A Department of Fish and Wildlife boat ramp with an access area and toilets is located on the north end of the lake. Food, gas, tackle, and lodging are available nearby in Lynnwood.

Contact: Ted's Sports Center, (206) 743-9505.

Species available: Rainbow trout, largemouth bass, yellow perch, brown bull-head catfish.

Fishing Stickney Lake: At only 26 acres, Stickney is a small lake with quite a lot to offer anglers. It receives an annual plant of about 1,000 legal-sized hatchery rainbows, which provide fair action through the spring, by which time bass fishing is good enough to draw interest from many Snohomish/King County bass enthusiasts. Perch fishing is good enough from early spring through late fall to make this a worthwhile bet as a place to take the kids for some can't-miss fishing. If the weather is good and the junk food holds out, stay into the night for catfish.

80. SILVER LAKE

Reference: **South of Everett; map A2 inset, grid g7.**

How to get there: South-bound on Interstate 5, take exit 189 and drive south on State Route 527 to 112th Street SW. Turn west (right) and drive a quarter of a mile to Silver Lake Road, then turn south (left) and drive 150 yards to the lake. Northbound on Interstate 5, take exit 186 and drive east to State Route 527. Turn north (left) and drive to 112th and turn left, then left again on Silver Lake Road.

Facilities: A city park with bank access and rest rooms is located on the west side of the lake, and it's possible to fish from the bank or launch a small boat in several spots along the lake's eastern shore. Silver Lake RV Park is on the west side of the lake and has both RV and tent sites, as well as a boat ramp and beach access for park guests. Food, gas, lodging, and tackle are available throughout the Everett area.

Contact: Silver Lake RV Park, (206) 338-9666; John's Sporting Goods, (206) 259-3056; Last Lure Bait and Tackle, (206) 359-0567.

Species available: Rainbow and cutthroat trout, kokanee.

Fishing Silver Lake: This 100-acre lake within casting range of Interstate 5 between Everett and Seattle is open to year-round fishing and has something to offer throughout much of that 12-month season. Hatchery rainbows, including a pretty good mix of one-pounders, draw most of the angler interest from March to May. Both boat and bank anglers score some good catches then, using just about all the old stand-by baits and lures that take trout everywhere else.

By May the kokanee usually turn on, although this isn't one of western Washington's top-ranked kokanee waters. As summer progresses, kokanee anglers sometimes find themselves gravitating toward the middle of the lake, where the small sockeye salmon may school in the cool depths that extend to 50 feet.

As kokanee fishing fades, usually by September, rainbows and some cutthroats become more readily available, providing fair stillfishing and trolling action until the cold winds of November send anglers looking for more comfortable places to spend their days.

81. MARTHA LAKE

Reference: **Northeast of Alderwood Manor; map A2 inset, grid g6.**

How to get there: Drive north from Seattle or south from Everett on Interstate 5 and turn east on 164th Street SW (exit 183 off the freeway). The lake is about half a mile off the freeway, on the north (left) side of the street.

Facilities: There's a Department of Fish and Wildlife access area with a boat ramp and toilets on the west side of the lake, with food, gas, and tackle available in Mill Creek or to the north in Everett. Lodging is available near the freeway exit.

Contact: Ted's Sports Center, (206) 743-9505.

Species available: Rainbow and cutthroat trout, largemouth bass, yellow perch, brown bullhead catfish.

Fishing Martha Lake: Yes, there are Martha Lakes all over the place, but this one is in Snohomish County. What's that you say? There are three Martha Lakes in Snohomish County? Well, this is the one that's just under 60 acres. Huh? There are two Martha Lakes in Snohomish County that are just under 60 acres? Well, this is the one near Alderwood Manor. Aha, now you know which Martha Lake I'm talking about. Who's in charge of naming these lakes, anyway?

This Martha Lake is stocked primarily with hatchery rainbows, although a few cutthroats make their way into the mix some years. Spring fishing produces better trout catches, but the ambience is better in fall, especially if you like more solitude.

The lake gives up a few large bass from time to time and is fairly famous for its summertime catfish action.

82. SNOHOMISH RIVER

Reference: **Enters Puget Sound immediately north of Everett: map A2 inset, grid g7.**

How to get there: Take Interstate 405 to State Route 522 at Woodinville and turn east. Drive 12 miles to the bridge that crosses the Snohomish just below the confluence of the Snoqualmie and Skykomish rivers. Turn north (left) on Elliott Road and drive two miles to the first of several roads leading to the east (right) toward the river at various points. An alternative is to take Interstate 5 to Everett and drive east on U.S. 2 to Snohomish, where two highway bridges cross the river. Cross the river and turn west (right) on River Road to fish the south side of the river between Snohomish and Everett.

Facilities: Boat ramps are located on the river in Everett, Snohomish, and off 115th Avenue SE, about mid-way between Snohomish and the State Route 522 bridge. Food, gas, lodging, and tackle are readily available in Snohomish and Everett.

Contact: John's Sporting Goods, (206) 259-3056; Last Lure Bait and Tackle, (206) 359-0567; Sky Valley Traders, (360) 794-8818.

Species available: Winter and summer steelhead; sea-run cutthroat trout; Dolly Varden; coho, chum, and pink salmon.

Fishing the Snohomish River: Two of western Washington's better steelhead and salmon rivers, the Skykomish and the Snoqualmie, join to form the big, slow-moving river known as the Snohomish. Since all the sea-run fish bound for the Sky and the Snoqualmie have to pass through the Snohomish, it stands to reason that it can be a productive fishing spot, and that it can.

The reason it isn't an even better producer is that it's so big, slow, and deep that it's difficult to "read." There aren't many distinguishable holding spots for salmon and steelhead, so many anglers come here, scratch their heads, and say to themselves, "Where do I start casting?" Veteran local anglers do alright, but visitors often have a tough time of it. The river's size and the nature of its shoreline give boat anglers a definite advantage, and it's those boat anglers who score the best catches from the Snohomish throughout the year.

The coho run is the backbone of the fall salmon fishery here, and October is the prime month to get in on the action. Back-trolling with various diving plugs or casting flashy spoons and spinners are the techniques that take them best. Catchable numbers of cohos continue to pass through the Snohomish in November, and some large chums are also available by then to add to the intrigue of a morning's fishing. Pink salmon are present in good numbers during odd-numbered years, and September is usually the best month to fish them.

September is also perhaps the most productive month for sea-run cutthroat and Dolly Varden, although both are available from mid-summer to late fall.

As for steelhead, the Snohomish shines brightest as a winter steelhead stream, often ranking among the state's top 10 as a winter steelie producer. Catches of 2,000 or more winter-runs per season are fairly common. December and January, when large numbers of hatchery fish pass through on their way to upstream hatchery facilities at Tokul Creek and the Reiter Ponds, are the top months to fish the Snohomish. Back-trolling plugs or diver-and-bait combinations account for good numbers of winter steelhead, as does plunking with fresh roe clusters, various winged bobbers, or combinations of the two. Summer steelheading is also a possibility here, but the numbers don't compare to the winter steelie catch. The best months for summer-runs are June and July.

83. BLACKMAN'S LAKE

Reference: **At Snohomish; map A2 inset, grid g7.**

How to get there: Take Interstate 5 to U.S. 2 at Everett and head east toward Snohomish. After about five miles, turn south on State Route 9 and follow it about 1.5 miles to the lake, which is on the left.

Facilities: A Department of Fish and Wildlife access area and boat ramp are located on the south end of the lake, and a city park provides access as well. A fishing pier located near the north end of the lake is wheelchair-accessible. Food, gas, lodging, and other facilities are nearby in Snohomish.

Contact: Last Lure Bait and Tackle, (206) 359-0567; Sky Valley Traders, (360) 794-8818.

Species available: Rainbow and cutthroat trout, largemouth bass, yellow perch.

Fishing Blackman's Lake: Located within the city limits of Snohomish, this 60-acre lake gets plenty of attention from local anglers throughout its year-round fishing season. Hatchery plants include some one-pounders, but most of the 3,000 or so planted rainbows are typical seven- to nine-inchers. April, May, and June are the best months for rainbows here, but cutthroats typically bite better a little later in the year. September and October offer good chances for catching both 'bows and cutts. Perch fishing is good all season, and all you need to catch them is a supply of garden worms.

84. FLOWING LAKE

Reference: **North of Monroe; map A2 inset, grid g8.**

How to get there: Take U.S. 2 to Snohomish, turn east on Three Lakes Road, and drive about five miles to the lake.

Facilities: The Department of Fish and Wildlife maintains a public access area with a boat ramp and toilets near the southeast corner of the lake. There's also a good deal of bank-fishing access and a boat ramp at the Snohomish County park at the north end of the lake. Food, gas, tackle, and lodging are available in Snohomish and Monroe.

Contact: Last Lure Bait and Tackle, (206) 359-0567; Sky Valley Traders, (360) 794-8818.

Species available: Rainbow trout, largemouth bass.

Fishing Flowing Lake: If there's such a thing as a western Washington lake that's perfectly suited to both trout and bass fishing, it might be Flowing Lake, which is open to fishing year-round. The lake's more than 130 acres can be roughly divided between the shallow east side and the deep west side, offering suitable water for both bass and trout.

If you want bass, head for the fast-warming shallows at the northeast or southeast corners of the lake in early spring, before the rest of the lake has even started to warm. Much of the water in these areas is less than 20 feet deep, and the shoreline offers lots of good bass-holding cover. Like many of the more popular Snohomish County lakes, Flowing Lake has a slot limit that allows anglers to kill only bass that are shorter than 12 inches or longer than 15 inches.

If you're after trout, fish virtually anywhere in the lake during the spring, but as the air and water temperature begins to climb in early summer, concentrate more of your effort in the western one-third of the lake. There the depth ranges to more than 60 feet in places, and you can stillfish near bottom or troll deep to continue catching rainbows after other trout lakes have quit producing. The lake is well-stocked with hatchery rainbows in the spring, and the plants often include some lunker brood fish in the two-pound range.

85. PANTHER LAKE

Reference: **Northeast of Snohomish; map A2 inset, grid g8.**

How to get there: Take U.S. 2 to Snohomish and drive east on Three Lakes Road. About three miles east of Snohomish, turn north (left) at Jamison Corner onto Panther Lake Road, which leads less than a mile to the west side of the lake.

Facilities: A Department of Fish and Wildlife access area with a boat ramp and toilets is located on the lake's west side. Food, gas, lodging, and tackle are available in Snohomish and Monroe.

Contact: Last Lure Bait and Tackle, (206) 359-0567; Sky Valley Traders, (360) 794-8818.

Species available: Rainbow and cutthroat trout, largemouth bass, crappies, brown bullhead catfish.

Fishing Panther Lake: This 45-acre lake near Snohomish is very much a typical mixed-species western Washington lake where nothing extraordinary ever seems to happen. It's stocked with legal-sized hatchery rainbows in the spring, and most of them get caught by early summer, at which time many anglers turn their attention toward bass and panfish. The bass fishing is fair for small bass, and if you locate a school of crappies, you can enjoy some worthwhile light-tackle action, too. Night-fishing for brown bullheads produces some good catches, most of them from the shallower waters at the north end of the lake. The lake holds a few cutthroat, some of them decent sized, and they offer fair angling opportunity during the spring and fall.

86. STORM LAKE

Reference: **North of Monroe; map A2 inset, grid g8.**

How to get there: Take U.S. 2 to Snohomish and drive east on Three Lakes Road about five miles to the lake.

Facilities: A public access area and boat ramp are located near the north end of the lake. Food, gas, lodging, and tackle are available in Snohomish and Monroe.

Contact: Last Lure Bait and Tackle, (206) 359-0567; Sky Valley Traders, (360) 794-8818.

Species available: Rainbow and some cutthroat trout.

Fishing Storm Lake: One of the great things about fishing 78-acre Storm Lake is that if the fishing is bad, you can go try your luck at Flowing Lake (see page 151) about 150 yards away. The good news, though, is that the fishing usually isn't bad at all. Storm Lake is stocked with something like 6,500 legal-sized hatchery rainbows every spring, providing steady angling action well into June. Cutthroats show in the catch from time to time, usually later in the summer and in the fall, but most are caught by accident rather than by design. October can be an excellent month to fish for Storm Lake trout, but few anglers take advantage of the opportunity.

87. LAKE ROESIGER

Reference: **Northeast of Monroe; map A2 inset, grid g9.**

How to get there: Take U.S. 2 to Monroe, turn north (left) on Woods Creek Road, and drive about 12 miles to the lake.

Facilities: Besides a Department of Fish and Wildlife access area and boat ramp near the south end of the lake, a county park offers a fishing pier and bank angling access on the east side. Food, gas, tackle, lodging, and other amenities are available in Monroe.

Contact: Sky Valley Traders, (360) 794-8818; Last Lure Bait and Tackle, (206) 359-0567.

Species available: Rainbow trout, kokanee, largemouth bass, yellow perch, bluegills, brown bullhead catfish.

Fishing Lake Roesiger: When it comes to fishing opportunity, this is one of Snohomish county's most impressive lakes. It's open year-round, and it would probably take you all 365 days to thoroughly probe its more than 350 acres and depths that range to more than 110 feet.

Lake Roesiger is really more like three lakes in one: The largest and deepest northern section, where trout and kokanee flourish; the shallow flats of the lake's narrow, wasp-like midsection, where bass and panfish thrive; and the south end of the lake, which is much like the north end but a little smaller and not quite so deep.

One of the best things about Roesiger is that the fishing holds up throughout so much of the year. You stand nearly as good a chance of catching trout in July as you do in May (you just have to fish a little deeper for them). Since the lake is stocked with as many as 10,000 legal-sized rainbows every spring, there are usually plenty of them still around in summer. And, if the trout aren't biting in July, maybe the kokanee will be. Use your depthsounder to locate them and be willing to troll deep if necessary. If all else fails on a warm summer morning, hit the lake's middle section and cast for bass, some of which top four pounds. Throw in perch, bluegills, and catfish in case you somehow get bored and it's easy to understand why Roesiger is so popular with Snohomish County anglers.

88. CHAIN LAKE

Reference: **North of Monroe; map A2 inset, grid g8.**
How to get there: Take U.S. 2 to Monroe and turn north (left) at the light on Lewis Street, which becomes 195th Avenue SE. The road turns left after three miles and becomes Chain Lake Road just before you get to the lake. Follow the signs about a mile from there.
Facilities: A small public access area with a rough boat ramp is located near the east end of the lake. All amenities are available in Monroe.
Contact: Sky Valley Traders, (360) 794-8818.
Species available: Rainbow and cutthroat trout, largemouth bass, crappies.
Fishing Chain Lake: When you consider the variety of species available and the fact that it has a year-round season, this little lake has quite a lot to offer anglers. Its 23-acre size is well-suited to fishing from a float tube, small boat, or canoe, whether you happen to be a trout, bass, or panfish angler. Rainbows are planted in March or April. Chain doesn't produce many lunkers of any species, but it's usually good for some kind of angling action anytime from about March to November.

89. WAGNER (WAGNER'S) LAKE

Reference: **Northeast of Monroe; map A2 inset, grid g8.**
How to get there: Take U.S. 2 to Monroe and turn north (left) on Woods Creek Road. Drive about 2.5 miles to Wagner Lake Road, turn left, and drive a mile to the lake, which is on the right.
Facilities: A public access area with a boat ramp and toilets is located on the lake's west side. Food, gas, tackle, and lodging are available in Monroe.
Contact: Sky Valley Traders, (360) 794-8818.
Species available: Rainbow trout, largemouth bass.
Fishing Wagner Lake: Though covering only about 20 acres, Wagner is a popular trout lake in the spring and a producer of some fairly good bass fishing in the summer. It's usually stocked with about 1,000 legal-sized

rainbows before the late-April opener, but there aren't many hiding places for them in this little lake that's only about 20 feet in its deepest spot. In other words, the term "fished out" may well apply here after the first few weekends of the season.

While not really a haven for trout, this shallow lake with a weedy shoreline is perfect for bass, and for bass anglers. It's easy to understand why someone took it upon himself or herself to "stock" bass here illegally.

90. WOODS CREEK

Reference: **Northeast of Monroe; map A2 inset, grid g8.**

How to get there: Take U.S. 2 to Monroe and turn north (left) on Woods Creek Road or Florence Acres Road to reach the two forks of Woods Creek. Both roads roughly parallel the stream for about six miles.

Facilities: Food, gas, tackle, and lodging are available in Monroe.

Contact: Sky Valley Traders, (360) 794-8818.

Species available: Cutthroat trout.

Fishing Woods Creek: This large tributary to the Skykomish River offers a little bit of something for every kind of trout angler, from those who never leave sight of the road to those who like to get out and do some hiking to find solitude and maybe even a couple of trout that haven't seen a bait or lure for at least a few days. Try casting small spinners, such as a Metric or Panther Martin, from July to September. If you fish it earlier (it opens June 1), bait might work better because of the still-cool water conditions. After Labor Day, when the creek is at its lowest and warmest, try a light-action fly rod and your favorite wet-fly patterns. Your best bet for a keeper trout of 14 inches or larger is probably in June.

91. COCHRAN LAKE

Reference: **Northeast of Monroe; map A2 inset, grid g8.**

How to get there: Take U.S. 2 to Monroe and turn north (left) on Woods Creek Road, following it about six miles to the lake, which is on the left.

Facilities: There's a rough access area where small boats and canoes can be launched, but it's not suitable for trailer boats. Food, gas, lodging, and tackle are available in Monroe.

Contact: Sky Valley Traders, (360) 794-8818.

Species available: Rainbow trout.

Fishing Cochran Lake: This 35-acre lake near Monroe doesn't get much attention from anglers, but it does have limited public access and offers fair spring and fall trout fishing. Carry your small boat, canoe, or float tube to the beach and go for it. After about the end of May, you shouldn't have much company.

The trout fishing remains fairly good even into the heat of summer, thanks to the fact that a large area around the middle of the lake is deep and cool, with depths plunging to 50 feet or more in some places.

92. SKYKOMISH RIVER

Reference: **Joins Snoqualmie River southwest of Monroe; map A2 inset, grid g9.**

How to get there: Take U.S. 2 through Monroe and continue east along the north side of the river, or drive south through Monroe, cross the bridge, and turn east (left) on Ben Howard Road to reach fishing spots along the south side of the river.

Facilities: There's a boat ramp and access area just below the Lewis Street bridge in Monroe, another about two miles upstream from the bridge, off Ben Howard Road, and two near the Mann Road bridge at Sultan. Food, gas, tackle, and lodging are available right along the highway in Monroe.

Contact: Sky Valley Traders, (360) 794-8818.

Species available: Winter and summer steelhead; Dolly Varden; coho, chum, and pink salmon.

Fishing the Skykomish River: Long one of the Puget Sound region's most popular, most publicized, and most productive steelhead rivers, it's probably impossible to say anything about the "Sky" that hasn't already been said hundreds of times and written at least once. But that's never stopped me before, so here goes.

This big, beautiful river is consistently among the top two or three winter steelhead producers in Washington, giving up at least 2,000 fish per winter season and some years more than doubling that output. Strong hatchery returns in December and January make those two months the best times to fish the Sky, but unlike many other Northwest streams, this one doesn't experience a February lull, so the fishing can be as good then as it is earlier in the winter. March and April see the winter steelie fishery here turn to a catch-and-release affair—one of the best and most popular of its kind in the Northwest. The biggest concentrations of winter steelheaders—and, often the biggest catches—are around the Reiter Ponds steelhead facility and from Sultan downstream to Monroe, but you might find a willing fish almost anywhere along the Sky during the height of the winter season.

Summer steelheading can also be extremely good on the Sky. The summertime catch sometimes tops the 2,000-fish mark, making the Skykomish an occasional entry on Washington's list of top 10 summer steelhead producers. June, July, August, and September all provide excellent summer steelheading possibilities. As on many Northwest streams, gearing down to lighter tackle and using a more subtle approach is often the key to summer steelhead fishing success here.

Cohos and chums share the salmon-fishing limelight on the Skykomish during a typical fall salmon season, with pinks playing a big part during odd-numbered years. Salmon angling is allowed up to the confluence of the forks, but it's hard to beat the numerous pools and drifts from Sultan down to Monroe, a stretch of river that is as good as any salmon stream in the country. Pinks show up in September (every other year), cohos in October, and chums are most numerous in November. Fish for all three and you'll quickly see the improvement in fish strength and stamina as the runs change.

The Skykomish—and the entire Snohomish system—is one of few places in Washington where it's legal for anglers to catch and keep Dolly Varden as part of the daily trout limit. Any Dolly you keep must be at least 20 inches long, but fish of legal size are certainly within the realm of possibility. The Sky, in fact, has produced much larger Dolly Varden. The state-record anadromous Dolly, a whopper of exactly 10 pounds, was pulled from the river back in 1982.

93. LITTLE QUILCENE RIVER

Reference: **Flows into Quilcene Bay near Quilcene, Jefferson County; map A2 inset, grid g2.**

How to get there: Take U.S. 101 north from Quilcene or south from Discovery Bay and turn west on Lords Lake Loop Road about 2.5 miles north of Quilcene. The road parallels the lower river, makes a jog away from it for two miles, then cuts back toward and crosses the river. Just before crossing, you can turn west (right) on Forest Road 2909 to reach upper sections of the river.

Facilities: The nearest food, gas, tackle, and lodging are in Quilcene.

Contact: The Fish In Hole, (360) 385-7031; Maple Grove Motel, (360) 765-3410; Quilcene Hotel, (360) 765-3447.

Species available: Resident and sea-run cutthroat trout, winter steelhead.

Fishing the Little Quilcene River: Near as I can tell from Department of Fish and Wildlife catch records, anglers caught a grand total of two steelhead from this river from 1991 to 1994, making it perhaps the state's worst winter steelhead stream. Why the Department of Fish and Wildlife bothers to leave the season open all winter is a mystery. You're better off fishing the Little Quilcene for sea-run cutthroat, which show in fair numbers from September to November. It's hard to find a legal-sized resident trout over the 14-inch minimum during the rest of the season.

94. QUILCENE RIVER

Reference: **Flows into Quilcene Bay near Quilcene, Jefferson County; map A2 inset, grid h2.**

How to get there: Drive south from Quilcene or north from Brinnon on U.S. 101 and turn west onto Big Quilcene River Road about two miles south of Quilcene. The road parallels the river upstream for several miles.

Facilities: The U.S. Forest Service's Falls View Campground, located between the highway and the river, has tent sites and rest rooms. The Cove RV Park and Grocery, north of Brinnon, has RV hookups, groceries, tackle, and fishing licenses. The nearest hotel/motel accommodations are in Quilcene.

Contact: Olympic National Forest, Quilcene Ranger Station, (360) 765-3368; The Cove RV Park and Grocery, (360) 796-4723.

Species available: Rainbow and cutthroat trout, sometimes winter steelhead.

Fishing the Quilcene River: Except for the summertime trout fishery centered on hatchery plants, the Quilcene doesn't have too much to offer visiting anglers. Once the scene of a fairly productive fall coho fishery and later a place where anglers could find decent fishing for chum salmon, the stream is now closed completely to salmon fishing.

The stretch of river from Falls View Campground downstream remains open to winter steelheading, but it's difficult to understand why. Department of Fish and Wildlife catch records indicate that steelhead anglers catch virtually nothing. The Quilcene National Fish Hatchery, which supposedly raises fish for this river system, seems to be another example of your tax dollars at rest.

Summertime trout plants provide fair put-and-take action for vacationing anglers, and fall provides a shot at some sea-run cutthroats.

95. DEVIL'S LAKE

Reference: **South of Quilcene, Jefferson County; map A2 inset, grid h2.**

How to get there: Take U.S. 101 to Quilcene and turn south off the highway onto Linger Longer Road toward Quilcene Bay. Turn right onto the secondary road about two miles south of town and follow it another 1.5 miles to the wide turn-out and trail leading west (right) off the road.

Facilities: There are no facilities at the lake itself, but Quilcene has food, gas, tackle, and lodging.

Contact: The Fish In Hole, (360) 385-7031; Maple Grove Motel, (360) 765-3410; Quilcene Hotel, (360) 765-3447.

Species available: Rainbow, cutthroat, and brook trout.

Fishing Devil's Lake: At only about 10 acres, Devil's Lake isn't a place where you can expect to go and load up on fat trout, but it's certainly far enough off the beaten path to provide some solitude and serenity in what looks like a wilderness setting. The short hike from roadway to water helps to keep the crowds down, but, unfortunately, also prompts some slobs to carry their food and drinks in but "forget" to pack their garbage out. You might want to take out a little more than you bring in to help keep the place tidy.

This is as good place to take a float tube or small boat to make it easier getting around the lake. Most of the trout are small, but now and then someone hooks a particularly large cutthroat, often in October, the final month of the season (the season opens in April).

96. LAKE BALLINGER

Reference: **West of Mountlake Terrace, just north of Snohomish-King county line; map A2 inset, grid h6.**

How to get there: Take Interstate 5 to the north end of Seattle and go west at exit 177 on State Route 104 (also known as 205th Street at this point). The road runs along the south shore of the lake about half a mile off Interstate 5.

Facilities: There's a city park with a boat ramp and fishing pier near the north end of the lake. Food, gas, lodging, and tackle are all available within a few minutes' drive in Mountlake Terrace.

Contact: Ted's Sports Center, (206) 743-9505.

Species available: Rainbow trout, largemouth bass, yellow perch, crappies, brown bullhead catfish.

Fishing Lake Ballinger: A spring stocking of about 5,000 hatchery rainbows provides most of the trout fishing here, but the warm-water species are self-sustaining and doing just fine. Troll or stillfish with any of your favorite trout offerings in April or May and you should catch your share of planted rainbows.

Ballinger can be an especially productive bass lake, coming on with some husky largemouths by the end of April and continuing to provide good fishing through the summer. If you're looking for bass and all else fails, spend some time casting around the small island on the west side of the lake; it may not produce, but it looks like it should. The standard bass slot limit is in effect here, making it illegal to keep any bass between 12 and 15 inches long.

The perch and crappies tend to be on the small side, but big and abundant enough to provide some good light-tackle possibilities. The bullhead catfish also run small, but late-spring and summertime fishing for them can be quite productive. Again, start around the island if you don't have a better idea.

97. DEVIL'S LAKE

Reference: **Southwest of Monroe; map A2 inset, grid h8.**
How to get there: Take Interstate 405 to State Route 522 and turn east. About 1.5 miles east of Maltby, turn south (right) on Echo Lake Road. Drive just under two miles to Devil's Lake Road, turn left, and drive a mile to the lake.
Facilities: A public access area and boat ramp are located on the lake. Food, gas, lodging, and tackle are available in Woodinville and Monroe.
Contact: Sky Valley Traders, (360) 794-8818.
Species available: Rainbow and cutthroat trout, yellow perch.
Fishing Devil's Lake: You may have a hell of a time trying to catch a limit of lunkers here, but Devil's Lake does offer some potential in the spring and fall. At under 15 acres, it's certainly small enough to afford some good float-tubing opportunity, but light plants of hatchery trout keep Devil's from being much more than a nice place to spend a little time on the water.

Perch are almost too abundant here, to the point of sometimes becoming pests for trout anglers. If you want perch, just cast a bobber-and-worm.

98. ECHO LAKE

Reference: **Southwest of Monroe; map A2 inset, grid h8.**
How to get there: Take Interstate 405 to State Route 522 and turn east. Pass through Maltby (watch closely or you'll miss it), continue about 1.5 miles to Echo Lake Road, turn right, and follow the road south to the lake.
Facilities: A public access area with boat ramp and toilets is located on the east side of the lake. Monroe has food, gas, tackle, and lodging.
Contact: Sky Valley Traders, (360) 794-8818.
Species available: Rainbow and cutthroat trout.
Fishing Echo Lake: You wouldn't think that a lake covering only 17 acres would offer much in the way of season-long angling opportunities, but Echo Lake might surprise you. Hatchery plants include a few rainbows and a few cutthroats, and as you might expect, the majority of them are caught during the spring invasion of eager anglers. But this year-round lake can also be productive in the summer and fall, which is something you can't say about too many small western Washington trout lakes.

Echo Lake's prolonged productivity each year is probably due to the lake's unusual depth. Some places in the middle of the lake are over 50 feet deep, and that's no doubt where some of the spring plants wind up. That's also where you should concentrate your angling efforts if you want to hook a decent trout or two during the summer or early fall.

99. FONTAL LAKE

Reference: **Southeast of Monroe; map A2 inset, grid h9.**

How to get there: Take U.S. 2 to Monroe and turn south on State Route 203. Drive 2.5 miles to High Rock Road and turn east (left). Turn east (left) again on Lake Fontal Road and follow it about six miles to the locked gate about two miles from the lake. The last leg of the trip must be completed on foot, bicycle, or horseback. The road belongs to the Weyerhaeuser Company.

Facilities: A rough boat ramp is located near the south end of the lake, but there are no other facilities. The nearest food, gas, and tackle are in Duvall, and the nearest lodging is in Monroe.

Contact: Sky Valley Traders, (360) 794-8818.

Species available: Rainbow, cutthroat, and brook trout.

Fishing Fontal Lake: Thanks to the rough logging road, poor boat ramp, and lack of easy bank access, you had to be somewhat of a pioneer to fish this 35-acre lake even in the "good old days" when the rough road extended all the way to the lake. Now, since the last two miles of the road are closed to vehicles, you have to be even more of a Lewis and Clark type to taste the pleasures of this tree-lined lake near the King-Snohomish county line.

Your trail-blazing efforts, however, could pay off with a Fontal Lake grand-slam—at least one rainbow, one cutthroat, and one brook trout in your daily five-fish trout limit. Some local anglers are more than a little ticked off about the road closure, but some of them may have been part of the reason for the gate. Littering and other slobbish behavior were part of the reason for Weyerhaeuser's decision to gate the road.

Energetic anglers who don't mind working harder to get away from the crowds are happy with the current situation, however, and if solitude is a factor in your decision to go trout fishing, Fontal may be worth investigating. One look at this jewel of a lowland lake will make you glad you put forth the effort.

100. LAKE HANNAN

Reference: **Southeast of Monroe; map A2 inset, grid h9.**

How to get there: Take U.S. 2 to Monroe and turn south on State Route 203. Drive about 2.5 miles to High Rock Road and turn east (left). Turn east (left) on Lake Fontal Road and drive seven miles to the west side of the lake, which is on the right.

Facilities: There are no facilities on the lake. Food, gas, tackle, and lodging are available in Monroe.

Contact: Sky Valley Traders, (360) 794-8818.

Species available: Rainbow and cutthroat trout.

Fishing Lake Hannan: Often overlooked by anglers scrambling to nearby Fontal Lake, this south Snohomish County lake is a worthwhile angling destination in its own right. It isn't a great place for large, trailer boats, but you can easily shoulder a small car-topper or canoe and launch on the west side of the lake. Lake Hannan is open year-round, and there's hardly every a crowd, so fish it whenever the urge strikes. Although you couldn't prove it by me, Hannan is reputed to hold some large carry-over rainbows.

May is the best time to visit if you like to troll or stillfish, with fly-fishing a good option in June, September, and October.

101. LAKE MARGARET

Reference: **Northeast of Duvall, near the King-Snohomish county line; map A2 inset, grid h9.**

How to get there: Take State Route 203 to Duvall and, just north of town, turn east on Cherry Valley Road and follow it out of town. Turn north (left) on Kelly Road and drive about three miles to the lake.

Facilities: The west side of the lake has a public access area with a boat ramp and toilets. The nearest food and gas are in Duvall. Lodging and tackle are available to the north in Monroe.

Contact: Sky Valley Traders, (360) 794-8818.

Species available: Rainbow and cutthroat trout.

Fishing Lake Margaret: A heavy dose of hatchery trout every spring before the April opener draws a lot of anglers for the first month of the season to small, 44-acre Margaret Lake. Rainbows provide a bulk of the angling action, but spring plants usually include a few cutthroats, some of which survive the early season onslaught and are available to take baits and lures during the last few weeks of the season in October. If you want solitude and a chance to use your float tube here, fish Margaret in the fall.

102. LAKE JOY

Reference: **Northeast of Stillwater; map A2 inset, grid h9.**

How to get there: Take State Route 203 south from Duvall or north from Carnation to Stillwater. Turn east on Kelly Road, drive about three miles to Lake Joy Road, and turn right. The road circles the lake.

Facilities: The lake has no formal access area, but boats may be carried to the water near its north end. The nearest food and gas are in Duvall and Carnation. Lodging and tackle are in Monroe.

Contact: Sky Valley Traders, (360) 794-8818.

Species available: Rainbow and cutthroat trout, yellow perch.

Fishing Lake Joy: Covering more than 100 acres and reaching depths of 50 feet, this is a lake with lots of trout-producing potential that has never been realized. There's no public access area, and fish-planting efforts over the years have been sporadic. Some large trout may be lurking in the lake's chilly depths, but few anglers come to search for them. Deep-trolling or even vertical jigging are logical options. Fishing worms, nightcrawlers, or maggots around the edge of the lake will take some respectable yellow perch.

103. LAKE CONSTANCE

Reference: **Near the forks of the Dosewallips River, Jefferson County; map A2 inset, grid h2.**

How to get there: Take U.S. 101 north to Brinnon and turn west (left) on Dosewallips Road, following it some 14 miles to the Olympic National Park boundary. Just inside the park boundary, on the right, is the trailhead for the Lake Constance Trail. From there it's a steep two-mile hike to the south end of the lake.

Facilities: Dosewallips Campground, about two miles west of the Lake Constance trailhead, has camp sites and water, but other necessities are back at Brinnon, on U.S. 101.

Contact: Olympic National Forest, Staircase Ranger Station, (360) 877-5569; Olympic National Park, (360) 452-0330.

Species available: Rainbow and brook trout.

Fishing Lake Constance: You'll love this high-country trout lake once you reach it. But getting to it isn't a particularly easy task. The two-mile trail is steep, almost vertical in spots, and certainly not for anglers with too much stomach hanging over their belts or two-pack-a-day habits. (The pan-sized trout in Lake Constance aren't worth risking a heart attack.) If you're fit and energetic, though, the beauty of this place is worth a little huffing and puffing—actually, a lot of huffing and puffing.

Take your fly rod and a good selection of dry and wet patterns to fish the edges of the lake, or pack a light spinning rod to cast quarter-ounce spoons and spinners toward the middle of the lake. If you plan to stay overnight, you'll need a permit in advance, and there's a limit of 20 campers per night. To reserve a permit, call Staircase Ranger Station at the number listed above.

104. DOSEWALLIPS RIVER

Reference: **Enters Hood Canal at Brinnon; map A2 inset, grid h2.**

How to get there: Drive north from Shelton on U.S. 101 to Dosewallips State Park or continue past the park and turn west (left) on Dosewallips Road to parallel the north side of the river for several miles.

Facilities: Dosewallips State Park is one of the newer, more modern facilities in the Washington State Parks system and offers 40 RV sites with complete hookups, as well as rest rooms and showers. It also offers several hundred yards of river access for anglers. Nearby Brinnon General Store has groceries, tackle, and fishing licenses. The Bayshore Motel is right on the highway at the intersection of Dosewallips Road for folks who want a permanent roof over their heads.

Contact: Dosewallips State Park, (360) 796-4415; Brinnon General Store, (360) 796-4400; Bayshore Motel, (360) 796-4220.

Species available: Winter steelhead, chum salmon, sea-run cutthroat trout.

Fishing the Dosewallips River: I have fond memories of the first time I ever fished this small, clear stream on the eastern flank of the Olympics, and those positive thoughts remain even though the fishing really isn't that good here anymore. I caught a chrome-bright winter steelhead just above the U.S. 101 bridge that January morning in 1975, and I re-live that moment every time I pass the "Dosey."

I haven't caught a steelhead from the river since that first one, nor have most other steelhead anglers who have fished the Dosewallips in the past 10 years or so. This was once a stream that gave up 250 to 300 winter-runs every season, but a good year now sees about 25 steelhead caught from the Dosewallips, most of them by local anglers who can run out and fish it when conditions are right. The lower river, near the state park, has some good steelhead holes and drifts, and the steep canyon farther upstream is also an intriguing and beautiful place to fish, even if you go fishless.

The Dosey has a good run of chum salmon in November and December, and there's usually a short Chum season during that time. Chum fishing usually is open only from the U.S. 101 bridge downstream, though. Be sure to check out the regulations pamphlet for complete details on this short chum salmon fishery.

Sea-run cutthroats are lightly fished here, but can provide good action after a fall rain storm. The problem is that all wild cutthroats must be released, and the river isn't stocked with hatchery cutts. This combination makes the Dosewallips cutthroat fishery a catch-and-release affair.

105. DUCKABUSH RIVER

Reference: **Enters Hood Canal near Pleasant Harbor; see map A2 inset, grid i2.**

How to get there: Drive north from Shelton on U.S. 101, cross the river and turn west on Duckabush Road.

Facilities: A U.S. Forest Service campground is located about six miles upstream on Duckabush Road. Dosewallips State Park, about five miles north, has 40 RV sites with complete hookups, rest rooms, and showers. Brinnon General Store, on U.S. 101 at Brinnon, has groceries, tackle, and fishing licenses. The Bayshore Motel, six miles away, offers the nearest lodging.

Contact: Olympic National Forest, Hood Canal Ranger Station, (360) 765-2200; Dosewallips State Park, (360) 796-4415; Bayshore Motel, (360) 796-4220.

Species available: Chum salmon, winter and summer steelhead, sea-run cutthroat trout.

Fishing the Duckabush River: A quick look at the menu might lead you to think that the Duckabush is a pretty hot river, but the fishing is fair at best. Although both summer and winter steelhead do enter the river, they arrive in drips and trickles, not floods. Anglers catch half a dozen summer-runs and a dozen-and-a-half winter-runs in a typical year. Fall chum salmon fishing is considerably better, but the season is short, lasting only about six weeks in November and December.

Sea-run cutthroat fishing can also be productive, with September and October the best months. Wild cutthroats (and wild steelhead) must be released here.

The lower river has a lot of private land, greatly limiting angler access. If you're the adventurous and energetic type, drive up the road to about a mile past Collins Campground and hit the trail upriver to fish some beautiful trout water. You won't find many trout over the minimum size limit of 12 inches, but you'll enjoy yourself while trying.

106. UPPER HOOD CANAL

Reference: **Foulweather Bluff south to Triton Head, west side of Kitsap Peninsula; map A2 inset, grid h3.**

How to get there: Take U.S. 101 north about 11 miles from Shelton or south 10 miles from Discovery Bay to reach much of the west side of the canal. To reach Dabob Bay and the west side of the canal along the Toandos Peninsula, take State Route 104 to the west side of the Hood Canal Floating Bridge and turn south on South Point Road. To get to the east side of the canal, take State Route 3 or State Route 16 to Bremerton and drive north on State Route 3 to Seabeck Highway, which runs west to Warrenville and Seabeck. Another route is to continue north from Bremerton on State Route 3, which parallels the east shore of the canal from Kitsap Memorial State Park north to Port Gamble. Other roads off State Route 3 and State Route 104 provide further access to the canal's east side.

Facilities: There's a boat ramp at Triton Cove, another near Wawa Point (about three miles north of Brinnon), a third near the Point Whitney Shellfish Lab (south of Quilcene Bay), and two just south of Quilcene. The Point Whitney and Quilcene ramps offer free launching, but Hjelvik's ramp at Wawa Point requires a $2 launch fee. Free boat ramps are located off Shine Road and Paradise Road, on either side of the west end of the Hood Canal Bridge. A roomy, well-maintained ramp is also available free of charge at Salisbury Point County Park, near the east end of the Hood Canal Floating Bridge. Other launch facilities on the east side of the canal include the free ramp at Misery Point and the sling launch at Seabeck Marina, where launch fees depend on the size of your boat. Moorage is available at Triton Cove, Pleasant Harbor, Quilcene, and Seabeck. Camping facilities on and around the northern half of the canal include Dosewallips State Park (off U.S. 101 near the mouth of the Dosewallips River), Cove Park (at Wawa Point, north of Brinnon), Scenic Beach State Park (near Seabeck), and Kitsap Memorial State Park (at Lofall, south of the Hood Canal Floating Bridge). Dosewallips and Cove Park have RV sites, while Scenic Beach and Kitsap Memorial have tent sites and group camping sites only. Food, gas, tackle, and lodging are also available in Shelton, Quilcene, Poulsbo, and Bremerton.

Contact: Seabeck Marina, (360) 830-5179; Dosewallips State Park, (360) 796-4415; Cove Park, (360) 796-4723; Scenic Beach State Park, (360) 830-5079; Kitsap Memorial State Park, (360) 779-3205. For nautical charts of this area, contact Captain's Nautical Supply, (206) 283-7242.

Species available: Chinook and chum salmon, sea-run cutthroat trout, various rockfish, Pacific cod, pile perch and striped seaperch, various sole and flounder, a few lingcod.

Fishing the upper end of Hood Canal: In the hearts and minds of many Hood Canal visitors, fish with fins have long taken a back seat to fish with shells. For those of you asking yourself, "What the hell does that mean?" it means that crabbing, shrimping, and clam digging tend to draw a lot more interest here than fishing. And, with only one real exception, a general decline in angling opportunities has left some anglers wondering why they should even bother taking a rod along when they head out for a weekend of fun on the waters of upper Hood Canal. But some decent possibilities do still exist if you're willing to search them out.

Summertime salmon fishing has pretty much become a thing of the past here. Wild coho and chinook runs are dismal in Hood Canal streams, and sport closures are in place to protect them throughout the summer and fall. Although some areas of Puget Sound and the Strait of Juan de Fuca have special pink salmon-only seasons during odd-numbered years to allow at least some summer salmon fishing, that's not the case on Hood Canal. If 1995 was an example of what we can continue to expect, even abundant pink salmon runs will go un-caught by anglers in an effort to help protect other species.

All these regulations leave limited salmon-fishing opportunities for anglers in the north half of the canal. Fall runs of chum salmon headed for the Hoodsport Hatchery, the Dosewallips, Duckabush, Hamma Hamma, and Skokomish rivers, and other streams provide some saltwater fishing action, although anglers have been slow in figuring out how to catch them and to capitalize on the fishing opportunities they might provide. Fishing for immature "blackmouth" chinooks is fair from November to March, with much of the action coming from a few time-proven spots scattered along the east and west sides of the canal. Sprawling Dabob Bay is perhaps the best possibility. The west side of the bay, including Red Bluff, Point Whitney, and Jackson Cove, offers fair numbers of winter chinooks and is fairly well protected from the wind. Nearby access is available at Quilcene and Wawa Point. Mooching with plug-cut herring is most popular here, but both jigging and trolling will also take winter blackmouth. Other spots likely to produce a chinook or two from late fall to early spring include Hazel Point and Oak Head (both at the south end of the Toandos Peninsula) and Misery Point (near Seabeck).

Dabob Bay also offers some decent fishing opportunities for sea-run cutthroat trout, especially in the shallows around the edges of Quilcene and Tarboo bays and Jackson Cove. The Dosewallips and Duckabush river estuaries also have sea-runs for anglers on the west side of the canal. On the east side, there's fair cutthroat fishing available from Seabeck Bay up to and including Big Beef Harbor. Chances are you could find sea-run cutts in many other places along both sides of the canal. If you feel a little adventurous, I would recommend that you simply take off trolling along the beach anywhere, staying in five to 10 feet of water and paying special attention wherever a small stream flows into the canal. Remember, though, that throughout Hood Canal you must release wild cutthroats and may kill only hatchery fish that sport at least one clipped fin.

Smaller rockfish, particularly coppers, are available almost wherever you can find shallow, rocky humps along the bottom. Many are caught accidentally by anglers fishing for salmon and cutthroats, but you can improve your chances of putting a few sweet, white-meat fillets in the deep-fryer if you concentrate your efforts around rocky points and submerged reefs that offer the kinds of solid bottom structure these fish like. Do the same kind of prospecting in deeper water and you might find a yelloweye, canary, or other, larger, deep-water rockfish.

The steeper, deeper, more jagged rock bottoms will also produce lingcod, but remember that these big, toothy bottom-dwellers are available only for about six weeks in May and June, and they're protected by very specific minimum and maximum size limits and other regulations. Lingcod habitat is limited in northern Hood Canal, but if you use your nautical chart and your depthsounder, you'll find a few. NOAA chart #18441 is a must for this kind of prospecting. If all the natural bottomfish habitat fails to produce, you might try the man-made structure placed in Hood Canal specifically for that purpose. I'm talking about the artificial reef constructed near Misery Point by the Department of Fisheries. Its exact location is 600 feet north of the Misery Point navigational light, and it's marked by a buoy. Lingcod, greenling, cabezon, and several species of rockfish call it home.

While the salmon, lingcod, and other large glamour fish may be somewhat hard to find, it's accurate to say that the north end of Hood Canal has its share of overlooked angling possibilities. Smallish flounder and sole can be found over sand and gravel bottoms in virtually every bay and estuary along either side of the canal, and they'll hit anything from garden worms, pieces of herring, or salad shrimp to small metal jigs and leadheads with plastic grubs. Those worms and shrimp will also take pile perch and striped seaperch from around the many docks, wharves, and pilings that line much of the canal. Fish them on the incoming tide, especially where the rising waters are just beginning to reach the exposed woody structure.

107. HALLER LAKE

Reference: **North of Northgate; map A2 inset, grid i6.**

How to get there: Take Interstate 5 to North 130th Street (exit 174) and drive west half a mile to North 125th Avenue. Turn south (left), drive two blocks, and the lake will be on the left.

Facilities: The lake doesn't have a public access area as such, but it's possible to carry a boat to the water off North 125th Avenue or Meridian Street. Food, gas, tackle, and lodging are available at Northgate, a few blocks to the east.

Contact: Warshal's Sporting Goods, (206) 624-7300.

Species available: Rainbow trout, largemouth bass, yellow perch.

Fishing Haller Lake: This 15-acre urban lake is open to year-round fishing, but your best chance to catch a couple of trout occurs in the spring, after the Department of Fish and Wildlife has stocked it with its annual plant of several hundred pan-sized rainbows. The bass fishing isn't worth a long trip from anywhere, but you might be able to catch enough decent-sized perch to keep you satisfied.

108. GREEN LAKE

Reference: **Within the city of Seattle; map A2 inset, grid i6.**

How to get there: Take State Route 99 north from Lake Union in Seattle, and at NW 65th Street watch for the lake on the east (right) side of the road.

Facilities: Green Lake doesn't have a boat ramp, but car-toppers and other small craft may be carried to the edge of the lake and launched. A concessionaire at the north end of the lake has boats for rent. There are several public fishing docks and piers around the lake, and bank-fishing is a possibility in numerous locations. Downtown Seattle is only a few miles away, and all amenities are also found along Aurora Avenue (State Route 99).

Contact: Warshal's Sporting Goods, (206) 824-7300.

Species available: Rainbow and brown trout, largemouth bass, yellow perch, brown bullhead catfish.

Fishing Green Lake: A year-round season, generous plants of hatchery trout, and hundreds of thousands of people living within walking distance combine to make Green Lake one of the Northwest's most heavily fished bodies of water. Fishing spots don't get much more urban than this 255-acre lake almost in the heart of Seattle, but it provides surprisingly good angling opportunity throughout much of the year.

Annual plants of brown and rainbow trout sometimes top 20,000 fish, most of them in spring and early summer. Angling crowds are smaller and the trout fishing is often better in the fall than in the spring. Thousands of browns and rainbows are caught here on worms, salmon eggs, marshmallows, and other standard fare, but a surprising number of anglers stroll to the shores of Green Lake with fly rods in hand and spend the early morning or evening casting wet, dry, and nymph patterns.

According to local mythology, Green Lake is home to some lunker largemouth bass, but like the sophisticated urbanites who inhabit the dry land around them, the bass here have seen it all and aren't particularly agreeable to chomping down on just any old spinnerbait, plastic worm, or crankbait that passes by within striking distance. If you want to catch big bass here, finesse is the key.

109. COTTAGE LAKE

Reference: **East of Woodinville; map A2 inset, grid h8.**

How to get there: Take Interstate 405 to State Route 522 and head east to Woodinville. Turn east (right) on Woodinville-Duvall Road about a mile north of Woodinville and follow it three miles, watching for signs pointing south (right) to the lake. If you come to Avondale Road, you've gone about a quarter of a mile too far.

Facilities: The new King County park on the lake has fishing piers and a launch site for small boats. Food, gas, and tackle are available in Woodinville, and there are numerous motels along Interstate 405.

Contact: The Fishin' Tackle Store, (206) 869-5117.

Species available: Rainbow trout, largemouth bass, yellow perch, crappies, brown bullhead catfish.

Fishing Cottage Lake: Although stocked with hatchery rainbows, Cottage has a long history of being among western Washington's best possibilities for lunker largemouth bass. This big-bass potential went unrealized for nearly 15 years, when Cottage was locked up in private ownership without any public access. The lake reopened to public fishing again in 1992, and the lunker bass are once more within reach of most anglers.

Bass fishing is best from May through July, which are also the best months for crappies and catfish. Perch and trout bite well in the spring and fall.

110. TOLT RIVER

Reference: **Flows into Snoqualmie River near Carnation; map A2 inset, grid i9.**

How to get there: Take State Route 203 to Carnation and turn east on Tolt River Road, which parallels the north side of the river.

Facilities: Food and gas are available in Carnation, and tackle and lodging can be found in Monroe.

Contact: Sky Valley Traders, (360) 794-8818.

Species available: Winter and summer steelhead, cutthroat trout.

Fishing the Tolt River: December, January, and February are the top months to fish this little Snoqualmie River tributary if you're looking for anything that resembles consistent fishing action. The Tolt is far short of a sure thing even then, but at least that's when the bulk of the adult steelhead from hatchery smolt plants usually return to the river.

Those plants, by the way, may vary considerably from year to year, which can have a drastic effect on steelheading success two years later. The total plant in 1992, for example, was only 8,000 fish, while in 1993 it was an impressive 40,000 fish. As for summer steelhead smolts, the river gets a few thousand some years, none at all other years. That might explain why the summer steelhead catch on the Tolt is barely worth talking about.

Special, selective fishery regulations are in effect here during the general summer season, and parts of the river are open to catch-and-release fishing during this time. Be sure to read the regulations pamphlet before embarking on a summer trout or steelhead fishing trip to the Tolt.

111. LANGLOIS LAKE

Reference: **Southeast of Carnation; map A2 inset, grid i9.**

How to get there: Take State Route 203 to Carnation and drive south through town. About a mile south of town, turn east (left) on Lake Langlois Road, also known as NE 24th Street, which runs about two miles to the east side of the lake.

Facilities: The lake has a public access area and boat ramp. Food, gas, and tackle are available in Carnation. Lodging can be found to the north in Monroe or to the south in Snoqualmie.

Contact: The Sport Shop, (206) 888-0715.

Species available: Rainbow trout.

Fishing Langlois Lake: Stocked with 4,000 to 5,000 legal-sized rainbows each spring, Langlois is a favorite of east King County anglers for the first several weeks of the season, from late April to late May. Large crowds are on hand through May, especially on weekends, but by June the mobs thin out and it's time for serious anglers to give this trout factory a try. June, September, and October offer excellent opportunities for patient anglers to do battle with some real trophy-class trout. The fish missed or lost by early season anglers wise up quickly in this extremely clear lake, where visibility in the water may exceed 20 feet, and once they realize the dangers, they get extremely wary. They also tend to go deep, and in Langlois, "deep" means some spots of nearly 100 feet.

To catch lunker trout from the clear depths, try trolling or stillfishing with as light a leader as you dare, and plan on spending some time playing any hooked fish as long it takes. The rewards for doing everything right could well be a rainbow of four pounds or larger.

If you're up to giving Langlois' trophy rainbows a try, you'll need a boat. The entire shoreline, except for the public access area, is privately owned, so bank fishing is a virtual impossibility.

112. LENA LAKES

Reference: **Near the Jefferson-Mason County line, north of the Hamma Hamma River; map A2 inset, grid i1.**

How to get there: Drive north from Shelton on U.S. 101 and turn west (left) onto Forest Road 25 about 2.5 miles north of the Hamma Hamma River bridge. Follow Forest Road 25 about eight miles to Lena Creek Campground. From there it's a 2.5-mile hike to Lena Lake and more than four more steep miles to Upper Lena Lake.

Facilities: Lena Creek Campground has 14 tent and RV sites, water, and vault toilets. The camping fee is $7 per night. Lena Lake has about 30 tent sites, plus vault toilets. There's no camping fee for this hike-in campground. There are also a few campsites at Upper Lena Lake. The nearest food, gas, and tackle are in Eldon, back on U.S. 101. Hoodsport and Shelton, to the south, have all amenities.

Contact: Olympic National Forest, Hood Canal Ranger District, (360) 877-5254.

Species available: Rainbow, cutthroat, and brook trout.

Fishing the Lena Lakes: Lena Lake, the larger, lower one of the two, has lots of visitors during the summer hiking season, but most are non-anglers or casual anglers, so the serious trout enthusiast has a chance of taking a respectable trout or two for a few hours' effort. Brookies are more abundant, but if you catch a cutthroat or rainbow, it's likely to be a little larger. Evening fishing with a fly rod or fly-and-bubble combination on a spinning rod might be your best bet.

You'll break a sweat and do some huffing and puffing to reach Upper Lena, but the fishing might be worth the effort. Even if you don't catch trout, the scenery (especially the early summer wildflowers) will make the trip worthwhile.

July, August, and September are prime fishing and viewing months.

113. ARMSTRONG LAKE

Reference: **West of U.S. 101, north of Eldon, Mason County; see map A2 inset, grid i1.**

How to get there: Drive north from Shelton on U.S. 101 and turn west on Forest Road 25 about two miles north of Eldon. Take the first gravel road to the right (about two miles up Forest Road 25) and follow it just under two miles to the lake, which is on the right after you've passed under a big power line the first time and just before the road goes under the line a second time.

Facilities: There's nothing at the lake except bank-fishing access. The nearest food, gas, tackle, and lodging are back on U.S. 101.

Contact: Eldon Store, (360) 877-5374.

Species available: Cutthroat and brook trout.

Fishing Armstrong Lake: Though there's nothing to get too excited about as far as hot fishing is concerned, Armstrong is a nice little lake for escaping from the crowds. At less than five acres—and far enough off the road to avoid detection by casual passers-by—Armstrong is fished primarily by a few regulars from Mason and Jefferson counties.

  Pack your float tube to the edge of the lake and you can easily reach all the spots with lots of fish. Try it with a fly rod and selection of small, dry patterns during a late-spring evening and you'll have some fun with small-ish trout. Be sure to take along your insect repellent—the mosquitoes here are the size of bats.

114. HAMMA HAMMA RIVER

Reference: **Flows into west side of Hood Canal at Eldon; map A2 inset, grid i2.**

How to get there: Drive north from Shelton on U.S. 101 and turn west (left) on Forest Road 24 (Jorsted Creek Road) or Forest Road 25 to reach upper sections of the river from the south or north side. If you take Forest Road 24, turn north (right) on Forest Road 2480 to reach the river. A short section of the lower river is accessible from U.S. 101, near the highway bridges.

Facilities: The U.S. Forest Service's Hamma Hamma Campground, on the north bank of the river, has 15 tent and RV sites, vault toilets, and drinking water. Food, gas, and tackle are available at the tiny town of Eldon, with lodging in Hoodsport and Shelton.

Contact: Olympic National Forest, Hood Canal Ranger District, (360) 877-5254; Eldon Store, (360) 877-5374.

Species available: Sea-run and resident cutthroat trout, rainbow trout, a few winter steelhead.

Fishing the Hamma Hamma River: The best fish runs in this small river with the repetitive name are the fall runs of chum salmon, but the Hamma Hamma is closed to all salmon fishing, so forget the chums if you're looking for fishing action. Fair numbers of sea-run cutthroats offer decent possibilities beginning in August. The chances of finding a legal-sized resident cutthroat over the minimum size of 14 inches are pretty slim. During some years, the

Hamma Hamma receives small plants of hatchery rainbows, but you can't always depend on it. The river isn't stocked with hatchery steelhead smolts, and it shows; anglers catch only a handful of winter steelies each season.

115. WILDCAT LAKE

Reference: **Northwest of Bremerton; map A2 inset, grid i3.**

How to get there: Drive north out of Bremerton on State Route 3 and turn west on the Seabeck Highway. Go about six miles and turn west (left) on Holly Road. Drive half a mile to Lakeview Road, turn south (left), and drive to the north side of the lake.

Facilities: The lake has a large public access area with a concrete boat ramp and a gravel ramp alongside it, plus pit toilets and plenty of room for bank anglers. Scenic Beach State Park is about 10 miles away, to the northwest. Food, gas, tackle, and lodging are available in Bremerton.

Contact: Kitsap Sport Shop, Bremerton, (360) 373-9589.

Species available: Rainbow and cutthroat trout, coho salmon, largemouth bass, brown bullhead catfish.

Fishing Wildcat Lake: Heavy plants of hatchery rainbows and the possibility of mixed-bag catches help to make this 110-acre lake near Bremerton one of Kitsap County's most popular. It's stocked with more than 8,000 legal-sized rainbows every spring before the opener, and occasional plants of sea-run cutthroats and pan-sized coho salmon keep the trout catch from becoming too predictable. Trout anglers are most likely to catch fish in the eight- to 10-inch range in the spring, but fall fish run about a foot apiece, and there's always the chance for a carry-over rainbow of 15 inches or larger.

If you prefer warm-water fish to salmonids, work your way slowly and carefully around Wildcat's many docks and floats for a crack at largemouth bass. Although not common, bass to four pounds and better can sometimes be found here.

Summertime fishing during the evening and dead of night provides fair fishing for brown bullheads.

116. KITSAP LAKE

Reference: **Immediately west of Bremerton; map A2 inset, grid i4.**

How to get there: Take the Seabeck Highway west out of Bremerton and turn south (left) on East Kitsap Lake Road a mile from town or West Kitsap Lake Road two miles from town.

Facilities: There's a blacktop public access area with rest rooms and a two-lane boat ramp at the southwest corner of the lake. Kitsap Lake Park, on the west side of the lake, has a boat ramp, lots of bank-fishing, and rest rooms. Bremerton has food, gas, tackle, and lodging.

Contact: Kitsap Sport Shop, Bremerton, (360) 373-9589.

Species available: Rainbow and cutthroat trout, largemouth bass, brown bull-head catfish, bluegills.

Fishing Kitsap Lake: Although the largest crowds of trout anglers turn out here in the spring, some folks will tell you that fall is the best time of year to fish for Kitsap Lake's rainbows and cutthroats. This large, 240-acres lake is open to year-round fishing and isn't heavily stocked with trout, so many people try it once or twice in the spring, find only fair fishing, and give up. The result is a light spring harvest and plenty of trout still around when the water begins to cool in the fall. You might find a two-pound rainbow here in September or October, and some of the cutthroats grow even larger.

As for bass, Kitsap has a pretty good reputation as a largemouth producer. There are lots of docks and floats to investigate around most of the lake's shoreline, but I hardly ever get past the fishy-looking water along the brushy, grassy south end of the lake. It has "The bass are right here!" written all over it, and I just can't resist. It's a great place to cast top-water plugs early in the morning and during the last hour of the evening. Those hours, by the way, are the best times to fish Kitsap Lake during the summer months, when water-skiers, personal water-craft riders, and other hot-rodders are not all over the lake.

The lake has some large bluegills, which will hit jigs or Beetlespins best in May and June. Those are also good months to fish nightcrawlers or worms at night for brown bullheads.

---

117. LAKE WASHINGTON

Reference: **Immediately east of Seattle; map A2 inset, grids h6 and i6.**

How to get there: There are so many ways to get to so many access points on this huge lake that it's impossible to list them all here. One is to take Interstate 405 north to Kirkland and turn west (left) on Central Way. Turn north on Market Street to reach some of the more northerly parts of the lake or turn south on Lake Washington Boulevard (which eventually becomes Bellevue Way) to reach fishing docks, parks, and boat ramps along the rest of the lake's east side.

Facilities: Boat ramps are located at Kenmore, Juanita Creek, Holmes Point, Moss Bay, Sweyolocken Park, Newport Shores, Gene Coulon Park, Cedar River Trail, Atlantic City Park, South Ferdinand Street Park, Stan Sayres Park, the west end of the Interstate 90 Bridge, Sunnyside Avenue, and Magnuson Park. More than two dozen parks and fishing docks provide access for shore-bound anglers. Food, gas, tackle, and lodging are available in Kirkland, Bellevue, Renton, and Seattle.

Contact: Fishin' Tom's Tackle, (206) 228-4552; Fishin' Tackle Store, (206) 869-5117.

Species available: Rainbow and cutthroat trout, largemouth and smallmouth bass, yellow perch.

Fishing Lake Washington: Before I get into the how-to information about the year-round fishing at this 22,000-acre lake on Seattle's doorstep, let's establish the fact that the species listed above are not the only fish that currently or previously inhabited the lake. Coho, chinook, and sockeye salmon, for example, pass through the lake on their way to various tributaries or hatchery facilities on the Lake Washington system, but salmon fishing is closed here these days. Likewise, fishing for some other species is on the down side and not worth mentioning.

That said, let's talk about the good fishing on Lake Washington. Trout fishing can pay big rewards, especially in the spring and fall, since there are some hefty rainbows and cutthroats inhabiting the lake. Both sometimes grow to 20 inches or larger. Unfortunately, rainbows over 20 inches have to be released. That's right, released, because steelhead fishing is closed here, and rainbows over 20 inches are considered steelhead. To catch a lunker cutthroat or rainbow, try trolling on the north side of the Highway 520 bridge or the Interstate 90 bridge, but don't get too close; regulations require anglers to stay at least 100 yards from either structure. The shallow flats near the north end of the lake at Kenmore can also be productive trolling grounds for big trout. Other good trolling possibilities include the East Channel near the mouth of Kelsey Creek, the Mercer Slough, Rainier Beach, and virtually all the way around Mercer Island.

If stillfishing is your preference, try fishing worms, red salmon eggs, marshmallows, or Power Bait at Waverly Park in Kirkland. Of all the fishing docks on the lake, it seems to provide the best trout action. Other possibilities include Logboom Park in Kenmore, Houghton Beach Park in Kirkland, and Chism Park in Bellevue.

Not much is left in the way of largemouth bass cover in the lake, except for the many docks and floats around its shoreline and the network of sloughs and shallow bays in and around the Washington Park Arboretum on the south side of Union Bay. This area offers lots of lily pads, submerged logs and stumps, old pilings, and other prime largemouth cover.

Smallmouth bass also inhabit the lake, but you probably won't find a lot of them in any one place. Try casting in spring and summer around docks and pilings and any of the many gravel beaches and rocky areas that dot the shoreline. All the shoreline development and the creation of smooth gravel beaches that eliminated largemouth habitat around this lake was better suited to the needs of the smallmouth, and they flourish in all those man-made gravel beds, concrete bulkheads, and other rocky structures.

Yellow perch may not be considered an angling highlight on most Northwest lakes, but they are here, because they grow to extremely impressive size. It isn't at all unusual to catch 12-inch perch from Lake Washington, and fish of 15 inches or larger are within the realm of possibility. Since perch of similar age and size often school together, you may be in big-fish perch business if you can locate the right spots. The best big-perch action is in the fall, from October to December, and some of the best fishing is in the northern part of the lake. Try a small leadhead jig with a piece of worm on the hook or, if the perch are quite deep, put a piece of worm on the hook of a Crippled Herring, Hopkins No=EQL, or similar jigging spoon and work it vertically through the depths.

118. PHANTOM LAKE

Reference: **Immediately west of Lake Sammamish; map A2 inset, grid i7.**
How to get there: Take Interstate 405 to Bellevue and turn east (right) on NE 8th Street. Drive about 2.5 miles to 156th Avenue and turn south (right). Follow 156th Avenue just under two miles to the lake, which is on the left.

Facilities: A Bellevue city park on the west side of the lake has a small fishing dock, and boats can be launched there. Before launching, you must get a launch permit from the Bellevue Parks Department. Food, gas, tackle, and lodging are available in Bellevue.

Contact: Bellevue City Parks, (206) 455-6881; The Fisherman, (206) 641-0083.

Species available: Largemouth bass, crappies, yellow perch, brown bullhead catfish.

Fishing Phantom Lake: Though overshadowed by nearby Lake Sammamish, this 63-acre lake is a good bass lake in its own right. Open throughout the year, it's at its best from April to June, when it commonly gives up large-mouths in the two- to three-pound range. A slot limit protects 12- to 15-inch bass from harvest.

Just in case you can't get the bass to hit, bring along a light spinning rod so you can spend a little time catching some of the lake's chunky crappies and yellow perch. Both can be caught on small leadheads with red-and-white plastic skirts. Add a small piece of worm to the jig and the perch will hit even faster.

Night-fishing is fair for foot-long catfish from May to September.

---

119. LAKE SAMMAMISH

Reference: **Northwest of Issaquah; map A2 inset, grid i7.**

How to get there: Take Interstate 90 southeast about six miles from Factoria or northwest 2.5 miles from Issaquah and turn north into Lake Sammamish State Park.

Facilities: A boat ramp and bank-fishing access are located at the state park, which encompasses the lake's entire south end. Several private parks also have boat ramps, docks, and bank fishing. Food, gas, tackle, and lodging are available in Bellevue and Issaquah.

Contact: The Fisherman, (206) 641-0083; Lake Sammamish State Park, (206) 455-7010.

Species available: Cutthroat trout, smallmouth and largemouth bass, yellow perch, brown bullhead catfish.

Fishing Lake Sammamish: The most important thing you need to know about Lake Sammamish is that the boat ramp at the state park isn't open 24 hours, so if you want to launch before daylight or fish until after dark, you should use one of the private parks instead.

The second thing you should know is that Sammamish is western Washington's premier smallmouth bass lake. Although these bronzeback fighters have been in the lake many years and there's absolutely no secret about it, Sammamish continues to provide good smallmouth fishing for those willing to work at it a little. The many old pilings and submerged trees around the south end of the lake are especially productive places to search for smallies, but fish may also be found around any of the dozens of docks and floats on the lake or over many of the gravel-bottom beaches where homeowners and Washington State Parks have dumped tons of sand and gravel to turn the once muddy lake bottom into an environment more pleasing to human water-lovers. While all this development has eliminated a lot of the largemouth habitat the lake once had, it's almost perfect for smallmouths. As for what to use, try small leadheads with green, gray, or clear plastic skirts to imitate the salmon fry on which Sammamish small-mouths have grown accustomed to feeding. The clean, generally snag-free bottom is also conducive to casting crankbaits, and be sure to take along at least a couple with crawfish finishes.

Sammamish is home to some big, beautiful cutthroat trout, some of them topping 20 inches and weighing well over two pounds. Casting or trolling Needlefish, Canadian Wonders, Dick Nites, and other minnow-imitating wobblers will take them, as will trolling nightcrawlers behind a string of trolling blades or stillfishing with nightcrawlers.

Many of the big lily pad beds and other vegetation that used to make Sammamish a top-notch largemouth lake are gone, but it's still possible to catch one here and there. Some of the bass caught are big ones, weighing in at three pounds or larger.

120. PINE LAKE

Reference: **North of Issaquah; map A2 inset, grid i7.**

How to get there: Take Interstate 90 to Issaquah and turn north on East Lake Sammamish Parkway, following it about two miles to SE 43rd Way. Turn right and follow SE 43rd Way about three miles to the lake, which is on the left.

Facilities: A King County park on the east side of the lake provides beach access, a fishing pier, a boat ramp, rest rooms, and picnic tables. Food, gas, tackle, and lodging are available in Issaquah, three miles south of the lake.

Contact: The Fisherman, (206) 641-0083.

Species available: Rainbow and cutthroat trout, largemouth bass.

Fishing Pine Lake: With sprawling Lake Sammamish less than two miles away, you might expect Pine Lake to be overlooked by King County anglers, but it gets at least its share of fishing pressure during its April-through-October season.

For Issaquah anglers, Pine is the nearest lake with spring plants of legal-sized hatchery trout, a big draw in and of itself. Although the plants usually total only about 1,000 fish, they include both rainbows and cutthroats for variety. A few trout somehow manage to survive the early season festivities and hang around long enough to provide fair fall fishing. That's perhaps the best time to fish specifically for cutts, and good places to find them are around the lake's three inlet streams, located at the southwest, southeast, and northeast corners of the lake.

Pine offers pretty good bass fishing in the spring and fall, especially in and around the shallow bays at the lake's southeast and southwest corners. Water in both is well under 10 feet, so it warms fast in the spring and tends to draw a bulk of the spawning bass during May and early June.

121. BEAVER LAKE

Reference: **Northwest of Fall City; map A2 inset, grid i8.**

How to get there: Take Interstate 90 to Issaquah and drive north out of town on Issaquah-Fall City Road. Signs pointing north about three miles out of town lead the way to the lake, which is 1.5 miles north of Issaquah-Fall City Road.

Facilities: The east side of the lake has a public access area with a boat ramp and toilets. Food, gas, tackle, and lodging are readily available in and around Issaquah.

Contact: The Sport Shop, (206) 888-0715.

Species available: Rainbow trout, largemouth bass, yellow perch, brown bullhead catfish.

Fishing Beaver Lake: Long a favorite of King County trout anglers and stocked with liberal doses of hatchery rainbows every spring, Beaver has also gained a well-deserved reputation for its fine largemouth bass fishing. This is actually a small chain of connected lakes, with the largest of the bunch getting a bulk of the attention from anglers. The smaller lakes at either end of the big lake, though, are also worth investigating, especially for bass and panfish.

The best trout fishing is in May and September, while top months for bass, perch, and bullheads are June, July, and August.

122. SNOQUALMIE RIVER

Reference: **Joins Skykomish River southwest of Monroe; map A2 inset, grid i9.**

How to get there: Take Interstate 90 to Preston and drive north four miles to Fall City, or take State Route 202 from Redmond east 14 miles to Fall City, cross the river, and either turn right and continue on State Route 202 upstream or turn left and take State Route 203 downstream.

Facilities: Boat ramps are located near the mouth of Tokul Creek and just upstream from Fall City. Food and gas are available in Fall City. Lodging and tackle can be found in Snoqualmie and North Bend.

Contact: The Sport Shop, (206) 888-0715.

Species available: Winter and summer steelhead, cutthroat trout, mountain whitefish.

Fishing the Snoqualmie River: Hatchery winter steelhead bound for the steelhead facility on Tokul Creek are the biggest draw to the Snoqualmie, and much of the fishing pressure occurs from Fall City upstream. The short stretch of river from the mouth of Tokul Creek to Fall City often produces hundreds of winter-runs from December to March, with both bank and boat anglers sharing in the fun. Many of the boaters back-troll Hot Shots, Wiggle Warts, and other diving plugs, but drift-fishing with roe, shrimp, and various drift bobbers also produces winter steelies. The bulk of the hatchery run returns early in the winter, and December and January provide the best fishing. The Snoqualmie receives about 150,000 winter steelhead smolts a year to keep things hopping.

Hatchery plants of summer steelhead aren't so liberal, totaling only about 30,000 smolts a year, but that's enough to provide anglers with the chance to catch 400 to 500 of these sun-burn steelies every summer. Unlike many Northwest summer steelhead streams, the Snoqualmie provides fairly consistent action from June to October, giving anglers plenty of time to get their summer-run fix.

Although anglers in search of bigger game don't think much about it, there's a fairly productive trout fishery on the upper reaches of the Snoqualmie, above the famous Snoqualmie Falls. Salmon and steelhead don't get past the falls, and the fisheries on the upper and lower Snoqualmie are as different as night and day. Interstate 90 crosses the South Fork Snoqualmie near North Bend and parallels it much of the way to the Snoqualmie Pass summit. The North Fork Snoqualmie is accessible via Weyerhaeuser Company roads out of Snoqualmie, while the Middle Fork is reached by logging roads running east from North Bend.

As in many western Washington rivers, mountain whitefish are fairly abundant but generally overlooked. There is a special winter season (no trout allowed) from December through March for them on the upper river and all forks.

---

123. RAGING RIVER

Reference: **Joins the Snoqualmie River at Fall City; map A2 inset, grid i8.**
How to get there: Take Interstate 90 to Preston and turn north onto Preston-Fall City Road, which parallels the river.
Facilities: Food, gas, tackle, and lodging are available in Fall City and Snoqualmie.
Contact: The Sport Shop, (206) 888-0715.
Species available: Winter and summer steelhead.
Fishing the Raging River: This small, fast-moving river that flows under Interstate 90 gets almost as little notice from Washington's anglers as it does from the thousands of travelers who race east or west along the busy freeway above it. That's really not too difficult to understand, since access to the river is limited, good fishing water is relatively scarce, and returning steelhead runs are only a fraction of what they are in some of the area's bigger and more popular rivers.

Still, thanks primarily to hatchery plants ranging from 5,000 to 10,000 smolts per year, the Raging does give up a few dozen winter-run steelhead and a handful of summer steelies every year. The most readily accessible part of the river is the stretch, several hundred feet long, immediately above where the Raging enters the Snoqualmie. Fish it with eggs, shrimp, small bobbers, bobber-and-yarn, or eggs-and-yarn combinations. And remember that in some places, especially if there's been a day or two of rain, the Raging lives up to its name. If you hook a hefty steelhead at the tail-end of a small poll and it takes off downstream, you'd better have on your running shoes.

124. LAKE ALICE

Reference: **South of Fall City; map A2 inset, grid i8.**

How to get there: Take State Route 202 or Preston-Fall City Road from Interstate 90 to Fall City. Drive south from Fall City on Lake Alice Road SE about three miles to the lake.

Facilities: The east side of the lake has a Department of Fish and Wildlife public access area with a boat ramp and pit toilets. Food, gas, tackle, and lodging are available in Fall City, Snoqualmie, and North Bend.

Contact: The Sport Shop, (206) 888-0715.

Species available: Rainbow, cutthroat, and brook trout.

Fishing Lake Alice: Variety and fairly generous plants from Department of Fish and Wildlife hatcheries help to make this small lake just north of Interstate 90 very popular among King County anglers. It's possible to catch rainbows, cutts, and brookies all in the same day, especially if you confine your fishing efforts to the fairly shallow water around the lake's shoreline during spring and early summer. As is usually the case in Northwest lakes, the brook trout are small here, but planted cutthroats run close to a pound apiece, and carry-over rainbows of a pound a half or larger are more common than you might expect from a lake of only about 25 acres.

125. TOKUL CREEK

Reference: **Enters Snoqualmie River southeast of Fall City; see map A2 inset, grid i9.**

How to get there: Take Interstate 90 to Preston and drive north to Fall City or take State Route 202 from Redmond to Fall City, cross the river, and turn right to continue on State Route 202 upstream to Tokul Creek.

Facilities: Food and gas are available in Fall City. The nearest lodging is in Snoqualmie and North Bend; the closest tackle is in North Bend.

Contact: The Sport Shop, (206) 888-0715.

Species available: Winter steelhead.

Fishing Tokul Creek: This is one of the few places I know of where anglers are not only allowed, but invited, to fish for anadromous fish within a few yards of their destination at a state-operated hatchery facility. As you might guess, there's nothing particularly charming or aesthetically pleasing about this fishery, with anglers crowding the shores of the rushing creek, trying to head off adult steelhead as they fight their way upstream toward the hatchery. This steelhead fishery has some of the earmarks of shooting fish in a barrel, but it's more challenging.

Tokul Creek goes like hell between the fishing boundary and the stream's confluence with the Snoqualmie River, with nothing that really looks like the holding water familiar to most steelheaders. The fast water also makes for tricky fish-fighting conditions; it's often a matter of setting the hook and then sprinting downstream in an attempt to keep up with the racing steelhead. Several hundred fish are caught this way each winter from Tokul Creek. December and January are usually the top months to fish it.

126. MILDRED LAKES

Reference: **Headwaters of the Hamma Hamma River, Mount Skokomish Wilderness, map A2 inset, grid i0.**

How to get there: Drive north from Shelton on U.S. 101 and turn west (left) on Forest Road 25, which runs along the north side of the Hamma Hamma River. Stay on Forest Road 25 all the way to its end at the concrete bridge over the Hamma Hamma, then hit the trail, hiking the last four-plus miles to the first of the three lakes.

Facilities: These are hike-in lakes with no developed facilities. Several good primitive camping spots can be found around the lakes. The nearest food, gas, tackle, and lodging are in Hoodsport back on U.S. 101.

Contact: Olympic National Forest Headquarters, (360) 956-2400.

Species available: Cutthroat and brook trout.

Fishing the Mildred Lakes: You'll earn your fish here, not because they're wise ol' trophies that know every trick in the book but because the hike into these lakes is a real expedition. You can lose the trail if you aren't paying attention, especially after reaching the first lake and forging on to find the other two. The westernmost lake is the largest and most productive, but also requires the longest hike. Since the round trip to these high-country lakes is about 10 miles, you'll need at least a weekend to fish them and still enjoy the scenery, which is as good as it gets anywhere. I recommend giving yourself three days and two nights, just so you have plenty of fishing time.

Take along a selection of Panther Martin or Bang Tail spinners, a few plastic floats, and several fly patterns and you should catch trout. Casting bubble-and-fly combos should work best in the evening.

127. ELK AND JEFFERSON LAKES

Reference: **West of Eldon, Mason County; map A2 inset, grid i1.**

How to get there: Drive north on U.S. 101 from Shelton and turn west (left) on Jorsted Creed Road (Forest Road 24). Drive 1.5 miles on Forest Road 2480 and follow it several miles to Forest Road 2441. Turn south (left) and drive 2.6 miles to a short spur road on the right. Elk Lake is less than 100 yards down a well-used trail. Drive another four miles past Elk Lake to Jefferson Lake, on the left.

Facilities: The nearest tent and RV sites are at Hamma Hamma Campground, about five miles north on Forest Road 25. The closest food, tackle, and gas are in Eldon on U.S. 101. Hoodsport has lodging.

Contact: Olympic National Forest, Hood Canal Ranger District, (360) 877-5254.

Species available: Brook, cutthroat, and rainbow trout.

Fishing Elk and Jefferson Lakes: You have to do quite a lot of driving but very little walking to reach these high lakes on the east side of the Olympic National Forest. They hold a mix of smallish trout that will, on a good day in June and July, take bait, hardware, or artificial flies. A small boat or float tube is very helpful in fishing these waters. These lakes are far enough off the highway that many anglers like to double their fishing opportunities by visiting both lakes on the same trip. I always do!

128. LAKE CUSHMAN

Reference: **Northwest of Hoodsport, Mason County; map A2 inset, grid j0.**

How to get there: Take U.S. 101 to Hoodsport, turn west on State Route 119 (Lake Cushman Road), and follow it about five miles to the lake, which is on the left.

Facilities: There are three boat ramps on the east side of the lake, one a Department of Fish and Wildlife ramp near the south end, one at Lake Cushman Resort a little farther north, and a third at Lake Cushman State Park. Lake Cushman Resort has cabins, RV and tent sites, a grocery store, and moorage floats. Lake Cushman State Park offers about 60 tent sites and 30 RV sites with full hookups, as well as rest rooms with showers and an RV pump-out. Lake Cushman Grocery, just west of the lake, has food and some tackle. Other amenities are in Hoodsport.

Contact: Lake Cushman Resort, (360) 877-9630; Lake Cushman State Park, (360) 877-5491.

Species available: Cutthroat trout, kokanee, a few brook and rainbow trout, chinook salmon, largemouth bass.

Fishing Lake Cushman: The most exciting thing about Lake Cushman may be the fact that its bull trout population, which spawns above the lake in the upper North Fork Skokomish River, has been making a slow but steady recovery in recent years, offering the possibility of a bull trout fishery once again occurring in this 4,000-acre impoundment. Over-fishing and illegal snagging almost wiped out this run of huge char—some of which top 10 pounds—but they're responding well to fishing closures and other measures that have been in place to protect them for several years. The Department of Fish and Wildlife hasn't made any promises yet, but if and when it decides to open the fishery again, these trophy-class fish with a taste for smaller fish will be susceptible to large wobbling spoons and plugs trolled through the depths. They would never provide hot fishing action, but it would only take one 10-pounder to make your day.

In the meantime, kokanee salmon and cutthroat trout continue to provide most of the angling action on Lake Cushman. Both fisheries have been up and down in recent years.

Most kokanee here are caught by trollers, with worms, maggots, or white corn usually added to the hooks of a Wedding Ring or similar spinner, which in turn is pulled behind a string of larger trolling blades. As in most kokanee fishing, locating a school and keeping your bait at the proper depth are the keys to success.

Cutthroats are often caught on the same rigs used by kokanee anglers throughout the spring and summer. But in fall, after the kokanee fishery has come to an end, cutthroat fishing remains a productive possibility, especially for anglers trolling Dick Nites, Triple Teazers, and similar wobbling spoons.

129. PRICE (PRICE'S) LAKE

Reference: **West of Lilliwaup, Mason County; map A2 inset, grid i1.**

How to get there: Take U.S. 101 to Hoodsport, turn west onto State Route 119 (Lake Cushman Road), and drive about eight miles, passing Lake Cushman State Park. About half a mile past the park, turn right onto a gravel logging road. The road splits, and you'll want to stay to the left, following it about two miles to a wide spot in the road that serves as a parking area. Take the trail from the parking area about one-eighth of a mile to the lake.

Facilities: No facilities are available at the lake, but Lake Cushman State Park has tent and RV sites, showers, and rest rooms. Lake Cushman Resort and Lake Cushman Store are near the south end of Lake Cushman, and food, gas, tackle, and lodging are available in Hoodsport.

Contact: Lake Cushman State Park, (360) 877-5491; Lake Cushman Resort, (360) 877-9630; Nelson's True Value Hardware, (360) 877-9834.

Species available: Rainbow, cutthroat, and brook trout.

Fishing Price Lake: Big, shallow Price Lake is full of brush, weeds, stumps, and some of Mason County's largest trout. Don't bother bringing your bobber-and-worm rigs along, though, because the lake has selective-fishery regulations requiring anglers to use artificial lures and flies with barbless hooks only. And you don't even need to bring your creel or your cooler, because this is strictly a catch-and-release fishery. That helps to explain why there are a few 20- to 24-inch trout available to Price Lake anglers. But, even if you get skunked, this is one of those place where you won't really mind. The peace, quiet, and lack of shoreline development are enough to make the trip well worth the effort. Bank access is tough, so bring along your float tube or a small boat that's light enough to be carried to the water's edge. Fishing can be excellent in spring and fall.

130. MELBOURNE LAKE

Reference: **Northwest of Lilliwaup, Mason County; map A2 inset, grid i1.**

How to get there: Drive north from Shelton on U.S. 101 and turn west (left) on Jorsted Creek Road (Forest Road 24). Drive 5.8 miles and turn left onto the rough road leading down the hill toward the lake. Stay on this road two miles and watch for the lake on your right, just past the second road to the right.

Facilities: There's absolutely nothing at the lake except a few spots along the shore where you can carry or drag a small boat to the water, and a couple of rough tent sites around the edge of the lake. The nearest food, gas, tackle, and lodging are in Hoodsport.

Contact: Olympic National Forest, Hood Canal Ranger District, (360) 877-5254.

Species available: Cutthroat trout.

Fishing Melbourne Lake: Visit Melbourne Lake in the spring to see the wild rhododendrons in bloom, but not for the great fishing. As with most cutthroat fisheries, Melbourne starts off slowly, and many early season anglers give up on it before it comes to life. Those who fish it in late April and May find only fair fishing, but those who wait until summer or fall often make good catches of 10- to 14-inch cutts. With no boat ramp and limited shore-line access, this shallow, 35-acre lake is well-suited to fishing from a float tube, canoe, or small inflatable.

Although pristine and well off the beaten path, the lake does draw some slobs, especially on holiday weekends. The boom-box and beer-bust crowd rolls in to shatter the solitude now and then. After Labor Day, though, you should find peace and quiet.

131. KOKANEE LAKE

Reference: **West of Hoodsport, Mason County; map A2 inset, grid j0.**

How to get there: Take U.S. 101 to Hoodsport and turn west onto State Route 119 (Lake Cushman Road). Drive just under three miles to Cushman-Potlatch Road and turn left. Go just under a mile to Lower Lake Road, turn right, and drive down the hill to the boat ramp near the south end of the lake.

Facilities: There's a small boat ramp with limited bank access near the dam at the south end of the lake. Lake Cushman Resort is less than three miles to the north, and Lake Cushman State Park is about six miles north. Lake Cushman Grocery is right across State Route 119, a mile from the lake. Food, gas, tackle, and lodging are available in Hoodsport.

Contact: Lake Cushman Resort, (360) 877-9630; Lake Cushman State Park, (360) 877-5491.

Species available: Rainbow and cutthroat trout, kokanee.

Fishing Kokanee Lake: Also known as Lower Cushman, this 150-acre reservoir is in some ways a miniature version of the real Lake Cushman (see page 179) immediately upstream. Narrow and fairly deep, it holds a few large trout that anglers seldom hook. Planted rainbows—some 4,000 of them in a typical year—provide most of the catch. All the usual baits and lures come into play here, but most of the locals prefer to troll gang troll-and-worm rigs for their fish.

May, June, and October are best for trout, with kokanee biting best in July and August.

132. SKOKOMISH RIVER

Reference: **Flows into the south end of Hood Canal, Mason County; map A2 inset, grid j1.**

How to get there: Take U.S. 101 north from Shelton and turn west (left) on Skokomish Valley Road to drive upstream. To reach lower portions of the river, turn east off U.S. 101 onto Purdy Cutoff Road and follow the river downstream.

Facilities: A Forest Service campground is located on the upper South Fork Skokomish, at the mouth of Brown Creek. Potlatch State Park, about five miles north of the river on U.S. 101, has two dozen camping sites, some with RV hookups. Food, gas, tackle, and lodging are available in Shelton to the south and Hoodsport to the north.

Contact: Verle's Sport Center, (360) 426-0933; Potlatch State Park, (360) 877-5361; Olympic National Forest, Hood Canal Ranger District, (360) 877-5254.

Species available: Winter steelhead; resident and sea-run cutthroat trout; chinook, coho, chum, and pink salmon.

Fishing the Skokomish River: The first time I ever fished the "Skoke" I was impressed, but not as impressed as steelheading companion Dave Borden, who hooked and landed a pair of bright January steelhead within an hour of parking alongside the river and starting to cast. We were returning from a fishless trip to the Dosewallips and Duckabush rivers, and decided to test the Skokomish simply because we had a couple of hours to kill before either of us had to be home. For Dave, at least, it was a successful test, and I got a few good photos for my efforts.

As it turned out, though, our first try at Skokomish River steelheading—some 20 years ago—would be our most successful, and any angler who catches two winter steelies from this badly abused Hood Canal tributary in a single outing these days has pulled off a minor miracle. Although stocked with 20,000 to 30,000 winter steelhead smolts each year, the annual sport catch seldom tops 20 fish for the entire season. The North Fork Skokomish, dammed (or is that damned?) in two places to form Cushman and Kokanee lakes, provides virtually no steelheading opportunity. The South Fork Skoke is paralleled by Skokomish Valley Road (Forest Road 23) and other forest roads cutting off the main road to the right.

As for salmon fishing, the best is provided by a catch-and-release chum salmon fishery on the lower river during November and early December. The stretch of river from the U.S. 101 bridge downstream is full of chums some years, providing excellent action, but all chums (and any coho you might hook) must be released. Depending on weather and water conditions, Thanksgiving weekend often marks the peak of this fishery, which is popular with fly rodders and those using conventional drift-fishing tackle. These big, tough chums, fresh in from Hood Canal, will really stretch your string.

Sea-run cutthroating is fair here, but all wild cutthroats must be released and there are no hatchery cutthroat plants to supplement the wild runs and provide a harvest. The upper portion of the South Fork has a few legal-sized cutthroats, but few anglers take advantage of them. Catch-and-release trout fishing is a possibility on the upper North Fork Skokomish, above Lake Cushman, but the season is short and special regulations apply.

---

133. LOWER HOOD CANAL

Reference: **Mason County; map A2 inset, grid j1.**

How to get there: Take U.S. 101 north from Shelton to reach the entire west side of the canal. To reach the south side from the "Great Bend" to the tip, take State Route 106 east from U.S. 101 or west from Belfair. To reach the north side of the canal from the tip to the Great Bend, take State Route 3 to Belfair and turn west on State Route 300.

Facilities: Mike's Beach Resort near Lilliwaup has a launch that will handle boats up to about 22 feet, while Rest-A-While Resort near Hoodsport offers a sling launch. Both are pay facilities where the bigger your boat, the more it costs to launch. A free launch is located farther south on the west side of the canal, at Potlatch. There's a free ramp with limited parking in the town of Union and an excellent ramp ($4 fee) at Twanoh State Park. Ramps on the north side of the lower canal, off State Route 300, include the free ramp at the Port of Allyn (just west of Belfair) and the pay ramp ($5 to $10) at Summertide Resort, about 16 miles west of Belfair. RV and tent sites are available at Rest-A-While Resort, Mike's Beach Resort, Potlatch State Park, Twanoh State Park, Belfair State Park, Summertide Resort, and other, smaller facilities along the south end of the canal. Motel accommodations and other amenities are available in and around Hoodsport, Union, and Belfair.

Contact: Mike's Beach Resort, (360) 877-5324; Rest-A-While Resort, (360) 877-9474; Summertide Resort, (360) 275-2268; Potlatch State Park, (360) 877-5361; Twanoh State Park, (360) 275-2222; Belfair State Park, (360) 275-0668; Rik's Marine, (360) 877-5244. For nautical charts of this area, contact Captain's Nautical Supply, (206) 283-7242.

Species available: Chinook, chum, and (sometimes) pink salmon; sea-run cutthroat trout; a few rockfish and lingcod; sole and flounder; pile perch; striped seaperch.

Fishing Lower Hood Canal: The most well-known and popular sport fishery in southern Hood Canal the past several years has been the chum salmon fishery in front of the Hoodsport Salmon Hatchery. Running for about two months from the middle of October to the middle of December, it gives hundreds of anglers the opportunity to do battle with perhaps the toughest salmon that swims, the chum or "dog" salmon.

Hooking a tough chum on drift tackle or a favorite fly rod is always great sport, but this fishery has taken somewhat of an ugly turn in recent years. Since fishing space is limited, anglers sometimes get into turf squabbles or resort to name-calling when someone's hooked fish tangles with the lines of other anglers. There's something of a grudge between anglers who fly fish and those using casting or spinning tackle. Some fish are killed and then thrown in the bushes or left to rot on the beach by anglers who decide they don't really want to take them home. There are even conflicts between anglers and Indian gill-netters who sometimes crowd in to fish the only place where anglers are allowed. Wear your chest waders, take along a good selection of small, green flies or small steelhead bobbers and green yarn, and fish during the week if you can, to avoid some of the crowds.

There is some blackmouth-fishing opportunity through the winter and early spring, but it's a hit-and-miss proposition at best. Spots near the beach at Lilliwaup, Hoodsport, Ayres Point, and east of Union offer a few fish, but even fewer anglers are enthused enough to give it much of a try.

You may recall that in 1995 there was a short pink salmon season near the Hoodsport Salmon Hatchery, an event that came as a pleasant surprise to many anglers. That's not something we can depend on every odd-numbered year, but let's keep our fingers crossed. When it happens, trolling or casting small, hot-colored spoons, spinners, and plastic hoochies just offshore from the hatchery will take fish. This season may or may not be listed in the fishing pamphlet, so listen and watch for special announcements in the newspaper and on the radio.

The south end of the canal offers a good deal of sea-run cutthroat fishing, but most of the fish are from wild stocks and must be released. All the major estuaries have sea-runs, but those at Lilliwaup, Dewatto, and the mouth of the Tahuya River can be especially worthwhile.

Sole, flounder, and perch are abundant and under-fished throughout the southern half of the canal. Look for sole and flounder in areas of fairly flat, soft bottom. Pile and striped perch may be found in the same areas, but are best caught around docks and pilings. All these species will take small baits of any kind.

If you're thinking about fishing southern Hood Canal, by the way, check the regulations pamphlet concerning crab season before you set out. Except from mid-April to mid-July, crab pots are usually legal, and it often pays to put out a couple of them as you set out for the day's fishing. Even if the fish aren't biting, a couple of big Dungeness crabs could make the day a success. Areas around Union, Tahuya, Potlatch, and the mouth of the Skokomish River can offer especially good crabbing. Check the regulation pamphlet closely for details about the legalities involved.

134. WOOD AND WILDBERRY LAKES

Reference: **Northwest of Tahuya, north of Hood Canal's Great Bend; map A2 inset, grid j1.**

How to get there: Take State Route 3 to Belfair and turn west on State Route 300, following it toward Tahuya. Go north near Tahuya on Belfair-Tahuya Road for about 1.5 miles to Jiggs Lake, which is on the right. Continue north half a mile past the lake and turn left at the next intersection. From there it's two miles to Wood Lake and just under three miles to Wildberry Lake, with small signs along the road pointing the way.

Facilities: Both lakes have bank-fishing spots, but little else. The nearest food and gas are back on State Route 300, and the closest tackle and lodging are in Belfair. Belfair State Park, which you'll pass as you make your way west on State Route 300, offers tent and RV sites, showers, and rest rooms.

Contact: Belfair State Park, (360) 275-0668.

Species available: Rainbow trout.

Fishing Wood and Wildberry Lakes: Spring plants of legal-sized rainbows provide most of the action at Wood and Wildberry lakes, and since the Department of Fish and Wildlife stocks only a few hundred of them, the action usually ends by June. These small lakes are fished primarily by local anglers, because out-of-towners are often unable to find them and end up at nearby Maggie Lake or one of the more well-known lakes to the north. I know, because it's happened to me. Their small size and lack of developed boat-launching facilities make Wood and Wildberry good candidates for float-tube fishing. Wildberry Lake, by the way, may show as Buck Lake on some older maps.

The season here is a standard late-April-through-October run.

135. DEWATTO-AREA LAKES

Reference: **Southwest of Belfair, east side of Hood Canal, Map A2 inset, grid j1.**

How to get there: Take State Route 3 to Belfair and turn west on State Route 300 (North Shore Road). Turn north (right) on Belfair-Tahuya Road at the town of Tahuya and drive about four miles to Dewatto Road. Turn west (left) and watch for Tee Lake Road on the right. West of Tee Lake, roads to the left lead to Cady, Don, U, Robbins, and Aldrich lakes. Watch closely for signs pointing to the respective lakes.

Facilities: Except for U Lake, all have small Department of Fish and Wildlife access areas with boat ramps suitable for car-toppers and other small boats. Small stores in the area have groceries and gas, and complete facilities are available in Belfair. Belfair State Park, between Belfair and the lakes on State Route 300, has 33 tent sites and 47 RV sites with water, electrical, and sewer hookups.

Contact: Belfair State Park, (360) 275-0668.

Species available: Rainbow trout in all six lakes; cutthroats in Cady Lake; largemouth bass and yellow perch in Tee Lake.

Fishing the Dewatto-Area Lakes: Aldrich, Cady, Don (also called Clara), Robbins, and U lakes, all 10 to 17 acres in size and within just over a mile of each other, are havens for small-boat anglers and float-tubers who like to get away from the hustle and bustle of big waters with lots of high-speed boating activity. Their small size and limited boat-launch facilities help to keep the high-speed thrill-seekers away and provide a quality experience for anglers. Tee Lake, which covers 38 acres and has a fair amount of development around it, is the exception, so don't be surprised if the water-skiers and personal water-craft jockeys try to buzz you. A large bass plug equipped with two or three treble hooks, cast in the direction of the culprits, may or may not help to keep them at bay.

Of the six lakes, Cady may be the gem of the bunch. Development around its shores is all but nonexistent, and fly-fishing-only regulations help to keep the crowds small. The other lakes are productive in May and June, but Cady provides fair-to-good fishing from spring through fall. All these lakes open in late April and close at the end of October.

136. DEWATTO RIVER

Reference: **Flows into Hood Canal east of Lilliwaup; map A2 inset, grid j2.**

How to get there: Take State Route 9 to Belfair and turn west on State Route 300. Turn north (right) at Tahuya onto Belfair-Tahuya Road, then west (left) on Dewatto Road to Dewatto, which is located at the river mouth. From there, follow Dewatto-Holly Road upstream.

Facilities: Tent and RV sites, rest rooms, and showers are available at Belfair State Park, on State Route 300. The town of Belfair has food, gas, lodging, and other amenities.

Contact: Belfair State Park, (360) 275-0668.

Species available: Sea-run cutthroat trout, a few winter steelhead.

Fishing the Dewatto River: Like the nearby Tahuya (see below), this small Hood Canal tributary is hardly worth a long trip just for the fishing. Wild cutthroats and wild steelhead must be released, and there aren't any hatchery plants, so don't expect fast action.

137. MAGGIE LAKE

Reference: **Southwest of Belfair, Mason County; map A2 inset, grid j2.**

How to get there: Take State Route 3 to Belfair and turn west onto State Route 300 (North Shore Road), following it to Tahuya. Turn north (right) at Tahuya onto Belfair-Tahuya Road and drive about 2.5 miles to the lake, which is on the right.

Facilities: A public access area with a boat ramp is located near the south end of the lake. Belfair State Park, about 12 miles away on State Route 300, has tent and RV sites, rest rooms, and showers. Other accommodations, along with food, gas, tackle, and lodging are available in Belfair.

Contact: Belfair State Park, (360) 275-0668.

Species available: Rainbow trout.

Fishing Maggie Lake: Some 2,000 legal-sized rainbow trout from Department of Fish and Wildlife hatcheries are on hand to greet anglers when this 25-acre lake opens to fishing in late April every year. Most of those trout are gone by the end of May, and as soon as the fishing slows, most early season anglers go looking for greener pastures. But if you like warm-weather trout fishing, don't be afraid to stick with this one all summer long. Maggie Lake sits in a deep basin and has spots more than 70 feet deep, making it one of Mason County's deepest lakes and one of the most likely to provide decent trout fishing even during the warm spells of summer. Things may get a little busy with swimmers and the like from June through August, but if you get on the water early in the day, they won't be a problem.

138. TAHUYA RIVER

Reference: **Flows into the south end of Hood Canal at the Great Bend; map A2 inset, grid j2.**

How to get there: Take State Route 9 to Belfair and turn west onto State Route 300, following it to Tahuya. Turn north (right) on Belfair-Tahuya Road, then east (right) on Tahuya River Road, which parallels the west side of the river.

Facilities: Belfair State Park is the nearest place with tent and RV sites. Food, gas, lodging, and tackle are available in Belfair.

Contact: Belfair State Park, (360) 275-0668.

Species available: Resident and sea-run cutthroat trout, some winter steelhead.

Fishing the Tahuya River: Though it's called a river, the Tahuya becomes little more than a small creek during the summer months, providing decent trout-fishing opportunity, except that all wild cutthroat must be released. Sea-run cutthroating becomes a good possibility when fall rains raise the river level, but, again, only fin-clipped hatchery sea-runs may be killed. Wild-fish-release rules also are in effect during the winter steelhead season, but the river doesn't always receive plants of hatchery steelhead smolts.

As you might guess, the steelheading gets pretty slow under those circumstances. But if you like small-stream steelheading, Tahuya River is a pretty good place to get away from the crowds. If you're really lucky, you might even hook a fish.

139. HOWELL LAKE

Reference: **West of Belfair, Mason County; map A2 inset, grid j2.**

How to get there: Take State Route 3 to Belfair and turn west on State Route 300. Drive about half a mile past Belfair State Park and turn north (right) at the sign pointing the way to nearly a dozen area lakes. About half a mile after crossing the Tahuya River bridge, turn left on the road with signs pointing to Howell, Tee, and other area lakes. Drive two miles to Howell Lake Road, turn left, and drive about half a mile to the lake.

Facilities: A rough boat ramp is located at the northwest corner of the lake. Food, gas, lodging, and tackle can be found back toward Belfair. Belfair State Park is on the south side of State Route 300, just west of Belfair, and has tent and RV sites, showers, and rest rooms.

Contact: Belfair State Park, (360) 275-0668.

Species available: Rainbow trout.

Fishing Howell Lake: Pan-sized rainbows from Department of Fish and Wildlife plants provide some pretty good action here for a few weeks in the spring. Then things drop off and most anglers forget about Howell for another year. Some of the old-timers who fish here say the lake contains a few brook trout, but I have yet to see anybody catch one.

140. HAVEN LAKE

Reference: **Northwest of Belfair, Mason County; map A2 inset, grid j2.**

How to get there: Take State Route 3 to Belfair and turn west on State Route 300. Drive about half a mile past Belfair State Park and turn north (right) at the sign pointing the way to Haven and other area lakes. Continue about seven miles to the lake.

Facilities: The lake has a public access area with a boat ramp and toilets. The nearest gas, food, lodging, and tackle are in Belfair and the vicinity. Belfair State Park has tent and RV sites, rest rooms, and showers.

Contact: Belfair State Park, (360) 275-0668.

Species available: Rainbow and cutthroat trout.

Fishing Haven Lake: Often one of Mason County's better early season trout producers, Haven is stocked with enough hatchery rainbows and cutthroats to keep everyone happy, at least for a while. This 70-acre lake with lots of homes and development around its shores usually produces a good per-rod catch average during the first few weeks of the April-through-October season, but like any good thing, it doesn't last. The trout fishing is tough by June and stays slow all summer, picking up somewhat in September.

141. LAKE WOOTEN

Reference: **Northwest of Belfair, Mason County; map A2 inset, grid j2.**

How to get there: Take State Route 3 to Belfair and turn west on State Route 300. Drive about half a mile past Belfair State Park and turn north (right) at the sign pointing the way to Wooten and other area lakes. Drive about seven miles to Haven Lake and continue along its east side another mile to Lake Wooten. The road runs completely around the lake.

Facilities: The lake has a boat ramp and access area. Belfair State Park, about a mile to the southeast, has 33 tent sites and 47 sites for RVs that are complete with water, electrical, and sewer hookups. Belfair offers the nearest food, gas, tackle, and lodging.

Contact: Belfair State Park, (360) 275-0668.

Species available: Rainbow and cutthroat trout.

Fishing Lake Wooten: Both spring and fall fishing can be good here, but the lake gets pretty busy with swimmers, skiers, and other sun-seekers throughout the summer, so fishing opportunities drop off at that time of year. If you do decide to fish it in July or August, get on the water early in the morning and try stillfishing the 35-foot-deep hole about 200 feet offshore near the east end of the lake. Rainbows, including some hefty carryovers, provide most of the action, but Wooten is also planted with some large cutthroats for variety.

142. TWIN LAKES

Reference: **Northwest of Belfair, Mason County; map A2 inset, grid i2.**

How to get there: Take State Route 3 to Belfair and turn west on State Route 300. About half a mile past Belfair State Park, turn right at the sign pointing to Twin and other area lakes. Drive just under three miles to Elfendahl Pass Road, turn north (right), drive three miles, and turn west (left) on the gravel road leading past Camp Spillman to Twin Lakes. A sign marks the right turn to the lakes.

Facilities: A primitive campground and small boat ramp are located on Big Twin, the eastern of the two lakes. Belfair State Park, about 20 minutes away, has tent and RV sites, rest rooms, and showers. Food, gas, tackle, and lodging are available in Belfair.

Contact: Belfair State Park, (360) 275-0668.

Species available: Rainbow trout.

Fishing Twin Lakes: Although they total only about 20 acres, Twin Lakes are heavily stocked with legal-sized rainbows by the Department of Fish and Wildlife. Would you believe about 8,000 seven- to 10-inch rainbows each spring? All those hungry hatchery trout provide good fishing throughout the spring, and it doesn't matter too much whether you like to dunk worms, troll spinners, or cast flies, although fly casters seem to be in the minority around here most of the time.

The lakes are virtually connected so you can fish either or both in one trip. The best trout action is from the opener in late April until about mid-June.

143. PANTHER LAKE

Reference: **Kitsap-Mason county line, north of Belfair; see map A2 inset, grid i3.**

How to get there: Take State Route 3 to Belfair and turn west on State Route 300. About a mile west of Belfair, turn north (right) on Sand Hill Road and drive about seven miles to Gold Creek Road. Turn left and almost instantly you're on Panther Lake Road, which encircles the lake.

Facilities: A gravel boat ramp is located on the south side of the lake, and the parking area and rest rooms are across the road. Belfair offers the nearest grocery stores, gas stations, and other facilities. Belfair State Park, with tent and RV sites, is about eight miles south of the lake.

Contact: Kitsap Sport Shop, Bremerton, (360) 373-9589; Belfair State Park, (360) 275-0668.

Species available: Rainbow trout, brown bullhead catfish.

Fishing Panther Lake: Most of the trout-catching activity on this 100-acre lake just west of Tiger Lake (see page 190) occurs from late April through early June, during the first six weeks or so of the season. By the start of summer, anglers have caught most of the 5,000 or so legal-sized rainbows stocked here, but a few may still be around to provide fair fishing in the fall. The lake also has enough brown bullheads to provide fair catfish opportunities during the spring and summer.

144. MISSION LAKE

Reference: **West of Gorst, Kitsap Peninsula; map A2 inset, grid i3.**

How to get there: Drive to Belfair on State Route 3, turn west on State Route 300, and drive about a mile to Sand Hill Road. Turn north (right) and drive about seven miles to Tiger Lake. Turn right to Tiger-Mission Road and drive 1.5 miles to the south end of Mission Lake.

Facilities: A small, gravel access area and boat ramp for car-toppers and small trailer boats is located at the southeast corner of the lake. Belfair, about seven miles to the south, has the nearest food, gas, tackle, and lodging.

Contact: Kitsap Sport Shop, Bremerton, (360) 373-9589.

Species available: Rainbow and cutthroat trout, brown bullhead catfish.

Fishing Mission Lake: Pretty little Mission Lake and its small access area get lots of fishing pressure early in the season, but the crowds disappear by June and forget to come back for the good fall angling opportunities. Fishing closes at the end of October, but the last month of the season offers a good chance for rainbows averaging a foot long and sometimes pushing a foot and a half. Making autumn even more attractive is the occasional stocking of large cutthroats in the lake. Cutts often come on strong in the fall, and Mission Lake cutthroats are no exception. Take a fly rod and a good selection of wet flies and nymph patterns to get the most from your trip.

145. TIGER LAKE

Reference: **North of Belfair, Kitsap Peninsula; map A2 inset, grid i3.**

How to get there: Drive to Belfair on State Route 3, turn west on State Route 300, and drive about a mile to Sand Hill Road. Turn north (right) and drive about seven miles to the lake, which has roads all the way around it.

Facilities: The large, gravel access area at the north end of the lake offers room to launch at least three boats at a time, with plenty of space for casting from the bank. Belfair offers the nearest food, gas, tackle, and lodging. Belfair State Park is about seven miles south of the lake.

Contact: Kitsap Sport Shop, Bremerton, (360) 373-9589; Belfair State Park, (360) 275-0668.

Species available: Rainbow and cutthroat trout.

Fishing Tiger Lake: Thanks to one of those wonderful quirks of geography, you have to launch in Kitsap County to fish this Mason County trout lake. The public access area and boat ramp at the north end of Tiger lies just across the Mason-Kitsap county line, while most of the lake's 100 acres are in Mason County. Okay, so that may have been a big deal back in the old days of county fishing licenses, but it isn't now.

What's really important is the fact that Tiger is heavily stocked with about 8,000 legal-sized rainbows every spring just before the April opener, and early season fishing here is often some of the best in Mason (and Kitsap) County. The Department of Fish and Wildlife often throws a few large cutthroats into the spring mix, adding variety and a fair chance for a bragging-sized trout. Come back in the fall; you'll find good fishing and small crowds.

---

146. UNION RIVER

Reference: **Flows into the tip of Hood Canal near Belfair, Mason County; map A2 inset, grid j3.**

How to get there: Take State Route 3 to Belfair and turn north on Old Belfair Highway, which parallels much of the river for about four miles.

Facilities: Restaurants, grocery stores, tackle, gas stations, and motels are abundant in Belfair. RV and tent sites, rest rooms, showers, and other amenities are available at Belfair State Park, just west of Belfair.

Contact: Belfair State Park, (360) 275-0668.

Species available: Winter and summer steelhead, sea-run and resident cutthroat trout.

Fishing the Union River: Though the Department of Fish and Wildlife says it stocks about 10,000 winter steelhead smolts a year into this little Hood Canal tributary, try to find someone who's caught an adult steelhead here in the past five years. And it's not just me; WDF&W catch statistics for the last several years show that the annual winter steelhead catch from the Union ranges from none to about a dozen fish per winter. That's not enough action to warrant a visit to the river unless you live just down the road and have nothing else to do with your winter days.

Although not stocked with summer-run steelhead, those same catch statistics show that anglers hook a few here. I have to assume that anglers are releasing those non-hatchery summer-runs, since the Union is a wild-fish-release steelhead stream.

As for trout fishing, it's fair during the fall, when sea-run cutthroats enter the river on just about every decent high tide or heavy rain. Grab a can of nightcrawlers and give it a try anytime from mid-September on.

147. LONG LAKE

Reference: **South of Port Orchard, Kitsap County; map A2 inset, grid i4.**
How to get there: Take State Route 16 south from Port Orchard, turn east (left) on Sedgewick Road, and then south (right) on Long Lake Road, which parallels the east side of the lake.
Facilities: The lake has a public access area with boat ramps and toilets. Food, gas, tackle, and lodging are available in Port Orchard and a little farther north in Bremerton.
Contact: Kitsap Sport Shop, Bremerton, (360) 373-9589.
Species available: Largemouth bass, crappies, bluegills, some cutthroat trout.
Fishing Long Lake: This 315-acre lake south of Port Orchard is most productive after it has warmed in the spring. Good-sized largemouths can be caught during spring and summer, but be sure to check the fishing pamphlet for details about the slot limit that requires you to throw back bass in the 12- to 15-inch size range.

Summertime crappie fishing can be quite good. Be prepared for an encounter with a school of cooperative crappies by taking along your favorite ultralight spinning outfit or light-action fly rod.

Your best shot at hooking a big cutthroat here is in the fall, especially in October and November.

148. ANGLE LAKE

Reference: **Southeast of Seattle-Tacoma Airport; map A2 inset, grid j6.**
How to get there: Take the 200th Street exit off Interstate 5 near Des Moines and drive west on 200th to Pacific Highway South. Turn north (right) and drive about four blocks to the lake, which is visible on the right.
Facilities: A King County park on the west side of the lake has a boat ramp, and food, gas, lodging, and other amenities are available within casting distance along Pacific Highway South.
Contact: Auburn Sports and Marine, (360) 833-1440.
Species available: Rainbow trout, largemouth bass, yellow perch, crappies.
Fishing Angle Lake: This popular lake within sight of Seattle-Tacoma International Airport is open to year-round fishing. The annual spring plant of about 6,000 rainbow trout doesn't last too long, with your best shot at catching them from March through May.

But the bass and panfish action holds up all summer. Anglers catch some good-sized bass around the lake's many docks and floats beginning in May. Nice summer days bring out the crowds, so consider doing your summertime bass fishing early in the morning, late in the evening or, as some anglers prefer, during the night. Perch fishing is good throughout most of the year, and the lake has some whoppers.

149. GREEN RIVER

Reference: **Flows into Elliott Bay and Puget Sound at Seattle; map A2 inset, grid j6.**

How to get there: Take State Route 167 to State Route 18 and drive east through Auburn to Green Valley Road. Turn east (right) and follow Green Valley Road east along the river. To fish lower portions of the Green, follow State Route 167 between Auburn and Kent and take any of several crossroads off the freeway to reach the river. The Meeker Street exit, for example, will take you to some deep pools right along the freeway.

Facilities: Food, gas, lodging, tackle, and all other facilities are available in Auburn and Kent.

Contact: Auburn Sports and Marine, (206) 833-1440.

Species available: Winter and summer steelhead, coho and chum salmon, cutthroat trout.

Fishing the Green River: Once one of Washington's top winter steelhead rivers, the Green has been a tough nut for anglers to crack in recent years. It hasn't even made the top 10 among the state's winter steelhead streams lately, even though it used to consistently rank near the head of that list. Although it's planted with nearly 200,000 winter steelhead smolts annually, the winter catch in recent years has hovered down around the 1,000 mark. During the winter of 1993-94, Green River anglers caught only 862 steelhead, a dismal total for this stream.

When winter steelhead are in the Green, the stretch of river from Kent upstream to Flaming Geyser State Park is one of the most popular among anglers. Several good bank-fishing spots are found along the Green River Road, which runs along the east side of the river between Kent and Auburn. Green Valley Road, which runs upriver several miles east of Auburn, is also a good bet for access to lots of potentially productive steelhead water. One of the favorite fishing spots along this stretch is immediately upstream and downstream from the State Route 18 bridge. To reach it, take the Green Valley Road exit off State Route 18 and turn left almost immediately into the gravel parking area between the road and the river. A trail leads downriver, under the bridge.

There's nothing special you need to know about fishing the Green for winter steelhead. When it's low and clear you can take fish on small spoons and metal-finish spinners, and during normal flows you can fish roe, shrimp, bobbers, and all the other offerings you might throw at winter fish on your favorite stream. One thing you can't do here during the winter is fish from a boat. You can use a drift boat or other craft for transportation, but if you want to fish you have to get out and cast from the bank.

The boat-fishing regulation doesn't apply during the summer, and many anglers launch near the Whitney Bridge or farther upstream at Flaming Geyser State Park and make the day-long float down to the State Route 18 bridge. Fishing for steelhead holds up pretty well on the Green throughout the summer, with decent catches from June through August. While the Green Valley Road area is a favorite with many summer steelheaders, the waters farther upstream, near the rearing ponds at Palmer, are also productive for summer-runs.

Fall salmon fishing can also be productive on the Green, especially around the Kent area and along the Green River Road between Kent and Auburn. Once a good chinook producer, the river is now closed for chinooks, but coho fishing can be good in October. The usual metallic spoons and spinners that work elsewhere will do the job here. Early in the fall, when the silvers first move into the river, you might also get them to take a cluster of fresh roe or a ghost shrimp, especially if it's enhanced with a small tuft of nylon yarn or a brightly colored steelhead bobber. Fall is also the time for sea-run cutthroat fishing, and the entire lower river (from Kent downstream) holds trout in September and October. Try rolling nightcrawlers along the bottom to tempt them.

150. PANTHER LAKE

Reference: **Northeast of Kent; map A2 inset, grid j7.**

How to get there: Take the Benson Highway (State Route 515) north from Kent and go through the intersection at South 208th Street. Turn right on the next street north of South 208th Street, drive less than half a mile to a "Y" in the road, and go right to the lake.

Facilities: A rather rough boat ramp is located on the east side of the lake. Other amenities are available in Kent and Renton.

Contact: The Reel Thing, (206) 941-0920.

Species available: Largemouth bass, rainbow trout, brown bullhead catfish.

Fishing Panther Lake: Although stocked with a few hatchery rainbows in the spring, this small lake between Kent and Renton is better known for its bass fishing. If you like fishing weeds, brush, and other vegetation, this is the place for you. Panther Lake is no more than seven or eight feet deep and filled with all sorts of greenery in which bass can hide. Bring an assortment of spinnerbaits, buzzbaits, Texas-rigged plastic worms, and other weedless or at least moderately weedless bass baits. The thick tangles produce some good-sized largemouths. The lake covers only about 33 acres, small enough to fish effectively from a float tube. You can also get small car-toppers into the lake, but the primitive launch isn't adequate for larger trailer boats. Because of all those weeds, catfishing is best accomplished with a nightcrawler suspended from a bobber, so that it hangs just over the tops of the weeds.

151. LAKE WILDERNESS

Reference: **East of Kent; map A2 inset, grid j7.**

How to get there: Take State Route 18 north from Auburn and turn east (right) on State Route 516 (Kent-Kangley Road). Drive about 3.6 miles and turn north (left) at the signs pointing the way to Lake Wilderness Park and Lake Wilderness Golf Course. Drive about 1.5 miles to the lake, which is on the right.

Facilities: A Washington Department of Fish and Wildlife access area and boat ramp, along with a King County park, provide lots of bank access. The nearest food, gas, tackle, and lodging are in Kent.

Contact: The Reel Thing, (206) 941-0920.
Species available: Rainbow trout, some kokanee.
Fishing Lake Wilderness: This one can be a little unpredictable when it comes to trout fishing. Some years it provides excellent early season catches of eight- to 10-inch hatchery rainbows and a few 15-inch carry-overs, while other years it starts off slow and then tapers off quickly. Although the lake is fairly shallow, its clean waters support a kokanee population, and trolling for these tasty little sockeye salmon can be fairly productive in June and July.

If you fish it, take a boat or float tube, because the water is quite shallow around the public beach-fishing spots and it takes an impressive cast to get your bait or lure out into water more than about 10 feet deep.

152. SHADY LAKE

Reference: **Northeast of Kent, map A2 inset, grid j7.**
How to get there: Drive east from Renton on Petrovitsky Road and turn north (left) on 196th Drive, which leads to the lake.
Facilities: The south end of the lake has a public access area with a boat ramp. Other amenities are in Renton, Kent, and Maple Valley.
Contact: The Reel Thing, (206) 941-0920.
Species available: Rainbow and cutthroat trout.
Fishing Shady Lake: This south King County lake has an unusually short season, opening to fishing on June 1 and closing at the end of October. It covers only about 21 acres and is a favorite with float-tubers and small-boat anglers. The planting of various-sized trout and some carryover from year to year means you never really know whether the next fish you catch will be an eight-incher or a three-pounder.

Because of the lake's small size, short season, and relatively light plant of legal-sized trout, Shady gets less fishing pressure than many other lakes in this part of King County. You probably won't catch a limit here, but you will enjoy some peace, quiet, and solitude, which is certainly part of what fishing is all about.

153. LAKE DESIRE

Reference: **Southeast of Renton; map A2 inset, grid j7.**
How to get there: Drive east from Renton on Petrovitsky Road, turn north (left) on 184th Avenue SE, and follow it half a mile to Lake Desire Drive. Turn left and drive just under a mile to the lake.
Facilities: The lake has a public access area with a new fishing dock and boat ramp at its north end. Other facilities are available in Renton.
Contact: The Reel Thing, (206) 941-0920.
Species available: Rainbow and cutthroat trout, largemouth bass, yellow perch.
Fishing Lake Desire: This popular south King County lake is now open year-round, and spring plants of legal-sized rainbows and a few larger cutthroats provide consistent angling action. Spring and fall are the best times to fish it for trout. Anglers catch rainbows and cutthroats by trolling most of the standard offerings or stillfishing with worms, marshmallows, salmon eggs, Power Bait, or cheese.

Bass fishing can be good during the spring and summer, and the lake produces a few hefty largemouths.

The entire lake is quite shallow, and that goes for the boat ramp. Be careful when launching, especially if you have a larger boat that requires a trailer.

154. OTTER (SPRING) LAKE

Reference: **Southeast of Renton; map A2 inset, grid j7.**

How to get there: Drive east from Renton on Petrovitsky Road and turn north (left) on 196th Avenue SE. Turn left again on SE 183rd Street and drive to Spring Lake Drive. The lake is on the left.

Facilities: A public access area and boat ramp are located near the northeast corner of the lake. The nearest amenities are in Kent, Renton, and Maple Valley.

Contact: The Reel Thing, (206) 941-0920.

Species available: Rainbow and cutthroat trout, largemouth bass, yellow perch, brown bullhead catfish.

Fishing Otter Lake: Some folks call it Otter Lake, some call it Spring Lake, and others really don't care one way or the other. What's important here is that this 67-acre lake between Renton and Maple Valley offers a wide range of fishing possibilities throughout much of the year. It sometimes gives up rainbows to four pounds, although liberal spring plants of hatchery trout make nine-inchers a more likely possibility. The trout fishing can be quite good in April and May.

While the rainbow fishery here is well-known, the lake's fair-sized cutthroats are a more well-kept secret, according to Tom Pollack at The Reel Thing tackle shop, who happens to live fairly close to the lake. Anglers who latch onto a large cutthroat just don't make too big a deal of it, he says.

The gently sloping flats near the south end of the lake warm quickly in the spring and stay warm all summer, providing some good fishing opportunities for bass, perch, and catfish. Try top-water plugs early and late in the day for bass, and dark-colored spinnerbaits or plastic worms while the sun is high. A bobber-and-worm rig will take the perch and catfish.

155. SHADOW LAKE

Reference: **Northeast of Kent; map A2 inset, grid j7.**

How to get there: Drive east from Renton on Petrovitsky Road and turn south (right) on 196th Avenue SE, then east (left) on 213th Street. Drive half a mile and the lake is on the left.

Facilities: A boat ramp is located at the north end of the lake. All other facilities are available in Renton.

Contact: The Reel Thing, (206) 941-0920.

Species available: Rainbow trout, largemouth bass, yellow perch, crappies.

Fishing Shadow Lake: One of many King County lakes that have gone from an April-to-October season to year-round in recent years, Shadow offers good spring trout fishing and fair action again in the fall.

Planted rainbows of eight to 10 inches are standard fare, but the spring plants often include a few brood stock trout that run a pound and a half to three pounds each. Trolling is more popular here than stillfishing, but if you have your heart set on staying in one place and waiting for the trout to come to you, try anchoring at the north end of the lake, just west of the entrance to the canal that leads to the boat ramp.

That 1,200-foot canal that connects the boat ramp to the main lake, by the way, is a pretty good place to fish for Shadow Lake bass. Tom Pollack, who operates The Reel Thing tackle shop in Federal Way, says he always makes his way slowly through the narrow canal when boating in and out of the lake, casting to both sides as he goes. The strategy pays off with a large-mouth or two more often than not, he says.

Perch are found throughout the lake and will hit worms or small jigs all spring and summer. Crappies also like little leadheads, fished around sub-merged wood or weedy cover.

156. LAKE MERIDIAN

Reference: **Southeast of Kent; map A2 inset, grid j7.**
How to get there: **Take Kent-Kangley Road (State Route 516) east from Kent** about three miles until you see the lake right alongside the road on your left. Turn left into the county park at the lake's southeast corner or go a block past it to the light and turn left to reach the Department of Fish and Wildlife boat ramp on the east end of the lake.
Facilities: **The county park has bank access and a boat ramp that closes at** sunset, while the WDF&W ramp is open 24 hours. The nearest food, gas, lodging, and tackle are in Kent.
Contact: **The Reel Thing, (206) 941-0920.**
Species available: **Rainbow trout, largemouth and smallmouth bass, yellow** perch, brown bullhead catfish.
Fishing Lake Meridian: **Spring hatchery plants of 8,000 to 9,000 legal-sized** rainbows draw most of the angling attention on this 150-acre lake near Kent, but fishing for bass and other warm-water fish can be good during the late spring and summer. Largemouth bass are fairly abundant, and the lake has a few smallmouths as well. Try surface plugs around the docks first thing in the morning and during the last few minutes of light in the evening, or work spinnerbaits and crankbaits around the many docks and floats during the day for largemouths. Smallmouths may also be caught on the surface early and late, or fish small plastic grubs on one-sixteenth- or one-eighth-ounce leadheads during the day. The bass fishery here often holds up into and through the night. If you need incentive to give bassing a try, how about a 5$1/2$-pound smallmouth caught here during the spring of 1995. I thought that might work.

157. WALSH LAKE

Reference: **Southeast of Hobart; map A2 inset, j8.**
How to get there: **Take State Route 18 to Hobart and drive south on 276th** Avenue SE, then east (left) on SE 216th Street. The road soon turns to gravel, then splits. Go left at the "Y" and the lake will be on your right.

Facilities: No facilities are available at the lake, but food and gas can be found in and around Hobart. Lodging and tackle are in Maple Valley, to the south.

Contact: The Sport Shop, (206) 888-0715.

Species available: Cutthroat trout, yellow perch, brown bullhead catfish.

Fishing Walsh Lake: Though Walsh Lake is large at 100 acres, the fishing opportunity is limited. But it's peaceful and quiet in this part of King County, so you'll enjoy the solitude. Chances are good that even the fish will leave you alone.

---

158. BENSON LAKE

Reference: **Southwest of Allyn, Mason County; map A2 inset, grid j2.**

How to get there: Take State Route 3 north from Shelton or south from Belfair and turn west on Mason Lake County Park Road. Turn left on East Benson Road and almost immediately turn right into the public access area at the lake.

Facilities: The gravel access area on the east side of the lake has a gravel boat ramp and room for several cars and boat trailers. When boating activity isn't too heavy at the ramp, there's room for about half a dozen bank anglers to try their luck. Twanoh State Park, to the north on Hood Canal, offers tent and RV sites, rest rooms, and showers. The nearest food, gas, tackle, and lodging are available in Belfair and Shelton.

Contact: Verle's Sport Center, (360) 426-0933; Twanoh State Park, (360) 275-2222.

Species available: Rainbow and cutthroat trout.

Fishing Benson Lake: This 80-acre lake just east of Mason Lake (see below) drops off steeply from the bank on both its east and west side, providing bank anglers a good opportunity to catch trout. That helps to explain why the public access area on the east side of the lake is often crowded with shore anglers—they catch fish there! But sometimes there are so many bank anglers at the access area that boaters have a tough time getting in and out of the water. It's a minor problem, since both boat and bank anglers catch their share of Benson Lake rainbows and cutthroats. The lake, which is open from late April through October, gets a generous plant of 6,000 legal-sized rainbows and a few large cutts every spring, providing good trout-fishing opportunities well into summer.

---

159. MASON LAKE

Reference: **Southwest of Allyn, Mason County; map A2 inset, grid j2.**

How to get there: Take U.S. 101 to Shelton and exit east onto State Route 3, through Shelton, and continue northeasterly on State Route 3 to Mason-Benson Road, about 11 miles out of Shelton. Turn left and drive about three miles to the lake.

Facilities: There's a Department of Fish and Wildlife access area and boat ramp on the lake, as well as a county park with a boat ramp and room for bank fishing. Twanoh State Park is only a few miles to the north and has more than 60 tent and RV sites. The nearest food, gas, tackle, and lodging are in Belfair and Shelton.

Contact: Verle's Sport Center, (360) 426-0933; Twanoh State Park, (360) 275-2222.

Species available: Kokanee, rainbow trout, largemouth bass, yellow perch, brown bullhead catfish.

Fishing Mason Lake: Kokanee fishing can be quite good here, but in July and August, when this fishery is at its peak, you had better plan on arriving early in the morning or fishing late in the evening. Mason Lake gets very busy during the rest of the day. At nearly 1,000 acres, it's one of the area's biggest lakes, and it's very popular with water-skiers, swimmers, and other non-angling water enthusiasts. Anglers don't have much chance against all that competition on a warm summer day.

If you do go kokanee fishing, try trolling a Wedding Ring spinner or other small, flashy offering behind a string of trolling blades. Add a maggot, a kernel of white corn, or a small piece of worm to the lure's hooks and you're in business. As in all kokanee fishing, use your depthsounder to pinpoint the depth at which the fish are concentrated or keep varying your trolling depth until you find the first fish, then stay with that depth to locate others. And, speaking of depth, this lake has plenty, with some spots plunging 80 to 90 feet.

You may also catch a few rainbow trout as you troll for kokanee. Trolling small wobblers and spinners near the shoreline also produces rainbows, as does stillfishing near the bottom with various baits or suspending a worm, salmon egg, or combination of the two beneath a bobber.

Shoreline areas of the lake also offer largemouth bass, some of them growing to impressive size. Most of the perch are small, but if you find a pocket of large ones, stick with it for a while and see if you can come out with enough of them for a fish fry. The same goes for the bullheads, which are available around the edge of the lake throughout the summer.

Small perch are abundant here and bite throughout the year-round season. Catfish action is best at night from June through August.

---

160. PRICKETT (TRAILS END) LAKE

Reference: **West of Allyn, Mason County; map A2 inset, grid j2.**

How to get there: Drive south from Belfair or north from U.S. 101 near Shelton on State Route 106 and turn east on Trails Road (a sign at the start of the road points the way toward Mason Lake Road). Go 1.5 miles on Trails End Road, turn left on Trails End Road (rather than going straight on what at that point becomes Mason Lake Road), and proceed half a mile to the lake's access area, which is on the left.

Facilities: The access area has a small, gravel parking lot and gravel boat ramp. Both have very limited room, and the boat ramp tends to clog with dollar pads and other vegetation late in the summer. Twanoh State Park, about six miles to the west on State Route 106, has 47 tent sites and 18 RV spaces with hookups, rest rooms, and showers. Restaurants, fast food, lodging, tackle, and other facilities are available in Belfair.

Contact: Twanoh State Park, (360) 275-2222.

Species available: Rainbow trout, black bullhead catfish.

Fishing Prickett Lake: Stocked with about 4,000 legal-sized rainbows every spring, this 75-acre lake with a year-round season provides its best fishing in April and May. Since most of the lake is less than 20 feet deep, it warms quickly in the summer, but the 30-foot hole about 300 yards off the boat ramp might be worth investigating if you need a trout fix during the warmer months. Trout fishing picks up again in September and October.

For catfish, try the shallow north end of the lake from May through July.

---

161. DEVEREAUX LAKE

Reference: **North of Allyn, Mason County, map A2 inset, grid j3.**

How to get there: Take State Route 3 south from Belfair or north from Allyn and turn west onto Devereaux Road, then drive about one-quarter of a mile to the lake, which is on the left.

Facilities: The Department of Fish and Wildlife has a large access area with a concrete boat ramp near the north end of the lake, and the big fir log next to the boat ramp is a perfect spot to sit and fish from the access area. Both Belfair and Twanoh state parks are within reasonable driving range, 6 and 10 miles, respectively, and both have tent and RV sites, rest rooms, and showers. Food, gas, and lodging are available both to the north and south on State Route 3. Tackle is available in Belfair.

Contact: Belfair State Park, (360) 275-0668; Twanoh State Park, (360) 275-2222.

Species available: Rainbow trout, kokanee.

Fishing Devereaux Lake: Except for a boat ramp and a Girl Scout camp, you might think you're on a wilderness lake out in the middle of nowhere when you're in the middle of this large Mason County Lake surrounded by trees and with no residential development. You have to like that in a lake, even on days when the fishing is lousy.

But the fishing at Devereaux is usually several cuts above the lousy category. Spring plants of 4,000 rainbows help to provide decent trout fishing well into June, and by that time the kokanee action is starting to pick up. Then, just as the kokanee fishing falls off, fall rainbows go on the bite. While pan-sized fish comprise most of the catch, Devereaux has a pretty good reputation for its lunker carry-overs, and Department of Fish and Wildlife personnel like to talk about the possibility of hooking rainbows to five pounds here. It's never happened to me, but my excuse is that I don't fish the lake very often.

Oh yes, a word of warning is in order. If you fish Devereaux in the summer, watch out for the mob (school?) of girls who have to swim across the lake as part of their stay at the scout camp. They don't move very fast, but they could certainly interfere if you're trying to troll around the middle of the lake. You would never land one of them, especially on light tackle, so you might as well avoid them.

162. COULTER CREEK

Reference: **Flows into North Bay, at the extreme north end of Case Inlet, near Allyn; map A2 inset, grid j3.**

How to get there: Take State Route 3 south from Belfair or north from Shelton and turn east onto State Route 302 at the town of Allyn. Drive about three miles to the Coulter Creek fish hatchery and turn north (left) to follow the east side of the creek.

Facilities: Food and gas are available in Allyn, with the nearest lodging and tackle in Belfair. Belfair State Park is about nine miles from the creek via State Route 3 and State Route 300.

Contact: Belfair State Park, (360) 275-0668.

Species available: Sea-run and resident cutthroat trout.

Fishing Coulter Creek: Forested and green, this is a pretty little stream in one of the prettiest parts of the entire Northwest, especially in the fall, when fishing is at its best. Coulter Creek has a fairly good population of resident trout, but few ever achieve the 14-inch minimum size required of a "keeper." Fall runs of sea-run trout, though, often contain fish of 14 to 16 inches. Since the creek is small, it usually takes a good rain to draw sea-run fish in, so fish it in foul weather if you can.

163. WYE LAKE

Reference: **Southwest corner of Kitsap County, southeast of Belfair; map A2 inset, grid j3.**

How to get there: From the east, take State Route 16 to Bethel and turn west (left) on Lider Road, drive about two miles to Lake Flora Road, and turn left. Drive about four miles to Dickenson Road and turn south (left), following it about three miles to where it makes a hard right and becomes Carney Lake Road. Another hard right in the road quickly follows, and at that point, turn right onto Wye Lake Boulevard. Take the first left and drive down the hill about 200 yards to the boat ramp, on the right. From the west, take State Route 3 south from Bremerton or north from Belfair and turn east onto Lake Flora Road. Turn south (right) onto Dickenson Road and follow it to Wye Lake Boulevard.

Facilities: There's a gravel access area and concrete boat ramp at the south end of the lake, with pit toilets and enough room to park maybe a dozen cars. The nearest food and gas are about four miles to the south in Vaughn. Food, gas, tackle, and lodging are available in Belfair.

Contact: Kitsap Sport Shop, Bremerton, (360) 373-9589.

Species available: Rainbow trout, largemouth bass, brown bullhead catfish.

Fishing Wye Lake: Some fishing memories have little to do with fishing, and I can't think about Wye Lake without remembering what I saw there one Sunday morning in the summer of 1995. It was cool and rainy, and even at 8 A.M. I couldn't hear or see any sign of human activity on or around the lake. But as I stepped out of my car in the lake's small, gravel public access area, I discovered I wasn't alone. I was sharing the boat ramp with thousands— that's right, thousands—of little brown frogs. I don't know where they were coming from or where they were going, but they obviously had spent the night camping out in the Wye Lake access area, and I couldn't take a step for fear of crushing about a half-dozen of them beneath my size thirteens. Luckily, I had parked well back away from the water, where most of the major toad frenzy was taking place, so I back-tracked carefully toward the car and went somewhere else to fish, leaving the Wye Lake boat ramp to the great hordes of mini-frogs (or maybe they were toads) that had claimed it.

Although the idea of launching into some Stephen King-esque tale about little amphibious creatures invading Kitsap County is mighty tempting, it's time to get back to the subject at hand, which happens to be fishing. The shores of this alphabetically shaped lake, originally called Y Lake for obvious reasons, are lined with homes, cabins, docks, and floats, which might lead you to suspect that this is one of those raucous, busy places where no self-respecting angler would be caught dead. But despite all the development, care has been taken to leave the lake as natural as possible. You feel as if you're fishing somewhere wild and natural, even though the signs of humanity are everywhere.

The lake is stocked with legal-sized rainbows in the spring, and some "midnight biologist" has started a pretty good culture of largemouths, too. What this means is that you can find good trout fishing through May and fair bass fishing from May until early fall.

Gas motors are prohibited on the lake, and it's an excellent place to prospect for either trout or bass from a float tube.

Just watch out for the little toads in the access area.

164. CARNEY LAKE

Reference: **Kitsap-Pierce county line, southeast of Belfair; map A2 inset, grid j3.**

How to get there: Take State Route 16 to Purdy and turn west on State Route 302. Less than a mile after passing the sign pointing to the Minter Creek Salmon Hatchery, turn west (right) at the intersection where the sign points toward Shelton. Drive about three miles to Wright-Bliss Road and turn north (right). Drive just over two miles to the lake, which is on the right.

Facilities: A rather rough, gravel access area and boat ramp are located on the west side of the lake, but there are no other facilities in the immediate area. The nearest gas and groceries are at the BP station where you turn onto Wright-Bliss Road. Tackle and lodging are available in Belfair and Purdy.

Contact: Kitsap Sport Shop, Bremerton, (360) 373-9589.

Species available: Rainbow trout.

Fishing Carney Lake: Except for opening day of the season in late April, this is a quiet and peaceful place to fish, thanks in part to its location well off the beaten path and some distance away from most western Washington population centers. The boat ramp is small, the lake is in a rural setting with only a handful of homes around its shores, and there's lots of wildlife. Canada geese are more or less full-time residents here. Throw in the fact that the lake has a prohibition against internal combustion engines and you have yourself a mighty fine place to fish.

The 2,000 or so legal-sized rainbows stocked in the spring get anglers through the first segment of Carney's split season, which closes at the end of June. Fishing reopens September 1, and for the next two months, until the season closes on October 31, there's a pretty good chance of finding a bragging-sized rainbow or two. Fall fly-fishing can be especially good, but bait and hardware enthusiasts also catch their share.

165. HORSESHOE LAKE

Reference: **Kitsap-Pierce county line, northwest of Purdy; map A2 inset, grid j4.**

How to get there: Take State Route 16 to Purdy and turn west on State Route 302. Cross the tip of Henderson Bay at Wauna and continue about two miles to 94th Avenue NW. Turn north (right) and drive 1.4 miles to the boat ramp, which is immediately past the county park, on the right.

Facilities: A large, gravel access area and boat ramp are located at the southwest corner of the lake, and nearby Horseshoe Lake County Park offers bank fishing and rest rooms. Food and gas are available on State Route 302, near the junction with 94th Avenue. Tackle and lodging are a few miles away in Purdy.

Contact: Kitsap Sport Shop, Bremerton, (360) 373-9589.

Species available: Rainbow trout, brown bullhead catfish.

Fishing Horseshoe Lake: Moderate plants of legal-sized hatchery rainbows provide fair fishing here in the spring, and there are enough small bullheads available for you to catch a pail of them for a catfish fry.

One of the highlights of a visit to Horseshoe Lake is the big bed of lily pads near the boat ramp at the public access area. The pink and white lilies are gorgeous in early summer, so take your camera and lots of color film along even if you forget the bait and potato chips. Those pad fields, by the way, are good places to start looking for catfish.

With a late-April-through-October season, Horseshoe offers good trout fishing in May and early June. Catfish action is best from May through July.

166. CRESCENT LAKE

Reference: **East of Purdy, near Pierce-Kitsap county line; map A2 inset, grid j4.**

How to get there: Take State Route 16 to Purdy and drive east (right) on Crescent Lake Road about two miles to the west shore of the lake.

Facilities: The west side of the lake has a public access area with a boat ramp. Food and gas are available in Purdy, and food, gas, tackle, and lodging can be found a few miles to the south in Gig Harbor.

Contact: Gig Harbor Chamber of Commerce, (360) 851-6865.

Species available: Rainbow trout.

Fishing Crescent Lake: This 47-acre lake is open to year-round fishing, but your best chance of success is during the spring, following the visit by the Department of Fish and Wildlife's fish-stocking truck. Fish it in May and you'll do alright on eight- to 10-inch rainbows, but fishing can be pretty lackluster the rest of the year.

167. CENTRAL PUGET SOUND

Reference: **Marine waters from the King-Snohomish county line south to the Tacoma Narrows; Map A2 inset, grid j5.**

How to get there: Launch at Shilshole Bay (off Seaview Avenue, Ballard), Don Armeni Ramp (off Harbor Avenue, West Seattle), Dockton Park (off Dockton Road, Vashon Island), Des Moines Marina (off State Route 509), Redondo (off Redondo Beach Drive), Ole and Charlie's Marina (off Marine View Drive, Tacoma), Asarco Ramp (off Ruston Way, Tacoma), Point Defiance (off Pearl Street, Tacoma), Gig Harbor (at the foot of Randall Street, Manchester (off Main Street), Port Orchard (off Bay Street), Evergreen Park (off 14th Street, Bremerton), or Lion's Field Park (off Ledo Street, Bremerton) to fish any of several potentially productive spots in these areas.

Facilities: Launching is free at Shilshole, where there are rest rooms, restaurants, and other facilities nearby. Food is within walking range of the Armeni launch, which is also free. Moorage, picnic areas, and plenty of parking are available at the free Dockton Park ramp. The launch sling at Des Moines Marina has fuel, rest rooms, restaurants, and stores within walking distance, with launch fees starting at about $6 (round trip). The free launch ramp at Redondo has rest rooms and a restaurant nearby, but is open only during limited hours. The sling at Ole and Charlie's also has limited hours of operation, and launch fees vary with boat length. Boat and motor repairs are available at the site. The launch ramp at the old Asarco plant doesn't have any facilities, but it's free and offers ample parking. There's room to launch three boats at a time at the Point Defiance ramp, with fuel, bait, and groceries available at the nearby boat house. The launch fee here is $3 round trip. The free Gig Harbor ramp has no facilities on site, but all are available nearby. The same is true at Manchester. The free, double-wide ramp at Port Orchard has fuel and rest rooms close by. The Evergreen Park ramp in Bremerton is also free, with ample parking, picnic areas, and clean rest rooms. The ramp at Lion's Field Park is free and has plenty of parking.

Contact: Shilshole Bay Marina (Seattle), (206) 728-3385; Seacrest Marina (Seattle), (206) 932-1050; Des Moines Marina, (206) 824-5200; Point Defiance Boat House (Tacoma), (206) 591-5325; Kitsap Sport Shop (Bremerton), (360) 373-9589. For nautical charts of this area, contact Captain's Nautical Supply, (206) 283-7242.

Species available: Chinook, coho, pink, and chum salmon; lingcod; various rockfish; Pacific cod; pollack; saltwater perch; sole; flounder.

Fishing Central Puget Sound: Some of the Northwest's most famous saltwater fishing spots are located here, places such as Tacoma's Point Defiance, Seattle's Elliott Bay, and the Kitsap Peninsula's Point Jefferson, affectionately known by generations of anglers as "Jeff Head." Although these and other traditional central Puget Sound salmon-fishing spots may not always be as productive as they were in past decades, there are times when they provide action that's as good as anything the region has to offer. Season restrictions in some areas have taken large bites from what used to be year-round salmon fishing, but others parts of the central Sound remain open throughout the year, providing realistic opportunities for anglers to catch chinooks, cohos, pinks, or chums 12 months of the year.

The waters from the Tacoma Narrows Bridge to the northern tip of Vashon Island have (so far) escaped most of the serious season-cutting measures and serve as a good example of the salmon fishing still available in central Puget Sound. Point Defiance and the waters immediately to the east—known locally as the Clay Banks—at times provide excellent fishing for resident chinooks, or blackmouth, from fall through winter. These same places once were hot spots for summertime kings of 20 to 40 pounds, but such piscatorial brutes are much more rare these days. Farther east, Commencement Bay—more famous for its toxic bottom sediments than for its fishing—still provides some solid summer and fall salmon as silvers bound for the Puyallup River stage in the bay before moving into the river. During odd-numbered years, pink salmon congregate off the mouth of the Puyallup, often providing even hotter angling action than that offered by the annual coho extravaganza.

Other decent salmon spots open to year-round fishing include Point Dalco (at the south end of Vashon Island), Quartermaster Harbor (between the south end of Vashon and Maury islands), and the waters around Redondo, where anglers casting from the Redondo Pier catch almost as many salmon as nearby boat anglers catch.

And, while we're on the subject of piers, there are lots of them available to anglers throughout central Puget Sound, providing angling access to a range of fish species that includes everything from rock crab and pile perch to coho and chinook salmon. They include the Point Defiance, Les Davis, and Old Town Dock piers along the south side of Tacoma's Commencement Bay, the Dash Point Pier between Tacoma and Federal Way, south King County's Des Moines and Redondo piers, Blake Island Pier at the island's north end, the First Street Dock, Park Avenue, Waterman, Annapolis, and Port Orchard piers on Sinclair Inlet, the Silverdale Pier and the Coal Dock on Dyes Inlet, the Keyport, Brownsville, and Illahee piers along the west side of Port Orchard, Indianola and Suquamish piers on the shores of Port Madison, Elliott Bay's Pier 86, the Duwamish Head pier, Shilshole Bay's A Dock, and the Edmonds Pier.

Back to the topic of salmon fishing, the waters of Puget Sound around Seattle and Bremerton are in a different management area than those to the south, and salmon-fishing regulations here have been somewhat more restrictive. Summertime closures have come into play in some areas, at times keeping anglers from getting a crack at mature kings and silvers in some spots and keeping them guessing about season openings and closings in others. In a nutshell, it's gotten complicated. Elliott Bay, for example, until a few years ago offered excellent chinook fishing right at Seattle's front door, but in recent years it's been illegal for anglers to keep chinooks in the bay, even while gill-net fisheries continued to take their toll. Jefferson Head, by the same token, is a year-round chinook producer, but in 1995 a closed season from early July until the middle of October kept anglers from getting a crack at any of them.

Winter fishing, however, is another story, and there are still places out of Seattle and Bremerton where feeder blackmouth are plentiful at various times from fall to spring. Allen Bank, between Blake Island and the northern tip of Vashon Island, often provides excellent winter blackmouth fishing, as does the Manchester area in the entrance to Rich Passage. The Port Orchard area is another spot that's sometimes red-hot for five- to 10-pound chinooks during the late fall and winter. Various spots along the east side of Bainbridge Island can also be good for winter chinooks, most notably Skiff Point and Point Monroe. Point Jefferson (Jefferson Head) can be an excellent blackmouth spot all fall and winter, especially on an incoming and high tide.

Rockfish and lingcod aren't as abundant here as they were before anglers "discovered" them when the salmon fishing began to drop off, but there are still places in the central Sound where fair bottomfishing can be found. Rock breakwaters, such as those found at Shilshole Bay and Edmonds, are home to both and are often overlooked as anglers head for deeper, more distant bottomfishing spots. These rock jetties also have greenling and the occasional cabezon, both worthy light-tackle adversaries and welcomed additions on the dinner table.

Natural rock piles and rocky drop-offs, such as those fairly well-known spots around the south end of Bainbridge Island and offshore from Jefferson Head, show on any Puget Sound nautical chart. In addition, this part of the sound has several artificial reefs constructed by the Department of Fisheries during the 1970s and 1980s. They include underwater rock piles near Point Heyer (east side of Vashon Island), just off the south end of Blake Island, south of Seattle's Alki Point, and near Edmonds (two miles south of Point Wells). All are marked with buoys to make them easy to locate.

Small-boat anglers and those without a boat may be overlooking some of the best saltwater angling action the central Sound has to offer if they aren't spending lots of time around the area's thousands of docks and bulkheads. These structures, which serve as homes to barnacles and mussels, draw large schools of striped seaperch and pile perch during the spring and summer, and these hard-fighting, sweet-eating fish will take almost any small bait you put in front of them. The waterfront areas of Tacoma, Seattle, and Bremerton are teeming with these cooperative fish—sometimes topping three pounds—and they're just waiting for anglers to come along with light enough tackle and a soft enough touch to catch them.

168. LAKE FENWICK

Reference: **Southwest of Kent; map A2 inset, grid j6.**

How to get there: Take Interstate 5 to the South 272nd exit north of Federal Way and drive east on 272nd. As you start down the hill, look for Lake Fenwick Road, turn north (left), and watch for the lake on the right.

Facilities: The city of Kent has a boat ramp and fishing dock on the lake, with other amenities available to the east in Kent and to the southwest in Federal Way.

Contact: The Reel Thing, (206) 941-0920.

Species available: Rainbow trout, largemouth bass, yellow perch, brown bull-head catfish.

Fishing Lake Fenwick: Okay, it's time for another quiz. In 10 words or less, what's this lake's biggest claim to fame? I'll give you a big hint: It has something to do with fishing tackle. No, the lake isn't perfectly round like a spool of monofilament, but nice try. If you guessed that this lake is named after the famous tackle company, you're very close. In fact, the famous tackle company is named after this lake. Yes, one of the founders of Fenwick Tackle lived near here and named his fledgling rod company after this little King County lake. Isn't some of the information in this book absolutely fascinating?

But what you really want to know about is the fishing, right? Well, I can help you out there, too. This 18-acre lake is open to year-round fishing and is stocked with hatchery rainbows of about seven to 10 inches each spring. Carry-overs to the next spring, or even through the summer, were pretty much an impossibility until recently, when an aeration system was installed to keep Fenwick oxygenated. If it works as expected, look for better opportunities to catch some bigger rainbows from the lake.

Fenwick has lots of natural cover in the form of brush, submerged trees, and weeds, offering bass anglers plenty of chances to do their thing. Good perch and catfish populations provide added angling variety. Along with the trout, these warm-water species may be caught from the fishing dock at the City of Kent's park near the north end of the lake.

The boat ramp is on the lake's west side, and if you're going to use your boat here, remember that gasoline motors aren't allowed.

---

169. STEEL (STEELE) LAKE

Reference: **In Federal Way, west of Interstate 5; map A2 inset, grid j6.**

How to get there: Take Interstate 5 to Federal Way and take the South 320th Street exit. Exit to the west on 320th and drive several blocks to Pacific Highway South, turn north (right), and go eight blocks to South 312th Street. Turn east (right) on 312th and follow it to the lake, which is on the left.

Facilities: A City of Federal Way park has a boat ramp and roomy fishing dock. All other facilities are available in the area.

Contact: The Reel Thing, (206) 941-0920.

Species available: Rainbow trout, largemouth bass, crappies, yellow perch, brown bullhead catfish.

Fishing Steel Lake: As with the other lakes around Federal Way, leave the big gas-burner home if you fish Steel. Internal combustion motors aren't allowed here. You don't really need one to get around here anyway, since the lake covers only about 47 acres. For its size, though, it offers lots of fishing variety.

Planted rainbows of seven to 10 inches draw much of the angler interest when Steel first opens in late April, but it isn't long before the lake's large-mouth bass, perch, and other warm-water fish are commanding most of the attention. The shallow west end of the lake warms first and is the first to start providing good bass fishing, but by June anglers are usually catching bass from the many docks and floats that line much of the lake's shoreline. This lake is capable of producing some hefty bass, with fish of seven and eight pounds being caught more often than most people might expect.

Perch fishing can be very good from spring to fall, and during the heat of the summer, Steel Lake offers good fishing for brown bullheads.

170. STAR LAKE

Reference: **Northeast of Federal Way; map A2 inset, grid j6.**

How to get there: Take Interstate 5 to the South 272nd exit, go east on 272nd to Military Road and turn south (right). Drive several blocks to Star Lake Road, turn left, and follow it to 37th Avenue South, which dead-ends at the lake.

Facilities: The lake has a rough boat ramp and limited beach access. All amenities are available in Federal Way.

Contact: The Reel Thing, (206) 941-0920.

Species available: Rainbow trout, largemouth bass.

Fishing Star Lake: Now open to year-round fishing, Star is one of the deeper lakes in the south King County area, so the trout fishing here holds up well into the summer. You'll have to switch from near-surface trolling or fishing a worm beneath a bobber to anchoring a marshmallow or Berkley Power Nugget to the bottom with a sliding sinker, but you can catch rainbows here into July if you want.

You can also catch warm-water fish in July. The 34-acre lake has a few largemouth bass, which can be caught around any of the many docks and floats, and it also has a fair population of brown bullheads to provide summer-time night-fishing possibilities.

171. LAKE DOLLOFF

Reference: **In Federal Way, just east of Interstate 5; map A2 inset, grid j6.**

How to get there: Take Interstate 5 to Federal Way and exit onto South 320th Street. Turn east on 320th and drive to Military Road. Go north (left) on Military Road and drive about a mile to where the road passes under the freeway. Turn right just before you drive under the freeway on South 310th and follow it completely around the lake to the south side.

Facilities: The south side of the lake has a Department of Fish and Wildlife boat ramp and access area, and other amenities are nearby in Federal Way.

Contact: The Reel Thing, (206) 941-0920.

Species available: Rainbow trout, largemouth bass, yellow perch, brown bull-head catfish.

Fishing Lake Dolloff: Although visible from Interstate 5, this 21-acre lake is just hard enough to reach to keep fishing pressure down compared to the other lakes in the area. Maybe that's why the legal-sized rainbows—along with a few big brood-stock trout thrown in for excitement—tend to provide decent fishing action a little further into the summer than some other King County lakes. Whatever the reason, you can usually find fairly good trout fishing here through June and again in September and October. This lake, by the way, is open year-round.

Something else that seems to be a fairly well-kept secret (at least until now) is the fact that Dolloff produces some big largemouth bass during the course of a typical summer. The top fish recorded for 1994, for example, was a whopping nine-pound, 12-ouncer, officially weighed at The Reel Thing tackle store in Federal Way. That's a trophy-class largemouth anywhere in the Northwest.

The shallow pothole area at the west end of the lake provides not only good bank-fishing access, but is also a good place to fish for the lake's abundant yellow perch and to try your luck at night-fishing for brown bullheads. If all else fails, try worms for both.

172. NORTH LAKE

Reference: **West of Auburn; map A2 inset, grid j6.**

How to get there: Take Interstate 5 to the South 320th Street exit in Federal Way and turn east on 320th Street. Drive half a mile, turn south (right) on Weyerhaeuser Way, and go another half a mile to the lake's access area, on the left.

Facilities: The lake has a boat ramp with beach access for fishing. Food, gas, lodging, and other amenities are nearby in Federal Way.

Contact: The Reel Thing, (206) 941-0920.

Species available: Rainbow trout, largemouth bass, yellow perch.

Fishing North Lake: North Lake is often crowded during the first few weekends of the season, but the trout fishing often gets better after those crowds taper off. Be patient and start fishing it in mid-May and you might do alright on 10- to 12-inch rainbows. Springtime plants of legal-sized rainbows usually include a few brood stock trout, some of which may top three pounds. If you don't have a boat to get out and troll all the usual things, try casting from the bank along the trail that extends south from the boat ramp. A bobber-and-worm or bobber-and-jig might work best when the water is still cool, but as the lake warms, you might try casting a bobber-and-fly combination with your spinning rod.

Bass and perch populations have grown considerably here in recent years, and the lake produces some fairly hefty largemouths. The numerous docks dotting the edge of the lake provide plenty of places for bass anglers to try their luck. As for perch, you may not have to go looking for them; they may find you, especially while you're prospecting for trout with that bobber-and-worm rig around the edge of the lake.

173. LAKE MORTON

Reference: **East of Auburn; map A2 inset, grid j8.**

How to get there: Drive east from Covington on Covington-Sawyer Road and take the second road to the south (right) to the lake.

Facilities: The northwest corner of the lake has a good boat ramp with beach fishing.

Contact: The Reel Thing, (206) 941-0920.

Species available: Rainbow and cutthroat trout, kokanee, yellow perch.

Fishing Lake Morton: The Department of Fish and Wildlife stocks this popular southeastern King County lake with about 4,000 rainbow trout each year to keep anglers happy, and the fishery holds up fairly well until about June. Now and then the department throws in a few larger cutthroat for variety, and these fish may average 14 inches and weigh a pound each. Summertime trolling may also turn up a kokanee or two, although these small landlocked salmon are not planted in the lake. As for perch, try fishing a garden worm or leadhead jig-and-worm combination under a bobber at the north end or narrow south end of the lake. Morton produces some hefty perch that are well worth pursuing. Remember that gas motors are not allowed on this 66-acre lake, so confine your means of locomotion to oars or electric motors.

174. LAKE SAWYER

Reference: **Northwest of Black Diamond; map A2 inset, grid j8.**

How to get there: Drive east from Kent on Kent-Kangley Road (State Route 516) and turn south (right) on 216th Avenue, which is about three miles east of State Route 18. Just over a mile down 216th, turn east (left) on Covington-Sawyer Road to the lake.

Facilities: There's a paved boat ramp at the northwest corner of the lake and a resort that has rental cabins and trailers, RV sites, boat and canoe rentals, and a country store. Lake Sawyer Store a short distance away has tackle and sells fishing licenses.

Contact: Sunrise Resort, (206) 630-4890.

Species available: Largemouth and smallmouth bass, rainbow and cutthroat trout, kokanee, yellow perch, crappies, brown bullhead catfish.

Fishing Lake Sawyer: At first glance, Lake Sawyer is an average-sized, average-looking western Washington suburban lake, complete with nice homes, beach cabins, and diving boards, but don't let first impressions fool you. Beneath all those trappings of suburbia is a lake that offers year-round fishing for a wide range of cold-water and warm-water species.

Perhaps best-known among Sawyer's many possibilities is its bass fishery. It isn't the kind of place where you can hang a plastic worm or spinnerbait from your line and start hooking bass one after the other, but if you're patient enough to fish all morning or all evening to hook a couple of bass, those fish might be three- to five-pounders. Odds are that most of the bass you'll hook will be largemouths, but don't be surprised if your efforts produce a smallmouth from time to time. Smallies to four pounds are occasionally caught.

Although much of the lake is developed, there are plenty of docks, floats, and other forms of man-mad cover to prospect for bass. If you like fishing weeds and heavier cover, try the southeast corner of the lake, which is the only part that is still pretty much undeveloped. If you're looking for your best crack at hooking (and hopefully releasing) a really large bass, you might do your fishing during the spawn, which usually takes place here from late May through June.

The lake has some fairly large perch and crappies, and if you can locate a school of either, you can expect some hot fishing and sweet eating. Small leadhead jigs will take both of these popular panfish, but if you want perch, you might try tipping the jigs' hooks with a small piece of worm.

Trolling the middle portions of the lake during the spring or fall may produce rainbow or cutthroat trout as well as kokanee. During the summer months, anglers who want to avoid the water-skiers and speed-boaters might want to fish the lake early or late in the day. That's when the speed limit on the lake is a mere eight miles per hour. During the middle of the day, that limit goes up to 30 mph, so the water may get churned up pretty well. Those faster boats, however, aren't allowed inside the string of marker buoys that line the shallows about 100 feet offshore, so you can get away from some of the craziness by staying close to the beach while fishing.

175. RAVENSDALE LAKE

Reference: **North of Black Diamond; map A2 inset, grid j8.**

How to get there: Drive east out of Kent on Kent-Kangley Road to Georgetown. Turn south on Black Diamond Road and drive about half a mile to Ravensdale. The lake is a 50-yard hike off Black Diamond Road, immediately west of Ravensdale.

Facilities: The lake has no facilities. Kanaskat-Palmer State Park, about seven miles east via Lake Retreat-Kanaskat Road, has limited tent and RV sites. The nearest food, gas, lodging, and tackle are in Kent and Enumclaw.

Contact: Kanaskat-Palmer State Park, (360) 886-0148.

Species available: Cutthroat trout.

Fishing Ravensdale Lake: Without a road running right to its shores, this 18-acre lake offers float-tubers and anglers willing to carry small boats to the water a chance to escape the crowds. There is some bank-fishing opportunity, but a small craft of some kind certainly offers an advantage.

A more-or-less self-sustaining population of cutthroats provides decent spring and fall fishing, and every now and then someone hooks a trout of 15 or 16 inches. This is a no-bait lake, so take along only your favorite spoons, spinners, nymph patterns, and other artificials, and if you want to keep a trout for the table, it has to be at least 12 inches long.

176. LAKE TWELVE

Reference: **Northeast of Black Diamond; map A2 inset, grid j8.**

How to get there: Take State Route 169 north from Enumclaw to Black Diamond and turn east (right) on Green River Gorge Road. Turn north (left) on Lake Twelve Road (270th Street SE) about 1.5 miles out of Black Diamond and drive half a mile to the lake.

Facilities: The lake has a boat ramp and toilets at its public access area. Food and gas are available in and around Black Diamond. Kanaskat-Palmer State Park, about four miles to the east, has limited tent and RV sites, rest rooms, and showers. The nearest lodging and tackle are found in Enumclaw.

Contact: Kanaskat-Palmer State Park, (360) 886-0148.

Species available: Rainbow and cutthroat trout, largemouth bass, yellow perch, brown bullhead catfish.

Fishing Lake Twelve: It's a fairly long drive for most folks—except, of course, those who happen to live in Black Diamond—but the angling variety available in this 45-acre lake can make the trip worthwhile. Open year-round, Lake Twelve offers its best trout fishing in May and June, after the Department of Fish and Wildlife has made its annual plant of 2,000 eight- to 10-inch rainbows and a sprinkling of cutthroats pushing a pound apiece. Fall trout fishing can also be fairly productive.

In the summer, bass fishing draws some interest, and there are good numbers of perch to catch if the largemouths have lock-jaw. Bring along a can of nightcrawlers and stay until dark to catch a string of brown bullheads, most of which run 10 to 13 inches.

---

177. RETREAT LAKE

Reference: **Northeast of Black Diamond; map A2 inset, grid j8.**

How to get there: Take Kent-Kangley Road east from Kent to Georgetown. About 1.5 miles east of Georgetown, turn south (right) on Lake Retreat-Kanaskat Road and drive half a mile to the lake, which is on the left.

Facilities: The lake has no facilities, but Kanaskat-Palmer State Park, with a few tent and RV sites, rest rooms, and showers, is about six miles away, to the east. Enumclaw and Kent offer the nearest food, gas, tackle, and lodging.

Contact: Kanaskat-Palmer State Park, (360) 886-0148.

Species available: Rainbow and cutthroat trout, largemouth bass, yellow perch.

Fishing Retreat Lake: Although it covers more than 50 acres, this King County lake with a year-round season near the base of Sugarloaf Mountain isn't anything to get excited about. Public access is limited since there's no boat ramp or Department of Fish and Wildlife access area, and the lake doesn't receive any hatchery plants. Still, a small population of trout survives here, and panfish action can at times provide worthwhile results during the summer.

MAP A3

WASHINGTON MAP .... see page 5
Adjoining Maps
NORTH .... no map
EAST (map A4) .... see page 256
SOUTH (map B3) .... see page 432
WEST (map A2) .... see page 100

61 Listings
PAGES 212-255

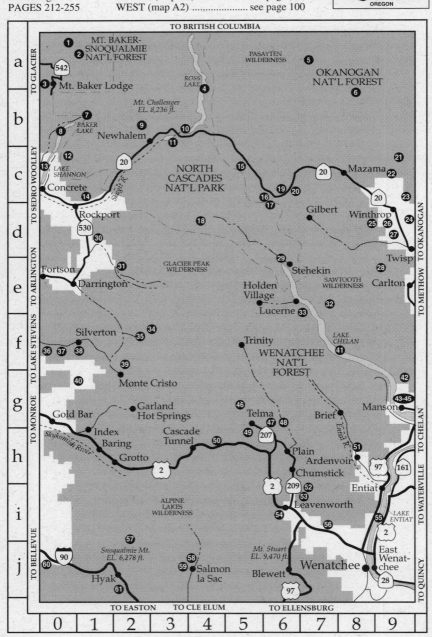

Map Section A3 features:

1. Tomyhoi Lake
2. Twin Lakes
3. Galena Chain Lakes
4. Ross Lake
5. Hidden Lakes Chain
6. Black Lake
7. Baker River
8. Baker Lake
9. Thornton Lakes
10. Diablo Lake
11. Gorge Lake
12. Watson Lakes
13. Lake Shannon
14. Upper Skagit River
15. Granite Creek
16. Lake Ann
17. Rainy Lake
18. Trapper Lake
19. Cutthroat Lake
20. Early Winters Creek
21. Chewack (Chewuch) River
22. Buck Lake
23. Pearrygin Lake
24. Davis Lake
25. Patterson Lake
26. Twin Lakes
27. Twisp River
28. Black Pine Lake
29. Stehekin River
30. Sauk River
31. Suiattle River
32. Lake Chelan-Sawtooth Wilderness Lakes
33. Domke Lake
34. Glacier Peak Lakes
35. White Chuck River
36. Heather Lake
37. Lake Twentytwo (or Twenty-Two, or even 22)
38. Boardman Lake, Upper Boardman (Island) Lake, and Lake Evan
39. Goat Lake
40. Spada Lake (Sultan Reservoir)
41. Lake Chelan
42. Antilon Lake
43. Dry Lake
44. Wapato Lake
45. Roses Lake
46. White River
47. Fish Lake
48. Chiwawa River
49. Lake Wenatchee
50. Nason Creek
51. Entiat River
52. Eagle Creek
53. Chumstick Creek
54. Icicle Creek (Icicle River)
55. Columbia River
56. Wenatchee River
57. Alpine Lakes Wilderness
58. Upper Cle Elum River
59. Cooper Lake
60. Rattlesnake Lake
61. Keechelus Lake

1. TOMYHOI LAKE

Reference: **Northeast of Shuksan, in Mount Baker Wilderness; map A3, grid a0.**

How to get there: Take Interstate 5 to Bellingham and exit east on State Route 542. Follow State Route 542 about 52 miles up the North Fork Nooksack River beyond Glacier to Forest Road 3065. Turn north (left) and follow Forest Road 3065 four miles to the trail on the left, which leads to the lake. From there it's a four-mile hike to the water.

Facilities: There's nothing at the lake but bank access and primitive campsites. Silver Fir Campground (U.S. Forest Service) is located at the junction of

State Route 542 and Forest Road 3065. The nearest food, gas, tackle, and lodging are in Deming.

Contact: Mount Baker-Snoqualmie National Forest, Mount Baker Ranger District, (360) 856-5700; Mount Baker-Snoqualmie National Forest, Glacier Public Service Center, (360) 599-2714.

Species available: Rainbow and brook trout.

Fishing Tomyhoi Lake: If you're expecting to hike four miles one-way to a little alpine lake where you can cast from one end to the other, you'll be surprised at what you find. Tomyhoi is better than three-quarters of a mile long and covers nearly 100 acres. What's more, it's quite deep, so your favorite spoon, spinner, or artificial fly will, quite literally, only scratch the surface. But that may be enough to catch a couple of pan-sized brookies from around the edge of the lake. Catching two or three rainbows may require a little more effort and some longer casts, but it can certainly be done. It wouldn't be a bad idea to take along a jar of salmon eggs, Power Bait, or even a few dozen worms, and if the weather is warm and sunny, don't be shy about fishing bait on the bottom for a chance at a large rainbow.

Snow and ice are usually gone from the lake by late June, with July and August offering the best weather and fishing conditions.

---

2. TWIN LAKES

Reference: **Northeast of Shuksan, in Mount Baker Wilderness; map A3, grid a0.**

How to get there: Take Interstate 5 to Bellingham and exit east on State Route 542, following it 52 miles up the North Fork Nooksack River beyond Glacier to Forest Road 3065. Turn north (left) and follow Forest Road 3065 about five miles to its end, where the lakes are on the left.

Facilities: The U.S. Forest Service's Silver Fir Campground is about five miles to the south of the lakes and has tent and trailer sites, rest rooms, picnic tables, and drinking water. Other amenities are available in Deming, 32 miles west on State Route 542.

Contact: Mount Baker-Snoqualmie National Forest, Mount Baker Ranger District, (360) 856-5700; Mount Baker-Snoqualmie National Forest, Glacier Public Service Center, (360) 599-2714.

Species available: Rainbow trout.

Fishing Twin Lakes: This pair of 20-acre lakes nestled between Goat Mountain and Winchester Mountain has lots of visitors during an average summer season, and the fishing pressure keeps trout populations in check. Since the lakes are quite deep, someone occasionally hauls a bragging-size fish onto the beach. I would suggest fishing a marshmallow-and-salmon-egg combination or adding a lively worm to a marshmallow or Power Nugget and fishing the combination near bottom to have a crack at one of these Twin Lakes trophies. Use a quarter-ounce slip-sinker, and when it's time to cast, don't be afraid to really let it fly.

These high-country lakes are open and fishable from late June to about mid-September.

3. GALENA CHAIN LAKES

Reference: **Southwest of Mount Baker Ski Area; map A3, grid a0.**

How to get there: Take Interstate 5 to Bellingham and exit east on State Route 542, following it up the North Fork Nooksack River to the Mount Baker ski area. Continue on to the end of the road and the parking area, where a six-mile loop trail will take you to the five lakes.

Facilities: The lakes have no facilities, but Silver Fir Campground, managed by the U.S. Forest Service, is about eight miles away. Food, tackle, gas, and lodging are available at Deming, to the west on State Route 542.

Contact: Mount Baker-Snoqualmie National Forest, Mount Baker Ranger District, (360) 856-5700; Mount Baker-Snoqualmie National Forest, Glacier Public Service Center, (360) 599-2714.

Species available: Brook trout.

Fishing the Galena Chain Lakes: You might find a large brookie or two in Iceberg Lake, the largest of the five major lakes in this system, but trout of seven to 10 inches provide the bulk of the angling action on these small and relatively easy-to-reach high lakes on the northeastern flank of Mount Baker. Upper and Lower Bagley lakes, the easternmost lakes in the chain and the closest to Mount Baker ski area, get quite a lot of fishing pressure, but you're a little more likely to beat the crowds if you hike west to Iceberg, Hayes, or Galena lakes. No matter which of the lakes you fish, you'll be treated to some of the most fantastic scenery in the North Cascades, including birds-eye views of Mount Baker. All of these lakes are best fished late in the summer, after the deep snows have had time to melt away.

4. ROSS LAKE

Reference: **East end of Whatcom County; map A3, grids a4 and b4.**

How to get there: Take Exit 230 off Interstate 5 at Burlington and drive 68 miles east on State Route 20 to Diablo. Catch the Seattle City Light tugboat to the base of the dam, where you'll be picked up and ferried to Ross Lake Resort. Hikers may continue east on State Route 20, past Diablo to the trailhead east of the lake. Some 10 camp sites are scattered along the trail to about two-thirds of the way up the lake. (A water taxi service from the resort is also available to take you to any of these camp sites.) If trailering a boat to the north end, take Interstate 5 to Bellingham and turn east on State Route 539 to Sumas. From there continue east on Canada Highway 401 to the Silver Creek cutoff, two miles west of Hope, then drive south to Hozomeen, on the east side of the lake.

Facilities: The only boat ramp on the lake is at the north end, but Ross Lake Resort, near the dam at the south end, has cabins and bunkhouse units for more than 80 guests, plus boat rentals and other amenities. There are also U.S. Park Service campsites at Green Point, Cougar Island, Big Beaver Creek, Little Beaver Creek, and Silver Creek, all on the west side of the lake. Campsites on the east side include those at Roland Point, McMillan Creek, May Creek, Rainbow Point, Devil's Junction, Ten-Mile Island, Ponderosa, Lightning Creek, Cat Island, and Boundary Bay. Ross Lake Resort offers food, gas, tackle, and lodging.

Contact: Ross Lake Resort, Rockport WA 98283, (206) 386-4437 (Seattle phone number).

Species available: Rainbow, cutthroat, and brook trout; Dolly Varden.

Fishing Ross Lake: It's one of western Washington's biggest lakes, but only a tiny segment of the angling population has fished it. This may sound like a "Jeopardy" answer, but it's really Ross Lake, the 21-mile-long Skagit River impoundment behind Ross Dam that backs up from near the North Cascades Highway to the British Columbia border and beyond. You really have to want to fish Ross Lake, since there aren't any perfectly simple ways to go about it. Invest the time and effort, though, and you might be rewarded with good summertime trout fishing.

Ross is managed as a quality fishery with special "selective" regulations, which means you can't use bait and all lures and flies must have single, barbless hooks. The daily limit is three trout, and the minimum size is 13 inches. Unlike most of the state's smaller lakes with selective fishery regulations, it's okay to use boats equipped with gas motors when you're fishing this long lake where the wind sometimes comes booming down the canyon. Besides having special regulations, Ross Lake has a special season, opening July 1 and closing at the end of October.

Rainbows provide most of the fishing action, and trolling with small spoons or spinners takes many of them. Trolling with a variety of fly patterns is also effective. You'll catch a few cutthroats for your efforts and an occasional brook trout. Although they must be released, the lake also has some large Dolly Varden, and from time to time someone brings a huge one to the boat.

5. HIDDEN LAKES CHAIN

Reference: **In the Pasayten Wilderness, northwest Okanogan County; map A3, grid a7.**

How to get there: Take State Route 20 to Winthrop and drive 10 miles north up the Chewack River on Forest Road 51. Turn west (left) on Forest Road 5130 and follow it 17 miles to the trailhead at the end of the road. From there it's a 12-mile hike to the first lake.

Facilities: This is wilderness, so take everything you need. The last chance for food, gas, and other necessities is in Winthrop.

Contact: Okanogan National Forest, (509) 826-3275.

Species available: Rainbow, cutthroat, and brook trout.

Fishing the Hidden Lakes Chain: This is one of the most interesting places that I've never fished. That's right, I said "never" fished, and since I'm not getting any younger, I may never make it. Of course, if I do try, the 12-mile trek to these wilderness lakes could do me in before my time, so I may have to pass. If you plan to hike to these four productive trout lakes, you'd better be tough or have plenty of time to make the trip. Although not a steep hike, it's a long one. May I recommend saddling up ol' Scout or booking a trip with an outfitter who spends considerable time in these hills? That way, your backside will be sore, but you'll reduce wear and tear on your legs and feet. Plan your trip for sometime between early July and mid-September, when you're least likely to encounter snow.

Once you make it to the general area, you'll have four lakes to choose from, each with its own distinctive personality. Cougar Lake is the southern-most of the bunch, and the first you'll reach as you hike or ride in from the south. Next in line is First Hidden, then Middle Hidden, and finally, Big Hidden Lake. Those who have been there say that each is a wonderful place to cast a small, red-and-white Dardevle spoon or Panther Martin spinner into the depths, let it sink several feet, then retrieve it just fast enough to keep it working enticingly through the clear water. Early and late in the day, find a shoreline log or boulder to cast from and try your hand with the dry fly of your choice, either on a light-weight fly rod or cast with your favorite spin-ning outfit about five feet down the line from a clear, plastic casting bubble.

Most of the rainbows you'll catch from any of these lakes will run 9 to 12 inches, the cutts a little smaller. Brook trout will average about eight inches.

---

6. BLACK LAKE

Reference: **North of Winthrop, Okanogan National Forest; map A3, grid b8.**

How to get there: Take State Route 20 to Winthrop and drive north on Chewack River Road (Forest Road 51). Stay on the main road past Camp 4 and turn west (left) on Forest Road 100. Follow Forest Road 100 to the end and hit the trail for nearly four miles to the lake.

Facilities: Several primitive campsites can be found around the lake. The near-est "formal" U.S. Forest Service campground is Camp 4, 10 miles back down the road. The closest food, gas, lodging, and tackle are in Winthrop.

Contact: Okanogan National Forest, Winthrop Ranger District, (509) 996-2266.

Species available: Rainbow and cutthroat trout.

Fishing Black Lake: If you get an early start, you can hike in, fish the lake several hours, and make it out the same day, but why hurry? This deep, 66-acre lake has plenty to offer, both in terms of decent fishing and above-average scenery.

Black Lake produces some large rainbows late in the summer, after the water has had ample time to warm. Take a fly rod to get the most from your stay, but if all you take is a spinning outfit, you'll probably score a couple of nice trout to fry over the campfire.

Although the lake is open year-round, the best fishing and weather con-ditions are from mid-May to early October.

---

7. BAKER RIVER

Reference: **Flows into the north end of Baker Lake near the center of Whatcom County; map A3, grid b1.**

How to get there: Take State Route 20 east from Interstate 5. About five miles east of Hamilton, turn north (left) on Baker Lake Road and follow it about 28 miles to the upper end of the lake and the Forest Service road that follows the river a short distance upstream. From there you can hike up the east side of the river.

Facilities: Three U.S. Forest Service campgrounds are located near the north end of Baker Lake, along the west side, providing good take-off points for anglers heading up the river. All other facilities are back down on State Route 20 in Hamilton and Concrete.

Contact: Mount Baker-Snoqualmie National Forest, Mount Baker Ranger District, (360) 856-5700.

Species available: Rainbow and a few cutthroat trout.

Fishing the Baker River: It's a long drive for only fair fishing, but the clear water and steep-sided canyons of the Baker River valley help to make it a worthwhile trip. If you lace up your hiking boots and work your way upriver to go boldly where you think no one has ever gone before, the scenery will get better but you may not notice much improvement in the fishing.

Fishing opens here in June, and the first two months of the season offer the most productive angling action.

8. BAKER LAKE

Reference: North of Concrete in the Mount Baker National Forest; map A3, grid b0.

How to get there: Take State Route 20 east from Interstate 5. About five miles east of Hamilton, turn north (left) on Baker Lake Road and follow it about 17 miles to the first of several roads leading right toward the lake.

Facilities: U.S. Forest Service campgrounds and boat ramps are located at Horseshoe Cove, Panorama Point, Park Creek, and Shannon Creek, all on the west side of the lake, and Maple Grove, on the east side. The nearest food, gas, tackle, and lodging are back on State Route 20 in Hamilton and Concrete.

Contact: Mount Baker-Snoqualmie National Forest, Mount Baker Ranger District, (360) 856-5700.

Species available: Kokanee, rainbow trout.

Fishing Baker Lake: Kokanee draw most of the attention at this 3,600-acre Baker River impoundment, where koke anglers can be rewarded generously. The waters down around the south end of the lake, near the two dams, often produce the best kokanee catches, but if you pay close attention to your depthsounder as you explore the lake, you may find a school of these little salmon almost anywhere. All the usual trolling and stillfishing strategies take Baker Lake kokes, but check the fishing regulations pamphlet closely before going after them. Among other unusual rules here, there's an 18-inch minimum size limit, established to help protect a depleted population of ocean-run sockeye salmon that still trickles into the lake.

As with kokanee, you might find a respectable rainbow trout almost anywhere on this big reservoir, but I recommend fishing around the mouths of the many streams that flow into the lake. Maybe I just have a prejudice for such spots and spend more time around the creek mouths than anywhere else, but I've found that the fresh, moving water, like that near the mouths of Sandy, Little Sandy, Boulder, Park, Shannon, Noisy, Anderson, and the other creeks entering Baker, are hard to beat when you're searching for a trout on the prowl. Try trolling a Triple Teazer, Dick Nite, Canadian Wonder, or similar wobbling spoon in silver/red head, and don't be afraid to troll it at the middle depths or deeper if you're looking for a bragging-sized rainbow. Even if you don't catch one, you'll enjoy the grand view of Mount Baker (if you can ignore all the clearcuts in the foreground).

9. THORNTON LAKES

Reference: **Northwest of Newhalem, southern Whatcom County; map A3, grid b2.**

How to get there: Take Interstate 5 to Burlington and drive east on State Route 20. Go about 10 miles past Marblemount and turn north (left) on Thornton Creek Road, which ends at the trailhead to Thornton Lakes. From there it's about a three-mile hike to the first lake.

Facilities: Lots of primitive campsites can be found around the shores of all three lakes. The nearest food, gas, and lodging are back on State Route 20 and in the Marblemount area.

Contact: North Cascades National Park, (360) 856-5700.

Species available: Cutthroat and brook trout.

Fishing the Thornton Lakes: Lower Thornton is the biggest and easiest to reach of the three lakes, and therefore the most heavily fished. I'm not particularly proud to admit that I've never caught a trout there, but it's true. I'm sure that other, more skilled anglers have more positive stories to relate. Middle Thornton is the smallest lake in the chain, and it's not particularly productive, either, but the upper lake does give up some fairly good catches now and then. If you're thinking about going to the trouble of hiking to any of these waters, I recommend you go for broke and hike all the way to the uppermost of the three and concentrate your angling efforts there. Spend at least one morning or evening casting flies around the shoreline, where hungry cutthroats and an occasional brook trout are likely possibilities.

Although open to year-round fishing, these lakes are best fished from May through October.

10. DIABLO LAKE

Reference: **On the Skagit River, immediately south of Ross Lake, southeast corner of Whatcom County; map A3, grid b4.**

How to get there: Exit Interstate 5 at Burlington and drive east about 68 miles on State Route 20 to the lake.

Facilities: Diablo Lake Resort has a boat ramp, tackle, tent and RV sites, rest rooms, and showers. There is also a public access area with a boat ramp. Marblemount and Concrete are the nearest places offering lodging, food, and gas.

Contact: Diablo Lake Resort, (206) 386-4429 (Seattle).

Species available: Rainbow and cutthroat trout.

Fishing Diablo Lake: The first time I ever stopped to try my luck at Diablo was in late summer, and it made sense to me when one of the anglers I talked to at the boat ramp suggested that I should "fish deep." Stopping near one of the spots he recommended, I tied a half-ounce Krocodile spoon to my line and dropped it over the side of the boat. This was back in the early 1970s, and I didn't even own a depthsounder, so I didn't know what I was getting myself into. My plan was to pay out line until the heavy wobbler found bottom, reel up a couple of feet, and put the motor in gear to begin some serious deep-trolling. But three minutes later the Krocodile was still dropping and the spool of my old Mitchell 300 spinning reel had only four or five wraps of line left on it. Undaunted, I reeled the lure back to the surface, replaced the reel's low-capacity spool for the one that held over 200 yards of 10-pound monofilament, and started the whole process over again. I don't know if that half-ounce Krocodile ever hit bottom, but when I estimated that I had let out 250 feet of line, I decided that was deep enough. When I engaged the motor, of course, the lure began to climb toward the surface, and I never did really "fish deep" in Diablo Lake. Nor did I catch any trout that September afternoon. I did, however, make one very important discovery: Diablo is one damned deep lake. This reservoir resulting from a dam in one of the Skagit River's steepest canyons reportedly has places more than 300 feet deep.

The moral of this story is that if you plan to fish deep at Diablo, you'd better take along your downrigger. The good news is that during most of Diablo's year-round season, it isn't necessary to ply the deep, dark depths in order to catch rainbows and cutthroats. Shallower shoreline areas, such as the two large bays along the north side of the reservoir, can be adequately productive. The ever-popular gang troll-and-worm combination works as well here as anything for trout that range from eight to 18 inches.

11. GORGE LAKE

Reference: **On the Skagit River, immediately downstream from Diablo Lake, southeastern Whatcom County; map A3, grid b3.**

How to get there: Take Interstate 5 to Burlington and turn east on State Route 20, following it 65 miles to the lake.

Facilities: A U.S. Forest Service campground and a boat ramp are both near the upper end of the lake. Diablo Lake Resort, three miles east, has tent and RV sites, showers, rest rooms, and tackle. Marblemount and Concrete offer complete facilities.

Contact: Mount Baker-Snoqualmie National Forest, (360) 775-9702.

Species available: Rainbow and cutthroat trout.

Fishing Gorge Lake: This lowermost and smallest of three back-to-back reservoirs on the upper Skagit River is stocked with hatchery trout and also offers the very real possibility of hooking a lunker carry-over from its green depths. Those cool depths are certainly worth fishing for trout throughout the summer, when many western Washington lakes are too warm for productive trout action. Much of Gorge Lake's bottom is more than 100 feet beneath the surface, and the water is plenty cool to keep rainbows and cutthroats actively feeding through the hottest days of July or August. Drop a couple of salmon eggs down there, use a downrigger to take your favorite trout lure into the depths, or try vertical jigging with a three-quarter-ounce Crippled Herring or Krocodile spoon.

12. WATSON LAKES

Reference: **East of Baker Lake, southern Whatcom County; map A3, grid c1.**

How to get there: Drive east from Interstate 5 on State Route 20. At the town of Concrete, turn north (left) on Baker River Road and drive up the east side of Lake Shannon about 11 miles to the south end of Baker Lake and Forest Road 1107. Turn right, drive to spur road 1107-022, and turn left, driving to the end of the road and the beginning of the 2.5-mile trail to the lakes.

Facilities: The lake has no facilities. The nearest food, gas, tackle, and lodging are in and around Concrete.

Contact: Mount Baker-Snoqualmie National Forest, Mount Baker Ranger District, (360) 856-5700.

Species available: Rainbow trout.

Fishing the Watson Lakes: Okay, so you have to hike a few miles, but for your efforts you can fish any of six lakes in fairly close proximity. Big and Little Watson are the largest of the bunch and the main attractions for anglers, but the smaller Anderson lakes a half-mile hike to the south may also strike your fancy. There are four Anderson lakes, named 1, 2, 3, and 4 by some highly creative hiker.

A dry fly, fished along the shoreline at daylight or dusk, will take trout from all these lakes. When the sun is higher in the sky, cast a small spoon, spinner, fish salmon eggs, or egg-and-marshmallows on the bottom.

13. LAKE SHANNON

Reference: **Immediately north of Concrete, Skagit County; map A3, grid c0.**

How to get there: Drive east from Interstate 5 on State Route 20. At the town of Concrete, turn north (left) on Baker River Road, which parallels the east side of Lake Shannon.

Facilities: A boat ramp is located on the southeast corner of the lake, at the end of a gravel road to the left off Baker River Road. Unless some repair work has been done on it lately, it's a rather steep and rough launch, so think twice about bringing your 20-footer. There's a motel in Concrete and an RV park just off State Route 20 on Baker Lake Road. Food, gas, and tackle are also available in Concrete.

Contact: North Cascade Inn, (800) 251-3054; Creekside Camping, (360) 826-3566.

Species available: Kokanee.

Fishing Lake Shannon: Get out your leaded line, downriggers, Wedding Ring spinners, Glo-Hooks, or whatever it is you like to use for kokanee and be sure to take them along if you plan on fishing this 2,100-acre reservoir. Kokanee fishing is the name of the game for anglers on this lower of two impounds on the Baker River. The kokes aren't particularly big here, but they are usually plentiful (especially from June through August), so a little searching with your depthsounder or taking some time to watch where and how other anglers are catching them should put you into some action.

If you happen to hook a lunker kokanee over 18 inches, it's probably a sea-run sockeye rather than a kokanee, and it must be released unharmed.

14. UPPER SKAGIT RIVER

Reference: **From Concrete upstream to Diablo; map A2, grid c1.**

How to get there: Take Interstate 5 to Burlington and turn east on State Route 20. The highway follows the Skagit upriver nearly 60 miles to Diablo Dam.

Facilities: Boat ramps are located near Van Horn, Rockport, and Marblemount. Rockport State Park has about 50 RV sites and 10 tent sites, plus rest rooms and showers. There are also two private RV parks/resorts near Rockport. The Totem Trail Motel is also in Rockport. Rockport Country Store has groceries, tackle, and fishing licenses, as well as fishing information, and gas is also available in Rockport.

Contact: Rockport Country Store, (360) 853-8531; Rockport State Park, (360) 853-8461.

Species available: Winter and summer steelhead, Dolly Varden.

Fishing the Upper Skagit River: It's still possible to catch steelhead from the upper Skagit, but you'll have to work a lot harder at it than in the good old days. Back then, some Skagit fishing guides ran two trips a day, getting steelhead limits for their clients in the morning and taking a second group in the afternoon, often finding limits for them, too. Catching a two-fish steelhead limit is no longer a sure thing here, and even catching one fish isn't guaranteed, whether you're fishing during the summer or the winter. The best months for winter-runs are January, February, and March, and there's a fair possibility of finding a summer-run steelhead if you fish from June through August.

Casting fresh shrimp, back-trolling plugs, or pitching weighted spinners into the deep-green pools and drifts of the upper Skagit may also draw strikes from the river's big Dolly Varden, some of which exceed the river's 20-inch minimum size limit.

15. GRANITE CREEK

Reference: **Parallels the North Cascades Highway through eastern Skagit County; map A3, grid c5.**

How to get there: Take State Route 20 east from Marblemount or west from Winthrop. The highway parallels and crisscrosses the creek for about 15 miles between Rainy Pass and the south end of Ross Lake.

Facilities: There's nothing in the immediate area. Food, gas, tackle, and lodging can be found in Concrete and Hamilton.

Contact: North Cascades National Park, (360) 856-5700.

Species available: Rainbow and brook trout.

Fishing Granite Creek: Thousands of people drive right by Granite Creek on any given summer's day, but only a handful ever stop to fish it. Those who keep going may be doing the right thing, since the aesthetics aren't all that great and the trout aren't all that big or all that abundant. It's not that the North Cascades aren't beautiful, but on Granite Creek you can't quite get far enough away from the highway traffic to escape the sound of cars and RVs racing by.

16. LAKE ANN

Reference: **West of State Route 20 at Rainy Pass, just south of Okanogan-Skagit county line; map A3, grid c5.**

How to get there: Take State Route 20 east from Ross Lake or west from Winthrop to Rainy Pass, drive to the southern end of the parking areas, and hit the trail heading west about 1.5 miles to the lake.

Facilities: The nearest camping area is the Forest Service's Lone Fir Campground, about 11 miles east on State Route 20, which has tent sites and a few RV sites, water, and rest rooms.

Contact: Okanogan National Forest, Winthrop Ranger District, (509) 996-2266; North Cascades National Park, (360) 856-5700.

Species available: Cutthroat trout.

Fishing Lake Ann: Although a relatively short hike away from one of Washington's busy summertime highways, the trail to Lake Ann doesn't host nearly as many anglers as it does casual hikers, photographers, and other outdoor enthusiasts. It's worth the half-hour walk to try for seven- to 10-inch cutthroats in the gin-clear water. Arm yourself with a few of your favorite weighted spoons and spinners and plenty of insect repellent. Western Washingtonians on their way to or from the popular trout lakes of the Okanogan country might consider stopping here for two or three hours to break up the long drive over the North Cascades.

Open year-round, Lake Ann is best fished from June through September.

17. RAINY LAKE

Reference: **West of the North Cascades Highway at Rainy Pass, northern Chelan County; map A3, grid d6.**

How to get there: Drive east from Ross Lake or west from Winthrop on State Route 20 to the large parking area at Rainy Pass, on the south side of the highway. It's an easy stroll of about half a mile to the lake from the south end of the parking lot.

Facilities: The U.S. Forest Service campground at Lone Fir has 21 tent sites and six RV sites, as well as water and rest rooms. The nearest amenities are in Winthrop.

Contact: Okanogan National Forest, Winthrop Ranger District, (509) 996-2266; North Cascades National Park, (360) 856-5700.

Species available: Cutthroat trout.

Fishing Rainy Lake: Although not a place where you can really escape humanity, Rainy Lake has all the other qualities of a high-country lake, including crystal-clear water and magnificent scenery. What's more, you can stop near the highway to straighten out after several hours behind the wheel, walk to the lake for two hours of exercising your arms with a fly rod, and still get to where you're going on schedule. You might even hook a couple of sassy cutthroat trout for your efforts. You'll probably encounter other anglers, but at 54 acres, this lake is big enough to give you plenty of elbow room throughout the June-to-September period when most folks visit.

18. TRAPPER LAKE

Reference: **Three miles southeast of Cascade Pass; map A3, grid d4.**

How to get there: Take State Route 20 to Rockport and turn south on State Route 530 (Sauk Valley Road). After crossing the Skagit River, drive about 1.5 miles to Rockport-Cascade Road and turn east (left). Cross the Cascade River near the Skagit Fish Hatchery, turn right at the "T" on Cascade Road, and continue east to Cascade Pass. From there it's about a four-mile hike by trail to the north side of the lake. From the east, take the passenger-only ferry up Lake Chelan to Stehekin and head north on the only road out of town. Go to Cottonwood Campground and hike up the hill to the south about three-quarters of a mile to the lake.

Facilities: Cottonwood is the nearest campground, but there are several others along the road from Stehekin. The closest stores, food, lodging, and tackle are in Stehekin.

Contact: North Cascades National Park, (360) 856-5700; North Cascades Stehekin Lodge, (509) 682-4494; Stehekin Valley Ranch, (509) 682-4677.

Species available: Rainbow and cutthroat trout.

Fishing Trapper Lake: As you can tell from the directions, you really have to want to fish this 145-acre, high-elevation lake, since it's not the kind of place you stumble on by accident. Although Trapper is a beautiful lake in an even more beautiful setting, it offers only fair fishing for small rainbows and an occasional cutthroat. As in the case of many Washington lakes, over-use has taken its toll on the once-impressive cutthroat fishing Trapper Lake used to offer. But if you use fishing as your excuse to lace on the hiking boots and don a day-pack, this one is worth visiting. Just stay on the trails, pack out everything you take in, and enjoy the experience.

This is a summertime fishery in a place that's snow-covered and iced-up from October to May.

19. CUTTHROAT LAKE

Reference: **Northwest of Washington Pass, near Okanogan-Chelan-Skagit county line; map A3, grid c6.**

How to get there: Take State Route 20 east from Ross Lake or west from Winthrop to Forest Road 400 (also known as Cutthroat Creek Road), which is about mid-way between Lone Fir and Washington Pass. Turn west on Forest Road 400 and drive about 1.5 miles to its end, where a one-mile trail leads southwesterly to the lake.

Facilities: The U.S. Forest Service's Lone Fir Campground has 21 tent sites and six RV sites, but the nearest concentration of food, gas, lodging, and other amenities is in Winthrop.

Contact: Okanogan National Forest, Winthrop Ranger District, (509) 996-2266.

Species available: Cutthroat trout.

Fishing Cutthroat Lake: True to its name, you'll find cutthroat trout here, lots of them. In fact, according to the Department of Fish and Wildlife, you'll find too many of them. This is one of those places where, on a good day, you'll hook smallish cutts cast after cast, and you may even get tired of casting before they get tired of biting. Though they won't be large fish, feel free to catch a limit for the frying pan. If you're a less-than-adequate fly caster and want to do something to bolster your self-esteem, Cutthroat Lake could be the place for you.

Although the fish season here is year-round, the best action is in the spring and again in the fall.

20. EARLY WINTERS CREEK

Reference: **Parallels the North Cascades Highway from Washington Pass to the Methow River; map A3, grid c7.**

How to get there: Take State Route 20 west from Winthrop. The highway parallels the creek for about 15 miles.

Facilities: Early Winters, Klipchuck, and Lone Fir campgrounds (all U.S. Forest Service) are scattered along State Route within casting distance of the creek. They offer tent sites, toilets, and drinking water. Winthrop has food, gas, tackle, and lodging.

Contact: Okanogan National Forest, (509) 826-3275.

Species available: Rainbow and cutthroat trout.

Fishing Early Winters Creek: This fast-moving stream right along the highway is tough to fish and produces only fair catches at best. Try it in late-June or early July with worms and you might catch a keeper or two, but don't expect too much.

21. CHEWACK (CHEWUCH) RIVER

Reference: **Flows into Methow River at Winthrop; map A3, grid c9.**

How to get there: Take State Route 20 to Winthrop and drive north up Chewack Road (Forest Road 51) or Eastside Chewack Road (Forest Road 5010), both of which closely parallel the river.

Facilities: Five U.S. Forest Service campgrounds are scattered along the river between Winthrop and Thirtymile Campground. Winthrop has several motels and a couple of RV parks, as well as food, gas, and tackle.

Contact: Okanogan National Forest, (509) 826-3275; Pine-Near Trailer Park, (509) 996-2391; Methow Valley KOA Campground, (509) 996-2255; Chewuch Inn, (509) 996-3107.

Species available: Rainbow and cutthroat trout, summer steelhead, mountain whitefish.

Fishing the Chewack River: Special regulations on this Methow River tributary mean you have to leave the worms and salmon eggs home during the general summer season. Although you can find success by fishing a small nymph pattern on a sink-tip line, many anglers prefer to work a small spinner through the deeper pools and medium-depth runs. Whether you go with flies, spinners, or some other form of artificial, be sure it has a single, barbless hook. You'll probably have to release lots of trout before you come up with the daily limit of two fish over 12 inches. But since the river is stocked with a few thousand summer steelhead smolts, there's always the chance you'll hook a fish that's well over that minimum. You never know when an eager steelie may come along, so you might want to gear up accordingly.

You can forget the special no-bait regulations during the winter, when the Chewack is open to fishing for whitefish only. Some of the deeper pools on the lower end of the river are best-suited to winter whitefish action, and limits are possible once you locate them.

22. BUCK LAKE

Reference: **North of Winthrop, Okanogan National Forest; map A3, grid c9.**

How to get there: Take State Route 20 to Winthrop and drive north on Chewack River Road (Forest Road 51), then turn west (left) on Forest Road 100, and drive about 2.5 miles to the lake.

Facilities: The U.S. Forest Service's Buck Lake Campground has four tent sites and five sites that are suitable for small RVs. Other amenities can be found in Winthrop.

Contact: Okanogan National Forest, Winthrop Ranger District, (509) 996-2266.

Species available: Rainbow trout.

Fishing Buck Lake: Although well off the heavily traveled highways, this forest lake is actually pretty accessible, so it gets a little busy during the summer, especially on long holiday weekends. The fishing is just fair for pan-sized trout from intermittent hatchery plants. They'll take small spinners, salmon eggs, marshmallows, and an assortment of artificial flies.

23. PEARRYGIN LAKE

Reference: **Northeast of Winthrop; map A3, grid c9.**

How to get there: Take State Route 20 to Winthrop and turn north on County Road 9137, following it 1.5 miles to County Road 1631. Turn east (right) on 1631 and drive half a mile to the lake.

Facilities: There's a state park, a public access area, and a private resort on the lake offering boat ramps, beach-fishing areas, tent and RV spaces, rental cabins, fish-cleaning facilities, rest rooms, and showers. Other amenities are available in Winthrop.

Contact: Pearrygin Lake State Park (509) 996-2370, Derry's Pearrygin Lake Resort, (509) 996-2322.

Species available: Rainbow trout.

Fishing Pearrygin Lake: Generous loads of hatchery rainbow fingerlings that grow to good size in a hurry help to make this one of eastern Washington's favorite trout lakes. Most of the rainbows run nine to 10 inches when the lake opens to fishing in late-April, but Pearrygin also offers a better-than-average shot at carry-overs that may range from 14 to 20 inches. These "bonus" trout are beautiful, red-meated fish that are as good in the frying pan or oven as they are in front of a camera lens.

The usual trout-fishing goodies are all popular here, with anglers who stillfish favoring Berkley Power Bait, worms, salmon eggs, and marshmallows, not necessarily in that order. Trollers like Rooster Tail and Bang Tail spinners, small Hot Shot plugs, Flatfish, Kwikfish, Triple Teazers, Dick Nites, and Canadian Wonders.

24. DAVIS LAKE

Reference: **Southeast of Winthrop; map A3, grid d9.**

How to get there: Take State Route 20 to Winthrop and drive southeast out of town on County Road 9129 to Bear Creek Road. Turn east (left) on Bear Creek Road and continue to Davis Lake Road, where you should turn south (right). Drive about a mile on Davis Lake Road to the lake, which is on the right.

Facilities: The lake has a public access area with a boat ramp. Motels, RV parks, restaurants, grocery stores, and other facilities are nearby in Winthrop.

Contact: Pine-Near Trailer Park, (509) 996-2391; Methow Valley KOA Campground, (509) 996-2255; Chewuch Inn, (509) 996-3107.

Species available: Rainbow trout.

Fishing Davis Lake: Like Campbell and Cougar lakes to the east and north (see pages 117 and 274), Davis Lake has for many years had a fishing season that opens in September and runs through March. This 40-acre lake southeast of Winthrop is sometimes still a little too warm for great fishing when it first opens, but by October the rainbows usually come alive, offering good open-water fishing until early December and then sometimes decent ice fishing for a few weeks in January and February. Late-season trout action may be good when the ice opens up.

Stillfishing with red salmon eggs has long been a favorite method of taking Davis Lake rainbows, but in recent years more and more anglers have been finding success with Berkley's various Power Bait offerings.

25. PATTERSON LAKE

Reference: **Southwest of Winthrop; map A3, grid d9.**

How to get there: Take Twin Lakes Road (County Road 9120) southwest from Winthrop, then turn west on Patterson Lake Road (County Road 1117) and drive four miles to the lake.

Facilities: The lake has a public access area with rest rooms and a boat ramp as well as a long-established private resort. Winthrop, three miles to the east, has all the other amenities.

Contact: Patterson Lake Resort, (509) 996-2226.

Species available: Rainbow trout, some brook trout.

Fishing Patterson Lake: This 130-acre lake usually stays cool well into the spring, which sometimes translates into slow early season fishing and better action as May turns to June. (The season runs from late April through October.) Most of Patterson's rainbows (the result of fingerling plants the previous year) average about 10 inches on opening day, growing to 11 or 12 inches by the end of the summer.

Trolling with Wedding Rings or worms behind a string of trolling blades is popular here, and if you prefer lighter gear, try a green Rooster Tail, which has long been a Patterson Lake producer. Berkley's Power Bait in a variety of colors has taken this area by storm in recent years, but you'll also find anglers taking trout on salmon eggs, marshmallows, and combinations of the two. I can tell you from personal experience that stillfishing with a couple kernels of yellow corn on a small egg hook is also effective. Add one small split shot to make it sink to the bottom, leave the bail open on your reel, and give the fish plenty of time to take it. I spent several days catching limits of fat rainbows with this technique back when I was a kid, fishing Patterson for the very first time, and it still works today.

Artificial flies are also effective at Patterson, both cast with standard fly rods and trolled on monofilament with spinning tackle. Productive fly patterns here are nymphs and wet flies in olive green, brown, and black color schemes. Those tied on size 8 or 10 hooks seem to work best.

One of the pleasant things about fishing here is that water-skiers and speed-boaters are kept at bay by a 10-mile-per-hour speed limit. That means you can stay on the water to enjoy the fishing and the view of the nearby pine-covered hills all day long, even during those warm days of summer.

26. TWIN LAKES

Reference: **South of Winthrop; map A3, grid d9.**
How to get there: Take State Route 20 south from Winthrop, drive about two miles to Twin Lakes Road, and turn west (right). Follow Twin Lakes Road about 1.5 miles to Big Twin Lake. Little Twin is reached by a road that runs along the east side of Big Twin.
Facilities: Both lakes have public access areas and boat ramps, with a resort on Big Twin that offers limited groceries, tackle, boats, tent and RV sites, showers, and rest rooms. Lodging and other amenities are available in Winthrop.
Contact: Big Twin Lake Resort and Campground, (509) 996-2650.
Species available: Rainbow trout.
Fishing Twin Lakes: These popular lakes receive healthy plants of hatchery rainbows, which put on ounces and inches quickly. Both Big Twin (80 acres) and Little Twin (23 acres) have special regulations or seasons. Big Twin has what the Department of Fish and Wildlife calls "selective fishery regulations," which means you have to use artificial lures or flies only, and the daily limit is just one fish. That's okay, of course, if the one trout you keep happens to be a plump 17-inches, which is well within the realm of possibility. I like to fish a green Carey Special fly on Big Twin during May or early June, but you can catch rainbows here on a wide range of artificials.

Little Twin is one of several Okanogan County lakes to have a winter-only fishing season, which usually runs from the first of December through March. Like its bigger neighbor, Little Twin offers up some nice trout throughout the winter, with 11-inchers common and carry-overs to 16 inches or bigger a good possibility. Try fishing a single red salmon egg or Berkley Power Bait near the bottom for best results at Little Twin.

27. TWISP RIVER

Reference: **Joins the Methow River at the town of Twisp; map A3, grid d9.**
How to get there: Take State Route 20 to Twisp and turn east on Twisp River Road, which follows the river upstream for miles.

Facilities: U.S. Forest Service campgrounds at War Creek, Mystery, Poplar Flat, and South Creek offer a total of about three dozen tent and trailer sites, with the largest number available at War Creek and Poplar Flat. These two larger campgrounds also have drinking water, which isn't available at South Creek or Mystery. Food, gas, lodging, RV parks, and other amenities are available in and around Twisp, including Riverbend RV Park, just north of town.

Contact: Okanogan National Forest, Twisp Ranger District, (509) 997-2131; Riverbend RV Park, (509) 997-3500.

Species available: Rainbow trout, summer steelhead.

Fishing the Twisp River: This pretty and popular Okanogan County stream is stocked with hatchery steelhead smolts, but anglers catch few, if any, returning adult steelies. Selective fishery regulations requiring the use of artificial lures only are in effect here, and there's a 12-inch minimum size limit that means most trout have to be released. Despite angling action that's fair at best, this is a pleasant destination for summertime fishing and camping, and a good place to teach the kids the fine art of stream fishing with artificials. June through September is the best time to visit.

28. BLACK PINE LAKE

Reference: **Southwest of Twisp; map A3, grid e8.**

How to get there: Take State Route 20 to Twisp and go west on Poorman Creek Road about 3.5 miles to Forest Road 300. Turn south (left) here and drive about six miles to the lake. Rough, bumpy Forest Road 300 is best-suited for pickups and four-wheel-drive rigs, so take it slow and easy.

Facilities: The lake has a U.S. Forest Service campground, a boat ramp, and a fishing dock. All other necessities can be found in Twisp.

Contact: Okanogan National Forest, Twisp Ranger District, (509) 997-2131; Riverbend RV Park, (509) 997-3500.

Species available: Brook trout.

Fishing Black Pine Lake: Neither the lake nor its brook trout are particularly large, but they draw a fair amount of attention from both local and visiting anglers. Black Pine is a pretty lake in a pretty setting, which makes the fishing good whether the brookies are biting or not. The lake is a favorite of float-tube anglers who work the shoreline casting flies or hardware into the weed beds at the edge of the crystal-clear lake. If you pay attention, you can sometimes see the fish before they strike. Small Canadian Wonders, Triple Teazers, and other little wobbling spoons in silver, bronze, or half-and-half combinations are effective lures here. May, June, September, and October tend to produce the largest numbers of trout.

For larger fish, try trolling these offerings as deep as possible in some of the lake's deeper water. Trolling flies can also be effective. A favorite technique is to troll as deeply and as slowly as possible with a fly pattern appropriately called a Stick. It's nothing more than a hook wrapped with green chenille on a number 10 hook, no tail, no hackle, nothing else, but the Black Pine brookies seem to like it, and that's all that really counts.

29. STEHEKIN RIVER

Reference: **Flows into the north end of Lake Chelan; map A3, grid d6.**

How to get there: Take U.S. 97 to the south end of Lake Chelan and the town of the same name, then take the $21 passenger ferry ride to Stehekin, at the north end of the lake. Work your way upstream on foot or catch the shuttle bus at Stehekin, ride it 12 miles to the mouth of Agnes Creek, and work your way downstream from there. The river is closed above Agnes Creek.

Facilities: Lodging is available at North Cascades Stehekin Lodge and Stehekin Valley Ranch. Half a dozen National Park Service campgrounds are scattered along the river to as far upstream as Bridge Creek. Food, lodging, and some tackle are available in Stehekin.

Contact: North Cascades National Park, (360) 856-5700; North Cascades Stehekin Lodge, (509) 682-4494; Stehekin Valley Ranch, (509) 682-4677.

Species available: Rainbow and cutthroat trout.

Fishing the Stehekin River: Like Domke Lake to the south (see page 233), the Stehekin is a popular spot during the summertime tourist season. It has lots of special regulations, so be sure to check the fishing pamphlet very carefully before even making a cast. The river is, for all intents and purposes, a catch-and-release fishery. This out-of-the-way end of Lake Chelan does offer some decent-sized trout for the persistent angler, and there are a lot of "touristy" things to do, such as shopping and touring historic Stehekin. The fishing may keep you occupied for only a day, but plan on spending at least a couple more exploring the Stehekin Valley.

If you are serious about trying to catch a "keeper" of 15 inches or larger, work a small nymph or wet-fly pattern slowly along the bottom of some of the deeper pools, but do it after July 1, since the river is all catch-and-release earlier in the year.

30. SAUK RIVER

Reference: **Flows northward to join the Skagit River near Rockport; map A3, grid d1.**

How to get there: Take Interstate 5 to Burlington and turn east on State Route 20, following it 32 miles to Rockport. Turn south (right) on State Route 530 at Rockport and follow it 19 miles up the Sauk River Valley to Darrington. An alternate route is to turn east off Interstate 5 on State Route 530 near Arlington and follow it to Darrington. The Mountain Loop Highway and Darrington-Clear Creek Road parallel the east and west sides of the Sauk, respectively, upstream from Darrington.

Facilities: Rockport State Park, located near the mouth of the Sauk on the north bank of the Skagit River, has 50 RV sites with hookups and a limited number of tent sites, as well as rest rooms with showers. U.S. Forest Service campgrounds located at Clear Creek and Bedal also have tent and RV sites. Food, gas, tackle, and fishing licenses are available in Darrington.

Contact: Sauk River Sporting Goods, (360) 436-1500; Mount Baker-Snoqualmie National Forest, Darrington Ranger District, (360) 436-1155; Rockport State Park, (360) 853-8461.

Species available: Winter and summer steelhead, Dolly Varden, cutthroat trout.

Fishing the Sauk River: There was a time, about two decades ago, when the Sauk was one of Washington's top two or three big-fish steelhead streams. Winter-run steelies in the 20-pound class were a distinct possibility, and every once in a while, someone boated or beached a monster of 25 pounds or better. I remember a newspaper item that told of an angler's first trip to the Sauk, during which he landed not one, but two steelhead over 20 pounds in a single day. Such catches might be a virtual impossibility these days, but the Sauk still has a trophy-fish mystique that makes it special to those old-timers (like me) who remember it at its best.

If you caught a trophy-class steelhead from the Sauk now, chances are pretty good that you'd have to release it, since those big wild fish tend to return in March and April, a time when steelhead regulations here now allow catch-and-release angling only. During the regular (catch-and-keep) winter season, anglers catch several dozen steelhead, most of them during January and February. Both boat and bank fishing are effective, and Sauk River anglers use pretty much all the usual steelhead baits and lures to take fish.

The river also has a small run of summer steelhead, and anglers find them scattered throughout the river from the summer season opener in June through the end of August. They catch a few summer-runs in September and October also, but during those months all steelhead caught from the Sauk have to be released.

It's okay to keep a Dolly Varden from the Sauk if it's over 20 inches long, and the river gives up a fair number of these big predator fish. Try nightcrawlers or large spoons to fool them. Luhr Jensen's Krocodile in virtually any of the metallic finishes is a good Dolly Varden-getter.

---

31. SUIATTLE RIVER

Reference: **Joins the Sauk River north of Darrington; map A3, grid e1.**

How to get there: Take State Route 530 east from Interstate 5, through Arlington, then through Darrington. Right after the highway crosses the Sauk River, about seven miles north of Darrington, take the first right, on Forest Road 26, which follows the Suiattle River upstream.

Facilities: A U.S. Forest Service campground with tent and RV sites, rest rooms, and picnic tables is located at Buck Creek, about 16 miles upriver. Food, gas, lodging, and tackle are available in Darrington.

Contact: Sauk River Sporting Goods, (360) 436-1500; Mount Baker-Snoqualmie National Forest, Darrington Ranger District, (360) 436-1155.

Species available: Summer steelhead, cutthroat trout, Dolly Varden.

Fishing the Suiattle River: The good news is that the Suiattle is one of several streams on the Skagit River system where it's still okay to keep a Dolly Varden should you happen to hook one, and there still are some to hook. The bad news is that September and October are traditionally the top summer steelhead months on the Suiattle, and the river is closed to steelheading during that two-month period. Fish it in the summer, before the change in steelhead regulations, and take your chances. To cover all the bases, fish nightcrawlers; they're effective for Dolly Varden and will attract the larger cutthroats, and the occasional summer steelhead you might encounter may also show an interest.

Avoid some of the summertime angling pressure and improve your chances of hooking fish by getting away from the road, which is easier to do downstream from Buck Creek than it is farther upstream.

32. LAKE CHELAN-SAWTOOTH WILDERNESS LAKES

Reference: **East of Lake Chelan; map A3, grid e8.**

How to get there: To reach the northern lakes, drive west from Twisp on Twisp River Road to Buttermilk Creek Road and turn south (left). Drive about 4.5 miles to Forest Road 4300-500 and turn west (right), driving about three miles to the end of the road and a trail continuing west about eight miles to the first lake. To reach the central lakes in the long chain, drive north from Pateros or south from Twisp on State Route 153 and turn west on Gold Creek Road (Forest Road 4340). Stay to the right on Forest Road 4340 for about seven miles and turn left on Forest Road 300, which is a dirt road. Follow the road just under five miles to its end and hit the trail at the Crater Creek trailhead. From there it's a 3.5 mile hike to Crater Lake. An alternate route to the southernmost lakes in the chain is to turn left off Gold Creek Road onto Forest Road 200 (at Foggy Dew Campground) and follow it about four miles to the end, where the trail up Foggy Dew Creek begins.

Facilities: The U.S. Forest Service campground at the junction of Foggy Dew Creek and North Fork Gold Creek is the nearest roadside camping area. It has a dozen tent sites and pit toilets, but no drinking water. The nearest food, gas, tackle, and lodging are in Twisp and Pateros.

Contact: Okanogan National Forest, Twisp Ranger District, (509) 997-2131.

Species available: Rainbow and brook trout.

Fishing the Lake Chelan-Sawtooth Wilderness Lakes: If you're the kind of hiker/angler who likes to get your money's worth out of a trip, you could easily spend two weeks on the trail and/or on the water here. There are about a dozen and a half named lakes along Sawtooth Ridge, including (north to south) West, Middle, East Oval, Star, Bernice, Libby, Upper and Lower Crater, Surprise, Upper and Lower Eagle, Boiling, Cub, the two Martin lakes, Cooney, and Sunrise lakes. How productive a particular lake might be when you get there—and even what species of trout the lake produces—might well depend on how recently (or if) the lake has been planted by fish and wildlife personnel or by volunteers who have packed fish in on their backs. But no matter what, you'll soon find a lake that offers trout willing to take your bait or lure. Although individual lakes or even two or three lakes may be within reach of a one-day hike, you'll greatly increase your odds of finding good fishing if you plan on spending at least a couple of days sampling what this spectacular part of Washington has to offer.

The best time to visit this area is in June and July or after Labor Day weekend in September.

33. DOMKE LAKE

Reference: **South of Lucerne, west side of Lake Chelan; map A3, grid f7.**

How to get there: Take U.S. 97 to the town of Chelan and catch the ferry up Lake Chelan to Lucerne ($21 round-trip). From there it's less than a two-mile hike on the clearly marked trail to the north end of the lake.

Facilities: There are six U.S. Forest Service camp sites at Domke Lake, two at Lucerne, and four at nearby Refrigerator Harbor. Food, lodging, tackle, and other necessities are available in Chelan.

Contact: Wenatchee National Forest, Chelan Ranger District, (509) 682-2576.

Species available: Rainbow and some cutthroat trout.

Fishing Domke Lake: A popular side-trip for summertime visitors to Lake Chelan, Domke sees lots of camping and angling activity from about mid-June to Labor Day. It holds some large trout, but you may have to fish long and hard to catch one. Pan-sized rainbows will hit dry flies during the first and last two hours of daylight, but you may have to break out the spinning rod to find success during the rest of the day. I would recommend hiking in one day, spending the night, and coming out the next afternoon. That should give you enough time to fish and explore this beautiful corner of Wenatchee National Forest.

---

34. GLACIER PEAK LAKES

Reference: **Immediately north and west of Glacier Peak, Mount Baker-Snoqualmie National Forest, near Snohomish-Chelan county line; map A3, grid f3.**

How to get there: To reach the Lime Mountain lakes, drive north from Granite Falls on State Route 530 about seven miles and turn east (right) on Forest Road 26. Follow it 25 miles to the end and hike up Milk Creek Trail. After two miles, secondary trails to the right lead one to three miles to the lakes. Meadow Mountain area lakes are reached by driving south from Granite Falls on Mountain Loop Highway and turning east (left) on Forest Road 23. Turn left onto Forest Road 27 and right onto Forest Road 2710, drive to the end, and hike five to eight miles to the various lakes. To reach Lake Byrne, stay on Forest Road 23 to the end and hike five miles to the lake.

Facilities: U.S. Forest Service campgrounds are located throughout the area, including Buck Creek and Sulphur Creek campgrounds on the Suiattle River; White Chuck Campground at the confluence of the White Chuck and Sauk rivers; and Bedal Campground at the confluence of the North Fork and South Fork Sauk River. All have campsites, toilets, and drinking water. The nearest food, gas, tackle, and lodging are in Darrington.

Contact: Mount Baker-Snoqualmie National Forest, Darrington Ranger District, (360) 436-1155.

Species available: Rainbow trout.

Fishing the Glacier Peak Lakes: Anglers who visit any of 18 or so lakes above the headwaters of the Suiattle and White Chuck rivers near Glacier Peak get a chance to fish some beautiful little lakes and take in fabulous alpine scenery at the same time. What's more, these lakes are stocked regularly (but not annually) with tiny rainbow trout fingerlings, most of which are packed in on the backs of Department of Fish and Wildlife personnel and volunteer hiker/anglers. If you ever meet any of these folks along the trail, be sure to thank them, because if it weren't for their efforts, most of Washington's high-country lakes would be barren of fish.

Although there isn't much of a trail system to them, the cluster of lakes near Lime Mountain (south of Sulphur Creek Campground on the upper Suiattle) are close enough together that they can all be fished in a single day. This chain of nine lakes includes the three Box Mountain lakes, Rivord Lake, Twin lakes, and the two Milk lakes. A few miles to the southeast, and accessible from trails off Forest Roads 2550, 2710, and 2710-011, are Indigo, Crystal, Meadow, Emerald, and Diamond lakes, all of which offer good summertime fishing. Farther south are Round Lake, Camp Lake, and Lake Byrne. These three can be reached from the south by a trail off Forest Road 49 or from the north by a trail starting at the end of Forest Road 23.

Lake Byrne is not only the biggest lake of the entire bunch at 50 acres, but it's also the closest to Kennedy Hot Springs, a popular muscle-soothing stop for hikers near the west flank of Glacier Peak. Depending on your priorities, you can either stay an extra hour to cast for trout at the end of your soak or you can stay an extra hour to soak at the end of your fishing trip. Either way, you win!

The fishing season here is determined by the snow pack and ice cover, which usually recede by late June. July and August are the only sure-thing months. Take along a selection of small Flatfish, Daredevil spoons, and Metric Spinners, as well as several dry flies, which can be cast with the addition of a small plastic bobber about four feet up the line.

35. WHITE CHUCK RIVER

Reference: **Flows into the Sauk River southeast of Darrington; map A3, grid e2.**

How to get there: Take State Route 530 east from Interstate 5 to Darrington, cross the Sauk River just east of town, and turn south (right) on the Mountain Loop Highway (Forest Road 22). Cross the White Chuck River at its confluence with the Sauk River and turn east (left) upstream.

Facilities: U.S. Forest Service campgrounds with tent and trailer sites are located to the north at Clear Creek and to the south at Bedal, both on the Sauk River. The nearest food, gas, tackle, and lodging are in Darrington.

Contact: Sauk River Sporting Goods, (360) 436-1500; Mount Baker-Snoqualmie National Forest, Darrington Ranger District, (360) 436-1155.

Species available: Cutthroat trout and Dolly Varden.

Fishing the White Chuck River: Fish it during most of the summer and you'll understand how the White Chuck (or Whitechuck, depending on where you see it written) got its name. It's often a milky white or gray color, making for tough fishing if you aren't the patient type. But if you fish it with small salmon egg clusters or lively nightcrawlers and let the bait soak a few seconds in every likely spot, you'll find success. You can keep Dolly Varden from the White Chuck, provided they're at least 20 inches long. Despite a road that provides easy access to most of the river, the colored water helps to keep angling pressure fairly light.

36. HEATHER LAKE

Reference: **East of Granite Falls, Snohomish County; map A3, grid f0.**

How to get there: Take State Route 9 to Lake Stevens and turn east on State Route 92, following it to Granite Falls. Continue east out of Granite Falls on the Mountain Loop Highway to Verlot, and after crossing the South Fork Stillaguamish River, turn south (right) on 102nd Street NE (Forest Road 42). Drive about 1.5 miles to the trailhead, on the left. It's a steep, one-mile hike to the lake. If you come to the Heather Creek bridge on 102nd Street NE, you've gone about three-tenths of a mile past the trail.

Facilities: U.S. Forest Service campgrounds at Turlo and Verlot have both tent and RV sites, while a third campground at Gold Basin has tent sites only. The Forest Service's Verlot Public Service Center has maps of the area and other useful information. Food, gas, tackle, and lodging are available in Granite Falls and along the Mountain Loop Highway.

Contact: Mount Baker-Snoqualmie National Forest, Darrington Ranger District, (360) 436-1155; Mount Baker-Snoqualmie National Forest, Verlot Public Service Center, (360) 691-7791.

Species available: Rainbow trout.

Fishing Heather Lake: This is one of those high-country lakes that you can fish without devoting four days of your life to it and without crawling on hands and knees over 10 miles of broken rock with a 60-pound pack on your back. You will gain about 800 feet in elevation over the one-mile trail, so it's no stroll through the park. But you can hike in, fish several hours, and hike out in a single day if you stay on the move.

The shallow, 15-acre lake doesn't produce many lunkers, but the steep, rugged cliffs surrounding it and the snow banks that linger well into summer make Heather Lake a nice place to spend the day casting small spinners or dry flies to the pan-sized rainbows.

Snow and ice have usually melted by late May, and the fishing can be worthwhile anytime from then until late September.

37. LAKE TWENTYTWO
(OR TWENTY-TWO, OR EVEN 22)

Reference: **East of Granite Falls, Snohomish County; map A3, grid f0.**

How to get there: Take State Route 9 to Lake Stevens and turn east on State Route 92 to Granite Falls. Continue east from Granite Falls on the Mountain Loop Highway. After crossing the South Fork Stillaguamish River about a mile east of the Verlot Campground, continue just under another mile to the parking lot and trailhead, on the right. From there it's a hike of just under two miles up Twentytwo Creek to the lake.

Facilities: U.S. Forest Service campgrounds at Turlo and Verlot have both tent and RV sites, while a third campground at Gold Basin has tent sites only.

The Forest Service's Verlot Public Service Center has maps of the area and other useful information. Food, gas, tackle, and lodging are available in Granite Falls and along the Mountain Loop Highway.

Contact: Mount Baker-Snoqualmie National Forest, Darrington Ranger District, (360) 436-1155; Mount Baker-Snoqualmie National Forest, Verlot Public Service Center, (360) 691-7791.

Species available: Rainbow trout.

Fishing Lake Twentytwo: This is one of those high-country lakes that's definitely worth the effort it takes to reach it. Although the trail is fairly steep, it's only about two miles each way and you should be able to make it in two hours even if you stop to wet a line in the creek along the way. But don't spend too much time fishing for the finger-length stream trout, because there's bigger game up ahead in Lake Twentytwo.

At 45 acres and more than 50 feet deep in places, this little jewel nestled in a steep basin has its share of bragging-sized trout. And though the size and depth help the lake grow good-sized trout, they also make it more difficult to fish than most other high lakes. Take along some bait and some fairly large egg sinkers, which will allow you to ply the depths for bigger fish. Stillfishing with bait also allows you more time to sit back and take in the scenery. Be sure to take your camera as well as your favorite spinning or fly rod.

---

38. BOARDMAN LAKE, UPPER BOARDMAN (ISLAND) LAKE, AND LAKE EVAN

Reference: East of Granite Falls, Snohomish County; map A3, grid f0.

How to get there: Take State Route 9 to Lake Stevens and turn east on State Route 92 to Granite Falls. Take the Mountain Loop Highway east from Granite Falls and turn south (right) on Forest Road 4020 (about 4.5 miles after crossing the South Fork Stillaguamish River near Verlot Campground). Stay on Forest Road 4020 for about four miles to where it more or less ends at Lake Evan. Boardman Lake is about three-quarters of a mile south of Lake Evan, via a trail. Follow the creek uphill from the southeast corner of Boardman to reach Upper Boardman, also called Island Lake.

Facilities: The U.S. Forest Service campgrounds at Terlo, Verlot, and Gold Creek all have tent sites, and all but Gold Creek have trailer sites. The nearest food, gas, tackle, and lodging are in Granite Falls.

Contact: Mount Baker-Snoqualmie National Forest, Darrington Ranger District, (360) 436-1155; Mount Baker-Snoqualmie National Forest, Verlot Public Service Center, (360) 691-7791.

Species available: Rainbow, brook, and cutthroat trout.

Fishing Boardman Lake, Upper Boardman Lake, and Lake Evan: Since the road runs right to its shores, Lake Evan is the best bet if you're looking for easy access and a place to take the kids for an afternoon getaway. Expect to catch an occasional cutthroat and small brook trout.

But larger and more out-of-the-way Boardman is more likely to produce a couple of keepers. At 50 acres and with depths as great as 25 feet, it holds some fair-sized rainbows.

You'll probably break a sweat getting farther up the hill to Upper Boardman (also called Island Lake), but the fishing and scenery make it worth the effort. The 10-acre lake features a small island, and it has fair numbers of pan-sized cutthroats and brookies to keep you casting.

The snow and ice are gone from these lakes from about Memorial Day to the end of September, so plan your trip during that period, unless you want to work harder than necessary.

39. GOAT LAKE

Reference: **In Henry M. Jackson Wilderness, Snohomish County; map A3, grid f2.**

How to get there: Take State Route 9 to Lake Stevens and turn east on State Route 92 to Granite Falls. Take the Mountain Loop Highway east from Granite Falls, and about three miles east of Monte Cristo Road, turn south (right) on Forest Road 4080. Follow Forest Road 4080 for five miles to the end, where a trail heads uphill just over a mile to the lake.

Facilities: The U.S. Forest Service's Bedal Campground, located on the Mountain Loop Highway about three miles past the turn-off to Forest Road 4080, has both tent and RV sites, plus rest rooms and drinking water. The nearest food, gas, tackle, and lodging are in Granite Falls.

Contact: Mount Baker-Snoqualmie National Forest, Darrington Ranger District, (360) 436-1155; Mount Baker-Snoqualmie National Forest, Verlot Public Service Center, (360) 691-7791.

Species available: Brook and a few rainbow trout.

Fishing Goat Lake: Fairly easy to reach by way of a trail that isn't all that steep, this high-country lake gets substantial fishing pressure during the summer and early fall. Still, it provides decent fishing for mostly pan-sized brookies that are within easy reach around the lake's shoreline. Since the main trail peters out near the lake's north end, the fishing often improves as you work your way around to the south end and southeast corner of the lake.

While brookies are the main attraction, Goat Lake reportedly holds some large rainbows as well, and such stories are easy to believe. The lake is large (64 acres) and one of the deepest in Washington's high country (100 feet in spots), providing plenty of places for a shy old lunker rainbow to hide. Take along some deep-running lures or even a supply of bait for fishing the depths if you want to try for one.

Fish Goat Lake from June through September, when the ice and snow are gone.

40. SPADA LAKE (SULTAN RESERVOIR)

Reference: **Northeast of Startup, Snohomish County; map A3, grid g0.**

How to get there: Take U.S. 2 to Sultan and, about a mile east of town, turn north on Sultan Basin Road, following it about 15 miles to the lake.

Facilities: A boat ramp is located near the east end of the lake. The nearest food, gas, lodging, and tackle are back on U.S. 2 in the towns of Sultan and Monroe.

Contact: Sky Valley Traders, (360) 794-8818; Mount Baker-Snoqualmie National Forest, Skykomish Ranger District, (360) 677-2414.

Species available: Rainbow and cutthroat trout.

Fishing Spada Lake: This big, deep, cool reservoir has a lot to offer the patient angler in search of quality trout fishing. Under "selective fishery" management by the Department of Fish and Wildlife, Spada Lake has no-bait regulations and all lures must have single, barbless hooks to accommodate safe catch-and-release until an angler kills his or her limit and has to quit for the day. Another noteworthy regulation is that the minimum size limit is 12 inches, which is unusual for a Washington lake or reservoir. You can have a motor on your boat, but it must be electric and not gas-powered.

Because of Spada's rather restrictive regulations—plus its distance from a major highway—fishing pressure is light compared to other western Washington lakes. Many anglers come here simply to practice catch-and-release, so Spada doesn't become "fished out" by early summer. June and July, in fact, are very good months to fish it. Don't be too surprised if you have the good fortune of hooking a husky rainbow of 18 inches or better.

The fishing season here runs from late April through October.

---

41. LAKE CHELAN

Reference: Stretches from town of Chelan to Stehekin, Chelan County; map A3, grid f7.

How to get there: Take Interstate 97 north from Wenatchee about 31 miles, all the way to the south end of the lake or turn north (left) on Navarre Canyon Road at about the 24-mile mark and follow it to Lake Chelan State Park, about a quarter of the way up the lake.

Facilities: The Caravel Resort is right on the lake and within walking distance of the Riverfront Park boat ramp and all the shops and restaurants in downtown Chelan. Many of the units have fully equipped kitchens and all are a few steps from the lake. If you want to soak away sore muscles after playing all those fish, try one of their Jacuzzi suites. Reservations are recommended for the summer months. Write or call Caravel Resort, P.O. Box 1509, Chelan WA 98816; (509) 682-2582 or 1-800-962-8723. RV and tent spaces are available at Lake Chelan State Park, but in summer most spaces are reserved far in advance. There are also private RV parks and campgrounds in and around Chelan. Gas, tackle, and other necessities also are available in Chelan.

Contact: The Chelan Chamber of Commerce, 1-800-4-CHELAN. To book a salmon/lake trout trip, write or call Rick Graybill at Graybill's Guide Service, P.O. Box 2621, Chelan WA 98816; (509) 682-4294.

Species available: Chinook salmon, lake and rainbow trout, kokanee, smallmouth bass, burbot.

Fishing Lake Chelan: Talk about summertime at Lake Chelan and most people think of hot boats, cold drinks, and cool sun glasses. It's a place to zip around on water skis and lounge about coated in suntan lotion. Yes, Chelan is all these things, but it's also one of north-central Washington's most popular fishing spots.

The chinook salmon fishing is so good that it's beginning to draw anglers away from the traditional fisheries over on Puget Sound. Chelan was first stocked with chinook in 1974, and for the past several years, the Washington Department of Fish and Wildlife has planted 100,000 chinooks annually. If all goes according to plan, those plants will continue for the next couple of years.

Unlike most of the chinook salmon that saltwater anglers are used to chasing, Lake Chelan salmon are seldom concentrated around schools of baitfish. In fact, smaller fish make a up only a slight part of their diet, according to Rick Graybill, one of the area's premier fishing guides.

"They feed primarily on freshwater shrimp," Graybill told me the first time I fished the lake with him. "That makes for the sweetest, reddest salmon flesh you'll ever put on a barbecue, but it also means you have to cover a lot of water in search of scattered fish that only have to cruise around with their mouths open whenever they want a meal."

Covering a lot of water in search of fish means trolling, and that's the technique that accounts for most Lake Chelan chinooks. Early and late in the day, when the light-sensitive shrimp are nearer the surface, trolling in the top 60 feet of water will pay off. But as the sun gets higher in the sky, the shrimp and the salmon that feed on them get deeper in the water, and anglers have to take their baits or lures deeper and deeper to find fish. In a lake that plunges to 1,500 feet in places, you'd better be equipped with downriggers or forget about catching salmon throughout most of the day. You may have to fish 200 to 250 feet down to catch them.

Downrigger trolling at depths of 200 feet or more is challenging to say the least, and Lake Chelan salmon anglers have to be on their toes at all times. Line stretch is a problem when there's that much monofilament between the rod tip and the downrigger weight, and these salmon are notoriously light biters, so many strikes go unnoticed. To help improve the odds, watch the tip of your trolling rod constantly, and when you notice the slightest signs of a bump on the rod tip, take the rod from its holders and jerk the heck out of it to release the line and set the hook. Whole and plug-cut herring account for many Lake Chelan chinooks, as do herring strips fished behind flashers. A variety of plugs and wobbling spoons are also effective.

Rick Graybill says the same trolling methods that catch salmon also account for good numbers of lake trout, or Mackinaw. Chelan is one of only a handful of Washington lakes where this largest member of the char family can be found. Lake trout were first stocked here around 1980, and tens of thousands of them have been planted since that time. Graybill thinks the next state record will come from Lake Chelan, although most of the lakers caught here so far have been fish of 10 to 16 pounds. Some have topped the 20-pound mark, and they continue to add inches and pounds. The best fishing for salmon and lake trout is from March to July, but you might catch one virtually any month of the year.

The lake is open to year-round fishing, and if you're not into trolling for lunkers, you can always find other fisheries to keep you occupied. Chelan, for example, is stocked with as many as 100,000 rainbow trout each year, and both bank and boat anglers make good catches of them all around the south end of the lake. Bank anglers catch some good-sized rainbows at Riverfront Park, at the extreme south end, as do guests at the nearby Caravel Resort.

Kokanee are among Washington's most popular freshwater fish, and Lake Chelan has 'em. The freshwater shrimp have had a negative impact on kokanee, but anglers still make some good catches of these sweet-eating little sockeye salmon. Trolling produces most of them, and like the salmon and lake trout, you often have to troll quite deep to catch Lake Chelan kokanee. Your best shot at a Kokanee here is from June through August.

Although it's a fairly well-kept secret, Lake Chelan also offers good smallmouth bass fishing. The warmer waters at the south end of the lake provide some of the best action. There's no shortage of rocky points, submerged boulder piles, and gravel beaches for smallmouth anglers to try their luck. May, June, and July are the best bass months.

If you want to try something really different, ask some of the locals about burbot, commonly known as freshwater lings. These somewhat prehistoric-looking denizens of deep water provide year-round action at Chelan, although some of the best fishing is during the winter and early spring. They're long, slim, and ugly, but the white-meated burbot is always a hit at the dinner table.

42. ANTILON LAKE

Reference: **North of Manson, east side of Lake Chelan; map A3, grid g9.**

How to get there: Drive northwest out of Chelan on State Route 150 toward Manson. Turn right five miles from Chelan on Swartout Road, then right on Wapato Lake Road, and right on Grade Creek Road, which runs up the east side of the lake.

Facilities: An undeveloped campground is located on the lake. Food, RV sites, gas, and tackle are available in Manson. Lodging is available in Chelan.

Contact: Paradise Resort, (509) 687-3444; Kamei Resort, (509) 687-3690.

Species available: Brown and cutthroat trout, largemouth bass, crappies, bluegills.

Fishing Antilon Lake: Once a natural lake, the lower end of Antilon was dammed many years ago and the water level now fluctuates with the seasons. Spring and early summer fishing offer the possibility of hooking a brown trout of two or three pounds. Although most of the locals stillfish with eggs, worms, marshmallows, and all the usual stuff, if you really want a big brown, you might try offering it something a little more in line with its big-fish appetite. A small Rapala or Jensen Minnow might do the trick.

The same minnow-imitating plugs, if twitched along the surface early and late in the day or retrieved in a series of short jerks and stops, might also turn up a largemouth bass. Antilon reportedly has some fair-sized largemouths in it, according to local angler Dave Graybill, although I've never seen anyone catch one. But then, I've never fished here specifically for bass, so my expertise on the subject is limited at best. Try it for yourself to be sure.

Several small streams enter the upper portion of the lake, and they offer fair to good fishing for wild cutthroats and some brook trout. This would be a good place to take that light-weight fly rod you've been longing to use.

Antilon's location well off the beaten path makes it a good place to do some wildlife watching while you fish. Ospreys nest near the lake and there are mule deer throughout the area. But be careful, especially if you wander too far away from other anglers. While you're watching wildlife, some of the wildlife may be watching you, especially the big cats. The area has a healthy cougar population, and they get hungry, too. Rattlesnakes can also be a problem here.

43. DRY LAKE

Reference: **North of Manson, east side of Lake Chelan; map A3, grid g9.**
How to get there: Drive northwest out of Chelan on State Route 150 toward Manson, turn north (right) on Totem Pole Road as you're entering town, and follow it northwesterly about 3.5 miles to the south end of the lake.
Facilities: Food, camping, and gas are available in and around Manson, while lodging and other amenities can be found in Chelan.
Contact: Paradise Resort, (509) 687-3444; Kamei Resort, (509) 687-3690.
Species available: Largemouth bass, crappies, yellow perch, bluegills, brown bullhead catfish.
Fishing Dry Lake: Contrary to its name, Dry Lake isn't at all dry. It has enough water to support a thriving population of bass and panfish, and the bassing is good enough to draw the attention of serious anglers from throughout central Washington. If all the stories are true, Dry Lake has produced a few large-mouths in the seven- to nine-pound range.

The abundance of small panfish not only provides easy pickin's for hungry bass, but makes this lake a good one for kids and other not-too-patient anglers. A bobber and worm will provide all the action any youngster could want, or suspend a Mini Jig or similar leadhead below the bobber for variety.

The lake also has brown bullheads, according to surveys conducted by the Department of Fish and Wildlife, so those bobber-and-worm rigs might also come in handy for a little night fishing.

A word of warning is in order if you're planning to fish Dry Lake—or any of those nearby (including Antilon and Wapato, described on page 240 and below)—from the bank. This is rattlesnake country, so pay attention to what you're doing and where you're walking. One wrong move could really ruin your day. Be especially careful if you have youngsters in tow.

44. WAPATO LAKE

Reference: **North of Manson, east side of Lake Chelan: map A3, grid g9.**
How to get there: Take State Route 150 from Chelan toward Manson for about five miles and turn right on Swartout Road. Go two miles and turn right on Wapato Lake Road, which parallels the entire southwest side of the lake.
Facilities: The lake has a public access area and a boat ramp, plus two private campgrounds, one at each end, which have RV hookups, tent sites, rest rooms,

and showers. Food, gas, and tackle are available in Manson. More amenities can be found in Chelan.

Contact: Kamei Resort, (509) 687-3690; Paradise Resort, (509) 687-3444.

Species available: Rainbow trout, largemouth bass, bluegills, crappies.

Fishing Wapato Lake: Wapato provides some of central Washington's best spring trout fishing, with limits and near-limits of plump rainbows more the rule than the exception. The trout sometimes run to 20 inches or more, but 10- to 16-inchers make up a bulk of the catch. The best fishing occurs during the first two months of the season, from late April to late June, but the lake also offers good fall fishing. If you do decide to visit Wapato after August 1, be advised that the trout-fishing regulations change on that date to selective fishery regs, which means you can fish only with artificial lures and flies with single, barbless hooks. Those regulations remain in effect until the end of the season on October 31.

Both trolling and stillfishing work here for trout, so do some experimenting until you find the hot combination. One effective technique is to drift a Carey Special fly well behind the boat in 10 to 15 feet of water. Use the oars as little as possible to keep the surface disturbance to a minimum. The Carey Special is tied in many variations, and those with either red or chartreuse bodies seem to work best here.

Wapato has long been home to a thriving population of warm-water fish, including some lunker largemouth bass. Over the past few years, the lake has produced some bass in the nine-pound range, so we're talking trophy bass. Here's a tip that may help warn you when it's time to pick up your bass rod and make a cast or two: The lake is full of small panfish, and you can see them milling around in the shallows. If they suddenly disappear, it means a big predator is nearby. The primary big predator in this lake is the largemouth bass, so take the hint. Cast a crankbait or plastic worm out and see what happens.

The little bass, crappies, and sunfish have grown somewhat out of control here in recent years, so you're more likely to find small, stunted panfish than fish big enough to eat, and they're beginning to make inroads into the trout population by out-competing the trout for food. If you fish Wapato, take home a bucket of little panfish if you get the chance. Your cat or rosebushes will love you for it.

Although not something you'd want to hook, Wapato Lake is full of turtles, and for someone who isn't used to seeing a lot of these armored reptiles in the wild, it's a hoot.

---

45. ROSES LAKE

Reference: **North of Manson, east side of Lake Chelan; map A3, grid g9.**

How to get there: Take State Route 150 from Chelan toward Manson. Turn right on Swartout Road, right again on Wapato Lake Road, and then take the first left, a short access road, which leads a quarter mile to the east side of the lake.

Facilities: The southeast end of the lake has a boat ramp and access area, and nearby facilities in Manson include food, tackle, camping, and gas. Everything else you may need is available in Chelan.

Contact: Kamei Resort, (509) 687-3690; Paradise Resort, (509) 687-3444.

Species available: Rainbow trout.

Fishing Roses Lake: One of just a handful of Washington lakes that offers fishing during the winter only, this December-through-March fishery provides anglers with an opportunity to fish through the ice for rainbows that range from pan-sized to two pounds or more. Red salmon eggs, used alone or in combination with corn, marshmallows, or other baits, account for many of the fish. If the ice forms late or breaks up early, there's a chance for open-water fishing, and when anglers can get their boats in the water, they enjoy excellent trolling success.

---

46. WHITE RIVER

Reference: **Flows into the west end of Lake Wenatchee; map A3, grids g5 and g6.**

How to get there: Drive east from Monroe or west from Leavenworth on U.S. 2 and turn north onto State Route 207, following it 12 miles along the north side of Lake Wenatchee and eight more miles up the White River.

Facilities: A state park with about 200 tent sites is located near the east end of Lake Wenatchee, and two U.S. Forest Service campgrounds can be found near the west end, each with a few tent sites, rest rooms, and drinking water. U.S. Forest Service campgrounds at White River Falls and Napeequa Crossing have five tent sites each. Food, gas, tackle, and lodging are available in Leavenworth.

Contact: Wenatchee National Forest, Lake Wenatchee Ranger District, (509) 763-3103; Lake Wenatchee State Park, (509) 763-3101.

Species available: Rainbow and cutthroat trout, Dolly Varden.

Fishing the White River: This glacial stream is often milky from summer run-off, but you can still catch trout if you stick with salmon eggs, worms, and Berkeley Power Bait. The part of the river above the mouth of the Napeequa River has selective regulations where bait isn't allowed, however, adding considerable challenge to the game.

Once stocked with generous loads of hatchery trout, the White is pretty much self-sustaining now, so the action isn't as fast and furious as it used to be. You might still hook an occasional Dolly Varden here, but if you do, you have to release it. June and July are the best months to fish the White River.

---

47. FISH LAKE

Reference: **Northeast of Lake Wenatchee; map A3, grid h6.**

How to get there: Take U.S. 2 over Stevens Pass or east from Wenatchee and turn north on State Route 207 about 14 miles northwest of Wenatchee. Stay on 207 past the intersection of State Route 209 and over the river on the steel bridge, and then bear right at the "Y." From there it's a short distance to the lake, which is on the left.

Facilities: The lake has no public boat ramp, but for a small fee, you can launch at The Cove Resort, which also has rental boats and motors, a couple of cabins, and tent and RV sites. There's a small cafe with good food on U.S. 2, just west of the State Route 207 intersection. Food, gas, lodging, and tackle are available in Leavenworth, to the east.

Contact: The Cove Resort, (509) 763-3130.

Species available: Rainbow and brown trout, largemouth and smallmouth bass, yellow perch.

Fishing Fish Lake: This 500-acre lake has a reputation for its trophy-class browns, some of which top five pounds. Now and then someone lands a really big one, in the eight to 10 pounds range. As with any trophy fishery, it's more complicated than going out, catching a couple of monsters, and going home. Trollers usually drag Rapalas and other minnow-imitating plugs around for hours at a time between strikes, and the fly anglers who work the west end and north and south sides of the lake with various streamers and wet flies typically go even longer between one fish and the next. Of course, if the next fish turns out to be a five-pounder, it's always worth the wait and the extra effort.

The rainbows are more cooperative and dependable than the browns. Spring trolling or drifting with the wind, using a small string of gang trolls ahead of a Wedding Ring spinner, Triple Teazer, or worm, may catch you a quick limit of fat 10- to 12-inchers. The rainbow fishery can be good almost all year, even during the winter, when anglers commonly catch some nice ones through the ice.

Most anglers come to this 500-acre lake for the trout fishing, but if you stay more than a day and don't try to catch a mess of perch, you're missing out on some fine eating. The perch are also in a biting mood throughout the year, and some anglers brave winter storms and icy roads just to fish them through the ice of January. Although always good eating, a yellow perch caught in winter is the best of all, and when they run nine to 12 inches, as they do here, they're almost worth risking your neck on treacherous highways.

The lake also offers largemouth and smallmouth bass, although the numbers aren't as good as they were a few years ago. But you still stand a chance of hooking a big fish of either species.

---

48. CHIWAWA RIVER

Reference: Flows into the Wenatchee River southeast of Lake Wenatchee; map A3, grids g6 and h6.

How to get there: Drive east from Stevens Pass or west from Leavenworth on U.S. 2 and turn north on State Route 207 near Lake Wenatchee. At Nason Creek Campground, turn east (right) onto State Route 206 and follow it about four miles southeast to Plain. Turn north (left) on Chiwawa River Road (Forest Road 62) and follow it for about 20 miles up the river.

Facilities: Lake Wenatchee State Park, about five miles west of the river, is the closest thing to a "full-service" campground in the area, with about 200 tent sites but no hookups. The Forest Service's Nason Creek Campground offers an additional 75 tent sites, plus water and rest rooms. The nearest food, gas, lodging, and other facilities are in Leavenworth.

Contact: Wenatchee National Forest, Lake Wenatchee Ranger District, (509) 763-3103; Lake Wenatchee State Park, (509) 763-3101.

Species available: Rainbow and cutthroat trout.

Fishing the Chiwawa River: No, it's not Chihuahua, as in the Mexican dog, but Chiwawa, as in the small tributary stream to the Wenatchee River. This is another stream where hatchery plants once provided the fishery but have dried up in recent years. Artificial-lures-only regulations help to get the most out of the stream's rather limited trout population, but Chiwawa is a place where you can definitely expect to spend several hours without hooking a decent trout. It's nice country, though, and there are certainly worse ways of spending a July or August morning than casting spinners or small wet flies to the trout scattered along the Chiwawa's many miles.

---

49. LAKE WENATCHEE

Reference: **North of Leavenworth; map A3, grid h5.**

How to get there: Drive east from Monroe or west from Leavenworth on U.S. 2 and turn north on State Route 207, which parallels the north side of the lake.

Facilities: There are about 30 tent sites (no hookups) at Lake Wenatchee State Park, located just off State Route 207 near the west end of the lake. The state park also has a boat ramp. Glacier View Campground, on the south side of the lake via Forest Road 6607, has 20 campsites and a boat ramp. Dirty Face Campground (U.S. Forest Service) is at the northwest corner of the lake and has three campsites. The nearest restaurant is on U.S. 2, just west of the intersection of U.S. 2 and State Route 207. Other food, gas, lodging, RV parks, and supplies are located in Leavenworth.

Contact: Wenatchee National Forest, Lake Wenatchee Ranger District, (509) 763-3103; Lake Wenatchee State Park, (509) 763-3101.

Species available: Kokanee, sockeye salmon.

Fishing Lake Wenatchee: It would be nice to be able to say that Lake Wenatchee offers huge bull trout and sockeye salmon along with its abundant kokanee, but both have had their ups and downs in recent years and are currently down. I vividly remember stories coming from the old Telma Resort 20 years ago, stories of big, dumb bull trout that sometimes topped 10 pounds and would readily inhale a slowly trolled plug-cut herring or large, minnow-imitating plug. The only problem back then was that very few anglers bothered to spend time fishing for these big but somewhat lethargic trophies. Now bull trout populations throughout the Northwest are in trouble, and you can't keep one even if you're lucky enough to hook and land it.

Anadromous sockeye salmon may show up in good numbers one year but not the next, so you can't count on getting a chance at them most of the time. The sockeye season was closed in 1995, and you should check the current fishing regulations pamphlet before deciding to try for sockeyes this year. When there is a season, anglers troll bare hooks in black or red finishes behind a slowly revolving flasher, the same technique that works on Seattle's Lake Washington when the sockeye runs are good over there.

That leaves the kokanee, and in recent years Lake Wenatchee has risen to the top as a kokanee producer. The fish aren't particularly large, but they've been abundant enough lately to allow for a 16-fish daily limit, a limit that many veteran anglers may achieve in a couple of hours. Trolling a Wedding Ring, Needlefish, or other small, flashy spinner or spoon behind a string of trolling blades is one way to catch them, and don't forget to add that kernel of white corn to the lure's hooks for added appeal. Summertime is kokanee time, with July usually the top fishing month.

50. NASON CREEK

Reference: **Parallels U.S. 2 east of Stevens Pass; map A3, grids h4 and h5.**
How to get there: Take U.S. 2 about 60 miles east from Monroe or west 26 miles from Leavenworth and use various turnouts and side roads to stop and fish the creek.
Facilities: White Pine Campground (U.S. Forest Service) has nine tent sites, plus rest rooms and drinking water. Food, gas, tackle, and lodging are available in Leavenworth, and there's a good restaurant at the intersection of U.S. 2 and State Route 207.
Contact: Wenatchee National Forest, Lake Wenatchee Ranger District, (509) 763-3103.
Species available: Rainbow and cutthroat trout.
Fishing Nason Creek: No longer stocked with hatchery trout by the Department of Fish and Wildlife, Nason has ceased to be the put-and-take trough it used to be every summer. Now you have to work at it if you want to find success in this easy-access stream. In fact, you have to work at it even harder than you do on most Washington trout streams, since this is a no-bait fishery where you have to use artificial flies and lures with single, barbless hooks.

The creek opens to fishing June 1 of every year, but fishing conditions are often tough at that time, thanks to spring run-off and cool water. Wait until late-June or July and you'll probably enjoy the experience a lot more. By September the creek is quite low, but the first precipitation of fall may provide some decent angling action. The season closes at the end of October.

51. ENTIAT RIVER

Reference: **Enters Columbia River at Entiat; map A3, grid h8.**
How to get there: Take U.S. 97 to the town of Entiat and turn west on Entiat River Road, which follows the river upstream for well over 30 miles.
Facilities: Cottonwood, North Fork, Silver Falls, Lake Creek, and Fox Creek campgrounds (all U.S. Forest Service facilities) are scattered along the upper half of the Entiat and offer nearly 100 campsites among them. For anglers visiting the lower Entiat, there's a city park in town with 31 RV sites, showers, and a trailer dump. Food, tackle, and gas are also available in Entiat.
Contact: Wenatchee National Forest, Entiat Ranger District, (509) 784-1511.
Species available: Rainbow trout, summer-run steelhead.

Fishing the Entiat River: If it's trout fishing you're after, plan your trip for July, when the river gets some hefty plants of hatchery rainbows from the Department of Fish and Wildlife. This is one of the few central Washington streams that's still receiving hatchery plants, but who knows when the practice may be stopped here as well? Selective fishery regulations requiring the use of artificial lures and flies with single, barbless hooks are in effect all summer from the mouth of Fox Creek downstream, and that stretch of the Entiat also has a 12-inch minimum size limit and a two-fish daily bag limit. Keep all those things in mind as you work your way through the Entiat River canyon.

As for steelhead, September and October are the top months, though the steelheading isn't nearly as good as it was 10 or 15 years ago, when this little river often gave up several dozen steelies a week during the height of the fall fishery. A few dozen fish for the entire season is more like it these days. Wild steelhead runs are in tough shape here—if they exist at all—so you can keep only hatchery steelhead from the Entiat. The best way to catch one? I'd use a small Okie Drifter or Corky bobber in pink or some other subtle color, with a small tuft of nylon yarn on the hook immediately below the bobber.

52. EAGLE CREEK

Reference: **Joins Chumstick Creek north of Leavenworth; map A3, grids i6 and i7.**

How to get there: Take U.S. 2 to Leavenworth and turn north on State Route 209. Drive about two miles to Eagle Creek Road (Forest Road 7520) and turn east (right) to follow the creek upstream.

Facilities: Food, gas, lodging, tackle, and other facilities are available in Leavenworth.

Contact: Wenatchee National Forest, Leavenworth Ranger District, (509) 782-1413.

Species available: Rainbow and cutthroat trout.

Fishing Eagle Creek: Like the Chumstick into which it flows (see below), Eagle Creek is readily accessible from the road that runs much of its length. It provides a few pan-sized trout early in the season and then dries up as a worthwhile angling possibility. The season runs from June 1 through October 31.

53. CHUMSTICK CREEK

Reference: **Joins the Wenatchee River near Leavenworth; map A3, grid i7.**

How to get there: Take U.S. 2 to Leavenworth and turn north on State Route 209, which parallels the creek for several miles.

Facilities: Everything you need, including a wide range of motels, hotels, and bed and breakfasts, all with a Bavarian theme, are available in Leavenworth. Food, gas, and tackle are also available.

Contact: Wenatchee National Forest, Leavenworth Ranger District, (509) 782-1413.

Species available: Rainbow and cutthroat trout.

Fishing Chumstick Creek: The good news is that a state highway provides plenty of easy access to this bubbling stream just north of Leavenworth. The bad news is that a state highway provides plenty of easy access to this bubbling stream just north of Leavenworth. Chumstick gets quite a lot of fishing pressure and seldom produces a trout of noteworthy (or even worthwhile) size. It's a nice, cool little creek, but not worth too much of your time if you're a serious angler.

---

54. ICICLE CREEK (ICICLE RIVER)

Reference: **Southwest of Leavenworth; map A3, grid i6.**

How to get there: Take U.S. 2 to Leavenworth and turn south on East Leavenworth Road or Icicle Road to parallel the lower end of Icicle Creek. Icicle Road (Forest Road 7600) continues upstream some 15 miles past the national fish hatchery on the lower end of the creek.

Facilities: Seven U.S. Forest Service campgrounds are scattered along the creek, all with at least some campsites. Working upstream, Eightmile Campground has 45 sites, Bridge Creek Campground has six, Johnny Creek Campground has 56, Ida Creek Campground has 10, Chatter Creek Campground has 12, Rock Island Campground has 22, and Blackpine Creek Horse Camp has eight. There's also a large private RV park and campground about three miles up Icicle Road. Motels, bed and breakfasts, gas, food, and other facilities are available nearby in Leavenworth.

Contact: Wenatchee National Forest, Leavenworth Ranger District, (509) 782-1413; Icicle River RV Park and Campground, (509) 548-5420.

Species available: Chinook salmon, summer steelhead, rainbow trout.

Fishing Icicle Creek: Impressive returns of hatchery-run spring chinook salmon really put the Icicle on Washington's angling map in the early 1990s, but it also drew some pretty large crowds of anglers to this pretty small stream on the eastern flank of the Cascades. All of those anglers were crowded into the two miles of stream from the fish hatchery down to the mouth, which certainly added to the congestion. When it was hot, it gave up more than its share of 10- to 25-pound salmon, the vast majority of them during the month of May. June catches ran a distant second. Anglers who got in on that excellent spring fishing are hoping that the season closure in 1995 represented only a temporary lull in one of eastern Washington's hottest salmon fisheries. When the season is open, all the usual spring chinook rigs work here, including salmon egg clusters, fresh ghost shrimp, egg-shrimp combinations, and diving plugs.

Steelhead fishing takes a back seat to salmon fishing here, despite some very generous plants of hatchery steelhead smolts some years. The 1994 plant was nearly 140,000 fish, which could bode well for Icicle Creek angling over the next few years, but we'll have to wait and see. In recent years the catch has been a dismal dozen or so steelhead annually, hardly providing enough steelheading opportunity to make the creek a worthwhile bet. Although steelheading is allowed every month but April and May, there's no pattern as far as hot fishing months. Anglers find a fish or two at various times throughout the summer, fall, and winter.

55. COLUMBIA RIVER

Reference: **North and south of Wenatchee; map A3, grid i8.**

How to get there: Drive east on U.S. 2 or west on State Route 28 to Wenatchee and turn north on U.S. 97 to follow the river upstream.

Facilities: Three boat ramps are located in and around Wenatchee, plus one at Lincoln Rock State Park and another at the town of Entiat. Lincoln Rock State Park has about 70 RV sites with hookups and a limited number of tent sites without hookups. Wenatchee has a wide range of motels, bed and breakfasts, restaurants, and other facilities.

Contact: Lincoln Rock State Park, (509) 884-8702; Washington Department of Fish and Wildlife, Wenatchee Office, (509) 662-0452.

Species available: Summer steelhead, walleyes.

Fishing the Columbia River (from Rock Island Dam upstream to Chelan Falls): Although the past few years indicate otherwise, this stretch of the Columbia sometimes provides fairly good steelhead fishing. Summer-run steelies bound for the Entiat, Methow, and Okanogan rivers and upstream hatchery facilities show here in late summer and often peak from September to November, but may provide action throughout the winter. January and February are often slow months, but as the water warms again in March, things often pick up for a few weeks. This is big water—half a mile wide in places—and boaters catch most of the steelhead. Areas around the mouths of the Wenatchee and Entiat rivers, as well as several parts of Entiat Lake, are good bets. Trolling deep-diving plugs often provides most of the steelhead action.

This portion of the big river may not be one of the most well-known walleye spots on the vast Columbia River system, but it does give up some trophy-class fish. Trolling with some of the same diving plugs that work for steelhead will also take walleyes, or you can troll spinner-and-worm rigs near bottom to find fish.

56. WENATCHEE RIVER

Reference: **Joins the Columbia at Wenatchee; map A3, grid i7.**

How to get there: Take U.S. 2 east from Wenatchee and you'll parallel more than 25 miles of the lower Wenatchee River. To reach the middle stretch of the river, turn east off U.S. 2 onto River Road near Tumwater Campground and drive upriver. To fish the Little Wenatchee, above Lake Wenatchee, turn north off U.S. 2 onto State Route 207 and drive up the north side of the lake. About a mile west of the lake's west end, turn south (left) on Forest Road 6500, which runs along the river's north side for about 15 miles.

Facilities: Four U.S. Forest Service campgrounds along the river above the lake provide a total of 23 campsites. Tumwater Campground, on the lower river just off U.S. 2, has 80 campsites, including some that are large enough for trailers and other RVs. Lake Wenatchee State Park, with its 30 tent sites, plus rest rooms and a picnic area, is another good possibility. Additional RV sites, as well as motels, restaurants, grocery stores, gas stations, and other facilities, are available in Leavenworth, Cashmere, and Wenatchee.

Contact: Wenatchee National Forest, Lake Wenatchee Ranger District, (509) 763-3103; Wenatchee National Forest, Leavenworth Ranger District, (509) 782-1413; Lake Wenatchee State Park, (509) 763-3101; Wenatchee Area Visitor and Convention Bureau, (509) 662-4774.

Species available: Summer steelhead, chinook salmon, rainbow trout.

Fishing the Wenatchee River: Take one look at the numbers of summer-run steelhead smolts planted in the Wenatchee every year and you might come to the immediate conclusion that it has to be one of the most productive steelhead factories in the Northwest. Unfortunately, all those steelhead smolts have to pass through all those dams between the mouth of the Wenatchee and the mouth of the Columbia. Each of those dams—Rock Island, Wanapum, Priest Rapids, McNary, John Day, The Dalles, and Bonneville—chews up tens of thousands of those six-inch steelhead and spits them out on the other side, meaning only a fraction of the fish released in the Wenatchee actually make it to the Pacific Ocean to begin a saltwater stay that will last two to five years. The survivors of that marine odyssey then have to make their way up the Columbia and through the dams all over again. Between dams they must also escape marauding marine mammals, eager anglers, and a maze of tribal gill nets. When they finally make it back to the Wenatchee, the number of survivors from a plant of about 350,000 smolts is enough for anglers to catch maybe 300 to 350 fish, roughly one for every 1,000 planted. Talk about tough odds! But without those hundreds of thousands of hatchery smolts planted each year, this big Columbia tributary would probably have no steelhead fishery at all.

Wild steelhead runs also take a terrible pounding as they try to live their life cycle in the unfriendly environment of a twentieth century river. Returns of wild steelhead to the Wenatchee are so weak that they're protected from anglers by a wild-steelhead-release regulation. No-bait and barbless-hook rules on the river help to ensure that those wild steelies are released in good condition. What's more, the steelhead fishery on the Wenatchee is pretty much confined to that part of the river from the Icicle River Road bridge downstream, since all "trout" over 20 inches caught upstream from there must be released (and what's a steelhead if not a rainbow trout over 20 inches long?).

The lower Wenatchee offers so many likely looking steelhead-fishing places that your first visit will make you drool. U.S. 2/97 provides fair access to this entire section of river, some of it at points where the highway crosses the water and the rest via side roads that lead down to and across the river. But even better access is available to those anglers who float the river in rafts or drift boats, and there are places to launch in and around Leavenworth, Peshastin, Dryden, and Cashmere.

All the usual plugs, spinners, and steelhead bobbers will work, but this is a wonderful place to fly-fish for steelhead, and more and more anglers are coming to the Wenatchee equipped with fly rods and their favorite patterns of fur and feathers. Whether you cast flies or spinners, you'll have your best luck on the Wenatchee from September through November, with a flurry of activity often occurring in February and March.

The Wenatchee River chinook salmon season—when there is one—is a spring affair, with May providing the hottest action by far. The spring chinook season targets on hatchery fish bound for the Icicle River, and the open area is the short section of river from the mouth of the Icicle to the U.S. 2 bridge just east of Leavenworth. When conditions are right, this mile or two of river gives up several hundred fat and sassy chinooks in only four or five weeks. All the usual spring chinook offerings will work, but be sure to check the current fishing regulations pamphlet to be sure about when and whether the season is open.

Trout anglers needn't feel left out on the Wenatchee, especially if they confine most of their efforts to the upper portion of the river, above the lake. This "Little Wenatchee" stretch of river is still stocked with several thousand hatchery rainbows each year. Depending on weather and water conditions, these plants usually come in three or four installments sometime between the end of June and the first week or two of August. The rainbows aren't big, but like hatchery trout everywhere, they're cooperative as can be.

---

57. ALPINE LAKES WILDERNESS

Reference: **South of Skykomish, eastern King County; map A3, grid i2.**

How to get there: There are nearly as many trails and potential travel routes into this area as there are lakes within its vast boundaries, so I won't take up several pages of this book describing the many possibilities. I will say that you can get to some of the various lake trails off U.S. 2 via Forest Roads 6412, 68, and 6830, Icicle Road, and several trails off the south side of the highway; off Interstate 90 via Taylor River Road, Lake Dorothy Road, Forest Road 9030, and several major trail systems beginning near the highway and Kachess and Salmon la Sac roads; and even off back roads leading north and west from U.S. 97 (Blewett Pass Highway). To nail down details on various trails into this wilderness area, buy a map of the Mount Baker-Snoqualmie National Forest and another of the Wenatchee National Forest ($3 each) from any U.S. Forest Service office and most ranger district offices. You would also be smart to invest $18.95 in a copy of Foghorn's *Pacific Northwest Hiking* by Ron C. Judd and Dan A. Nelson, which provides complete details on hikes to many lakes in the Alpine Lakes Wilderness, as well as other high-country lakes and streams throughout Washington and Oregon.

Facilities: This is a wilderness area, so don't even bother asking about restaurants or motels. Stay on the trails and make camp where others have gone before you. Note: Day-use and camping permits are required for everyone entering the Alpine Lakes Wilderness. They're free and are available from local ranger district offices and information centers and at most trailheads. Food, gas, lodging, and tackle are available at several locations along U.S. 2 and Interstate 90, including Monroe, Sultan, North Bend, and Cle Elum.

Contact: Mount Baker-Snoqualmie National Forest, Skykomish Ranger District, (360) 677-2414; Mount Baker-Snoqualmie National Forest, North Bend Ranger District, (206) 888-1421; Wenatchee National Forest, Cle Elum Ranger District, (509) 674-4411; Wenatchee National Forest, Leavenworth Ranger District, (509) 782-1413.

Species available: Rainbow, brook, golden, and cutthroat trout.

Fishing the Alpine Lakes Wilderness: Would you believe this area has something in the neighborhood of 200 lakes, ranging in size from a couple of acres to nearly 300 acres, most of them holding at least one species of trout, and all located within some of the most spectacular alpine country to be found anywhere in the world? If you don't mind getting out and working up a sweat to get to your little piece of heaven, this is the place for you. Of course, other people want a piece of heaven, too, so don't plan on having it all to yourself during the narrow window of opportunity when these lakes are ice-free and the snow has melted out of the trails enough to allow passage. "Fishing season" on most of the lakes opens when Mother Nature says it does, and can close in a hurry any time after Labor Day, so everyone has to get what they can out of the wilderness area during only a few weeks in June, July, August, and September.

Some of the lakes are within relatively short hiking distances of forest roads and even major freeway systems. Olallie, Talapus, Rainbow, Island, and Blazer lakes, for example, all lie within a mile and a half of each other at the southwest corner of the wilderness and are within a three- to five-mile hike of Interstate 90 near the Bandera Airstrip. If you continue on past Olallie, you'll soon come to Pratt Lake, then Lower Tuscohatchie and tiny Melakwa lakes. I fished several of these in a mere two days back when I was about 13 years old (shortly after lakes were first invented). Immediately north of these are My Lake (love that name), Kaleetan, Snow, Upper and Lower Wildcat, Caroline, Big and Little Derrick, Hatchet, Horseshoe, Shamrock, and Emerald lakes, even the smallest of which is stocked periodically.

Lake Dorothy, one of the wilderness area's biggest lakes, can be reached and fished in a morning's time via Forest Road 6412 (Miller River Road) near the northwest corner of the wilderness. A short distance beyond Dorothy are Bear, Deer, and Snoqualmie lakes. South of this popular group lie a number of smaller but productive lakes, including Nordrum, Judy, Carole, Charlie Brown, Upper and Lower Garfield Mountain, Rock, Lunker, Green Ridge, Hi-Low, Pumpkinseed, Le Fay, Myrtle and Little Myrtle, Merlin, Nimme, Goat, Horseshoe (another one), Hester, Little Hester, and Big Snow lakes. A couple of miles east are several of the area's biggest lakes, including Copper, Big Heart, Angeline, Chetwoot, Otter, Locket, and Iswoot lakes.

Many of the lakes in the Alpine Lakes Wilderness are only for the accomplished, experienced hiker/angler. Grace, Charles, Margaret, Cup, Larch, and some of the other lakes in the northeastern portion of the wilderness are far from the nearest road, and you have to know where you're going in order to find them. Waptus, Spade, Shovel, Venus, Rowena, and other lakes in the Chelan County portion of the wilderness are also well back from any roads, as are many of the King County lakes in the system. Not only are many of the lakes a long way from the nearest road, but many don't even have particularly good trails leading to them. Some of these off-the-trail lakes may offer better trout fishing, but you'd better be a pro with map and compass if you plan to visit any of them.

Lakes or streams located more than a mile or two off the road require a little special planning on the part of any angler headed that way. Traveling light is, of course, one of the keys, whether you're going in only for the day or for an extended stay of several days or even weeks. I'll assume that any-one planning an extended trip already knows the do's and don'ts of high-country hiking. For the rest of you, though, think seriously about what you'll need and what you won't, and take only the necessities.

Unless you're an avid fly-fishing fanatic, take along only one rod for all-purpose fishing, and make it a lightweight spinning rod. With a six-foot rod and small spinning reel spooled with four or six-pound monofilament, you can fish flies as well as baits and lures; just take along a couple of plastic floats (bobbers) for additional casting weight. By the same token, if you like fishing with salmon eggs and think you may need several different shades to cover all the possibilities, dump part of the contents of several jars into one or two jars, rather than packing a jar of each color. Each jar you eliminate is that much less weight you'll have to carry. Remember, too, that even a two-piece spinning rod is three feet long when it's broken down, and that's long enough to catch on overhanging limbs and other obstacles if it's carried vertically on your back pack. Seriously consider a four- or five-piece pack rod or buy a light-weight rod tube for any pack trip you might take. There's nothing worse than hiking five miles to a trout-filled lake and discovering that you've broken six inches off your only fishing rod on the way in.

58. UPPER CLE ELUM RIVER

Reference: **Flows into the north end of Lake Cle Elum south of Salmon la Sac; map A3, grid j4.**

How to get there: Take Interstate 90 to Cle Elum and turn north on State Route 903, staying on it all the way up the east side of Lake Cle Elum and parallel-ing the river upstream.

Facilities: The U.S. Forest Service campground at Salmon la Sac has more than 100 campsites for tents and RVs. The Forest Service's Red Mountain and Cle Elum River campgrounds also have campsites, water, and rest rooms. The town of Cle Elum has food, gas, tackle, and lodging.

Contact: Wenatchee National Forest, Cle Elum Ranger District, (509) 674-4411.

Species available: Rainbow trout.

Fishing the Upper Cle Elum River: Once well-stocked with hatchery trout throughout the summer, the upper Cle Elum no longer receives hatchery plants, which means pretty tough fishing these days. You'll find a respectable rainbow here and there from late spring to mid-fall, but the angling action certainly isn't anything to get worked up about. The pine-covered hills around Salmon la Sac, however, are mighty pretty, and the scenery is good enough to keep your mind off the slow fishing—at least for a few hours.

59. COOPER LAKE

Reference: **Northwest of Salmon la Sac; map A3, grid j3.**

How to get there: Take Interstate 90 to Cle Elum and turn north on State Route 903. Drive three miles past the north end of Lake Cle Elum and turn west (left) on Forest Road 46. Follow it about five miles to Forest Road 4616, turn north (right), and follow the road along the north side of Cooper Lake.

Facilities: A launch ramp and nearly 30 tent sites are available at the U.S. Forest Service's Owhi Campground, on the lake's north shore. Food, gas, tackle, and lodging are available in and around Cle Elum.

Contact: Wenatchee National Forest, Cle Elum Ranger District, (509) 674-4411.

Species available: Rainbow and brook trout, kokanee.

Fishing Cooper Lake: Sometimes a slow starter, this high-country lake above Kachess Lake (see page 433) often provides good brook trout fishing beginning around the end of May or early June. Most of the brookies here run seven to nine inches, but occasionally the measuring tape is stretched to double figures. Casting wet or dry flies, small Super Dupers, and other bite-sized artificials will take them, but you can also use salmon eggs or worms successfully.

Now and then, rainbows are caught from the shoreline areas that produce brookies. If you want to improve your chances for a fat "bow," however, troll farther out toward the middle of the lake. That's also where you'll find the kokanee, which come on strong from about the middle of June to the middle of August. Like the trout, Cooper Lake kokanee are on the small side.

60. RATTLESNAKE LAKE

Reference: **South of North Bend; map A3, grid j0.**

How to get there: Take Interstate 90 to North Bend and turn south on Cedar Falls Road SE, following it three miles to the lake.

Facilities: The east side of the lake has a rough boat ramp (leave the trailer boat home) with pit toilets and plenty of room for bank-fishing. Food, gas, lodging, tackle, and other facilities are available in North Bend.

Contact: The Sport Shop, (206) 888-0715.

Species available: Rainbow and cutthroat trout.

Fishing Rattlesnake Lake: Leave the salmon eggs and Power Bait behind when you head for Rattlesnake; it's had special, no-bait angling regulations for years. Something else it's had for a long time is a reputation for fluctuating greatly in size depending on winter and spring weather conditions, and we're not talking subtle differences. Rattlesnake may be as large as 110 acres in April and as small as 10 or 15 acres in September. The size (and depth) may also change during the same season from one year to the next. You could say that Rattlesnake is worth fishing whether you like to do your trout fishing in little ponds or full-sized lakes; it might be either from one trip to the next.

But whatever the water conditions, the lake is stocked by the Department of Fish and Wildlife. Along with a mix of legal-sized rainbows and foot-long cutthroats planted every spring, Rattlesnake receives several thousand fingerling rainbows that grow to keeper size in the lake. The season here opens in late April and runs through October.

61. KEECHELUS LAKE

Reference: **Alongside Interstate 90 at Hyak; map A3, grid j2.**

How to get there: Take Interstate 90 to Snoqualmie Pass and exit to the south at Hyak onto Forest Road 9070, following it to the northwest corner of the lake and the boat ramp. To reach the southwest corner of the lake, turn south off Interstate 90 at Crystal Springs (Exit 62). Turn west on Forest Road 5480 and follow it two miles to the lake. If you want to fish the east side of Keechelus, stay on Interstate 90 to where the freeway parallels the shoreline and look for wide highway shoulders where there's ample room to pull over and park.

Facilities: The rough boat ramp near the northwest corner of the lake also has rest rooms and a picnic area. The U.S. Forest Service campground at Crystal Springs has about two-dozen campsites, some of which are large enough for RVs. Restaurants, motels, gas, and groceries are available at Snoqualmie Summit. Tackle can be found in Cle Elum and North Bend.

Contact: Mount Baker-Snoqualmie National Forest, North Bend Ranger District, (206) 888-1421; Wenatchee National Forest, Cle Elum Ranger District, (509) 674-4411.

Species available: Kokanee, burbot, a few rainbow trout.

Fishing Keechelus Lake: Located at an elevation of more than 2,500 feet and covering some 2,560 acres at full pool, Keechelus certainly qualifies as one of Washington's biggest "alpine lakes." Actually an impoundment on the headwaters of the Yakima River, fluctuating water levels throughout the year and a lack of good facilities along its shores keep Keechelus from becoming a major destination of Washington anglers.

The lake does offer fairly good kokanee fishing in the spring and summer, but as the water level drops in late-summer, anglers have a tougher and tougher time getting boats in the water to get at the fish. Find the kokes, though, and get set to enjoy some excellent fishing, since populations have been up in recent years. A 16-fish bonus limit has been in effect on Keechelus kokanee lately. Both stillfishing and trolling will work once you locate a school of fish.

Although it's an opportunity that is almost universally overlooked, Keechelus offers perhaps the best chance for western Washington anglers to catch burbot, those long, skinny, slithering bottom-feeders commonly referred to as freshwater lings. Keechelus has a large burbot population, and a few anglers—most of them from the eastern slope of the Cascades—put out set lines for them throughout much of the year. Such "trotline" tactics are legal for burbot, and the results can be quite good. Nightcrawlers, strips of sucker meat, and smelt are among the baits used by set-line anglers here. The same baits will also work at the ends of rod-and-reel rigs, and you certainly don't have to go the set-line route to catch these fine-eating fish.

MAP A4

WASHINGTON MAP .... see page 5
Adjoining Maps
NORTH .... no map
EAST (map A5) .... see page 300
SOUTH (map B4) .... see page 462
WEST (map A3) .... see page 212

59 Listings
PAGES 256-299

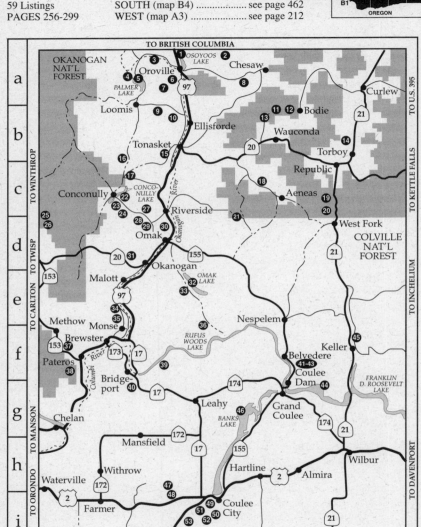

Map Section A4 features:

1. Osoyoos Lake
2. Sidley and Molson Lakes
3. Similkameen River
4. Chopaka Lake
5. Palmer Lake
6. Blue Lake
7. Wannacut Lake
8. Muskrat Lake
9. Spectacle Lake
10. Whitestone Lake
11. Lost Lake
12. Beth, Beaver, and Little Beaver Lakes
13. Bonaparte Lake
14. Curlew Lake
15. Aeneas Lake
16. Blue Lake (Sinlahekin Valley)
17. Fish Lake
18. Long, Round, and Ell Lakes
19. Ferry Lake
20. Swan Lake
21. Crawfish Lake
22. Conconully Lake
23. Conconully Reservoir
24. Salmon Creek
25. Cougar Lake
26. Campbell Lake
27. Lime Belt Lakes
28. Brown Lake
29. Green Lakes
30. Duck Lake
31. Leader Lake
32. Omak Lake
33. Cook and Little Goose Lakes
34. Okanogan River
35. Rat Lake
36. Big Goose Lake
37. Methow River
38. Alta Lake
39. Columbia River (Lake Pateros and Rufus Woods Lake)
40. Foster Creek
41. Buffalo Lake
42. Rebecca Lake
43. McGinnis Lake
44. Lower Lake Roosevelt
45. San Poil River
46. Banks Lake
47. Grimes Lake
48. Jameson Lake
49. Dry Falls Lake
50. Deep Lake
51. Perch Lake
52. Vic Meyers (Rainbow) Lake
53. Park Lake
54. Blue Lake
55. Alkali Lake
56. Lake Lenore
57. Billy Clapp Lake
58. Middle Crab Creek
59. Lake Creek Chain

1. OSOYOOS LAKE

Reference: **North of Oroville; map A4; grid a3.**

How to get there: Take U.S. 97 to Oroville and continue through town along the west side of the lake.

Facilities: Osoyoos Lake State Park, located at the south end of the lake, has 80 tent sites, rest rooms with showers, a boat ramp, and picnic tables. Food, gas, lodging, and other amenities are available in Oroville.

Contact: Darrell's Sporting Goods, (509) 476-2112; Osoyoos Lake State Park, (509) 476-3321.

Species available: Largemouth and smallmouth bass, kokanee, rainbow trout, black crappies, brown bullhead catfish, yellow perch.

Fishing Osoyoos Lake: Good catches of smallmouth bass and an occasional lunker largemouth have helped to put Osoyoos on the fishing map in recent years. This lake with a year-round season offers excellent smallmouth action, and anglers seem to have good luck with everything from crankbaits and spinnerbaits to jig-and-grub combinations or even skirted spinners. May, June, and July are the top bass months.

That same time frame is also good for trolling or stillfishing for Osoyoos kokanee, most of which range in size from 10 to 14 inches. Wedding Ring spinners with a kernel of white corn on the hooks will take them as well as anything, assuming you locate a good school and get your lure down to the right depth.

Spring fishing is also fair to good for rainbow trout, most of which are the result of hatchery plants. Spring and fall can produce good caches of crappies for anglers casting small leadheads, usually suspended two to four feet beneath a bobber. The same jig-and-bobber combination will also take perch during the warm months. In winter, fishing a perch eye or small strip of perch meat near bottom may produce a bucket of plump perch in short order.

2. SIDLEY AND MOLSON LAKES

Reference: **Northeast of Oroville, just south of the Canadian border; map A4, grid a5.**

How to get there: Take U.S. 97 to Oroville and turn east on Tonasket Creek Road. About eight miles east of Oroville, turn north (left) on County Road 9485, which leads to the town of Molson. Drive about a mile northeast from town, first to Molson Lake, then to Sidley, both of which are on the left.

Facilities: The north side of Sidley Lake has a public access area with a boat ramp and toilets. Limited services are available in Molson, but everything you'll need can be found in Oroville. The high point at Molson is the pioneer museum.

Contact: Darrell's Sporting Goods, (509) 476-2112.

Species available: Rainbow trout.

Fishing Sidley and Molson Lakes: The fishing is a whole lot better than it used to be here, thanks to the installation of an aerator that cuts down on wintertime trout loss at Sidley Lake, the more productive of the two lakes. Foot-long rainbows provide much of the action in this shallow, 120-acre lake, and don't be too surprised if your spring or fall angling efforts turn up a trout in the 16- to 18-inch range. Try casting or trolling a small, silver-and-red Super Duper if all else fails. It might not be a bad idea to take along your favorite fly rod, especially if you plan to be on the lake early or late in the day. Sidley is a favorite of bait-dunkers, hardware trollers, and dry-fly purists alike, and all three groups seem to hook their share of fat rainbows.

At Molson Lake, spring plants of hatchery rainbow fingerlings provide most of the action. The catch consists primarily of pan-sized trout, which are caught on salmon eggs, Power Bait, bobber-and-worm rigs, and all the usual spoons, spinners, and small wobbling plugs.

3. SIMILKAMEEN RIVER

Reference: **West of Oroville; map A4, grid a3.**

How to get there: Take U.S. 97 to Oroville and turn west on County Road 9425, which parallels the river upstream for miles.

Facilities: Food, gas, lodging, tackle, and other amenities are available in Oroville.

Contact: Darrell's Sporting Goods, (509) 476-2112.

Species available: Steelhead, mountain whitefish, kokanee.

Fishing the Similkameen River: Steelhead fishing downstream from Enloe Dam is the biggest draw for local anglers on the Similkameen, and some years the river produces good catches. October and March traditionally provide the best fishing, but there are steelhead in the river throughout the winter, and when conditions are mild, there's some good fishing to be had even in December and January. As is the case on many upper Columbia River tributaries, much of the fishing here is done with leadhead jigs fished beneath a float. Some anglers tip their jigs with shrimp, others don't, but the locals recommend changing jig color until you find the combination that works. Be sure to check the fishing regulations pamphlet before using shrimp, since it's illegal on the lower Similkameen during part of the season.

Whitefish provide some excellent wintertime angling opportunity on the Similkameen, both above and below the dam. The summertime counterpart of whitefish action is the kokanee fishery above the dam, where the relatively still waters of the impoundment produce some decent catches in June, July, and August. Kokanee to 18 inches are available.

4. CHOPAKA LAKE

Reference: **Southwest of Oroville; map a4, grid a2.**

How to get there: Take U.S. 97 to Ellisforde and turn west, over the Okanogan River, to County Road 9437, which parallels the west side of the river. Turn south (left), drive just over a mile to Loomis-Oroville Road (County Road 9425), and turn west (right). Drive past Whitestone and Spectacle lakes to the town of Loomis and bear right on Stehekin Road. A little over two miles north of Loomis, turn west (left) on Loomis Lake Road, marked by a clearly visible sign. The road gets pretty steep and ugly at this point and stays that way for about five miles, so drive slowly and take it easy. When you come to a "Y" five miles farther up the road, go to the right and you'll wind your way down to the edge of the lake, which is on the right.

Facilities: The west side of the lake has a fairly well-used camping area, boat ramp, and toilets. Chopaka Lodge and Sully's Trailer Park and RV offer lodging and camping, respectively. The nearest food, gas, tackle, and lodging are in Tonasket and Oroville.

Contact: Chopaka Lodge, (509) 223-3131; Sully's Trailer Park and RV, (509) 223-2303; Darrell's Sporting Goods, (509) 476-2112.

Species available: Rainbow and a few cutthroat trout.

Fishing Chopaka Lake: About the time you think you've arrived at one of the most desolate, out-of-the-way trout lakes in Washington, you'll arrive at the

Chopaka Lake access area and wonder where all the float tubes and fly rods came from. This fly-fishing-only lake with a one-fish limit is extremely popular during the late-spring and summer, and there's little chance you'll ever have it to yourself during that time of year. Weekends, in fact, are downright busy. Once you get through the bottleneck on shore and make it to the water in your car-topper or float tube, you'll realize why Chopaka is so popular— it's simply a quality fishery for quality trout.

Though anglers are allowed to keep one trout per day, most of the Chopaka regulars release everything, and that includes even the beautiful 18- to 20-inch trophies that are hooked here more often than you might suspect. Bring along a selection of leech and freshwater shrimp patterns, and maybe some mosquitoes if you want to work the surface, but be prepared for the Mayfly hatch, because when it happens, it provides some of Washington's best fly-fishing action. Newcomers to Chopaka should note that most of the fishing pressure is concentrated on the shallower southern half of the lake, but you can catch trout virtually everywhere, except in the 60- to 70-foot depths in the middle of the north end, where fly fishing is just a little tough.

5. PALMER LAKE

Reference: **Southwest of Oroville; map A4, grid a2.**

How to get there: Take U.S. 97 to Ellisforde and turn west, over the Okanogan River, to County Road 9437, which parallels the west side of the river. Turn south (left), drive just over a mile to Loomis-Oroville Road (County Road 9425), and turn west (right). Drive past Whitestone and Spectacle lakes to the town of Loomis and turn right on Stehekin Road. From there it's about five miles to the lake.

Facilities: Lodging is available at Chopaka Lodge and there are RV and tent sites at Sully's Trailer Park and RV, both within easy driving range of the lake. Additional amenities are abundant in Oroville.

Contact: Chopaka Lodge, (509) 223-3131; Sully's Trailer Park and RV, (509) 223-2303; Darrell's Sporting Goods, (509) 476-2112.

Species available: Largemouth and smallmouth bass, burbot, crappies, yellow perch, brown bullhead catfish, brook trout.

Fishing Palmer Lake: Covering more than 2,000 acres, Palmer is one of Okanogan County's biggest lakes, but trout-fishing purists don't consider it one of the best. That's because the trout-fishing possibilities are limited to a few pan-sized brookies that take a distant back seat to a variety of other angling opportunities.

The hottest action these days is dished up by spunky smallmouth bass that were stocked in the lake a few years ago. Bronzebacks have reproduced well and grown quickly, and the only thing that keeps Palmer from being ranked among Washington's best smallmouth lakes is the fact that it's so darned far away from where most people happen to live. Those who live in the population centers of the Puget Sound region have to give themselves the better part of a full day just to get to Palmer, and the trip home isn't any shorter. But if you have the time, bring along a selection of your favorite crawfish crankbaits, lots of leadheads and two to three-inch grubs, or whatever happens to be your favorite smallmouth medicine, and plan on spending at least two or three days to make the trip worthwhile. You'll like what you find.

As for the other fish Palmer has to offer, largemouth bass fishing is fair during the late-spring and summer, with fish of three and four pounds a likely possibility. The lake has a set limit on both largemouth and smallmouth bass, which allows anglers to keep only bass under 12 inches and over 15 inches, a common slot limit for Washington bass lakes. Crappie fishing is also good around the edge of the lake, and there are some keeper-sized perch. For a change of pace, bring along some nightcrawlers or cut strips from a couple of small perch and soak them in the depths for burbot. Or, if you're really serious about catching a few of these good-eating but homely looking "freshwater lings," use a multi-hook set line that might enable you to catch several at a time. Check the Palmer Lake regulations in the fishing pamphlet for details on what you can and can't do when set-line fishing.

Although abundant, the brown bullheads in the lake are pretty much overlooked. Catch them at night on bobber-and-nightcrawler rigs.

---

6. BLUE LAKE

Reference: **Southwest of Oroville, near Wannacut Lake; map A4, grid a3.**
How to get there: Take U.S. 97 to Ellisforde, turn west onto the bridge that crosses the Okanogan River (you can't miss it), and turn north (right) on County Road 9437, which parallels the west side of the river. Drive north about eight miles to Blue Lake Road (County Road 4510) and turn west (left). Drive about two miles to the lake, which is on the right.
Facilities: There's nothing here but a wide spot along the road and a dirt road that leads off along the east side of the lake, but you can get a car-top boat or float tube in the water. Food, gas, lodging, tackle, and other amenities are available in Oroville. Sun Cove Resort, on nearby Wannacut Lake, has lots of tent and RV sites, plus rest rooms, showers, and a small store.
Contact: Sun Cove Resort, (509) 476-2223; Darrell's Sporting Goods, (509) 476-2112.
Species available: Lahontan cutthroat trout.
Fishing Blue Lake: Okanogan County alone has at least three Blue Lakes, and I don't know how many there are in all of Washington, but I think this is the only Blue Lake that offers anglers a crack at Lahontan cutthroats. It hasn't always been that way. I vividly remember camping on the shores of this Blue Lake for several October days back in the late-seventies, hunting mule deer in the morning and late-afternoon and wishing the lake had something to fish for during the heat of the day. But its alkaline waters were fishless, so I had to occupy my time playing pinochle with my family and listening to Saturday afternoon Huskies football and Sunday afternoon Seahawks football.

But the introduction of Lahontan cutts a few years ago has changed all that, and fall is now a good time to cast a wet fly or a brightly colored wobbling spoon for husky cutthroats. Regulations require the use of artificial flies and lures only, with barbless, single hooks, and the daily bag limit is one fish. Although you can get a small boat into the water, it's also possible to hook trout by casting from the wide-open shores of the lake.

7. WANNACUT LAKE

Reference: **Southwest of Oroville; map A4, grid a3.**

How to get there: Take U.S. 97 to Ellisforde, turn west across the Okanogan River, and then turn north (right) on County Road 9437, which parallels the west side of the river. Drive north about eight miles to Blue Lake Road (County Road 4510) and turn west (left). Drive about four miles (past Blue Lake) to the "T," turn left, and drive about a mile to the lake, which is on the left.

Facilities: Sun Cove Resort has a boat ramp and moorage, tent and RV sites, cabins, a store with tackle, rest rooms with showers, and other facilities. The lake also has a public access area with a boat ramp and toilets. Additional amenities, including gas, are available in Oroville.

Contact: Sun Cove Resort, (509) 476-2223; Darrell's Sporting Goods, (509) 476-2112.

Species available: Rainbow trout.

Fishing Wannacut Lake: One look at the steep hillside bordering the east side of Wannacut might provide a hint about the character of this popular trout lake near the Canadian border. Spots near the lake's north end are well over 150 feet deep, and while you're not likely to be looking for rainbows 150 feet below the surface, the deep, cool waters provide good summertime trout survival and are part of the reason why Wannacut is one of the best. Not only does it produce a lot of trout, but a high percentage of the catch is comprised of big, strong carryovers that have spent at least a year in the lake.

Both trolling and stillfishing produce good catches of Wannacut rainbows from spring to early fall. Berkley Power Bait is a favorite among anglers who stillfish, while trollers often favor Supper Dupers. Much of the activity is centered around the many points that jut out from the east and west sides of the lake, but be sure to ask around when you arrive. The "hot spots" seem to change regularly, so you might be wasting your time if you go directly to the place that produced fish for you on the last trip to Wannacut.

If fly-fishing is your sport of choice, you might want to first investigate the shallow north and south ends of the lake. Nymphs and other wet patterns work well here throughout the day, but take along a floating line and a selection of dry patterns to cover the bases. Evening dry fly-fishing can be exceptional around the shallow weed patches at both ends of the lake.

The season runs from late April through October.

8. MUSKRAT LAKE

Reference: **Southeast of Oroville; map A4, grid a5.**

How to get there: Take U.S. 97 north from Tonasket toward Oroville. About four miles north of Ellisforde, turn east (right) on Mount Hull Road, following it east to Havillah, where it becomes Havillah-Tonasket Road. Drive northeast on Havillah-Tonasket Road and turn north (left) on Kipling Road. Drive about 1.5 miles to the lake, which is on the right.

Facilities: The lake has no facilities. The nearest food, gas, tackle, and lodging are at Bonaparte Lake, to the southeast, and in Tonasket and Oroville, to the west.

Contact: Cascade Toys and Sports, (509) 826-4148.

Species available: Brook and a few rainbow trout.

Fishing Muskrat Lake: There's nothing particularly notable about the fishing here, but anglers do take fair numbers of pan-sized brookies and an occasional rainbow by casting small spoons and spinners, salmon eggs and worms, even artificial flies. Fall fishing can be especially attractive, since the angling crowds are gone and the brookies are at their brightly colored best. The season opens in late April and runs through October.

---

9. SPECTACLE LAKE

Reference: **Northwest of Tonasket; map A4, grid b3.**

How to get there: Take U.S. 97 to Ellisforde and turn west, over the Okanogan River, to County Road 9437, which parallels the west side of the river. Turn south (left) here, drive just over a mile to Loomis-Oroville Road (County Road 9425), and turn west (right). Drive past Whitestone Lake and continue on to Spectacle, which is on the left side of the road.

Facilities: The lake has not one, not two, but three private resorts on it, and among them they have everything you'll need for a weekend (or month-long) visit. There's also a public access area with a boat ramp and toilets.

Contact: Spectacle Lake Resort, (509) 223-3433; Spectacle Falls Resort, (509) 223-4141; Rainbow Resort, (509) 223-3700.

Species available: Rainbow trout.

Fishing Spectacle Lake: After becoming infested with various fish species that anglers didn't particularly want to catch, Spectacle was given the rotenone treatment in 1994, so it's once again all rainbows. At least that's the case until some barroom biologist once again takes it upon himself to dump something into the lake that doesn't belong.

As of the 1995 season, Spectacle now opens to fishing earlier than most Okanogan County lakes, kicking off the season on March 1 and staying open through the end of July. During that time, anglers who stillfish, trollers, and fly-casters all enjoy productive trout action. Most prefer the deeper waters along the south side of the lake, where they take plump rainbows on everything from nightcrawlers, marshmallows, and Power Bait to Super Dupers, black Rooster Tails and frog-pattern Flatfish. Artificial flies are also popular here, and many anglers simply troll them at the end of a monofilament line. Favorite patterns include green or black Woolly Worms and green Carey Specials.

10. WHITESTONE LAKE

Reference: **Northwest of Tonasket; map A4, grid b3.**

How to get there: Take U.S. 97 to Ellisforde and turn west, over the Okanogan River, to County Road 9437, which parallels the west side of the river. Turn south (left) here, drive just over a mile to Loomis-Oroville Road (County Road 9425), and turn west (right). Drive about three miles to the lake, which is alongside the road on the left.

Facilities: The public access area on the lake has a good boat ramp and toilets. Three resorts with virtually everything an angler might need are located at Spectacle Lake, a few miles to the west.

Contact: Spectacle Lake Resort, (509) 223-3433; Spectacle Falls Resort, (509) 223-4141; Rainbow Resort, (509) 223-3700; Cascade Toys and Sports, (509) 826-4148.

Species available: Largemouth bass, crappies, yellow perch, brown bullhead catfish.

Fishing Whitestone Lake: Known to most Northwest anglers as a place to catch rainbow trout, Okanogan County also has some very good largemouth fishing, and Whitestone stands as one of the best examples, with bass to five pounds and over. It's an excellent place to practice your technique with plastic worm, jig-and-pig, crankbait, spinnerbait, or buzzbait. The afternoon wind sometimes causes problems for anglers on this long, narrow lake, so think about fishing it early in the day rather than late in the evening. Be sure to check the fishing pamphlet for details on the bass slot limit in effect here.

Whitestone used to be one of north-central Washington's better crappie lakes, but the (illegal) introduction of perch and sunfish has made things tough for the crappies. You're much more likely to find stunted, five-inch panfish than you are a half-dozen of the fat, 11-inch crappies for which the lake was once famous.

11. LOST LAKE

Reference: **Northwest of Wauconda, Okanogan County; map A4, grid b6.**

How to get there: Take U.S. 97 to Tonasket and turn east on State Route 20. Drive east to County Road 4953 and turn north (left), going about six miles to Bonaparte Lake and continuing another 10 miles to the short spur road leading to the north end of Lost Lake.

Facilities: The U.S. Forest Service's Lost Lake Campground has about 20 tent and trailer sites. Bonaparte Lake Resort, a few miles to the south, has tent and RV sites, cabins, and other amenities. The nearest food, gas, tackle, and lodging are in Tonasket.

Contact: Cascade Toys and Sports, (509) 826-4148; Okanogan National Forest, Tonasket Ranger District, (509) 486-2186; Bonaparte Lake Resort, (509) 486-2828.

Species available: Brook trout.

Fishing Lost Lake: This 47-acre lake, located in the high country of Okanogan National Forest near Strawberry Mountain, is a haven for brightly colored brook trout, hence brook trout anglers. Although it opens in late April, the fishing gets good here around Memorial Day and stays productive into early fall, with eight- to 10-inch brookies providing most of the fun. But there are enough larger carryovers around to keep you guessing whether the next cast will produce trout of 13 inches or larger.

Many anglers fish worms, salmon eggs, or Power Bait for their trout, but brookies are active feeders that don't mind chasing down a shiny spinner or small wobbling spoon. Casting dry flies early in the morning or during the last hour of daylight can pay off, or you can try small wet patterns during the day to entice trout.

12. BETH, BEAVER, AND LITTLE BEAVER LAKES

Reference: **West of Bodie, Okanogan National Forest; map A4, grid b6.**

How to get there: Take U.S. 97 to Tonasket and turn east on State Route 20, following it about 18 miles to Bonaparte Lake Road (County Road 4953). Continue about six miles past Bonaparte Lake to Beaver Lake. Little Beaver Lake is immediately to the east, and Beth Lake is about 1.5 miles to the northwest.

Facilities: The U.S. Forest Service maintains two campgrounds in the area. Beaver Lake Campground has five tent/trailer spaces, while Beth Lake Campground has eight sites. Both campgrounds have drinking water and vault toilets. Small boats can be launched on all three lakes. Bonaparte Lake Resort has cabins, RV and tent sites, groceries, tackle, and other amenities.

Contact: Okanogan National Forest, Tonasket Ranger District, (509) 486-2186; Bonaparte Lake Resort, (509) 486-2828.

Species available: Rainbow and brook trout.

Fishing Beth, Beaver, and Little Beaver Lakes: The pan-sized brookies stocked here every spring provide most of the angling action in all three lakes, at least as far as numbers are concerned. But the real excitement is generated by the occasional rainbow that's winched from these small lakes nestled in the pine-covered hills of the Okanogan National Forest. Some of them weigh in at three, four, even five pounds. Like the brook trout, the big 'bows can be caught on all the usual baits, lures, and artificial flies.

Since the lakes are small and shallow, they warm rather quickly in summer, which slows the trout fishing. Plan to visit in June, September, or October for the greatest success.

13. BONAPARTE LAKE

Reference: **Northwest of Wauconda, Okanogan County; map A4, grid b6.**

How to get there: Take U.S. 97 to Tonasket and turn east on State Route 20, following it about 18 miles to County Road 4953 (Bonaparte Lake Road) and signs pointing to Bonaparte Lake. Turn north (left) and drive about six miles to the lake.

Facilities: Bonaparte Lake Resort has a boat ramp, tent and RV sites, cabins, tackle, and groceries. There's also a boat ramp and about two dozen campsites at the U.S. Forest Service's Bonaparte Lake Campground.

Contact: Bonaparte Lake Resort, (509) 486-2828; Okanogan National Forest, Tonasket Ranger District, (509) 486-2186.

Species available: Rainbow and brook trout, kokanee, lake trout.

Fishing Bonaparte Lake: We're talking cold, clear, and deep, the ideal ingredients for trout and trout fishing. That certainly helps to explain why this 160-acre lake in the "Okanogan Highlands" offers so much trout-fishing variety. Open year-round, you can find some kind of salmonid to catch here virtually 12 months out of the year. But the biggest of the bunch is the lake trout, or Mackinaw, which occasionally grows to more than 20 pounds in Bonaparte's chilly waters. Although Washington's official state-record Mackinaw is a fish of just over 30 pounds, folks around Bonaparte Lake like to tell the story of the monster 38-pounder that was caught here but not submitted for record consideration. If the scales were accurate and the story hasn't been embellished over the years, that's the largest trout or char ever caught from a Washington lake. The best time of year for a trophy lake trout is shortly after the ice cover disappears from the lake, usually some time in April. Vertical jigging with Buzz Bombs and other metal jigs is one productive technique, but trolling with large Rapalas, Flatfish, Kwikfish, and other big plugs is also effective. Get on the water around first light and/or last light to improve your chances of catching one of these trophies.

As for Bonaparte's "smaller" trout, the rainbows here sometimes grow to five pounds or more, which is substantially larger than the average lake rainbow. Trollers pull Pop Geer-and-worm rigs for them, while anglers who stillfish prefer orange Berkley Power Bait and salmon eggs. The same offerings also turn up an occasional brook trout. Kokanee can also be caught by trolling or stillfishing, but practitioners of either method should be willing to experiment a little until finding the right combination. Wedding Ring spinners and Triple Teazers are a couple of the old stand-by offerings for trolling, but trolling blades with worms also take kokanee. Some anglers score good catches by substituting a Berkley Power Wiggler or two for the worm. Again, experiment until you find the right combination of bait, lure, and color. Use your depthsounder to locate schools of these sweet-eating fish, and you may need a downrigger to get your bait or lure down to the strike zone.

---

14. CURLEW LAKE

Reference: **Northeast of Republic, Ferry County; map A4, grid b8.**

How to get there: Take State Route 20 or State Route 21 to Republic and continue north on State Route 21, which parallels the east side of the lake. To reach the west side of the lake, turn west (left) on West Curlew Lake Road about six miles north of Republic.

Facilities: Four private resorts and a state park provide a wealth of facilities for visiting anglers, including boat ramps, moorage, boat rentals, fishing docks, cabins, RV and tent sites, rest rooms with showers, and small stores with tackle and groceries. Other services are available in Republic.

Contact: Curlew Lake State Park, (509) 775-3592; Pine Point Resort, (509) 775-3643; Tiffany's Resort, (509) 775- 3152; Black's Beach Resort, (509) 775-3989; Fisherman's Cove, (509) 775-3641.

Species available: Rainbow and brook trout, largemouth bass.

Fishing Curlew Lake: The term "fish factory" probably applies here as well as anywhere in the Pacific Northwest. Curlew has long been a favorite of Washington trout anglers, and the addition of largemouth bass in the 1980s (compliments of the midnight biologist corps, not the old Department of Game), has added a new dimension to the fishery without causing any noticeable problems for the trout population.

But rainbow trout still rule the roost in this 870-acre lake bordered by pine-covered hills around much of its perimeter. Between Department of Fish and Wildlife plants and net-pen facilities on the lake, Curlew is stocked with something like 300,000 rainbows a year, and they grow quickly in its food-rich waters. Ten- to 14-inch trout provide much of the angling action, but pot-bellied lunkers of 18 to 22 inches are common enough to be a realistic possibility for anyone fishing here. Slow-trolling with various gang trolls is standard operating procedure, and anglers typically hang Rooster Tails, Wedding Rings, Flatfish, or Triple Teazers off the back end of those blade strings. Another productive trolling technique involves leaded line, a long monofilament leader and a green Carey Special or other streamer fly of some kind, pulled very slowly through the depths. Stillfishing also accounts for some good catches, and the fishing docks at the various resorts are some of the most productive spots on the lake. Night-fishing can be especially productive from these structures, primarily because the dock lights are left on, and that attracts freshwater shrimp and other aquatic organisms, which in turn draw the trout.

Casting flies, small spinners, or wobbling spoons or fishing a plain ol' bobber-and-worm rig around the edge of the lake are all good ways to catch brook trout from Curlew. Like brookies everywhere, they're generally small but brightly colored, full of fight, and quite tasty if you keep 'em cool and cook 'em the same day you catch 'em.

Although Curlew is open to year-round fishing and provides at least fair trout fishing during every season, the bass fishery is pretty much a late spring and summer affair. The limited number of docks and other man-made structures usually have trout anglers on them, so bass anglers have to confine most of their efforts to natural cover around the edges of the lake. Luckily, such cover is abundant, taking the form of submerged logs and trees, overhanging and submerged brush, and some fairly thick patches of grass and scattered weeds. There are lots of smaller bass (under half a pound) but enough big fish to make it worth your while.

---

15. AENEAS LAKE

Reference: Southwest of Tonasket; map A4, grid b3.

How to get there: Take U.S. 97 to Tonasket and turn west on Pine Creek Road (Forest Road 9400). Be sure to take the hard left about three miles west of town to stay on Pine Creek Road. The lake is on the right, just under a mile from that 90-degree turn.

Facilities: The lake has a few primitive campsites, a boat ramp, and toilets. Food, gas, lodging, and other amenities are available a few miles away in Tonasket.

Contact: Cascade Toys and Sports, (509) 826-4148.

Species available: Rainbow trout.

Fishing Aeneas Lake: This is one of relatively few Washington lakes that's reserved for fly-casters only, and it's long been a favorite of fly-tossers from all over the Pacific Northwest. Since I'm well down any existing list of accomplished fly-casters, my success here has been limited, and I'm always out-fished by the ospreys that work the lake daily. But anglers who know what they're doing with a fly rod catch some beautiful rainbows from Aeneas, including the occasional trout to 20 inches or better. The "average" rainbows here run 12 to 16 inches.

Although this 60-acre lake is not large, it is quite deep, with spots in the middle plunging to more than 60 feet. Needless to say, fly-anglers don't spend much time trying to ply these depths with their feathery offerings. Most regulars fish the relatively shallow waters near the north end, using various leech patterns or a local favorite known as the Stick, which is little more than olive or black chenille wrapped around a size 10 hook. It may look like a stick to us, but it looks like food to a hungry trout.

The season here runs from late April through the end of October, with May and June providing the best trout action. Late September and the entire month of October are also productive fishing times.

16. BLUE LAKE (SINLAHEKIN VALLEY)

Reference: Southwest of Tonasket; map A4, grid b2.

How to get there: Take U.S. 97 to Riverside and continue north about 5.5 miles to Pine Creek Road (County Road 9410). Turn west (left) here and drive about 10 miles to Fish Lake. Turn north (right) just past Fish Lake onto Sinlahekin Road. Continue about four miles north to Blue Lake.

Facilities: The lake has an access area and boat ramp. Although there's not an official campground, lots of people camp in primitive sites around the lake. The nearest campgrounds and other amenities are in and around Conconully, 10.5 miles to the south.

Contact: Liar's Cove Resort, (509) 826-1288; Shady Pines Resort, (509) 826-2287; Conconully Lake Resort, (509) 826-7408; Conconully State Park, (509) 826-7408; Okanogan National Forest Headquarters, (509) 422-2704.

Species available: Rainbow trout.

Fishing Blue Lake: If you like to do your trout fishing with artificial lures and flies, this 160-acre lake in the Sinlahekin Valley is worth visiting any time during the spring, early summer, or fall. Selective fishery regulations keep it from being hammered too heavily, and it seems as if a few foot-long rainbows are always in a biting mood. Patient anglers are sometimes rewarded with trout of 17 to 20 inches. The daily limit is one trout, but don't feel like you have to kill one; the fishing stays good because most anglers release everything they catch. If you're planning to toss feathers and fur for your trout, be sure to take along a selection of Muddlers and various leech patterns. The "strike zone" here is often quite deep, so include a fast-sink fly line in your arsenal.

17. FISH LAKE

Reference: **Northeast of Conconully; map A4, grid c2.**

How to get there: Take U.S. 97 to Riverside and continue north about 5.5 miles to Pine Creek Road (County Road 9410). Turn west (left) here and continue just under 10 miles to the lake.

Facilities: The lake has two public access areas with a boat ramp and toilets. The U.S. Forest Service's Sugar Loaf Campground, with five campsites that have room for small trailers and RVs, is two miles south of the lake on Sinlahekin Road. Other amenities can be found in Conconully, about seven miles to the south.

Contact: Liar's Cove Resort, (509) 826-1288; Shady Pines Resort, (509) 826-2287; Conconully Lake Resort, (509) 826-7408; Conconully State Park, (509) 826-7408; Okanogan National Forest Headquarters, (509) 422-2704.

Species available: Rainbow trout, a few largemouth bass.

Fishing Fish Lake: Unlike many Okanogan County waters, this long, narrow lake produces trout pretty well for about the first month of the season and then tapers off quickly. Yearling rainbows from plants made the previous spring run about 10 inches long on opening day, but anglers do catch fair numbers of two-year carryovers that range in size from 15 to 19 inches. Try trolling a small Flatfish or Kwikfish, preferably one in some shade of green, or still with the tried and true gang troll-and-worms combination.

Although bass fishing isn't a big deal for most Okanogan County anglers, a few do visit Fish Lake after the trout action tapers off in May or June to try for largemouths. Most work Rapalas on the surface for their fish, but don't hesitate to work a white or chartreuse spinnerbait along the shoreline if the fish aren't hitting on top.

18. LONG, ROUND, AND ELL LAKES

Reference: **Southeast of Tonasket; map A4, grid c6.**

How to get there: Drive east from Tonasket on State Route 20 and turn south (right) on Aeneas Valley Road. Drive about five miles to Long Lake, then Round Lake and Ell Lake, all on the east (left) side of the road.

Facilities: All three lakes have access areas and launch sites for smaller boats. The nearest food, gas, lodging, and other amenities are in Tonasket.

Contact: Cascade Toys and Sports, (509) 826-4148.

Species available: Rainbow trout.

Fishing Long, Round, and Ell Lakes: All three of these lakes offer anglers a pretty good shot at pan-sized yearling rainbows with a few husky carryovers mixed in for good measure. But Ell Lake now has different regulations and even a different open season from the other two, so anglers headed for these three neighboring lakes in the Aeneas Valley need to remember which lake they're fishing and act accordingly.

Ell Lake is the only one of the three that remains open to fishing past the end of September, closing October 31. But angling regulations on Ell Lake are also more restrictive, with selective fishery rules now in effect. That means you can't use bait and all lures must have single, barbless hooks. Ell also has a one-fish daily limit, while the other two have standard, five-fish limits.

19. FERRY LAKE

Reference: **Southwest of Republic; map A4, grid c7.**

How to get there: Take State Route 21 north from Wilbur or south from Republic and turn west on Swan Lake Road (Forest Road 53) about eight miles south of Republic. Drive about 6.5 miles and turn west (right) on Forest Road 500, then take the next right to Ferry Lake.

Facilities: The U.S. Forest Service's Ferry Lake Campground has tent and RV sites, rest rooms, drinking water, and picnic areas, as well as a boat ramp. The nearest food, gas, lodging, and other amenities are in Republic.

Contact: Colville National Forest, Republic Ranger District, (509) 775-3305.

Species available: Rainbow trout.

Fishing Ferry Lake: At just under 20 acres, this lake in the high country of western Ferry County often suffers fish losses due to winter-kill, so the fishery depends on annual plants of hatchery rainbows. Ferry Lake is a popular destination of hikers, ORV enthusiasts, partiers, and other campers during the summer, so perhaps not the best choice for serious summertime anglers. But in spring and fall, when the crowds are light, it's worth a couple days of your time. The proximity of Swan Lake (see below) makes it easy to fish two different spots in the same day.

20. SWAN LAKE

Reference: **Southwest of Republic; map A4, grid c7.**

How to get there: Take State Route 21 north from Wilbur or south from Republic to Swan Lake Road (Forest Road 53), which is about eight miles south of Republic. Turn west and drive about 6.5 miles to Forest Road 500, then turn west (right) and continue about two miles to the lake.

Facilities: Swan Lake Campground (U.S. Forest Service) has tent and RV sites, drinking water, a boat ramp, rest rooms, and picnic tables. Other amenities are available in Republic.

Contact: Colville National Forest, Republic Ranger District, (509) 775-3305.

Species available: Rainbow and brook trout, largemouth bass.

Fishing Swan Lake: Regular plants of hatchery brookies and rainbows offer some pretty good trout fishing in this 50-acre lake located at the 3,600-foot mark near Swan Butte. Early summer and early fall provide some of the best fishing, and when the bite is on, it doesn't seem to matter much what you throw at 'em. A big trout here is a fish of maybe 13 inches, but now and then someone takes a lunker brook trout of two pounds or better. The cool, clear water helps to make them excellent table fare.

A down side here, according to the Department of Fish and Wildlife, is that some mental midget has dumped largemouth bass in the lake. Besides growing slowly and seldom getting big enough to provide much angling action, the bass are dining on the small brook trout.

21. CRAWFISH LAKE

Reference: **Northeast of Omak; map A4, grid d5.**

How to get there: Take State Route 155 east from Omak and turn north (left) on Lyman Lake Road. Continue another seven miles to Crawfish Lake Road and turn north (left). When you cross the Okanogan National Forest border, the road becomes Forest Road 100, and it leads right to the lake.

Facilities: Crawfish Lake Campground (U.S. Forest Service) has 22 tent and trailer sites and a boat ramp. Omak has food, gas, tackle, and lodging.

Contact: Okanogan National Forest, Tonasket Ranger District, (509) 486-2186; Cascade Toys and Sports, (509) 826-4148.

Species available: Rainbow and brook trout.

Fishing Crawfish Lake: Since both rainbows and brookies do well here, this 80-acre lake straddling the border between the Colville Indian Reservation and the Colville National Forest is stocked with both species on a regular basis. Pulling worms behind a string of gang trolls is an effective way to get the rainbows. Move into shallower shoreline areas and cast or troll a Super Duper and you'll be fishing for brookies the way most of the locals do.

As you might have guessed from its name, the lake is home to a fairly healthy crawfish population, at least it's becoming more healthy after a die-off a few years ago that nearly wiped them all out. If you want to try something a little different, drop a crawfish trap and catch a few of the little crustaceans while you fish. Boil the larger ones just like crab for the dinner table, peeling and eating only the tail section. Save a few of the smaller ones to use for trout bait. Don't boil them, but break them in half, peel the tail section, and use the little gray morsel of meat on a size six or eight worm hook. It's an excellent bait. What's more, the crawfish is one of the few critters you're still allowed to harvest without any kind of license or permit.

22. CONCONULLY LAKE

Reference: **Immediately east of the town of Conconully; map A4, grid c2.**

How to get there: From the south, drive north on U.S. 97 to Okanogan and turn north (right) on State Route 215 (Conconully Road), which continues north to the town of Conconully. You'll first past Conconully Reservoir. The lake is just northeast of the reservoir. From the north, drive south on U.S. 97 to Riverside and turn west (right) on Riverside Cutoff Road, which joins Conconully Road six miles west of U.S. 97. Turn right on Conconully Road and continue north to the town of Conconully and the lake.

Facilities: Conconully Lake Resort has RV and tent sites, rest rooms and showers, a boat ramp and moorage, boat rentals, and a small grocery store with fishing tackle. Nearby Conconully State Park has more than 80 tent sites, plus rest rooms and showers.

Contact: Conconully Lake Resort, (509) 826-0813; Conconully State Park, (509) 826-7408.

Species available: Rainbow trout, kokanee, some largemouth and small-mouth bass.

Fishing Conconully Lake: Like the reservoir immediately to the southwest (see below), this long, narrow lake provides excellent rainbow trout fishing from the time it opens in late April until about the middle of June. After slowing somewhat in the summer, it comes on strong with hefty strings of trout again in the fall. But during that partial lull in trout action, kokanee take up much of the slack.

Trolling with Wedding Rings, Triple Teazers, Double Whammys, Needle Fish, and other small spoons and spinners will take both trout and kokanee. Many anglers come to the Conconully area year after year because they know that even if the trout go on a hunger strike in the lake, they can drop down to the reservoir and pick up where they left off, and vise-versa. There's real security in knowing that you have two of Washington's top trout lakes within a few hundred feet of each other.

Although most anglers come here for trout, a growing population of both largemouth and smallmouth bass is starting to interest some anglers. The bass are mostly small, but will hit leadhead jigs adorned with three- or four-inch plastic grubs, small crankbaits, or spinnerbaits. Fish weedy cover for largemouths and rocky spots for smallmouths.

---

23. CONCONULLY RESERVOIR

Reference: **Immediately south of the town of Conconully; map A4, grid c2.**

How to get there: From the south, take U.S. 97 to Okanogan and turn north (right) on State Route 215, also called Conconully Road, which eventually runs along the east side of the reservoir. From the north, drive south on U.S. 97 to Riverside and turn west (right) on Riverside Cutoff Road, which joins Conconully Road about six miles west of U.S. 97. Turn right on Conconully Road and follow it to the reservoir.

Facilities: Liar's Cove Resort and Shady Pines Resort offer a wide range of facilities, including RV sites with hookups, rest rooms and showers, boat ramps, boat rentals, and tackle. Conconully State Park has more than 80 tent sites, plus rest rooms with showers, picnic areas, and a boat ramp.

Contact: Liar's Cove Resort, (509) 826-1288; Shady Pines Resort, (509) 826-2287; Conconully State Park, (509) 826-7408.

Species available: Rainbow trout, kokanee.

Fishing Conconully Reservoir: When you call a particular body of water one of the best trout fisheries in Okanogan County, you're saying quite a lot, but that description can be used here without fear of exaggeration. This impoundment on Salmon Creek has long been a great place to catch rainbow trout, and over the decades few anglers have been disappointed. Both stillfishing and trolling are effective, and along with the yearlings from spring plants of fingerling rainbows, you'll hook a surprising number of husky carryovers measuring 16 inches and over. All the usual baits and lures have been known to take Conconully trout, but the hot number may change from week to week or even day to day, so be sure to ask around when you arrive.

Besides rainbows, the reservoir also has decent kokanee populations, which come on strong about the time the trout fishery begins to slow a little in early summer.

24. SALMON CREEK

Reference: **Northwest of Okanogan; map A4, grid d2.**

How to get there: Take U.S. 97 to Okanogan and turn west on Salmon Creek Road, which follows the stream northwest for several miles. At the tiny town of Ruby, turn east (right) to Conconully Road and turn north (left) to the town of Conconully. Continue north out of town on Salmon Creek Road (Conconully Road turns into Salmon Creek Road) to fish the North Fork Salmon Creek or turn south along the west side of Conconully Reservoir to reach the West Fork Salmon Creek.

Facilities: Conconully State Park and the several private resorts in the Conconully area are good centers of operation for a Salmon Creek angling assault. The U.S. Forest Service's Cottonwood, Oreille, Kerr, and Salmon Meadows campgrounds also have tent sites for anglers who may want to camp along the North Fork Salmon Creek. Food, gas, tackle, and lodging all are available in and around Conconully.

Contact: Liar's Cove Resort, (509) 826-1288; Shady Pines Resort, (509) 826-2287; Conconully Lake Resort, (509) 826-7408; Conconully State Park, (509) 826-7408; Okanogan National Forest Headquarters, (509) 422-2704.

Species available: Rainbow, brook, and some brown trout.

Fishing Salmon Creek: This little stream that heads into the heart of Okanogan National Forest and eventually merges with the Okanogan River at the town of Okanogan is important to thousands of Washington anglers, many of whom don't even realize it. That's because the North Fork and West Fork of Salmon Creek provide most of the water for Conconully Reservoir, one of north-central Washington's most productive and popular trout waters. Fishing in the creek itself is overshadowed by the action available in the reservoir and nearby Conconully Lake, but the North Fork, West Fork, and main Salmon Creek below the reservoir are productive trout fisheries in their own right and certainly worth some of your time if you happen to be in this steep, pine-covered part of the Pacific Northwest.

The lower 15 miles of the creek, much of which runs through private property where it's a must to get permission to fish, holds some nice rainbows and a few trophy-class browns. Those brown trout, by the way, are just myths as far as I'm concerned, but a few local anglers insist they really exist. When and if you get permission from the local landowners to fish on the lower creek, it's okay to use your favorite baits, and nightcrawlers account for some of the big trout to come from this part of the creek.

On the North Fork and South Fork, selective regulations are in effect, so it's artificial lures and flies with single, barbless hooks only. These waters produce mostly pan-sized brookies and rainbows, and many of the brook trout don't make the eight-inch minimum size limit that's in effect here. Still, they're eager biters and lots of fun to catch and release. Both forks are popular with fly-casters, and productive fly patterns here include small gnats, ant imitations, and grasshopper imitations. Grasshopper patterns are also popular with fly-casters who work the lower end of the creek for browns and rainbows, since the long-legged insects become a staple of the trout diet throughout the summer.

25. COUGAR LAKE

Reference: **East of Winthrop; map A4, grid c0.**

How to get there: Take State Route 20 to Winthrop and drive north out of town on County Road 9137. Go 1.5 miles and turn east (right) on County Road 9137 (Bear Creek Road). You'll come to a "T" about four miles up this road, and you'll want to go left. From there it's about 1.5 miles to the lake, which is on the right side of the road.

Facilities: The lake has a rough boat ramp. All other amenities are available in Winthrop.

Contact: Okanogan National Forest, Winthrop Ranger District, (509) 996-2266; Pine-Near Trailer Park, (509) 996-2391; Methow Valley KOA Campground, (509) 996-2255; Chewuch Inn, (509) 996-3107.

Species available: Rainbow trout.

Fishing Cougar Lake: Like Campbell and Davis lakes to the south (see pages 117 and 227), Cougar Lake has had a "reverse" season for many years, opening to fishing in September and closing at the end of March. Fall fishing can be good for anglers who stillfish and troll, and decent catches are made off and on through the winter and spring as well. Spring plants of six- to seven-inch rainbows grow to worthwhile size during the summer and greet anglers as eager 10-inchers in the fall. Mixed in with those pan-sizers are fair numbers of carry-over trout measuring 14 to 18 inches. There's nothing fancy about the things folks use or the way they use 'em here, so bring along your favorite trout goodies and give it a try.

26. CAMPBELL LAKE

Reference: **East of Winthrop; map A4, grid d0.**

How to get there: Take State Route 20 to Winthrop and drive out of town southeast on County Road 1631 (Bear Creek Road) past the golf course. Turn east (right) on Lester Road and follow it about three winding miles to the lake.

Facilities: The lake has a rough boat launch and plenty of bank-fishing space. Other amenities are available in Winthrop and Twisp.

Contact: Methow Wildlife Area, (509) 996-2559; Pine-Near Trailer Park, (509) 996-2391; Methow Valley KOA Campground, (509) 996-2255; Chewuch Inn, (509) 996-3107.

Species available: Rainbow trout.

Fishing Campbell Lake: Fishing for rainbows can be fairly good at Campbell Lake for the first couple of months after the September 1 opener. Trolling with Pop Geer and worms is popular, but stillfishing with salmon eggs, cheese, corn, marshmallows, and Power Bait also accounts for good numbers of fish. Most of the trout run 10 to 11 inches, but there's a chance you'll find an occasional carryover to 18 inches. Wintertime fishing can be off and on, depending on whether and when the lake freezes over with a good coat of ice. Spring plants of about 4,000 hatchery rainbows each year help to keep the fishing worthwhile. The lake closes to fishing at the end of March.

27. LIME BELT LAKES

Reference: **Northeast of Omak; map A4, grid c3.**

How to get there: Take U.S. 97 to Okanogan and turn north on State Route 215 (Conconully Road). After passing the Riverside Cutoff Road, watch for Lime Belt Road and turn north (right). Lime Belt Road goes directly to Blue Lake and Sutton Lake, with side roads leading to other lakes in the area.

Facilities: Blue Lake has a fairly good boat ramp, but the other lakes offer little or nothing in the way of amenities. Food, gas, tackle, and lodging are available to the south in Omak and Okanogan.

Contact: Cascade Toys and Sports, (509) 826-4148.

Species available: Brook trout, maybe a few rainbow trout.

Fishing the Lime Belt Lakes: Of the dozen and a half lakes scattered around the hills between U.S. 97 and Conconully Lake, only one is stocked regularly with hatchery trout. That one is Blue Lake, the most readily accessible of the lot. But accessibility can be relative, and even the main road to Blue Lake can give you trouble early in the season or whenever a pouring rain hits the area to turn the road into a slimy mess. Assuming you can reach it, Blue Lake will provide fair spring and early summer action on brook trout of eight to 10 inches. They'll hit flies, hardware, or bait, but most of the locals fish for 'em with good ol' worms.

Some of the other lakes in the group are fishless, some have remnant populations of brookies or rainbows from plants in years go by, and a few have populations of various panfish courtesy of the midnight planting truck. High alkalinity is a problem in some of these lakes, and they may not ever provide much of a fishery unless the Department of Fish and Wildlife should decide to try stocking Lahontan cutthroats. If you want to try your luck anyway, the largest lakes in the group are Alkali (46 acres), Medicine (38 acres), Horseshoe (29 acres), Evans (27 acres), and Booher (25 acres). Castor, Price, Frye, Shellberg, and Sutton lakes might be a waste of time, but you can always investigate them if you feel like exploring.

All of these lakes are best fished in May or late September.

28. BROWN LAKE

Reference: **Northwest of Omak; map A4, grid d3.**

How to get there: Take State Route 20 or U.S. 97 to Okanogan and drive northwest from town on Salmon Creek Road. Turn right on Green Lake Road and drive about a mile past Green Lake to Brown Lake, on the left.

Facilities: There's nothing at the lake but some bank access for fishing or boat-launching. The nearest food, gas, tackle, and lodging are available in Omak.

Contact: Cascade Toys and Sports, (509) 826-4148.

Species available: Some bass and panfish, an occasional rainbow trout.

Fishing Brown Lake: Don't bother unless you have lots of spare time on your hands. This little lake doesn't offer much except a few small fish. Driving a half hour to Conconully (see page 271) would be a better use of your time.

29. GREEN LAKES

Reference: **Northwest of Omak; map A4, grid d3.**

How to get there: Take U.S. 97 or State Route 20 to Okanogan and drive northwest from town on Salmon Creek Road. Turn right on Green Lake Road and drive about 1.5 miles to the lake.

Facilities: A public access area with a boat ramp and toilets is located on the upper lake, and there are other spots where it's easy to get a boat in the water. Food, gas, lodging, and other amenities are available in nearby Okanogan and Omak.

Contact: Cascade Toys and Sports, (509) 826-4148.

Species available: Rainbow and brook trout, a few largemouth bass.

Fishing Green Lakes: If you show up on the shores of Upper or Lower Green Lake on a sunny May morning and wonder why you have both lakes all to yourself, stop in your tracks and consult the current fishing pamphlet. What you'll notice when you run down the alphabetical listing in the "Eastside Lakes" section is that these lakes aren't open during the regular spring-to-fall season, nor are they open to year-round fishing, as are more and more Washington lakes. Like a few other waters scattered around various parts of eastern Washington, Upper and Lower Green are open only during the winter, from December 1 through March 31. Don't feel stupid if you've made this mistake, because it's happened to others before you and will no doubt happen to others after you. It's even happened to someone who's very close to me, but I won't mention any names.

Anyway, winter fishing can be quite good here, especially on the 45-acre Upper Green. At nine or 10 inches, the rainbows aren't big, but they do well in the chilly Okanogan County winters and have a reputation for being among the hardest-fighting trout around. Occasionally you'll reel in a pan-sized brook trout along with your catch of rainbows. Wintertime trout don't have big appetites, so whatever you use, make it small. Tiny flies work well, as do the small Berkley Power Nuggets, single salmon eggs, and marshmallows.

30. DUCK LAKE

Reference: **North of Omak; map A4, grid d3.**

How to get there: Take U.S. 97 or State Route 155 to Omak and drive north from town on U.S. 97. About 2.5 miles north of town, turn west (left) on Cherokee Road, drive two miles to Airport Road, and turn north (right). Drive half a mile to Bide-A-Wee Road and turn left, then continue a mile to the lake, which is on the right.

Facilities: The lake has a rough boat ramp. Other amenities are available in Omak and Okanogan.

Contact: Cascade Toys and Sports, (509) 826-4148.

Species available: Largemouth and a few smallmouth bass, black crappies, bluegills.

Fishing Duck Lake: If there's such a thing as a favorite local warm-water fish lake around the Okanogan-Omak area, this is it. Anglers like to cast Rapalas and similar minnow-type lures for their bass, and they're sometime rewarded with fish to three pounds. Most of the bass, however, are on the small side. If you want to work at it and try a jig-n-pig, plastic worm in the weeds, or perhaps a spinnerbait, you might find enough worthwhile largemouths to make for a good day. If prospecting for bass doesn't pay off, try BeetleSpins for bluegills or small leadheads suspended beneath a bobber for crappies, both of which grow to respectable size here.

31. LEADER LAKE

Reference: **West of Okanogan; map A4, grid d2.**

How to get there: Drive east from Twisp or west from Okanogan on State Route 20. About nine miles west of Okanogan, turn north on Leader Lake Road and follow it about half a mile to the lake.

Facilities: There's a boat ramp and camping area at the west end of the lake and lots of good bank-fishing access around most of its shoreline. The nearest food, gas, lodging, and other amenities are in Okanogan and Omak.

Contact: Cascade Toys and Sports, (509) 826-4148.

Species available: Rainbow trout.

Fishing Leader Lake: Anglers who stillfish, troll, and fly-cast all do fairly well at Leader Lake during a normal year. But some years aren't "normal," or at least aren't conducive to good trout survival. This 160-acre lake is actually an impoundment built to help provide irrigation for local farms and ranches, and things get tight when the lake is drawn down too far during a dry summer. The effects are felt the next spring and summer, when poor trout survival and carryover result in lackluster fishing. Rainbows that do make it through the low-water period are fat 12- to 14-inchers the following spring. Stillfishing with Power Bait, salmon eggs, marshmallows, and combinations of the three is popular here. Most trollers go with the tried-and-true combination of a fat worm behind a string of trolling blades, especially for the first few weeks of the April-through-October season.

32. OMAK LAKE

Reference: **Southeast of Okanogan; map A4, grid e4.**

How to get there: Take U.S. 97 to Omak and turn east on State Route 155, then south (right) on Omak Lake Road through Antoine Pass to the lake.

Facilities: A boat ramp is located near the north end of the lake. Food, gas, lodging, and other amenities are available in Omak and Okanogan.

Contact: Cascade Toys and Sports, (509) 826-4148; Colville Confederated Tribes, Fish and Wildlife Department, (509) 634-8845.

Species available: Lahontan cutthroat trout.

Fishing Omak Lake: The Lahontan cutts were first stocked in Omak Lake in the mid-seventies, but it wasn't until the summer of 1993 that anglers really began to take notice of the cutthroat fishery here. That's when Omak Lake regular Dan Beardslee smashed the lake and state record for Lahontans with a whopping 18-pound trout. Beardslee used a Ross Swimmer Tail spoon to fool his record-breaker, and that's a good choice for anyone whose sights may be set on a monster cutthroat. Other large spoons and wobbling plugs—the kind of stuff commonly associated with saltwater salmon fishing—will also work. You can't use bait at Omak, only artificial flies and lures with barbless hooks. Although the lake is open to year-round fishing, some of the best catches of big fish come during the summer and early fall, when it's legal to keep trout following a catch-and-release-only period from March through June. This is a huge lake, covering well over 3,000 acres, and you could waste a lot of valuable time trolling and casting to areas that don't hold fish. A sensitive depthsounder that will mark fish is a valuable tool.

Most anglers coming to Omak Lake are already well aware of the fact that the lake is on the Colville Indian Reservation, where tribal regulations are in effect and where tribal angling permits are required. In case you didn't know, a three-day permit is available for $15, a seven-day permit for $20, and a season-long (calendar year) permit for $30. Kids under 16 years of age can fish without a license if they're with a licensed adult. Tribal permits are available in all towns on and around the Colville Reservation.

33. COOK AND LITTLE GOOSE LAKES

Reference: **Northeast of Brewster; map A4, grid e3.**

How to get there: Take U.S. 97 to Okanogan and then Wakefield-Cameron Lake Road east from town. Drive about nine miles to Cook Lake and another 1.5 miles to Little Goose Lake.

Facilities: It's possible to launch a small boat or canoe at both lakes. The nearest food, gas, lodging, and tackle are available in Okanogan and Omak.

Contact: Colville Confederated Tribes, Fish and Wildlife Department, (509) 634-8845; Cascade Toys and Sports, (509) 826-4148.

Species available: Rainbow and brook trout, crappies.

Fishing Cook and Little Goose Lakes: These two Colville Indian Reservation lakes don't really have too much in common, except that they're both under 15 acres and are located within about a mile and a half of each other on the same road. Cook Lake is known for its warm-water fishery, especially for crappies, while Little Goose Lake is a trout lake with good populations of rainbows and brookies.

If you want Cook Lake crappies, simply suspend a small, plastic-skirted jig from a bobber and fish around any cover you can find. If you can't locate cover, try working the bobber-and-jig rig in six to 10 feet of water wherever you feel like it until you locate a school of these cooperative panfish. For Little Goose rainbows and brookies, troll or cast any of your favorite trout goodies or fish a marshmallow-and-salmon-egg combination near bottom.

34. OKANOGAN RIVER

Reference: **Joins the Columbia River east of Brewster; map A4, grid e2.**

How to get there: Take U.S. 97 east or State Route 17 north to the confluence of the Okanogan and Columbia rivers, and continue north on U.S. 97 to follow the Okanogan upstream.

Facilities: Plenty of motels and RV parks can be found in the major towns along the river—Okanogan, Omak, Tonasket, and Oroville. Restaurants, grocery stores, gas stations, tackle shops, and other amenities also are available in all four. Osoyoos Lake State Park is in Oroville, at the upper end of the Okanogan.

Contact: Cascade Toys and Sports, (509) 826-4148; Darrell's Sporting Goods, (509) 476-2112; Osoyoos Lake State Park, (509) 476-3321.

Species available: Smallmouth bass, steelhead.

Fishing the Okanogan River: With the possible exception of the much-larger Snake River (see page 486), the Okanogan offers the best stream smallmouth fishing in Washington. (With all its dams, it's not very accurate to call the Snake a river, at least not in Washington.) Anyway, the Okanogan has been a favorite destination of smallmouth enthusiasts since the 1970s, and it's just as good now as it was then, perhaps better. Although not something you'll hook every day, the river has bronzebacks of five pounds and over, and while you're looking for them, you'll hook and release a number of smaller fish. What's more, U.S. 97 and side roads off it provide miles of good river access for bank anglers. The season is open year-round, but the best bass action occurs as the water begins to warm substantially, usually around the end of June, and holds up well into September. Leadhead-and-grub combinations, small crankbaits, size 1 or size 0 bucktail spinners, even wet flies and streamers will take them. If you don't have any smallmouth tackle, invest in a few one-eighth- to three-eighths-ounce leadheads and a dozen three-inch Berkley Power Grubs in the pumpkinseed color. If that doesn't take smallmouths, you're probably fishing where there aren't any fish.

Steelheading on the Okanogan has been an up-and-down proposition in recent years, but it's usually "up" enough to make the trip worthwhile. The lowest annual catch in recent years was the rather poor 175 fish taken in 1993–94, but during the two previous seasons, the Okanogan gave up more than 500 fish each year. If you have to pick just one month of the year to fish the river for steelhead, make it October. That single month typically produces half of the total catch for the entire year. September, November, and March may also provide some pretty good steelheading. Spoons, spinners, diving plugs, fresh roe clusters, ghost shrimp, and most of the popular steelhead bobbers all account for their share of fish.

---

35. RAT LAKE

Reference: North of Brewster; map A4, grid e1.

How to get there: Take U.S. 97 to Brewster and turn north on Paradise Mill Road. Take Rat Lake Road to the right about 3.5 miles north of town and continue another two miles to the lake.

Facilities: The south end of the lake has a boat ramp. Food, gas, lodging, RV sites, and other amenities are available in Brewster.

Contact: Columbia Cove RV Park, (509) 689-2994; Brewster Chamber of Commerce, (509) 689-2517.

Species available: Rainbow and (a few) brown trout.

Fishing Rat Lake: This lake with the unusual name has an unusual fishing season, opening December 1 and staying open through March. When the water is open—as in no ice—anglers like to troll over the big flat along the western shore. Interestingly, fly-casters also do well here. As you might guess, this cold-weather fishing calls for various wet patterns, and the Carey Special and the Stick are both popular at Rat Lake. Rainbows account for most of the catch, but the lake has a few trophy-sized browns.

As for the history of the lake's name, it has nothing at all to do with rodents, but with reptiles. This is serious rattlesnake country, and the "Rat" is short for "Rattler." Are we learning some neat stuff here or what?

36. BIG GOOSE LAKE

Reference: **South of Omak Lake, Colville Indian Reservation; map A4, grid e4.**

How to get there: Drive northwest from Nespelem on State Route 155. About nine miles from town, turn south (left) on Omak Lake Road. Drive 11 miles and turn south (left) at Kartar Creek (there are no road signs). Continue southwesterly about six miles to the lake.

Facilities: It's possible to launch a boat from the road along the east side of the lake, but there are no real facilities of any kind. The nearest food, gas, lodging, and other amenities are to the north in Okanogan and Omak, to the southwest in Brewster and Bridgeport, and to the southeast in the Coulee Dam area.

Contact: Colville Confederated Tribes, Fish and Wildlife Department, (509) 634-8845.

Species available: Largemouth bass.

Fishing Big Goose Lake: If you're looking for a place to catch lots of little bass and get plenty of hook-setting practice, Big Goose Lake could be the place for you. Some years—1995 was a good example—this large, shallow lake is over-populated with smallish largemouths. Would you believe a daily bag limit of 25 fish was in effect in 1995? But check the Colville tribal regulations pamphlet before killing two dozen small bass, since a hard winter can knock down the population considerably and prompt a change in the limits and fishing rules. A tribal fishing permit is required. They cost $15 for three days, $20 for seven days, and $30 for the calendar year. These permits are available in Nespelem, Inchelium, Republic, Colville, Kettle Falls, Elmer City, and Brewster.

37. METHOW RIVER

Reference: **Enters Columbia River at Pateros; map A4, grid f1.**

How to get there: Take State Route 20 east to Mazama and drive downstream along the river. Near Twisp, turn south on State Route 153 to stay near the Methow. From the south, take U.S. 97 to Pateros and turn north on State Route 153.

Facilities: Alta Lake State Park, near the mouth of the river west of Pateros, has tent and RV sites, rest roo ms, showers, and picnic areas. Food, gas, lodging, and other amenities are available in Pateros, Twisp, and Winthrop.

Contact: Methow Wildlife Area, (509) 996-2559; Pine-Near Trailer Park, (509) 996-2391; Methow Valley KOA Campground, (509) 996-2255; Chewuch Inn, (509) 996-3107; Alta Lake State Park, (509) 923-2473.

Species available: Summer steelhead, some rainbow trout.

Fishing the Methow River: You'll find some trout-fishing activity scattered along the Methow, particularly on the upper reaches around Twisp, Winthrop, and farther upstream, but the most serious angling effort is centered on the adult steelhead that travel hundreds of miles through the Columbia River system to return to this clear, cold mountain river. Hatchery-run steelies provide most of the action—in fact, all wild steelhead must be released—but it's amazing how many hatchery steelhead smolts must be stocked here in order to provide even a mediocre sport fishery. Would you believe plants of 400,000 smolts from the Wells Hatchery just to produce enough returning adults for a sport catch that's ranged from about 500 to 1,400 fish a year? Oh, the joy of trying to get salmon and steelhead through a river system that's clogged with hydroelectric dams and gill nets. Maybe the real wonder is that any steelhead return at all.

When they finally make it back to the Methow, they begin providing worthwhile catches in August, with September and October almost always the best fishing months. Although technically summer steelhead because of the time they enter the Columbia, they hang around all winter and are available to Methow anglers whenever conditions allow. During some mild winters, good catches are made straight through from September to March. Other years, when there's lots of ice and snow in the Methow Valley, the fishery all but dies in the winter, coming to life again for a few weeks when conditions improve in March.

Much of the Methow River steelhead catch comes from the slow water at the river's mouth, where boat anglers have the advantage. Some troll diving plugs or spinners along the bottom for their fish, but for many years the standard technique has been to troll or drift with the wind, trailing a leadhead jig that's suspended from a small float. Yes, that's right, it does sound a lot like crappie fishing, and some anglers still use the small, plastic crappie jigs that anglers used in the late-seventies when they discovered this somewhat unorthodox steelheading method. Farther upstream, where moving water allows for more traditional drift-fishing applications, the river is shared by hardware and fly anglers, and both catch their share of fish.

It's safe to say that the crystal-clear Methow is one of Washington's most popular steelhead streams among fly-casters. But if you're thinking about rolling a cluster of salmon eggs or a fresh ghost shrimp along the bottom, forget it; most of the river is under selective fishery regulations that prohibit bait and limit lures to those with a single, barbless hook.

---

38. ALTA LAKE

Reference: **Southwest of Pateros; map A4, grid f0.**

How to get there: Take U.S. 97 to Pateros and turn north on State Route 153. Drive two miles to Alta Lake Road, turn west (left), and drive two miles to the lake.

Facilities: Alta Lake State Park has 15 tent sites and more than 30 RV sites with full hookups, rest rooms with showers, picnic tables, and a boat ramp. Whistlin' Pines Resort has 75 tent and RV sites, rest rooms with showers, and a small store with groceries and fishing tackle.

Contact: Alta Lake State Park, (509) 923-2473; Whistlin' Pines Resort, (509) 923-2548.

Species available: Rainbow trout.

Fishing Alta Lake: The easy access off U.S. 97, full array of facilities, large size, and productive trout fishing make Alta one of Okanogan County's more popular lakes. Heavily stocked with hatchery rainbows, it provides good fishing into the early summer and again in the fall. One drawback is that Alta closes earlier than most lakes, with the season ending on the last day of September. Another problem is that shortly after the first warm weather hits, the water-skiers and personal water-craft terrorists show up, and they pretty much take over the lake from late morning to early evening. If you're a summertime angler, get up early or stay late to do your fishing.

Most of the trout are pan-sizers of eight to 13 inches, but Alta always produces a few husky carryovers in the spring, some of them ranging to a brawny 20 inches. Try trolling a Wedding Ring spinner behind a string of larger trolling blades and you'll probably be happy with the results. If there's such a thing as a local favorite for Alta Lake rainbows, that's it. If you don't have something matching that description, go with a Flatfish or Kwikfish in green or your favorite small spoon and see what happens. For many years, anglers who stillfished here favored a single red salmon egg or a marshmallow-and-egg combination, but Berkley's various Power Baits have become very popular among Alta Lake anglers the past few years.

---

39. COLUMBIA RIVER (LAKE PATEROS
AND RUFUS WOODS LAKE)

Reference: **From Pateros upstream to Grand Coulee Dam; map A4, grid f3.**

How to get there: Take State Route 155 north from Coulee City or State Route 174 north from Wilbur to Grand Coulee to fish the part of the river directly downstream from Grand Coulee Dam. To reach the other end of this section of the Columbia, drive east from Pateros on U.S. 97 and turn south on State Route 17 near Fort Okanogan. State Route 17 parallels several miles of the river's northern shoreline.

Facilities: Boat ramps are located near the town of Elmer City, which is downstream from Grand Coulee Dam, and at Bridgeport State Park, at the lower end of Rufus Woods Lake. Ramps at Bridgeport, Brewster, and Pateros provide access to Lake Pateros. Food, gas, RV parks, lodging, and other amenities are available in Pateros, Brewster, Bridgeport, Coulee Dam, and Grand Coulee. Bridgeport State Park, at the lower end of Rufus Woods Lake, offers about three dozen tent and RV sites.

Contact: George's Tackle, (509) 633-1163; Coulee Playland Resort, (509) 633-2671; Big Wally's, (509) 632-5504; Bridgeport State Park, (509) 686-7231; Columbia Cove RV Park, (509) 689-2994; Brewster Chamber of Commerce, (509) 689-2517.

Species available: Rainbow trout, steelhead, walleyes, smallmouth and large-mouth bass.

Fishing Lake Pateros and Rufus Woods Lake: Compared to most of the Columbia River system, the many miles of largely still water between Wells and Grand Coulee dams are rather lightly fished by Washington anglers. Road access to much of this stretch—especially Rufus Woods Lake—is limited, and boat ramps are relatively few and far between. It's accurate to say that much of this portion of the Columbia holds angling secrets that few anglers ever discover.

The upper reaches of Rufus Woods have some large, heavy rainbows, many of them escapees from Lake Roosevelt, and they can be caught by both anglers who troll and those who stillfish. Try rolling nightcrawlers along the bottom or slow-trolling with gang troll-and-worm combinations. Flatfish, Kwikfish, and Hot Shots in some of the larger sizes may also take these broad-shouldered rainbows, some of which will top three pounds.

As is the case throughout much of the Columbia, walleyes can be found here, too. The walleye fishery in Rufus Woods Lake and Lake Pateros continues to provide new surprises as to where and how the fish may be caught. Because of the vast area available to walleye anglers, those who cover the most water often make the best catches. Try trolling along rocky points with diving Rapalas or Power Dive Minnows or with the "standard" Columbia River walleye trolling rig, which includes a half-ounce to two-ounce sinker, a spinner, and a nightcrawler stretched out straight on a two-hook rig.

Diving plugs similar to those used for walleyes are also effective for steelhead on some of this stretch of river. Lake Pateros is a popular destination for fall steelhead anglers, many of whom troll driving plugs for their fish. The waters around the mouth of the Methow River are some of the most popular, but trolling for steelhead can also be good in other places, including off the mouth of the Okanogan River. September and October are usually the best months, but steelhead may be caught until ice becomes a problem in December or January.

---

40. FOSTER CREEK

Reference: **Flows into the Columbia near Bridgeport; map A4, grid g2.**

How to get there: Drive south from Bridgeport on State Route 17 and turn west (right) on Bridgeport Hill Road to reach the Middle Fork and West Fork of the creek. Continue south (the road signs say you're going south, but at this point you're really driving east) on State Route 17 to fish the East Fork.

Facilities: Food, gas, lodging, and other amenities are available in Bridgeport, and Bridgeport State Park, with both tent and RV sites, is eight miles to the north.

Contact: Bridgeport State Park, (509) 686-7231.

Species available: Rainbow and brook trout.

Fishing Foster Creek: You won't find great fishing and you aren't likely to find any trophy-sized trout, but this rather expansive stream system offers miles of worthwhile trout water where you can stretch your casting arm a little. Small spinners work well, or simply roll a salmon egg or garden worm along the bottom. Fly fishing with small nymph patterns can also be effective. Be on your toes for rattlesnakes.

41. BUFFALO LAKE

Reference: **Northeast of Coulee Dam, Colville Indian Reservation; map A4, grid f7.**

How to get there: Take State Route 155 north from Coulee Dam or south from Nespelem and turn east on Rebecca Lake Road. Drive about 3.5 miles, past Rebecca Lake, to Buffalo Lake Road and follow it two miles to the lake.

Facilities: The lake has a public access area with a boat ramp as well as a resort with tent and RV sites, showers, and other amenities. Food, gas, tackle, and lodging are available to the south in Grand Coulee and Coulee Dam.

Contact: Reynolds' Resort, (509) 633-1092; Colville Confederated Tribes, Fish and Wildlife Department, (509) 634-8845.

Species available: Rainbow and brook trout, kokanee, largemouth bass.

Fishing Buffalo Lake: This is a big, deep lake with a lot of fishing variety. Since more than half of the water in the 500-acre lake is more than 100 feet deep, it warms rather slowly and continues to provide decent fishing well into the summer. Stillfishing with Berkley Power Bait, salmon eggs, or worms accounts for most of the rainbows and brookies, some of which are large, thick-bodied fish. Most of the kokanee action comes to trollers, who use Wedding Rings, Double Whammys, Dick Nites, Triple Teazers, and other small spoons and spinners behind larger dodgers or flashers to attract fish. Tipping the hooks with Berkley Power Wigglers or maggots usually helps draw more kokanee strikes. The lake produces some fairly husky largemouth bass, most of them coming from the shallower north end of the lake. While all the usual bass offerings will work, many of the locals stick with a bass bait that's readily available in the lake—crawdads. And, if you want to enjoy some sweet eating yourself, take along a crawdad trap and catch a mess of them for yourself.

Besides the regular, summertime season, Buffalo is one of few lakes on the Colville Reservation that offers a winter season, and anglers catch some trophy-sized trout here from January to March. Stillfishing with the baits mentioned above is the way to go during the cold months.

Buffalo Lake is within the boundaries of the Colville Indian Reservation, where a tribal angling permit is required. The cost is $15 for a three-day permit, $20 for a seven-day permit, and $30 for a season permit that's valid from January 1 through December 31. A winter-fishing permit costing $5 is also required for fishing during the lake's special winter season, which runs from January 1 to March 15. The permits, as well as tribal angling regulations, are available from some resorts and businesses in Nespelem, Inchelium, Republic, Colville, Kettle Falls, Elmer City, Brewster, Omak, and other towns in and around the Colville Indian Reservation.

42. REBECCA LAKE

Reference: **Northeast of Coulee Dam, Colville Indian Reservation; map A4, grid f7.**

How to get there: Take State Route 155 north from Coulee Dam or south from Nespelem and turn east on Rebecca Lake Road, following it about 2.5 miles to the lake.

Facilities: Small boats can be launched along the north side of the lake, but there isn't much else in the way of facilities. Reynolds' Resort on nearby Buffalo Lake is your best bet for overnight accommodations and other needs. Motels, restaurants, gas, food, and tackle are available to the south in the Coulee Dam area.

Contact: Reynolds' Resort, (509) 633-1092; Colville Confederated Tribes, Fish and Wildlife Department, (509) 634-8845.

Species available: Largemouth bass.

Fishing Rebecca Lake: Small Rebecca Lake has a fairly healthy bass population and provides fair fishing even for bank anglers. But the best fishing is available to boat anglers who can get away from the road and work the southern and eastern shoreline. Arrive early or stay late and you'll find decent surface action on largemouths to two or three pounds. Now and then someone pulls a lunker out of here, but such catches are rare.

The lake is within the boundaries of the Colville Indian Reservation, so don't forget the fishing permits, available in towns throughout the area. The cost is $15 for a three-day permit, $20 for a seven-day permit, and $30 for a season permit that's valid from January 1 through December 31.

43. McGINNIS LAKE

Reference: **Northeast of Coulee Dam, Colville Indian Reservation; map A4, grid f7.**

How to get there: Take State Route 155 north from Coulee Dam or south from Nespelem and turn east on Rebecca Lake Road. About a mile past Rebecca Lake, turn south (right) on Buffalo Lake Road and drive about 2.5 miles to the sign pointing left to McGinnis Lake.

Facilities: The north side of the lake has a small boat ramp, and camping facilities are available to the north at Buffalo Lake. Motels, restaurants, and other services can be found in and around Coulee Dam.

Contact: Reynolds' Resort, (509) 633-1092; Colville Confederated Tribes, Fish and Wildlife Department, (509) 634-8845.

Species available: Brook trout.

Fishing McGinnis Lake: Good numbers of brook trout make McGinnis Lake a worthwhile possibility early and late in the season, when the water is cool enough for the brookies to be active. Try it from mid-April to about the first of June, or from the middle of September until the lake closes at the end of October. Casting small spinners and wobblers around the edge of the lake will produce pan-sized brookies, as will wet flies throughout the day and dry flies in the morning and evening. As in many Colville Reservation lakes, the daily trout limit here is six pounds plus one fish, not to exceed eight fish.

This is another lake where a Colville tribal fishing permit is required. They're available for three days, seven days, or the entire season, with prices of $15, $20, and $30, respectively, and can be purchased in resorts and businesses throughout the area.

44. LOWER LAKE ROOSEVELT

Reference: **From Grand Coulee Dam up to Lincoln; map A4, grid g7.**

How to get there: Take State Route 155 north from Coulee City, State Routes 174 or 21 north from Wilbur, or State Route 25 north from Davenport to reach major access areas on the lower lake.

Facilities: Campgrounds are located at Crescent Bay, Spring Canyon, Plum Point, Keller Ferry, Penix Canyon, Jones Bay, Halverson Canyon, and Hawk Creek, all of which are on the south side of the lake. Of these, Crescent Bay, Spring Canyon, Keller Ferry, Jones Bay, and Hawk Creek have boat ramps. Houseboat rentals are available in Keller Ferry (reservations required). On-the-water fuel docks can be found at Crescent Bay and Keller Ferry. A full range of services are available at Grand Coulee and Coulee Dam.

Contact: Coulee Dam National Recreation Area, (509) 633-0881; Keller Ferry Marina, (509) 647-5755; George's Tackle, (509) 633-1163.

Species available: Rainbow, cutthroat, and brook trout; kokanee; smallmouth bass and largemouth bass; walleye; lake whitefish; yellow perch; crappies; brown bullhead catfish.

Fishing Lower Lake Roosevelt: Except for the whitefish and perch, every species available in this huge Columbia River reservoir has stolen the angling limelight for some period of time during the past two decades. Throughout the late-seventies and early eighties, it was the walleye that drew most anglers to Roosevelt, and walleye fishing is still popular and productive here. Troll diving plugs or spinner-and-worm rigs along the bottom or cast leadheads adorned with plastic grubs around the many rock slides and rocky coves that border the lake.

When the walleye action tapered off somewhat in the mid- to late-eighties, many anglers started focusing their attention on the lake's rainbow trout, which grow to impressive size. Casting from the bank around the lower end of the lake or trolling various spoons, spinners, or wobbling plugs farther up the lake all were found to take trout, and those same techniques continue to be effective today. Don't be too surprised if your efforts pay off with a rainbow or two in the 18-inch, 2 1/2-pound range. I like fall for trout, but anglers catch them here year-round.

The late-eighties also saw smallmouth bass populations blossom in the lake, and by the early nineties, anglers were coming from all over the Northwest to fish Roosevelt for fat and sassy smallies ranging from a few ounces to several pounds. The rocky structure throughout the lower lake is near-perfect smallmouth habitat, and the fish continue to do very well. Try casting crawfish-finish crankbaits around rocky points or bounce leadheads with two- or three-inch plastic grubs or tube skirts down the face of submerged rock piles or cliffs. Berkley's three-inch Power Grub in pumpkinseed has produced my best smallmouth catches here, but such colors as came ouflage) and smoke also can be effective.

The last few years have seen interest in kokanee increase dramatically, thanks in great part to the fact that Roosevelt produced a couple of new state-record kokanee during the spring and summer of 1993. The year's second record-breaker—a fish of 5.47 pounds—still stands as the state's best-ever kokanee. Many kokanee of four pounds and over have been caught since, and some of the Lake Roosevelt regulars feel that it's only a matter of time before the record is topped again. Besides running large, these fish are strong and lively, sometimes stripping reels before an angler can react to save his or her tackle. Perhaps the best part is that it isn't always necessary to troll deep to find these lunker landlocked sockeyes. During the spring and summer of 1995, anglers were catching lots of them only a few feet beneath the surface without the need for downriggers or any other deep-trolling equipment. Small spoons and spinners, such as Luhr Jensen's Super Duper and Needlefish and Yakima Bait's Rooster Tail, are among the favorite kokanee-getters, and they're usually fished with white corn and/or maggots on the hooks.

With walleyes, rainbows, smallmouths, and kokanee available, it's easy to understand why lake whitefish are almost totally overlooked by Lake Roosevelt anglers. The fish provide good angling opportunities when they move into the shallows early in the spring, and some of them range to three or four pounds, but they hardly draw a second thought from anglers with other fish on their minds.

45. SAN POIL RIVER

Reference: **Flows into Lake Roosevelt near Keller; map A4, grid f8.**

How to get there: Drive north from Wilbur or south from Republic on State Route 21. The road parallels the river for well over 30 miles.

Facilities: Tent and RV sites are available at Keller Ferry, on the south side of Lake Roosevelt and a ferry ride away from the mouth of the river. Beyond that, the nearest amenities are in Republic to the north and Wilbur to the south.

Contact: Colville Confederated Tribes, Fish and Wildlife Department, (509) 634-8845.

Species available: Rainbow and brook trout, mountain whitefish, walleyes.

Fishing the San Poil River: Although a state highway runs right along its banks for easy access, this pretty little river provides surprisingly good trout catches. Pan-sized rainbows constitute most of the action on the lower portion of the river, with a few brookies mixed in along the upper part of the main river and the West Fork. But don't be too surprised if you turn up an occasional rainbow of two or three pounds. This food-rich stream with lots of good trout cover does produce more than its share of what most Northwesterners would consider trophy-class trout. The section of the San Poil from Nineteen Mile Bridge north to the reservation boundary is open to catch-and-release fishing only, with artificial lures and barbless hooks required.

Besides trout, the creek has a fair population of whitefish, but since it's closed in the winter, the fishery isn't what it might be. Walleyes have made their way up into the lower reaches of the river from Lake Roosevelt, and a nightcrawler rolled along the bottom of a deep pool might just turn up one of these hungry predators.

Most of the San Poil is within the boundaries of the Colville Indian Reservation, where a tribal angling permit is required. The cost is $15 for a three-day permit, $20 for a seven-day permit, and $30 for a season permit valid from January 1 through December 31. The permits, as well as tribal angling regulations, are available in Nespelem, Inchelium, Republic, Colville, Kettle Falls, Elmer City, Brewster, and other nearby towns.

46. BANKS LAKE

Reference: **Between Grand Coulee at the north and Coulee City at the south; map A4, grid g5.**

How to get there: Take State Route 17 or U.S. 2 to Coulee City and turn north on State Route 155 to parallel the east side of the lake all the way to Electric City.

Facilities: Anglers at the south end of the lake will find a boat ramp, camping, food, gas, and lodging in and around Coulee City. The best source for fishing tackle and information at this end of the lake is Big Wally's, which is right along the highway, just north of town. A guide service is also available there. Steamboat Rock State Park, at the north end of the lake, has tent and RV sites (reservations required), boat ramps and floats, rest rooms with showers, and a small store with ice, snacks, and groceries. A little farther north, in Electric City, are Coulee Playland and the Skydeck Motel, both right on the water. Groceries, restaurants, watering holes, gas stations, and motels are also available in Electric City. For tackle and angling information, check out George's Tackle, which is right along the highway. Between the north and south ends of the lake is a big Department of Fish and Wildlife access area and boat ramp, where self-contained RVs sometimes stay for a night or two. This is one of the few WDF&W access sites where overnight camping is permitted, but it's not particularly pretty.

Contact: Big Wally's, (509) 632-5504; George's Tackle, (509) 633-1163; Steamboat Rock State Park, (509) 633-1304; Coulee Playland Resort, (509) 633-2671; Skydeck Motel, (509) 633-0290.

Species available: Largemouth and smallmouth bass, walleyes, crappies, yellow perch, rainbow trout, lake whitefish, brown bullhead catfish, burbot.

Fishing Banks Lake: It's not always easy to find a place where both the anglers and non-anglers in a family can be totally content for a week-long vacation, but Banks Lake is one such place. The fishing variety and quality are enough to keep any angler busy and happy, while those who aren't so dedicated to the piscatorial pursuits can swim, water ski, hike, bike, golf, play tennis, or simply lounge around the beach reading a good book and working on that tan.

Walleye fishing isn't as good here as it was a few years ago, but it's still pretty decent. Most anglers troll spinner-and-nightcrawler rigs along the bottom for their fish, but when the walleyes are feeding along the broken rock and boulders so common along the lake's shoreline, pitching a small grub into the rocks and bouncing it across the bottom will also take fish. In spring and early summer, before most of the lake warms, the shallow flat on the east side of Steamboat Rock—known as the Devil's Punchbowl—is usually a good place to troll for walleyes.

"The Punchbowl" can also be a good bet for bass, especially largemouths that move into its shallow, weedy bays to spawn in late-spring. Farther north is Osborne Bay, another big, shallow flat that draws lots of bass, especially largemouths. Smallmouths, which were stocked in Banks by the then-Department of Game back in 1980, are found throughout much of the lake, from the rocky islands down by the lower dam at the south end of the lake to the broken rock that comprises the upper dam at the north end. Wherever you find rocks or gravel—which means about 98 percent of the Banks Lake shoreline—you may find smallmouths large enough and abundant enough to make you a very happy angler.

The trout grow large in Banks, but they get relatively little attention from anglers. Many are caught accidentally by bass and walleye anglers, but you can catch them on any of the usual trolling gadgets or by stillfishing worms, salmon eggs, Power Bait, or marshmallows. When you catch one, it's likely to be a dandy 15- to 18-incher, red-meated and in prime shape for the dinner table.

All the shallow bays and coves have panfish of some kind. Crappies are much sought-after but not as abundant as perch. Prowl around a little and you should be able to find a few of one or the other large enough for a fish-fry.

Night fishing in the shallows will produce brown bullheads, but hardly anyone bothers. Winter fishing for barbot is similarly overlooked.

47. GRIMES LAKE

Reference: **Southeast of Mansfield; map A4, grid h3.**

How to get there: Take State Route 172 to Mansfield and turn south out of town on Mansfield Road. Just over three miles from town, the road makes a 90-degree left. A mile farther along, it merges with Wittier Road and you make a 90-degree right. You'll reach the bottom of Moses Coulee three miles farther down the road, and the road turns left. From there it's a dirt road for 1.5 miles to the south end of the lake. That 1.5 miles is no place for the family station wagon.

Facilities: The nearest food, gas, tackle, and lodging are in Waterville and Mansfield.

Contact: Jameson Lake Resort, (509) 683-1141.

Species available: Lahontan cutthroat trout.

Fishing Grimes Lake: On a calm morning, chances are you can see the husky cutthroats cruising just beneath the surface, and it's enough to get any angler worked up. As you row or paddle through the narrow canal connecting the lower pool to the main body of the lake, the locals recommend you have a Woolly Bugger fly soaked and ready for that first cast. The water is only three or four feet deep and you'll see the trout tailing before you. If you're careful and if your cast is true, you could be in business right off the bat. If you don't hit fish right away, drift with the breeze and let your little offering of fur and feathers slip along a couple of feet off the bottom. Mend the line often to keep the slack out, and be on your toes for light strikes.

Grimes Lake has large Lahontan cutthroats, special regulations, and a very short season. It all starts June 1 and ends August 31, so you have to fish hard for only a few weeks during the heat of the Douglas County summer. Is it worth the trouble? You bet! Remember that selective fishery regulations here mean no gas-powered motors, single, barbless hooks, no bait, and a one-fish daily bag limit. There aren't even any pit toilets here, so you'll have to hide behind a patch of sagebrush when nature calls. Be careful, though, because the rattlesnakes also like to hide in that sage.

48. JAMESON LAKE

Reference: **Southeast of Mansfield; map A4, grid h3.**

How to get there: Take State Route 2 west from Waterville or east from Coulee City and turn north on Jameson Lake Road, following it a little over six miles to the lake. A road leading around the east side of the lake to the north isn't always passable, so a different route may be in order if you want to reach the north end of Jameson by road. Take State Route 172 to Mansfield and turn south (right) from town on Mansfield Road. Just over three miles from town, where Berg Road begins, turn left and follow Wittig Road toward the north end of Jameson Lake.

Facilities: Besides the public access area and boat ramp, there are resorts at both ends of the lake that have tent and RV sites, boat ramps, small stores with groceries and tackle, rest rooms, and other amenities.

Contact: Jack's Resort, (509) 683-1095; Jameson Lake Resort, (509) 683-1141.

Species available: Rainbow trout.

Fishing Jameson Lake: Perhaps eastern Washington's most famous and most popular trout lake, Jameson has been pumping out plump rainbows for as long as I can remember, and I've been around a while. The lake gets quite warm and has an expansive algae bloom during the middle of the summer, so it has a split season that's open during the spring and fall. Both the early and late segment of the season provide some excellent trout-fishing opportunities.

Although a majority of Jameson Lake's trout anglers are what you might call conventional trollers and stillfishers who use all the standard salmon eggs, worms, Power Bait, marshmallows, Triple Teazers, Flatfish, and Rooster Tails to catch their fish, this is an exceptional fly fishing lake. Favorite patterns include Carey Specials, Peacock Specials, Woolly Buggers, leech patterns, and a local favorite called a Jameson Shrimp. Whether you stillfish bait, troll hardware, or cast flies, expect the trout you catch to be thick-bodied, red-meated, and hard-fighting specimens, the kind of fish for which this 330-acre Douglas County jewel has long been famous. A typical spring rainbow here measures about 11 inches, but one-year carryovers will measure 16 to 18 inches and older fish may top 20 inches and weigh in at three pounds.

49. DRY FALLS LAKE

Reference: **Southwest of Coulee City; map A4, grid i4.**

How to get there: Take State Route 17 south from Dry Falls Junction or north from Soap Lake to the Sun Lakes State Park entrance and turn east into the park. About 1.2 miles off the highway, turn left at the sign pointing to Dry Falls Lake. Continue following signs to the lake for about three miles, passing Rainbow and Perch lakes on the left. The last mile to Dry Falls is over a rough dirt road, where pickups or four-wheel-drive vehicles are recommended.

Facilities: There is no boat ramp on the lake, but it's fairly easy to carry a car-topper, canoe, or float tube to the edge of the water. Nearby Sun Lakes State Park has 18 RV sites and 175 tent sites for campers, as well as rest rooms, showers, and picnic areas. Food and gas are available in Coulee City, and there's plenty of lodging available to the south in Soap Lake.

Contact: Sun Lakes State Park, (509) 632-5583.

Species available: Rainbow and brown trout.

Fishing Dry Falls Lake: This must have been an incredible place back when the flood waters and icebergs of Lake Missoula were crashing over the basalt cliffs and gouging out the bowl where Dry Falls Lake now lies. Had any of us been around, we likely could have heard the thundering falls from miles away, and we would have been awestruck by the amount of water coursing through the Grand Coulee. Actually, we're probably better off being around now, because the trout fishing at what we now call Dry Falls Lake is a whole lot better than what was available back when the ice-diverted Columbia River surged through this huge canyon.

Plenty of anglers think the fishing opportunities at Dry Falls are pretty awesome in their own right. This 99-acre lake at the head of the so-called Sun Lakes Chain is shallow and filled with aquatic vegetation, perfect conditions for huge populations of aquatic insects that provide rapid growth and high energy to the rainbows and browns that gorge on them. Fly-casters flock to Dry Falls throughout its April-to-October season, and they return with broad smiles and happy stories of trout topping 20 inches and weighing three, four, even five pounds. Fish of that size aren't the average Dry Falls trout, but they're common enough to keep it interesting. This isn't a fly-fishing-only lake, but it is a no-bait lake, where flies and lures must have only a single, barbless hook, and where the daily bag limit—should you choose to kill any trout at all—is one fish.

And, while you're casting, it's okay to let your mind wander back to what it must have been like when the lake was being formed, and to take a minute to thank Ma Nature for a job well-done.

50. DEEP LAKE

Reference: **Southwest of Coulee City; map A4, grid i4.**

How to get there: Take State Route 17 north from Soap Lake or south from Dry Falls Junction to the Sun Lakes State Park entrance and turn east into the park. After dropping down the hill into the bottom of the Grand Coulee, follow the signs eastward to Deep Lake. It gets pretty rough the last couple of miles.

Facilities: Although there is no boat ramp on the lake, you can get a car-topper or canoe to the water quite easily. Nearby Sun Lakes State Park has 18 RV sites and 175 tent sites for campers, as well as rest rooms, showers, and picnic areas. Food, tackle, and gas are available in Coulee City, and there's plenty of lodging available to the south in Soap Lake.

Contact: Sun Lakes State Park, (509) 632-5583; Big Wally's, (509) 632-5504.

Species available: Rainbow trout.

Fishing Deep Lake: At just over 100 acres, Deep is one of the largest but perhaps least-famous lakes in the Sun Lakes Chain. The reason for its low profile is its location farthest from the highway and the condition of the road that leads to its banks. Unlike some of the nearby waters that draw anglers from all over the state, Deep is fished mostly by locals. The lake is stocked with about 20,000 rainbow fingerlings every spring, and by the following season, they're running a chunky 10 to 12 inches. Casting from the bank or from a small boat with a bobber-and-worm combination or a slip-sinker rig baited with a marshmallow-and-salmon egg combo or Berkley Power Bait is an effective weapon here. Trollers go with the standard trolling blades-and-worm offering, small Flatfish and Kwikfish, Triple Teazers, Dick Nites, Rooster Tails, and Canadian Wonders.

Spring fishing is best on this lake with an April-to-October season.

51. PERCH LAKE

Reference: **Southwest of Coulee City; map A4, grid i4.**

How to get there: Take State Route 17 north from Soap Lake or south from Dry Falls Junction to the Sun Lakes State Park entrance and turn east into the park. After dropping down the hill into the bottom of the Grand Coulee, turn left at the sign pointing to Perch, Rainbow, and Dry Falls lakes. Perch is the second lake on the left.

Facilities: There is no boat ramp on the lake, but you can get a car-topper or canoe to the water quite easily. Nearby Sun Lakes State Park has 18 RV sites and 175 tent sites for campers, as well as rest rooms, showers, and picnic areas. Food, gas, and tackle are available in Coulee City, and there's plenty of lodging available to the south in Soap Lake.

Contact: Sun Lakes State Park, (509) 632-5583; Big Wally's, (509) 632-5504.

Species available: Rainbow trout (and you thought I was going to say "perch").

Fishing Perch Lake: This little lake often provides some of the hottest opening-day trout action in Grant County, but its annual plant of about 10,000 rainbows is usually removed within a few days, after which Perch Lake resembles a 16-acre biological desert. Fish it early in the season if you want trout, or fish it later in the spring if you want to simply get out on the water to enjoy the beauty of the Columbia Basin.

52. VIC MEYERS (RAINBOW) LAKE

Reference: **Southwest of Coulee City; map A4, grid i4.**

How to get there: Take State Route 17 north from Soap Lake or south from Dry Falls Junction to the Sun Lakes State Park entrance and turn east into the park. After dropping down the hill into the bottom of the Grand Coulee, turn left at the sign pointing to Perch, Rainbow, and Dry Falls lakes. Vic Meyers is the second lake on the left.

Facilities: There is no boat ramp on the lake, but you can get a car-topper or canoe to the water quite easily. Nearby Sun Lakes State Park has 18 RV sites and 175 tent sites for campers, as well as rest rooms, showers, and picnic areas. Food and gas are available in Coulee City, and there's plenty of lodging available to the south in Soap Lake.

Contact: Sun Lakes State Park, (509) 632-5583; Big Wally's, (509) 632-5504.

Species available: Rainbow trout.

Fishing Vic Meyers Lake: Since this lake is even smaller than Perch Lake, when the crowds flock here on opening day, they make even quicker work of the 5,000 or so yearling rainbows stocked as fingerlings the year before. If you're going to fish for Vic Meyers' 11-inch rainbows, arrive early on opening weekend (or even before to get a good spot near the water) and be prepared for some elbow-to-elbow "combat fishing."

53. PARK LAKE

Reference: **Southwest of Coulee City; map A4, grid i4.**

How to get there: Drive south from Dry Falls Junction or north from Soap Lake on State Route 17, which parallels the lake's southwestern shoreline. Turn east at the Sun Lakes State Park entrance to reach the resort, boat ramp, and state park at the northeast end of the lake.

Facilities: Sun Lakes State Park has a large number of tent sites and a few RV sites with hookups. Sun Lakes Park Resort has more than 100 RV sites, a store, rental boats, rest rooms with showers, a boat ramp, and other facilities.

Contact: Sun Lakes State Park, (509) 632-5583; Sun Lakes Park Resort, (509) 632-5291.

Species available: Rainbow trout, yellow perch.

Fishing Park Lake: Every time I think of Park Lake I remember the June morning many years ago when, as a boy of about 10, I set out in a rental boat with my dad at the oars to try for eastern Washington trout for the very first time. It was quite a lesson. About the only thing I ever trolled with back then was a string of Ford Fender trolling blades and a juicy garden worm, so that's what I was using. My dad decided to take a more sophisticated approach, tying some kind of artificial fly to the monofilament on his spinning outfit. Half an hour into the trip, Dad's rod lurched toward the boat's stern and he was into a good fish, one that put a terrific bend in his spinning rod and would have no doubt peeled several yards of line off the reel if the drag had been adjusted downward even the slightest bit from the "Power Winch" setting. When the tight line snubbed its efforts to swim, the fish launched itself skyward, and we got a good look at what was then the largest rainbow trout I had ever seen. The sight of the huge trout made Dad turn the reel handle even faster than before, and certain laws of physics began to seep into my young brain for the first time. Before I could utter anything about unstoppable forces and immovable objects, though, the monofilament snapped and the fun ended. Dad and I agreed that the 18-inch trout must have weighed at least six pounds, since it had broken his six-pound line, and he tied on another fly. Minutes later the entire episode was repeated, right up to and including the dull "ping" that rang through the still morning air as the line snapped. Without even considering backing his reel's drag off a little to the "Dredge" or "Pull Stumps" setting, Dad cussed his lousy line and tied on a third fly. Perhaps 15 minutes later it met the same fate as its two predecessors, and Dad was starting to think he had a starring role in "Rainbows from Hell, The Series." Luckily, the trout quit biting before my dad ran out of flies, and we eventually returned to the dock fishless. Although I hadn't hooked a single fish, I had learned a lot about fishing Park Lake, not the least of which was that its husky, hard-fighting rainbows demand respect.

Generous plants of hatchery fingerlings make Park and nearby Blue Lake (see below) a couple of the best trout lakes in the Columbia Basin. Crowds of anglers show up here days before the opener to get a good spot, and limit catches are as common among bank anglers crowding the edges of Highway 17 as they are among boaters who troll Flatfish, Triple Teazers, or Ford Fenders-and-worm rigs. The fishing holds up well into June, slows a little during the heat of summer, and picks up again in September. Although they aren't particularly welcomed by anglers and are in fact causing some problems for the trout population, the lake also has an abundant supply of perch, which can provide fast action for youngsters or anyone who wants to catch fish when the trout aren't biting. Like other lakes in this popular chain, Park closes to fishing at the end of September.

54. BLUE LAKE

Reference: **Southwest of Coulee City; map A4, grid i4.**

How to get there: Take State Route 17 north from Soap Lake or south from Dry Falls Junction. The road runs right along the west side of the lake, with side roads at the north and south end leading to resort facilities on the lake.

Facilities: Blue Lake has a large public access area with a boat ramp and toilets. Coulee Lodge, at the north end of the lake, has RV sites, a small store, rest rooms and showers, a boat ramp, a dock, boat rentals, and other accommodations. Similar facilities are available at both Blue Lake Resort and Laurent's Sun Village Resort, at the lake's south end. Sun Lakes State Park is nearby, with 175 tent sites and a few RV sites.

Contact: Coulee Lodge, (509) 632-5565; Blue Lake Resort, (509) 632-5364; Sun Village Resort, (509) 632-5664; Sun Lakes State Park, (509) 632-5583.

Species available: Rainbow trout.

Fishing Blue Lake: Like Park Lake to the immediate north (see page 293), Blue is a real trout factory, giving up limit catches of chunky rainbows from the opening bell until early summer, when the hot-rod traffic starts to make for tougher fishing. The speed-boaters all go home after Labor Day, and trout fishing comes on strong again until the season closes at the end of September.

Bank fishing is excellent along the west side of the lake, where State Route 17 provides hundreds of yards of access and a wide, gravel parking area. Berkley Power Bait has become one of the favorite enticements among bank anglers, and the hot colors during the 1995 season were chartreuse and pink. The usual worms, salmon eggs, marshmallows, cheese, and combinations of these are also effective.

Troll a dry fly along the surface early in the morning or in the evening if the wind isn't a problem. During the day, gang troll-and-worm combos account for good catches, as do Triple Teazers and Needle Fish in silver/red-head finishes or various shades of green. Green is also a good choice in Flatfish and Kwikfish, both of which are popular here.

55. ALKALI LAKE

Reference: **North of Soap Lake; map A4, grid i3.**

How to get there: Drive south from Dry Falls Junction or north from Soap Lake on State Route 17, which crosses the lower end of the lake. A gravel road to the east runs a short distance up the eastern shoreline.

Facilities: A boat ramp is located near the southeast corner of the lake. The nearest food, gas, and lodging are in Soap Lake, famous for its cabins and motels with "healing waters" mineral tubs. Resorts to the north, along with Sun Lakes State Park, offer tent and RV sites, showers, limited groceries, and tackle.

Contact: Blue Lake Resort, (509) 632-5364; Coulee Lodge, (509) 632-5565; Sun Lakes State Park, (509) 632-5583.

Species available: Walleyes, largemouth bass, crappies, bluegills, yellow perch, brown bullhead catfish.

Fishing Alkali Lake: With trout everywhere around it, Alkali may seem a little out of place in this part of the Columbia Basin, but anglers need warm-water fish, too, and this lake certainly provides variety along those lines. Until recently, about the only thing Alkali lacked for a "spinyray grand slam" was walleyes, and now it has them, too. The Department of Fish and Wildlife stocked about 1,400 baby walleyes in the lake in June of 1994, with more added in 1995, and with a little luck it shouldn't be long before anglers can enjoy year-round, all day and all night warm-water fishing action.

56. LAKE LENORE

Reference: **North of Soap Lake; map A4, grid i3.**

How to get there: Drive south from Dry Falls Junction or north from Soap Lake on State Route 17, which parallels the east side of the lake.

Facilities: There are several public access areas on the east side of the lake where launching a small car-topper or float tube is an easy chore. Resorts and the state park to the north provide RV and tent sites, showers, groceries, tackle, and other necessities. Food, gas, and lodging are available in Soap Lake, a few miles to the south.

Contact: Blue Lake Resort, (509) 632-5364; Coulee Lodge, (509) 632-5565; Sun Lakes State Park, (509) 632-5583.

Species available: Lahontan cutthroat trout.

Fishing Lake Lenore: This highly alkaline lake in the long chain of waters near the south end of the Grand Coulee was once thought to be a lost cause as far as angling opportunities were concerned, but then along came the Lahontan cutthroat, which is known to thrive in some of the alkaline lakes of Nevada and other western states. Lahontans introduced into Lenore in the late-seventies and early eighties not only survived, but thrived, and it wasn't long before anglers were catching two, three, even five-pounders and larger, creating one of central Washington's most successful trout fisheries. The stocking of Lahontan cutts continues today, and so does the productive trout fishing.

This isn't a place where anglers are encouraged to catch and kill a limit of fish. In fact, catch-and-release regulations apply during the early part of the season, from March 1 through the end of May. Beginning June 1 and through the end of the season in November, there's a one-fish daily bag limit. This is a selective fishery lake, where bait is prohibited and where single, barbless hooks are required on all lures and flies. Fishing is excellent in the spring and fall, but drops off to only "good" during the summer. Most people don't seem to mind.

---

57. BILLY CLAPP LAKE

Reference: **Northeast of Soap Lake; map A4, grid i5.**

How to get there: Take State Route 28 east from Soap Lake to Stratford and turn north on J Road NE. Turn right on the second gravel and dirt road to the south end of the lake.

Facilities: The southwest corner of the lake has a good gravel boat ramp. Food, gas, tackle, and lodging are available in Soap Lake.

Contact: Big Wally's, (509) 632-5504.

Species available: Walleyes, largemouth and smallmouth bass, rainbow trout, kokanee, crappies, yellow perch.

Fishing Billy Clapp Lake: The last time I called Big Wally's in Coulee City, I wound up talking to Jack Calhoun in the store's expansive tackle shop, and the conversation eventually turned to the subject of Billy Clapp Lake. After telling him that I hadn't heard many reports about the lake and assumed the fishing was slow, Calhoun said, only half-jokingly, "Well, us locals have a few good spots that we don't talk about very much." If you haven't heard much about the fishing variety available in Billy Clapp, maybe it's because you aren't one of the locals. All you really need to know is that the lake produces good numbers of walleyes, a mixed bag of largemouth and small-mouth bass, regular limits of rainbow trout, and some decent catches of kokanee to anglers who take a little time to learn its secrets. There were lots of sub-legal walleyes (under 18 inches) in the lake during the 1995 season, which should bode well for anglers these days, and enough net-pen rain-bows from the south end of Banks Lake make their way through the Bacon

Canal and into Billy Clapp to provide consistent trouting throughout much of the year.

Some anglers fish the lake specifically for bass, catching fair numbers of decent-sized largemouths and/or smallmouths, depending on where and how they fish. If you want faster action, a bobber-and-jig combination will take some large crappies, or tip the jig with half a worm to tip the balance more toward perch.

58. MIDDLE CRAB CREEK

Reference: **From Moses Lake upstream to Odessa; map A4, grid j5.**
How to get there: Take Interstate 90 to Moses Lake and turn north on State Route 17, following it three miles to J Road NE. Turn right on J Road NE and drive six miles to reach parts of the creek near Moses Lake. Areas a little farther upstream are accessible by taking State Route 28 to Soap Lake and turning east on Road 20 NE to Adrian and turning south toward the Willow Lakes. To reach areas farther upstream, take State Route 28 to Wilson Creek or Odessa and explore various side roads that cross and parallel the creek.
Facilities: Food, gas, tackle, and lodging are available in Moses Lake and Soap Lake, with limited services available in Wilson Creek and Odessa.
Contact: Big Wally's, (509) 632-5504.
Species available: Rainbow and brown trout.
Fishing Middle Crab Creek: A few years ago I stumbled across a tidbit of information that I found rather fascinating. According to whatever source it was, Washington's Crab Creek is the longest creek in the country, or in all of North America, or maybe it was the entire northern hemisphere. As you can tell, I don't recall the details, but the revelation did send me scrambling for a map, and I found that Crab Creek is certainly the longest creek in Washington. Beginning south of U.S. 2 near the town of Reardan and eventually finding its way into the Columbia a few miles south of Vantage, the creek's course is roughly equivalent to 40 percent of the distance across Washington at its widest point. That makes it a mighty long creek.

The section of Crab Creek upstream from Moses Lake is stocked with trout every year, providing decent fishing for pan-sized rainbows and browns through the summer. But in places where you can get away from the road some distance, you stand to catch some large carry-over fish, especially browns that have lived long enough to figure things out and not strike at just any old bait or lure that passes by within range. Browns of 16 or 18 inches are available from this part of the creek, but you have to be sneaky, stealthy, and sophisticated to catch them consistently (or even occasionally).

59. LAKE CREEK CHAIN

Reference: **North of Odessa, Lincoln County; map A4, grid j8.**
How to get there: Take State Route 28 or State Route 21 to Odessa and drive north on State Route 21. Lakeview Road, Trejabel Road, and several unmarked dirt and gravel roads about five miles north of Odessa, leading

east and west, provide access to the various lakes in the chain. Coffeepot Lake, at the north end of the chain, is accessible from the north by driving east off State Route 21 on Coffeepot Road about 20 miles south of Wilbur.

Facilities: Food, gas, lodging, and RV facilities are available in and around Odessa, but the lakes have nothing except limited bank access.

Contact: Odessa Chamber of Commerce, (509) 982-0049.

Species available: Largemouth bass, yellow perch, crappies, brown bullhead catfish, some rainbow trout.

Fishing the Lake Creek Chain: Coffeepot Lake, at the north end of the chain, is the biggest and best-known of the dozen lakes in this chain, but Deer, Browns, Tavares, Neves, Wederspahn, Pacific, Walter, Waukesha, Bob's, and the smaller lakes in this long chain offer similar angling opportunities. All of them contain a mixed bag, so take along gear for bass, panfish, and trout. The only one that's stocked regularly with rainbows is Deer Lake, also known as Deer Springs Lake.

Some of these lakes are on private property, where permission from the nearest landowner is required before you can gain access to fish. No two of the lakes are exactly alike, so you can spend a couple of days exploring and learning as you cast. All are open to year-round fishing, but April, May, and June offer the best angling opportunities.

Large lingcod like this will take a wide variety of offerings, from metal jigs and leadheads to herring and even smaller lingcod.

WASHINGTON MAP .... see page 5
Adjoining Maps
NORTH .... no map
EAST .... no map
SOUTH (map B5) .... see page 482
WEST (map A4) .... see page 256

60 Listings
PAGES 300-337

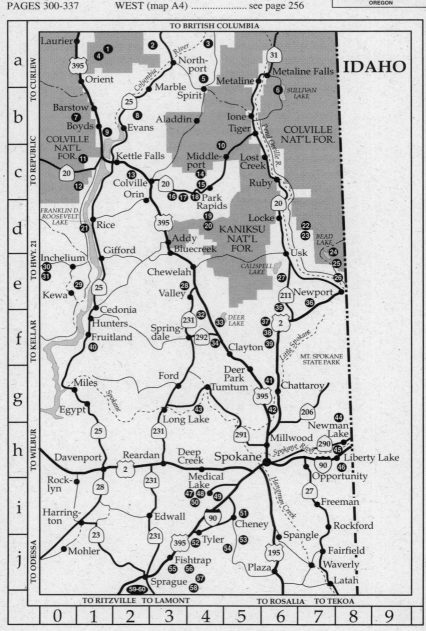

Map Section A5 features:

1. Summit Lake
2. Big Sheep Creek
3. Cedar Lake
4. Pierre Lake
5. Deep Lake
6. Sullivan Lake
7. Davis Lake
8. Williams Lake
9. Kettle River
10. Little Pend Oreille Chain of Lakes
11. Trout Lake
12. Ellen Lake
13. Colville River
14. Little Twin Lakes
15. Black Lake
16. Rocky Lake
17. Hatch Lake
18. Starvation Lake
19. McDowell Lake
20. Bayley Lake
21. Upper Lake Roosevelt
22. Browns Lake
23. Skookum Lakes
24. Bead Lake
25. Marshall Lake
26. Pend Oreille River
27. Davis Lake
28. Waitts Lake
29. Borgeau Lake
30. North Twin Lake
31. South Twin Lake
32. Jumpoff Joe Lake
33. Deer Lake
34. Loon Lake
35. Sacheen Lake
36. Diamond Lake
37. Horseshoe Lake
38. Fan Lake
39. Eloika Lake
40. Mudgett Lake
41. Bear Lake
42. Little Spokane River
43. Long Lake
44. Newman Lake
45. Spokane River
46. Liberty Lake
47. West Medical Lake
48. Medical Lake
49. Silver Lake
50. Clear Lake
51. Fish Lake
52. Hog Canyon Lake
53. Chapman Lake
54. Badger Lake
55. Fishtrap Lake
56. Amber Lake
57. Williams Lake
58. Downs Lake
59. Sprague Lake
60. Fourth of July Lake

1. SUMMIT LAKE

Reference: **Southeast of Laurier, Stevens County; map A5, grid a1.**

How to get there: Take U.S. 395 north from Kettle Falls and drive about four miles past Orient. Turn east (right) on Sand Creek Road, drive four more miles to Box Canyon Road, and turn north (left). Drive three miles to the lake, which is on the left.

Facilities: The lake has a boat ramp, and there's a U.S. Forest Service campground about five miles south at Pierre Lake. The nearest food, gas, tackle, and lodging are in Kettle Falls.

Contact: Colville National Forest, Kettle Falls Ranger District, (509) 738-6111.

Species available: Brook trout.

Fishing Summit Lake: Although covering only seven acres, Summit is stocked every year with hatchery brookies. They provide decent action through the summer for boat and bank anglers alike. Fishing pressure becomes virtually nonexistent after Labor Day, but fishing can be productive here in late September and October. Cast small spoons, spinners, or artificial flies around the edge of the lake. The season runs from late April through October.

2. BIG SHEEP CREEK

Reference: **Flows into the Columbia River near Northport; map A5, grid a3.**

How to get there: Take State Route 25 to Northport, cross the Columbia River, and turn west (left) on Sheep Creek Road, which parallels the creek for several miles.

Facilities: Food, gas, tackle, and lodging are available in Northport.

Contact: The Sport Spot, (509) 738-6711.

Species available: Rainbow, brook, and cutthroat trout.

Fishing Big Sheep Creek: The upper stretches of the river offer some beautiful pools that just beg you to stop and spend some time fishing for the pan-sized brookies and cutthroats in them. Farther downstream you're likely to find more rainbows than brook trout and cutts, and some of them will be respectable-sized fish. As summer progresses, the creek gets a little harder to fish because of the abundant foliage that chokes off access to some areas. That doesn't stop die-hard anglers, many of whom are fly-casters who use a variety of small, dark patterns to catch good numbers of trout here.

Fishing is best right after the season opens on June 1.

3. CEDAR LAKE

Reference: **Northwest of Northport, Stevens County; map A5, grid a4.**

How to get there: Take U.S. 395 to Colville and turn east on State Route 20. Just east of town, turn north (left) at the sign pointing toward Northport (Colville-Aladdin-Northport Road) and follow it to the small town of Spirit. Go east (right) on Deep Lake-Boundary Road and follow it north, past Deep Lake, to the east side of Cedar Lake.

Facilities: The lake has a public access area and boat ramp, but no other facilities. The nearest food, gas, tackle, and lodging are in Northport.

Contact: Wilderness West Resort, (509) 732-4263.

Species available: Rainbow trout.

Fishing Cedar Lake: Since this is another one of those northeast Washington lakes that you aren't likely to pass on your way to somewhere else, anglers who fish Cedar Lake are there to fish Cedar Lake. Not only is this a pretty lake in a pretty part of the state, but Cedar also produces some pretty nice rainbows. Fry plants grow to about a foot long by the following spring, but two-year carryovers of 17 to 19 inches are fairly common. Try trolling a green Carey Special fly very slowly during the day. Night-fishing is also popular here, and most anglers use Glo Hooks with Berkley Power Bait for their night-time trouting.

Spring and fall are the best times to fish, but the season runs from late April through early October.

4. PIERRE LAKE

Reference: **Northeast of Orient; map A5, grid a1.**

How to get there: Take U.S. 395 to Barstow and turn east onto Barstow-Pierre Lake Road, which soon turns north and leads about 10 miles to the west side of the lake.

Facilities: The west side of the lake has a U.S. Forest Service campground and a boat ramp. The nearest food, gas, tackle, and lodging are in Kettle Falls.

Contact: The Sport Spot, (509) 738-6710; Colville National Forest, Kettle Falls Ranger District, (509) 738-6111.

Species available: Rainbow, brook, and cutthroat trout; kokanee; crappies; large-mouth bass; brown bullhead catfish.

Fishing Pierre Lake: Stocked with fingerling rainbows, this 106-acre lake is also home to such a wide variety of fish species that it has something for virtually every angler. The lake used to produce some hefty cutthroats, but cutts over 12 inches or so are now rare. Casting or trolling for rainbows might also turn up an occasional brook trout. As the water warms in May, many anglers fish Pierre in the evening for trout and then stick around into the night to catch catfish (brown bullheads). They aren't big, but they are abundant, and it's possible to fill a five-gallon bucket with them on a good night. Some anglers use nightcrawlers, others prefer chicken livers, but the catfish don't seem to care one way or the other. While bass and crappies are available here, too, there are better places to fish for both.

5. DEEP LAKE

Reference: **Southeast of Northport, Stevens County; map A5, grid a4.**

How to get there: Take U.S. 395 to Colville and turn east on State Route 20. Just east of town, turn north (left) at the sign pointing toward Northport (Colville-Aladdin-Northport Road) and follow it to the small town of Spirit. Go east (right) on Deep Lake-Boundary Road and follow it for four miles to the east side of the lake.

Facilities: The east side of the lake has a private resort with boats, campsites, rest rooms, a small store, and other amenities. The lake also has a public access area with a boat ramp and toilets. The nearest food, gas, tackle, and lodging are in Northport.

Contact: Wilderness West Resort, (509) 732-4263.

Species available: Rainbow, brook and cutthroat trout.

Fishing Deep Lake: Since it covers nearly 200 acres but is only about 45 feet deep in its deepest spot, maybe it should be called Big Lake rather than Deep Lake. Who comes up with these names? Anyway, Deep is a steady trout producer and a popular spring and summer destination of anglers from all over northeastern Washington. It's a long drive from most places, but worth it.

The best angling advice from the folks at Wilderness West Resort is to "think green." A green Carey Special fly with a red tail is so popular here that it's referred to as a "Deep Lake Special." Troll it fairly deep, behind five or six colors of leaded line, and you'll probably do just fine. Flatfish and Kwikfish in various shades of green are also effective. As a general rule, fish around the north end of the lake—near the mouth of Cedar Creek—if you want brookies. Cutthroats, on the other hand, are more abundant at the lake's south end, especially in the fall, before they head up into the lower reaches of Deep Creek to spawn.

6. SULLIVAN LAKE

Reference: **Southeast of Metaline Falls, Pend Oreille County; map A5, grid b6.**

How to get there: Take State Route 20 to the small town of Tiger and turn north on State Route 31. Just south of Ione, turn east (right) on Sullivan Lake Road and follow it to the lake.

Facilities: There are boat ramps and U.S. Forest Service campgrounds at the north and south ends of the lake. Food, gas, tackle, motels, trailer parks, and bed and breakfast inns are available in Ione.

Contact: Colville National Forest, Newport Ranger District, (509) 447-3129; Ione Chamber of Commerce, (509) 442-3200.

Species available: Brown, rainbow, cutthroat, and brook trout; kokanee.

Fishing Sullivan Lake: Over three decades ago, an angler named R. L. Henry coaxed a whopping 22-pound brown trout from the deep, clear waters of this 1,300-acre lake near the northeastern corner of the state, and Sullivan has been somewhat of a mythical, mystical place ever since. Henry's trophy trout still stands as Washington's best-ever brown, and it's a record that may never be broken. It probably isn't very likely that you'll catch a 22-pounder, or even a 10-pounder, but the lake still does hold some trophy-class brown trout, and there's always a chance of hooking a real lunker. Besides big browns, the lake also offers the possibility of taking a bragging-sized cutthroat or even a rainbow over five pounds. The brook trout and kokanee don't grow nearly as large, and may in fact serve as menu items for the bigger trout as well as providing opportunities for anglers to catch pan-sizers for the table.

Standard trolling and stillfishing techniques work for the kokanee and smaller trout, but if you want a crack at a fish big enough for a trip to the taxidermist, try trolling large plugs and wobbling spoons that are large enough to impersonate the kokanee on which the bigger trout often feed.

7. DAVIS LAKE

Reference: **Southwest of Barstow, Ferry County; map A5, grid b1.**

How to get there: Take State Route 20 north from Kettle Falls and turn west (left) on Deadman Creek Road (County Road 460). Turn north (right) on County Road 465, east (left) on County Road 480, and north (right) on Forest Road 080 to the lake.

Facilities: The west side of the lake has a U.S. Forest Service campground and a boat ramp for small boats.

Contact: Colville National Forest, Kettle Falls Ranger District, (509) 738-6111.

Species available: Cutthroat trout.

Fishing Davis Lake: This 17-acre lake seems to have been custom-built for cutthroat trout. Hatchery cutthroats stocked by the Department of Fish and Wildlife flourish here, providing good fishing from late-spring until the dog days of summer. After the summertime lull, they come on strong again for the final few weeks of the season in October. Davis is a good place to troll small wobbling spoons, Flatfish, Kwikfish, or other small plugs, but anglers casting bobber-and-worm rigs also make some good catches of eight- to 12-inch cutts.

8. WILLIAMS LAKE

Reference: **Northeast of Evans, Stevens County; map A5, grid b2.**

How to get there: Take State Route 25 north from Kettle Falls and turn east (right) on Williams Lake Road, following it about four miles to the lake.

Facilities: The lake has a public access area with a boat ramp, but that's about it. The nearest food, gas, tackle, and lodging are in Colville and Kettle Falls.

Contact: The Sport Spot, (509) 738-6710.

Species available: Rainbow trout.

Fishing Williams Lake: Though this 38-acre lake east of Lake Roosevelt (see page 311) may look mighty inviting on a calm Saturday morning in mid-May, try to resist the temptation. Unlike most Washington lakes and reservoirs, Williams is closed to fishing in the spring. The season opens December 1 and runs through the end of March. But before you feel cheated, you should know that wintertime fishing here can be excellent. Depending on the winter conditions, you may get a chance to fish "open water" early in the season, but by the first of the year, you can usually plan on fishing through the ice. That ice cover may be nearly a foot thick some years, so don't forget your ice auger or a good ax for chopping holes. Your chances of catching a fat rainbow on top of the ice are about as close to zilch as you can get. Red salmon eggs account for a high percentage of the catch here, but if the bite is off and red eggs don't work, don't be afraid to experiment with Power Bait, marshmallows, yellow corn, or other baits.

9. KETTLE RIVER

Reference: **Enters north end of Lake Roosevelt north of Kettle Falls; map A5, grid b1.**

How to get there: Take U.S. 395 north from Kettle Falls to parallel the west side of the river all the way to the Canadian border.

Facilities: The highway provides a great deal of access to the river. Food, gas, tackle, and lodging are available in Kettle Falls, with limited facilities available in the several small towns along the river.

Contact: The Sport Spot, (509) 738-6710.

Species available: Rainbow trout, mountain whitefish, walleye.

Fishing the Kettle River: Once the scene of some pretty good spring and fall trout fishing, the Kettle now has some special regulations in place to give native rainbows added protection, especially at spawning time. While most of the river is open to year-round fishing, it's catch-and-release-only for trout from November through May. Selective fishery regulations are in effect above the Napoleon Bridge throughout the year. Those no-bait and barbless-hook regulations don't apply to anglers fishing specifically for whitefish during the winter. That's good, because the Kettle offers some of Washington's best whitefish action in February and March. If you fish the lower end of the river, where it flows into Lake Roosevelt, don't be too surprised if you catch a walleye or two for your efforts. Trolling a spinner-and-worm combination or a diving plug near bottom is most likely to take these sweet-eating members of the perch family.

10. LITTLE PEND OREILLE CHAIN OF LAKES

Reference: **Northeast of Colville; map A5, grid c5.**

How to get there: Drive west from Tiger or east from Colville on State Route 20, which runs right along the north or west shore of most of the Little Pend Oreille lakes.

Facilities: A private resort on Gillette Lake offers tent and RV sites, boat rentals, a boat ramp, fishing docks, and a grocery store. The public access area and boat ramp for several of the lakes is located on Gillette Lake. U.S. Forest Service campgrounds can also be found on Gillette, Thomas, and Leo lakes. The nearest food, gas, tackle, and lodging are in Ione and Colville.

Contact: Beaver Lodge, (509) 684-5657.

Species available: Cutthroat, brook, and rainbow trout.

Fishing the Little Pend Oreille Chain of Lakes: These beautiful little lakes in the pine forests along the Stevens-Pend Oreille county line would be worth visiting even if they were fishless. This is gorgeous country, far away from the hustle and bustle of the rest of the world, where lots of folks come just to get away. Luckily, the lakes of the upper Little Pend Oreille chain also offer some excellent trout fishing. Cutthroats of nine to 13 inches provide a bulk of the angling opportunity, but some of the lakes also have rainbows, some have brookies, and some have all three species. Heritage, Thomas, Gillette, and Sherry lakes are all connected by narrow channels, while Leo, Frater, and Nile lakes are nearby, just to the northeast. Coffin Lake, located about three miles south of Sherry, is the southernmost lake in the chain and also the smallest.

While the lakes are open to hardware and bait, fly-fishing is a worthwhile possibility on every lake in the chain. It's especially effective for cutthroat during the late spring and summer. If you aren't too good at casting a fly, try trolling a red or green Carey Special tipped with a grub, moving along fast enough to keep the fly just under the surface. Rooster Tails, Super Dupers, and Wedding Rings all are popular here. Anglers who stillfish prefer corn, salmon eggs, marshmallows, and Berkley Power Bait, not necessarily in that order.

These lakes all open in late April and close at the end of October.

11. TROUT LAKE

Reference: **West of Kettle Falls, Ferry County: map A5, grid c1.**

How to get there: Take State Route 20 east from Kettle Falls and turn north (right) on Trout Lake Road, which runs for five miles right to the south end of the lake.

Facilities: The south end of the lake has a U.S. Forest Service campground and a boat ramp. The nearest food, gas, tackle, and lodging are in Kettle Falls.

Contact: Colville National Forest, Kettle Falls Ranger District, (509) 738-6111; The Sport Spot, (509) 738-6710.

Species available: Rainbow trout.

Fishing Trout Lake: Spring plants of hatchery trout provide most of the action at Trout Lake, but a few rainbows carry-over through the winter to give anglers a crack at some 14- to 16-inchers. Casting spoons, spinners, and flies from the bank is effective, but trollers usually have better luck.

12. ELLEN LAKE

Reference: **North of Inchelium, Ferry County; map A5, grid c1.**

How to get there: Take State Route 20 east from Republic or west from Kettle Falls and turn south at Sherman Creek onto Kettle Falls Road. Drive four miles to Lake Ellen Road (County Road 412) and turn west (right). Follow Lake Ellen Road for four miles to the lake.

Facilities: The lake has a U.S. Forest Service campground with tent and trailer sites, drinking water, rest rooms, a boat ramp, and shore access. The nearest food, gas, tackle, and lodging are to the north in Kettle Falls.

Contact: The Sport Spot, (509) 738-6710; Colville National Forest, Kettle Falls Ranger District, (509) 738-6111.

Species available: Rainbow trout.

Fishing Ellen Lake: If you fished this 80-acre lake just north of the Colville Indian Reservation up to and including 1994, you may have caught large-mouth bass, but they've been eliminated and the lake (at least for now) is back to a trout-only fishery. Rainbows are stocked every year and provide fairly good fishing throughout the spring and early summer. During the early season, when the water is still cool, focus your attention on the southern half of the lake, where water depths range from five to 25 feet, but as the water temperature rises, work your way toward the "deep" end, where you'll find 30 to 40 feet of water in places. By mid-summer this lake gets pretty busy, so if you want to avoid the crowds, visit Ellen before Memorial Day or after Labor Day.

13. COLVILLE RIVER

Reference: **Flows into Lake Roosevelt south of Kettle Falls; map A5, grid c2.**

How to get there: Take U.S. 395 north from Chewelah or south from Kettle Falls to parallel most of the river. The upstream portions of the river are accessible via State Route 231, which turns west off U.S. 395 about five miles south of Chewelah.

Facilities: Food, gas, tackle, and lodging are available in Kettle Falls and Chewelah.

Contact: The Sport Spot, (509) 738-6710.

Species available: Rainbow and brown trout throughout the river; some walleyes, largemouth and smallmouth bass, and yellow perch in the lower river.

Fishing the Colville River: The Colville has long had a reputation for producing some hefty brown trout, and they're still here, though catching them isn't always easy. The trout seem to be getting wiser all the time, and to complicate matters a little more, much of this river runs through private property, limiting angler access. But if you're willing to work at your fishing and to cultivate a few property owners, you might be rewarded with a trout of five pounds or more. If you're fly-fishing, try a grasshopper pattern of some kind. Hardware anglers might try a spinner painted in a grasshopper finish, such as Luhr Jensen's grasshopper BangTail. If you're not a fly or hardware angler, try a real grasshopper.

14. LITTLE TWIN LAKES

Reference: **Northeast of Colville; map A5, grid c4.**

How to get there: Take U.S. 395 to Colville and turn east on State Route 20. About 11 miles out of town, turn north (left) on Black Lake-Squaw Creek Road. Turn right on Forest Road 150 after four miles and follow it for one mile to the lake.

Facilities: The lake has a U.S. Forest Service campground with tent and trailer sites, rest rooms, and drinking water, and it's possible to launch a small boat from the bank. The nearest food, gas, tackle, and lodging are in Colville.

Contact: Colville National Forest, Colville Ranger District, (509) 684-4557.

Species available: Cutthroat trout.

Fishing Little Twin Lakes: The Department of Fish and Wildlife stocks cutthroat fry here every spring after the late April opener, and by the following spring, these fish range from 10 to 14 inches long. Cast small spinners or bobber-and-worm combinations from the bank and you'll do okay, but troll a small Triple Teazer, Dick Nite, or Flatfish from a boat and you'll probably do even better. Like most other cutthroats, these will readily take an artificial fly, so work the shoreline with your favorite fly pattern during the morning and evening hours. Twin Lakes is a great destination for summertime family camping/fishing vacations. These "twins," by the way, are actually one lake with a rather narrow channel connecting the larger eastern and much smaller western portions.

15. BLACK LAKE

Reference: **East of Colville; map A5, grid c4.**

How to get there: Take U.S. 395 to Colville and turn east on State Route 20. About two miles east of Park Rapids, turn north (left) on Black Lake-Squaw Creek Road and follow it for two miles to the east side of the lake.

Facilities: There's a boat ramp on the lake, and a U.S. Forest Service campground with tent and trailer sites, water, and rest rooms a couple of miles away at Little Twin Lakes. Other amenities are available in Colville.

Contact: The Sport Spot, (509) 738-6710.

Species available: Rainbow and brook trout.

Fishing Black Lake: Rainbows and brookies are stocked here every year, and such variety is one reason anglers keep coming to Black Lake. But the sheer beauty of the place is every bit as good a reason to visit. This 70-acre lake in the high country east of Colville is one of the Northwest's prettiest, and the pan-sized trout you might catch are merely a bonus. Fishing sometimes gets off to a slow start in this cold, clear, sub-alpine lake, but by June things are usually hopping, and the good fishing holds up well into the summer.

16. ROCKY LAKE

Reference: **Southeast of Colville; map A5, grid c3.**

How to get there: Take U.S. 395 to Colville and go southeast on Graham Road for three miles to Rocky Lake Road, which leads to the lake.

Facilities: The south end of the lake has a Washington Department of Natural Resources campground with tent sites, picnic tables, rest rooms, an access area, and a boat ramp. Food, gas, tackle, and lodging are available in Colville.

Contact: The Sport Spot, (509) 738-6710.

Species available: Rainbow trout.

Fishing Rocky Lake: Stocked with hatchery fry every spring, this 20-acre lake gives up pan-sized rainbows at a pretty good clip through May and early June. Don't expect anything spectacular here, just decent trout fishing early in the season. After school gets out in June, you might have trouble finding a campsite. Rocky Lake regulars like to stillfish with Berkley Power Bait and red salmon eggs, but all the usual baits and hardware will take trout.

17. HATCH LAKE

Reference: **Southeast of Colville; map A5, grid c3.**

How to get there: Take U.S. 395 to Colville and turn east on State Route 20. About six miles from town, turn south (right) on Artman-Gibson Road, which leads about 1.5 miles to the lake.

Facilities: The north end of the lake has a public access area and boat ramp. Food, gas, tackle, and lodging are available in Colville.

Contact: The Sport Spot, (509) 738-6710.

Species available: Rainbow trout, yellow perch.

Fishing Hatch Lake: You'd better bundle up before hitting the water at Hatch Lake. Actually, you'll probably hit the ice rather than the water, since most of the trout caught here are taken through the winter ice cover. The season runs from the first of December through the end of March, and there's usually an ice lid on Hatch during much of that time. Since wintertime trout tend to have subdued appetites, anglers prefer small baits, such as a single salmon eggs, a kernel of corn, one or two maggots on a hook, or a couple of "golden grubs," the small larvae found inside the goldenrod stalk.

18. STARVATION LAKE

Reference: **Southeast of Colville; map A5, grid c4.**

How to get there: Take U.S. 395 to Colville and turn east on State Route 20. After eight miles, turn south (right) on Narcisse Creek Road, which is marked by a sign announcing the Little Pend Oreille Wildlife Area, and follow it two miles to Starvation Lake Road.

Facilities: The lake has a public access area and a boat ramp suitable for small boats. Colville has food, gas, tackle, and lodging.

Contact: The Sport Spot, (509) 738-6710.

Species available: Rainbow trout.

Fishing Starvation Lake: The name may not sound too promising, especially if you're hankering for a dinner of freshly caught trout fried over an open fire, but it's nowhere near as bad as it sounds. Yes, the trout population does sometimes take a pounding from low water levels and the winter ice cover, but the Department of Fish and Wildlife is usually standing by to plant more rainbows when that happens. During the years that Mother Nature is kind, trout fishing in this 30-acre lake can be excellent. That's how it was in 1995, when anglers had a very good year at Starvation.

Read the angling regulations pamphlet before fishing the lake, especially if you plan to visit after the end of May. Catch-and-keep rules change to catch-and-release at that time, so don't kill any trout unless you know it's okay to do so. The regulations after June 1 also call for no-bait and barbless hooks, so that's when many fly casters prefer to start fishing here. Starvation is considered by some to be one of eastern Washington's top fly-fishing lakes, and it's not unusual to see half a dozen float-tubers casting dry flies along the shoreline lily pads on a summer weekend.

19. McDOWELL LAKE

Reference: **East of Arden, Stevens County; map A5, grid d4.**

How to get there: Take U.S. 395 to Colville and turn east on State Route 20. After eight miles, turn south (right) on Narcisse Creek Road (marked by a Little Pend Oreille Wildlife Area sign) and follow it to the bridge crossing the Little Pend Oreille River. Just past the bridge, turn right and park at the gate. From there it's an easy quarter-mile hike to the lake.

Facilities: The lake has no facilities. Food, gas, tackle, and lodging are available in Colville.

Contact: The Sport Spot, (509) 738-6710.

Species available: Rainbow, brown, and brook trout.

Fishing McDowell Lake: Don't even think about bringing the worms and salmon eggs to this one, since McDowell has fly-fishing-only regulations. What's more, it's all catch-and-release, which makes it easier to understand why the trout fishing can be so good here at times, especially early in the season. Rainbows provide most of the action, but the lake has long had a fair population of brookies, and browns were introduced a few years ago. Since the lake is accessible only by a trail and has a no-motors regulation, it stays peaceful and quiet most of the time. The fact that there are no homes or any kind of development around the lake makes it even better. One word of warning: You'll have to share the lake with several Canada geese, numerous species of ducks, and other wildlife. Hope you can handle that.

20. BAYLEY LAKE

Reference: **North of Chewelah; map A5, grid d4.**

How to get there: Take U.S. 395 to Colville and turn east on State Route 20. Drive eight miles to Narcisse Creek Road (marked with a Little Pend Oreille Wildlife Area sign) and turn south (right). Follow the road for two miles to a "T" and turn left on Bear Creek Road for just over 4.5 miles to a dirt road leading right. Take that dirt road and drive another mile to the north end of the lake.

Facilities: The lake has a public access area and a boat ramp. The nearest food, lodging, and other amenities are in Colville.

Contact: The Sport Spot, (509) 738-6710.

Species available: Rainbow and brook trout.

Fishing Bayley Lake: Bayley is another of several lakes in the immediate area where any angling method is okay as long it's fly-fishing. No worms, no salmon eggs, no weighted spinners, and no wobbling spoons, period. Since the lake is small, covering only about 17 acres, the regulations no doubt help to get the most out of a trout population that would quickly be caught if standard rules were in effect. You can keep a couple of trout per day early in the season, but in early July the lake goes to catch-and-release regulations. No-motor rules and the size of the lake make this a great place to kick around in a float tube. If you arrive here for the first time and can't decide what to tie on the end of your leader, the locals suggest a green Woolly Bugger. That should get you by at least until some kind of hatch occurs. You're on your own from there.

21. UPPER LAKE ROOSEVELT

Reference: **From Kettle Falls south to the mouth of the Spokane River; map A5, grid d1.**

How to get there: Take State Route 25 north from Davenport for 20 miles to parallel much of the east side of the lake.

Facilities: Boat ramps and campgrounds with tents and trailer sites, rest rooms, and drinking water are located at Fort Spokane, Hunters, Gifford, and Kettle Falls. Davenport to the south and Kettle Falls at the north end of the lake are the best bets for groceries, restaurants, motels, gas, and other amenities.

Contact: The Sport Spot, (509) 738-6710.

Species available: Rainbow trout, kokanee, walleyes, smallmouth bass, yellow perch, crappies, lake whitefish.

Fishing the upper end of Lake Roosevelt: The waters of Lake Roosevelt around the entrance to the Spokane Arm were the birthplace of the Northwest walleye fishery. If you don't remember that, you're either a kid or a relative newcomer to this part of the world. The lake still has walleyes, but it's safe to say that the fishing isn't as good as it was, say, 15 years ago. Oh, there are still some husky walleyes to be caught from the upper end of the big lake, but they aren't all concentrated in one spot and just waiting around with their mouths open like they used to be. If you want to catch walleyes now, you may have to do some trolling with diving plugs or spinner-and-nightcrawler rigs to locate cooperative fish, then work them with a leadhead-and-grub combination or continue trolling the area.

Trolling for rainbows or kokanee might be more productive, especially during the spring and early summer months. Two- to five-pound rainbows can be found throughout the lake, including this more lightly fished northern half. The same goes for kokanee. The lower end of Roosevelt (see page 286) has earned a reputation in recent years for being one of the best big-kokanee producers in the Northwest, but the kokanee fishery up in this area is either lightly exploited or so good that the few locals taking advantage of it are keeping their mouths shut.

Smallmouth bass are also abundant throughout the big lake, but the smallies in the northern half don't get all that much attention from anglers. Working a three-inch Berkley Power Grub along the rocky shoreline and submerged gravel piles will coax them to life, as will a small crankbait of some kind, especially if it happens to be painted in the general color scheme of a crayfish.

The fishing season here runs year-round.

---

22. BROWNS LAKE

Reference: **Northeast of Usk, Pend Oreille County; map A5, grid d7.**
How to get there: Take State Route 20 along the Pend Oreille River to Kings Lake Road and the sign pointing east to Usk. Drive through town and stay on Kings Lake Road across the river and north past the Skookum Lakes. Turn left on Forest Road 5030 and follow it to the campground on the shores of Browns Lake.
Facilities: The south side of the lake has a U.S. Forest Service campground with tent and trailer sites, water, rest rooms, and a boat ramp. The nearest lodging and other amenities are back on State Route 20.
Contact: Colville National Forest, Newport Ranger District, (509) 447-3129.
Species available: Cutthroat trout.
Fishing Browns Lake: If you want to capture the true essence of what fly-fishing is really supposed to be all about, you owe it to yourself to visit Browns Lake. Located between two steep, timbered hillsides and with no development except the Forest Service campground on its south shore, this 88-acre lake is a haven for anglers who think that sport fishing should be peaceful, quiet, and relaxing. If you take your fly-fishing seriously, you might even be happy that you won't run into any bait-soakers or spinner-casters here, since the lake is open to fly-fishing only.

Cutthroats provide all the angling action at Browns, and most of them are pan-sized fish in the eight- to 12-inch class. But don't be too surprised if you stumble into a much bigger fish, say something in the 16- or 18-inch class.

The lake has its share of these husky carryovers, and they always provide a pleasant surprise when they decide to inhale one of those fur-and-feather offerings a fly caster throws their way.

Because the lake's shoreline is so steep, bank fishing is tough, so you really should consider using a boat or float tube to fish Browns Lake effectively (and safely).

23. SKOOKUM LAKES

Reference: **Northeast of Usk, Pend Oreille County; map A4, grid d7.**

How to get there: Take State Route 20 along the Pend Oreille River to Kings Lake Road and the sign pointing east to Usk. Drive through town and stay on Kings Lake Road across the river and north six miles to the Skookum Lakes.

Facilities: Both lakes have boat ramps and U.S. Forest Service campgrounds on or near their shores. Those campgrounds have tent and trailer sites, drinking water, picnic tables, and rest rooms. The nearest food, gas, tackle, and lodging are back on State Route 20.

Contact: Colville National Forest, Newport Ranger District, (509) 447-3129.

Species available: Rainbow trout.

Fishing the Skookum Lakes: Take your pick when it comes to fishing North Skookum and its twin to the south, where the trout fishing quality is about the same. Both lakes are open year-round and are stocked with hatchery rainbows that provide decent fishing in the spring, early summer, and again in the fall. Whether you like to troll, cast hardware, or simply sit and wait for a trout to come along and take a liking to whatever bait you might happen to be soaking, you'll probably do okay at either lake.

While you're fishing, be sure to take in the scenery. The pine-covered hills and clean, high-country (3,500 feet) air, make fishing a pleasure even when the trout aren't biting. The season here runs from late April through October.

24. BEAD LAKE

Reference: **East of Usk, Pend Oreille County; map A5, grid e7.**

How to get there: Take U.S. 2 to Newport and across the Pend Oreille River. Then take the first left onto LeClerc Creek Road and continue north up the east side of the river. A little over three miles from the bridge, go right on Bead Lake Road and follow it for six miles to the lake.

Facilities: The lake has a boat ramp at its north end, but there isn't much else in the way of facilities anywhere in the vicinity. The nearest food, gas, tackle, and lodging are on State Route 20 near Usk.

Contact: Marshall Lake Resort, (509) 447-4158; Washington Department of Fish and Wildlife, Spokane Regional Office, (509) 456-4082.

Species available: Burbot, lake trout (Mackinaw), kokanee.

Fishing Bead Lake: Long open to the public, the most often-used access to Bead Lake has been eliminated, and about the only way you can get at the water now is to trudge over the bank. The footing is steep and nasty, so think about it and plan your strategy carefully. If visiting the lake for the first time, ask around for tips and shortcuts.

Although open to year-round fishing, much of the angling action at Bead takes place during the winter when the lake freezes over and anglers converge here to fish for burbot. These long, skinny, freshwater bottomfish are abundant in the big (over 700 acres) lake, and they're easiest to catch during the winter months. Jigging with various metal jigs or heavy spoons accounts for most of the fish, and a majority of anglers tip their jigs with nightcrawlers, strips of sucker meat, smelt, or some other natural bait. Working the jig-and-bait combination just off the bottom is often the key to success.

Variety comes when a big lake trout decides it likes the looks of one of the baitfish-imitating jigs and decides to inhale it. A 10-pound lake trout (Mackinaw) may not be a common catch, but it's certainly within the realm of possibility. These big Mackinaws can also be caught in early spring, after the ice lid has melted away. Like lake trout everywhere in Washington, they're best fished with large plugs and spoons that imitate the smaller fish on which lake trout feed. Fish them near the surface soon after the ice melts, but as the water warms, you'll have to work deeper and deeper, using downriggers or leaded line to take your lure down where the fish are living.

Trolling is also the way most anglers fish for kokanee here, and they make fair catches through the late spring and summer.

25. MARSHALL LAKE

Reference: **North of Newport, Pend Oreille County; map A5, grid e8.**

How to get there: Take U.S. 2 to Newport and cross the Pend Oreille River on the east side of town. Take the first left onto LeClerc Creek Road after crossing the bridge and drive about three miles to Bead Lake Road. Turn right on Bead Lake Road, drive three miles, and turn right on Marshall Lake Road, which leads one mile to the lake.

Facilities: A public access area with a boat ramp and a private fishing resort with tackle, campsites, showers, and moorage are both at the south end of the lake. Food, gas, tackle, and lodging are available in Newport.

Contact: Marshall Lake Resort, (509) 447-4158.

Species available: Cutthroat trout.

Fishing Marshall Lake: This deep, clear, cold lake about eight miles north of Newport with an April-through-October season offers excellent cutthroat trout fishing, especially in the spring and fall. Although it has standard regulations that allow the use of bait and hardware, many anglers prefer to pursue Marshall's cutthroats with artificial flies. Dry fly-fishing can be very good here in the spring, but in fall, when the cutts are gorging in preparation for the long, cold Pend Oreille County winter, wet flies and nymph patterns get heavy play. Dragonfly nymphs, Renegades, Black Leeches, and Black Ant patterns are among the favorites. Some anglers use flies whose hooks are tipped with a meal worm, just for a little real protein to sweeten the pot.

26. PEND OREILLE RIVER

Reference: **Flows south from British Columbia, through Pend Oreille County and into Idaho at Newport; map A5, grid e8.**

How to get there: Take State Route 20 north from Newport and drive about 40 miles to the town of Tiger. From Tiger upstream, State Route 31 parallels several miles of the river.

Facilities: Boat ramps are located at several points along the river, including near Newport, Dalkena, Usk, Ruby, Blueside, Ione, and Metaline. Food, gas, tackle, and lodging are available in Newport, Usk, Metaline, Ione, and at other points along the highway.

Contact: Newport Chamber of Commerce, (509) 447-5812; Keo's Korner, (509) 445-1294; Ione Chamber of Commerce, (509) 442-3200; Circle Motel, (509) 446-4343; Z Canyon Motel, (509) 446-4935.

Species available: Rainbow and some brown trout, largemouth bass, crappies, yellow perch.

Fishing the Pend Oreille River: One of eastern Washington's largest rivers—more than 100 yards wide in spots—the Pend Oreille is in many ways an untapped angling resource. Although popular with many local anglers, it doesn't get the publicity and attention it deserves.

The river itself is big and wide, and when you add the many sloughs and side channels, it becomes a virtual potpourri of warm-water and cold-water fishing possibilities. Pen-raised rainbows are abundant, and if you're willing to put in the time and effort, you might be rewarded with a hefty brown trout. The bass fishing is some of eastern Washington's best, especially in the warmer sloughs where largemouths congregate to spawn in the late spring and early summer. These same sloughs offer large numbers of crappies, and there are places where a few hours casting a bobber and a worm will produce all the yellow perch you need for a neighborhood fish-fry. The Pend Oreille is best fished by boat, but don't get careless and forget that it's a moving, ever-changing river.

The season here runs year-round, but trout fishing is best in May and June. Bass and panfish action tops from July through August.

27. DAVIS LAKE

Reference: **South of Usk; map A5, grid e6.**

How to get there: Drive north from Spokane on U.S. 2 for about 25 miles and turn left (north) on State Route 211, following it about 10 miles to the lake, which is on the left.

Facilities: A public access area with a boat ramp is located on the lake. The nearest lodging and RV facilities are in Usk, to the north. Food, gas, lodging, and tackle are available in Newport.

Contact: The Inn at Usk, (509) 445-1526; Keo's Korner, (509) 445-1294.

Species available: Rainbow and brook trout, kokanee, largemouth bass.

Fishing Davis Lake: Though not very well known to most Washington anglers, this 150-acre lake is easily accessible and offers a wide variety of angling opportunities. The lake is a long drive away for western Washington anglers, and those living in the Spokane area have plenty of other productive trout and bass lakes from which to choose for their weekend activities. As a result, Davis usually offers plenty of elbow room, especially if you fish it during the week. Spring and fall provide the best fishing, but the season is open year-round.

Fish your favorite baits and lures during April and May for trout. For kokanee, pull trolling blades with Wedding Ring spinners behind or stillfish with maggots on Glo Hooks in July and August. Early morning and evening fishing for bass are also best in July and August.

---

28. WAITTS LAKE

Reference: **West of Valley, Stevens County; map A5, grid e3.**

How to get there: Take U.S. 395 north from Spokane, and after 23 miles turn west (left) at Loon Lake on State Route 292, following it seven miles to Springdale. Proceed north from Springdale on State Route 231 to the town of Valley and turn west (left) on Waitts Lake Road, following it about four miles to the lake.

Facilities: The lake has a public access area and public boat ramp, as well as two privately owned resorts that offer RV and tent sites, cabins, boat rentals, groceries, tackle, and other facilities. Gas is available on U.S. 395.

Contact: Silver Beach Resort, (509) 937-2811; Waitts Lake Resort, (509) 937-2400.

Species available: Rainbow and brown trout, largemouth bass, yellow perch.

Fishing Waitts Lake: If asked to name the lake that produced the state-record rainbow trout, most Evergreen State anglers would fail the quiz. The fact that I'm mentioning it here should be a really good clue. Bill Dittner caught a whopping 22 ½-pounder at Waitts Lake back in 1957, and it's a state record that in all likelihood will never be broken. Waitts, however, does continue to give up some big trout even to this day, although nothing approaching 22 pounds has been recorded lately.

The 450-acre lake is stocked with both rainbows and browns, and they put on weight and inches quickly. Carryovers are common, and many of them range to 17 inches and larger. If you don't have trophies on your mind, go with a string of trolling blades and a Wedding Ring spinner tipped with worms. But if you want a crack at a lunker, try trolling a Rapala or similar plug in a perch pattern, gold, or some shade of brown. The most popular trolling area is around the Winona Beach outlet. If stillfishing is your bag, stay well into the evening and soak green or pink Power Bait on a Glo Hook. Like to cast flies for your browns and 'bows? The locals recommend a green Muddler Minnow tied on a fairly large hook.

While Waitts is known to most as a trout lake, it also produces its share of husky largemouth bass, some of them topping five pounds. The docks and floats produce most of the big ones, and anglers like to coax them out from hiding with spinnerbaits, crankbaits, or various plastic worms.

The lake has an April-through-October season, but trout fishing is best in May. Largemouths hit best from May through July.

29. BORGEAU LAKE

Reference: **South of Inchelium, Ferry County; map A5, grid e0.**

How to get there: Take State Route 20 east from Republic or west from Kettle
Falls, turn south at Sherman Creek onto Inchelium-Kettle Falls Road, and
follow it 22 miles to Inchelium. From there turn right on Twin Lakes Road
and drive about two miles west, then turn south (left) on Silver Creek Road.
Drive another three miles and turn west (right) on Apex Road, following it
two miles to the lake, which is on the right.

Facilities: There isn't much at the lake, but limited facilities are available in
Inchelium. Food, gas and lodging are available in Kettle Falls.

Contact: Colville Confederated Tribes, Fish and Wildlife Department, (509)
634-8845.

Species available: Rainbow trout, largemouth bass.

Fishing Borgeau Lake: This little, 12-acre lake doesn't get nearly as much
angling attention as some of the bigger, more famous lakes on the Colville
Reservation, but it does offer decent trout and bass fishing. The season usually opens in mid-May and runs through October, with trout fishing best
through June and bass hitting from June through August. Tribal fishing permits are required and can be obtained from businesses in the area. The cost
is $15 for three days, $20 for seven days, and $30 for the calendar year.

30. NORTH TWIN LAKE

Reference: **West of Inchelium, Colville Indian Reservation; map A5,
grid e0.**

How to get there: Take State Route 20 east from Republic or west from Kettle
Falls, turn south at Sherman Creek onto Inchelium-Kettle Falls Road, and
follow it for about 22 miles to Inchelium. From there go west (right) on
Twin Lakes Road, following it a little over eight miles to the lake.

Facilities: A privately owned fishing resort on the north side of the lake offers
all the necessities.

Contact: Rainbow Beach Resort, (509) 722-5901.

Species available: Rainbow and brook trout, largemouth bass, some kokanee.

Fishing North Twin Lake: Sprawling over more than 700 acres, North Twin is
a big lake with some big trout. The thick-bodied rainbows grow to impressive size, and even some of the usually sleek brook trout are on the chunky
side. Trollers usually go with strings of trolling blades, followed by Wedding Ring spinners or any of the usual trout offerings in some shade of green.
Common wisdom around the lake also dictates using any lure "with a red
spot on it," so take along that bright red fingernail polish or fluorescent
paint and be ready to do some customizing if the rainbows and brookies
aren't showing enough interest in what you happen to be using. If you aren't
into painting your trout spoons and spinners, try stillfishing with such proven
trout-getters as Nightcrawlers and Berkley Power Bait.

   If bass fishing is your bag—or if you catch your eight-fish trout limit early
and are looking for something else to do—give North Twin largemouths a

try. Like other lakes on the Colville Indian Reservation, this one has a liberal, 25-bass daily limit, only two of which may be over 14 inches long. The idea is that there are lots of small, stunted bass in the lake, and the Colville fish managers would like to see them thinned out. The lily pads and weed beds along the north side of the lake provide some of the fastest bass fishing.

Colville fishing permits are required. They're available at the resort or from businesses throughout the area and cost $15 for three days, $20 for seven days, and $30 for the calendar year.

31. SOUTH TWIN LAKE

Reference: **Southwest of Inchelium, Colville Indian Reservation; map A5, grid e0.**

How to get there: Take State Route 20 east from Republic or west from Kettle Falls, turn south at Sherman Creek onto Inchelium-Kettle Falls Road, and follow it about 22 miles to Inchelium. From there go west on Twin Lakes Road and follow it about eight miles to the road turning south (right) to the lake.

Facilities: A private resort with campsites, showers, bait, tackle, boat rentals, and moorage is located near the north end of the lake. The nearest food, gas, tackle, and lodging are in Kettle Falls and Chewelah.

Contact: Log Cabin Resort, (509) 722-3543.

Species available: Rainbow and brook trout, largemouth bass.

Fishing South Twin Lake: At more than 900 acres, South Twin is one heck of a big lake, and you could spend the better part of a month really getting to know all of its secrets. Add North Twin Lake (see page 317) to the menu and you can plan on staying busy all summer. Both trolling and stillfishing produce good catches of husky rainbows and some larger-than-average brook trout. Bass fishing is also good, especially if you don't mind catching a lot of small fish for every lunker you manage to hook. The daily bass limit is a liberal 25 fish, established in hopes of encouraging anglers to harvest a lot of the smaller fish. Only two of those 25 fish you keep may be over 14 inches long. Tribal fishing permits—not state licenses—are required and are available from businesses throughout the area. The cost is $15 for three days, $20 for seven days, and $30 for the year.

32. JUMPOFF JOE LAKE

Reference: **Southeast of Valley, Stevens County; map A5, grid e4.**

How to get there: Take U.S. 395 north from Spokane for 32 miles to Beitey Road and turn east (left). Turn left again on Jumpoff Joe Road and follow it one mile to the east side of the lake.

Facilities: Jumpoff Joe Resort has tent and RV sites, cabins, boat rentals, moorage, and fishing docks. The lake also has a public access area and boat ramp. Food, gas, tackle, and lodging are available in Chewelah.

Contact: Jumpoff Joe Resort, (509) 937-2133.

Species available: Rainbow and brook trout, largemouth bass, yellow perch, bluegills.

Fishing Jumpoff Joe Lake: Rainbow and brook trout do well at Jumpoff Joe, and anglers, in turn, do well fishing for them. Both species carry-over well through the winter, giving anglers a chance to catch some large trout in the 14- to 17-inch range. Favorite stillfishing baits include white or yellow corn, Pautzke salmon eggs, nightcrawlers, marshmallows, and Berkley Power Bait. Trollers favor Rooster Tails in shades of green, brown, yellow, and orange, Dardevles, and Kastmasters of one-eighth to one-quarter-ounce size. Carey Specials and other fly patterns are also popular with some trollers. As for bass, they seem to prefer plastic worms fished around the docks, piers, and floats, especially if those worms are black or another dark color.

33. DEER LAKE

Reference: **Northeast of Loon Lake; map A5, grid f5.**

How to get there: Drive north from Spokane on U.S. 395 for 26 miles and turn east (right) on Deer Lake Loop Road. Follow it about two miles to the lake.

Facilities: The lake has a public access area with a boat ramp, as well as two private resorts.

Contact: Deer Lake Resort, (509) 233-2081; Sunrise Point Resort, (509) 233-2342.

Species available: Rainbow, brook, and lake trout; kokanee; smallmouth and largemouth bass; brown bullhead catfish; yellow perch; crappies.

Fishing Deer Lake: Whether trout and kokanee ring your chimes or bass and panfish are your idea of worthy opponents, you'll find worthwhile angling action at Deer Lake, where there's something to fish for from the opening bell in April until the season comes to a close at the end of October.

Lake trout, or Mackinaw, are a big draw when the season opens, especially if the spring has been cool and the water temperatures are down far enough to keep the big lakers near the surface. Trolling with big plugs and spoons, like those used for saltwater salmon, will do the job if the Big Macks are on the bite. If April weather is warm and the fish have gone deeper, you'll have to use leaded line or downriggers to take your plugs and spoons down to the action. Using your depthsounder to locate the fish is a big plus in giving you some idea at what depth you should be trolling.

Kokanee fishing has also been a big draw at Deer Lake for many years. The lake, in fact, gave up several record-class kokanee during the seventies, and it still offers the chance for a koke in the three-pound class or larger. Trolling Kokanee Killers, Triple Teazers, Wedding Rings, and all the other popular kokanee spoons and spinners works; just remember to lace those hooks with a kernel of shoepeg corn or a couple of maggots. Corn and maggots are also popular for stillfishing, which becomes the method of choice for summertime kokanee fishing. Many anglers concentrate their efforts during the night, when Glo Hooks (a brand of hook painted with luminescent paint) are an important part of the arsenal.

Brook trout can be found throughout much of the lake, especially around the edges where they're easy to get at with fly rods, spinning outfits, or trolling gear. You can even catch brookies from the bank at the resorts and public access area.

Rainbow trout are stocked in Deer every year, and they're caught on a variety of trolled and stillfished offerings. The Triple Teazers and Wedding Rings that work for kokanee will certainly take rainbows, as will Flatfish and Kwikfish in metallic finishes, Rooster Tail and BangTail spinners, or plain ol' gang troll-and-worm combinations. Salmon eggs, marshmallows, Berkley Power Bait, and yellow corn will also do the job.

Largemouth and smallmouth bass are fairly abundant, especially around the narrow arm at the north end of the lake and in the relatively shallow flats near the southeast corner.

34. LOON LAKE

Reference: **At the town of Loon Lake; map 5A, grid f4.**

How to get there: Drive north from Spokane on U.S. 395 for 25 miles until you see the lake on the left. Turn at the "Granite Point Park" sign along the highway or turn left on State Route 292 to get to the north and west sides of the lake.

Facilities: While the west side of the lake has a public access area and boat ramp, both sides of the lake have privately owned resorts with boat rentals, moorage, RV and tent sites, cabins, and groceries.

Contact: Granite Point Park, (509) 233-2100; Shore Acres Resort, (509) 233-2474.

Species available: Rainbow, brook, brown, and lake trout; kokanee; largemouth and smallmouth bass; yellow perch; crappies; brown bullhead catfish.

Fishing Loon Lake: Like Deer Lake a few miles away (see page 319), Loon has something to offer every angler. The biggest fish in the lake are Mackinaws, or lake trout, and they sometimes top 20 pounds. (Loon gave up the state-record Mackinaw about 30 years ago, a whopper that weighed in at more than 30 pounds.) Trolling large plugs accounts for most of them. Sutton spoons, blue Flatfish, and Kwikfish are popular, but other offerings in various shades of blue or pink are also effective. You can troll near the surface the first week or two of the season, but as the water warms, break out the downrigger and take that plug into the cool depths. If you're not a troller, use your depthsounder to locate fish, position your boat over them, and work a metal jig up and down until you coax them into striking.

Rainbows, browns, and brookies are all stocked with varying regularity, so you shouldn't have much trouble finding productive trout fishing throughout the spring. Troll the open water for rainbows and browns, the shallow shoreline areas for brookies. Rooster Tail spinners in brown or black shades seem to work best, or at least they're the favorite of local trout anglers.

Both trolling and stillfishing are top methods for taking Loon Lake kokanee, perhaps the most popular fish in the lake. As a general rule, trolling works better in the spring and early summer, with stillfishing gaining popularity about mid-summer. Some anglers fish at night and report better catches than many of the daytime anglers. Favorite trolling rigs include leaded line, Kokanee Killers, or Luhr Jensen Cherry Bombs and hooks tipped with maggots or white corn.

Largemouth bass are found along much of the lake's west side, while smallmouths are often found hanging close to the rocky shoreline near the southwest corner of the lake. Fishing the docks and floats around the lake may take either or both.

35. SACHEEN LAKE

Reference: **Near Highway 211, west of Newport; Map A5, grid e6.**

How to get there: Take U.S. 2 north from Spokane for about 25 miles and turn north (left) on State Route 211. The lake is on the left, about four miles off U.S. 2.

Facilities: The lake has a public access area and boat ramp. Diamond Lake Resort is a few miles away, to the southeast, off U.S. 2. Food, gas, tackle, and lodging are available in Newport.

Contact: Diamond Lake Resort, (509) 447-4474.

Species available: Rainbow and brook trout.

Fishing Sacheen Lake: This cool, clear lake provides very good fishing for both rainbow and brook trout throughout the spring and early summer, with the brookies coming on strong again in the fall. All the usual stillfishing and trolling techniques work, and fly-fishing is also popular on warm spring and summer evenings.

The lake is rather unusual in that it offers steep banks where the water drops right off from shore to 30 or 40 feet in many areas, the kind of shoreline many anglers—especially trollers—like to explore. Adding to the intrigue are the many bays and shallow reefs, especially around the south end of the lake. Perhaps the lake's most interesting feature, though, is the deep hole at its extreme south end, where the shoreline drops away quickly into an abyss more than 70 feet deep. It might be a good place to look for trout in July or August.

36. DIAMOND LAKE

Reference: **Southwest of Newport; map A5, grid f7.**

How to get there: Take U.S. 2 north from Spokane for 32 miles until you pass within casting distance of the lake's south side. Diamond Lake Road runs almost completely around the lake.

Facilities: The lake has a public access area and boat ramp as well as a privately owned resort with tackle, RV and tent sites, boat moorage, fuel, and some groceries. Food, gas, tackle, and lodging are available in Newport.

Contact: Diamond Lake Resort, (509) 447-4474.

Species available: Rainbow and cutthroat trout, largemouth and smallmouth bass, yellow perch, brown bullhead catfish.

Fishing Diamond Lake: Once primarily a trout lake offering lunker-class cutthroats and rainbows, the Department of Fish and Wildlife says that illegally stocked bass and panfish have added variety but had a negative impact on the trout fishery. The fishing is still pretty good for 10- to 14-inch rainbows, and an occasional trophy-class cutthroat may still be found. The rule of thumb for trout anglers is to "think deep, think green," especially as the water warms in the summer. A deep-trolled Carey Special fly in green or fluorescent green is a local favorite for rainbows and cuts. If you prefer stillfishing, go with a nightcrawler or green Berkley Power Bait, and fish it deeper and deeper as the season progresses. If you can locate one of the many underground springs that feed the lake, so much the better for summertime fishing.

37. HORSESHOE LAKE

Reference: **North of Eloika Lake, southwestern Pend Oreille County; map A5, grid f5.**

How to get there: Take U.S. 2 north from Spokane for 20 miles and turn west (left) on Eloika Lake Road, following it three miles to Division Road. Turn north (right) on Division Road, which becomes Horseshoe Lake Road somewhere along the line, and follow it 7.5 miles to the lake.

Facilities: The lake has a public access, boat ramp, and toilets, as well as resort facilities that include cabins, RV hookups, tent sites, boat rentals, fuel, and a small store with groceries and tackle.

Contact: Westbrook Resort, (509) 276-9221.

Species available: Rainbow and a few lake trout, kokanee, largemouth bass, yellow perch, crappies.

Fishing Horseshoe Lake: If you like a little bit of everything when you visit a lake, and pretty scenery to boot, this spot off the beaten path is worth a few days of your time. Planted rainbows draw much of the attention from anglers, but trolling for kokanee with Wedding Ring spinners tipped with maggots is also productive. Limited numbers of lake trout don't get a lot of publicity, but hooking a 10-pounder is a possibility. When the weather warms in summer, work the shoreline shallows for bass, crappies, and other warm-water fish. The lake has a year-round season, and it produces fish during all but the dead of winter.

38. FAN LAKE

Reference: **Northeast of Deer Park; map A5, grid f6.**

How to get there: Take U.S. 2 north from Spokane for 20 miles and turn east (left) on Eloika Lake Road. After about three miles, the road makes a 90-degree left, then a 90-degree right, and another 90-degree left. At that second left, bear right onto the gravel side road that leads about 1.5 miles to Fan Lake.

Facilities: The lake has a public access area and a boat ramp. The nearest food, gas, tackle, and lodging are in Deer Park.

Contact: Jerry's Landing, (509) 292-2337.

Species available: Rainbow and cutthroat trout.

Fishing Fan Lake: Liberal plants of hatchery trout make Fan Lake a good bet for anglers who want to get away from most of the crowds to do their trout fishing. Although not overlooked by local anglers, Fan certainly doesn't get the fishing pressure of the bigger and better-known trout lakes in the Stevens/Spokane/Pend Oreille County area. The ban on gas-powered boats may be part of the reason, or maybe it's the fact that Fan Lake closes to fishing at the end of September, about a month earlier than most other lakes in the area. Whatever the reason, you'll find less competition and decent trout fishing. I think it's just about perfect for evening fly-fishing, but feel free to take along your hardware or bait; it all works here.

39. ELOIKA LAKE

Reference: **Northeast of Deer Park; map A5, grid f6.**
How to get there: Take U.S. 2 north from Spokane for 22 miles and turn west (left) on Bridges Road or Oregon Road to reach the east side of the lake.
Facilities: There's a public access area and boat ramp near the southeast corner of the lake and a resort about half-way up the east side that offers tent and trailer sites, fuel, moorage, tackle, and some groceries. Food, gas, tackle, and lodging are also available to the south in Deer Park.
Contact: Jerry's Landing, (509) 292-2337.
Species available: Largemouth bass; yellow perch; crappies; brown bullhead catfish; brown, rainbow, and brook trout.
Fishing Eloika Lake: This has been one of my favorite lakes since I caught my first decent-sized Eloika bass back in the late 1970s, and I'm sure lots of other anglers feel the same way. Eloika is a bass and panfish angler's paradise, with very little shoreline development and lots of cattails, weed beds, and over-hanging brush to explore. The largemouths can run well in excess of five pounds, but it takes them a long time to get that big. That's part of the reason why most anglers release their bass here. The other reason is that they like to catch them over and over again. Among the effective bass-getting techniques are pitching plastic worms and plastic lizards into the shoreline cover and working spinnerbaits along the edges of the weeds and around the brush piles.

Both the perch and crappies are big enough to interest anglers, which you can't say about the panfish populations in all Washington lakes. Suspending a small leadhead with a plastic skirt or tube body will take the crappies, and you can add a piece of worm to the same rig and draw lots of interest from the perch. Stick around until darkness sets in and pitch a nightcrawler or chicken liver around until you find a few cooperative catfish.

This is one of the few eastern Washington lakes where trout fishing takes a back seat to warm-water species. Some respectable brookies and planted brown trout are available; the best fishing for them is in the spring and fall.

Oh yes, Eloika is open year-round, so you can fish it whenever you feel the urge. But most people don't feel the urge too much during cold Spokane County winters.

40. MUDGETT LAKE

Reference: **South of Fruitland, Stevens County; map A5, grid f1.**
How to get there: Drive north from Davenport on State Route 25, across the Spokane River Arm of Lake Roosevelt for about 20 miles. Turn east (right) on the Old Highway 22 Cutoff Road, drive a mile, and turn north on Old Highway 22. Drive 2.5 miles to the lake, which is on the left.

Facilities: The lake has a public access area where it's possible to launch a small boat. The nearest food, gas, tackle, and lodging are to the south in Davenport and to the north in Kettle Falls.

Contact: The Sport Spot, (509) 738-6711.

Species available: Rainbow trout.

Fishing Mudgett Lake: The lake is stocked quite generously with hatchery rainbows, and they provide good fishing for a few weeks after the late-April opener. From then on things get pretty tough, although thanks to easy access and light traffic, this is a pleasant place to take the kids for an afternoon of laid-back fishing any time during the season. That season, by the way, runs through October.

41. BEAR LAKE

Reference: **North of Chattaroy, Spokane County; map A5, grid g6.**

How to get there: Drive north from Spokane on U.S. 2. The lake is 2.8 miles north of Chattaroy, on the west (left) side of the highway.

Facilities: There's bank access and a fishing dock near the north end of the lake, and it's easy to carry a small boat to the water for launching.

Contact: Big 5 Sporting Goods, (509) 533-9811.

Species available: Rainbow trout, largemouth bass, yellow perch, crappies.

Fishing Bear Lake: This little, 34-acre lake is so handy that everyone passing by on the highway should stop in and make a few casts. If you want trout, try casting a one-eighth-ounce Panther Martin spinner in black or brown or a Rooster Tail in silver or red, a couple of the favorites here. If you're into fly-fishing, break out the long rod and tie on a mosquito or leech pattern and work it around the shoreline. Although anglers don't seem to catch many big bass at Bear Lake, there are enough smaller largemouths to make spending a few hours pitching plastic worms or spinnerbaits around the shoreline cover worthwhile. And, if it's panfish you want, suspend a worm about four feet beneath a bobber and cast for perch. A few crappies call the lake home, too; replace that worm with a red-and-white Mini Jig below the bobber to catch them.

42. LITTLE SPOKANE RIVER

Reference: **Joins the Spokane River at Nine Mile Falls; map A5, grid g6.**

How to get there: To reach the lower portion of the river, take U.S. 395 north from Spokane about three miles and turn west (left) on Hawthorne Road, following it two miles and turning south (left) to Waikiki Road, which crosses and parallels parts of the river. To reach areas farther upstream, drive north from Spokane on U.S. 2, turning west (left) on various county roads to reach the river downstream from Chattaroy. Roads to the east reach the river above Chattaroy, where the highway crosses over the river. Bridges, Oregon, and Scotia roads are among the possibilities on this upper stretch of the Little Spokane.

Facilities: Riverside State Park, located near the mouth of the Little Spokane, has a limited number of tent and RV sites. Resorts on Eloika and Diamond lakes are good possibilities for the upper reaches of the river. In-between are lots of motels in and around Spokane, as well as restaurants and other amenities.

Contact: Riverside State Park, (509) 456-3964; Big 5 Sporting Goods, (509) 533-9811.

Species available: Rainbow, brook, and brown trout; mountain whitefish.

Fishing the Little Spokane River: Although it doesn't receive large plants of hatchery trout, the Little Spokane does offer the possibility of decent catches, and some of the trout are surprisingly large. Try your hand with a fly rod and you'll have a good time even if you don't catch any fish. But plenty of 10- to 12-inch rainbows and eager seven to 10-inch brookies are available to practically guarantee you'll find something in a biting mood. And, just to keep you on your toes, the Little Spokane does have a few 20- to 24-inch trout, making for the possibility of a fantastic day if one of them comes to life on your visit. Trout season here runs from late April through October.

If you get the fishing bug during the dead of winter, the Little Spokane has a winter whitefish season that provides some good fishing opportunity from December 1 through March 31.

A lot of private property borders this pretty little stream, and many of the landowners are unwilling to allow angling access, so you won't be able to fish wherever you want along the Little Spokane. Ask permission and don't foul it up for the rest of us by trespassing.

---

43. LONG LAKE

Reference: Spokane River impoundment, west of Spokane; map A5, grid g3.

How to get there: Take Interstate 90 to Sprague and turn north on State Route 231, following it for 26 miles to U.S. 2. Turn east on U.S. 2 and drive about three miles to Reardan, then continue north on State Route 231 for 12 miles, all the way to the Spokane River below Long Lake Dam. Cross the river and immediately turn east (right) on Corkscrew Canyon Road. Drive five miles and turn right on the gravel road that drops down the hill and leads to the boat ramp.

Facilities: The lake has a public access area with a boat ramp and a resort, both of them on the north side, off State Route 291. The resort has moorage, tackle, RV sites, and showers. Riverside State Park is also within fairly easy driving range of about 18 miles. Food, gas, tackle, and lodging are available in Davenport.

Contact: Willow Bay Resort, (509) 276-2350; Riverside State Park, (509) 456-3964.

Species available: Largemouth and smallmouth bass, crappies, rainbow and brown trout, walleyes, northern pike.

Fishing Long Lake: Some people come to Long Lake to troll gang troll-and-worm rigs or spoons and spinners for trout, while others come to work spinnerbaits, plastic worms, crankbaits, and other offerings along the shoreline for bass, and both groups consider this lower Spokane River impoundment a pretty good fishery. Now and then an angler hooks some-thing unusual, such as a big, nasty northern pike, though that's probably not something you'd come here specifically to do. But then again, if you're the patient type who doesn't mind casting all weekend for the possibility of a single strike, you might want to gear up and try your luck on northerns. Long Lake is a big impoundment with miles and miles of shoreline, so at least you'll get to see a lot of scenery as you work your way along the shore in search of that toothy trophy. The best time to fish Long Lake is during the spring and early summer, from about April through June.

44. NEWMAN LAKE

Reference: **Northeast of Spokane, near the Idaho border; map A5, grid h8.**
How to get there: Drive east from Spokane on State Route 290 for about 12 miles and turn north (left) on Newman Lake Road.
Facilities: The lake has a public access area and boat ramp as well as private resort facilities with all the amenities.
Contact: Cherokee Landing Resort, (509) 226-3843; Sutton Bay Resort, (509) 226-3660; Big 5 Sporting Goods, (509) 533-9811.
Species available: Rainbow and brown trout, largemouth bass, tiger muskies, crappie, yellow perch, bluegills, yellow bullhead catfish.
Fishing Newman Lake: Talk about 1,200 acres of fishing variety and you can only mean Newman Lake, perhaps one of Spokane County's best-kept fish-ing secrets. Not only is the lake huge, but it's one of those places where you never really know what you're going to pull out of the water next. Both rainbows and browns are stocked in the lake for trout anglers, while bass anglers come in search of trophy-class largemouths and are often rewarded handsomely for their efforts. Fish during the day and you'll find good num-bers of crappies, bluegills, and perch; fish at night and you'll find bullhead catfish in a biting mood. And, the pot has become even sweeter with the addition of tiger muskies to the Newman Lake angling menu. The fast-growing, mean-spirited tigers were stocked to help eliminate a pesky sucker population, but they'll also provide some wonderful trophy fishing in the coming years, just as they've done in western Washington's Mayfield Lake (see page 405). They'll hit large bucktail spinners and plugs similar to those used for bass, only a little bigger.

With all this angling variety, you can expect to have one serious problem if you're heading for Newman Lake for the first time: You may not have enough room in your car for all the tackle you might need.

45. SPOKANE RIVER

Reference: **Flows westerly through Spokane and into the east side of Lake Roosevelt at Fort Spokane; map A5, grid h7.**
How to get there: Drive north out of Spokane on U.S. 395, then turn east (left) to reach portions of the river from downtown Spokane to the upper end of Long Lake. Drive east from town on Interstate 90 and take roads to the north to reach the section of river between Spokane and the Idaho state line.

Facilities: Boat ramps are located at Nine Mile Falls (downstream from Spokane) and Myrtle Point (upstream from town). Food, gas, lodging, and tackle are available throughout the area. Riverside State Park, about seven miles west of Spokane on the north side of the river, has a limited number of tent and RV sites, showers, and other facilities.

Contact: Sportsmen's Surplus, (509) 467-5970; The Outdoor Sportsman, (509) 328-1556; Riverside State Park (509) 456-3964.

Species available: Rainbow and some brown trout.

Fishing the Spokane River: Special regulations, including wild-fish-release rules and restrictions on the use of bait, have helped to make the Spokane a respectable trophy-trout fishery in recent years. The stretch of river east of Spokane, which offers some beautiful trout water, is where I would recommend going if you really want to sample what this pretty river has to offer.

The problem may be getting to the water, since brush crowds the bank in many areas. There are man-made trails through it in some places, but in other spots you avoid the brush by staying in the river.

Take along a good selection of Muddler Minnows and other streamer patterns if you plan on fly-fishing in search of a bragging-sized fish. If you prefer casting hardware for your trout, try a quarter-ounce BangTail or Rooster Tail spinner or a three-eighths-ounce Krocodile spoon. And remember that the lure must have a single, barbless hook, so replace that treble or clip off two of the points. A limited number of hatchery rainbows are planted here every year to provide some put-and-take harvest.

The river is open to year-round fishing, but some of the best trout action is in the very early spring—March and April—and late fall—October and early November.

46. LIBERTY LAKE

Reference: **East of Spokane; map A5, grid h8.**

How to get there: Take Interstate 90 east from Spokane for 12 miles and turn south (right) at the signs pointing the way to Liberty Lake. The lake is about 1.5 miles off the freeway, on the left side of the road.

Facilities: The lake has a public access area and boat ramp, with RV parks, food, gas, tackle, and lodging available in Liberty Lake and Spokane.

Contact: Sportsmen's Surplus, (509) 467-5970; The Outdoor Sportsman, (509) 328-1556.

Species available: Rainbow and brown trout, largemouth bass, yellow perch, crappies, bluegills, brown bullhead catfish.

Fishing Liberty Lake: Liberty used to be one of the Spokane area's top trout producers, but now warm-water species provide a mixed-bag fishery and trout fishing is only part of the picture. The lake produces some big bass, many of them caught from the numerous docks and floats that dot much of the lake's shoreline. Perch, crappies, and bluegills are abundant around many of the same docks and floats, but don't be surprised if you locate a school of them just about anywhere around the edges of the lake. The put-and-take trout fishery provides fish for anglers using any and all of the usual trout baits and lures, so practice your favorite technique and you'll be satisfied with the results.

If you're into night fishing, you'll find good numbers of brown bullheads available in the spring and summer. The Liberty Lake season runs from late April through September.

47. WEST MEDICAL LAKE

Reference: **West of the town of Medical Lake; map A4, grid i4.**

How to get there: Take Interstate 90 east from Sprague for 16 miles or west from Spokane for 14 miles and turn north on Salnave Road (State Route 902). Go about six miles. Before getting to the town of Medical Lake, turn west (left) on Fancher Road and drive 0.4 miles to the south end of the lake.

Facilities: A public access area with a boat ramp is located on the west side of the lake, while the south end has a privately owned resort with rental boats, a fishing dock, tackle, a cafe, showers, RV hookups, and snacks. The nearest gas is in the town of Medical Lake.

Contact: West Medical Lake Resort, (509) 299-3921.

Species available: Rainbow trout.

Fishing West Medical Lake: Food-rich West Medical Lake has many times been described as one of Washington's top trout producers, and I've been among those praising it. The lake bottom is alive with freshwater shrimp, Dobsonfly larvae, and other creepy-crawlers too numerous to mention, and the rainbows gorge on them, growing as fast as an inch a month during certain times of the year.

West Medical has so much food that the trout don't even have to work at it, and that's why some regulars say that trolling isn't all that productive. "Why should the trout go out of their way to chase down a moving lure when there's all this stuff just sitting around for the taking?" they reason. Makes sense. Whatever the reason, stillfishing produces some of the best catches of rainbows, and the bait of choice is a live Dobsonfly larva, fished by itself or in conjunction with a salmon egg, worm, or marshmallow.

If you simply can't stand to sit still for stillfishing, some trolling lures seem to work better than others here. They include Luhr Jensen Needlefish in red and rainbow finishes, red-head Triple Teazers, Wedding Ring spinners, red Rooster Tails, and nickel/red-head or fire Super Dupers.

Lots of West Medical anglers do their fishing with flies, either the dry kind that float on the surface or the nymphs that sink toward the bottom and imitate the Dobsonflies and other natural inhabitants of the lake upon which the rainbows feed. Speaking from personal experience, I can tell you that you don't have to be very good at fly-fishing to catch trout here on artificials.

One more important word of advice: The undeveloped west side of the lake always seems to provide better fishing than the east side. You may want to prospect around a little, but chances are you'll end up along the lake's eastern shoreline, like most everybody else.

48. MEDICAL LAKE

Reference: **West of the town of Medical Lake; map A5, grid i4.**

How to get there: Take Interstate 90 east from Sprague for 16 miles or west from Spokane for 14 miles and turn north on Salnave Road (State Route 902). Drive about six miles, and before getting to the town of Medical Lake, turn west (left) on Fancher Road and then take an immediate right into the public access area of Medical Lake.

Facilities: The south end of the lake has a public access area and boat ramp. Food, gas, tackle, and lodging are available in the town of Medical Lake.

Contact: West Medical Lake Resort, (509) 299-3921.

Species available: Brown trout.

Fishing Medical Lake: Rarely are two of the best trout lakes in the state within a few hundred yards of each other, but that's the case with Medical Lake and West Medical Lake (see page 328), both of which offer quality trout fishing. The main differences are that Medical Lake has browns instead of rainbows and selective fishery regulations that require the use of artificial lures and flies with single, barbless hooks for all fishing. Medical also discourages taking home a creel full of fish, with a two-fish limit and a 14-inch minimum size limit. Many anglers come here to catch and release, not to kill a meal of fresh trout.

A haven for fly-fishing, Medical is a place where you can bide your time catching foot-long browns on nymphs and wet patterns until some kind of hatch occurs, and then you might be able to get your fill of dry-fly-fishing for a few minutes or a few hours. My advice is to plan a trip to West Medical, give yourself an extra day to fish its neighbor, and vice versa.

The season here opens in late April and closes at the end of September.

49. SILVER LAKE

Reference: **Southeast of Medical Lake; map A5, grid i4.**

How to get there: Take Interstate 90 west from Sprague for 21 miles or east from Spokane for 9 miles and turn north onto Four Lakes Road, following the signs for 3 miles toward the town of Medical Lake. Silver Lake is on the left, about three miles off the freeway.

Facilities: The lake has a public access area and a boat ramp, as well as several private resorts and campgrounds that have rental boats, fishing docks, bait and tackle, some groceries, RV sites, and moorage. Food, gas, tackle, and lodging are available in nearby Medical Lake.

Contact: Picnic Pines Resort, (509) 299-3223; Bernie's Last Resort, (509) 299-7273.

Species available: Rainbow and brook trout.

Fishing Silver Lake: Stocked with both legal-sized fish and hatchery fry, Silver Lake produces large numbers of trout throughout much of the season, which runs from late April through October. Resort fishing docks provide some of the best catches of all, especially early in the season when stillfishing is the most productive angling method. By May the trollers are catching their share, too. Carry-over rainbows and browns are common here. If there's a down side to fishing Silver Lake, it's the fact that low water sometimes causes problems for anglers trying to get their boats in and out of the water. If you have a small car-topper craft or even a canoe, that might be the rig to consider using when the water levels are low.

50. CLEAR LAKE

Reference: **South of Medical Lake; map A5, grid i4.**

How to get there: Drive west from Sprague for 16 miles or east from Spokane for 14 miles on Interstate 90 and turn north on Salnave Road, also known as State Route 902. Less than a quarter of a mile from the freeway, turn right on Clear Lake Road and follow it for two miles to the east side of the lake.

Facilities: Besides a public access area and boat ramp, the lake has resorts with boat rentals, moorage, bait and tackle, and other facilities. The nearest gas, food, and lodging are in the town of Medical Lake.

Contact: Rainbow Cove Resort, (509) 299-3717; Barber's Resort, (509) 299-3830.

Species available: Rainbow and brown trout, largemouth bass.

Fishing Clear Lake: If you're looking for a place with easy access off the freeway and a good mixed bag of angling possibilities, Clear Lake may be the answer. It's planted with liberal doses of hatchery rainbow and brown trout, which means plenty of trout trolling and stillfishing opportunities. Stillfish with grubs and yellow corn, like many of the locals do from their boats or from the resort docks. If you like to troll, try a Jake's Spinalure, a Wedding Ring-and-worm combination, a green or brown Carey Special, or a Woolly Bugger fly for rainbows. The browns seem to prefer green or brown Flatfish or Kwikfish, Rooster Tails in the same colors, or Mepps spinners.

If your timing is good—as in sometime during the second half of May— you may even be around when the mayflies begin to hatch, providing some of the best fly-fishing you'll ever find. The north end of the lake is usually the scene of the best action during one of these hatches.

If you should get tired of trout, stick around into the evening and work your way around the edge of the lake with a spinnerbait, plastic worm, or crankbait and see what's happening with the bass. Chances are you'll come up with a few nice largemouths for your efforts. The best bassing is from May through July.

Clear Lake's fishing season opens in late April and runs through October.

51. FISH LAKE

Reference: **Northeast of Cheney; map A5, grid i5.**

How to get there: Take Interstate 90 east from Sprague for 21 miles or west from Spokane for 6 miles and exit onto State Route 904 to Cheney. Drive northeast out of Cheney on Cheney-Spokane Road, which is the "main drag" out of town to the east. The lake is on the right, about 2.5 miles from Cheney.

Facilities: The north side of the lake has a county park with a boat ramp and beach access, as well as a privately owned resort with bait, tackle, snacks, campsites, and a fishing dock.

Contact: Myers Park, (509) 235-2391.

Species available: Brook trout.

Fishing Fish Lake: This has been Spokane County's most well-known brook trout producer for decades, and the fishing can be as good now as it was 30 years ago. While most of us think of brookies as skinny little seven-inchers, Fish Lake brook trout are the exception. Sure, they all originate in Department of Fish and Wildlife hatcheries, and many are caught shortly after release while they're still skinny little seven-inchers. But lots of fish carry-over here through the winter, providing a high percentage of fat, 11- to 14-inch fish that are well worth anyone's time and effort.

Stillfishing with garden worms or nightcrawlers rates as the number one trout-getter, but trolling one of the slick little wigglers behind a string of trolling blades will also pay off. If you do fish the lake in a boat, remember that the lake has a prohibition on gas-powered motors, so use your electric or your oars.

The best trout fishing is in May and June, but the season runs from late April through September.

52. HOG CANYON LAKE

Reference: **Northeast of Sprague; map A5, grid j4.**

How to get there: Drive east from Sprague for nine miles or west from Spokane for 20 miles on Interstate 90 and exit south at Fishtrap. Drive south just over half a mile to the first gravel road and turn east (left). Go another half-mile to the stop sign and railroad track, continuing straight ahead from the stop sign and following the rough dirt road about 1.5 miles to the south end of the lake. People take their cars to the lake on this road, but as far as I'm concerned, this is a four-wheel-drive-only road, especially right after it rains or snows.

Facilities: The lake has a rough boat ramp at its south end. The nearest food, gas, tackle, and lodging are in Sprague.

Contact: Four Seasons Campground, (509) 257-2332; Purple Sage Motel, (509) 257-2507.

Species available: Rainbow trout.

Fishing Hog Canyon Lake: This winter-season lake with the unusual name offers some good trout fishing from the time it opens on December 1 until it closes at the end of March. Open-water fishing is usually possible early in the season, but the lake might freeze over any time after Christmas. Though the fishing can be just as good through the ice, the angling strategy obviously changes. Trolling is good in open water, but when the ice forms, nobody seems willing to cut large enough holes to keep the trolling paths open. That's when it's time to dangle a red salmon egg, a couple of kernels of yellow corn, or a small wad of Berkley Power Bait near the bottom. Be on your toes for light, subtle strikes, even from the 16-inch rainbows that are quite common. And on those chilly days when the fishing is good, remember that the regulations require that no more than two trout in your five-fish limit may exceed 14 inches.

53. CHAPMAN LAKE

Reference: **South of Cheney; map A5, grid j5.**

How to get there: Drive south from Cheney on Cheney-Spangle Road for seven miles and turn west (right) on Pine Grove Road. Drive a little over three miles to Cheney-Plaza Road and turn right. Continue 1.5 miles and turn right again down the gravel road leading half a mile to the south end of the lake.

Facilities: A boat ramp with an access area is located on the east side of the lake, near the south end, and the lake also has a fishing resort with cabins and RV hookups. Food, gas, tackle, and lodging are available in Cheney.

Contact: Chapman Lake Resort, (509) 523-2221.

Species available: Largemouth and smallmouth bass, rainbow trout, kokanee, yellow perch, crappies, brown bullhead catfish.

Fishing Chapman Lake: Chapman has long been one of Spokane County's top bass lakes, featuring both largemouths and smallmouths in good numbers. Arrive early in the morning or stay late into the evening and you may get in some good top-water action. But if the bass aren't on top, you'll still get in some quality fishing time, whether you work plastics around shoreline cover, snake spinnerbaits or crankbaits over and around underwater structure, or do whatever it is you like to do for bass.

Kokanee are in good enough supply here to warrant a sort of revised bonus limit on them. You can keep up to 10 "trout" per day, but at least five of those must be kokanee. Trolling Wedding Ring spinners whose hooks are tipped with maggots or white corn is the favored kokanee-catching technique, and it also accounts for many of the rainbow trout caught here. Stillfishing with worms, Berkley Power Bait, marshmallows, and yellow corn is also popular with trout anglers.

Perch and crappies are abundant here, and both will hit small leadheads adorned with plastic skirt bodies. Perch hit throughout the April-to-October season; crappies bite best in May and October.

54. BADGER LAKE

Reference: **South of Cheney; map A5, grid j5.**

How to get there: Drive south from Cheney on Mullinix Road for five miles and turn east (left) on Dover Road, following it to the west side of the lake.

Facilities: The lake has a public access area with a very steep boat ramp where launching is sometimes a struggle, especially during times of low water. Resort facilities on the west side of the lake include rental boats, RV hookups, moorage, tackle, and food. The nearest gas stations and motels are in Cheney.

Contact: Badger Lake Resort, (509) 235-2341.

Species available: Rainbow and cutthroat trout, smallmouth bass.

Fishing Badger Lake: Long a favorite Spokane County trout lake, Badger was illegally stocked with bass several years ago, which provided variety to the catch but was, according to Department of Fish and Wildlife biologists, very tough on the trout. The lake was scheduled for treatment with rotenone at the end of the 1995 season to eliminate everything and start over. This means that heavy hatchery plants will be the rule in 1996 and 1997 to provide what amounts to a put-and-take fishery until the trout fully re-establish themselves and things get back to "normal." I included bass as one of the species available just in case the plan doesn't work out as scheduled.

Assuming a trout-only fishery again, I recommend trolling with gang troll-and-worm combinations, green Flatfish or Kwikfish, silver/red-head Triple Teazers, and Dick Nites. Stillfishing with worms, Power Bait, marshmallows, and red salmon eggs should continue to take fish, as in the past. And the mayfly hatch always provides good fly-fishing opportunity later in the spring and into early summer.

Badger is open to fishing from late April through September.

55. FISHTRAP LAKE

Reference: **Northeast of Sprague; map A5, grid j3.**

How to get there: Take Interstate 90 east from Sprague for 9 miles or west from Spokane for 20 miles and take the Fishtrap exit to the south. Drive three miles to Scroggie Road and turn east (left), continuing for one mile to the north end of the lake.

Facilities: The north end of the lake has a public access area with a boat ramp and a privately owned resort offering food, fuel, tackle, rental boats, showers, and rest rooms. Additional facilities are in Sprague.

Contact: Fishtrap Lake Resort, (509) 235-2284.

Species available: Rainbow trout.

Fishing Fishtrap Lake: Fishtrap offers some of the best early season fishing in eastern Washington, at least in terms of catch-per-angler. Anglers catch limits of plump rainbows with uncanny consistency during the first few weeks of the season from late April through May. Stillfish with worms and/or marshmallows, or troll one-quarter-ounce and one-sixth-ounce Panther Martins in black, Rooster Tails spinners in frog or rainbow patterns, or small Flatfish or Kwikfish in a frog finish.

56. AMBER LAKE

Reference: **Southwest of Cheney; map A5, grid j4.**

How to get there: From the west, exit Interstate 90 at Sprague and drive east out of town on Old State Highway. After two miles, turn south (right) on Martin Road and follow it about 11 miles to Mullinex Road. Turn north (left) on Mullinex and follow it about six miles to Pine Spring Road. Turn west (left) on Pine Spring and follow it to the lake. From the east, exit Interstate 90 at Tyler and drive south on Pine Spring Road, staying on it all the way for eight miles to the lake.

Facilities: A public access area with a boat ramp is located on the north side of the lake. The nearest food, gas, tackle, and lodging are in Sprague and Cheney.

Contact: Four Seasons Campground, (509) 257-2332; Purple Sage Motel, (509) 257-2507.

Species available: Rainbow and cutthroat trout.

Fishing Amber Lake: If you want peace, quiet, and a laid-back atmosphere while trout fishing, you'll probably like Amber Lake. Selective fishery regulations prohibiting bait and barbed hooks are now in effect, which leads many anglers hungry for fresh trout to go elsewhere. A two-fish daily limit also helps reduce the size of the crowds, and an electric-motors-only rule helps in the peace and quiet category. Anglers thin out even more after the end of September, when Amber's regulations switch to catch-and-release fishing only until the end of the season on November 30.

The catch consists of both rainbows and cutthroats, and both grow to pretty good size under Amber's restrictive regulations. Trolling various spoons and spinners is effective, and fly-fishing is also productive beginning with the mayfly hatch in late-May.

57. WILLIAMS LAKE

Reference: **Southwest of Cheney; map A5, grid j4.**

How to get there: Take Martin Road east from Sprague for 10 miles, turn north (left) on Mullinex Road, and then east (right) on Williams Lake Road to the lake. From Cheney, follow Mullinex Road south for 10 miles to Williams Lake Road and turn east (left) to the lake.

Facilities: The lake has a public access area and boat ramp, along with two resorts that offer tent and RV sites, restaurants, boat rentals, moorage, fishing docks, groceries, and tackle. Gas, food, and lodging are available in Sprague and Cheney.

Contact: Williams Lake Resort, (509) 235-2391; Bunker's Resort, (509) 235-5212.

Species available: Rainbow and cutthroat trout.

Fishing Williams Lake: Here's another lake where some self-appointed fish biologist decided to add bass to the mix, with less than positive results. But fair numbers of rainbows and cutthroats are still available, and fishing can be good at times.

Like other lakes in this part of the state, the mayfly hatch causes lots of excitement among trout and trout anglers alike around the end of May, providing a couple of weeks of the best fly-fishing you could want. If you're not into fly-fishing, try stillfishing near the bottom with orange or red Power Bait, red Pautzke salmon eggs, or a combination of the two. Trolling is also effective, especially for anglers who use frog-finish Flatfish, Kwikfish, or Hot Shots. Another trolling tactic is to trail a Muddler Minnow, Carey Special, or some other streamer or wet fly pattern behind a leaded line and a 30-foot leader.

58. DOWNS LAKE

Reference: **Southeast of Sprague; map A5, grid j4.**

How to get there: Take Interstate 90 to Sprague, exit the freeway onto the Old State Highway east (left), and drive 2.5 miles to Martin Road, following it about six miles to the gravel road turning south (right) to the lake.

Facilities: The north side of the lake has a private resort with camping sites, bait, and tackle, a boat ramp, and other facilities. The nearest food, gas, and lodging are in Sprague and Cheney.

Contact: Downs Lake Resort, (509) 235-2314.

Species available: Rainbow trout, largemouth bass, yellow perch, brown bull-head catfish.

Fishing Downs Lake: This big, shallow lake warms quickly in the spring sun, providing some of its best trout fishing during the first few weeks of the season. Most anglers troll here, using the full range of standard goodies. But don't troll too slowly or use something too heavy, since much of the lake is only a few feet deep; you don't want to spend all your time dredging the bottom or trying to un-hook your bottom-snagged lure. Downs is also well-suited to fly-fishing, and you can easily spend a weekend working around the weeds and reeds in search of rainbows without casting to the same place twice.

Bass fishing can also be very good here as soon as the water warms in spring, and some years that means good bassing as soon as the lake opens in late-April. Largenmouths provide the action, and Downs produces its share of bigmouths of five pounds and over.

You can almost always catch a few perch here—even when you're trying to catch something else—and catfish action is good at night from May to August.

59. SPRAGUE LAKE

Reference: **Southwest of Sprague, south side of Interstate 90; map A5, grid j2.**

How to get there: Take Interstate 90 to the town of Sprague, hit main street, and follow it out of town to the southwest for about four miles. The road parallels the lake for several miles.

Facilities: The east side of the lake has a public boat ramp and the northeast end has a private resort with RV hookups, a store with groceries, bait, and tackle, a fishing dock, and other amenities. Restaurants, gas, and lodging are available in Sprague.

Contact: Sprague Lake Resort, (509) 257-2864.

Species available: Rainbow and cutthroat trout, largemouth and smallmouth bass, bluegills, channel catfish, crappies, yellow perch, brown bullhead catfish.

Fishing Sprague Lake: Sprague is another one of those eastern Washington lakes that has almost everything an angler could want. But unlike most of the others, the mixed bag here was created by design, not by accident. In 1985, Sprague was a big mud hole, filled with tens of thousands of carp and little else. An energetic program to treat the lake with rotenone and re-stock it with trout, bass, and panfish was undertaken that year, and Sprague has been a piscatorial highlight film ever since. Rainbow and Lahontan cutthroat trout were stocked early in the process, and within months were providing year-round trout fishing that was above and beyond everyone's expectations. A year and a half after the rotenone treatment, beautiful rainbows of 20 inches were coming from the lake with amazing regularity, and the cut-throats were measuring a good 14 inches each. Even though the lake is shallow, it's fed by numerous underground springs that keep water temperatures surprisingly cool, even in summer, so anglers were catching limits of big trout when all the other lakes in the area were dead for trout fishing.

But the trout were only a stop-gap to provide angling action while various warm-water species were established, and as the trouting tapered off in the late eighties, it wasn't long before good catches of smallmouth and largemouth bass were coming from Sprague—and they continue to provide excellent fishing from early spring to late fall. The lake is full of crawdads, so the bass grow fast, fat, and strong. There's no end to the weedy largemouth cover and the rocky hideaways that smallmouths like, so you can fish your brains out and never cover it all in a single trip.

Walleyes have responded pretty much the same as all the other species, and so have the bluegills and channel cats. Sprague may now be the best bluegill lake in Washington, which was part of the plan back when the lake was poisoned and the lake-rehabilitation program started. Perch, crappies, and bullhead catfish tend to be overlooked in the excitement.

Be sure to check the regulations pamphlet before fishing Sprague, especially in the spring. Although the season runs year-round, special spring closures are in effect on part of the lake, and you'll want to know the details before fishing rather than finding out the hard way.

60. FOURTH OF JULY LAKE

Reference: **South of Sprague; map A5, grid j2.**

How to get there: Take Interstate 90 to Sprague and turn south onto State Route 23. Drive a mile and turn west (right) on the gravel and dirt road that begins at the one-mile marker. Head straight for about one mile to the lake.

Facilities: The north end of the lake has a rough boat ramp. Food, gas, tackle, lodging, and RV facilities are available in and around Sprague.

Contact: Four Seasons Campground, (509) 257-2332; Purple Sage Motel, (509) 257-2507; Sprague Lake Resort, (509) 257-2864.

Species available: Rainbow trout.

Fishing Fourth of July Lake: Fourth of July is another winter-only lake that's open to fishing only from the first of December through the end of March. Although this is a mighty cold time of year in the Inland Empire, the winter fishing here can be hot as a firecracker. You may be able to fish by boat early in the season, but it doesn't take long for a thick ice cover to form on the lake, and from that time on it's strictly a through-the-ice proposition.

The rainbows here run 10 to 16 inches, with a few two-year carryovers of 18 inches or more. Pautzke's red salmon eggs have long been favorite bait among Fourth of July ice anglers, but Berkley's Power Bait gets more popular every season. Take both along and see which works best for you. Just to cover all the bases, throw in some whole-kernel corn and maybe a few miniature marshmallows. With all those supplies, if the trout aren't biting, at least you won't starve.

The resort fishing dock on West Medical Lake is a popular and productive spot for rainbow trout.

MAP B1

WASHINGTON MAP .... see page 5
Adjoining Maps
NORTH (map A1) .... see page 70
EAST (map B2) .... see page 366
SOUTH .... no map
WEST .... no map

36 Listings
PAGES 338-365

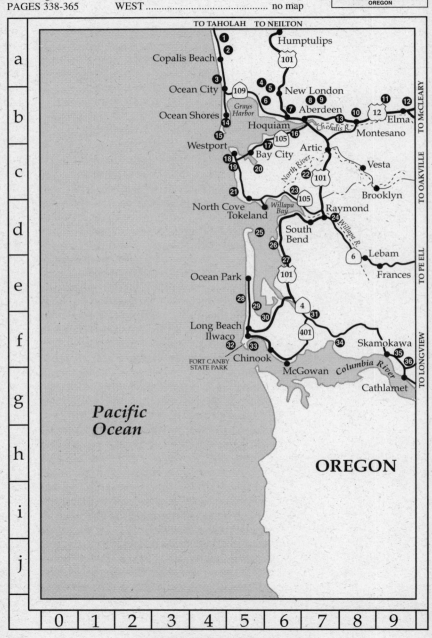

Map Section B1 features:

1. Moclips River
2. Copalis River
3. North Beach Surf
4. Humptulips River
5. Failor Lake
6. Chenois Creek
7. Hoquiam River
8. Wishkah River
9. Lake Aberdeen
10. Wynoochee River
11. Satsop River
12. Cloquallum Creek
13. Lower Chehalis River
14. Duck Lake
15. Grays Harbor North Jetty and Point Brown
16. South Grays Harbor Streams
17. Johns River
18. Westport Inshore
19. Westport Offshore
20. Elk River
21. South Beach Surf
22. North River
23. Smith Creek
24. Willapa River
25. Willapa Bay
26. Palix River
27. Nemah River
28. Long Beach Peninsula Surf
29. Long Beach Peninsula Lakes
30. Bear River
31. Naselle River
32. Ilwaco Offshore
33. Columbia River Estuary
34. Grays River
35. Skamokawa Creek
36. Elochoman River

1. MOCLIPS RIVER

Reference: **Flows into Pacific Ocean at Moclips; map B1, grid a5.**

How to get there: Take State Route 109 west out of Hoquiam and follow it up the coast 30 miles to Moclips and the mouth of the river. The only road leading east out of town parallels the south side of the river.

Facilities: The nearest place to find a full complement of amenities is Ocean Shores, 17 miles to the south, but Moclips has lodging, RV parks, groceries, gas, and tackle.

Contact: All Seasons Sports, (360) 538-7033.

Species available: Sea-run cutthroat trout, a few winter steelhead.

Fishing the Moclips River: Although this coastal stream is open during the winter to allow for a steelhead season, the winter fishery doesn't amount to anything at all. During the winter of 1993-94, for example, anglers didn't catch a single winter steelie, according to Washington Department of Fish and Wildlife catch records. For most folks, the Moclips is too far away and the steelheading too poor to be worth a wintertime trip.

Fall fishing for sea-run cutts, on the other hand, can be a worthwhile endeavor. Like many other streams around the Grays Harbor area, the best cutthroating occurs within about 24 hours of the end of a heavy rain that causes a good rise in water levels. Roll a nightcrawler or small clusters of salmon eggs along the bottom to catch them.

2. COPALIS RIVER

Reference: **Enters Pacific Ocean near Copalis Beach; map B1, grid a5.**

How to get there: Take State Route 109 west from Hoquiam and follow it up the coast for 20 miles to Copalis Beach and the mouth of the river. To reach the upper river, drive east out of Copalis on Copalis Beach Road for about five miles, turn north (left) on Ocean Beach Road, and drive just under four miles to the Copalis River Bridge. An unimproved road leads a short distance downstream and several miles upstream from the bridge.

Facilities: In Ocean Shores, seven miles south.

Contact: All Seasons Sports, (360) 538-7033.

Species available: Coho salmon, sea-run cutthroat trout, seaperch, flounder and sole, winter and summer steelhead (maybe).

Fishing the Copalis River: If there's such a thing as a big-draw fishery on the Copalis, it has to be the flurry of activity generated by the fall coho run. It starts in September, ends in October, and for the rest of the year, there isn't a heck of a lot to do around here. The locals catch a few sea-run cutts, but for folks living around the population centers of Puget Sound, this stream is a long way from home for a shot at cutthroats.

> You can catch flounder, sole, and perch by casting pieces of shrimp, clam, or small crabs at the river mouth at the start of an incoming tide.

3. NORTH BEACH SURF

Reference: **From Copalis Beach south to Ocean Shores; map B1, grid a4.**

How to get there: Take State Route 109 west from Hoquiam and turn west (left) on any of the public roads leading to the beach. Access roads at Ocean City, Copalis Beach, Pacific Beach, Moclips, and other areas are well-marked.

Facilities: Food and gas are available at Copalis Beach, and all other amenities can be found at Ocean Shores. Ocean City State Park has tent sites, RV spaces, and rest rooms with showers.

Contact: Ocean City State Park, (360) 289-3553.

Species available: Redtail surfperch.

Fishing the North Beach Surf: This stretch of beach, especially the northern portion, gets lighter fishing pressure than beaches to the south, and the perch fishing can be very good. Spring and early summer often produce best, but perch are available virtually all year. Fish the incoming tide, concentrating on spots with lagoons, channels, and other noticeable bottom structure. Perch like to forage in these deeper spots where tiny food items collect.

4. HUMPTULIPS RIVER

Reference: **Flows into Grays Harbor's North Bay northwest of Hoquiam; map B1, grid a6.**

How to get there: Take U.S. 101 north from Hoquiam, driving about 22 miles to the middle portion of the river. To reach the lower Humptulips, turn west (left) off U.S. 101 onto Ocean Beach Road about three miles north of Hoquiam and follow it for 10 miles to the river.

Facilities: There are boat ramps of various quality off East Humptulips and McNutt roads, both of which are upstream from the U.S. 101 bridge, and several spots off Copalis Crossing Road, which runs along the west side of the river between U.S. 101 and Copalis Crossing. There's also a good paved ramp off Ocean Beach Road a mile or so above the mouth of the river. Food and gas are available at Humptulips. Tackle, lodging, and other facilities can be found in Hoquiam.

Contact: Big Mouth John's Tackle, (360) 533-0144.

Species available: Winter and summer steelhead; fall chinook, coho, and chum salmon; sea-run cutthroat trout.

Fishing the Humptulips River: If you like catching fish fresh from the ocean, this may be the place for you. Many freshwater salmon and steelhead anglers count the "Hump" as their favorite, and the cutthroat fishing can be every bit as good. The best cutthroat fishing is in October, while the sea-run trout are available from August to November.

Winter steelheading is best in December and January, when good numbers of hatchery fish return to the river, and again in March and April, when the catch includes a high percentage of big and tough wild fish. If a 20-pound steelhead is your heart's desire, fish the Humptulips in March from now until the time you die and you just might achieve your goal. Boat fishing offers definite advantages, but there are plenty of good places to fish from the bank as well, including right under the U.S. 101 bridge (where I hooked my first Humptulips winter-run many years ago), and near the fish hatchery about two miles downstream from the highway bridge.

Although summer steelhead smolts are planted in the Humptulips, summer steelheading here is nothing to write home about. Persistent anglers catch a few dozen steelhead a month from June to September.

Salmon fishing is another matter, since the Humptulips ranks up among the Northwest's best fall salmon streams. Things start hopping in September, when good numbers of chinooks take over the river. Some of them are brutes, topping 40 pounds, and they're strong enough to knock you down and stomp all over you if you give them half a chance. This chinook run lasts longer than any other on the Washington coast, as anglers continue to catch big kings well into November. Long before they disappear, both coho and chum salmon show in the river, and there are days when you may hook all three species. The coho and chum fishing usually tapers off by Thanksgiving, but don't be too surprised to find stragglers of both species in the river as late as January.

---

5. FAILOR LAKE

Reference: **North of Hoquiam and west of Highway 101; map B1, grid a6.**

How to get there: Drive north about nine miles from Hoquiam on U.S. 101 and turn west (left) on Failor Lake Road. The lake is about 2.5 miles off the highway.

Facilities: The public access area has a boat ramp. All other amenities are in Hoquiam and Aberdeen.

Contact: Big Mouth John's Tackle, (360) 533-0143.

Species available: Rainbow and cutthroat trout.

Fishing Failor Lake: At 65 acres, Failor Lake isn't very big, but it's a favorite of Grays Harbor County anglers. Stocked with both rainbow and cutthroat trout to the tune of about 6,000 fish annually, there are plenty of eight- to 10-inchers to go around. The carry-over of fish from the previous year is fair, so there's always a chance you'll find a 14- to 16-incher early in the season. Fishing is good throughout May and June, slows during July and August, and picks up again in September and October.

    Stillfishing with all the standard baits works pretty well for Failor Lake rainbows, but worms are your best bet if you want a chance of catching a cutthroat or two along with the 'bows. As for trolling, gang trolls with worms trailing behind account for many of the fish, but you might try a silver/red head Triple Teazer or a small Flatfish or Kwikfish in any light or metallic finish. The season here opens in late April and runs through October.

6. CHENOIS CREEK

Reference: **Enters Grays Harbor's North Bay northwest of Hoquiam; map B1, grid b6.**

How to get there: Take State Route 109 west from Hoquiam about eight miles to the bridge that crosses over Chenois Creek.

Facilities: There isn't much here except a small grocery store along the highway at the mouth of the creek. Food, gas, tackle, and lodging are available in Aberdeen and Hoquiam.

Contact: Big Mouth John's Tackle, (360) 533-0143.

Species available: Sea-run cutthroat trout.

Fishing Chenois Creek: Local anglers, many of them Copenhagen-chewing loggers and mill-workers, call this "Snoose Creek," perhaps because the word "Chenois" sort of looks like "Snoose," or it may be that they spit in the creek and the water actually does contain a high percentage of snoose. Whatever the reason for the nickname, Chenois Creek is a pretty fair little sea-run cutthroat stream. Fish it anytime between the first of September and the end of October, but if you can get there at the tail end of a good rain, you'll at least double your chances of hooking fish. The season opens on June 1 and runs through October.

7. HOQUIAM RIVER

Reference: **Enters the east end of Grays Harbor at Hoquiam; map B1, grid b6.**

How to get there: Take U.S. 101 north from Hoquiam for about five miles to parallel the west side of the river. East Hoquiam Road out of Hoquiam parallels the East Fork of the Hoquiam and provides good access.

Facilities: A boat ramp is located on the East Fork Hoquiam and several places to fish from the bank are scattered along all the forks. Food, gas, lodging, and tackle are just a few minutes away in Hoquiam and Aberdeen.

Contact: Big Mouth John's Tackle, (360) 533-0143.

Species available: Winter steelhead, coho salmon, sea-run and resident cut-throat trout, seaperch, pile perch.

Fishing the Hoquiam River: Although it's stocked with a few hatchery steelhead smolts and is open for fall salmon fishing, the Hoquiam doesn't fit anyone's definition of a hot spot for either species. Winter steelheaders—mostly locals who know their way around and who can drop what they're doing to fish when conditions are right—catch a couple of dozen fish a year, and the fall coho fishery is even less productive.

Sea-run cutthroats offer more action, and the Department of Fish and Wildlife releases hatchery cutts here to enhance the opportunities. If you decide to keep a trout or two for the table, be sure to take only fin-clipped hatchery fish; all wild cutthroat have to be released.

The piers, bridge abutments, and old pilings at the mouth of the Hoquiam offer decent perch fishing on an incoming tide, but few anglers fish for them. Both pile perch and striped seaperch are available.

8. WISHKAH RIVER

Reference: **Flows into the east end of Grays Harbor at Aberdeen; map B1, grid b7.**

How to get there: Take U.S. 12 to Aberdeen and turn north (right) on Wishkah Road, which parallels the river.

Facilities: Food, lodging, gas, tackle, and plenty of watering holes are available in Aberdeen.

Contact: Big Mouth John's Tackle, (360) 533-0143.

Species available: Winter steelhead; coho, chinook, and chum salmon; resident and sea-run cutthroat trout; seaperch.

Fishing the Wishkah River: Though only one valley away from the Hoquiam (see page 342), the Wishkah is a much better salmon and steelhead stream, thanks to its better fish habitat and access to the water. Though your chances of hooking a keeper chinook aren't all that great, work your way up Wishkah Road to the mouth of the West Fork Wishkah during October or early November and you just might locate a cooperative coho or two. The winter steelheading is up and down from year to year, but some seasons the Wishkah gives up 150 to 200 fish. The best part is that the steelheading usually remains fairly consistent from December until the end of the season in March (the season open on June 1). Sea-run cutthroat fishing is fair here in October. Like the nearby Hoquiam, the regulations call for the release of all wild (not fin-clipped) cutthroats.

9. LAKE ABERDEEN

Reference: **Northeast of Aberdeen; map B1, grid b7.**

How to get there: Driving west on U.S. 12 toward Aberdeen, turn north (right) at the "Fish Hatchery-Aberdeen Lake" sign, which is about a mile west of the Central Park drive-in theater.

Facilities: The east side of the lake has a city park boat ramp, with all other amenities in Aberdeen.

Contact: Balcombe's Reel and Rod Service, (360) 249-6282.

Species available: Rainbow and cutthroat trout.

Fishing Lake Aberdeen: Spring plants of legal-sized rainbows from the Aberdeen Hatchery only a few hundred feet away, along with some resident cutthroats that have been around ever since the lake was created, provide the excitement here. Fishing is fair as long as the rainbows hold out, but the action is slow after that, so plan your visit for some time before the first of June for best results. Standard gang troll-and-worm rigs will take both rainbows and cutthroats, and that's what most of the regulars at Aberdeen like to use.

10. WYNOOCHEE RIVER

Reference: **Joins the Chehalis River at Montesano; map B1, grid b8.**

How to get there: Take State Route 8/U.S. 12 west from Olympia for 31 miles and turn north (right) on Wynoochee Road, about 1.5 miles past Montesano.

Facilities: Several boat ramps are located along the Wynoochee Road. Montesano has food, gas, lodging, and tackle.

Contact: Balcombe's Reel and Rod Service, (360) 249-6282.

Species available: Winter and summer steelhead; chinook, coho, and chum salmon; sea-run cutthroat trout.

Fishing the Wynoochee River: Although it doesn't get the praise or publicity accorded many other western Washington steelhead streams, this lower Chehalis tributary produces steelhead 10 months out of the year. Not bad, since it's closed to fishing in April and May. The annual sport catch of about 3,000 steelies is pretty equally divided between winter and summer fish. If you don't have the luxury of being able to fish the Wynoochee throughout the year, concentrate your efforts during March and June, the months anglers always seem to score the best catches, according to statistics compiled by the Department of Fish and Wildlife.

Fall fishing for salmon is fair in the Wynoochee, with a few big chinooks taken on roe clusters or ghost shrimp in October and larger numbers of coho caught on spinners and wobbling spoons in November and December.

Sea-run cutthroat fishing gets under way on the Wynoochee as early as mid-July and runs well into the fall. The best fishing is in September and October, especially right after a drenching rain that raises the river level a few inches. This is one of many Olympic Peninsula streams where anglers can keep only hatchery cutthroat marked with a fin-clip.

Wynoochee Road provides access for both bank and boat anglers. A boat ramp is located about three miles upriver from U.S. 12, near Black Creek, and another can be found about six miles farther upstream. Drift-boat anglers also launch at two or three other points along the road farther upriver, including a spot near Schafer Creek, about mid-way between Wynoochee Dam and the mouth of the river.

11. SATSOP RIVER

Reference: **Joins the Chehalis River west of Elma; map B1, grid b9.**

How to get there: Take State Route 8/U.S. 12 west from Olympia to Satsop, which is about four miles west of Elma. Turn north (right) onto East Satsop Road and follow it upriver.

Facilities: Schafer State Park, located on the East Fork Satsop, has tent sites and a few spaces with RV hookups, plus rest rooms. Gas, food, lodging, and tackle are available in Elma.

Contact: Schafer State Park, (360) 482-3852; Balcombe's Reel and Rod Service, (360) 249-6282.

Species available: Winter and summer steelhead; coho, chinook, and chum salmon; sea-run cutthroat trout.

Fishing the Satsop River: Fall salmon fishing is now a big draw at the Satsop, but this once-productive steelhead producer is hardly worth fishing during the steelhead season these days. Skimming the steelhead catch figures compiled every year by the Washington Department of Fish and Wildlife and seeing that the Satsop produces only a handful of winter-run steelies every year is enough to bring a tear to the eye of those who were on hand to fish it in the 1950s, 60s, and early 70s. I had that opportunity only once, but it was a day of steelheading I'll never forget, as fishing partner Dave Borden and I floated the lightly fished West Fork Satsop on a rainy January day. We hooked three fish, all of them over 10 pounds, and landed a pair that weighed in at 14 and 18 pounds. We only saw one other angler, and he was fishing within sight of where we took the boat out of the water at the end of that special day.

As I said, few people bother coming to the Satsop for steelhead now, but hundreds of them come for the salmon fishing. October can be good for coho, many of them quite large. The real circus, though, starts when the chum salmon surge into the river from late October to January. Much of the action is centered around two or three drifts on the East Fork Satsop, where it isn't unusual to see a flock of anglers hook several dozen fish in a morning. The crowds make this sort a of "combat fishing" spot, so bring your hard hat and safety goggles. Smarter anglers fish the lower Satsop from boats to see a little scenery and get away from the mobs.

12. CLOQUALLUM CREEK

Reference: **Flows into the Chehalis River near Elma; map B1, grid b9.**

How to get there: Take State Route 8 west from Olympia for 21 miles and either turn right at the "Grays Harbor County Fairgrounds" sign just east of Elma or take the Elma exit and go south (left) to the bridge that crosses the creek just south of town.

Facilities: Food, gas, tackle, and lodging are available in Elma.

Contact: Balcombe's Reel and Rod Service, (360) 249-6282.

Species available: Winter steelhead, sea-run cutthroat trout.

Fishing Cloquallum Creek: Timing is everything here, as it is on many small Northwest streams where water levels are the key to whether or not there are fish. A couple of days of rain that raises the water level a foot or two will bring a run of winter steelhead or sea-run cutts surging out of the Chehalis and into Cloquallum Creek, but they soon scatter through the system and are hard to find. That explains why a few local anglers—who can get to the creek on short notice when conditions are right—catch most of the fish here. February and March are the best months for steelheading, while November is tops for cutthroat fishing.

13. LOWER CHEHALIS RIVER

Reference: **Enters the east end of Grays Harbor at Aberdeen; map B1, grid b7.**

How to get there: Take Interstate 5 to Grand Mound and turn west onto U.S. 12, following the river downstream. Or take State Route 8 west from Olympia and either turn south to follow the Chehalis upstream toward Oakville or continue west to parallel the river downstream to Aberdeen.

Facilities: Boat ramps are located at Cosmopolis, as well as off State Route 107 just south of Montesano, just upstream from the mouth of the Satsop River, at Porter, and at Cedarville.

Contact: Balcombe's Reel and Rod Service, (360) 533-0143.

Species available: Winter and summer steelhead; chinook, coho, and chum salmon; sea-run cutthroat trout; white and green sturgeon; largemouth bass.

Fishing the lower Chehalis River: Early in this decade, the lower Chehalis was a hot bed of salmon-fishing activity, but the action has cooled significantly due to weaker returns of kings and silvers. When the runs are booming, boat anglers flock to the popular boat ramp beneath the State Route 107 bridge just south of Montesano and work both upstream and downstream. Trolling with Wiggle Warts, Hot 'N Tots, Hot Shots, Flatfish, Kwikfish, and other diving plugs often works best for the kings, which sometimes top 35 pounds. Trolling Flash Glos, Metrics, Mepps, and other spinners does a good job of drawing strikes from the silvers. Most of this action takes place in September and October.

Chum salmon runs have been more dependable than the chinook and coho returns lately, and trollers on the lower Chehalis also take a fair number of these so-called "dog salmon," many of which are bound for the Satsop River. Chums will also hit diving plugs, especially those plugs that happen to be some shade of green or chartreuse. Drift-fishing with green bobber-and-yarn combinations may also be effective for chums, which sometimes reach 20 pounds here.

Both bank and boat anglers take winter steelhead from the lower Chehalis, with the best fishing usually occurring from January through March. As with the river's salmon, many of the steelhead caught here are bound for the river's two major tributaries, the Wynoochee and Satsop rivers. Trolling plugs or diver-and-bait rigs accounts for many of the winter-runs, but plunkers fishing shrimp, roe, or Spin-N-Glos from the bank also take a few fish.

While catch statistics compiled by the Department of Fish and Wildlife show that the river produces a few summer-run steelhead, many of these fish are taken incidentally by early fall salmon anglers, and there isn't much of a targeted sport fishery on summer steelies.

There is, however, a target sport fishery on sturgeon. The stretch of river from Montesano downstream to Cosmopolis is the main focus of sturgeon-fishing activity. The chance of catching a monster eight- or nine-footer probably isn't as great here as it might be on the Columbia, but there are enough legal-sized 42- to 66-inchers to make this a very worthwhile sturgeon fishery that extends pretty much throughout the year. Boat fishing certainly has advantages, and most boaters launch at the Highway 107 launch or at Cosmopolis. Smelt are the most commonly used baits, but ghost shrimp, herring, and other offerings might work. Some Chehalis River sturgeon anglers do their fishing during the day, while others prefer night-fishing, but in either case the best action may occur immediately before or immediately after a tide change.

The Chehalis has been stocked with as many as 14,000 sea-run cutthroat smolts a year in recent years, but such plants aren't something anglers can necessarily depend on. Since all wild cutthroats must be released, the availability of hatchery cutts is pretty much a necessity if cutthroat anglers are to find any fish in the river that they can take home for the table. There's certainly nothing wrong with catch-and-release fishing for sea-runs, but it would be nice if anglers could count on those hatchery plants every year. The lower Chehalis has the look of a "natural" sea-run cutthroat trout stream, with lots of slow water, undercut banks, and submerged trees to provide near-perfect cutthroat cover. If you can't find them down around Elma and Montesano, or if the salmon-fishing crowd on the extreme lower end of the river makes it impossible to fish in solitude, try going up to Cedarville or Porter to try your luck. These areas are usually lightly fished during the fall.

Although often overlooked because of the many other possibilities, the lower Chehalis offers some fairly good bass fishing, especially in some of the slow-moving sloughs downstream from Montesano. Largemouths are the main target of anglers' efforts, but local rumor has it that some spots hold smallmouths as well.

---

14. DUCK LAKE

Reference: **South of Ocean Shores; map B1, grid b5.**

How to get there: Take State Route 109 west from Hoquiam for 14 miles to State Route 115. Turn south (left) and drive through Ocean Shores. Turn left on either Chance A La Mer and drive three blocks to the boat ramp near the north end of the lake or continue south for one mile to Ocean Lake Way, turn left, and drive a quarter of a mile to Duck Lake Drive. Turn right and follow Duck Lake Drive one mile to the southern boat ramp.

Facilities: The ramp nearest the north end of the lake is suitable for launching trailer boats of a decent size, while the southern ramp is better for car-toppers and smaller craft. Food, gas, tackle, and lodging are available in Ocean Shores.

Contact: Ocean City State Park, (360) 289-3553; Big Mouth John's Tackle, (360) 533-0143.

Species available: Rainbow and cutthroat trout, largemouth bass, bluegills, crappies.

Fishing Duck Lake: This long, shallow lake with coffee-colored water offers an interesting mix to any angler who takes the time to learn a few of its secrets. Both the bass and the trout sometimes grow to lunker proportions in the rich waters.

For rainbows, try trolling with small Kwikfish or Flatfish or stillfishing with Power Bait on the bottom or a bobber-and-worm rig near the surface. The few anglers who come to fly fish also do fairly well with various nymph patterns during the day or with dry flies in the evening. Spinnerbaits and various plastics work well for bass, and during the summer it's easy to coax them to the surface for a plug, popper, or buzz bait.

If you want bluegills, try casting a Beetle Spin or Berkley Power spin to shoreline brush piles and overhanging willows, especially when they congregate for spawning in the spring and early summer. Some of the bluegills grow to good size.

---

15. GRAYS HARBOR NORTH JETTY
AND POINT BROWN

Reference: **South of Ocean Shores; map B1, grid b4.**

How to get there: Take State Route 109 west from Hoquiam to State Route 115, turn south, and drive through Ocean Shores. Bear west on any of the major cross streets to get on Sand Dune Drive and take it to Ocean Shores Boulevard, which ends at the North Jetty.

Facilities: Everything you need is in Ocean Shores.

Contact: All Seasons Sports, (360) 538-7033.

Species available: Black rockfish, redtail surfperch, pile perch, cabezon, lingcod, greenling, various sole and flounder, coho salmon.

Fishing the Grays Harbor North Jetty and Point Brown: The jetty and the sandy beach to the northeast receive moderate fishing pressure during the summer and fall, but they go virtually unfished the rest of the year, which means many Washington anglers are missing out on about nine months of fishing opportunity each year. There's always something to catch here, since every high tide brings in a fresh supply of hungry customers.

Spring fishing can be especially good for lingcod, cabezon, and perch, and if you fish here in March or April, you'll probably have them all to yourself. Try leadhead jigs, herring, or live perch for lingcod, and small beach crabs or live shrimp for cabezon. Small baits such as limpets or pieces of clam, marine worms, or shrimp work best for perch. The early stages of the incoming tide are best for perch, while lings and cabezon may bite best just before and during the high slack.

The perch, lings, and cabezon continue biting through the summer, but other species also become important to anglers here, including black rockfish. They like leadhead jigs with small, plastic grub bodies, fished on an incoming and high tide.

Greenling, sole, and flounder are available around the North Jetty throughout most of the year, so you can fish for them whenever the mood strikes you and the weather isn't too rough. The same small baits that work for perch will also take these cooperative bottomfish.

Most anglers around here turn their attention to salmon fishing in the fall. A net-pen project started in the late-eighties has produced varying returns of adult cohos that make their way into the Ocean Shores boat harbor from September to November. These fish will sometimes hit herring baits that are either cast and retrieved or suspended beneath a large bobber, but more active artificial lures tend to be more productive for these fast-maturing silvers. Buzz Bombs and Blue Fox spinners are good bets.

16. SOUTH GRAYS HARBOR STREAMS

Reference: **Flow into the southeast side of Grays Harbor between South Aberdeen and Markham; map B1, grid b6.**

How to get there: Drive southwest from Aberdeen on State Route 105 and either stop at roadside turnouts near the bridges or turn south (left) on the various side roads that lead up the creeks.

Facilities: Everything you need is available in Aberdeen.

Contact: All Seasons Sports, (360) 538-7033; Big Mouth John's Tackle, (360) 533-0143.

Species available: Resident and sea-run cutthroat trout.

Fishing the South Grays Harbor Streams: Resident cutthroat trout seem capable of living in the darnedest little ponds and ditches, so it should come as no surprise to find them in the many streams that flow out of the hills south of Grays Harbor. The names include Charley, Newskah, Chapin, Indian, Stafford, and O'Leary creeks. All of these creeks have fishable populations of trout, but don't expect any lunkers; a mature fish may measure only nine or 10 inches. Be sure to read the regulations pamphlet before fishing, since stream-fishing rules and limits are very conservative in Washington.

The trout will readily inhale a squirming garden worm, but where there's room to cast and fish them, why not offer up a small Metric, Mepps, or Panther Martin spinner? If you hunger to use your fly rod, try a small wet pattern or nymph and you'll find the cutthroat will oblige.

The fish get bigger in the fall, when the sea-run member of the cutthroat clan invades these streams. That's when you have a real chance of catching a two-fish limit of keepers over 12 inches. Nightcrawlers and small clusters of salmon roe will entice them.

17. JOHNS RIVER

Reference: **Flows into the south side of Grays Harbor at Markham; map B1, grid c6.**

How to get there: Drive southwest out of Aberdeen on State Route 105 for 10 miles and turn east (left) on Johns River Road.

Facilities: A good boat ramp is located near the mouth of the river. Food, lodging, and other amenities are available in Westport and Aberdeen.

Contact: Washington Department of Fish and Wildlife, Montesano Office, (360) 249-4628; All Seasons Sports, (360) 538-7033.

Species available: Winter steelhead, sea-run cutthroat trout.

Fishing the Johns River: The fishing regulations pamphlet lists the Johns as being open for salmon fishing, but for the handful of coho and chums it produces, they might as well not bother. Fishing for winter steelhead is only slightly better, even though the river is planted with hatchery smolts. If you do decide to give it a try during the winter season, you're better off fishing in December or January and looking for greener pastures later in the season.

Hatchery plants of sea-run cutts make the Johns a pretty good bet in the fall, and there are some fairly good walk-in spots on the middle and upper river that should produce trout in October. The boat ramp at the mouth of the river makes trolling for cutthroats a good possibility as well. Use your favorite small wobbling plugs or trout spoons, especially a size 960 Triple Teazer. If that fails, catch a couple of small sculpins and cut strips off their sides, then fish the sculpin strips on a short leader behind a single or double-blade spinner. Cutthroats are located throughout the Johns River estuary. Remember that regulations allow you to keep only fin-clipped hatchery cutthroats.

18. WESTPORT INSHORE

Reference: **South entrance to Grays Harbor; map B1, grid c5.**
How to get there: Take State Route 105 west from Aberdeen for 18 miles and turn north (right) at the "Y" as you approach the coast.
Facilities: A boat ramp, public rest rooms, food, lodging, gas, bait, and tackle all are available in and around Westport.
Contact: The Hungry Whale, (360) 268-0136; Westport/Grayland Chamber of Commerce, (800) 345-6223. For nautical charts of this area, contact Captain's Nautical Supply, (206) 283-7242.
Species available: Lingcod, rockfish, cabezon, redtail surfperch, pile perch, greenling, sole, flounder, chinook and coho salmon, Dungeness crab.
Fishing the Inshore Waters around Westport: The vast South Jetty and the half-dozen shorter "finger jetties" that protect the Westport boat harbor offer a wealth of angling opportunities for the more adventurous rock-hopper, but there's also good fishing available to more restrained anglers on the long fishing pier near the north end of the boat harbor. Black rockfish provide excellent angling at all of these locations during the spring and early summer. With a small boat, you can fish these spots even more effectively, and get to other piers and bulkheads that shore-bound anglers can't reach. Fish quarter-ounce to three-quarter-ounce leadheads with two- or three-inch plastic curl-tail grubs for best results on rockfish; they seem to shy away from the bigger lures that some anglers use.

Early spring provides a good chance to do battle with big, toothy lingcod on the South Jetty and finger jetties. Fish leadheads with large, dark-colored plastic grubs for lings, or offer them a living snack in the form of a lip-hooked greenling, sole, or shiner perch. Lings to 20 pounds have been caught off the rocks here, and much larger ones have broken off to fight again.

The jetties and fishing pier also offer lots of smaller species that are just as good to eat as the big guys. Kelp greenling are abundant and will take almost any small bait or lure you might offer them. Cabezon will take shrimp or small crabs, and you might catch starry flounder and other flatfish species on just about any bait you offer.

Pile perch and redtail surfperch are popular with coastal anglers, and both are available in good numbers here. The pile perch population could use a little more fishing pressure, since many of the docks and piers around the boat harbor are inaccessible by land and can be reached only by boat anglers. Surfperch fishing is best in Half Moon Bay, the sandy beach on the northwest side of the peninsula on which Westport rests. The west side of the peninsula, on the ocean beach, is also a good place to fish for redtails.

Jetty fishing for salmon can be productive and is a specialized sport worth mentioning. Most commonly practiced near the end of the South Jetty, it involves the use of a whole or plug-cut herring on a standard, two-hook mooching leader with a spin sinker four to six feet above the bait. A large float made of wood or foam slides up and down the line above the sinker, with a bobber stop on the line wherever it needs to be to allow the angler to fish the proper depth. Some years (when salmon season is open along the coast) this rig accounts for good catches of both chinook and coho salmon.

A more dependable salmon fishery in recent years has taken place inside the Westport boat harbor. A successful net-pen project has resulted in large numbers of coho returning to the Westport docks, where anglers cast Buzz Bombs, spinners, and wobbling plugs for them. The fishing can be hot at times during September and October, but some so-called anglers have turned this fishery into somewhat of a snag-fest.

Catch Dungeness crab with a rod and reel by casting a small tangle of line with a piece of fish tied into it. The crabs take the bait, become entangled, and you have 'em!

19. WESTPORT OFFSHORE

Reference: **South entrance to Grays Harbor; map B1, grid c5.**
How to get there: Take State Route 105 west from Aberdeen for 18 miles and turn north (right) at the "Y" as you approach the coast.
Facilities: Charters, restaurants, motels, RV parks, watering holes, and anything else you might need are available within walking distance of the boat harbor.
Contact: Westport Charters, (800) 562-0157; Washington Charters, (800) 562-0173; Westport/Grayland Chamber of Commerce, (800) 345-6223. For nautical charts of this area, contact Captain's Nautical Supply, (206) 283-7242.
Species available: Chinook and coho salmon, albacore tuna, lingcod, halibut, black rockfish and several other varieties of rockfish.
Fishing the Pacific Ocean out of Westport: The area commonly referred to as the Salmon Capital of the World in the 1960s and 1970s just may be a better place to fish now than it was then. There's plenty of room to park, it's easy to find a spot on a charter boat, and anglers have a better opportunity to explore the vast fishing variety available along the eastern edge of the Pacific Ocean. Yes, those wonderful days of wide-open coastal salmon fishing are gone forever, but now there's an opportunity to fish for lingcod, black rockfish, halibut, even albacore when the salmon seasons are closed. These fish

were for the most part overlooked back in the hey-days when the salmon were biting like crazy.

Some charter offices run bottomfish trips virtually year-round, concentrating mostly on black rockfish and lingcod during the winter and spring. Weather sometimes causes trip cancellations, but if the water is relatively flat, even in January or February, anglers stand to catch some husky lingcod this time of year. Halibut seasons have been very restrictive on the coast in recent years, but when they occur the Westport fleet has little trouble getting its charter anglers into fish, most of them caught from halibut grounds to the north.

There really isn't too much to say about the Westport salmon fishery that hasn't already been said hundreds of times before, except to note that when the season is open and the kings and silvers are biting, no better fishing can be found anywhere. It might be the excitement generated when four or five people on the same boat are playing fish at once, multiplying the thrill not only for those involved, but for all the others onboard, each knowing that he or she is going to be the next to hook-up.

Albacore tuna pass by the Northwest coast every summer, but not always within range of the Westport charter fleet. Those years when they do get close enough, they provide from a few days to several weeks of red-hot angling action. August is the most likely month for this long-fin tuna madness, but it could start as early as July and some years lasts well into September. These 15- to 30-pound fish are as fast and tough as they come, and excellent table fare as well. Just as in bottomfish and salmon trips, all tackle is included in the price of an albacore trip.

With the exception of albacore and those trips north for halibut, anglers with their own boats can get in on much of Westport's offshore angling action. Larger, seaworthy boats equipped with all the necessary electronic and safety equipment are recommended, not only because this is open-water fishing in every regard, but because the sometimes-rough bar at the entrance to Grays Harbor can become as rough and unpredictable as any water you'd ever want to run. Westport has a roomy boat ramp with plenty of parking space for those boat-owners who know what they're doing.

20. ELK RIVER

Reference: **Flows into Grays Harbor's South Bay near Bay City; map B1, grid c6.**

How to get there: **Drive southwest out of Aberdeen on State Route 105 and turn east (left) on Johns River Road. After two miles, there will be a "Y" in the road. Turn right (west) and drive for about one mile to the Elk River.**

Facilities: **The nearest food, gas, motels, tackle, and other amenities are in Westport and Aberdeen.**

Contact: **Washington Department of Fish and Wildlife, Montesano Office, (360) 249-2648; All Seasons Sports, (360) 538-7033.**

Species available: **Winter steelhead, sea-run cutthroat, seaperch, various sole and flounder.**

Fishing the Elk River: This is another stream where an open salmon season provides virtually no angling action. Annual steelhead plants produce a few fish in December and January, but certainly not enough to generate much excitement. Sea-run cutthroat smolts are also stocked, and fishing for them is fair from September to November. Check the fishing pamphlet for details on wild-cutthroat-release rules. In spring and summer, fish around the highway bridge at the mouth of the river for striped seaperch and pile perch, which may be abundant on an incoming tide. Starry flounder and various species of sole are also possibilities if you let your bait sink to the bottom.

21. SOUTH BEACH SURF

Reference: **Coastal beach from Westport south to Cape Shoalwater, northern entrance to Willapa Bay; map B1, grid c5.**

How to get there: Take State Route 105 southwest from Aberdeen for 25 miles or northwest from Raymond for 17 miles and turn west at any of the well-marked beach-access roads.

Facilities: Twin Harbors State Park to the north and Grayland Beach State Park to the south have tent spaces, RV hookups, and rest rooms with showers; other facilities are available in Westport and Tokeland.

Contact: Twin Harbors State Park, (360) 265-9565; or Grayland Beach State Park, (360) 268-9717.

Species available: Redtail surfperch.

Fishing the South Beach Surf: Several roads lead off the highway toward the beach, and any of them may lead to productive perch fishing. Although the best fishing usually occurs on the incoming tide, arriving early to check out the beach is a good idea. Look for deep ruts, humps, and lagoons that will draw fish as they move in with the tide. Pieces of razor clam neck make good bait, and if the clam season isn't open, you may be able to buy bait at local grocery and bait shops. If a particular spot doesn't produce right away, be patient. Take a coffee break and keep casting until the perch find you.

22. NORTH RIVER

Reference: **Enters Willapa Bay east of Tokeland; map B1, grid c6.**

How to get there: Take U.S. 101 south from Aberdeen or north from Raymond and turn east at Artic on North River Road to reach the upper river. Turn west off U.S. 101 onto Lund Road and follow it downriver to American Mill Road to explore lower portions of the river. To fish the two miles of river at the mouth, take State Route 105 west from Raymond and turn north (left) near the west end of the highway bridge to the access area and boat ramp.

Facilities: A good boat ramp is located at the mouth of the river, right off State Route 105. Artic has a store and a tavern, and other facilities are available in Raymond and Aberdeen.

Contact: Balcombe's Reel and Rod Service, (360) 249-6282; Washington Department of Fish and Wildlife, Montesano Office, (360) 249-4628.

Species available: Winter steelhead, coho salmon, sea-run cutthroat trout.

Fishing the North River: This small river in the heart of Washington's timber country gets little publicity and is fished mostly by locals who would just as soon keep the river a secret. It's not so much that the river offers red-hot salmon, trout, or steelhead fishing; folks around here just aren't all that wild about outsiders stomping up and down their favorite rivers.

The North has been known to give up 200 to 300 fish a winter, the bulk of them in January. December and February offer fair steelheading as well. Lots of logs and stream-side brush make this a challenging place to play and land an angry winter steelhead. I wouldn't make a special trip here for salmon, but anglers who time it right in October may find some bright silvers in the lower river. By November these fish are scattered throughout the river, where they provide spotty action. Sea-run cutthroat fishing is good in October, especially on the lower river. The North is stocked with hatchery sea-run cutts, but it's okay to keep wild trout, too, as long as they're at least 14 inches long.

23. SMITH CREEK

Reference: **Flows into the north end of Willapa Bay northwest of Raymond; map B1, grid c6.**

How to get there: Take U.S. 101 north from Raymond for five miles or south from Aberdeen for 18 miles and turn east on Smith Creek Road to reach about 12 miles of the creek between the highway and the small town of Brooklyn. Turn west off U.S. 101 on Dixon Road to reach part of the lower section of the creek. To fish the waters near the creek mouth, drive west from Raymond on State Route 105 for eight miles and turn right into the boat ramp and access area just across the Smith Creek bridge.

Facilities: A good boat ramp is located at the mouth of the creek. Other amenities are available in Raymond.

Contact: Washington Department of Fish and Wildlife, Montesano Office, (360) 249-4628.

Species available: Winter steelhead, coho salmon, sea-run cutthroat trout.

Fishing Smith Creek: For its size, this little Willapa Bay tributary receives a pretty generous helping of hatchery steelhead smolts, helping to provide a fair fishery from December through February. Department of Fish and Wildlife records show that anglers catch 60 or 70 winter steelhead here every year. Anglers willing to get off the back roads and do some exploring on foot along the middle and lower sections of the creek are often rewarded for their efforts. Salmon fishing is fair for adult and jack coho on the lower portion of the creek in October, and there are also fair numbers of sea-run cutthroats in the creek at that time. All cuts in Smith Creek are wild, but it's okay to keep a couple of them each day, as long as they're at least 14 inches long.

24. WILLAPA RIVER

Reference: **Enters the northeast corner of Willapa Bay near South Bend; map B1, grid d7.**

How to get there: Take U.S. 101 to Raymond and turn east on Willapa Road at the north end of the highway bridge just north of town to reach some of the boat-fishing areas at the lower end of the river. To reach upstream sections of the Willapa, take State Route 6 east from Raymond for six miles or west from Chehalis for 22 miles.

Facilities: There's a boat ramp near the river mouth, at the west end of South Bend, and another at Old Willapa, on Willapa Road about 3.5 miles upstream from the U.S. 101 bridge. A fair selection of restaurants and some lodging, along with tackle, gas, and grocery stores, are available in Raymond and South Bend.

Contact: Big Mouth John's Tackle, (360) 533-0143; Washington Department of Fish and Wildlife, Montesano Office, (360) 249-4628.

Species available: Winter steelhead, chinook and coho salmon, sea-run cutthroat trout.

Fishing the Willapa River: This is arguably the best steelhead river among all Willapa Bay tributaries, and it's no slouch as a salmon river, either. The river is stocked with about 50,000 winter steelhead smolts every year, and anglers catch anywhere from 500 to 1,000 adult Willapa steelhead each winter. Hatchery fish, as most steelheaders know, return earlier in the winter, and the rule holds true here. December and January are the top months, but don't give up completely in February and March. Leave your drift boat home when you visit the Willapa during the winter, since you can't fish from the boat on most of the best steelhead water from November through March.

The lower few miles of the Willapa produce good numbers of chinook salmon in September and October, especially for boat anglers who launch at the Old Willapa launch area near the mouth of Ward Creek. Many of them try to time their trips so that they launch at high tide and fish as the tide ebbs. Flash Glo spinners are favorites of many of these anglers, but back-bouncing with roe clusters or back-trolling with Kwikfish or diver-and-roe combinations also works. The catch often includes a large percentage of jack chinooks weighing two to five pounds, but 25- to 35-pounders are also possibilities. Coho salmon are scattered through the Willapa from September through December, filling the gap between the height of the chinook fishery and the start of winter steelhead action.

If you need to warm up your arm before the salmon action gets hot, try your luck on Willapa sea-run cutthroats. Anglers start catching them in July, and by the middle of August, you can find them pretty much throughout the river, where they provide excellent fishing through October. If things get too crowded on the lower Willapa, take State Route 6 up to Oxbow Road and cast a nightcrawler, small spinner, or small streamer and wet fly patterns with your favorite fly rod and a sink-tip line.

25. WILLAPA BAY

Reference: **West of Raymond; map B1, grid d5.**

How to get there: The north side of the bay is accessible by State Route 105 from Aberdeen or Raymond, the south end and east side via U.S. 101.

Facilities: Tokeland has a boat ramp and bait shop, as well as motels. If you stay there, eat at the Tokeland Hotel, which has some of the best home cookin' in Pacific County. There's also a boat ramp at the mouth of Smith Creek, one about two miles above the mouth of the Willapa River near South Bend, and another near the mouth of the Palix River at Bay Center.

Contact: Warren's Bait and Tackle, (360) 642-5463. For nautical charts of this area, contact Captain's Nautical Supply, (206) 283-7242.

Species available: Chinook and coho salmon, sturgeon, sea-run cutthroat trout, seaperch and surfperch.

Fishing Willapa Bay: Salmon bound for the Willapa, Naselle, and other river systems all have to pass through Willapa Bay to get home, but anglers have to compete for them with commercial fishermen netters. Depending on the length and timing of the commercial seasons, sport fishing for chinooks can be good here from the time the season opens around the middle of August until late September. Long before the chinooks taper off, the coho move in to take up the slack. Most of the salmon fishing is confined to the waters near the bay entrance, just west of Tokeland. Drift-mooching with whole or plug-cut herring right up near the beach produces most of the kings, some of which top 30 pounds. Most of the silvers are caught farther from shore, usually by trollers.

Sea-run cutthroats are available here throughout much of the year and can be caught by trolling near the shoreline or around any of the islands. The mouths of all rivers and creeks are especially good places to look for them. If Triple Teazers, Dick Nites, Canadian Wonders, and similar spoons don't work, try a strip of sculpin meat behind a spinner, worked just off bottom at a slow troll. Regulations in recent years have allowed anglers to keep only two trout per day from Willapa Bay, and they must be at least 14 inches long.

Willapa Bay in general and the mouths of such major tributaries as the Willapa and Naselle rivers in particular also provide fairly good sturgeon fishing from late winter through the summer months. The sturgeon fishery is primarily a boat fishery.

26. PALIX RIVER

Reference: **Enters the east side of Willapa Bay southwest of South Bend; map B1, grid d6.**

How to get there: Drive south from South Bend on U.S. 101 for 12 miles and take the left just before your cross the Palix River bridge or turn left on South Palix Road about a mile south of the bridge.

Facilities: There's a boat ramp near the river mouth, just south of the U.S. 101 bridge. The nearest major facilities are in South Bend and Raymond, both within 12 to 14 miles.

Contact: Warren's Bait and Tackle, (360) 642-5463.

Species available: Sea-run cutthroat trout, winter steelhead.

Fishing the Palix River: You won't find a heck of a lot going on here except for some fair to good fall cutthroat fishing. Although open for both fall salmon and winter steelhead fishing, you could waste a lot of time fishing for both. September and October are the prime times for cutts, and anglers get them by casting a whole nightcrawler weighted with a sinker just heavy enough to roll it along the bottom.

27. NEMAH RIVER

Reference: **Flows into the east side of Willapa Bay at Nemah; map B1, grid e6.**

How to get there: Drive south from South Bend on U.S. 101 for 18 miles and turn east on North Nemah Road or any of the next three gravel roads to the east, all of which reach upper portions of the Nemah. You can also fish some parts of the river by parking near the highway bridges and walking upstream or downstream.

Facilities: You'll find some necessities at Bay Center, but most facilities are to the north in South Bend and Raymond.

Contact: Warren's Bait and Tackle, (360) 642-5463.

Species available: Winter steelhead; sea-run cutthroat trout; chum, coho and chinook salmon.

Fishing the Nemah River: The busiest time of the year for Nemah River anglers is in October, when larger runs of scrappy chum salmon invade from Willapa Bay. This fishery is hot but short-lived, providing several hundred fish in a few weeks. The three forks of the Nemah also give up a few chinook and coho salmon, most of them also caught in October. Stocked with about 10,000 hatchery steelhead smolts a year, the various forks of the Nemah provide fair winter steelheading from December through February. More like a creek than a river throughout, it's a pretty stream system that's fun to fish even when the action isn't hot, which is most of the time. Cutthroat fishing can be good beginning in August and lasting as late as Thanksgiving or beyond.

28. LONG BEACH PENINSULA SURF

Reference: **Leadbetter Point south to Cape Disappointment; map B1, grid e5.**

How to get there: Take U.S. 101 west to the small town of Seaview and go north on State Route 103. Several roads to the west lead to the beach.

Facilities: Campgrounds, RV parks, motels, tackle, gas, and restaurants are located in Long Beach and Ocean Park.

Contact: Warren's Bait and Tackle, (360) 642-5463.

Species available: Redtail surfperch.

Fishing the Long Beach Peninsula Surf: Perch are as readily available here as they are in beach areas to the north, but fishing pressure is quite light. Fish pieces of clam neck or ghost or sand shrimp on an incoming tide, and remember to fish just beyond the first line of breakers.

If you have time during the low tide before or after you fish, venture across to the east side of the Long Beach Peninsula and the port town of Nahcotta, where you'll find Nahcotta Tidelands Interpretive Center and several acres of public tidelands on Willapa Bay where you can gather oysters and dig clams. That way, even if the fishing is slow, you can still return home with enough fresh seafood for a delicious meal.

29. LONG BEACH PENINSULA LAKES

Reference: **Long Beach Peninsula, from Ocean Park south to Ilwaco; map B1, grid f5.**

How to get there: Take U.S. 101 to the extreme southwest corner of Washington and turn north at Seaview at State Route 103.

Facilities: Loomis Lake has a boat ramp, but most of the other lakes don't. Food, gas, RV and tent sites, tackle, and lodging are readily available on the Long Beach Peninsula. If you're around at dinner time, make reservations at the 42nd Street Cafe in Seaview (great home-cooked meals and fantastic service) or at the Ark Restaurant in Nahcotta (excellent food and a wonderful view of Willapa Bay).

Contact: Warren's Bait and Tackle, (360) 642-5463.

Species available: Rainbow trout, yellow perch, largemouth bass.

Fishing the Long Beach Peninsula Lakes: Loomis Lake, at about 170 acres, is the largest and best-known of the Long Beach lakes, and probably the most productive for anglers. It's stocked with about 7,000 legal-sized rainbows before the April opener and provides good fishing into early summer, even though it's only about 10 feet deep in its deepest spot. Loomis is a good fly-fishing lake, but most anglers troll hardware or stillfish with bait. Though trout fishing is the big draw, the lake also offers some decent-sized perch.

Immediately east of Loomis Lake is Lost Lake, which covers only a couple of acres and produces more perch than anything else. Then comes Island Lake, within walking distance to the south of Lost. Island has a rather rough boat ramp on its east side, where anglers launch car-topper boats and canoes to go after largemouth bass and yellow perch. Like other lakes in the area, it's very shallow, but it produces some largemouths of three pounds and larger. Next come Tape, Cranberry, and Litschke lakes, all under 20 acres and all containing both largemouths and perch. A little farther south are Clam and Gile lakes, at 10 and 18 acres respectively, both containing bass and perch. Gile now and then produces a trophy-class bass. Briscoe, Breaker, Clear, and Tinker lakes, all connected by a small stream, run north to south along the west side of the peninsula, and all offer largemouths and perch.

About three miles south of the rest of the pack, between Seaview and Ilwaco, lies Black Lake, a 30-acre lake that has rainbow trout and black bullheads along with its bass and perch. Black is stocked with several hundred legal-sized rainbows every spring. An excellent fishing dock alongside the road offers a place to park and fish.

Most of these lakes have some kind of public access, but be sure to ask around if you aren't sure. Even the lakes with public access, though, don't necessarily have a good place to launch a boat. While few anglers use them, float tubes would be the perfect way to fish virtually all of these lakes, so if you have one, bring it along next time you head for the Long Beach Peninsula.

30. BEAR RIVER

Reference: **Enters south end of Willapa Bay; map B1, grid f6.**

How to get there: Take U.S. 101 south from South Bend or follow State Route 4 west from Longview to its junction with U.S. 101 and follow it south. The highway crosses over Bear River about six miles northeast of Ilwaco.

Facilities: Food, gas, lodging, tackle, and other amenities are available in Ilwaco.

Contact: Warren's Bait and Tackle, (360) 642-5463.

Species available: Chum salmon, sea-run cutthroat trout, a few coho salmon and winter steelhead.

Fishing the Bear River: A good run of brawling chum salmon disrupts the serenity of this otherwise placid little river at the south end of Willapa Bay. The wildest chum fishing usually occurs in October, but good fishing is a possibility during the first two weeks of November. You might find an occasional coho mixed in with all the chums. Winter steelheading here is a matter of fishing for wild fish, and there aren't many of them. But wild cutthroat runs are fairly healthy, so bring your light spinning rod or favorite fly rod in September to try for them.

---

31. NASELLE RIVER

Reference: **Enters the southeast corner of Willapa Bay; map B1, grid e6.**

How to get there: Take State Route 4 west from Longview to Naselle or drive south from South Bend on U.S. 101, turn southeast on State Route 4, and drive about six miles to Naselle.

Facilities: You'll find food and gas in Naselle, and there's a campground on State Route 4 about three miles east of town. Long Beach has tackle, lodging, and restaurants.

Contact: Warren's Bait and Tackle, (360) 642-5463.

Species available: Winter steelhead; chinook, coho, and chum salmon; sea-run and resident cutthroat trout.

Fishing the Naselle River: It's not a big river, but the Naselle is a consistent producer of good winter steelhead and fall salmon catches. Hatchery-stock steelhead pour into the river throughout the winter, providing the possibility for good fishing from early December until the end of March. Roads upstream and downstream from State Route 4 offer lots of bank-fishing access throughout the winter. Chinook salmon fishing can be excellent for both boat and bank anglers on the lower Naselle in September and early October, and an even bigger run of cohos moves into the river as the chinook fishery wanes. Some large chums join in for added variety and excitement about the same time the silvers arrive. Through it all, sea-run cutts trickle in at a fairly steady pace from August to November.

32. ILWACO OFFSHORE

Reference: Outside the mouth of the Columbia River, southwest of Ilwaco; map B1, grid f5.

How to get there: Take U.S. 101 south about 41 miles from Raymond or take State Route 4 west from Kelso to State Route 401 at Naselle, turn south (left), and follow State Route 14 about 21 miles to Ilwaco.

Facilities: Charters, boat ramps, gas, restaurants, groceries, lodging, and other accommodations are available in Ilwaco. Fort Canby State Park, one of the state's largest campgrounds, is just south of town.

Contact: Pacific Salmon Charters, (360) 642-3466; Fort Canby State Park, (360) 642-3078. For nautical charts of this area, contact Captain's Nautical Supply, (206) 283-7242.

Species available: Chinook and coho salmon, lingcod, rockfish, halibut, albacore tuna.

Fishing Ilwaco Offshore: Like Westport (see page 350), Ilwaco has a long-standing reputation for its excellent salmon fishing. And, also like Westport, the charter and private boat fleet out of Ilwaco has had to find other fish to catch during at least part of the season now that salmon-fishing restrictions have become a way of life along the Northwest coast.

Bottomfish trips fill a big void for Ilwaco-area anglers before the salmon seasons open—and those openers have been very unpredictable lately. Spring trips for lingcod and rockfish produce well, and the catch often includes a few of those big, brightly colored yelloweye rockfish that are as impressive to the veteran saltwater angler as they are to the novice who has never seen one before. Much of the bottomfish activity for the Ilwaco fleet takes place to the south, over several rock pinnacles that lie off the Oregon coast.

As in Westport, the halibut fishing for Ilwaco anglers could be a whole lot better if the season were longer and more liberal, but that's not the way it is. Charters don't have much trouble finding halibut for their customers, but they don't get much opportunity to do it during a season that may last only a few days in July.

If and when the albacore show up within range of the Ilwaco charter fleet, trips are available from mid to late summer. Most are overnight affairs, and the rewards can be impressive. The problem with albacore is that they're not dependable enough to allow much advanced planning, so trips are scheduled on short notice and everyone has to scurry to get in on the action.

Even though salmon seasons have been restrictive in recent years, at least anglers know in advance that they're going to occur, and when the seasons are open, anglers know they can usually catch kings and silvers off the mouth of the Columbia. The only question may be whether the boat will make a 20-minute run or a two-hour run to where the fish are located. That's not a big problem where most anglers are concerned.

I consider charter fishing the safest and easiest way to fish off the mouth of the Columbia, but many anglers fish here in their own boats. If you're thinking about doing so for the first time, do your homework first. Crossing the bar here can be about as tricky and as potentially dangerous as anywhere on the West Coast. Monstrous energy is released when coastal winds and the mighty Columbia collide, and since the river is shallow, there's no place for the water to go but up. Some very good boaters have lost it all here, so don't take chances.

33. COLUMBIA RIVER ESTUARY

Reference: **Mouth of Columbia River near Ilwaco; map B1, grid f5.**

How to get there: Take U.S. 101 south from Raymond for 41 miles or drive west on State Route 4 from Kelso about 56 miles and turn south (left) on State Route 401 to the river.

Facilities: Fort Canby State Park has RV and tent sites, rest rooms with showers, and other amenities. The park also has a large boat ramp and a store with food, beverages, bait, and tackle. Restaurants, motels, gas stations, and watering holes are easy to find in Ilwaco and to the north in Long Beach. Several charter companies work out of Ilwaco.

Contact: Fort Canby State Park, (360) 642-3078; Dave's Shell, (360) 642-2320; Warren's Bait and Tackle, (360) 642-5463. For nautical charts of this area, contact Captain's Nautical Supply, (206) 283-7242.

Species available: Chinook and coho salmon, white sturgeon, green sturgeon, lingcod, rockfish, cabezon, greenling, Dungeness crab.

Fishing the Columbia River Estuary (including the North Jetty): The angling variety available in and around the mouth of the Columbia River is similar to that of Grays Harbor and the Westport area (see page 350), except that sturgeon fishing is a much bigger deal here. Not only do dozens of private boats and hundreds of bank anglers stake out their claims to what they hope will be productive sturgeon water every morning, but a number of charters out of Ilwaco also explore the Columbia estuary for "Ol' Diamond Sides." White sturgeon are more numerous and grow substantially larger than green sturgeon, but anglers catch both species. Now and then someone catches a monster white of nine feet, 10 feet, 12 feet, or even larger, but all of these huge females must be released unharmed. The high point of any sturgeon trip is to see one of these prehistoric behemoths jump completely out of the water, looking and sounding every bit like a Douglas fir log when it crashes back into the river. Some of the best spots to anchor and wait out a big sturgeon are places where the bottom breaks away quickly from shallow to deep water, and it may take some exploring with a depthsounder to find such spots. An easier way for the newcomer is to watch where other boats anchor and pull in nearby (but not too near) to investigate. Smelt, ghost shrimp, and shad (when they're running through the lower river) are among the top sturgeon baits here.

As for salmon, the world-famous "Buoy 10" fishery takes place here—at least it takes place most years. When the season is open and the fishing is good, the waters near the mouth of the Columbia become one of the world's biggest aquatic traffic jams, as boats of all sizes and styles jockey for a crack at incoming kings and silvers. Slow-trolling with herring at the start of an outgoing tide is often the most productive combination, but be willing to do some experimenting.

Anglers also catch their share of salmon right off the North Jetty, a spot that has been known to give up a few kings of 40 pounds and larger. Subduing an angry chinook on those slick, barnacle-encrusted boulders, with the waves crashing at your feet, is no easy chore, but veteran jetty-jumpers can do it. Fishing a whole anchovy or plug-cut herring below a big slip-bobber accounts for most of the salmon.

The North Jetty is also a good place to fish for lingcod, rockfish, greenling, cabezon, and crab, not to mention smaller perch, sole, and flounder. Herring, anchovies, leadhead jigs with plastic grub bodies, even small metal jigs work well here. If you want perch, sole, or flounder, cast pieces of clam, blood worm, or shrimp with a light sinker and fairly small hook.

---

34. GRAYS RIVER

Reference: **Enters the lower Columbia River west of Skamokawa; map B1, grid f8.**

How to get there: Take State Route 4 west from Cathlamet or east from Naselle. To reach much of the middle portion of the river, take Loop Road south off the highway (midway between the little town of Grays River and the highway bridge over the river), or turn south on State Route 403 near Rosburg to reach the lower river.

Facilities: Ilwaco, the nearest town of any size, is about 20 miles to the southeast and offers food, gas, tackle, and lodging. About 30 miles to the west is Fort Canby State Park, which has tent and RV sites, rest rooms with showers, and a small store.

Contact: Warren's Bait and Tackle, (360) 642-5463.

Species available: Winter steelhead, sea-run and resident cutthroat trout, chinook and coho salmon.

Fishing the Grays River: Once a pretty well-respected winter steelhead stream, the Grays has slipped a few notches over the past 10 years or so. Although stocked with 40,000 to 50,000 steelhead smolts a year, the steelhead catch bounces up and down between only 150 and 400 fish a winter. That's probably enough to provide a ray of hope for any visiting angler, but you have to wonder what happened to those other 49,600 smolts, don't you? When the few adult steelhead that survive their oceanic adventure finally make it back to the Grays, most of them show up in December and January, so those are the months to fish here if you entertain any hope of catching steelhead. Fall salmon fishing is a whole lot worse and only open on parts of the river system, so be sure to read the latest copy of the regulations pamphlet before even considering it.

Unless you hit it right for fishing, the high point of a trip to the Grays might be getting an opportunity to gawk at Washington's only remaining covered bridge. Though there weren't many of them to begin with, now there's only one. Maybe that's why no one ever bought the movie rights to "Bridges of Wahkiakum County."

35. SKAMOKAWA CREEK

Reference: **Enters the Columbia River at Skamokawa; map B1, grid f9.**

How to get there: Take State Route 4 to Skamakawa and turn north on Maki Road to follow the creek upstream.

Facilities: There are limited visitor facilities in Skamokawa and Cathlamet.

Contact: Bob's Merchandise, (360) 425-3870.

Species available: Winter steelhead.

Fishing Skamokawa Creek: Here's another stream where several thousand winter steelhead smolts are planted every year but nobody knows what happens to them. Very few have made it back to provide any decent winter steelheading during the past few years. You might get lucky and hook a fish in December or January, but the odds are against you.

---

36. ELOCHOMAN RIVER

Reference: **Joins the Columbia River near Cathlamet; map B1, grid f9.**

How to get there: Take State Route 4 to about a mile west of Cathlamet and turn north on State Route 407.

Facilities: Food and gas are available in Cathlamet.

Contact: Bob's Merchandise, (360) 425-3870.

Species available: Winter and summer steelhead, chinook and coho salmon, sea-run cutthroat trout.

Fishing the Elochoman River: After three hours of driving, fishing partner Dave Borden and I unfolded slowly from the cab of the pickup and strolled to the edge of the muddy parking area for a closer look at the river.

"It's not much, is it?" Dave observed. Going largely by the river's reputation as a steelhead producer, we both expected a bigger stream than the one that purred by so gently a few yards below. But we had driven more than 150 miles, there were no other anglers in sight, and the small pocket of potential steelhead holding water just upstream looked pretty good, so we walked back to the camper for hip boots, rods, and bait boxes.

Dave's a lot smaller and a little quicker than I am, so he was rigged, ready, and standing at the edge of the river several minutes ahead of me. As I made my way down the steep bank toward the water, he reared back on the rod and let out a holler.

"There's one," he said, quite unnecessarily, as a silver-sided buck steelhead of about six pounds rolled violently on the surface for a couple of seconds and then blasted downstream, through a short riffle and into a long stretch of flat water below. Dave followed, I went along for moral support, and a couple minutes later our first steelhead of the day was on the bank.

But it wouldn't be our last. My partner hooked and lost another steelhead on his next cast into that little pocket of slick water before turning it over to me for a few casts. I pulled out a mint-bright nine-pounder, told Dave to take another shot, and darned if he didn't hook and land another fish that was a near dead-ringer to his first. Seven hours later, after exploring a few miles of river upstream and returning to finish the day where we had started, our tally was 10 hatchery steelhead hooked, seven landed, and four killed for the table, and I felt that I had found the place I had been looking for all my life.

As it turned out, we had simply timed our first visit to the Elochoman perfectly. A couple of hours of rain the evening before had raised the river a few inches, attracting a fresh run of bright steelhead in from the Columbia, and since it was the middle of the week and most normal people were working, Dave and I had several stretches of the small stream pretty much to ourselves. By the next day the river had dropped back down to normal flow and below, and a full day of fishing produced only two fish.

But we had seen enough to know that southwest Washington's Elochoman can be red-hot when conditions are right, and that very first trip to this little river with the big name was enough to convert me and my long-time fishing partner into confirmed Elochoman addicts. We're not alone in that regard. During the peak of the winter steelhead season, finding elbow room along the banks of this small steelie producer is a tough proposition, especially on a weekend. Word has gotten out, and some of the more productive and popular stretches of river draw plenty of angler interest.

Despite its small size, the Elochoman regularly ranks among the state's top winter steelhead producers. During the 1993-94 season, it gave up just over 1,600 winter steelies, pretty much an average year, but some years it has been known to produce more than 6,000 steelhead in a single winter. The vast majority of those thousands of winter-run steelhead caught by Elochoman River anglers have been hatchery fish. The Beaver Creek Hatchery, operated by the Washington Department of Fish and Wildlife about six miles upstream from the river mouth, releases about 100,000 winter steelhead smolts a year into the river, and it's the adult fish returning to the hatchery a couple of years after their release that provide a bulk of the Elochoman's winter steelhead action. Because hatchery steelhead tend to return early in the winter season, December and January are the best months to fish the Elochoman.

This tiny river also provides worthwhile summer steelheading, producing 200 to 300 fish each year during the warm months from June to September. June, when the river is still running fairly high, is the top month for summer-runs, but July also can be worthwhile. By August and September the river is so low and clear that out-smarting one of these spooky, ocean-run rainbows becomes a real challenge.

As on many western Washington streams, fall means salmon and sea-run cutthroat fishing on the Elochoman. Anglers should check the regulations, especially where chinook salmon are concerned, but October and November coho fishing can be quite productive.

The Department of Fish and Wildlife stocks 30,000 to 40,000 sea-run cutthroat smolts in the Elochoman every year, helping to provide excellent fall trout fishing. This is one of those streams where anglers may keep only hatchery (fin-clipped) cutthroat.

Spring-run chinooks provide fantastic action for anglers along many Olympic Peninsula and lower Columbia River tributaries.

MAP B2

WASHINGTON MAP .... see page 5
Adjoining Maps
NORTH (map A2) .... see page 100
EAST (map B3) .... see page 432
SOUTH .... no map
WEST (map B1) .... see page 338

97 Listings
PAGES 366-431

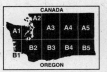

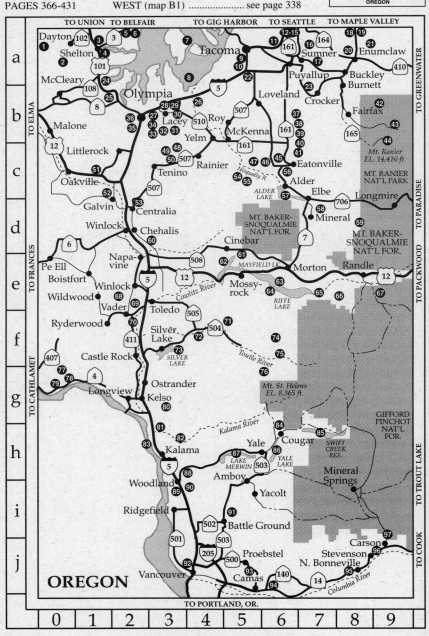

Map Section B2 features:

1. Lake Nahwatzel
2. Lost Lake
3. Island Lake
4. Lake Isabella
5. Spencer Lake
6. Phillips Lake
7. Bay Lake
8. South Puget Sound
9. Steilacoom Lake
10. American Lake
11. Puyallup River
12. Lake Killarney
13. Lake Geneva
14. Five Mile Lake
15. Trout Lake
16. White River
17. Lake Tapps
18. Fish Lake
19. Deep Lake
20. Bass Lake
21. Walker Lake
22. Spanaway Lake
23. Carbon River
24. Kennedy Creek
25. Summit Lake
26. Nisqually River
27. Chambers Lake
28. Hicks Lake
29. Long Lake
30. Lake St. Clair
31. Pattison (Patterson) Lake
32. Ward Lake
33. Munn Lake
34. Deschutes River
35. Black Lake
36. Capitol Lake
37. Kapowsin Lake
38. Whitman Lake
39. Tanwax Lake
40. Clear Lake
41. Ohop Lake
42. Coplay Lake/Clearwater Wilderness Lakes
43. Carbon Glacier Lakes
44. Mowich Lake
45. Rapjohn Lake
46. Silver Lake
47. Harts Lake
48. Offut Lake
49. Deep Lake
50. McIntosh Lake
51. Black River
52. Upper Chehalis River
53. Skookumchuck River
54. Lawrence Lake
55. Clear Lake
56. Mashel River
57. Alder Lake
58. Mineral Lake
59. Skate Creek
60. Newaukum River
61. Tilton River
62. Mayfield Lake
63. Riffe Lake
64. Swofford Pond
65. Lake Scanewa
66. Cispus River
67. Yellowjacket Ponds
68. Olequa Creek
69. Lacamas Creek
70. Cowlitz River
71. Green River
72. Toutle River
73. Silver Lake
74. Upper Green River Lakes
75. Coldwater Lake
76. Castle Lake
77. Abernathy Creek
78. Germany Creek
79. Mill Creek
80. Coweeman River
81. Kress Lake
82. Kalama River
83. Lower Columbia River
84. Merrill Lake
85. Swift Creek Reservoir
86. Yale Lake (Reservoir)
87. Lake Merwin
88. North Fork Lewis River
89. Horseshoe Lake

90. East Fork Lewis River
91. Battle Ground Lake
92. Vancouver Lake
93. Lacamas Lake

94. Washougal River
95. Hamilton Creek
96. Rock Creek
97. Wind River

1. LAKE NAHWATZEL

Reference: **Northwest of Shelton; map B2, grid a0.**

How to get there: Take U.S. 101 to Shelton and turn west on Shelton-Matlock Road, following it about 11 miles to the lake, which is on the north (right) side of the road.

Facilities: Lake Nahwatzel Resort has two cabins and a trailer for rent, plus RV sites, a restaurant and bar, and bait. A Department of Fish and Wildlife boat ramp with an access area is located near the resort. Other facilities are in Shelton.

Contact: Lake Nahwatzel Resort, (360) 426-3823.

Species available: Rainbow trout, largemouth bass.

Fishing Lake Nahwatzel: This large, 270-acre lake provides good trout fishing from spring to fall and worthwhile opportunities for bass in the summer. The rainbows, mostly nine- and 10-inchers from spring plants, are caught by both trolling and stillfishing in April and May, but by June stillfishing may be the better bet, especially around the 25-foot hole near the northwest side of the lake. Bass are found pretty much all around the lake's shoreline.

2. LOST LAKE

Reference: **Southwest of Shelton; map B2, grid a0.**

How to get there: Take Lost Lake Road west off U.S. 101 near Shelton and drive about 8.5 miles to the sign pointing to the lake. Turn north (right) and drive about a mile to the lake.

Facilities: A boat ramp and rest rooms can be found at the access. Food, gas, tackle, and lodging are available in Shelton.

Contact: Verle's Sport Center, (360) 426-0933.

Species available: Rainbow trout, brown bullhead catfish.

Fishing Lost Lake: A liberal dose of hatchery rainbows helps to keep fishing interesting on this 120-acre Mason County lake. The Department of Fish and Wildlife stocks about 5,000 legal-sized trout here each spring, and they provide decent action into the summer months. Lost is much like two lakes in one, connected by a narrow neck in the middle. The north end is quite deep—much of it over 50 feet—while the southern half is only 10 to 20 feet deep and features a large island. The entire lake offers fair to good trout fishing in April and May, but by mid-summer you're better off fishing the cooler waters of the north half. Conversely, if you want to try your hand at night-time catfishing, you should concentrate most of your efforts at the lower end of the lake.

3. ISLAND LAKE

Reference: **North of Shelton; map B2, grid a1.**

How to get there: Follow U.S. 101 north about two miles past Shelton and turn east (right) on Shelton Springs Road, also known as the Dayton Cutoff. Drive one mile to Island Lake Road, turn left, and the road circles Island Lake.

Facilities: A Department of Fish and Wildlife boat ramp is located on the west end of the lake. Groceries and gasoline are available at the intersection of U.S. 101 and Shelton Springs Road. All other amenities are available in Shelton.

Contact: Verle's Sport Center, (360) 426-0933.

Species available: Rainbow trout, largemouth and smallmouth bass, yellow perch, brown bullhead catfish, pumpkinseed sunfish.

Fishing Island Lake: Legal-sized rainbows are stocked in this lake every spring, providing good action until about mid-June, when trout fishing gives way to some very good warm-water fishing. Although I've caught trout here by stillfishing a bobber-and-worm rig around the south end of the small island near the center of the lake, trollers seem to score more consistently. Many of them use worms behind a string of trolling blades, but those fishing lighter with Dick Nites, Triple Teazers, Flatfish, Kwikfish, and Rooster Tails also make some good catches.

Perhaps Island Lake's biggest claim to fame is that it's one of very few western Washington lakes with a fishable population of smallmouth bass. Some are caught from the rocky areas around the island, but the shallow flats along the lake's northeastern shoreline may be the best places to fish for them. If you keep your eyes open, you may spot them feeding in the clear, shallow water, but seeing them is one thing, catching them quite another. The water's clarity makes for wary bass, so cast well ahead as you work your way along the shoreline and move as quietly and carefully as possible. Just to get you enthused, I'll warn you that I have seen smallmouth bass of perhaps five pounds in this lake.

Because Island Lake is so clear and its bass so wary, many bass anglers prefer to fish it at night. The docks and floats along the northern shoreline produce both largemouths and smallmouths for night-time anglers, and the brushy areas at the extreme south end of the lake and along the western side may also produce bass at night.

If you're looking for perch or brown bullheads, concentrate your efforts around the south end of the lake.

4. LAKE ISABELLA

Reference: **South of Shelton; map B2, grid a1.**

How to get there: Turn west off U.S. 101 onto Delight Park Road, just south of Shelton (the Golden Pheasant Tavern is the landmark to look for), drive a mile, and watch for the "Public Fishing" sign on the right.

Facilities: The south side of the lake has a public access area with a boat ramp. Other amenities are available in Shelton and Olympia.

Contact: Verle's Sport Center, (360) 426-0933.

Species available: Rainbow trout, largemouth bass, black bullhead catfish.

Fishing Lake Isabella: Open year-round, Isabella is a decent bet for 10- to 12-inch rainbows almost any time. Don't depend on it for hot "opening day" fishing in late April; because of its year-round season, the lake isn't always stocked with legal-sized catchables during the spring. Troll with all the standard trout-getters, or if you're the patient type, anchor somewhere around the edge of the lake and stillfish with a marshmallow or Power Bait on a slip-sinker rig. In the summer, when this relatively shallow lake warms up, concentrate your stillfishing efforts in the 22- to 25-foot "hole" located about two-thirds of the way up toward the north end of the lake.

Summer is bass-fishing time here, and the many docks that line the shore offer good chances for a decent largemouth. Pitching plastic worms, lizards, or tube baits around and under the docks will eventually pay off.

5. SPENCER LAKE

Reference: **Northeast of Shelton; map B2, grid a2.**

How to get there: Take State Route 3 northeast from Shelton about 10 miles and turn east (right) on Pickering Road, then right on Spencer Lake Road.

Facilities: The west side of the lake has a public access area and boat ramp. Other amenities can be found in Shelton.

Contact: Verle's Sport Center, (360) 426-0933.

Species available: Rainbow trout, largemouth bass.

Fishing Spencer Lake: With a long tradition of being one of Mason County's top opening-day trout producers, this 230-acre lake north of Shelton continues to provide excellent catches of rainbows now that it's open year-round. Stocked with legal-sized trout in the spring, some of them weighing more than a pound apiece, Spencer is a worthwhile bet right on through much of the summer. Its deep water—with spots more than 35 feet deep near the southeast corner of the lake—remains cool and keeps the trout active. This deep area is a good spot for summertime stillfishing with a slip-sinker rig and a marshmallow or Power Bait combination of some kind.

As for bass, the lake is gaining a reputation for producing some husky ones. Largemouths of five pounds and better are possible, and there are also good numbers of smaller fish to keep you busy as you cast for something in the trophy range. The large, shallow bays at the east end and the north side of the lake are good places to start casting.

6. PHILLIPS LAKE

Reference: **Northeast of Shelton; map B2, grid a2.**

How to get there: Take State Route 3 northeast from Shelton for about 10 miles and turn east (right) on Pickering Road. Drive about two miles (past Spencer Lake), turn south (right) on Phillips Lake Loop, and follow it about a mile to the lake.

Facilities: The lake has a Department of Fish and Wildlife boat ramp and access area. Food, gas, tackle, and lodging are available in Shelton.

Contact: Verle's Sport Center, (360) 426-0933.

Species available: Rainbow and cutthroat trout.

Fishing Phillips Lake: This is another of several Mason County lakes where a year-round fishing season is a fairly new change in the regulations. Spring-planted rainbows average about nine inches in May but grow quickly to 12 inches or so by fall. There's a fairly good carryover of trout through the winter, which means early spring fishing might also produce a 14- to 16-inch rainbow for you. Planted cutthroats are larger, weighing about a pound each when they're stocked.

Both rainbows and cutts are caught on all the standard trolling rigs and on worms fished a few feet below a bobber. Salmon eggs, cheese baits, Power Bait, and marshmallows will take rainbows but few, if any, cutthroats.

7. BAY LAKE

Reference: **Longbranch Peninsula; map B2, grid a3.**
How to get there: Take State Route 302 southwest from Purdy to Lakebay. Cross the bridge, drive up the hill about 100 yards, and turn left at the sign pointing to Penrose Point State Park. Wind up and over the hill and turn right at the "T" intersection. The lake's public access area is on the right, about half a mile from the "T."
Facilities: The large, gravel access area has a boat ramp and rest rooms. Penrose Point State Park has tent sites for camping. Food, gas, tackle, and lodging can be found in and around Lakebay.
Contact: Penrose Point State Park, (360) 884-2514.
Species available: Rainbow trout.
Fishing Bay Lake: Spring plants of hatchery rainbows provide pretty good fishing for the first few weeks of the season, but by mid-summer things are just about done for at Bay Lake. Although, at 115 acres, it's a fairly large lake, it's also extremely shallow, so the 6,000 or so rainbows planted annually get caught in a hurry. The shallow waters also heat up quickly with the summer sun, becoming too warm for good trout fishing by mid-June most years. The moral here, of course, is to fish Bay Lake soon after it opens to fishing in late April.

8. SOUTH PUGET SOUND

Reference: **Marine waters from the Tacoma Narrows south to Olympia and Shelton; map B2, grid a4.**
How to get there: Launch at Narrows Marina (off 19th Street in Tacoma, just south of the Narrows Bridge), Wollochet (off Point Fosdick Drive, south of Gig Harbor), Steilacoom (off Commercial Street, near the McNeil Island ferry landing), Luhr's Beach (off 46th Avenue, on the west end of Nisqually Flats), Zittel's Marina (off 92nd Avenue NE, north of Olympia), Boston Harbor (off 73rd Avenue NE, north of Olympia), or East Bay Marina (off Marine Drive, north end of Olympia).
Facilities: Narrows Marina has bait, fuel, and one of the most complete tackle shops in western Washington, and most of the other marinas have everything an angler might need. Exceptions are Wollochet and Luhr's Beach, which have no amenities at all.

Contact: Narrows Marina, (206) 564-4222; Point Defiance Boat House, (206) 591-5325; Zittel's Marina, (360) 459-1950. For nautical charts of this area, contact Captain's Nautical Supply, (206) 283-7242.

Species available: Chinook, coho, and chum salmon; lingcod; rockfish; sole; flounder; seaperch.

Fishing South Puget Sound: The south end of Puget Sound has been a real roller-coaster ride for salmon anglers in recent years, providing good fishing for a time and then going dead for months, even years. The good news is that salmon action has been on a sharp upswing since 1993, especially for chinooks.

The most popular year-round salmon fishing spot in south Puget Sound is Lyle Point, at the south end of Anderson Island. Located about two miles northeast of the Luhr's Beach boat ramp, it's an especially good spot for resident chinooks, known to most of us as blackmouth. On an ebb tide, try starting your drift in about 10 fathoms of water off Thompson Cove, drifting southeast out to about 30 fathoms, always checking the depthsounder for signs of baitfish. On the flood tide, start in 25 or 30 fathoms of water just east of the buoy and drift in toward Thompson Cove. While these are good general guidelines, the productive fishing pattern can change quickly, so be on your toes and watch where and how other anglers are fishing. The shoreline to the immediate east of Lyle Point can be good for coho as well. Try trolling or drifting small, plug-cut herring or casting wobbling spoons or small, baitfish-imitating plugs toward the shoreline and retrieving it at a fast clip. Johnson Point is another popular south-sound salmon spot, especially for blackmouth. It's best fished on an ebb tide, and most chinook are caught from eight to 15 fathoms.

Point Gibson, at the south tip of Fox Island, is another popular fishing spot among south Puget Sound blackmouth anglers. It's good on the ebb tide and is an excellent mooching spot. Fish in 15 to 30 fathoms of water here.

Other traditionally productive spots worth investigating by south-sound salmon anglers include Dugall Point (at the north end of Hartstene Island), the northeast corner of McMicken Island, Cooper Point (where Eld and Budd Inlets converge), the South Bay Light (southwest of John Point, near the entrance to Henderson Inlet), Devil's Head (south end of the Key Peninsula), Eagle Island (between Anderson and McNeil islands), Nearns Point (at the north end of Fox Island) the entrance to Wollochet Bay, and Point Evans (just north of the Narrows Bridge on the west side of the Narrows). During the summer of 1995, the waters around the "Green Buoy" near the mouth of the Nisqually turned into a real hot spot for summertime kings, and that action could be repeated.

I won't make any friends with this disclosure, but there's at least one productive bank-fishing spot for salmon in southern Puget Sound. Well, it's not really bank-fishing; a more accurate description would be bridge-fishing. The Steamboat Island Bridge, which connects Steamboat Island with the tip of the mainland at the confluence of Totten Inlet with Squaxin Passage, can be a productive fishing spot for chinook salmon in the spring and summer and for adult coho and chum salmon from September through November.

Most anglers fish Blue Fox spinners or Buzz Bombs here, casting off the west side of the bridge as the tide begins to ebb.

The opportunities for catching bottomfish aren't as great in southern Puget Sound as they are in other marine areas of the Northwest. Much of the bottom is sand, mud, and gravel, so lingcod, rockfish, and other rock-dwelling species are hard to find. Exceptions include the waters immediately below the Narrows Bridge, where the skeletal remains of its predecessor lie in a tangled heap, providing good habitat for lingcod and rockfish. Fish it only on a slack tide or you'll be snagged on the bottom constantly, and remember that the lingcod season in this area is open only for about six weeks in May and early June. Other spots worth fishing for springtime lings and rockfish throughout the year are the artificial reefs at Toliva Shoal and Itsami Ledge. The Toliva Shoal Reef is south of Point Gibson, 1,300 feet northwest of the Toliva Shoal navigational buoy and 2.4 miles from the Steilacoom boat ramp. The Itsami Ledge Reef, near Olympia, is southwest of Johnson Point, 1,100 feet northwest of the South Bay Light. The nearest boat ramp is at Zittel's Marina, 2.4 miles away.

If you want sole and flounder, you'll have little trouble finding them in southern Puget Sound. Virtually every sandy-bottom bay has lots of them, and all you need to catch them is a supply of garden worms and a few small sinkers. The Nisqually River estuary is home to a fairly good summertime population of starry flounder, and you'll also find these large flatfish near the south end of Budd Inlet, where the Deschutes River empties into the south end of Puget Sound.

Pile perch and striped seaperch are an overlooked resource in southern Puget Sound. They're available around docks, piers, and pilings from Tacoma to Shelton, and are best fished as the incoming tide first reaches these structures.

One of the mainstays of the south-sound sport fishery has long been the sea-run cutthroat trout. Even though it's not as common as it once was and more restrictive regulations are now in effect, the sea-run is still a popular fish here. You can catch them from Point Evans to the mouth of Kennedy Creek, and the best fishing is right up next to the beach during an evening high tide.

9. STEILACOOM LAKE

Reference: **In Lakewood, southwest Tacoma; map B2, grid a5.**
How to get there: Take Exit 127 off Interstate 5, drive north of South Tacoma Way, and turn west on Steilacoom Boulevard, following it about three miles to the north end of the lake, on the left.
Facilities: The north end of the lake has a boat ramp. Food, gas, lodging, and tackle are available throughout the area.
Contact: Washington Department of Fish and Wildlife, (206) 775-6211.
Species available: Largemouth bass, rock bass, brown bullhead catfish.
Fishing Steilacoom Lake: This large, shallow lake is well-suited to the needs of largemouth bass, and it grows some hefty ones. With more than 300 acres to explore, you'll never run out of places to cast. If you fish "small," with

two- or three-inch plastic grubs, quarter-ounce crankbaits, or little spinnerbaits, you might catch an occasional rock bass as you cast around the edges of the lake. Good catfish action can be had by fishing nightcrawlers, chicken livers, or various stinkbaits at night. Steilacoom Lake is open year-round, but the hottest fishing is in the spring and early summer, with some good bass catches possible into the fall.

10. AMERICAN LAKE

Reference: **Southwest of Tacoma; map B2, grid a5.**

How to get there: Take Exit 122 off Interstate 5 just south of Tacoma and head west, across the tracks, on Berkley Street. Drive half a mile to the "T" and turn right on Portland Avenue SW, following it four blocks to the lake, which is on the left.

Facilities: Bill's Boat House has a fishing dock, boat rentals, snacks and beverages, tackle, and rest rooms. The lake also has a Department of Fish and Wildlife boat ramp and access area. Gas and lodging are only a few blocks away, along Interstate 5.

Contact: Bill's Boat House, (206) 588-2594.

Species available: Rainbow and cutthroat trout, landlocked steelhead, kokanee, smallmouth bass, yellow perch, rock bass, brown bullhead catfish.

Fishing American Lake: One of Pierce County's largest lakes at more than 1,100 acres, American also offers some of the area's finest angling variety. Read the list of species above and it's easy to understand why there's something to catch here throughout the entire year-round season.

This is a lake that's known for big trout. I was talking with Genevieve Anderson, the owner of Bill's Boat House, one sunny Saturday afternoon in May of 1995 when an angler who had been fishing on the dock all morning strolled in to weigh the rainbow he had just caught. It weighed 7½ pounds, not large enough to replace the 8½-pounder that topped the list of trophies from the dock that spring, but an impressive trout nonetheless. Talk of those fish prompted me to ask Mrs. Anderson about the largest trout she had ever seen caught from the lake. She told the story about another dock angler who came in with a big fish wrapped in his coat one day in the early nineties. That fish pulled the scale pointer to 11 pounds, five ounces, and upon closer examination Mrs. Anderson noticed that it had already been cleaned. It might well have weighed 13 pounds when it was first caught.

American Lake, of course, doesn't treat everyone to a shot at its trophy trout, but the odds of catching a big one here are perhaps better now than they have been in a long time, thanks to the stocking of more than 40,000 young steelhead from 1993 to 1995. Fish from the 1993 plant were running two pounds or better in the spring of 1995 and are certainly larger now, adding a great deal of angling excitement at the lake. True to their bloodline, these fish tend to stay quite deep, and one of the most consistent ways of catching them is trolling with two or three-ounce sinkers with 100 to 150 feet of line off the reel. Small Wedding Ring spinners with maggots on the hooks are among the offerings that will take them.

Those same Wedding ring-and-maggot combinations are commonly used by kokanee anglers at American. One of the area's top kokanee lakes, it gives up fish to two pounds or more from mid-summer until these land-locked kokanee move inshore to spawn in the fall. Trolling is also a good way to catch cutthroats here, but don't waste your time out in deep water. As is typical with these shallow-water trout, they're most often caught around the edges of the lake. Some of the largest cutthroats are caught in the fall, often by fly anglers working leeches and other wet-fly patterns in the shore-line weed beds.

If you like fish with red eyes, American has two species that fall into that category. Both smallmouths and rock bass are available here, and some of the best fishing for both is found at the lake's north and south ends and in the wide bay at the northwest corner of the lake. Casting around the several islands in the lake also produces bass.

---

11. PUYALLUP RIVER

Reference: **Enters Commencement Bay at Tacoma; map B2, grid a6.**

How to get there: Take the Puyallup exit off Interstate 5 near the north end of Tacoma to reach the lower Puyallup, which is paralleled by River Road on the south and North Levee Road on the north. To reach upper portions of the river, take Pioneer Avenue east out of Puyallup to State Route 162 (the Sumner-Orting Highway). Side roads to the east off State Route 162 provide river access at Alderton, McMillan, and other places along the way toward Orting. McCutcheon Road runs along the east side of the river from Sumner to McMillan.

Facilities: The towns of Puyallup and Sumner have all the amenities you need.

Contact: The Ultimate Fisherman, (206) 845-1202.

Species available: Winter steelhead, chinook and coho salmon, cutthroat trout, mountain whitefish.

Fishing the Puyallup River: Some of the best fishing on the Puyallup is found from Sumner upstream to the mouth of the Carbon River, a few miles north of Orting. This is true of both steelhead and salmon. Many anglers float this stretch of the river, but McCutcheon Road provides plenty of access at more than a half-dozen points.

Chinook start showing in the Puyallup in August, and by mid-September the salmon fishery is going full-speed. The hottest action is in October, when coho fill the river, most of them bound for the state salmon hatchery on Voight Creek, a Carbon River tributary near Orting. Boat anglers score good coho catches by back-trolling Hot Shots, Wiggle Warts, and other plugs, while bank anglers do well with Blue Fox, Metric, and Flash Glo spinners.

A few steelhead still trickle into the upper reaches of the Puyallup above the mouth of the Carbon, but you're much better off concentrating your efforts from McMillan downstream. If you're a drift-angler, you'll find plenty of good water between Sumner and McMillan, with no areas better than the others. If plunking is your bag, stay downstream of Puyallup. Plunkers do well along the North Levee Road, where there's plenty of bank access and a good chance of catching fish right after a period of high water.

12. LAKE KILLARNEY

Reference: **Southeast of Federal Way; map B2, grid a6.**

How to get there: Take Military Road south from S 320th Street in Federal Way and drive three miles to 352nd Street; turn west (right), then north (right) on 34th Avenue. Drive two blocks to the lake, which is on the left. (The lake on the right is Lake Geneva, mentioned below.)

Facilities: The lake has a boat ramp for craft of limited size. The nearest food, gas, tackle, and lodging are in Federal Way.

Contact: The Reel Thing, (206) 941-0920.

Species available: Rainbow trout, largemouth bass, brown bullhead catfish, yellow perch, bluegills.

Fishing Lake Killarney: This shallow, 31-acre lake is best noted for its panfish and fair largemouth bass fishing, but it also offers decent possibilities for rainbow trout stocked in the lake every year. The marshy north end is a good place to fish spinnerbaits and various plastics for bass. Killarney also has yellow perch and bluegills, but you may have trouble finding any large ones. If you're into night-fishing, try the south end of the lake for brown bullheads, some of which run 15 inches or so. As the water drops in late summer and fall, the northern and southern portions of this small lake may separate when a shoal in the middle becomes dry land.

13. LAKE GENEVA

Reference: **Southeast of Federal Way; map B2, grid a6.**

How to get there: Take Military Road south from S 320th Street in Federal Way. Drive three miles and turn west (right) on 352nd Street and north (right) on 34th Avenue. Drive two blocks to the lake, which is on the right. (Lake Killarney, mentioned above, is on the left.)

Facilities: A narrow boat ramp provides access on the west side of the lake. Federal Way has food, gas, tackle, and lodging.

Contact: The Reel Thing, (206) 941-0920.

Species available: Rainbow trout.

Fishing Lake Geneva: Stocked with hatchery trout just prior to the April season opener, Geneva usually offers good fishing for a few weeks and then slows considerably. It's only about 29 acres in size and very popular with South King County anglers, which explains why it succumbs to fishing pressure so quickly. Because the carryover of fish from season to season is low, the Department of Fish and Wildlife often includes a few large trout in its spring plant, just to help provide excitement. A few warm-water species are also available to help provide summertime angling activity.

14. FIVE MILE LAKE

Reference: **Southeast of Federal Way; map B2, grid a6.**

How to get there: Take Military Road south from S 320th Street in Federal Way. The lake is on the west side of Military, about three miles south of 320th Street.

Facilities: There's a King County park and boat ramp near the south end of the lake. Food, gas, tackle, and lodging can be found in Federal Way.

Contact: The Reel Thing, (206) 941-0920.

Species available: Rainbow trout.

Fishing Five Mile Lake: This lake is now open to year-round fishing and produces fair catches from March to June and again in the fall. A large public fishing dock is popular and fairly productive, but trolling the north end and east side of the lake pays off better. Fishing gets tough in the summer, but a large 30-foot hole near the south end continues to produce some rainbows even in hot weather. Stillfishing on the bottom often works best in this spot.

15. TROUT LAKE

Reference: **Southeast of Federal Way; map B2, grid a6.**

How to get there: Take Military Road south from S 320th Street in Federal Way. Drive about 4.5 miles and turn east (left) on S 366th Street, which is about a quarter of a mile south of the south end of Five Mile Lake.

Facilities: The lake has a public boat ramp. All other amenities are available in Federal Way.

Contact: The Reel Thing, (206) 941-0920.

Species available: Rainbow trout, largemouth bass.

Fishing Trout Lake: Trolling and stillfishing for trout is fairly good here in the spring. June, July, and August provide some fair catches of largemouth bass, including an occasional trophy-sized fish. The lake covers only 18 acres, but much of it is more than 20 feet deep, with several spots nearly 30 feet deep. Stay along the edges if you want bass, but troll or stillfish the middle for rainbows.

16. WHITE RIVER

Reference: **Joins the Puyallup River near Sumner; map B2, grid a7.**

How to get there: Take State Route 164 or the East Valley Highway south from Auburn about two miles to the river.

Facilities: Food, gas, tackle, and lodging are available in Auburn and Sumner.

Contact: Al's Sporting Goods, (360) 829-0174; Auburn Sports and Marine, (206) 833-1440.

Species available: Winter and summer steelhead, cutthroat trout, mountain whitefish.

Fishing the White River: This glacial stream that heads on the eastern flank of Mount Rainier is a glaring example of man's infinite lack of wisdom. Once a tributary to the Green River, somebody back in the good old days at the start of the 1900s determined that it would be more convenient if the White flowed into the Puyallup instead, so it was diverted. Imagine the impact a little change like that would have on the stream's salmon and steelhead runs. The White, which is also referred to as the Stuck River along its lower reaches, really hasn't been worth a darn for fishing since. Much of the river is closed to fishing during the summer months, and only rarely does someone catch anything worth keeping during the time it is open.

17. LAKE TAPPS

Reference: **Northeast of Sumner; map B2, grid a7.**

How to get there: Take State Route 410 east from Sumner and turn north on the Sumner-Tapps Highway, which parallels the northwest, north, and east shoreline of the lake.

Facilities: Boat ramps are located near the northeast and northwest corners of the lake. Other amenities can be found in Sumner and Auburn.

Contact: Auburn Sports and Marine, (206) 833-1440.

Species available: Rainbow trout, largemouth bass, yellow perch, Dolly Varden.

Fishing Lake Tapps: Anglers using gang trolls with worms or small wobbling spoons behind them catch some rainbows at Lake Tapps, but this huge reservoir is not a particularly productive trout fishery. Patient or lucky anglers will occasionally take a real lunker, though it's not an everyday occurrence. A few big largemouth bass are also caught but, again, this certainly isn't one of the area's hot bass lakes. The water level is drawn way down from winter to early spring, and by the time it comes back up, water-skiers, drag-boaters, and jet-ski enthusiasts take over much of the lake.

18. FISH LAKE

Reference: **Northeast of Enumclaw; map B2, grid a8.**

How to get there: Take Veazie-Cumberland Road north from Enumclaw for six miles and turn west (left) onto 295th Avenue SE. Turn left again on 371st Street and drive half a mile to the lake.

Facilities: The lake has a public boat ramp and access area. The nearest food, gas, tackle, and lodging are in Enumclaw.

Contact: Al's Sporting Goods, (360) 829-0174.

Species available: Rainbow and cutthroat trout.

Fishing Fish Lake: A small plant of hatchery rainbows and cutthroats is enough to provide year-round fishing on little, 16-acre Fish Lake, located just east of Nolte State Park. The lake gets quite low and hard to fish by mid-summer, but fills again with the fall rains. Float-tubes work well here, since you can easily make your way around in a few hours of casting small spinners or flies. The lake has a boat ramp where car-toppers and inflatables can be launched. Private property surrounds the water, so confine your efforts to the access area or stay in your boat.

19. DEEP LAKE

Reference: **Northeast of Enumclaw; map B2, grid a8.**

How to get there: Take Veazie-Cumberland Road north from Enumclaw for 6.5 miles and watch for the Nolte State Park sign on the left.

Facilities: The east end of the lake has a narrow boat ramp. Nolte State Park, where the lake is located, has picnic tables but no overnight camping. The closest food, gas, tackle, and lodging are in Enumclaw.

Contact: Nolte State Park, (360) 825-4646; Al's Sporting Goods, (360) 829-0174.

Species available: Rainbow and cutthroat trout, kokanee, crappies, yellow perch, brown bullhead catfish.

Fishing Deep Lake: Although now open year-round, April and May are still the best months to fish this 40-acre lake for rainbows, most of which are legal-sized hatchery fish planted in March or April. A few cutthroat are also stocked, and they may provide some fall fishing action. During the summer, troll a Wedding Ring spinner with white corn on the hooks behind a string of larger trolling blades for the kokanee. Stillfishing with maggots, white corn, or small pieces of worm may also be effective. Perch can be caught here pretty much year-round on worms or jig-and-worm combinations.

20. BASS LAKE

Reference: **North of Enumclaw; map B2, grid a8.**

How to get there: Take State Route 169 north from Enumclaw for 3.5 miles and turn west (left) onto 264th Avenue SE, which runs right by the north side of the lake.

Facilities: The lake has a public access area and boat ramp. The nearest food, gas, tackle, and lodging are in Enumclaw.

Contact: Al's Sporting Goods, (360) 829-0174.

Species available: Yellow perch, crappies.

Fishing Bass Lake: Although it doesn't have much in the way of a bass population, as its name would suggest, this small, 24-acre lake does offer decent spring and summer panfish action. Take your favorite ultralight spinning rod and a few plastic-skirted or marabou leadheads and you're in business.

The boat ramp on the east side of the lake isn't suited to that big bass boat, but you can launch a car-topper or small inflatable here with little trouble. This is also a good lake for float-tubers to investigate, except that by mid-summer the milfoil gets so thick that you might not be able to get through it.

21. WALKER LAKE

Reference: **Northeast of Enumclaw; map B2, grid a8.**

How to get there: Drive north from Enumclaw on Veazie-Cumberland Road, turn east (right) a mile past Nolte State Park onto Walker Lake Road, and drive about two miles to the lake.

Facilities: The south side of the lake has a public access area and boat ramp. Food, gas, tackle, and lodging can be found in Enumclaw.

Contact: Al's Sporting Goods, (360) 829-0174.

Species available: Rainbow and cutthroat trout.

Fishing Walker Lake: At only 11 acres, this probably should be called Walker Pond, but it's stocked with about 1,200 trout a year and provides fairly good spring trout fishing. The small boat ramp is a good place to drop a car-topper in the water or to wade in with your float-tube cinched firmly around your waist. Arrive early or stay late in the evening and fish the edge of the lake with your favorite fly rod. The access area offers the only public beach on the lake, so stay off the surrounding private property.

22. SPANAWAY LAKE

Reference: **In Spanaway, Pierce County; map B2, grid a5.**

How to get there: Take Interstate 5 to State Route 512 and turn east. Head south on State Route 7 and drive south about three miles to Military Road. Turn west (right), go one-quarter of a mile to Breezeman Boulevard, and turn south (left) into the park entrance.

Facilities: The county park has a boat ramp, free fishing pier, rowboat rentals, and cooking facilities for picnickers. Lodging and other amenities are available nearby in Spanaway.

Contact: Spanaway Park Boat House, (206) 531-0555.

Species available: Rainbow trout, largemouth and smallmouth bass, rock bass, yellow perch, brown bullhead catfish.

Fishing Spanaway Lake: Spring plants of about 15,000 rainbows annually provide fair to good fishing for eight- to 14-inch trout, with a few carryovers to about 18 inches. Stillfishing with Berkley Power Bait is popular here. In the spring good catches are made this way from the public fishing dock at the north end and for boaters around the south end. As the water warms in summer, move toward the 20- to 25-foot-deep waters in the middle one-third of the lake.

The shallow flats at the south end of the lake are best for bass, perch, and bullheads. Spanaway produces some big largemouths from time to time.

23. CARBON RIVER

Reference: **Joins the Puyallup River northwest of Orting, Pierce County; map B2, grid a7.**

How to get there: Take State Route 162 (Sumner-Orting Highway) south from Sumner toward Orting. Drive five miles from Sumner to the concrete bridge and continue another quarter of a mile to the gated gravel road to the left. Park at the gate and walk to the river. Another option is to continue two miles past the concrete bridge on State Route 162 to a second gated road on the left. Park at the gate and walk a quarter of a mile to the river. Continue on State Route 162 about a mile and a half past this second access road and you'll come to the town of Orting, where you can turn left on Bridge Street and drive four blocks to the river.

Facilities: Food and gas are available in Orting, while tackle and lodging can be found in Sumner.

Contact: The Ultimate Fisherman, (206) 845-1202.

Species available: Winter steelhead, fall chinook and coho salmon, mountain whitefish.

Fishing the Carbon River: Fish bound for the Puyallup River Salmon Hatchery on Voight Creek often provide good coho fishing and a crack at a 30-pound chinook on the Carbon. The three-mile stretch of river from Orting down to the mouth is most productive. Although the Carbon is a relatively small stream, it often produces good coho catches in October, especially after a decent rain draws fresh runs in from the Puyallup. As for steelheading, the Carbon can be quite good in December and January, but many of the 100 or so fish it gives up each winter are caught by locals who can get to the river when conditions are right. As with salmon, the right time to fish the Carbon is immediately after a good rain. Although overlooked by all but a few locals, the Carbon's whitefish population is worth exploiting during the winter. A couple of deep pools immediately behind Orting produce some good catches.

24. KENNEDY CREEK

Reference: **Flows into Oyster Bay south of Shelton; map B2, grid a1.**
How to get there: Follow U.S. 101 north from Olympia to the Kennedy Creek bridge, about three-quarters of a mile past the Thurston-Mason county line. The creek is mid-way between Olympia and Shelton.
Facilities: Food, gas, and cold beer are available at the intersection of U.S. 101 and Steamboat Island Road, about two miles south of the creek. Lodging and tackle are available to the south in Olympia and to the north in Shelton.
Contact: Verle's Sport Center, (360) 426-0933.
Species available: Chum salmon, winter steelhead, sea-run cutthroat trout.
Fishing Kennedy Creek: One of western Washington's best-kept secret steelhead holes in the late-seventies, Kennedy Creek is now best-known for its fall chum salmon fishery. November is the top month for chums, and when conditions are right, as many as 100 anglers may line the banks at the mouth of this small stream. They cast small offerings of green yarn, green steelhead bobbers, or combinations of the two and score their best catches as the water drops after a high tide has brought fresh fish into the creek. Salmon fishing is allowed only at the mouth, downstream of the freeway bridge.

Winter steelhead can still be found in Kennedy Creek from December until the season closes at the end of February, but certainly not in the numbers available back in the "good old days" when employees of what was then the Washington Game Department used to release "extra" steelhead smolts into this tiny stream. Adult steelhead returning from those lightly publicized hatchery plants provided some wild and woolly steelheading for the few anglers who caught on. But these days your best chance of hooking an occasional steelie will occur if you fish the lower half-mile of the creek immediately after a high tide or the day the water level begins dropping after a heavy rain puts it out of fishing condition.

25. SUMMIT LAKE

Reference: **West of Olympia; map B2, grid b1.**
How to get there: Take State Route 8 west from Olympia about 12 miles to Summit Lake Road, turn north (right), and follow it about 1.5 miles to the lake.
Facilities: A large, paved boat ramp and access area is located near the southwest corner of the lake. All other amenities are in Olympia.
Contact: Tumwater Sports, (360) 352-5161.
Species available: Rainbow and cutthroat trout, kokanee, yellow perch, brown bullhead catfish, largemouth bass.

Fishing Summit Lake: At more than 500 acres, Summit is one of Thurston County's largest lakes, and it once was home to some of western Washington's largest resident cutthroat trout. If any of the whopper cutthroat still inhabit the lake, no one seems to catch them anymore, but Summit is one of the south Puget Sound region's favorite fishing lakes just the same.

Liberal plants of hatchery rainbows are what keep most Summit Lake anglers interested during the first several weeks of the season, which opens in late April. Trolling is popular, and the tried-and-true gang troll with a worm trailer probably catches more rainbows here than anything else. But stillfishing is very effective, especially around the west end of the lake. In May and early June it's very possible to catch a limit of plump rainbows by simply anchoring in 20 to 30 feet of water and suspending a garden worm about six feet beneath a small bobber. If the day is bright and sunny or the water unseasonably warm, try a slip-sinker rig with a marshmallow or glob of Berkley Power Bait floating up two feet off the bottom.

By the time the trout fishing begins to slow, some Summit Lake anglers are getting serious about catching kokanee. June and July are the most productive months for these landlocked sockeye salmon, which run about eight to 11 inches here. Trolling Wedding Ring spinners and similar lures accounts for some of them, but many Summit Lake kokanee are caught by stillfishing at the lake's west end and northwest corner. In warm weather, get on and off the lake before the skiers, knee-boarders, and other thrill-seekers become active.

Perch fishing can be quite good at Summit, but the fish are usually on the small side. You may have to put up with three or four small ones for every perch large enough to be worth filleting, but keep the small ones, too, if you want to increase your odds of getting bigger fish next time.

As in other Northwest lakes, the brown bullheads here draw relatively little interest from anglers. But if you want to give it a shot, the odds would be in your favor if you were to launch your boat about sunset and row or motor into the shallows at the extreme west end of the lake. Much of the water here is in the four- to eight-foot depth range, shallow enough to warm several degrees on a warm summer day and stay that way well into the night. Suspend a juicy nightcrawler, gob of beef or chicken liver, or other tasty catfish treat beneath a bobber for an hour or two and you should be in business.

---

26. NISQUALLY RIVER

Reference: **Enters Puget Sound between Tacoma and Olympia; map B2, grid b4.**

How to get there: Take Interstate 5 to the Old Nisqually exit and follow Pacific Avenue south two miles to Reservation Road. Turn left on Reservation Road and left again on State Route 510 (Olympia-Yelm Highway), which roughly parallels the south side of the river before crossing over it at the small town of McKenna.

Facilities: Groceries, gas, and tackle are available in Yelm, and lodging can be found nearby in Olympia.

Contact: Jayhawks, (360) 458-5707 (sporting goods department).

Species available: Winter and summer steelhead, chum salmon, sea-run cutthroat trout.

Fishing the Nisqually River: Illegal netting by tribal anglers all but wiped out the wild winter steelhead here a few years ago, and sport fishing has been closed during the peak of the steelhead runs ever since. With luck, worthwhile March and April steelheading will return to the Nisqually some day, but it could take a while.

In the meantime, chum salmon are the biggest draw for anglers on the Nisqually these days. Chums come on strong with the first high waters of November and provide fishing action well into January most years. Favorite fishing spots are the long drift immediately above the Pacific Avenue Bridge, and a few miles upstream near the mouth of Muck Creek. Nisqually River chums are fond of green yarn, small, green steelhead bobbers, or bobber-and-yarn combinations.

Sea-run cutthroat trout are available in the Nisqually from about August through November, but get relatively little attention from anglers. The best cutthroat fishing is on the lower river, between Yelm and the river mouth.

27. CHAMBERS LAKE

Reference: **Southwest side of Lacey; map B2, grid b3.**
How to get there: Take the Sleater-Kinney Road South exit off Interstate 5 at Lacey and drive south to 14th Avenue SE. Turn west (right) and drive about half a mile to the public access area, on the left.
Facilities: There's a boat ramp at the access area, and all other facilities are in Lacey.
Contact: Tumwater Sports, (360) 352-5161.
Species available: Largemouth bass, yellow perch.
Fishing Chambers Lake: This flat, shallow lake on the outskirts of Lacey is another favorite of some Olympia-area bass anglers. Much of the lake is four to seven feet deep, offering a wealth of bass-fishing possibilities. It's a good place to fish surface lures early and late in the day, and plastics or spinnerbaits the rest of the time.

As if the 72-acre main lake didn't have enough to offer bass anglers, there's another smaller lake attached to its southeast corner. Little Chambers Lake covers some 50 acres and offers about the same kind of fishing as the main lake. You probably won't want to attempt getting your $20,000 bass boat from one lake to the other, but it's possible to drag a car-topper or other small craft back and forth between the two if you feel adventurous.

28. HICKS LAKE

Reference: **In Lacey; map B2, grid b3.**
How to get there: Take the Pacific Avenue exit of Interstate 5 at Lacey and drive east to Carpenter Road, turn right, and follow Carpenter about two miles to Shady Lane. Turn right, drive to the "T" at Lilac Street, turn left, go a block and a half, and turn left again on Hicks Lake Road. The boat ramp and access area are about one-quarter of a mile down Hicks Lake Road, on the left.

Facilities: The lake has a single-lane boat ramp with ample parking and about 100 feet of gravel beach, plus a chemical toilet. Other facilities can be found in nearby Lacey.

Contact: Sports Warehouse, (360) 491-1346.

Species available: Rainbow trout, largemouth bass, rock bass, warmouth, yellow perch.

Fishing Hicks Lake: Fairly large and quite deep by Puget Sound standards, this 170-acre lake south of Lacey warms rather slowly, so the rainbow trout fishing may be slow early in the season and get better in May and early June. Legal-sized rainbows stocked just prior to the opener provide most of the action, but carryovers to about 17 inches are a real possibility. Some trout are caught by bank anglers at the access area, but the first warm weather of the spring brings out the local kids who seem to think the gravel beach is their personal swimming area. Although anglers pay for this and other access areas throughout the state and have a legal priority here, it doesn't always work out that way.

Although lakeside development over the past several decades has eliminated much of the brushy shoreline and other suitable habitat for warmwater fish, Hicks produces some nice largemouth bass and fair numbers of panfish. The best fishing for these species is near the shallow south end, where there's still some weedy and brushy cover.

29. LONG LAKE

Reference: **East side of Lacey; map B2, grid b3.**

How to get there: Take the Pacific Avenue exit off Interstate 5 at Lacey. Go east (right) on Pacific to Carpenter Road, turn right, and follow Carpenter about three miles to the south end of the Thurston County Fairgrounds. Go left on Boat Launch Road just past the fairgrounds and follow it 200 yards to the lake.

Facilities: The lake has a large Department of Fish and Wildlife access area with a boat ramp and outhouses. Food, gas, lodging, and other amenities are available in Lacey.

Contact: Sports Warehouse, (360) 491-1346.

Species available: Rainbow trout, largemouth bass, rock bass, warmouth, crappies, yellow perch.

Fishing Long Lake: Pre-season plants of legal-sized rainbows at this 300-acre lake make for fair fishing from the late April opener until about mid-June. The lake, which is really more like two lakes connected by a narrow channel, treats trollers quite well, but anglers living around the lake also do fine stillfishing from their docks and floats. Stillfishing for rainbows is also popular on the beach alongside the boat ramp. Decent bass fishing can be found along much of the lake's east side and wherever there's shoreline brush and trees. The many docks and floats also produce bass early and late in the day. Perch and crappies can be found throughout the lake, and anglers fishing for both occasionally score a rock bass or warmouth.

30. LAKE ST. CLAIR

Reference: **Southeast of Lacey, map B2, grid b3.**

How to get there: Take State Route 510 southeast from Lacey or northwest from Yelm and turn east on the Yelm Highway. Several roads and streets going north of the Yelm Highway, beginning 1.5 miles from SR 510, lead to the lake.

Facilities: The lake has two public access areas, each with rest rooms and boat ramps. Food, gas, tackle, and lodging can be found in Lacey.

Contact: Sports Warehouse, (360) 491-1346.

Species available: Rainbow trout, kokanee, largemouth, rock bass, warmouth, yellow perch, crappies.

Fishing Lake St. Clair: A year-round fishing season and wide variety of fish species make St. Clair an interesting lake to fish. It offers fair trout fishing after the Department of Fish and Wildlife stocks it with about 5,000 legal-sized rainbows each spring, but there are also some chunky, winter carry-over rainbows in the lake from fall plants of large fingerlings. The lake's self-sustaining kokanee population provides fairly good fishing from June to August, mostly for trollers using Pop Geer and Wedding Ring spinners or similar small, flashy offerings. Largemouth bass fishing can be good in the spring and summer, and there are plenty of docks, floats, and brushy shoreline areas to prospect for bass. The lake's two most unusual species are warmouth and white crappies, neither of which is found in more than a handful of Northwest lakes, and you'll also find rock bass, a fairly rare catch in its own right. Fairly good perch fishing is also available here, and even though nobody but the kids seems to notice, the lake also has a lot of pumpkinseed sunfish to round out the angling menu. Grab a fishing rod and take your pick.

31. PATTISON (PATTERSON) LAKE

Reference: **South of Lacey; map B2, grid b3.**

How to get there: Drive south out of Lacey on Ruddell Road for about 1.5 miles and turn east (left) on Mullen Road. Drive another 1.5 miles and turn south (right) on Carpenter Road. Drive half a mile and watch for the brown sign pointing to the public access area at the lake.

Facilities: The east side of the lake has a Department of Fish and Wildlife access area and boat ramp. Food, gas, tackle, and lodging are available in Lacey.

Contact: Sports Warehouse, (360) 491-1346.

Species available: Rainbow and brown trout, largemouth bass, rock bass, crappies, yellow perch, bluegills.

Fishing Pattison Lake: A wide variety of cold-water and warm-water fish makes this 250-acre lake just south of Lacey a treat to fish. Although huge plants of legal-sized rainbows stocked just prior to the fishing season in late April provide most of the spring sport for trout anglers, you have a decent chance of hooking a carry-over rainbow in the 15- to 18-inch class or a couple of brown trout that may be almost any size. Most anglers troll the usual spoons, spinners, and small wobblers, but give stillfishing a try and you might improve your chances of hooking one of the big carryovers.

Largemouth bass and yellow perch are also worth fishing for here, with the lake usually giving up a few really large bass during the course of a summer. Although not rare, rock bass always provide an interesting twist, and they're usually caught near shore by anglers who happen to be fishing for something else, including trout.

32. WARD LAKE

Reference: **East of Tumwater; map B2, grid b3.**

How to get there: Take Interstate 5 to Tumwater and exit at the Olympia Brewery onto Custer Way. Drive east on Custer Way to the four-way blinking light and turn sough (right) on Cleveland Avenue, which becomes the Yelm Highway. Turn north (left) on Boulevard Road, drive seven blocks to 42nd Way SE, turn left, and drive about three blocks to the lake.

Facilities: The east side of the lake has a boat ramp and access area. Other amenities can be found in Tumwater.

Contact: Tumwater Sports, (360) 352-5161.

Species available: Rainbow trout, kokanee, largemouth bass.

Fishing Ward Lake: At perhaps 65 acres, Ward is probably an average-sized lake for the Puget Sound area. But what sets it apart from most of the rest is that it's unusually deep. It's more than 50 feet down in several spots, and nearly 70 feet in one place near the west side. This depth, plus the clearness of the water, help to make Ward a worthwhile prospect for trout throughout the summer, a rather rare quality among lakes in this area. Troll it with your favorite spoons, spinners, wobblers, or even flies early in the season, but by June and July make your way into the deeper waters around the south end or west side to try your hand at stillfishing on or near the bottom. As summer turns to fall and the water begins to cool, the rainbows will move back up into the more shallow areas where trolling will again be productive until the season comes to a halt at the end of October.

The clear, cool waters also offer an opportunity to catch kokanee, although this fishery seems to vary somewhat from year to year. Your best shot at these little landlocked sockeye salmon is during the summer. Try either trolling with a small, beaded spinner behind a string of larger trolling blades or stillfishing with white corn or maggots on brightly colored hooks. As always when trying for kokanee, try to locate the fish with your depthsounder or vary your fishing depth until you catch a fish, then concentrate your efforts on that depth to find others.

Ward Lake also has some good-sized largemouth bass, but they can be a little shy and hard to fool in the lake's clear waters. That's probably why they're as big as they are here.

33. MUNN LAKE

Reference: **Southeast of Tumwater; map B2, grid b2.**

How to get there: Take the Airdustrial Avenue exit off Interstate 5 just south of Tumwater and drive east to the second stop light. Turn south (right) on Capitol Boulevard (which becomes Pacific Highway SE at about this point) and drive less than a mile to Henderson Boulevard. Turn left and drive about two miles on Henderson to 65th Avenue. Turn right and go about half a mile to the public access area, on the right.

Facilities: The public access area has a boat ramp and rest rooms, but there are no other facilities on the lake. The nearest restaurants, accommodations, tackle, and gas are in Tumwater.

Contact: Tumwater Sports, (360) 352-5161.

Species available: Rainbow trout, largemouth bass.

Fishing Munn Lake: A spring plant of about 3,000 rainbows provides fair trout fishing here in May and early June. Most of the rainbows are seven to nine-inchers. After trout fishing drops off in the summer, there's another flurry of activity in the fall, especially from about the middle of September to early October. By this time the rainbows have grown to about 11 inches and are well worth catching.

The main warm-weather fishery is for largemouth bass, and this 40-acre lake (including Susan Lake, which is really just an extension of Munn), is a favorite of many Olympia-area bass anglers. Much of the lake is less than 15 feet deep, so there are plenty of places to look for largemouths. One good place to fish in the spring is the shallow channel that connects the main lake to Susan Lake. This channel begins just to the right (north) of the boat ramp.

34. DESCHUTES RIVER

Reference: **Flows into Capitol Lake at Olympia; map B2, grid b3.**

How to get there: Exit Interstate 5 at the Olympia Brewery in Tumwater and take Custer Avenue to Capitol Way. Turn south (right) on Capitol and then left at the first light, which is E Street, to fish a productive part of the lower river. Follow Capitol Way south to Henderson and turn left to reach another worthwhile section of the Deschutes. Continue south on Capitol Way (which becomes Pacific Highway SE) to Waldrick Road and turn east (left) to reach several miles of the Deschutes near Offut Lake.

Facilities: Food, gas, lodging, and tackle are available in Tumwater.

Contact: Tumwater Sports, (360) 352-5161.

Species available: Winter steelhead, chinook and coho salmon, sea-run and resident cutthroat trout.

Fishing the Deschutes River: Not to be confused with its larger and more famous Oregon counterpart, Washington's Deschutes flows through the town of Tumwater and into the south end of Puget Sound at Olympia. Just before reaching saltwater, it flattens out and becomes Capitol Lake for its final few hundred yards. While fishing on the Deschutes isn't all that well-known, the river does have one important claim to fame: It runs right by the Olympia Brewery, and its impressive falls are part of Olympia Beer's long-time logo.

As for the fishing, it's only fair. Although stocked with about 20,000 winter steelhead smolts annually, this little river doesn't provide much of a steelhead catch. It has some beautiful pools and drifts that look as though they should be full of fish all winter, but the average sport catch is only about a dozen steelhead a season.

A fair number of chinook and coho salmon make their way through the fish ladder and around the lower-river falls to a trapping facility operated by the Department of Fish and Wildlife. Fish that are allowed to pass by the facility and continue upstream provide some fishing action, but the river is often low and clear when the salmon are present, and they aren't too interested in what anglers have to offer.

Sea-run cutthroats also make their way into the Deschutes during the fall, and fishing for these little anadromous trout can be fairly good at times. Again, the clear water keeps them shy and spooky, so you may have to use stealth and patience to take them.

---

35. BLACK LAKE

Reference: **Southwest of Olympia; map B2, grid b2.**

How to get there: Take the Black Lake Boulevard exit off U.S. 101 in west Olympia and drive about two miles to the lake. Turn left on Black Lake-Belmore Road near the north end of the lake and bear right at the fire station. Drive about two miles to 66th Avenue, turn right, and follow it to the public access area and boat ramp near the south end of the lake.

Facilities: Besides the access area and ramp at the south end of the lake, there's a fishing dock and small store at Black Lake RV Park near the lake's northeast corner. Another store with gas pumps is located at the intersection of Black Lake-Belmore and Dent roads, on the east side of the lake.

Contact: Black Lake RV Park, (306) 357-6775.

Species available: Rainbow trout, cutthroat trout, chinook salmon, largemouth bass, yellow perch, black crappie, brown bullhead catfish.

Fishing Black Lake: When it comes to angling variety, Black Lake is Thurston County's biggest and best—biggest because it covers about 570 surface acres and best because there's something to catch here virtually all year.

The trout fishing is often best early and late in the year, when the water is quite cool. I've made good catches of rainbows by trolling a small Triple Teazer or Dick Nite in a chrome/red head finish along the east side of the lake as early as mid-March, and one chilly November afternoon, I stopped to visit a friend who lives on the lake and found both him and his son happily reeling in husky 12- to 14-inch rainbows on his dock. They were using salmon egg/worm combinations right on the bottom. Cutthroat are often caught along with the hatchery-stocked rainbows, and during the past few years, trout anglers have also been surprised to find what seems to be an ever-growing number of small chinook salmon in their catch. Although Black lake is connected to Puget Sound and the open Pacific Ocean via Percival Creek at one end and the Black River at the other, exactly how the chinook are getting into the lake remains somewhat of a mystery.

Black Lake begins to serve up pretty good largemouth bass catches by the first few warms days in April and remains productive through the summer. The weedy south end of the lake is a favorite stomping ground of local bass anglers, but respectable largemouths are caught all around the lake. By mid-summer, when swimmers, skiers, drag-boaters, jet-skiers, and other hell-raisers are flocking to the lake in raging hordes, you'd best plan on doing your bass fishing very early in the morning, very late in the evening, or during the black of night.

And, while we're talking about the black of night, that's the best time to fish for Black Lake's abundant brown bullheads. The lake provides some good catfish catches from mid-June through August. Start looking for them at the weedy south end of the lake. Most of them will weigh about a pound and measure 11 to 14 inches.

36. CAPITOL LAKE

Reference: **Southwest Olympia; map B2, grid b2.**

How to get there: Take exit 103 off Interstate 5 and follow Deschutes Parkway about three-quarters of a mile to Tumwater Historical Park, where the upper end of the lake is on the right. To reach the lower part of the lake, continue past the park and under the freeway on Deschutes Parkway, paralleling the lake's west shoreline.

Facilities: The upper end of the lake has a boat ramp and public fishing dock. Food, lodging, and other amenities are available in Olympia and Tumwater. Falls Terrace Restaurant, with good food and one of the best views anywhere, is half a mile south of the lake, overlooking Tumwater Falls.

Contact: Tumwater Sports, (360) 352-5161.

Species available: Chinook salmon, cutthroat trout.

Fishing Capitol Lake: Throughout most of the year, this wide spot at the mouth of the Deschutes River has little to offer anglers. But in August and September it can be a fairly good bet for chinook salmon. The best fishing is at the upper end of the lake, where it narrows down and starts turning into a river, directly beneath the Interstate 5 bridge. Some people anchor small boats here, others fish from the public fishing dock at the southwest corner of the lake. The boat launch and fishing dock are accessible from the Tumwater Historical Park. Most anglers fish roe elusters or fresh ghost shrimp for their kings, either suspended below a bobber or anchored to the bottom.

37. KAPOWSIN LAKE

Reference: **South of Orting; map B2, grid b6.**

How to get there: Take State Route 161 south from Puyallup for 14 miles and turn east (left) on the Kapowsin Highway. Drive three miles and, at the intersection of Kapowsin Highway and Orville Road, turn right to reach the south end of the lake or left to reach the north end.

Facilities: A boat ramp with outhouses can be found near the north end of the lake. Gas, food, and tackle are available in Kapowsin. Lodging can be found in Puyallup.

Contact: The Ultimate Fisherman, (206) 845-1202.

Species available: Rainbow trout, largemouth bass, rock bass, crappies, perch, brown bullhead catfish.

Fishing Kapowsin Lake: As someone who grew up fishing this stump-filled wonderland, I can tell you that it's one of those places that has something for virtually every angler. It's even been known to give up a few steelhead, although you probably wouldn't want to come here just for the steelheading. The trout fishing doesn't get the recognition it deserves, maybe because lots of newcomers come to Kapowsin, take off trolling across the lake, and don't have very good luck. For whatever reason, trolling produces only so-so results. If you insist on trolling, try a small Kwikfish or Flatfish in silver, gray, green, or yellow, or pull a nice, lively worm behind a string of small trolling blades. Stillfishing, though, usually pays off best at Kapowsin. The good ol' bobber-and-worm combination works as well as anything, both early in the spring and again in the fall. During the summer, when most trout anglers give up on Kapowsin completely, try fishing early morning and late evening with a sliding bait rig right on the bottom. Berkley Power Bait, marshmallows, salmon eggs, and yellow corn all work well for this kind of fishing.

Kapowsin is a haven for bass and bass anglers, with a limitless supply of submerged stumps and logs and lots of shoreline brush and weed patches. Although it seldom gives up much in the way of trophy-class largemouths, there are enough one- and two-pounders to make things worthwhile. The north end of the lake is especially good.

The brown bullheads often grow quite large here, sometimes topping 18 inches and two pounds. Casting nightcrawlers in the shallows at the north end of the lake—at night, of course—is the way to catch them.

Kapowsin is one of those dozen or so south Puget Sound lakes that has rock bass, so take along a few Beetle Spins and other small spinnerbaits or small wobbling plugs if you're interested in catching one. A place to start casting might be the shallow bay on the east side of the lake, where St. Regis Paper Company (now Champion International) used to dump its logs.

38. WHITMAN LAKE

Reference: **North of Eatonville; map B2, grid b6.**

How to get there: Take State Route 161 south from Puyallup and turn east (left) on Kapowsin Highway and follow it two miles to 144th Avenue. Turn right and follow 144th about 1.5 miles to the lake.

Facilities: There's a public access area and boat ramp on the south end of the lake. Food, gas, and tackle are available in Kapowsin, about two miles to the northwest. The nearest lodging is in Eatonville and Puyallup.

Contact: The Ultimate Fisherman, (206) 845-1202.

Species available: Rainbow trout, largemouth bass, crappies, perch, brown bullhead catfish.

Fishing Whitman Lake: Small plants of hatchery rainbows provide fair early season trout fishing on this 30-acre Pierce County lake. Trollers might try a trolling pattern that takes them around the island or along the western and northern shorelines, but stillfishing is often better around the shallow flats near the southeast corner of the lake.

The docks and floats dotting the shoreline all around the lake provide some of Whitman's best bass cover, but fish the lake's limited weed beds and brush, too. Crappie and perch may be scattered in almost any part of the lake, while some of the best brown bullhead action may be found near the boat ramp at the south end.

39. TANWAX LAKE

Reference: **North of Eatonville; map B2, grid b6.**

How to get there: Take State Route 161 south from Puyallup for 17 miles and turn left on Tanwax Drive to reach the resort on the north side. Go a quarter-mile past Tanwax Drive and take the next left to reach the public boat ramp near the south end of the lake.

Facilities: Rainbow Resort has a fishing dock, groceries, tackle, and tent and RV sites. Lodging and other amenities are available in Eatonville, five miles to the south.

Contact: Rainbow Resort, (360) 879-5115.

Species available: Rainbow trout, largemouth bass, yellow perch, bluegills, brown bullhead catfish, pumpkinseed sunfish.

Fishing Tanwax Lake: This popular Pierce County lake is a haven for trout anglers, thanks in part to a liberal plant of about 40,000 legal-sized rainbows every spring. Both trolling and stillfishing work well, with anglers who stillfish often catching the large, carry-over trout for which this lake is well-known.

The wide variety of warm-water fish available at Tanwax makes this as good a bet for bass and panfish anglers as for trout enthusiasts. The east side and north end of the lake provide some of the best bass fishing.

At more than 170 acres, Tanwax has plenty of elbow room for everybody, although things can get a little congested at the public boat ramp on a sunny weekend. The season here runs year-round, but the best trout fishing is in May and June. Bass and panfish bite best from June to August.

40. CLEAR LAKE

Reference: **North of Eatonville; map B2, grid c6.**

How to get there: Drive south from Puyallup for 15 miles on State Route 161 and watch for the lake on your left.

Facilities: A private resort near the south end of the lake has a small store, and there's a public access area with boat ramp and rest rooms at the northwest corner of the lake. Food, gas, lodging, and tackle can be found in Eatonville.

Contact: Eatonville Coast to Coast, (360) 832-3181; Ohop Valley Grocery, (360) 847-2141.

Species available: Rainbow trout, kokanee, brown bullhead catfish, a few largemouth bass.

Fishing Clear Lake: Liberal spring plants of legal-sized rainbow trout supplement a healthy, self-sustaining population of kokanee in this popular south Pierce County lake. Clear Lake is open to year-round fishing and produces fair to good rainbow action from April to June and again for several weeks after Labor Day. The center of the lake has a couple of spots over 85 feet deep, so trout fishing is also a possibility during the warm months, but by then most folks are turning their attention to kokanee. Trolling with leaded line or downriggers may be required to get down to the kokanee in the summer, especially during the middle of the day. If you're not a troller, find a concentration of these small sockeye salmon and drop a hook baited with a kernel of white corn or a maggot down to the appropriate depth. As always, a good depthsounder is a valuable tool in locating Clear Lake kokanee, but you can also look for concentrations of other kokanee anglers on the surface, which requires no special electronic equipment. This lake lives up to its name, so be willing to fish light lines and leaders.

Clear Lake has had brown bullheads in it since I fished it as a kid more than 30 years ago, and they'll always be there. Night fishing almost anywhere in the lake should provide enough of these 10- to 12-inch catfish for a meal. Use worms or chicken livers for bait.

Summertime fishing can be a little tough because of the lake's popularity with skiers and swimmers, so do your fishing early and late in the day to avoid some of the commotion. Summertime weekends can be particularly hazardous to your health.

---

41. OHOP LAKE

Reference: **North of Eatonville; map B2, grid c6.**

How to get there: Take State Route 161 south from Puyallup for about 24 miles and turn left on Orville Road, or take Orville Road south from Kapowsin for eight miles to reach the lake.

Facilities: A large public access area with rest rooms and a boat ramp is located near the south end of the lake. The nearest food, gas, lodging, and tackle are in Eatonville, a mile south of the lake.

Contact: Eatonville Coast to Coast, (360) 832-3181; Ohop Valley Grocery, (360) 847-2141.

Species available: Rainbow trout, largemouth bass, black crappies, yellow perch, brown bullhead catfish.

Fishing Ohop Lake: Although stocked with legal-sized rainbows every spring, this large, 235-acre lake offers only fair trout fishing. Trolling with Flatfish, Kwikfish, Triple Teazers, Dick Nites, and garden worms behind a string of trolling blades is most popular, but lakeside home owners often catch some nice fish while stillfishing from their docks and floats. Carryovers to about 18 inches are rare but possible.

Lots of largemouth bass have been caught from Ohop since I caught my first one there nearly four decades ago, many of them from the undeveloped southwest shoreline and the many docks, stumps, and brushy spots along the east side of the lake. A two-pounder is a pretty good sized bass here.

The perch, crappie, and brown bullhead fishing gets better as summer progresses, thanks in part to the fact that this big lake warms rather slowly.

42. COPLAY LAKE/CLEARWATER WILDERNESS LAKES

Reference: **East of Fairfax, northern Pierce County; map B2, grid b8.**

How to get there: Drive east from Sumner on State Route 410 and turn south on State Route 165 near Buckley. About four miles south of Carbonado (and a mile after crossing over the impressive high bridge over the Carbon River), turn left on Forest Road 7810 (Cayada Creek Road), which leads to Coplay Lake. Proceed past the lake a mile and take the trail that leads a mile to Twin Lakes, another mile west to Summit Lake, a mile northeast to Lily Lake, and 1.5 miles northwest to Coundly Lake.

Facilities: There are no facilities at Coplay or any of the nearby lakes, but food and gas are available in Carbonado. Lodging and tackle can be found in Buckley.

Contact: Al's Sporting Goods, (360) 829-0174.

Species available: Cutthroat, rainbow, and brook trout.

Fishing Coplay Lake and the lakes of the Clearwater Wilderness: Coplay offers anglers a sort of user-friendly version of the alpine lake experience, since it's a high-country lake with a road running virtually right to its shores. Coplay and the hike-in lakes to the north are stocked intermittently by the Department of Fish and Wildlife, so they offer only fair, take-what-you-get trout fishing. You may have company when you fish Coplay, especially on weekends, but if you hit the trail, there's a good chance you'll be fishing in solitude. Of all the hike-in lakes, Summit is the largest and deepest and offers the best potential for a couple of decent-sized trout. Spring and fall provide the best fishing at these lakes.

43. CARBON GLACIER LAKES

Reference: **North of Mount Rainier, within Mount Rainier National Park; map B2, grid b9.**

How to get there: Drive east from Sumner on State Route 410 and turn south on State Route 165 near Buckley. A mile past the high bridge over the Carbon River south of Carbonado, bear left on the well-marked road to the Carbon River entrance to Mount Rainier National Park and follow it toward Ipsut Creek Campground. The mile-and-a-half trail to Green Lake is on the right side of the road, about three miles past the entrance station. To reach lakes to the east, continue past the Green Lake trail to Ipsut Creek Campground, where the road ends. A seven- to eight-mile hike will take you to James, Ethel, Marjorie, Oliver, and Adelaide lakes.

Facilities: Ipsut Creek Campground has tent sites, water, and rest rooms. The nearest food and gas are in Carbonado. Lodging and tackle are available in Buckley.

Contact: Mount Rainier National Park, (360) 569-2211.

Species available: Brook, cutthroat, and rainbow trout.

Fishing the Carbon Glacier Lakes: Green Lake, about a mile and a half off the road by way of a good trail, gets the heaviest fishing pressure of all lakes in the area, but it isn't very generous with its trout. Some say the cutthroats and rainbows here have grown wary in the lake's extremely clear water, and it's hard to find anyone who will argue the point. But there are some large trout in Green Lake that should be susceptible to light leaders and a clever strategy.

The lakes past Ipsut Creek, which don't see as many offerings from anglers, hold trout that are apparently less sophisticated than those in Green Lake, and decent catches of brook trout, with an occasional cutthroat mixed in, are fairly common. Pack your favorite light spinning rod and a selection of small spinners, spoons, and both dry and wet fly patterns. You can fish the flies behind a clear, plastic float with the spinning rod in the morning and evening. The best fishing is in June and July, but September can also be good.

44. MOWICH LAKE

Reference: **Northwest of Mount Rainier, Mount Rainier National Park; map B2, grid c9.**

How to get there: Drive east from Sumner on State Route 410 and turn south on State Route 165 near Buckley. Stay on State Route 165 all the way to the lake, a distance of about 25 miles.

Facilities: The only facilities here are a parking area and a trail around the lake. Food and gas are available in Carbonado, lodging and tackle in Buckley.

Contact: Mount Rainier National Park, (360) 569-2211.

Species available: Rainbow and brook trout.

Fishing Mowich Lake: The lake is as pretty as it ever was, but decades of drive-to access and the Park Service's no fish-stocking policy have greatly diminished the fishing potential of this large alpine lake. I can remember drifting around Mowich in an inflatable raft as a kid and catching several of what seemed at the time like trophy-class trout, but that scene is seldom repeated these days. It's still a nice place to practice your fly-casting or to troll a small wobbling spoon around on a light line, but don't promise anyone that you'll be home with freshly caught trout for dinner.

45. RAPJOHN LAKE

Reference: **Northwest of Eatonville; map B2, grid c6.**

How to get there: Take State Route 7 south from Spanaway. Exactly two miles south of the State Route 702 (352nd Avenue East) intersection, turn east (left) at the brown "Public Fishing" sign onto the narrow road that leads to the lake.

Facilities: The west side of the lake has a Department of Fish and Wildlife public access area and boat ramp. The nearest food, gas, tackle, and lodging are in Eatonville, five miles to the south.

Contact: The Ultimate Fisherman, (206) 845-1202.

Species available: Rainbow and brown trout, largemouth bass, yellow perch, crappies, brown bullhead catfish.

Fishing Rapjohn Lake: The Department of Fish and Wildlife stocks about 4,000 pan-sized rainbows here before the April opener, and they provide most of the fishing action through May. After that, some serious trout anglers switch from bobber-and-worm rigs and small wobbling spoons to larger offerings in hopes of finding a cooperative brown trout. Browns were stocked at Rapjohn several years ago, and every now and then someone tangles with one in the five- to 10-pound range. Some of those encounters are by design, others quite accidentally. If you're fishing with your favorite ultralight outfit and four-pound line, you lose. Bass anglers casting crankbaits on 15-pound mono tend to come out a little better during these encounters of the brown trout kind.

Speaking of bass, Rapjohn has long been a favorite of largemouth enthusiasts, since the lake has plenty of productive bass cover to investigate and produces some large bass. If you haven't fished it before, check the regulations pamphlet for information about the slot limit on bass that's in effect here.

Evening fishing for perch and crappies can be excellent from late spring to fall, and if you're still on the water at dusk, you might stick around a couple of more hours to try your hand at catfish. Brown bullheads are abundant and will gladly accept your offering of a juicy nightcrawler suspended from a bobber. Explore the edges of the lake until you find action.

46. SILVER LAKE

Reference: **Northwest of Eatonville; map B2, grid c6.**
How to get there: Take State Route 7 south from Spanaway and watch for the Silver Lake Resort sign 3.5 miles south of the State Route 702 (352nd Avenue East) intersection. Turn west (right) to the lake.
Facilities: Henley's Silver Lake Resort has rental boats, a 250-foot fishing dock, a boat ramp, tackle, and tent and RV spaces. Food, gas, tackle, and lodging can be found in Eatonville, five miles away.
Contact: Henley's Silver Lake Resort, (360) 832-3580.
Species available: Rainbow, brown, and brook trout; largemouth bass; yellow perch; crappies; bluegills; brown bullhead catfish.
Fishing Silver Lake: If it's true that variety is the spice of life, Silver Lake is a mighty spicy place. From the time it opens to fishing in late April until the day it closes at the end of October, there's always something to fish for—and to catch—from this 138-acre south Pierce County gem.

Silver is one of few western Washington lakes that offers three species of trout, many of them raised and released by resort-owner George Henley in the large net pen at the resort. Rainbow, brown, and brook trout inhabit the lake, and depending on how and where you fish, you might catch all three as part of the five-fish daily limit. Troll Flatfish, Kwikfish, Dick Nites, Triple Teazers, or Pop Geer-and-worm combinations throughout the lake for all three, or stillfish Berkley Power Bait, garden worms, or meal worms off the resort dock, which may be the longest such freshwater fishing dock in the Northwest. To target brook trout, troll or cast small spoons and spinners close to shore, or catch them by casting your favorite wet- or dry-fly patterns in the shallows. Anglers in search of larger brown trout—some of which have grown to trophy proportions during several years in the lake—should troll with large, minnow-imitating plugs or wobbling spoons.

Silver Lake is one of Pierce County's best largemouth bass lakes, producing more than its share of fish in the five- to seven-pound range. They'll take surface plugs, buzzbaits, and other top-water goodies at first and last light. During the day, you'll find places to fish all your favorite things, whether they be plastics, crankbaits, spinnerbaits, or something else. A slot limit protects bass between 12 and 15 inches long.

The panfish possibilities include black crappies, yellow perch, and bluegills, all of which grow to worthwhile size in the lake's rich environment. This is also a popular catfish lake, with brown bullheads running 10 to 14 inches, sometimes larger. Most catfish anglers fish from boats, but the resort dock can also be a good place. Garden worms and meal worms are favorite baits.

47. HARTS LAKE

Reference: **Southwest of McKenna; map B2, grid c5.**

How to get there: Drive east out of McKenna on State Route 702 for a mile, turn south on Harts Lake Road, and follow it about 4.5 miles to the lake, which is on the right.

Facilities: There's a public access area and boat ramp on the lake, as well as a private resort. The resort has food, tackle, and RV hookups. Additional food, gas, tackle, and lodging are available in Yelm, six miles away.

Contact: The Ultimate Fisherman, (206) 845-1202.

Species available: Rainbow trout, largemouth bass, yellow perch, crappies, brown bullhead catfish.

Fishing Harts Lake: The season at Harts Lake is now year-round, and hatchery rainbows stocked in the spring provide a decent shot at trout throughout most of that time. Those rainbows run 11 to 12 inches by fall, making this a good place to try fly-fishing after the Labor Day weekend.

Like nearby Silver Lake (see page 395), Harts is a good one for bass, too, with seven-pound largemouths a possibility. As at other area lakes, a slot limit protects bass between 12 and 15 inches from harvest.

Yellow perch and crappies are abundant in the lake as well, and summertime provides some excellent catches of brown bullheads.

48. OFFUT LAKE

Reference: **Southeast of Tumwater; map B2, grid c3.**

How to get there: To reach the public access and boat launch on the north side of the lake, take Pacific Highway SE south from Tumwater and turn east (left) onto Waldrick Road about four miles south of the airport. Watch for the brown "Public Access" sign about 1.5 miles down Waldrick Road and turn right. To reach the south side of the lake, continue south past Waldrick Road on Pacific Highway SE for about 1.5 miles and turn left (east) on Offut Lake Road. That's where Offut Lake Resort is located.

Facilities: Offut Lake Resort has a fishing dock, boat rentals, tackle, groceries, rental cabins, an RV park, and tent sites, not to mention a restaurant that serves up some of the finest meals in Thurston County. There's a grocery store and gas station at the intersection of Pacific Highway SE and Offut Lake Road.

Contact: Offut Lake Resort, (360) 264-2438.

Species available: Rainbow trout, largemouth and (maybe a few) smallmouth bass, yellow perch, black bullhead catfish.

Fishing Offut Lake: This 192-acre lake has a reputation for producing some of the biggest trout anywhere in Thurston County, perhaps anywhere in Washington. Carry-over rainbows of three to five pounds aren't caught by everyone who wets a line here, but they are hooked often enough to keep things interesting. Now and then someone catches a real monster, such as the lake-record 10-pounder caught in 1976. Many of the biggest fish are caught by anglers stillfishing from the resort's fishing dock. But trolling and stillfishing in other parts of the lake are also effective.

Offut also provides good largemouth bass fishing, and some of the bucketmouths range from five to seven pounds. The docks along the northeast corner of the lake and the weed beds at the east end are good places to look for bass. No one is sure where the smallmouths came from, but they're in the lake, according to folks at the resort, and you might catch smallies to over three pounds if you're persistent (or lucky). The east end of the lake is also a good place to look for both perch and brown bullheads.

If you quit fishing early, stop by Wolf Haven on your way out. This wildlife park is home to wolves from all over North America, and the small entrance fee is money well spent for what you'll see and learn about these fascinating animals.

---

49. DEEP LAKE

Reference: **South of Tumwater; map B2, grid c3.**

How to get there: Take Interstate 5 to the 93rd Avenue exit south of Tumwater and drive east on 93rd about a mile and a quarter to Tilley Road. Turn south (right) on Tilley and drive about three miles to the lake, on the right.

Facilities: Deep Lake Resort has tackle, bait, fishing licenses, some groceries, boat rentals, cabins, and tent and RV sites. Millersylvania State Park has a boat ramp and a short fishing dock, tent and RV spaces, and picnic shelters. The resort and state park combined provide several hundred feet of beach access for fishing along the north side and east end of the lake. There's a gas station with groceries back at the 93rd Avenue exit off Interstate 5. Additional amenities are available in Tumwater.

Contact: Deep Lake Resort, (360) 352-7388; Millersylvania State Park, (360) 753-1519.

Species available: Rainbow trout, largemouth bass, bluegills.

Fishing Deep Lake: If you launch your boat here, turn on your depthsounder, and go looking for the cool depths that give this Thurston County lake its name, you'll eventually conclude that either your depthsounder has gone berserk or the lake is woefully misnamed. The latter happens to be the case. You would have to look a long time to find a spot in Deep Lake that's more than about 18 feet deep. Whoever named it either had a dry sense of humor or had been sipping his hair tonic before visiting the lake.

But just because the lake isn't really deep doesn't mean anglers should overlook it. Deep Lake provides fair to good fishing for rainbows from the time it opens in late-April until about the middle of June, when it becomes more of a haven for swimmers than for trout anglers. The trout action picks up again after Labor Day and can be quite good in September and October. Casting from the bank, either with small spoons and spinners or with bobber-and-worm or bobber-and-salmon egg combinations, can be effective. The small fishing dock near the boat ramp at the northwest corner of the lake is a good place to fish marshmallows, salmon eggs, Berkley Power Bait, and other offerings near the bottom. When the dock isn't crowded, fly anglers often cast to rising rainbows here in the morning and evening.

Although not noted for its bass fishing, Deep Lake produces some fair-sized largemouths. The brushy, weedy waters around the uninhabited west end of the lake offer the best bass-fishing opportunities.

The brush piles, weeds, and overhanging trees at the west end also provide the best shot at bluegills. Try a BeetleSpin or small leadhead laces with a piece of worm to catch them.

50. McINTOSH LAKE

Reference: **Northeast of Tenino; map B2, grid c3.**

How to get there: Take Interstate 5 to Grand Mound and exit east onto Pacific Highway SE, following it about eight miles to Tenino and the junction of State Route 507. Continue east on State Route 507 for about four miles to Military Road and turn north (left). Follow Military Road about 1.5 miles to the boat ramp, on the right. If you continue on State Route 507 past Military Road, you'll drive along the south side of the lake.

Facilities: The north side of the lake has a public access area with a boat ramp and rest rooms. Food and gas are available in Tenino, four miles away. The drive north a few miles to eat dinner at Offut Lake Resort is worth the trip. Lodging and tackle can be found in Tumwater.

Contact: Jayhawks, (360) 458-5707 (sporting goods department).

Species available: Rainbow trout.

Fishing McIntosh Lake: Hatchery plants do pretty well at McIntosh, and the lake is often one of the area's better producers throughout the spring. Although the trout planted here are often quite small, they grow quickly in the early spring and provide good fishing throughout May. But by June this shallow lake warms up considerably and trout fishing falls off until September. Trolling, stillfishing, and evening fly-fishing all work well here. Fly anglers should pay special attention to the brushy shoreline along the south side and the large patch of snags and stumps near the middle of the lake.

McIntosh Lake is also popular with nesting ducks and Canada geese, so watch out for them and their young during the spring.

51. BLACK RIVER

Reference: **Flows from Black Lake into the Chehalis River near Oakville; map B2, grid c1.**

How to get there: Take U.S. 12 west of Interstate 5 at Grand Mound and turn north on State Route 121 (Little Rock Road) at Rochester to go upriver, or continue west on U.S. 12 through Rochester to where the highway crosses the lower river.

Facilities: Rough boat launches are located about 1.5 miles north of Little Rock (off 110th Avenue), two miles south of Little Rock (off State Route 121), two miles west of Rochester (off Moon Road), and a little over four miles west of Rochester (on the south side of the U.S. 12 bridge). Food, gas, tackle, and lodging are available in and around Rochester.

Contact: Tumwater Sports, (360) 352-5161.

Species available: Cutthroat and rainbow trout, largemouth bass.

Fishing the Black River: This is one of the slowest, most gently moving streams in the Northwest, flowing nearly 30 miles from the south end of Black Lake to the Chehalis River with hardly a riffle along the way. It can be floated quite safely in a canoe or small inflatable, and that's how many anglers fish it. Most anglers fish for trout with spinning tackle or fly rods, but there are also bass in the river that probably made their way out of Black Lake.

Whether you fish for trout or bass, you can't use bait. This river has selective regulations, which means artificial lures and flies only, with single, barbless hooks. The same goes for Mima Creek, Waddell Creek, Beaver Creek, Salmon Creek, Dempsey Creek, and Blooms Ditch, all of which are tributaries to the Black River. The season here opens June 1 and runs through October.

52. UPPER CHEHALIS RIVER

Reference: From Oakville upstream; map B2, grid c1.

How to get there: Take Interstate 5 to Grand Mound, drive west on U.S. 12, and turn south on Albany Street to Independence Road to reach some of the river between Grand Mound and Oakville. Roads off Old Highway 99 between Grand Mound and Chehalis, including Prather Road and Cooks Hill Road, provide some river access. Take State Route 6 west of Interstate 5 at Chehalis to reach more than 20 miles of the river from Chehalis upstream to Pe Ell.

Facilities: Rainbow Falls State Park has tent sites and rest rooms. Food, gas, lodging, tackle, and other amenities are available in Centralia and Chehalis.

Contact: Sunbirds Shopping Center, (360) 748-3337 (sporting goods department).

Species available: Winter and (some) summer steelhead; coho, chinook, and chum salmon; sea-run and resident cutthroat trout, largemouth bass.

Fishing the upper Chehalis River: Like a number of western Washington rivers, the Chehalis assumes many faces as it winds its way northward from its humble beginnings in the hills of northwestern Cowlitz County to the low farmlands of Lewis, Thurston, and Grays Harbor counties, finally entering Grays Harbor and the Pacific Ocean near Aberdeen. While the lower Chehalis (see page 346) is a favorite among a broad range of Northwest anglers, the upper two-thirds of the river draw relatively little angler interest or fishing pressure.

Access is part of the problem. Much of the river runs through farmland and other private property, and some of the greetings you'll get if you go knocking on farmhouse doors asking permission to fish will give you a sense of what Burt Reynolds, Jon Voight, and Ned Beatty must have felt like at times during their little canoe trip a few years back. And, even where it is okay to fish, the river has a lot of high, steep banks and a serious shortage of gently sloping gravel bars where you can stroll casually up and down the river. Boating this stretch of the Chehalis might be the answer, but the river is too slow-moving for drift boats and rafts and there are no developed boat ramps where larger jet sleds or other power boats can be launched.

A rare exception to this generally dismal story is the short section of river around Rainbow Falls State Park, where deep pools and at least some gravel beach provide the opportunity to fish several hundred feet of beautiful stream. The fishing isn't all that productive, but at least it's pretty. And, if you take the time to explore some of the areas downstream, you're sure to find other short sections of the river where you can wet a line. I haven't found many such places, but maybe you will.

53. SKOOKUMCHUCK RIVER

Reference: **Flows into the Chehalis River at Centralia; map B2, grid c2.**

How to get there: Take State Route 507 north from Centralia to Bucoda, paralleling the lower river much of the way. Turn east onto Skookumchuck Road about 1.5 miles north of Bucoda to reach the section of river between State Route 507 and Skookumchuck Dam.

Facilities: Groceries and gas are available in Bucoda and Tenino, with other amenities in Centralia.

Contact: Sunbirds Shopping Center, (360) 748-3337 (sporting goods department).

Species available: Winter steelhead, sea-run and resident cutthroat trout.

Fishing the Skookumchuck River: Hatchery plants of one kind or another provide virtually all action for anglers on the lower Skookumchuck. At least 80,000 winter steelhead smolts a year are released from the hatchery facility at the base of the dam, and when adult fish from those plants return to the river, they provide a flurry of fishing opportunity. The best fishing is in March and April, and most of the steelhead are caught from a short stretch of river near the dam. Like the Blue Creek Hole on the Cowlitz or the Tokul Creek fishery on the Snoqualmie (see pages 411 and 175), what happens here is something short of an aesthetic angling experience, but the catching can be good. Several thousand hatchery cutthroat are also stocked in the lower Skookumchuck most years, providing a pretty good October and November fishery. The standard river regulation of allowing two trout per day, at least 12 inches long, is in effect here. Wild steelhead and wild cutthroats must be released whenever you fish the lower Skookumchuck.

Things are a little different on the upper Skookumchuck, above the reservoir. This stretch has selective fishery regulations, so you can't use bait or barbed hooks. It's also pretty tough to find a legal-sized trout here throughout most of the season. Access to this upper-river fishery is via logging roads running south from Vail.

54. LAWRENCE LAKE

Reference: **Southeast of Yelm; map B2, grid c5.**

How to get there: Take Bald Hills Road southeast off State Route 507 at a place called Five Corners, about a mile southeast of Yelm. Follow the road southward until you come to a three-way fork (about a mile after 138th Avenue SE), and go west (right). Drive half a mile to Lawrence Lake Road and turn south (left). Drive another mile and you'll see the lake on the right.

Facilities: The lake has an access area with a boat ramp and rest rooms. The town of Yelm offers the nearest food, gas, tackle, and lodging.

Contact: Jayhawks, (360) 458-5707 (sporting goods department).

Species available: Largemouth bass, yellow perch, brown bullhead catfish, brown trout.

Fishing Lawrence Lake: Even though Lawrence Lake covers 300 acres, it's fairly shallow, so it warms quickly in the summer—so quickly, in fact, that rainbow trout don't do particularly well here. The Department of Fish and Wildlife stocked brown trout in the lake in 1994, and they are expected to hold up well and provide decent trout fishing in the spring and fall. But even if they don't, anglers who are busy catching bass and other warm-water fish won't mind. Lawrence offers some good bass fishing, and largemouths of five pounds and bigger are caught here throughout the spring and summer. A special slot limit on bass is in effect, so check the fishing regulations pamphlet before fishing the lake for the first time.

In addition to trout and bass, perch fishing can be very good during the day. Brown bullheads bite equally well during the evening and at night.

If you plan to fish Lawrence Lake, do it from April until the end of October. The public access area and boat ramp are closed from early November until early April each year.

---

55. CLEAR LAKE

Reference: **West of La Grande, eastern Thurston County; map B2, grid c5.**

How to get there: Turn southeast on Black Hills Road from State Route 507 at Five Corners, a mile southeast of Yelm. Follow Black Hills Road just under 10 miles to the south end of the lake, on the left.

Facilities: Clear Lake Resort and the Department of Fish and Wildlife public access area have pretty much everything an angler might need.

Contact: Clear Lake Resort, (360) 894-2543.

Species available: Rainbow and brown trout.

Fishing Clear Lake: This is one of the most productive—and therefore one of the most popular—trout lakes in the south Puget Sound region. Long known for its husky rainbows, Clear Lake is generous with trout in the nine- to 11-inch range early in the season, and they just get bigger as time goes by. The rainbows carryover pretty well, too, meaning your catch might include a dandy of 18 to 20 inches. The addition of brown trout several years ago made things that much more interesting and prolonged the fishing action a little farther into the summer. Both trolling and stillfishing work well, and one local favorite is a small, green Triple Teazer.

56. MASHEL RIVER

Reference: **Joins Nisqually River southwest of Eatonville; map B2, grid c6.**

How to get there: Take State Route 161 to Eatonville. Logging roads leading east from town provide access to the upper river. State Route 161 itself parallels part of the river to the west of Eatonville.

Facilities: Food, gas, tackle, and lodging are available in and around Eatonville.

Contact: Eatonville Coast to Coast, (360) 832-3181.

Species available: Cutthroat trout.

Fishing the Mashel River: The Mashel provides a little trout-fishing activity after it opens to fishing in June, but finding a two-fish limit of a legal-sized cutthroat here can be a challenge. Local anglers fish it pretty thoroughly at the start of the season, and these trout grow to eight inches rather slowly. You might do well to wait and fish it in October, after the interest and fishing pressure have waned. The Mashel is open through October 31.

57. ALDER LAKE

Reference: **Southeast of La Grande, southeast corner of Thurston County; map B2, grid c6.**

How to get there: Take State Route 7 south from Spanaway about 25 miles or north from Morton about 18 miles. The lake is on the south side of the road.

Facilities: Alder Park, near the north end of the lake, has a two-lane boat ramp, tent and RV sites, picnic tables, showers and rest rooms, a moorage float, covered cooking areas, and a nearby store with groceries, bait, and other necessities. There's a public boat ramp and access area on the northeast side of the lake, just off the highway, and another on the south side, off Pleasant Valley Road. There's a gas station in Elbe, at the east end of the lake.

Contact: Alder Park Store, (360) 569-8824.

Species available: Rainbow and (a few) cutthroat trout, kokanee, yellow perch, crappies.

Fishing Alder Lake: Are you looking for the largest fish in the entire Northwest? Well, Alder Lake has it. That's right, I said "it," not "them." The fish in question is one-of-a-kind, and it resides near the northwest end of the lake, not far from the dam. Fly over the lake sometime and you'll see it. That's how I first spotted it, and I was so impressed that I shot several photos of it out the airplane window. Since then I've even seen the monster on a few good maps. Okay, before you start thinking that I've been sniffing too much Smelly Jelly, I should tell you that this "fish" is actually Bogucki Island, a fish-shaped high spot that managed to keep its head above water after the Nisqually River was dammed near the little community of Alder to form the reservoir we now call Alder Lake. It's the most fishy-looking landmark I know of around here.

There are also enough real fish in Alder Lake, which is open to fishing year-round, to draw anglers from all over western Washington. Kokanee are perhaps the biggest draw, providing plenty of excitement and fine eating for Alder Lake anglers. May, June, and July are the top months to fish for them, and most are caught by trollers. Wedding Rings and similar spinners, fished behind strings of trolling blades, are most popular for Alder Lake kokanee, which average about nine inches in May but sometimes top the 12-inch mark by mid-summer. Most anglers use bait on the hooks of those Wedding Rings, with worms being the most popular bait.

The lake is also planted with legal-sized rainbows in the spring, some of which are caught by the folks fishing for kokanee. If you want rainbows instead of kokanee, try small Kwikfish, Dick Nite or Triple Teazer spoons, Rooster Tails, or Mepps spinners near the surface, either cast or trolled. You might also pick up an occasional cutthroat this way.

Some people come here just for the excellent perch fishing, especially in the spring and summer. A bobber-and-worm rig or plastic-skirted Mini Jig with a piece of worm on its hook will take all you want, once you locate a school. Some of the perch grow impressively large.

Although this cool impoundment isn't what anyone would call perfect bass habitat, the lake does have a fair largemouth population. They can be found along the shoreline where rocks and boulders provide food and cover, or cast to spots where shoreline trees and brush hang into the water.

---

58. MINERAL LAKE

Reference: **At the town of Mineral, Lewis County; map B2, grid d7.**

How to get there: Take U.S. 12 east from Interstate 5 to Morton and turn north on State Route 7, following it about 13 miles to Mineral Road. From there it's a two-mile drive to the town of Mineral and Mineral Lake.

Facilities: The lake has a public boat ramp. Mineral Lake Resort offers boat rentals, cabins and RV sites (no tent sites), a large and productive fishing dock ($4 per day), bait, tackle, and snacks. A small market in town sells fishing licenses, and gas is available in Mineral.

Contact: Mineral Lake Resort, (360) 492-5367.

Species available: Brown trout, rainbow trout.

Fishing Mineral Lake: People in these parts still haven't gotten over the monster rainbows a few anglers caught from this lake in the spring of 1995, so that's what you may hear about whenever you ask about the fishing here. Mineral produced several rainbows of eight to 14½ pounds—that's right, "pounds," not inches—during that spring of monsters, greatly increasing the popularity of this already-popular Lewis County lake.

Not everyone fishing Mineral is going to catch a trout of such impressive proportions, but it does tend to treat anglers very generously. Both rainbows and browns put on weight fast in this rich lake, so anglers complain neither about the quality nor the quantity of their catch. Stillfishing with Berkley Power Bait produces some of the larger rainbows, but trolling is also lucrative. Since brown trout were added to the Mineral Lake menu a few years ago, the good fishing tends to last much longer, usually well into summer.

If there's a down side to fishing Mineral Lake, it's the fact that lots of folks converge on its tiny boat ramp and access area at about the same time every morning, sometimes creating traffic jams and tattered nerves. The key is to arrive early and be patient. The fishing is worth the wait.

59. SKATE CREEK

Reference: **Flows into the upper Cowlitz River west of Packwood; map B2, grid d8.**

How to get there: Drive east from Ashford for two miles on State Route 706 and turn south (right) on Forest Road 52 or take U.S. 12 to Packwood and turn north on Forest Road 52, which parallels the creek for about seven miles.

Facilities: Food, gas, tackle, and lodging are available in Packwood and Ashford.

Contact: Washington Department of Fish and Wildlife, Vancouver Office, (360) 696-6211.

Species available: Rainbow trout.

Fishing Skate Creek: This large back-country stream is easily accessible from Forest Road 52, and the liberal plants of hatchery rainbows make it very popular with summertime anglers. Skate Creek opens to fishing June 1 (closing at the end of October), but stocking may occur after the opener, depending on stream conditions. Because it gets hatchery plants, the creek has an eight-inch minimum size limit and anglers are allowed to keep five trout a day. Any bait, lure, or fly you use will work after the trout have been stocked.

60. NEWAUKUM RIVER

Reference: **Joins the Chehalis River northwest of Chehalis; map B2, grid d3.**

How to get there: Take Centralia-Alpha Road southeast from Centralia for about 11 miles and turn on North Fork Road (left to go upstream on the North Fork Newaukum, right to go downstream). To reach the South Fork Newaukum, take Interstate 5 south from Chehalis for six miles and turn east (left) on State Route 508, which parallels much of the river. To reach the lower Newaukum, turn south off Interstate 5 on Rush Road, about 3.5 miles south of Chehalis, then west on Newaukum Valley Road.

Facilities: Food, gas, tackle, and lodging are available in Centralia and Chehalis.

Contact: Sunbirds Shopping Center, (360) 748-3337 (sporting goods department).

Species available: Winter steelhead.

Fishing the Newaukum River: Wild steelhead runs on this small Lewis County tributary to the Chehalis have been in tough shape for many years, but a small-scale steelhead fishery is provided by hatchery fish that are stocked on a somewhat infrequent basis. A typical winter's catch from the entire Newaukum system is 40 to 50 winter steelies. Any wild steelhead (those without any clipped fins) must be released. The river is also open to summertime trout fishing, but few fish over the 14-inch minimum size are caught. The season here runs from June 1 through March 31.

61. TILTON RIVER

Reference: **Flows into the north arm of Mayfield Lake; map B2, grid e5.**

How to get there: Take U.S. 12 to Morton, turn north on State Route 7, drive a half mile, and turn west (left) on State Route 508 to follow the river downstream. Drive three miles and turn north (right) to reach the North Fork Tilton.

Facilities: Ike Kinswa State Park is located where the Tilton flows into Mayfield Lake, and has both tent and RV sites, rest rooms with showers, and other amenities. Food, gas, lodging, and tackle are available in Morton.

Contact: Morton Coast to Coast Hardware, (360) 496-6444; Ike Kinswa State Park, (360) 983-3402.

Species available: Rainbow trout, winter steelhead, coho salmon.

Fishing the Tilton River: Generous late-spring plants of hatchery rainbows provide most of the fishing action on this small tributary to the Cowlitz River system. While most of the planters are legal-sized eight- to 10-inchers, the Department of Fish and Wildlife also includes a number of so-called jumbo legals, which range up to 15 inches. Trout fishing is best in June and July. Liberal regulations on the main Tilton allow anglers to use bait and keep up to five trout per day and any trout eight inches or longer (only one of which can top 12 inches). On the North, South, East, and West forks of the river, selective fishery regulations are in effect, so you have to use artificial lures and flies with barbless hooks, and the limit is two trout per day.

Before the construction of Mayfield Dam in the 1960s, the Tilton flowed directly into the Cowlitz River, but now it enters the river system at the north end of Mayfield Lake. As dams tend to do, Mayfield cut off the once-healthy runs of salmon and steelhead into the Tilton. Fish are now trucked from the Cowlitz Trout Hatchery and Cowlitz Salmon Hatchery to provide some salmon and steelhead fishing. Unfortunately, only a small percentage of the fish hauled to the Tilton are caught by anglers. This little stream where anglers were accustomed to catching wild 10- to 20-pound winter steelhead with amazing frequency 40 years ago now produces only a few dozen "transplanted" hatchery steelies each season. The coho trucking operation is a little more successful, providing anglers with some decent salmon fishing from October to December.

62. MAYFIELD LAKE

Reference: **West of Mossyrock, Lewis County; map B2, grid e5.**

How to get there: Take U.S. 12 east from Interstate 5 about 17 miles to the lake. Turn north (left) at Silver Creek to reach Ike Kinswa State Park on the north side of the lake or cross over the lake on U.S. 12 and go just over a mile to Mayfield Lake County Park, on the left.

Facilities: Kinswa State Park has RV and tent spaces, rest rooms, and a boat ramp. Mayfield Lake County Park offers rest rooms and a boat ramp. Snacks and beverages are available at the small store next to the turn-off to the county park, with everything else available four miles to the east in Mossyrock.

Contact: Fish Country Sport Shop, (360) 985-2090; Ike Kinswa State Park, (360) 983-3402.

Species available: Tiger muskies, rainbow trout, coho salmon, a few smallmouth bass.

Fishing Mayfield Lake: Before making a tiger musky trip to Mayfield Lake, read the chapter about this big, ill-tempered trophy in the first section of this book. That's where you'll find the how-to information you'll need to effectively pursue this worthy adversary. If you have the choice, fish the lake in the evening, and plan on staying right up until dark, since that's when tigers are most likely to go on the prowl. This is especially true if the day has been clear and warm. Among the places you'll want to spend some time looking and casting are the entrance to the Tilton Arm on the north side, the Winston Creek Arm at the south end, the big weed beds along the shoreline east of the county park, and the shallow bay south of the hatchery near the upper end of the lake. If you launch at the county park and still have a few minutes of daylight left when you return to the ramp, make a few casts just outside the east end of the swimming area. That's where I caught my one and only tiger musky on a warm July evening in 1992, and I released it. If it's still there, it's a whopper by now.

Now that the tiger muskies have gotten a good start on reducing the once-abundant squawfish in Mayfield, Department of Fish and Wildlife biologists are once again planting rainbow trout in the lake. The trout fishery was in the dumps throughout the 1980s, but it's flourishing once again. Planted as fingerlings, they soon grow to catchable size, and you might have the good fortune of hooking a fish or two in the 12- to 14-inch range. Most of the locals troll Pop Geer and worms for their trout, but Kwikfish, Triple Teazers, Rooster Tails, and all the other usual trolling fare will work. Don't be too surprised if, along with the rainbows, you catch a small coho salmon or two. Coho from Riffe Lake and the Tilton River commonly make their way into Mayfield to mix with the trout population.

The smallmouths still remaining from a plant made several years ago are scattered all over the lake, but if you have your heart set on catching a couple of them, try fishing along the high bank on the north side of the lake, west of the state park. The submerged boulders found here and there around the entrance to the Cowlitz Arm also produce a few smallmouths.

---

63. RIFFE LAKE

Reference: **East of Mossyrock, Lewis County; map B2, grid e6.**
How to get there: Take U.S. 12 east from Interstate 5 about 23 miles to Mossyrock, turn south (right) into town and go east (left) on Aljune Road, which leads to Tacoma Public Utilities' Mossyrock Park Campground and boat ramps near the dam. To reach the upper lake, continue on U.S. 12 about five miles past Morton and turn south (right) on Kosmos Road. Bear right to reach the steep boat ramp at the northeast corner of the lake or turn left and drive about four miles to the entrance of the new Tacoma Public Utilities' Taidnapam Park near where the Cowlitz River enters the lake.
Facilities: Mossyrock Park at the lower end of the lake has RV hookups, tent sites, boat ramps, and rest rooms with showers, as does Taidnapam Park at the upper end. Groceries, restaurants, gas, tackle, and lodging are available in Mossyrock and Morton.
Contact: Fish Country Sport Shop, (360) 985-2090; Mossyrock Park, (360) 983-3900; Taidnapam Park, (360) 497-7707.
Species available: Coho salmon, cutthroat and brown trout, largemouth and smallmouth bass, brown bullhead catfish, crappies, perch.

Fishing Riffe Lake: The coho fishery is the biggest angling attraction at Riffe Lake, and it draws both boat and bank anglers from all over western Washington. In the spring and early summer, cohos are near the surface, where they can be caught by trollers using strings of trolling blades and worms, white corn, cocktail shrimp, or combinations of these three baits. Bank anglers catch them by suspending the same baits three or four feet beneath a bobber. As the summer progresses and the thermocline establishes itself in this big, deep reservoir, the coho go deep, where both boat and bank anglers typically fish them 100 feet down with slip-bobber rigs. Most of this coho action takes place at the west end of the lake, within sight of the dam. As for size, two-year-olds comprise most of the catch in the spring and early summer, and they average 12 to 14 inches. The one-year-old class begins to dominate the catch by July, and for the rest of the summer and fall, the average Riffe Lake coho is an eight- to nine-incher.

Another coho fishery that's really taken off the past couple of years is at the other end of the reservoir, where the Cowlitz River flows into the east end of the impoundment. The so-called "108 Bridge" on the Champion Haul Road near Taidnapam Park has become a mecca for anglers who stillfish using worms, salmon eggs, cocktail shrimp, and corn to catch coho to about 14 inches. Both spring and fall can be productive times to take part in this fishery, but leave your landing net at home; the bridge is about 40 feet above the water. Talk about flying fish!

Shortages of coho for planting in Riffe Lake have prompted Fish and Wildlife personnel to get creative and stock a few steelhead in the lake. Many anglers don't even notice the difference. Although rare, an occasional brown trout may grab one of the offerings meant for coho here. If you want to target specifically on these trophies—which may top 10 pounds—forget the worms and corn and offer them something like a slowly trolled Rapala or other large, bait fish-imitating plug or wobbling spoon.

Smallmouth bass are much more abundant than largemouths in this chilly reservoir, but you might catch both if you fish the upper end during May and June. As the creek channels fill with water that time of year, they draw hungry bass like a magnet, and the fishing with crankbaits or plastics can be very good. Another possibility for bass is Swofford Cove, on the north side, near the west end of the reservoir. Both largemouths and smallmouths tend to congregate in this shallow, warm bay in spring and summer.

Riffe has a healthy population of brown bullheads, and the best time and place to catch them is during spring, in the shallow flats at the upper end of the lake. Most catfish anglers launch at the Kosmos boat ramp in the evening and fish the shallow water nearby with worms or nightcrawlers. Although not large at an average of 10 or 11 inches, they're abundant enough to provide plenty of fast action and good eating for a few hours' effort.

64. SWOFFORD POND

Reference: **Southeast of Mossyrock; map B2, grid e5.**

How to get there: Take Aljune Road southeast from Mossyrock about 2.5 miles and turn south (right) on Swofford Road. Drive 1.5 miles, go left at the "T," and drive to the pond, which will be on your right.

Facilities: There's a boat ramp at the east end of the lake and plenty of bank-fishing access along the north side. The nearest food, gas, and tackle are in Mossyrock, and there's a Tacoma Public Utilities campground on nearby Riffe Lake.

Contact: Fish Country Sport Shop, (360) 985-2090.

Species available: Rainbow and brown trout, largemouth bass, bluegills, crappies, brown bullhead and channel catfish.

Fishing Swofford Pond: Few freshwater fishing spots in the Pacific Northwest can claim to have it all, but this 240-acre "pond" just south of Riffe Lake (see page 406) comes pretty close. Whether your preferences lean toward pan-sized bluegills, sweet-eating channel catfish, or hook-nosed brown trout, you might find them here.

Thousands of legal-sized rainbow and brown trout are stocked here every spring, and anglers have little trouble catching a limit of them. Trollers use small spoons, spinners, wobbling plugs, or trolling blades with worms, while most bank anglers do just fine with that time-proven favorite, a garden worm suspended several feet below a bobber. Although anglers fishing for eight- to 10-inch planters seldom encounter them, the lake does have some huge brown trout. Biologists conducting tests with electroshock equipment—used to stun and count fish in a test area—have captured and released browns of 10 pounds.

Long a productive bass pond, Swofford is home to some husky large-mouths. Unfortunately, it isn't home to many small bass, at least not lately, which could bode poorly for bass anglers in the future. But if you want a crack at a five-pounder, you have a realistic chance here. Hit it early in the morning or late in the evening with surface plugs or buzzbaits, or fish spinnerbaits or plastics during the day around the weedy shoreline.

Stocked long ago with bluegills, Swofford offers the possibility of excellent panfish action. Crappies are also abundant, and if you're willing to work at it with small leadheads or BeetleSpins, you'll catch enough for a family fish-fry.

Brown bullheads are also plentiful, and the many bank-fishing spots along the road on the north shore of the pond are good places to fish for them. Anglers who fish nightcrawlers well into the night during the late spring and summer make some impressive catches. Along with the bullheads, don't be too surprised if you catch a couple of large channel catfish. And, when I say "large," I'm not kidding. A 19½-pound channel cat was caught from the lake in 1995.

65. LAKE SCANEWA

Reference: **Southeast of Glenoma, Lewis County; map B2, grid e7.**

How to get there: Drive east from Interstate 5 on U.S. 12 about 40 miles and turn south at mile marker 111 on Savio Road. Drive 1.5 miles and turn south again on Kiona Road, which eventually becomes Peters Road, and follow it about four miles to the campground and the reservoir, on the right.

Facilities: The Lewis County Public Utility District operates a campground and a day-use park on the reservoir. The campground, which is closed in winter, offers tent and RV sites, rest rooms, showers, and a boat ramp. Food, gas, tackle, and lodging are available in Randle and Morton.

Contact: The Lake Scanewa Concessionaire, (360) 497-7175; Lewis County PUD, (360) 497-5351.

Species available: Rainbow trout, Kamloops-strain rainbow trout.

Fishing Lake Scanewa: This is Washington's newest lake, having filled in 1994 with the completion of Cowlitz Falls Dam on the Cowlitz River. But even though it's just a youngster, Scanewa (pronounced Scan-EE-wah) is already drawing enthusiastic reviews from trout anglers. Kamloops rainbows stocked in 1994 have done fairly well in the cool waters of this 600-acre impoundment, providing the opportunity for some bragging-sized fish. Subsequent plants of "regular" rainbows provide the bulk of the fishing action. This lake has a somewhat unusual season, designed to protect steelhead smolts migrating downstream in early spring, so be sure to check the regulations pamphlet for details before fishing this newest Cowlitz River reservoir. The fishing season runs from June 1 through February.

66. CISPUS RIVER

Reference: **Joins the Cowlitz River above Riffe Lake; map B2, grid e8.**

How to get there: Take U.S. 12 to Randle and turn south on Forest Road 25 (Woods Creek Road). Drive just over a mile and turn east (left) on Cispus Road (Forest Road 23), which follows the river upstream for more than 20 miles.

Facilities: There are a few Forest Service campgrounds along the river with campsites, rest rooms, and water, but the nearest food, gas, tackle, and lodging are in Randle.

Contact: Fish Country Sport Shop, (360) 985-2090.

Species available: Cutthroat, rainbow, and brook trout.

Fishing the Cispus River: Wild cutthroat and planted rainbows provide some action on the lower Cispus, below the mouth of the Muddy Fork. Above the Muddy Fork anglers will find a mix of small cutthroats and brook trout.The season here runs from June 1 through October 31, and you'll find small trout available all season. Fishing pressure gets fairly heavy during the height of the mid-summer camping season, but you'll have elbow room before mid-June and after Labor Day.

67. YELLOWJACKET PONDS

Reference: **About 10 miles southeast of Randle, Lewis County; map B2, grid e8.**

How to get there: Take U.S. 12 to Randle, turn south on Forest Road 25, and then east on Cispus Road. Turn east (left) on Forest Road 29 and drive about three miles to the road turning left to the first pond. The road to the second pond is on the right about a quarter-mile past the first.

Facilities: The nearest food, gas, tackle, and lodging are in Randle.

Contact: U.S. Forest Service Office in Randle, (360) 497-7565.

Species available: Rainbow trout.

Fishing Yellowjacket Ponds: Liberal plants of hatchery rainbows mean productive fishing for trout anglers on these two small ponds about 10 miles off U.S. 12. Most of the plants are eight- to 10-inchers, but the Department of Fish and Wildlife includes a few 12- to 14-inchers in the mix for added excitement. Fish your favorite here, whether it be a bobber-and-worm rig, small spoon or spinner, or even a dry fly. These ponds, by the way, have an interesting season, opening in late April and staying open through the fall and winter until the end of February.

68. OLEQUA CREEK

Reference: **Flows into the Cowlitz River south of Vader; map B2, grid e2.**

How to get there: Take State Route 506 west off Interstate 5, drive four miles through the town of Vader, and turn north (right) on Winlock-Vader Road, which parallels the west side of the creek for more than six miles.

Facilities: Gas and food are available in Vader and Winlock. Lodging, tackle, and other amenities are in Chehalis.

Contact: Sunbirds Shopping Center, (360) 748-3337 (sporting goods department).

Species available: Winter and summer steelhead, sea-run cutthroat trout.

Fishing Olequa Creek: Steelheading is tough on this pretty little stream, since it has wild-steelhead-release regulations and receives no hatchery plants. Still, anglers do manage to catch a few, both winter and summer. The best fishing here is for fall cutthroats, but weather is the key. A little rain is a good thing; too much rain muddies the creek and renders it unfishable. If you time it right, a well-placed nightcrawler in any of the slow, deep pools will bring quick results. The creek opens to fishing on June 1, closing at the end of February.

69. LACAMAS CREEK

Reference: **Flows into the Cowlitz River near Vader; map B2, grid e2.**

How to get there: Take State Route 506 west off Interstate 5, drive two miles, and turn north (right) on Telegraph Road, which parallels the river upstream for more than three miles.

Facilities: Gas and food are available in Toledo, Vader, and Winlock. Lodging and tackle can be found in Chehalis.

Contact: Sunbirds Shopping Center, (360) 748-3337 (sporting goods department).

Species available: Winter steelhead, resident cutthroat trout.

Fishing Lacamas Creek: Don't drive a long distance to fish this creek unless you have a lot of time on your hands. Winter steelhead fishing regulations require that all wild fish be released, but the creek isn't stocked with hatchery fish, so there just plain isn't a very good chance that you're going to catch one. There are cutthroat in the creek, but they're on the smallish side, and the minimum legal size for trout here is 14 inches. You might get a chance to do a little-catch-and-release fishing, but that's about it.

70. COWLITZ RIVER

Reference: **Flows into the Columbia River near Kelso; map B2, grid f2.**

How to get there: Interstate 5 parallels the east side of the river from Kelso upstream to Toledo. But the most popular stretch of river is upstream, between Toledo and the Cowlitz Salmon Hatchery. To reach this area, take U.S. 12 east from Interstate 5, turning south (right) on Tucker Road, left at the "Y" onto Classe Road, left on Spencer Road, and right onto the road leading past the state trout hatchery and to the river. To reach the salmon hatchery farther upstream, continue about four miles farther on U.S. 12 to Salkum and turn right at the "Salmon Hatchery" sign.

Facilities: Boat ramps can be found at the trout and salmon hatcheries, with well-stocked tackle stores, gas stations, and grocery stores at the junction of U.S. 12 and Tucker Road and at Blue Creek Bait and Tackle. Barrier Dam Campground, a short distance north of the salmon hatchery, has RV spaces.

Contact: Blue Creek Bait and Tackle, (360) 985-2495; Bob's Merchandise, (360) 425-3870.

Species available: Spring and fall chinook salmon, coho salmon, winter and summer steelhead, sea-run cutthroat trout, Columbia River smelt.

Fishing the Cowlitz River: Winter steelhead and spring chinook are the two biggest draws at this river, and for very good reason. The Cowlitz has been Washington's top winter steelie stream every winter but one since 1971, giving up as many as 30,000 fish in a single season, although in recent years the catch has been more like 10,000 to 16,000 fish per year.

Boat ramps at the salmon hatchery, trout hatchery, and other points downstream make this one of the Northwest's most heavily boated rivers. During the winter season, a bulk of the boat traffic is concentrated on the two miles of river immediately downstream from the trout hatchery ramp. Some boaters back-troll plugs or diver-and-bait combinations for their steelhead, but a technique called "free-drifting" has become very popular in recent years. It involves making long casts across and slightly upstream, using lighter sinkers than those commonly associated with drift-fishing, and allowing the boat to drift downstream while the line drags behind.

Bank anglers also make good catches of winter steelhead from the Cowlitz, but if you want to fish the best spots, plan on getting shoulder-to-shoulder with your fellow anglers. The mouth of Blue Creek, just downstream from the Cowlitz Trout Hatchery, may produce several hundred fish in a single morning, with several hundred anglers on hand to catch them. If you don't like the idea of fishing with 200 to 300 fishing buddies on a 300-foot stretch of river bank, you won't like Blue Creek. But if catching steelhead takes precedence over anything remotely resembling an aesthetic angling experience, this spot is for you. Grab a selection of leadhead jigs and a couple of sliding bobbers (floats), take the quarter-mile trail leading from the back corner of the trout hatchery parking lot, and join the crowd at the mouth of Blue Creek. And when you reach the creek mouth, don't be shy; this isn't a place for the meek.

A lot more elbow room can be found along the long stretch of public river bank upstream from Blue Creek, both above and below the boat ramp. Steelheading can be very good here, and the heavy boat traffic doesn't seem to bother the fish. There are those, in fact, who say the boats keep the steelhead stirred up and active, making them more likely to take a bait or lure. I'm not a fish psychologist, so I'm not sure about this theory.

Several miles upstream, below the salmon hatchery's barrier dam, is another spot where winter steelheaders like to congregate. You'll have a little more room to cast here than at Blue Creek, but on a winter weekend, it's still pretty busy.

The area below the barrier dam is also popular with spring chinook anglers, both those fishing from the bank and those who launch at the mouth of Mill Creek, where the gravel road ends in a two-lane boat ramp. Boaters can't fish between the ramp and the barrier dam, but they catch lots of chinook from the half-mile of river immediately downstream from the ramp. Back-trolling Kwikfish and Flatfish with a strip of sardine lashed to the belly of each lure is effective for boat anglers, as is back-bouncing with large clusters of salmon roe or shrimp-and-roe combinations. Bank anglers drift-fish shrimp, roe, and the shrimp-roe combos known locally as "Cowlitz Cocktails." Chinook fishing peaks in May.

Anglers fishing the lower section of the Cowlitz, around Kelso and Longview, get a crack at spring chinook several days to a week before the gang at the barrier dam, as fresh runs enter the river. Some plunking with roe, spinners, plugs, and herring occurs on this lower part of the river, but boaters still have the advantage. They also back-troll plugs with that same sardine wrap used upstream, but large spinners and whole or plug-cut herring play bigger roles in the fishery on the lower Cowlitz than they do up by the salmon hatchery.

As the spring chinook fishery tapers off, summer steelhead action picks up, and the Cowlitz often provides excellent summer steelheading from July through October. There are dozens of productive fishing spots between the trout hatchery and Toledo. Boat anglers probably account for 70 or more of those fish.

Coho returns have been so poor on the Cowlitz in recent years that I won't even talk about it.

Hatchery production of sea-run cutthroat has been good enough on the Cowlitz over the past decade to allow anglers what amounts to a bonus trout limit. While the daily limit on most Washington streams is only two fish, it's five on the Cowlitz, and limits are well within the realm of possibility during the height of the fishery in September and October. The mouth of Blue Creek is the hottest cutthroat hole, and the crowds are much smaller in the fall than during the height of the steelhead fishery in December and January. If you don't want to hike to Blue Creek, try any deep, slow pool downstream, especially those that contain downed trees, stumps, and other submerged wood cover. Rolling a nightcrawler along the bottom works best for Cowlitz sea-runs, some of which top 20 inches.

I can't leave the Cowlitz without talking about smelt. The best dip-netting for these succulent little eulachons usually occurs in February, but might start as early as the second week in January and run as late as early April. The Castle Rock and Kelso areas offer some of the best dipping, and you're more likely to net a 20-pound daily limit if you hit the river at night or on overcast days.

71. GREEN RIVER

Reference: **Joins the Toutle River near Kid Valley; map B2, grid f4.**

How to get there: Turn east off Interstate 5 at Castle Rock onto State Route 504 and drive 26 miles to 19 Mile Camp. Turn north (left) onto the Weyerhaeuser 1000 Road and follow it east to the 2500 Road, which parallels much of the upper Green.

Facilities: Food, gas, and tackle are available in Toutle and Kid Valley, both along State Route 504. Lodging can be found in Castle Rock.

Contact: Drew's Grocery, (360) 274-8920.

Species available: Summer steelhead.

Fishing the Green River: This little Toutle River tributary is stocked with hatchery steelhead smolts and provides pretty good fishing in June, July, and August. It's open only during the summer and fall, and only for hatchery steelhead; any salmon, trout, or wild steelhead you catch must be released.

Since the river is small and clear, fishing with a "light touch" helps, although you may find yourself hooked to an angry fish on tackle that seems woefully inadequate when the fish takes off downstream, through the brush, under the submerged trees, and around the boulders. Much of the river is small enough and shallow enough to wade, so all you can do is give chase. Good luck!

72. TOUTLE RIVER

Reference: **Flows into the Cowlitz River north of Castle Rock; map B2, grid f4.**

How to get there: Turn east off Interstate 5 onto State Route 504, which parallels much of the North Fork Toutle. Weyerhaeuser's 4100 Road from the town of Toutle, 11 miles east of the freeway, parallels the South Fork.

Facilities: Seaquest State Park, located right on State Route 504 near Silver Lake, has a limited number of tent and RV sites, plus rest rooms with showers and an RV sewage dump. There are also two private resorts on the lake, right alongside the highway. Other than those facilities, the nearest food, gas, tackle, and lodging are in Castle Rock.

Contact: Drew's Grocery, (360) 274-8920; Seaquest State Park, (360) 274-8633.

Species available: Winter and summer steelhead.

Fishing the Toutle River: After Mount St. Helens erupted in 1980, totally destroying the gorgeous North Fork of the Toutle and the main Toutle below the confluence of the North and South forks, fish biologists estimated that it might take decades before the river again provided a steelhead fishery. Well, Mother Nature, with at least some help from her human assistants, shortened that timetable considerably, and the Toutle River system was providing fair to good steelheading before the end of the 1980s. It's still not like the glory days, but there are fish to be caught.

Roles have been reversed between the once-great North Fork and the South Fork that received relatively little angler attention or publicity before the eruption. Now it's the South Fork, which was only lightly damaged by the volcano, that provides most of the steelheading opportunity. Although both are stocked with 25,000 to 30,000 summer steelhead smolts annually, the catch by anglers in 1993 (the latest year for complete catch statistics from the Department of Fish and Wildlife) was more than 1,300 on the South Fork but only 205 from the North Fork. Water clarity remains a problem on the North Fork, and anglers find relatively few days during the year when the river is in fishable condition. Wild steelhead, descendants from fish that started returning to the river shortly after the eruption and resulting mudflows, must be released, whether you fish the North Fork, South Fork, or main river.

June and July are the best months to fish for Toutle River steelhead, with anglers catching more steelhead from the South Fork in those two months alone than they catch during the rest of the year.

73. SILVER LAKE

Reference: **East of Castle Rock; map B2, grid f3.**
How to get there: Take State Route 504 east off Interstate 5 at Castle Rock and drive five miles to the lake, on the south (right) side of the highway.
Facilities: Three private resorts with tackle, groceries, and campsites are located on or near the lake, two of them just off State Route 504. There's also a Department of Fish and Wildlife boat ramp on the lake and a state park with limited tent and RV spaces right across the highway. Gas, food, tackle, and lodging are also available in Castle Rock.
Contact: Silver Lake Resort, (360) 274-6141; Streeter's Resort, (360) 274-6112; Volcano View Resort, (360) 274-7087; Seaquest State Park, (360) 274-8633.
Species available: Largemouth bass, black crappies, white crappies, yellow perch, warmouth, bluegills, brown bullhead catfish, yellow bullhead catfish, rainbow trout.
Fishing Silver Lake: A case could easily be made for calling Silver Lake Washington's best largemouth bass lake. Not only does it produce good numbers of bass for patient anglers, but it's also known for its big fish, giving up more than its share of eight-pounders. The lake is open year-round, and serious bass anglers never really quit fishing it, although the bassing is mighty slow and you can find plenty of solitude in December and January. The first few warm days of February, though, may generate some real activity, and you can find largemouths being caught from that point until the first cold weather of November.

This 3,000-acre lake is only a few feet deep and is very lightly developed, so bass are scattered throughout the water. If you tried to fish Silver's entire shoreline thoroughly, you would be at it for days, so many anglers concentrate their efforts on a few favorite spots that have produced before and are suited to their individual preferences. Whether you like to fish submerged rocks, docks, and floats, submerged trees and logs, shoreline weeds and brush, pad fields, or any other kind of bass cover and structure, you'll probably find plenty of it at Silver Lake.

As you might expect, the lake is a favorite with tournament anglers, so if you prefer a little solitude when you fish, especially during the spring and summer, either call ahead to inquire about weekend activities or fish it during the week.

Although bass get most of the publicity here, the fishing for other warmwater species can be every bit as impressive. Casting a tiny leadhead jig with a plastic skirt or marabou body can produce excellent catches of crappies, and perch fishing is also very good throughout the lake. Brown bullheads are abundant and provide good night-fishing opportunities from spring until early fall.

Until recently, Silver Lake was so overgrown with weeds that it was difficult to get around parts of it in a boat. But the Department of Fish and Wildlife stocked grass carp to help "graze" the vegetation down a bit, and the strategy worked. Now the lake has so much open water that in 1995 the WDF&W planted rainbow trout in the lake for the first time in many years.

---

74. UPPER GREEN RIVER LAKES

Reference: **North of Coldwater Lake, near Cowlitz-Skamania County line; map B2, grid f6.**

How to get there: Turn east off of Interstate 5 onto State Route 504 and drive 26 miles to 19 Mile Camp. Turn north (left) onto the Weyerhaeuser 1000 Road and follow it east to 2500 Road. Take 2500 Road to Shultz Creek and turn right on 2800 Road; follow it to 3500 Road and take it uphill to the lakes.

Facilities: Food, gas, and tackle can be found in Kid Valley and Toutle, both on State Route 504. The nearest lodging is in Castle Rock.

Contact: Drew's Grocery, (360) 274-8920.

Species available: Cutthroat, brook, and brown trout.

Fishing the upper Green River lakes: Ranging in size from eight to 30 acres, these five lakes on the upper Green River drainage are somewhat typical of high-elevation lakes throughout the Northwest except that all are reached by various logging roads. At 30 acres, Elk is the largest of the bunch, but Hanaford and Fawn lakes are just a little smaller. Forest Lake covers only eight acres and Tradedollar Lake is only 12 acres. Fawn Lake is well-known for its brook trout while Tradedollar has a good population of west-slope cutthroat.

Forest, Elk, and Hanaford are within easy walking distance of each other, and offer brown trout as well as cutthroats and brookies. All three species will take small spoons and spinners, or cast flies, either behind a bobber with your spinning rod or with your favorite fly rod. These lakes are open to fishing year-round, but May and June are the best months to fish them.

75. COLDWATER LAKE

Reference: **Northwest of Mount St. Helens; map B2, grid f6.**

How to get there: Take Interstate 5 to the town of Castle Rock and turn east on State Route 504, following it about 45 miles to the Coldwater Ridge Visitor Center and down the hill to the lake.

Facilities: A boat ramp and rest rooms are located at the southeast end of the lake, while the nearest stores are several miles west on State Route 504. Food, gas, and tackle are available in Toutle and Kid Valley, lodging in Castle Rock.

Contact: Mount St. Helens National Volcanic Monument Headquarters, U.S. Forest Service, (360) 750-5234.

Species available: Rainbow and cutthroat trout.

Fishing Coldwater Lake: This lake northwest of Mount St. Helens didn't exist before the mountain's violent eruption on May 18, 1980. That's when millions of tons of mud and debris created a natural dam that blocked the flow of Coldwater Creek and created the 700-acre lake. Biologists thought the lake was void of fish and in 1989 stocked it with rainbows, which are now reproducing on their own and no longer supplemented with hatchery plants. As it turns out, some resident trout apparently did survive the blast that buried the area in ash and mud, so Coldwater Lake also contains cutthroat trout. Most of the cutts are caught near the upper end of the lake, which is difficult to reach since gasoline engines are prohibited and float-tubes are the most common form of aquatic transportation.

Selective fishery regulations allowing anglers to use only artificial flies and lures with single, barbless hooks have been in effect since the lake opened to fishing in 1993. Most of the anglers fishing it are fly-rodders, and they have their best luck with dark leech patterns and other wet flies, although summertime insect hatches often provide fairly good dry fly-fishing. If a dark leech works for fly-casters, Jim Byrd of the Washington Department of Fish and Wildlife reasons that a black marabou jig might be just the ticket for spin anglers here.

Probably 90 percent of the fishing that occurs on Coldwater takes place at the south end, within sight of the U.S. Forest Service boat ramp. That makes sense if you recall that most of the fishing is done from float tubes, and it would take one heck of a pair of legs to kick all the way from the boat ramp to the north end of the lake and back. The wind that seems to blow here about 95 percent of the time would make the trip up-lake a miserable one, too. A trail parallels much of the lake's northern shoreline, but it's illegal to step off of it to reach the water. Those who try are cited for their efforts.

Leave enough time at the end of your fishing day to visit the Coldwater Ridge Visitor Center, which is at the edge of the hill overlooking the lake. And be sure to watch for the area's many elk herds as you drive along the Spirit Lake Highway. The lake is open to year-round fishing.

76. CASTLE LAKE

Reference: **Northwest of Mount St. Helens; map B2, grid g6.**

How to get there: Take State Route 504 (Spirit Lake Highway) east off Interstate 5 to the town of Toutle, turning east to follow Weyerhaeuser's 4100 Road up the South Fork of the Toutle River. At the second bridge over the river, turn left on 5600 Road and continue up the hill about four miles to a sign pointing the way to 3000 Road. Go east on 3000 Road about 10 miles to overlook where you can see the lake below. Park there and hike about half a mile down the steep hill to the lake.

Facilities: The nearest food, gas, and tackle are in Toutle and Kid Valley, with lodging in Castle Rock.

Contact: Mount St. Helens National Volcanic Monument Headquarters, U.S. Forest Service, (360) 750-5243.

Species available: Rainbow trout.

Fishing Castle Lake: Although never stocked by fish and wildlife agencies, this lake northwest of Mount St. Helens reportedly has produced a few eight- to 10-pound rainbows in recent years. This self-sustaining trout population is protected by selective fishery regulations and a one-fish daily limit. Although reaching Castle is a struggle, fishing your way around the lake's shoreline is pretty easy.

The lake is open to year-round fishing, but ice and snow limit fishing activity to the summer and early fall.

77. ABERNATHY CREEK

Reference: **Enters Columbia River west of Stella, southwestern Cowlitz County; map B2, grid g0.**

How to get there: Take State Route 4 west from Longview and turn north (right) on Abernathy Road about 2.5 miles west of Stella. Abernathy Road parallels the creek for about five miles.

Facilities: Everything you need, including food, gas, tackle, and lodging, is in Kelso and Longview.

Contact: Bob's Merchandise, (360) 425-3870.

Species available: Winter steelhead, sea-run cutthroat trout.

Fishing Abernathy Creek: Time it right, just after a soaking rain that raises the creek level a few inches during December or January, and you could find yourself right in the middle of some good small-stream winter steelheading on Abernathy Creek. The rest of the winter, though, the odds are against you. The fish come in with the rain, disperse, and are "gone" in a day or two.

It's pretty much the same with sea-run cutthroat, except that the months most likely to produce these little migratory trout are September, October, and November.

Abernathy is stocked with about 7,500 steelhead and an equal number of cutthroat. It's okay to catch and keep hatchery fish of either species, but wild steelhead and cutthroat must be released.

78. GERMANY CREEK

Reference: **Enters the Columbia River at Stella, southwestern Cowlitz County; map B2, grid g1.**

How to get there: Take State Route 4 west from Longview and turn north (right) onto Germany Creek Road at the town of Stella. This road parallels the creek for 4.5 miles.

Facilities: Available in Longview and Kelso.

Contact: Bob's Merchandise, (360) 425-3870.

Species available: Winter steelhead, sea-run cutthroat trout.

Fishing Germany Creek: Like nearby Abernathy and Mill creeks (see page 417 and below), this little Columbia River tributary provides winter steelhead and fall cutthroat action on the spur of the moment, usually in direct response to a slight rise in water levels that draws waiting fish in from the Columbia. Wild steelhead and wild cutthroat release rules are in effect, but enough hatchery fish are stocked to provide fisheries for both. Cutthroat fishing can be quite good in October and November.

79. MILL CREEK

Reference: **Enters Columbia River west of Stella, southwestern Cowlitz County; map B2, grid g0.**

How to get there: Take State Route 4 west from Longview and turn north (right) on Mill Creek Road about three miles west of Stella. The road parallels the creek for more than three miles.

Facilities: Food, gas, lodging, and other amenities can be found in Longview and Kelso.

Contact: Bob's Merchandise, (306) 425-3870.

Species available: Sea-run cutthroat trout.

Fishing Mill Creek: Hatchery sea-runs provide the fishing action at Mill Creek during the fall. Fairly good road access and the availability of those hatchery cutts make this a worthwhile bet in October and early November. Although the creek is open for winter steelhead fishing, it has wild-steelhead-release regulations but receives no hatchery plants.

80. COWEEMAN RIVER

Reference: **Enters Cowlitz River south of Kelso; map B2, grid g3.**

How to get there: Take Rose Valley Road off Interstate 5 about four miles south of Kelso and follow it northeast about five miles to the river.

Facilities: Food, gas, lodging, tackle, and other amenities are available in Longview and Kelso, near the mouth of the river.

Contact: Bob's Merchandise, (360) 425-3870.

Species available: Winter steelhead, sea-run cutthroat trout.

Fishing the Coweeman River: Although it receives generous plants of hatchery winter steelhead smolts, this little Cowlitz tributary either gives up only modest numbers of adult fish or lots of local anglers catch steelhead and don't bother to record them on their steelhead report cards. Department of Fish and Wildlife statistics show a steelhead catch of about 150 to 500 fish a year from the river. Most of those are caught above the confluence of Goble Creek, where Rose Valley Road parallels many miles of the Coweeman to afford lots of river-bank access. Access to the lower river is very limited. Wild steelhead caught from the Coweeman must be released.

If you're into sea-run cutthroat trout, the upper Coweeman is a good bet. Hatchery plants of Beaver Creek cutts provide good trout returns from September to November. Like sea-run cutthroating anywhere, the best fishing is with a lively nightcrawler right after a good rain. You can keep only hatchery (fin-clipped) cutthroat from the Coweeman.

81. KRESS LAKE

Reference: **Just east of Interstate 5 and north of the lower Kalama River, map B2, grid g3.**

How to get there: Take Kalama River Road east off Interstate 5 about 2.5 miles north of Kalama. Go left at the first turn (Kress Road) and drive about half a mile to the lake, which is on the right.

Facilities: The lake has a boat ramp that's suitable for small trailer boats and car-toppers. Food, gas, tackle, and lodging are available in Kalama, Kelso, and Longview.

Contact: Bob's Merchandise, (360) 425-3870.

Species available: Rainbow and brown trout, largemouth bass, crappies, bluegills, warmouth, brown bullhead catfish.

Fishing Kress Lake: It's hard to believe how much angling opportunity is available from a lake that covers only 26 acres and has a maximum depth of about 17 feet. Of course, the fact that this is the only lake for miles has a lot to do with Kress' popularity and productivity. Plants of hatchery trout totaling more than 20,000 fish a year don't hurt, either. Yes, that's 20,000 browns and rainbows a year, most of them stocked between the first of March and the end of April. As if those large numbers weren't enough, the plants include a few brood-stock trout ranging from two to four pounds.

Not everyone is a trout angler, and when it comes to warm-water fishing, Kress doesn't disappoint either. Bass, crappies, and bluegills grow to impressive size here, and there's enough of a brown bullhead fishery to keep some anglers at the lake all night.

The long season here—from late April through February—offers anglers plenty of opportunity to try their luck.

82. KALAMA RIVER

Reference: **North of Kalama; map B2, grid h3.**

How to get there: Take Interstate 5 to Kalama River Road, about 2.5 miles north of Kalama, and follow it east, up the north side of the river.

Facilities: Tackle, snacks, and lots of fishing talk can be found at Pritchard's Western Angler on the Kalama River Road, with other amenities in Kalama and Kelso.

Contact: Pritchard's Western Angler, (360) 673-4690.

Species available: Spring and fall chinook salmon, coho salmon, winter and summer steelhead, sea-run cutthroat trout.

Fishing the Kalama River: Long a favorite of boat and bank anglers alike, the Kalama is a gem among southwest Washington streams. Easy access via Interstate 5 and Kalama Road certainly doesn't diminish the popularity of this clear, green river. But popularity means fishing pressure, so there are times when solitude is difficult, if not impossible, to find.

Salmon and steelhead provide year-round angling opportunities. The river produces steelhead every month of the year, but summer-run fish dominate the catch. May, June, July, and August all offer excellent steelheading, with catches ranging from 250 to 900 fish during each of those four months. Anglers fishing from the mouth of Summers Creek downstream to the river mouth use ghost shrimp, roe clusters, crawfish tails, nightcrawlers, spinners, spoons, and all the usual steelhead bobbers to catch summer-runs. From Summers Creek up to the falls, the Kalama is open to fly-fishing only, and fly-rodders do as well on this stretch as the bait and hardware folks do downstream. Even though the Kalama was once considered a top-rate producer of both summer and winter steelies, and even though more winter than summer-run stealhead smolts are stocked here, winter steelheading has dropped off in recent years. December sees a little flurry of activity, but wintertime steelheading on the Kalama is fair at best these days.

As for salmon, the Kalama offers decent spring chinook fishing from April to June. Fish of 10 to 25 pounds comprise most of the catch, but now and then the river gives up a real bragging-sized springer of 30 pounds or more. Back-bouncing or drifting bait works here, as does back-trolling with plugs or diver-and-bait rigs. In the fall anglers catch both coho and chinook, but all adult chinook must be released from mid-August until mid-October.

83. LOWER COLUMBIA RIVER

Reference: **From Cathlamet upstream to Bonneville Dam; map B2, grid h3.**

How to get there: Take Interstate 5 to Longview and drive west on State Route 4 to reach the 22-mile-long Cathlamet-to-Longview stretch of river. Continue south past Longview on Interstate 5 to reach the 40-mile portion of the river between Longview and Vancouver. Drive east from Vancouver on State Route 44 as far as 43 miles to reach that part of the Columbia between Vancouver and Bonneville Dam.

Facilities: Good boat ramps are located at the Port of Kalama, Port of Camas ($3 fee), Beacon Rock State Park ($3 fee), and North Bonneville. For what it's worth, access is much easier from the Oregon side of the river, with about eight boat ramps on the Columbia and several more on Multnomah Channel. Beacon Rock State Park, several miles downstream from Bonneville Dam, is the best bet for tent-camping, but there are lots of private campgrounds with tent and RV sites along the river. Several motels can be found in Vancouver, with others in Longview, Kelso, Kalama, Camas, Washougal, and Stevenson. Food, gas, and tackle can also be found in Vancouver.

Contact: Bob's Merchandise in Longview, (360) 425-3870; Lewis River Sports in Woodland, (360) 225-9530; (360) 690-4351; Reeder Rods in Vancouver, (360) 690-4351; Camas Sport Center, (360) 834-4462; Dan's Specialty Guide Service, (360) 225-5910.

Species available: Summer and winter steelhead, chinook and coho salmon, sturgeon, shad, sea-run cutthroat trout, largemouth and smallmouth bass, walleyes.

Fishing the Lower Columbia River: This huge waterway and its many fish species and angling opportunities are worthy of an entire book in their own right, so I'm going to give you the short version here and send you off to find out more on your own. Let's get the bad news out of the way first, and when you talk bad news on the Columbia, you're talking about the current state of the salmon runs. Spring chinook fishing is a traditional possibility but no longer a foregone conclusion below the Interstate 5 bridge, a fishery that has closed at the end of March in recent years. The waters in and around the mouths of Washington's Cowlitz and Oregon's Willamette rivers have long been among the best places to find these early-season springers. Whole or plug-cut herring are productive, but in recent years more and more anglers have gone to large Flatfish and Kwikfish plugs with sardine strips wrapped to the lures' bellies.

Except for a month or two in the spring, this section of the Columbia is open to steelheading, and it should come as no surprise that it's one of the region's top steelie producers. Steelhead bound for dozens of rivers in Washington, Oregon, and Idaho all have to pass through the lower Columbia as they head for their upstream destinations, giving anglers lots of opportunity to practice their steelheading skills. Washington anglers alone caught 10,000 to 16,000 steelhead a year from the lower Columbia during the first few years of this decade, and Oregon anglers enjoyed similar success. Boat anglers throughout this stretch of the vast river enjoy obvious advantages, but bank anglers casting from the gravel bars and rock jetties along the river also take fish. This is plunking and trolling country when it comes to steelheading, so stock up on Bonneville Spinners, Spin N Glos, Hot Shots, and Wiggle Warts before hitting the river. You have to release all wild (not fin-clipped) steelhead here, but even hatchery fish might run 10 to 15 pounds, and most are beautiful, sleek, chrome-bright specimens.

This section of the Columbia produces more white sturgeon than all other Northwest waters combined. Even if you don't count the sturgeon that are too small or too large to keep, Washington sturgeon anglers boat more than 10,000 fish annually from the lower Columbia. That's a lot of legal-sized sturgeon and a lot of fantastic eating. Legal-sized, by the way, means fish between 42 and 66 inches long. Sorry, but those "little" three-footers have to go back. And those seven-footers, even though lots of fun to hook and play, also have to go back into the water unharmed. Sturgeon fishing is a waiting game, but one that's enjoyed by both boat and bank anglers throughout this stretch of river. Spring and early summer often provide the best chance at a catch-and-release monster, and the best bait that time of year is a whole shad. Smelt are good baits the rest of the year, and most sturgeon anglers rig "backwards," with the tail pointing up the line and the head pointing down. Anchor to the bottom at the edge of a deep drop-off and settle in to wait. Perhaps more than any other kind of fishing, the Columbia River sturgeon fishery is one where it's a great idea to hire a guide for the first day, or hang around watching a gang of local anglers to pick up all the little tricks that can make the difference between successful fishing and just standing around waiting for days at a time between strikes.

The year's hottest fishing on the lower Columbia occurs from the middle of May to the middle of June, when millions of American shad crowd into the river on their annual spawning migration. Boat anglers find good shad action in several locations along the lower river, including the waters around the mouth of Oregon's Sandy River and Washington's Washougal River, but the best bank fishing for shad is found within a mile or so downstream of Bonneville Dam. This fishery usually peaks in early June, when tens of thousands of shad pass over the Bonneville fish ladder every day. Your favorite trout, bass, or light steelhead rod will work here, but take along lots of terminal tackle to fish this "grabby" part of the river. Small Mini Jigs or bare hooks with a couple of colored beads above them will do the trick. Although there's no limit on shad, most anglers prefer to catch-and-release these hard-fighting but bony members of the herring family.

Most of the bass fishing on the lower Columbia is confined to the sloughs, bays, and side channels connected to the main river. The bay where the Beacon Rock boat launch is located, for example, provides some good small-mouth fishing during the spring and summer. The Camas Slough also offers decent bass fishing, and there are numerous side channels and sloughs between Vancouver and Woodland that are very popular with bass anglers. The stretch of river from Kalama downstream to Longview is also well-known for its excellent largemouth fishing. You can fish bass here for two weeks and never cast to the same place twice, and you'd probably be surprised at the number of bass over four pounds caught from this river traditionally known for its salmon and steelhead.

Columbia River walleye fishing isn't much of a secret anymore, but it might come as news to you to learn that these transplants from the Midwest are now found as far downriver as the Interstate 5 bridge. Trolling spinner-and-worm rigs and diving plugs accounts for some 10-pound-plus walleyes on the lower Columbia, and if you can locate a good concentration of fish, you might also take them on leadheads/grubs bounced along the bottom.

84. MERRILL LAKE

Reference: **North of Cougar, Clark County; map B2, grid h6.**

How to get there: Take Interstate 5 to Woodland, turn east on State Route 503, and drive 30 miles to Forest Road 81. Turn north (left) and drive four miles to the lake.

Facilities: The east side of the lake has a boat ramp and Washington Department of Natural Resources campground. There's also a private campground in Cougar, about five miles to the south. Food, gas, and tackle are also available in Cougar. Motels can be found in Woodland.

Contact: Cougar Store, (360) 238-5228; Lone Fir, (360) 258-5210; Yale Lake Country Store, (360) 238-5246; Jack's Sporting Goods, (360) 231-4276; Lewis River Sports, (360) 225-9530.

Species available: Brown, rainbow, cutthroat, and brook trout.

Fishing Merrill Lake: The lake has a year-round season, but the road to it doesn't, so you can't drive to Merrill once the snow piles up. Brown trout have been added to the lake's menu in recent years, partly because the rainbows, brookies, and cutthroats have fallen victim to some aquatic parasite that catches more fish than anglers do. Merrill has fly-fishing-only regulations and a two-fish daily limit. To protect older, trophy-class trout, the lake also has a 12-inch maximum size limit.

85. SWIFT CREEK RESERVOIR

Reference: **East of Cougar, western Skamania County; map B2, grid h7.**
How to get there: Take Interstate 5 to Woodland, turn east on State Route 503, and drive 35 miles to where the highway becomes Road 91013. Continue on this road several miles to parallel the north side of the lake.
Facilities: There's a public access area and boat ramp near the upper (east) end of the reservoir. Lone Fir, near Cougar, is the closest campground with both tent and RV sites. Food, gas, and tackle are available in Cougar, lodging in Woodland.
Contact: Cougar Store, (360) 238-5228; Lone Fir, (360) 258-5210; Yale Lake Country Store, (360) 238-5246; Jack's Sporting Goods, (360) 231-4276; Lewis River Sports, (360) 225-9530. Call (800) 547-1501 for information on water levels in the reservoir.
Species available: Rainbow trout.
Fishing Swift Creek Reservoir: This uppermost of the three big reservoirs on the North Fork Lewis River is stocked with rainbow fingerlings, but fluctuating water levels and varying water clarity keep things challenging for anglers. In the spring, when visibility may be down, fishing is often best around the mouths of creeks that bring clear water into the lake.

Trolling in and around the small bay at the mouth of Drift Creek, about a mile and a half west of the boat ramp, is popular in April and May. Most of the reservoir is clear by mid-summer, allowing anglers to catch fish pretty much throughout it. Although most anglers troll Triple Teazers, Needlefish, Dick Nites, and the like behind strings of trolling blades, stillfishing is also an option.

There are lots of places to park alongside the road and hike down the bank to fish along the north shore of the lake. Swift Creek Reservoir opens to fishing in late April and closes at the end of October.

86. YALE LAKE (RESERVOIR)

Reference: **Northeast of Woodland; map B2, grid h6.**
How to get there: Take Interstate 5 to Woodland, turn east on State Route 503, and drive about 25 miles to the lake, on the right.
Facilities: Four public access areas and boat ramps are located on the lake, the biggest and best of which is at Yale Park, near Cougar. It features a four-lane boat ramp that usually makes getting in and out of the water a snap. Food, groceries, and tackle are available at Yale Lake Country Store and the Cougar Store, both near the lake. If you need a place to camp, Lone Fir in Cougar has tent and RV spaces. Try Woodland for lodging.

Contact: Cougar Store, (360) 238-5228; Lone Fir, (360) 258-5210; Yale Lake Country Store, (360) 238-5246; Jack's Sporting Goods, (360) 231-4276; Lewis River Sports, (360) 225-9530.

Species available: Kokanee, cutthroat trout.

Fishing Yale Lake: Even though it's not on the blast-devastated north side of Mount St. Helens, Yale was greatly affected by the 1980 eruption. Sediment from the volcano flowed into the reservoir and caused a severe drop in the kokanee population. If you fished for kokanee here in the mid-eighties, you may think Yale is the biggest biological desert in the Northwest, but things have changed. Kokanee populations have expanded to what they were in the good old days before the eruption, and the lake even has a bonus daily kokanee limit of 16 fish.

Most anglers troll for their fish, using three- or four-blade gang trolls with a Kokanee Killer, Jeweled Bead spinner, or Needlefish behind the trolling blades. Add a kernel of white corn to the lure and you'll catch more fish. Yale Lake kokanee go on the bite around late-May, and fishing is good from June to September. Most of the cutthroat are caught along with the kokanee. You might also catch a bull trout here, but you must release it.

87. LAKE MERWIN

Reference: Northeast of Woodland; map B2, grid h5.

How to get there: Take Interstate 5 to Woodland, turn east on State Route 503, and drive about 12 miles to the lake, on the right.

Facilities: A public boat ramp is about the only facility on the lake itself, but gas, tackle, and groceries are available from small stores along the highway. Lodging can be found in Woodland.

Contact: Jack's Sporting Goods, (360) 231-4276; Lewis River Sports, (360) 225-9530.

Species available: Coho salmon, kokanee.

Fishing Lake Merwin: An annual plant of 200,000 cohos provides most of the fishing action on Merwin, the lowest of three large impoundments on the North Fork of the Lewis River. These cohos are about 10 to 11 inches long in the spring and early summer, when fishing is best here. Summertime trolling also produces some kokanee, which are "escapees" from Yale Reservoir, the impoundment immediately upstream of Merwin.

If there's an abundance of any one fish species here, it has to be squawfish, which most anglers really don't care to catch. The lake's cold temperatures and its hordes of small squawfish, in fact, make Merwin a good candidate for another introduction of tiger muskies, those squawfish-eating transplants that currently provide outstanding trophy-fishing opportunities in Mayfield Lake. Remember, you heard it here first.

88. NORTH FORK LEWIS RIVER

Reference: Joins the Columbia River south of Woodland; map B2, grid h4.

How to get there: Take Interstate 5 to Woodland and drive east on State Route 503 to parallel the north side of the river for more than 10 miles, or drive east on County Road 16 to parallel the south side.

Facilities: Boat ramps on the south side of the river include a rough one (four-wheel-drive only) at the end of Haapa Road and the popular launch farther upstream at Cedar Creek. Another launch on the north side of the river near the mouth, off Dike Road, gets a lot of use from anglers fishing the extreme lower river. Above Woodland on the north side of the river are the "Island" ramp (about three miles upstream from town) and the rough launch at the golf course, both of which are accessible off State Route 503. Restaurants, gas, tackle and motel accommodations are in Woodland.

Contact: Lewis River Sports, (360) 225-9530; Jack's Sporting Goods, (360) 231-4276; Dan's Specialty Guide Service, (360) 225-5910.

Species available: Winter and summer steelhead, spring and fall chinook salmon, coho salmon, sea-run cutthroat and rainbow trout.

Fishing the North Fork Lewis River: The Pacific Northwest has very few places where it's possible (and legal) to catch both salmon and steelhead 12 months out of the year. But the North Fork Lewis is one such place. Granted, the salmon numbers are mighty small in January, and the winter steelhead catch is rather unimpressive for a river of this size, but the fact that both adult salmon and steelhead inhabit this Columbia River tributary through-out the year says a lot for the river and its angling opportunities.

The North Lewis has a well-earned reputation as one of Washington's top spring chinook rivers. April and May are the peak months, but springers are caught as early as February and as late as July. A good month may see anglers take over 2,000 of these hard-charging, 10- to 30-pound fish from the river. The most famous and most popular spring chinook spot on the entire river is the slow, deep pool at the Cedar Creek boat ramp, but be warned: You won't have the place to yourself. When the fish are in, it's gunwale-to-gunwale. Affectionately known as "The Meat Hole," it often lives up to the nickname. Fortunately for those who like a little more elbow room, there are also productive springer holes upstream and downstream from Cedar Creek, including some excellent water near the salmon hatchery and the long, deep run a short distance downstream from the Haapa boat ramp. All the usual spring chinook goodies work, including roe clusters, live ghost shrimp, and combinations of the two. Many boaters back-troll sardine-wrapped Flatfish and Kwikfish plugs.

The North Fork Lewis also hosts fair runs of fall chinook, with September and October providing the best shot, but the coho run is what usually provides most of the fall fishing excitement here. These five- to 15-pound silvers begin hitting in September, with the runs peaking in October and continuing to provide fair fishing through November.

Summer-run steelhead do a good job of keeping anglers from dozing off between the spring chinook fishery and the start of fall salmon action. They actually show in the river by April, and many are caught by spring salmon anglers during May and June, but July and August are by far the top steelheading months. As with salmon fishing, the best steelhead action is had by boat anglers, but all the public bank-fishing spots also produce summer-runs. Casting spoons, spinners, various steelhead bobbers, roe clusters, and fresh shrimp all work for bank anglers. The summer steelhead catch here over the past few years has ranged from 2,000 to 4,000 fish annually.

Winter steelheading on the North Lewis is a tougher proposition, despite liberal plants of hatchery smolts. Anglers may catch as many as 2,000 winter-runs a year, but in some recent winters the catch has been a piddling 400 winter steelhead. When you consider annual plants of as many as 200,000 winter-run smolts, this small catch is a puzzler. Keep in mind that you have to release any wild-stock steelhead you catch.

Cutthroat trout also are protected by wild-fish-release regulations here, and fall cutthroat-fishing success may very well hinge on the size of recent hatchery cutthroat plants. Stocking efforts are impressive some years (more than 21,000 fish in 1993, for example), but too small to provide much action other years (only 2,500 fish in 1992).

Although overlooked by most serious anglers, the upper North Fork above Swift Creek Reservoir provides some fairly good trout fishing, with rainbows making up a bulk of the catch. The river also offers some huge Dolly Varden, which must be released. Forest Road 90 above Swift Creek Reservoir provides bank access, and some anglers use inflatables or kayaks to float various sections of the river.

---

89. HORSESHOE LAKE

Reference: **Immediately south of Woodland; map B2, grid i3.**

How to get there: Exit Interstate 5 to the west at Woodland and take the frontage road on the west side of the freeway south about two blocks to the lake.

Facilities: A boat ramp and lots of beach access can be found at the city park on the north side of the lake. Tackle, food, gas, and lodging are available in Woodland.

Contact: Lewis River Sports, (360) 225-9530.

Species available: Rainbow and brown trout, largemouth bass, yellow perch, brown bullhead catfish.

Fishing Horseshoe Lake: Trout fishing is very good at Horseshoe Lake the first few weeks of the late-April-through-October season, thanks to spring plants of both rainbow and brown trout. Some years the Department of Fish and Wildlife includes a few lunker brood stock trout in those plants, creating plenty of excitement when somebody hauls in one of these five- to 10-pound trophies.

Trout fishing gets tougher after those planters are gone, but summertime offers fair possibilities for largemouth bass to three pounds and some good catches of yellow perch and brown bullheads. Anglers occasionally catch yellow bullheads, too, but seldom notice the difference between them and the more common browns. To most folks who catch them, they're all just catfish.

90. EAST FORK LEWIS RIVER

Reference: **Meets the North Lewis three miles south of Woodland; map B2, grid i4.**

How to get there: Take the La Center exit off Interstate 5 south of Woodland and drive east on County Road 42 to County Road 48. Continue east on County Road 48 to NE 82nd Avenue and turn south (right). Drive about two miles to the Daybreak Bridge section of the river. To reach areas farther upstream, turn east off NE 82nd Avenue onto NE 299th Street, which intersects State Route 503. Turn south on State Route 503 and drive about two miles to reach Lewisville County Park. To reach areas upstream, turn north off NE 299th Street onto State Route 503 and east (right) on Lucia Falls Road.

Facilities: Boat ramps are located at Lewisville County Park, Daybreak Bridge County Park, and near the mouth of the river at Paradise Point State Park, which has about 80 campsites, rest rooms with showers, an RV pump-out, and other amenities. Food, gas, tackle, and lodging are available in Battle Ground, La Center, and Woodland.

Contact: Paradise Point State Park, (360) 263-2350; Lewis River Sports (360) 225-9530.

Species available: Winter and summer steelhead, chinook and coho salmon, sea-run cutthroat trout.

Fishing the East Fork Lewis River: The East Lewis was perhaps once Washington's premier big-steelhead river, giving up a surprising number of fish over 20 pounds, a few over 25, and an occasional monster of 30 pounds or larger. Washington's state-record winter steelhead, in fact, came from the East Lewis back in the spring of 1980. That behemoth buck steelie weighed in at 32 pounds, 12 ounces. A few whopping wild steelhead still inhabit the river, but special regulations are now in effect to protect them from anglers. Wild-steelhead-release rules apply here throughout the year, and spring fishing closures are in effect for varying times to provide further protection to the late-arriving wild runs.

But generous plants of both winter and summer hatchery steelhead smolts provide adequate angling opportunity these days, and if you work at it, you can hook steelhead every month of the year. June tends to be the best month for summer-runs, while December and January are the most productive winter-run months. The stretch of river between Lewisville Park and Daybreak Bridge is very popular among boat anglers, especially in winter, but there are lots of places along the East Lewis for bank anglers to try their luck.

91. BATTLE GROUND LAKE

Reference: **Northeast of the town of Battle Ground; map B2, grid i5.**

How to get there: Drive east off Interstate 5 on State Route 502 to Battle Ground, then north (left) on Heisson Road about three miles to the lake.

Facilities: Battle Ground Lake State Park has tent sites, rest rooms, and a boat ramp (with a $3 launch fee). Food, tackle, and gas are available in the town of Battle Ground, and there's at least one bed and breakfast in town.

Contact: Battle Ground Lake State Park, (360) 687-4621.

Species available: Rainbow and brook trout, largemouth bass.

Fishing Battle Ground Lake: This popular little lake, which opens to fishing in late April and closes at the end of October, is heavily planted throughout the spring with both rainbow and brook trout. The spring plants usually include a few lunker brood trout which may top five pounds. All the usual trolling lures and stillfished baits work as long as the trout last, which usually means into about the middle of June. After that, bass fishing is the best bet, but this isn't a great bass lake.

92. VANCOUVER LAKE

Reference: **Northwest of Vancouver; map B2, grid j4.**

How to get there: Take Interstate 5 to Vancouver, turn west on NW 78th Street, and drive 1.5 miles to the east side of the lake. To reach the west side, turn west off Interstate 5 in Vancouver onto State Route 501 and follow it four miles to the lake.

Facilities: There's a boat ramp near the south end of the lake, with all other amenities available in Vancouver.

Contact: Reeder Rods, (360) 690-4351.

Species available: Rainbow trout, crappies, yellow perch, channel and brown bullhead catfish.

Fishing Vancouver Lake: Trout fishing takes a back seat to warm-water angling action on this big (over 2,800 acres) Columbia River backwater. Vancouver is open year-round but is at its best from May through September. Nightfishing for both brown bullheads and channel cats can be especially worthwhile, but don't overlook the perch and crappie during the daylight hours.

93. LACAMAS LAKE

Reference: **North of Camas; map B2, grid j5.**

How to get there: Take Interstate 205 to State Route 14 and drive east to Camas. Take Everett Road north out of Camas and turn west (left) on Leadbetter Road. It's about a mile to the lake, on the left.

Facilities: A public boat ramp is located on the northeast side of the lake. Restaurants, tackle, gas, and other amenities are available in nearby Camas and Washougal.

Contact: Camas Sports Center, (360) 834-4462.

Species available: Brown trout, largemouth bass, yellow perch, brown bullhead catfish.

Fishing Lacamas Lake: Hidden away in the heart of Clark County, Lacamas is quite a ways off the beaten path for most Washington anglers, so it doesn't receive the publicity or the praise that it might deserve as a largemouth bass producer. The small, rough boat ramp and the jungle of aquatic weeds that sprouts throughout the lake don't do much to enhance its popularity, either. Maybe I'm prejudiced, since I caught my largest bass from this shallow, 300-acre lake, but I think Lacamas is worth fishing if you're a serious bass angler. It produces far too many four- to six-pound largemouths for any of them to be flukes. Although my best-ever bass fell for a crankbait, you're better off fishing something a little more snag-resistant in most of this vegetation-filled lake. Spinnerbaits, Texas-rigged plastics, and other offerings that are more-or-less snagless are your best bets. Lacamas is open year-round and provides bass-fishing opportunities from as early as February to as late as November.

This was the first western Washington lake to be stocked with brown trout, at least in modern times. Back in the early 1980s, biologists were looking for something that might work to provide a trout fishery in this lake that grows quite warm in the summer. The brown trout experiment proved successful, and browns have been providing most of the salmonid action here ever since. Although you might run into a carryover now and then, spring planters in the half-pound range provide most of the excitement. Small wobbling plugs, spinners, and spoons work well for them.

If you like catching crappies, perch, and catfish, Lacamas is a good bet during the spring and summer. Brown bullheads are especially abundant, and if you don't have a boat, you can catch them right off the bank at several points along the northeast side of the lake, where the road parallels the shoreline.

94. WASHOUGAL RIVER

Reference: **Joins the Columbia River at Camas; map B2, grid j6.**

How to get there: Take State Route 14 to Washougal and turn north on State Route 140, which parallels the main river for about 10 miles. Take Skye Road north off State Route 140 and turn east (right) on Washougal River Road to follow the main river upstream, or turn north on North Fork Road, past the Skamania Hatchery, to reach the West Fork Washougal.

Facilities: There are several public access spots and a couple of places to launch boats along State Route 140. Food, gas, lodging, tackle, and other amenities are available in Camas and Washougal.

Contact: Camas Sport Center, (360) 834-4462.

Species available: Summer and winter steelhead, coho and chinook salmon, sea-run cutthroat trout.

Fishing the Washougal River: The Washougal's biggest claim to fame is the fact that it produces steelhead 12 months out of the year. It has strong runs of winter and summer steelhead, thanks to generous annual plants totaling more than 100,000 of each. The summer run is by far the stronger of the two, and most years this relatively small Columbia tributary gives up at least 1,000 summer steelies. These are the famous Skamania Hatchery steelhead that were such a huge success and caused such a stir among anglers when they were transplanted to the Great Lakes system nearly two decades ago. May, June, and July produce the best catches, and the fishing often drops off considerably in August. Wild-steelhead-release regulations are in effect throughout the year.

The highway provides fairly good bank-fishing access to the lower Washougal, and there are three spots along the river where boat anglers launch to fish. This is a small river with plenty of boulders, so don't try boating it unless you know what you're doing and have a chance to check out the river before launching. The safest boating is when the river level is fairly high; during low flows boating is nearly impossible.

A state salmon hatchery on the upper Washougal produces good numbers of coho and chinook salmon that return to the river throughout the fall. Check the fishing pamphlet for detailed regulations concerning salmon fishing on the Washougal, but as a general rule, you can catch and keep two adult salmon a day here, and that's exactly what many anglers do when conditions are right.

Take your favorite trout rod along if you visit the Washougal for fall salmon, and if they aren't biting, try your hand at sea-run cutthroat fishing. Some 30,000 to 40,000 cutthroat smolts are released here every year, and the returning adults provide excellent fishing possibilities. Only the Elochoman and Cowlitz rivers (see pages 363 and 411) have been stocked with more cutthroat smolts than the Washougal over the past half-dozen years or so.

95. HAMILTON CREEK

Reference: **Joins the Columbia River at North Bonneville; map B2, grid j8.**
How to get there: Take State Route 14 east from Camas. The highway crosses Hamilton Creek about two miles east of Beacon Rock State Park. A gravel road leading north just west of the bridge goes upstream a short distance.
Facilities: Beacon Rock State Park has about 80 tent sites, plus rest rooms and showers. The nearest town is Stevenson, about eight miles to the east, and it has food, gas, lodging, and tackle.
Contact: Beacon Rock State Park, (509) 427-8267; Camas Sports Center, (360) 834-4462.
Species available: Winter steelhead, sea-run cutthroat trout.
Fishing Hamilton Creek: This little, steep-gradient creek that runs out of the hills north of Bonneville Dam has both wild and hatchery steelhead, but if you catch a wild one, you have to release it. Plants of about 5,000 hatchery steelhead a year, unfortunately, don't provide much of a return, and the biggest catch from the creek in recent years was about 50 fish. If there's such a thing as a best time to fish Hamilton, it's in December and January.

The cutthroat picture is about the same, with hatchery plants accounting for most of the catch and anglers required to release any wild cutthroats they hook.

96. ROCK CREEK

Reference: **Enters the Columbia River just west of Stevenson; map B2, grid j8.**
How to get there: Drive east from Camas on State Route 14 toward Stevenson. As you approach town, turn left on Rock Creek Road just before crossing the Columbia River backwater known as Rock Cove. Stay to the left to continue upstream along the west side of the creek.
Facilities: Food, gas, tackle, lodging, and camping are available in and around Stevenson. Beacon Rock State Park, about 10 miles to the west, has campsites and showers.

Contact: Beacon Rock State Park, (509) 427-8267; Camas Sport Center, (360) 834-4462.

Species available: Winter steelhead, sea-run cutthroat trout.

Fishing Rock Creek: Don't hop in your car and drive a long distance to fish Rock Creek unless you really have a lot of spare time on your hands. Anglers catch a few steelhead here in January and February, but the fishing is anything but hot. The catch is surprisingly small for a stream that's stocked with as many as 10,000 hatchery smolts a year. You might find decent catch-and-release cutthroat fishing in the fall, but all wild cutthroats must be released. Since the creek receives no hatchery cutthroat plants, you won't find many fish to keep.

97. WIND RIVER

Reference: **Enters the Columbia River at Carson; map B2, grid i9.**

How to get there: Take State Route 14 along the Columbia River to Carson and turn north on Wind River Road to reach the upper river. To fish lower portions of the Wind, drive east past Carson and turn left at the bridge crossing over the river mouth.

Facilities: Carson Hot Springs is a funky old place with a hotel, a campground, a restaurant, and hot mineral springs. Restaurants, gas stations, and other accommodations can be found throughout the area, including huge Skamania Lodge a few miles west in Stevenson. The best bet for tackle is in Camas, to the west on State Route 14.

Contact: Camas Sports Center, (360) 427-8267; Carson Hot Springs, (509) 427-8292.

Species available: Summer steelhead, chinook salmon.

Fishing the Wind River: Summer steelhead provide virtually all the angling opportunity on the Wind nowadays, thanks to restrictions that have all but eliminated the river's once-productive chinook fishery. Planted with about 40,000 summer steelhead smolts annually, the river is closed to the taking of wild steelhead. June, July, August, and September all provide decent chances to hook a keeper summer-run. If you're planning to fish the Wind for the first time, be sure to check the fishing pamphlet for details about angling closures around Shipherd Falls and other spots.

MAP B3

WASHINGTON MAP .... see page 5
Adjoining Maps
NORTH (map A3) .... see page 212
EAST (map B4) .... see page 462
SOUTH .... no map
WEST (map B2) .... see page 366

40 Listings
PAGES 432-461

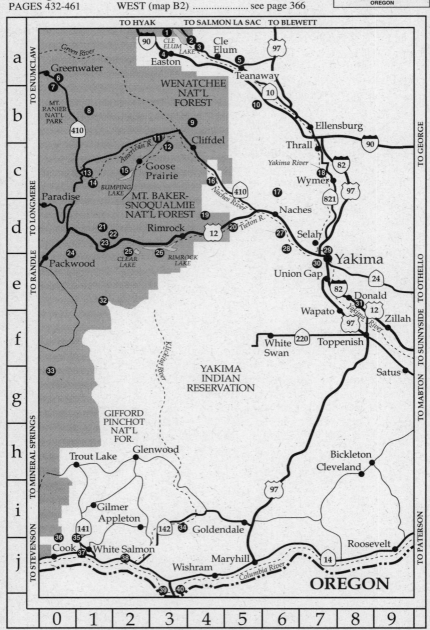

Map Section B3 features:

1. Kachess Lake
2. Lake Cle Elum
3. Lower Cle Elum River
4. Lake Easton
5. Teanaway River
6. Greenwater River
7. Upper White River
8. Echo and Lost Lakes
9. Manastash Lake
10. Taneum Creek
11. American River
12. Bumping River
13. Dewey Lake
14. Swamp and Cougar Lakes
15. Bumping Lake (Reservoir)
16. Rattlesnake Creek
17. Wenas Lake
18. Upper Yakima River
19. Oak Creek
20. Tieton River
21. William O. Douglas
    Wilderness Lakes
22. Dog Lake
23. Leech Lake
24. Packwood Lake
25. Clear Lake
26. Rimrock Lake (Reservoir)
27. Naches River
28. Cowiche Creek
29. Rotary Lake
30. Ahtanum Creek
31. I-82 Ponds (Freeway Ponds)
32. Walupt Lake
33. Horseshoe, Takhlakh, Council,
    Olallie, and Chain of Lakes
34. Klickitat River
35. White Salmon River
36. Little White Salmon River/
    Drano Lake
37. Northwestern Lake
    (Reservoir)
38. Rowland Lake(s)
39. Columbia River
40. Horsethief Lake

1. KACHESS LAKE

Reference: **North of Easton, Kittitas County; map B3, grid a3.**

How to get there: Drive east from Snoqualmie Summit or west from Cle Elum on Interstate 90. Turn north at Crystal Springs onto Forest Road 49 and go four miles to reach the upper end of the lake's west side. Forest Road 4828, which is accessible off Forest Road 49 or by turning north off the freeway near Lake Easton, provides access to six miles of the southern portion of the lake's west side. To reach the east side of the lake, turn north off Interstate 90 near Lake Easton onto Forest Road 4818 and drive two miles to the lake.

Facilities: The U.S. Forest Service's Kachess Campground, located at the northwest corner of the lake, has nearly 200 tent and RV sites, plus rest rooms, and a boat ramp. Crystal Springs Campground, three miles from the lake along Interstate 90, has about two dozen tent and trailer sites. The nearest food, gas, tackle, and lodging can be found in Easton and Cle Elum.

Contact: Wenatchee National Forest, Cle Elum Ranger District, (509) 674-4411.

Species available: Kokanee, rainbow, cutthroat and lake trout, burbot.

Fishing Kachess Lake: The kokanee fishery is the big deal at Kachess, and it's been good enough in recent years to prompt a "bonus" kokanee limit of 16 fish per day. Since the lake covers more than 4,500 acres, you may have to do some prospecting to find the fish, or maybe you'll just want to tune in to where all the other boats are congregated and join the crowd. Take along your favorite gang trolls, a selection of Wedding Rings, Double Wammys,

Needlefish, or other kokanee-getters, and go for it. Don't forget the white corn, maggots, or Power Wigglers to add to the hooks of whatever lure you use.

These same offerings will take rainbows and cutthroat now and then, but to increase your chances at these larger species, gear up a little and offer larger fish a bigger meal, something like a Kwikfish or Flatfish in a metallic finish or a Triple Teazer, silver with red head.

If you want lake trout, or Mackinaw, come to the lake early in the spring, when the water is still cold, and troll large plugs or wobbling spoons. These trophies can be caught later in the spring and even into early summer, but getting down to them in warmer weather makes trolling deep with a downrigger a virtual must.

The lake also has an abundance of burbot, or freshwater lings, and they'll take nightcrawlers or strips of sucker meat fished on the bottom. If you catch a big burbot, fillet it and either give it the deep-fryer treatment or let it bask in the warm glow of your barbecue. Delicious!

---

2. LAKE CLE ELUM

Reference: **Northeast of Easton, Kittitas County; map B3, grid a4.**
How to get there: Take Interstate 90 to Cle Elum and turn north on State Route 903, following it for six miles through Roslyn and up the east side of the lake.
Facilities: Boat ramps are located at Wish Poosh, Morgan Creek, and Dry Creek. Wish Poosh Campground (U.S. Forest Service) has about 40 campsites. Food, gas, tackle, and lodging are available in and around Cle Elum.
Contact: Wenatchee National Forest, Cle Elum Ranger District, (509) 674-4411.
Species available: Kokanee, lake trout, burbot.
Fishing Lake Cle Elum: Kokanee fishing has come on strong here, and as of 1995 there was a bonus limit of 16 kokanee per day. Those bonus limits are a good indicator of worthwhile fishing for these little, landlocked sockeye salmon. Although Lake Cle Elum kokanee have a reputation for running small, anglers were catching good numbers of plump 13- and 14-inchers in 1995, a good sign for kokanee anglers these days.

Trolling with all the usual kokanee gear works, but be willing to travel some for your fish; this eight-mile-long reservoir covers nearly 5,000 acres. The best kokanee fishing is from June through August, perfect timing for anglers looking to take a vacation in the high country of the central Cascades.

If you want lake trout, visit earlier in the season, when the water is still cold and the fish within easier reach. By May, you pretty much need a downrigger to have any chance of hooking a big laker. Like the other big reservoirs and lakes nearby, Cle Elum has a large population of burbot, which can be caught near the bottom with nightcrawlers, smelt, or strips of sucker meat. Regulations allow fishing with a set-line for burbot.

No visit to Lake Cle Elum would be complete without spending an hour or two in Roslyn, where the wacky but popular television show, "Northern Exposure" was filmed. You won't find any moose, but all the familiar buildings are there. The town feels like it's from another era, except for all the tourists in their Nikes and baseball caps.

3. LOWER CLE ELUM RIVER

Reference: **Joins the Yakima River southwest of Cle Elum; see map B3, grid a4.**

How to get there: Take Interstate 90 to Cle Elum and turn north on State Route 903, then left over the next seven miles on any of several roads leading southeast (left) toward the river.

Facilities: There are plenty of places to eat, sleep, buy gas and groceries, camp, and play tourist in and around Cle Elum. Lake Easton State Park is a few miles to the west.

Contact: Lake Easton State Park, (509) 656-2230.

Species available: Rainbow trout, mountain whitefish.

Fishing the Lower Cle Elum River: This small stream, which flows out of Lake Cle Elum and into the Yakima River near the town of Cle Elum, remains pretty constant and predictable as eastern Washington streams go. The dam holding back the water to form Lake Cle Elum keeps spring runoff from getting out of hand, keeping the water fairly clear and the water level fairly constant. This pretty little river with lots of pools, medium-depth runs, and noisy riffles provides fair fishing during the summer and early fall. Deeper pools near the lower end of the Cle Elum offer good winter fishing for mountain whitefish. If you fish it at that time of year, regulations dictate that you release any trout you hook.

4. LAKE EASTON

Reference: **Northwest of Easton, Kittitas County; map B3, grid a3.**

How to get there: Take Interstate 90 to Easton and follow the signs for a mile to Lake Easton State Park.

Facilities: Lake Easton State Park has nearly 100 tent sites and more than 40 RV sites with hookups, as well as rest rooms, showers, and a roomy boat ramp. There's also a private RV park right next to the state park. Food, gas, tackle, and lodging are available in Easton and Cle Elum.

Contact: Lake Easton State Park, (509) 656-2230; RV Town, (509) 656-2360.

Species available: Rainbow trout.

Fishing Lake Easton: Since this 235-acre lake on the eastern flank of the Cascades is slow to warm in the spring, the trout fishing takes its time to heat up as well. It's stocked with about 8,000 legal-sized rainbows every year, and they come to life around the end of May, in time for Memorial Day anglers and the start of the June vacation season. The roomy, forested state park and abundance of trout make this a great place to take the kids on an early summer fishing vacation as soon as school is out. Troll a Flatfish, Triple Teazer, Dick Nite, Canadian Wonder, or a gang troll-and-worm rig just about anywhere in the lake and you should catch a few fish.

5. TEANAWAY RIVER

Reference: **Joins the Yakima River southeast of Cle Elum; see map B3, grid a5.**

How to get there: Take Interstate 90 about two miles east from Cle Elum and turn north on State Route 970, which parallels the lower Teanaway and crosses it about three miles above the river mouth. Seven-tenths of a mile past the bridge crossing the river, turn north (left) on Teanaway Road, which parallels the river for several miles and has spurs running up the West, Middle, and East forks of the Teanaway.

Facilities: There are several primitive camp sites and a couple of public camping areas on the upper reaches of the river. Food, gas, tackle, and lodging are available in Cle Elum.

Contact: Washington Department of Fish and Wildlife, Yakima Regional Office, (509) 575-2740.

Species available: Rainbow and cutthroat trout.

Fishing the Teanaway River: Summertime plants of hatchery rainbows seem to be a thing of the past here, but there are a few pan-sized rainbows in the lower reaches of the Teanaway and small cutthroats in the upper reaches. The river is high and off-colored in the spring, drops into excellent fishing condition around the end of June and throughout most of the July, but continues to drop and clear through August. By September the fishing is often tough because of low water. Fly-fishing is a very good possibility during July. A lot of the river runs through private property, so be sure to get permission before fishing.

6. GREENWATER RIVER

Reference: **East of Greenwater, Highway 410; map B3, grid a0.**

How to get there: Drive east from Enumclaw on State Route 410. About two miles east of the small town of Greenwater, turn north (left) off the highway on Forest Road 70, which soon crosses the Greenwater River and then crisscrosses it for several miles upstream.

Facilities: Food and gas are available in Greenwater, and all other facilities can be found in Enumclaw.

Contact: Greenwater General Store, (360) 663-2357; Mount Baker-Snoqualmie National Forest, White River Ranger District, (360) 825-6585.

Species available: Rainbow and cutthroat trout.

Fishing the Greenwater River: Once stocked with hatchery trout to provide action for summertime anglers, the Greenwater is now managed as a wild-fish stream, with no-bait regulations, a two-fish daily limit, and 12-inch minimum size restriction on trout. That adds greatly to the challenge, but access is fairly easy and the stream has lots of inviting, fishy-looking pools. What's more, it's within fairly easy reach of anglers in the Seattle-Tacoma area. Cast small spinners or soak wet flies here during June or July for best results.

7. UPPER WHITE RIVER

Reference: **Southeast of Enumclaw; map B3, grid a0.**

How to get there: Drive east from Enumclaw on State Route 410 (Chinook Pass Highway) and after 19 miles take logging roads and Forest Service roads to the south (right) to reach various sections of the river. Take Forest Road 74 to reach the West Fork White River.

Facilities: Enumclaw has food, gas, lodging, and tackle, and food and gas are available in the small town of Greenwater.

Contact: Greenwater General Store, (360) 663-2357; Mount Baker-Snoqualmie National Forest, White River Ranger District, (360) 825-6585.

Species available: Cutthroat trout, mountain whitefish.

Fishing the Upper White River: Get away from the road and down into some of the canyon areas of the White and you'll find a few decent-sized trout. Living up to its name, the river is often off-color with snow runoff, so fishing with lures and artificial flies can be a tough proposition. Most anglers go with worms, salmon eggs, and other traditional trout offerings. You don't have to look too hard to find places where you can get away from the rest of the angling crowd.

The summer season here runs from June 1 through the end of October, with June and July often the most productive months.

8. ECHO AND LOST LAKES

Reference: **Southeast of Greenwater, extreme northeastern corner of Pierce County; map B3, grid b1.**

How to get there: Take State Route 410 to about two miles east of Greenwater and turn north on Forest Road 70. Drive just over eight miles to Forest Road 7030 and turn right, following the road about one-third of a mile to the start of Forest Trail 1176. Put on your hiking boots and hit the trail; it's about a seven-mile hike to Echo Lake. To reach Lost Lake, hang a right off Trail 1176 onto Trail 1185, about three miles from the trailhead, and hike just over 3.5 miles.

Facilities: The nearest food and gas are in Greenwater, with complete services in Enumclaw.

Contact: Mount Baker-Snoqualmie National Forest, White River Ranger District, (360) 825-6585.

Species available: Cutthroat and brook trout.

Fishing Echo and Lost Lakes: It seems as if Echo Lakes and Lost Lakes are scattered all over Washington, but the names are perhaps most accurate when describing these two high-country jewels in the Norse Peak Wilderness. You really could get lost if you weren't paying attention getting to and from Lost Lake, and you can certainly hear an echo ringing off the nearby hillsides if you talk loudly along the shores of Echo Lake.

Echo Lake covers 67 acres and Lost Lake about 25, both large enough to harbor decent populations of trout for visiting anglers. Cutthroats provide most of the action at Echo, although now and then someone reports catching a rainbow. Pan-sized brookies are the main targets at Lost.

Most folks visit these lakes in July and August, but you'll still enjoy good fishing and avoid most other anglers if you fish them after Labor Day weekend.

9. MANASTASH LAKE

Reference: **Northeast of State Route 410 near Cliffdel; map B3, grid b4.**

How to get there: Take State Route 410 (Chinook Pass Highway) to Forest Road 1708 (about three miles north of Cliffdel) and turn east (right), following the road abut 10 miles (it deteriorates more and more as you get closer to the lake). I wouldn't attempt the trip in anything but a four-wheel-drive rig.

Facilities: U.S. Forest Service campgrounds are located at Little Naches, Halfway Flat, and Sawmill Flat, all just off State Route 410 near the turn-off to Forest Road 1708 and all offering campsites, rest rooms, drinking water, and picnic tables. The nearest food, gas, tackle, and lodging are in Naches.

Contact: Wenatchee National Forest, Cle Elum Ranger District, (509) 674-4411; Wenatchee National Forest, Naches Ranger District, (509) 653-2205.

Species available: Brook trout.

Fishing Manastash Lake: It's a long, rough trip just to fish for pan-sized brook trout, but this 24-acre lake nestled among the pine-covered mountains of southwestern Kittitas County is a worthwhile reward for your effort. Casting Super Dupers, Panther Martin spinners, and other small lures from the bank will take fish, or wade out far enough to give yourself back-casting room and catch 'em with a fly rod. Either way, it's lots of fun.

June is the best month to fish here, but anglers find decent success all summer.

10. TANEUM CREEK

Reference: **Joins the Yakima River northwest of Ellensburg; map B3, grid b6.**

How to get there: Drive east from Cle Elum or west from Ellensburg on Interstate 90 and turn south onto Taneum Road (Forest Road 33), which parallels the river upstream for about 10 miles.

Facilities: There are 14 tent and trailer sites at the U.S. Forest Service's Taneum Campground, about seven miles east of the highway. The nearest food, gas, lodging, and tackle are to the east and west, near Cle Elum and Ellensburg.

Contact: Wenatchee National Forest, Cle Elum Ranger District, (509) 674-4411; L.T. Murray Wildlife Area (Department of Fish and Wildlife), (509) 925-6746.

Species available: Rainbow and cutthroat trout.

Fishing Taneum Creek: The Taneum isn't a particularly big stream, but it can provide fair trout fishing in June and July. Most of the trout are pan-sized, with an occasional fish of 12 inches or so. Selective fishery regulations mean no bait and single, barbless hooks. Since the river runs almost totally through state or national forest land, you'll find plenty of access to good fishing water.

11. AMERICAN RIVER

Reference: **Joins the Bumping River northwest of Cliffdel; map B3, grid c2.**

How to get there: Take State Route 410 east from Greenwater or west from Cliffdel. The highway parallels the river most of the way from Lodge Pole Campground on the west to American Forks Campground and its confluence with the Bumping River on the east, a distance of 12 miles.

Facilities: The U.S. Forest Service's Lodge Pole, Pleasant Valley, Hells Crossing, Pine Needle, American Forks, and Little Naches campgrounds all have campsites, rest rooms, and water, and they're all on or near the river. The nearest food, gas, tackle, and lodging are in Naches.

Contact: Wenatchee National Forest, Naches Ranger District, (509) 653-2205.

Species available: Rainbow, cutthroat, and brook trout; mountain whitefish.

Fishing the American River: Once planted with lots of pan-sized rainbows from the Naches Trout Hatchery, this easy-to-reach river is now pretty much self-supporting as far as its trout population is concerned, so don't expect hot fishing. No-bait regulations are in effect, and the clear, cold waters of the American are perfect for stream anglers who like to entice their fish with small spinners or wet flies. Easy access and the large numbers of summertime visitors using local campgrounds keep fishing pressure fairly high. If you want to escape other anglers, try parking along the highway just west of Lodge Pole and working your way upstream, away from the road. The season here opens in June, provides fair fishing all summer, and closes at the end of October.

12. BUMPING RIVER

Reference: **Joins the Naches River northwest of Cliffdel; map B3, grid c3.**

How to get there: Take State Route 410 (Chinook Pass Highway) to Bumping Lake Road (Forest Road 18) and turn south. The road runs alongside the river all the way from the highway to the east end of Bumping Lake. To reach the upper river, go south on Forest Road 174 along the east side of Bumping Lake, following it to the end, where a hiking trail continues upriver.

Facilities: U.S. Forest Service campgrounds at Little Naches, American Forks, Cedar Springs, Soda Springs, Cougar Flat, Bumping Crossing, and Bumping Dam all have campsites and other facilities. The closest food, gas, tackle, and lodging are in Naches.

Contact: Wenatchee National Forest, Naches Ranger District, (509) 653-2205.

Species available: Rainbow, cutthroat, and brook trout; mountain whitefish.

Fishing the Bumping River: The lower part of the river, downstream from the lake, gets fairly heavy fishing pressure through the summer and is no longer stocked with hatchery rainbows to bear the brunt of the onslaught. Fewer anglers put forth the effort to hike in and fish the upper river, so your odds are considerably better there. No-bait and barbless-hook regulations are in effect below the confluence of the American River, but standard rules apply upstream. Winter whitefish action can be good on the lower Bumping, but snow, ice, and resulting highway closures keep most anglers from ever giving it a try.

13. DEWEY LAKE

Reference: **Southeast of Chinook Pass; map B3, grid c1.**

How to get there: Take State Route 410 to the top of Chinook Pass and park in the Pacific Crest Trail parking lot. Hike south on the PCT about two miles to the Dewey Lake Trail, on the left. From there it's another mile to the lake.

Facilities: Several primitive campsites are located around the lake. The nearest food, gas, tackle, and lodging are in Greenwater (to the west) and Naches (to the east).

Contact: Wenatchee National Forest, Naches Ranger District, (509) 653-2205.

Species available: Brook trout.

Fishing Dewey Lake: You probably won't get lonely here in the northwest corner of the William O. Douglas Wilderness, since the nearby Pacific Crest Trail is often crowded with hikers, many of whom spend the night at Dewey Lake. The good news is that only about one out of 10 of them carries a fishing rod, and only about half of those know how to use it. If you're at least an average angler, you can out-fish the competition and catch your share of Dewey Lake's pan-sized brookies. Whether you cast flies, spoons, or spinners, two hours of casting should produce enough fish to fill the frying pan. The trout fishing is good enough to make the trip worthwhile; the scenery makes the trip memorable.

14. SWAMP AND COUGAR LAKES

Reference: **West of Bumping Lake, northwest portion of the William O. Douglas Wilderness, near Yakima-Pierce county line; map B3, grid c1.**

How to get there: Take State Route 410 to Bumping Lake Road (Forest Road 18) and turn south. When you get to Bumping Lake after driving ten miles, bear left on Forest Road 174 and follow it for eight miles to its end at the confluence of Cougar Creek and the upper Bumping River. From there it's a 2.5-mile hike to Swamp Lake and another two miles to Big and Little Cougar lakes.

Facilities: Primitive campsites can be found around the lakes. The nearest campgrounds are those at Bumping Lake and Bumping Dam (U.S. Forest Service). The closest gas, food, lodging, and tackle are in Greenwater and Naches.

Contact: Wenatchee National Forest, Naches Ranger District, (509) 653-2205; Cascade Toys and Sports, (509) 965-4423.

Species available: Rainbow and brook trout.

Fishing Swamp and Cougar Lakes: You might be able to find better fishing, but you'll have to look long and hard to find lakes in a prettier setting. Mount Rainier is only a few craggy ridges to the west, and there's usually snow on the nearby hillsides until August in this pristine corner of Yakima County. If you like to hike and catch pan-sized trout, you owe it to yourself to give these high-country gems a try.

At 82 acres, Big Cougar is the largest of the three lakes and offers perhaps the best fishing, but there are eager brookies in Little Cougar as well, and a mixed-bag catch of rainbows and brook trout is a possibility in Swamp Lake. All three lakes offer fly-fishing possibilities, but a spinning rod and selection of small spoons and spinners will also get you into fish. If you take a fly rod, be sure to include a few mosquito patterns in your fly box. Just as the mosquitoes here will feed on you, the trout feed heavily on the mosquitoes. The "season" at these lakes starts when the snow and ice melt, usually around the middle of June.

15. BUMPING LAKE (RESERVOIR)

Reference: **Southwest of Goose Prairie, Yakima County; map B3, grid c2.**
How to get there: Take State Route 410 to Bumping Lake Road (Forest Road 18) and turn south. Follow Bumping Lake Road about 11 miles to the east end of the lake.
Facilities: The east side of the lake has a good boat ramp and a Forest Service campground with tent and trailer sites, rest rooms, drinking water, and picnic tables. Several other campgrounds are within easy driving range along the Bumping River. For food, gas, tackle, and lodging, you'll have to go to Naches, about 30 miles away.
Contact: Wenatchee National Forest, Naches Ranger District, (509) 653-2205
Species available: Rainbow and cutthroat trout, kokanee.
Fishing Bumping Lake: Trolling for kokanee has long been a favorite pastime for Bumping Lake anglers, and most find the activity plenty rewarding. The fish aren't big, averaging maybe 10 inches, but all you have to do is locate a few of them, drop a gang troll rig equipped with a Wedding Ring or similar spinner over the side, and you're in business. Most anglers add a maggot or two to the hooks of the Wedding Ring, but white corn or Berkley's Power Wigglers should work just as well. Stillfishing with any of the same three baits, usually on a small, brightly painted hook, will also take Bumping Lake kokanee.

While the kokanee are more or less self-sustaining, both rainbows and cutthroats come by way of the Department of Fish and Wildlife planting truck, usually in the form of fall fingerling plants that winter-over in the lake to provide angling action the next spring and summer. These yearling trout average about 10 inches and can be suckered into biting all the usual baits and lures. Bumping Lake has a year-round season, but June and July are best for kokanee, with June and September good for rainbows and cutts.

16. RATTLESNAKE CREEK

Reference: **Joins the Naches River southeast of Cliffdel; map B3, grid c4.**
How to get there: Take State Route 410 to Forest Road 1500 (about nine miles northwest of the U.S. 12 junction) and turn east. The road follows the creek upstream for several miles.
Facilities: Eagle Rock Resort, located just off State Route 410 about 1.5 miles from the turn-off, has tent and RV sites, rest rooms, and a small store. The nearest food, gas, tackle, and lodging are in Naches.
Contact: Wenatchee National Forest, Naches Ranger District, (509) 653-2205; Eagle Rock Resort, (509) 658-2905; Cascade Toys and Sports, (509) 965-4423.
Species available: Rainbow and cutthroat trout.

Fishing Rattlesnake Creek: No longer stocked with hatchery trout, the Rattle-snake depends on catch-and-release and selective fishery regulations to continue providing decent angling opportunities. Pan-sized cutthroats and rainbows up to about 12 inches provide most of the action. The best time to fish it is during late June and July, and then again in September and October. The nearby Little Rattlesnake has standard regulations and provides fishing similar to the main creek. Access to Little Rattlesnake Creek is via Forest Road 1501, which turns south of the main road just over a mile east of State Route 410.

17. WENAS LAKE

Reference: **North of Naches; map B3, grid c6.**

How to get there: From Ellensburg, drive south on Umtanum Road to Wenas Road, turn west (right), and follow it for 22 miles to the lake. From Yakima, take State Route 823 north, through Selah, to Wenas Road, turn left, and follow it northwest for 12 miles to the lake.

Facilities: The lake has a large public access area with a boat ramp and toilets. Wenas Lake Resort has tent and RV sites, a small store, rest rooms, and other amenities. Food, gas, tackle, and lodging are available in Yakima.

Contact: Wenas Lake Resort, (509) 697-7670.

Species available: Rainbow and brown trout, channel catfish.

Fishing Wenas Lake: Being from the wet, green, west side of the state, I always think they should have built Wenas Lake in a better location, but I wasn't around when they decided to dam Wenas Creek and form this 61-acre reservoir, so I had no say in the matter. Luckily, most folks come here to fish rather than to check out the scenery, and they're usually happy with what they find. The truth is, Wenas has long been one of the best rainbow trout lakes on the east slope of the Cascades, and when the Department of Game—now the Department of Fish and Wildlife—decided to stock the lake with brown trout, they made it even better. Wenas is now home to some of the Evergreen State's biggest browns, a few of them reaching true trophy size of 10 pounds and over.

While trolling a little Triple Teazer or casting a bobber-and-worm rig might produce some nice rainbows, such simplistic techniques don't produce many of the big browns. That calls for trolling large, baitfish-imitating plugs and wobbling spoons—and for the kind of patience it takes to troll for hours at a time between strikes. The lake is open to year-round fishing, and some of the best brown trout action occurs early in the spring and late in the fall, times when most of the less-serious anglers have forsaken the lake for more comfortable spots next to living room fireplaces.

To extend the summertime angling opportunities, the Department of Fish and Wildlife has stocked channel catfish in the lake, and it shouldn't be long before the lake starts to produce some hefty channel cats. Stay tuned.

18. UPPER YAKIMA RIVER

Reference: **Easton downstream to Yakima; map B3, grid c7.**

How to get there: To reach the stretch of river between Cle Elum and Ellensburg from the west, take Interstate 90 to Cle Elum and exit onto State Route 907 as though you were headed for Blewett Pass. But instead of going left at the "Y" a few miles off the freeway, go right onto State Route 10, which parallels the river for several miles. Anglers headed west should follow Interstate 90 to a few miles west of Ellensburg, exit north onto U.S. 97, and then turn west (left) onto State Route 10 to go downstream along the river. To reach the "Canyon" portion of the river, drive south from Ellensburg on State Route 821 or drive north from Yakima on Interstate 82 and exit onto State Route 821 about five miles out of town.

Facilities: Several access sites and boat-launching spots are located along State Route 10 and State Route 821, most of them visible from the road. As for food, gas, lodging, tackle, and other facilities, you'll find everything you need in Easton, Cle Elum, Ellensburg, and Yakima. A few guides run float trips down the river.

Contact: Gary's Fly Shoppe, (509) 457-3474; Chinook Sporting Goods, (509) 452-8205; Cascade Toys and Sports, (509) 965-4423.

Species available: Rainbow trout, mountain whitefish.

Fishing the Upper Yakima River: The Yakima is Washington's best example of what can happen when a decision is made to manage a river for wild fish production and quality angling opportunity. The trend on the upper and middle portions of the Yakima since the early 1980s has been toward quality fishing, and it has paid off in a big way. Even though you can't kill a trout between Easton Dam and Roza Dam, you can certainly catch them, and some anglers experience days when they hook and release upwards of 50 wild rainbows or more. This part of the river is open year-round, and you may find excellent fishing during all but the coldest part of winter.

Although the majority of people who fish the Yakima do so with fly rods, spinning tackle and hardware are also used. In fact, small spinners such as the Luhr Jensen Metric or the Panther Martin are very effective. Just remember that the selective fishery regulations require that all lures be equipped with single, barbless hooks. Bait is prohibited for trout fishing on this stretch of the river.

Whether you fish flies or lures, casting precision is often a must on the Yakima. Much of the river is lined with grassy banks and overhanging brush or trees, and Yakima rainbows are notorious for hugging the river's edge and refusing to move more than a few inches into open water for a meal. That means, of course, that your spinner or fly has to touch down within an inch or two of the bank or it may be ignored. Sloppy casting under these conditions can quickly lead to frustration.

The Yakima is popular with both bank and boat anglers, and there are many places to reach the water along this stretch of the river. Several of those are along Interstate 90 between Easton and Cle Elum, but some of the most popular are off State Route 10 from Cle Elum downstream to Ellensburg and along State Route 821—also known as the Yakima Canyon Road—from Ellensburg downstream to Yakima.

The only time of year you may use bait for fishing the upper Yakima is during the winter, and then only for whitefish. Unlike many Northwest rivers, the Yakima is the scene of some fairly serious interest in whitefish among area anglers. Maggots, small grubs, and various aquatic larvae are the productive baits, but a few anglers stick with their fly rods and small nymph patterns to take whitefish throughout the winter. Any of the deeper, slower water upstream of Yakima is likely to produce good whitefish action.

19. OAK CREEK

Reference: **Joins the Tieton River at Oak Creek Wildlife Area, about two miles from the junction of U.S. 12 and State Route 410; map B3, grid d4.**

How to get there: Take U.S. 12 east from White Pass or west from Naches and turn north on Oak Creek Road, just east of the Oak Creek Wildlife Area. Oak Creek Road follows the creek upstream for more than 10 miles.

Facilities: Rest rooms and drinking water are available at Oak Creek Wildlife Area. The nearest variety of food, gas, lodging, and other amenities are to the east in Naches and Yakima.

Contact: Oak Creek Wildlife Area, (509) 653-2390; Cascade Toys and Sports, (509) 965-4423.

Species available: Rainbow, cutthroat, and brook trout.

Fishing Oak Creek: One of the few Yakima County streams that still gets plants of hatchery trout every summer, Oak Creek provides especially good fishing right after the hatchery truck visits, usually in June or July. With standard stream-fishing regulations and a five-fish daily trout limit, it's pretty much a put-and-take fishery. The season runs from June 1 to October 31.

20. TIETON RIVER

Reference: **Joins Naches River northwest of Naches; map B3, grid d5.**

How to get there: Take U.S. 12 east from White Pass or west from Naches to parallel the river between Rimrock Lake and the U.S. 12-State Route 410 junction. To reach the North Fork Tieton above Rimrock Lake, turn south off U.S. 12 near the west end of the lake onto Forest Road 12, then onto Forest Road 1207, which parallels the North Fork. To reach the South Fork Tieton, take Tieton Reservoir Road (Forest Road 12) off U.S. 12 about three miles east of the dam and follow it to the southeast corner of Rimrock Lake. Turn south (left) on Forest Road 100, which parallels the South Fork for several miles.

Facilities: Five U.S. Forest Service campgrounds are located along the river between the dam and the mouth of the river, all with tent and trailer sites, rest rooms, and water, and all easily accessible from U.S. 12. Forest Service campgrounds at Clear Lake are the primarily facilities for anglers on the North Fork Tieton. Stores, restaurants, tackle, motels, and cabins can be found along U.S. 12 on the north shore of Rimrock Lake.

Contact: Wenatchee National Forest, Naches Ranger District, (509) 653-2205; Getaway Sports, (509) 672-2239.

Species available: Rainbow and cutthroat trout, mountain whitefish.

Fishing the Tieton River: One look at the Tieton River makes it's hard to believe that this little stream was the scene of what turned out to be an historic battle between an angler and a monster bull trout of over 20 pounds. Like a goldfish in a bowl, it doesn't seem likely that a trout could grow to trophy proportions in such a small stream system. But on an April day back in 1961, Louis Schott found out that the Tieton was capable of growing huge bull trout, and the 22-pound, eight-ouncer he wrestled to the beach that day still stands as the Washington state-record bull trout. Since most of the state's waters are closed to the taking of both bull trout and the closely related Dolly Varden, it's very possible that Schott's record will never be broken.

Rainbow trout provide most of the summertime angling opportunity on the Tieton these days. They're hatchery fish stocked by the Department of Fish and Wildlife, and the Tieton is one of relatively few streams that still receives such plants. The Tieton system also has some cutthroat trout in it, and anglers find most of them in the North Fork and the extreme upper reaches of the South Fork. The lower 12 miles or so of the South Fork Tieton are closed to fishing. Standard angling regulations apply on the Tieton, so anglers use everything from salmon eggs and worms to dry flies. Grasshoppers are an important menu item to Tieton trout, and some anglers capture a handful of the long-legged insects to use for bait as they work their way from pool to pool. Grasshopper look-alikes are also effective, including Rooster Tail and Bang Tail spinners in various shades of brown, green, and yellow that imitate the insects. Fly fishing with various grasshopper patterns also takes trout. Other popular fly patterns include the Hare's Ear, caddis, and other nymphs.

Besides trout, the Tieton produces good numbers of mountain whitefish. A winter whitefish-only season on the main river (below the dam) extends from December through March, and 15-fish limits are fairly common for anglers who find schools of fish in some of the deeper pools and runs. Maggots, Berkley's Power Wigglers and other small baits are most effective for these small-mouthed fish. Fly fishing also accounts for good numbers of Tieton River whitefish, mostly on very sparsely tied, size 12 or 14 nymph patterns fished along the bottom on a sink-tip line or floating line with a long leader.

21. WILLIAM O. DOUGLAS
WILDERNESS LAKES

Reference: **North of White Pass, along Yakima-Lewis county line; map B3, grid d1.**

How to get there: From the north, take State Route 410 to Bumping Lake Road (Forest Road 18) and turn south, following the road along the east side of Bumping Lake to Forest Road 395, which follows Deep Creek upstream to Deep Creek Campground and the trail to Twin Sisters Lakes and beyond. From the south, take U.S. 12 (White Pass Highway) to the top of White Pass and White Pass Horse Camp, which is on the north side of the road.

The Pacific Crest Trail leads north from there, with the first lake about 1.5 miles up the trail.

Facilities: There are a few campsites at White Pass Horse Camp and a few more at Dog Lake Campground, about two miles to the east. Motels, restaurants, gas, groceries, and other amenities are available in White Pass and Packwood, which is several miles to the west.

Contact: Wenatchee National Forest, Naches Ranger District, (509) 653-2205; Cascade Toys and Sports, (509) 965-4423.

Species available: Rainbow, cutthroat, and brook trout.

Fishing the William O. Douglas Wilderness Lakes: About three dozen lakes offer decent trout-fishing opportunities in this area, and there are lots of smaller ponds that might produce a fish if your timing is good. The catch depends on the lake you fish. Twin Sisters lakes, the largest and among the easiest to reach, offer brook trout as a main course, although you might catch an occasional cutthroat or rainbow, especially in the bigger lake. The three Blankenship lakes are primarily cutthroat lakes, while nearby Apple and Pear lakes have both cutts and rainbows. Cramer, Dancing Lady, and Shellrock lakes, all near the south end of the chain, are best-known for their rainbows, with a few cutthroats mixed in. Other lakes well worth investigating and within reach of good hiking trails include Dumbbell, Otter, Long John, Beusch, Art, Hill, Pillar, Pipe, Jess, Penoyer, Bill, Henry, Snow, Jug, Fryingpan, Fish, and Lower and Upper Crag lakes. Two lakes at the south end of the chain, Deep and Sand lakes, are within easy reach of day-hikers from White Pass, so they receive a lot of summertime fishing pressure and may not be very productive.

If you're planning to fish seriously for a couple of days, be sure to bring a tackle selection to cover all the bases. You'd be smart to include a few salmon eggs or even some worms in your arsenal, as well as an assortment of small spinners and wobbling spoons, a selection of dry and wet flies, and a couple of bobbers for casting both bait and flies.

Two things you can expect for sure if you fish these lakes and hike these trails during the summer are other people and lots of bugs. This may be the mosquito capital of the world, and deer flies often add to the excitement. Take along some good insect repellant or expect to donate at least two pints of blood. Depending on how long the snow and rain hold off, you can escape the insect plague—and most of the other hikers and anglers—by visiting after mid-September.

---

22. DOG LAKE

Reference: **East of White Pass Summit; map B3, grid d2.**

How to get there: Take U.S. 12 (White Pass Highway) to White Pass and turn north off the road just east of the summit. The lake is within sight of the highway, on the north side.

Facilities: Dog Lake Campground (U.S. Forest Service) has about 10 campsites, and there's a rough boat ramp near the campground. Food, gas, tackle, and lodging are available nearby at White Pass Summit.

Contact: Wenatchee National Forest, Naches Ranger District, (509) 653-2205.

Species available: Rainbow and brook trout.

Fishing Dog Lake: It's not common to find a clear, cold, beautiful alpine lake right along a major highway, but Dog Lake is the exception to the rule. Except for the sound of the cars and RVs droning up and down the east slope of the White Pass summit, you might think you're a million miles from civilization as you cast small spinners along the big rock slide at the northeast corner of the lake. Then you remember that you're casting from the comfort of a small boat or float tube and look around to see a dozen other anglers working the shoreline around the 61-acre lake. No, you're not alone in the world after all, but the brook trout continue to bite, so you don't really mind. Now and then you hook a nice rainbow for variety, and it occurs to you that you can have it both ways, wilderness setting and easy access. That's what Dog Lake has to offer.

Tip of the day: Fish the lake right after the ice melts off in June or wait until late-September. The fishing pressure is lighter at both ends of the summer and the fishing is also better. Late-season at Dog Lake is especially rewarding, since the mosquitos are gone and the brook trout are at their brilliantly colored best.

---

23. LEECH LAKE

Reference: Near White Pass Summit; map B3, grid d2.

How to get there: From Morton or Naches, take U.S. 12 (White Pass Highway) to the top of White Pass, where the lake is located just north of the highway.

Facilities: Forest Service campgrounds with tent sites, rest rooms, and drinking water are located on and near the lake, with food, gas, tackle, and lodging available on the highway nearby. The lake has a boat ramp.

Contact: Wenatchee National Forest, Naches Ranger District, (509) 653-2205.

Species available: Brook trout.

Fishing Leech Lake: The name may not sound too attractive, but Leech provides pretty good fishing for a lake that's within casting distance of one of Washington's more popular mountain pass highways. The lake is open to year-round fishing, but few anglers come here to dig through the deep snow and chop a hole through the ice to try their luck in the dead of winter. Fly-fishing through the ice is next to impossible, and since Leech has fly-fishing-only regulations, wintertime angling is a non-event.

Most anglers wait until about mid-June, by which time the ice usually has melted away and the brook trout are within reach of fly-rodders. Both wet and dry flies are effective, and they produce some very respectable trout. Don't overdo it if you get into the lunkers, since only two fish among the daily bag limit of five may exceed 12 inches. Better yet, release everything you catch except maybe a couple of pan-sizers for the dinner table.

---

24. PACKWOOD LAKE

Reference: Southeast of Packwood; map B3, grid e1.

How to get there: Take U.S. 12 to Packwood and drive east on Forest Road 1260 for 3.5 miles. Park at the end of the road and hike about 2.5 miles to the lake.

Facilities: You can camp at any of several primitive sites around the lake. Food, gas, tackle, and lodging are available in Packwood.

Contact: Gifford Pinchot National Forest, Packwood Ranger District, (360) 494-5515.

Species available: Rainbow trout.

Fishing Packwood Lake: Although it's some distance away from the U.S. 12 traffic flow and even farther away from any of the state's population centers, this 450-acre lake in the mountains east of Packwood gets a surprising amount of foot traffic, mostly anglers who venture up here to try for the lake's foot-long rainbows. The trails and camping areas around the lake get pretty crowded on holiday weekends, but you can usually find plenty of elbow room to test your skills with a fly rod or spinning outfit during the rest of the summer.

Leave the worms and salmon eggs home, because Packwood is under selective fishery regulations, where only artificial lures and flies with single, barbless hooks are legal. Fishing usually picks up around the end of May or first of June and stays good through July. The first cool nights of September also bring on a good trout bite, and by then the angling crowds have gone home for the winter.

25. CLEAR LAKE

Reference: **East of White Pass Summit, at west end of Rimrock Lake; map B3, grid d2.**

How to get there: Take U.S. 12 from Morton or Naches to the east end of Rimrock Lake and turn south on Forest Road 12. A "Y" near the bottom of the hill will take you to the east or west side of the lake.

Facilities: U.S. Forest Service campgrounds located on the north and south sides of the lake have more than 60 campsites between them. The south side of the lake also has a boat ramp. Food, gas, tackle, and lodging can be found along U.S. 12, on the north side of Rimrock Lake.

Contact: Wenatchee National Forest, Naches Ranger District, (509) 653-2205.

Species available: Rainbow trout.

Fishing Clear Lake: The Department of Fish and Wildlife stocks hatchery rainbows in this 265-acre lake every spring to provide good fishing throughout most of the summer. Although these eight- to 10-inch planters provide most of the angling action, the catch also includes a fair number of carry-over rainbows from previous years' plants, some of which top 18 inches.

This high-country lake gets pretty busy during the height of the summer camping season, so you may want to beat the crowds by fishing Clear Lake before school gets out. Trolling Rooster Tails is popular here, but all the other popular trout offerings will also work. Stillfishing around the edge of the lake with Power Bait, worms, or marshmallow-salmon egg combinations is also effective.

26. RIMROCK LAKE (RESERVOIR)

Reference: **South side of White Pass Highway between White Pass Summit and Rimrock; map B3, grid d3.**

How to get there: Take U.S. 12 east from White Pass or west from Naches. The highway parallels the north shore of the reservoir for several miles. Turn south on Forest Road 12 at either end of Rimrock to reach the south side of the lake.

Facilities: Forest Service campgrounds that offer tent and RV sites, drinking water, and rest rooms, plus private lodges, boat ramps, stores, gas stations, and restaurants are scattered along the highway on the north side of the lake. Boat ramps and campgrounds are also available on the south side of the lake, near the east end.

Contact: Trout Lodge, (509) 672-2211; Silver Beach Resort, (509) 672-2500; Wenatchee National Forest, Naches Ranger District, (509) 653-2205; Getaway Sports, (509) 672-2239.

Species available: Kokanee, rainbow trout.

Fishing Rimrock Lake: Some years Rimrock is the most productive kokanee lake in Washington, giving up tens of thousands of the firm-fleshed little sockeye salmon in a single summer season. When it's prime, usually through July, anglers even catch kokanee from the bank, a rarity in most Northwest kokanee lakes. Unfortunately, the reservoir's valuable kokanee population takes a back seat to agricultural irrigation, which is why Tieton Dam was built and the lake was formed in the first place. A few years ago the lake was drawn down to little more than a river running through a wide basin, but the Department of Fish and Wildlife had time to plan for the event and "saved" large numbers of kokanee for re-planting after the reservoir re-filled. As a result, kokanee fishing now is nearly as good as it was during its heyday in the mid-eighties. The fish aren't too big, averaging eight to 11 inches, but there's a 16-fish daily bag limit and good anglers have little trouble reaching it in a few hours.

Strings of trolling blades, followed by Wedding Ring spinners, Needlefish, Double Whammys, and other flashy lures, account for many of the kokanee. Tip the hooks with maggots or Berkley Power Wigglers to improve your chances.

The lake is also stocked with rainbow trout, which can be caught on all the usual spoons, spinners, wobbling plugs, and baits. Rimrock holds a few hefty bull trout, but if you catch one, you have to release it unharmed as quickly as possible. Some of the trout caught here are taken on kokanee gear, but you can also stillfish for them with worms, salmon eggs, marshmallows, or Berkley Power Bait.

27. NACHES RIVER

Reference: **Joins the Yakima River at Yakima; map B3, grid d6.**

How to get there: Drive east on U.S. 12 from Yakima to parallel the lower Naches. Turn north on State Route 410 to continue upriver. To reach the Little Naches, turn north off State Route 410 onto Forest Road 19, which follows the river upstream for miles.

Facilities: Besides several U.S. Forest Service campgrounds with campsites, drinking water, and rest rooms along the upper river, there are also private resorts and RV parks near the river on State Route 410. Other amenities can be found in Naches and Yakima.

Contact: Squaw Rock Resort and RV Park, (509) 658-2926; Eagle Rock Campground, (509) 658-2905; Whistlin' Jack Lodge, (509) 658-2433; Wenatchee National Forest, Naches Ranger District, (509) 653-2205.

Species available: Rainbow and cutthroat trout, mountain whitefish.

Fishing the Naches River: The best advice for anyone headed to the Naches for the first time is to read the angling regulations pamphlet very carefully before wetting a line. Three different sections of the river—the mouth to Rattlesnake Creek, Rattlesnake Creek to the mouth of the Bumping River, and the Little Naches above the Bumping—all have different limits, different minimum size regulations, and different rules concerning legal tackle.

The most restrictive regulations are on the Little Naches, where no-bait rules and other selective fishery regs are in effect. The Little Naches is a great area to prospect along the river bank with a light-action fly rod, working various nymphs through the small runs and pools in search of a keeper rainbow or cutthroat. Bait fishing is popular on the middle stretch of the Naches, between the mouth of the Bumping and the mouth of Rattlesnake Creek, and an eight-inch minimum size limit allows anglers to keep many of the trout they catch in this area. This is bigger water than the Little Naches, easier to fish, and readily accessible from State Route 410.

The Naches begins to slow and widen a little below Rattlesnake Creek, and becomes a good-sized river downstream from the mouth of the Tieton. There are some excellent trout pool along this stretch, where anglers find a fair number of rainbows and a few cuts in excess of the 12-inch minimum size limit that's in effect along the lower river. But be careful if you catch a particularly large trout; there's a 20-inch maximum limit on the lower and middle stretches of the Naches to protect steelhead from harvest. Rolling a nightcrawler along the bottom or working a skirted spinner through the depths are good ways to catch trout here, but fly-fishing with various nymph and streamer patterns is also effective.

Like other rivers in the area, the Naches has a special winter whitefish season that provides good angling action during the cold months. Small flies, maggots, stonefly nymphs, and other tiny baits work best for whitefish. If you find one or two fish in a pool, stay with that spot for a while, because these are schooling fish.

28. COWICHE CREEK

Reference: **Joins the Naches River northwest of Yakima; map B3, grid d6.**

How to get there: Take Summitview Avenue west out of Yakima for six miles and bear left on Cowiche Mill Road to reach the South Fork Cowiche Creek. Go right on North Cowiche Road to work your way up the North Fork Cowiche Creek.

Facilities: The best bet for food, gas, lodging, tackle, and other amenities is Yakima.

Contact: Cascade Toys and Sports, (509) 965-4423.

Species available: Rainbow, cutthroat, and brook trout.

Fishing Cowiche Creek: Though there are bigger and better stream fisheries around Yakima County, this stream within an easy six-mile driving range of Yakima fills a niche for anglers in search of pan-sized trout that aren't too choosy about what they eat. With no special regulations in effect, the creek is open to bait, hardware, or fly-fishing, and anglers can keep two trout of eight inches or larger. The fishing is usually good by the end of June, and you'll find better fishing and fewer anglers if you work your way up the forks, away from town.

---

29. ROTARY LAKE

Reference: **Near confluence of Yakima and Naches rivers, north side of Yakima; map B3, grid e7.**

How to get there: Take Yakima's First Avenue about two miles from the center of town to the north end of the Greenway Trail and follow it a few hundred feet to the lake.

Facilities: Good bank access and a fishing dock are available at the lake, and you can easily pack a float tube or small boat to its shores. Food, gas, lodging, and tackle are within a few blocks of the lake in Yakima.

Contact: Cascade Toys and Sports, (509) 965-4423.

Species available: Rainbow and brown trout, largemouth bass.

Fishing Rotary Lake: The only time I ever visited this 23-acre pond on Yakima's north side I stopped to chat with three college-age guys who were obviously having a great time. They had pretty much finished off the large supply of beer they had brought along, the sun had burned them all to a bright shade of red, and the trout were in a fairly cooperative mood. Only problem was that the fish weren't drinking alcohol, and with full control of their physical and mental capacities, they were all managing to escape before the inebriated trio could get them to the bank and up onto the beach. The young anglers laughed every time they lost a trout because of their own ineptitude, and it occurred to me that everyone was having a good time, including the fish. Other anglers do fish Rotary Lake a little more seriously, and some come away with good catches of stocked browns and rainbows. Casting bobber-and-worm rigs, Berkley Power Bait, Rooster Tail spinners, and other offerings works well. The lake is open year-round, but trout fishing is best in April, May, and early June.

If you're not a trout angler, try working the shoreline with spinnerbaits, plastic worms, or various surface offerings to see if you can pick off one of the lake's many hefty largemouth bass. This small lake gives up a surprising number of bass over five pounds during the course of a typical summer.

30. AHTANUM CREEK

Reference: **Joins Yakima River south of Yakima; map B3, grid e6.**
How to get there: Take Interstate 82/U.S. 12 to Union Gap and turn west on Ahtanum Road. Roads to the south every few miles cross the creek. The road splits at Tampico, and you can go south to fish the South Fork Ahtanum Creek or north to fish the North Fork.
Facilities: Food, gas, tackle, lodging, and RV parks are easy to find in Yakima.
Contact: Cascade Toys and Sports, (509) 965-4423.
Species available: Rainbow and cutthroat trout, mountain whitefish.
Fishing Ahtanum Creek: Pan-sized trout provide most of the action for anglers at Ahtanum Creek. If you work your way up or down the entire length of the creek, you'll have a chance to fish everything from a high-country stream in the Cascade foothills to a slow-moving slough running through agricultural fields. There are some bigger trout in the lower portions of the creek, but you may have to get permission to fish, since much of it is bordered by private farmlands. Much of the land on the south side of the creek is on the Yakima Indian Reservation. The season here runs from June 1 through October 31, with fishing best during the first two months and last month of the season.

31. I-82 PONDS (FREEWAY PONDS)

Reference: **Along Interstate 82, east side of Yakima; map B3, grid e8.**
How to get there: Take Interstate 82 east from Union Gap or west from Zillah. From the west end, Ponds 1 and 2 are between Mellis and Donald roads, Pond 3 is east of Donald Road, Ponds 4 and 5 are near Finley Road, Pond 6 is off Buena Loop Road, and Pond 7 is east of Buena.
Facilities: The Yakima-Union Gap area has a full range of motels, RV parks, restaurants, grocery stores, tackle and fly shops, and other amenities.
Contact: Cascade Toys and Sports, (509) 965-4423; Chinook Sporting Goods, (509) 452-8205.
Species available: Rainbow and brown trout, largemouth bass, crappies, blue-gills, yellow perch, black bullhead catfish, walleyes, channel catfish.
Fishing the I-82 ponds: Pond 1 may soon offer anglers a decent chance at wall-eyes right in Yakima's backyard, but for now those walleyes are there to eat their little cousins the yellow perch. If they scarf down a few thousand pump-kinseed sunfish, that would also be okay with the Department of Fish and Wildlife biologists who planted the walleyes here. If things go as planned, some big walleyes will replace all the stunted panfish, eventually providing Yakima anglers with good fishing and great eating. For now, though, anglers have to release any walleyes they might catch from Pond 1.

In the meantime, largemouth bass are the best bet for Pond 1 anglers, and they can be caught on all the usual crankbaits, spinnerbaits, buzzbaits, and plastics that work for largemouths everywhere. You also have a chance of taking a trophy-class brown trout from Pond 1, as well as Pond 2, since both were stocked with hatchery browns a few years back. Pond 2's main claim to fame is that it produced the state-record black bullhead catfish in 1994, and biologists suspect that there may still be bigger black bullheads in the water.

Brown trout are stocked now and then in Pond 3, but if you don't catch one, you can busy yourself trying for some of the pond's husky largemouth bass. If the bass aren't biting either, try for yellow perch, since Pond 3 has some of the largest in the entire chain.

Ponds 4 and 5, which are connected by a culvert so that species may come and go from one to the other, offer a combined menu that includes rainbow and brown trout, largemouth bass, crappies, perch, bluegills, and channel catfish. Those channel cats were stocked in Pond 5 in 1994, and as of 1996 are big enough to draw interest from anglers. While they offer a wide variety, Ponds 4 and 5 are most often visited by anglers in search of trout. Pond 4 is close enough to the road so that some anglers carry or drag boats to it.

Pond 6, also called Buena Pond, is stocked with rainbows and is the most popular of the bunch among trout anglers. It also has bass and perch. Since it's possible to drive to the edge of Pond 6, it gets the most boat traffic of the seven.

Pond 7, on the other hand, is nearly a mile from the nearest road, so it gets the lightest angling pressure. Anglers willing to make the hike find some very good crappie fishing and a few good-sized largemouth bass.

---

32. WALUPT LAKE

Reference: **Southeast of Packwood, southeast corner of Lewis County; map B3, grid e1.**

How to get there: Take U.S. 12 to about three miles west of Packwood and turn east on Forest Road 21, staying on it about 15 miles to Forest Road 2160. Turn east (left) there and follow Road 2160 about 3.5 miles to the north side of the lake.

Facilities: The north side of the lake has a U.S. Forest Service campground. Food, gas, lodging, and other amenities can be found in Packwood.

Contact: Gifford Pinchot National Forest, Packwood Ranger District, (360) 494-5515.

Species available: Rainbow and cutthroat trout.

Fishing Walupt Lake: You have to venture to the extreme southeastern corner of Lewis County to find Walupt, but it's worth the trip because of all the lake's unusual qualities, beginning with the fact that it's a high-country lake you can actually drive to. Less than a mile from the Pacific Crest Trail at one point, it has a well-used gravel road running right to its shores. Walupt's size and depth are also unusual, even unique among Washington's high lakes. It covers more than 380 acres, and its clear, cold waters are reported to be 200 feet deep in spots—huge for a lake located nearly 4,000 feet above sea level. Walupt's angling regulations set it apart, too. Though selective fishery regulations (no bait, single barbless hooks only) are in effect, a standard, five-trout daily bag limit is allowed. Even the minimum size limit is an unusual 10 inches.

Whether anglers flock to Walupt despite of all these apparent contradictions or because of them, I don't know, but from about mid-June to Labor Day, this is one of western Washington's most popular camping/fishing/getaway destinations. Casting spinners, wobblers, or artificial flies from the banks takes fish, but a boat offers obvious advantages on a lake this big and deep. Unlike most lakes with selective fishery rules, it's okay to use a boat with a gas-powered motor, and many of the more successful anglers do.

Lots of anglers also put out crawdad traps. The lake is full of the little crustaceans, and they're large enough to make worthwhile hors d'oeuvres or a tasty addition to a green salad. Just boil 'em until they're red, break 'em in half, and peel the shell off the lower half. They taste and look just like lobster, only it takes a lot more of them to make a meal.

---

33. HORSESHOE, TAKHLAKH, COUNCIL, OLALLIE, AND CHAIN OF LAKES

Reference: **Northwest of Mount Adams, northeastern Skamania County; map B3, grid g0.**

How to get there: These lakes are accessible via U.S. Forest Service roads from several directions. One route is to take U.S. 12 to about three miles west of Packwood, and then turn south on Forest Road 21, following it to Forest Road 56. Turn south (left) on Forest Road 56, then right on Forest Road 5601, following it to Olallie and the rest of the lakes. Another option is to take U.S. 12 to Randle and turn south on Cispus Road, which is also called Forest Road 23. It runs directly to Takhlakh Lake. From the southwest, another way into these lakes is to take Interstate 5 to Woodland and follow State Route 503 up the Lewis River until it becomes Forest Road 90. Stay on Forest Road 90 all the way to Forest Road 23, turn north (left), and the lakes are a couple of miles ahead. From the southeast, take State Route 14 to White Salmon and turn north on State Route 141, following it to Trout Lake. Continue north up the White Salmon River on Forest Road 23 all the way to the lakes. Once you're in the area, use Forest Road 2334 to reach Council Lake, Forest Road 2329 to reach Takhlakh and Horseshoe lakes, Forest Road 5601 to reach Olallie Lake, and Forest Road 022 to reach Chain of Lakes. Whew!

Facilities: U.S. Forest Service campgrounds with tent and trailer sites, drinking water, and rest rooms are located on all but Chain of Lakes, and it's possible to get a boat into all of them. Bring everything else you need with you, since the nearest stores, motels, tackle, and gas stations are about 30 miles away.

Contact: Gifford Pinchot National Forest, Randle Ranger District, (360) 497-7565.

Species available: Cutthroat, brown, and brook trout.

Fishing Horseshoe, Takhlakh, Council, Olallie, and Chain of Lakes: These lakes a few miles northwest of Mount Adams are a long distance from anywhere and yet accessible from almost everywhere. Located near the center of a maze of U.S. Forest Service roads that extends along the eastern flank of the Cascades from Mount Rainier to the Columbia River, these sub-alpine lakes are popular with anglers from Yakima to Vancouver, Goldendale to Tacoma. If they weren't stocked regularly by the Department of Fish and Wildlife, they would most likely be depleted of trout in no time.

Olallie Lake, the smallest of the bunch, is only 16 acres, and Council Lake, at 48 acres, is the largest. All receive steady angling pressure from the time they clear themselves of ice in the late spring until fall snows blanket the roads in October. The relative closeness of the lakes to each other and the network of roads connecting them makes it possible for an angler to fish all five lakes in a single day if desired. In case you have preferences about the type of trout you want to catch, Olallie has brown and brook trout, as does 30-acre Chain of Lakes; Council and 35-acre Takhlakh (pronounced Tak-a-lak) have brookies and cutthroats; and 24-acre Horseshoe Lake offers brook trout.

---

34. KLICKITAT RIVER

Reference: **Joins the Columbia at the town of Lyle; map B3, grid i3.**

How to get there: Take State Route 14 to the town of Lyle and turn north on State Route 142, which follows the river upstream for nearly 20 miles. Continue up State Route 142 a few more miles and turn north at the sign pointing to Glenwood to follow the river several miles more.

Facilities: Primitive camping areas are scattered along the river. There are several places along the highway where boats can be launched and where bank-fishing access is available. Groceries can be found in Klickitat, with more amenities to the east in Goldendale. A few fishing guides work various parts of the river.

Contact: Klickitat Wildlife Recreation Area, (509) 773-4459; Garrett's Guide Service, (509) 493-3242.

Species available: Summer steelhead, fall chinook and coho salmon, rainbow trout.

Fishing the Klickitat River: Take some of Washington's best summer steelhead fishing, put it in one of the state's prettiest rivers, then run that river through some of the region's most spectacular scenery, and what do you get? The Klickitat, a stream that I would rank right up there among the best the Northwest has to offer. In a part of the world where rivers seem to be running in every direction, that's quite a statement, but then the Klickitat is quite a river.

Summer steelheading is the biggest attraction, and even though the Klickitat doesn't often rank up there among the state's top 10 summertime steelie streams, it's a consistent producer that gives up 1,000 or more fish virtually every year. Summer steelhead are in the river when it opens to fishing on June 1, and the fishing gets better right on through July, then holds up pretty well into October. The action slows during the hottest periods of the summer, when snow-melt dirties the river and reduces visibility to an inch or two. But as soon as the weather cools, the river clears and fishing improves again.

All the usual steelhead baits and lures work, but for years Klickitat steelhead have had a reputation for favoring freshly caught grasshoppers for breakfast. Today's hatchery steelies may not have quite the same appetite for 'hoppers as the Klickitat's wild-run steelhead, but they're still worth a try if all else fails. And if you should happen to hook a wild steelhead with not-clipped fins, it has to be released unharmed.

As for salmon, fall chinook runs in the Klickitat the past few years have been good enough to draw the attention of many anglers. September is the top chinook month, and most of the fish are caught around the mouth of the river and upstream several hundred yards into the slow water at the bottom end of the Klickitat Canyon. Trolling large Kwikfish and Flatfish plugs can be productive, but many anglers bounce large roe clusters or fresh ghost shrimp along the bottom for their fish.

There are some large resident rainbows throughout much of the Klickitat all season long, and many are caught accidentally by steelhead anglers. Hatchery rainbows are also stocked in the Little Klickitat, above the town of Goldendale. If you want to target them, work a small spoon or spinner through the tail-outs of the deeper pools or along the "edges" where fast and slow water meet. And remember, if the hardware doesn't work, those rainbows will take grasshoppers, too.

Drift boats are popular modes of transportation on the Klickitat, but if you haven't floated it before, be sure to do some research before you launch. Tight spots and heavy rapids are scattered here and there along the entire length of the river, and sloppy boating or failure to scout ahead can get you in deep trouble in a hurry. As for the lower part of the river, where the Klickitat narrows and squeezes through a steep-walled canyon only a few feet wide, don't even think about boating it.

35. WHITE SALMON RIVER

Reference: **Joins the Columbia River just west of the town of White Salmon; map B3, grid i1.**

How to get there: Take State Route 14 to the town of White Salmon and turn north on State Route 141 to parallel the river upstream. Several side roads in and around White Salmon provide access to some good fishing water on the lower reaches of the river.

Facilities: Food, gas, tackle, and lodging are readily available in White Salmon. For those who aren't on a diet, stay at the Inn of the White Salmon and enjoy a fantastic breakfast along with a comfortable bed in one of Washington's more interesting old hotel/B&B facilities.

Contact: Miller's Sports, (509) 493-2233; Inn of the White Salmon, (509) 493-2335.

Species available: Spring and fall chinook salmon, summer-run steelhead.

Fishing the White Salmon River: As on the Little White Salmon to the west (see page 457), the White Salmon provides its best steelhead fishing in August and September. Anglers drift-fishing the moving water above town make some good catches, but boaters fishing in and around the river mouth account for a bulk of the steelhead. Some of the best catches are made at night, with anglers using a variety of baits and diving plugs. Access is sometimes a problem for boaters, since the lone boat ramp at the mouth of the river is on tribal property and the Indians who own it sometimes close it down. When that happens, it's a long run in rough water to reach the productive fishing spots at the mouth of the river.

Fall also provides some fair chinook salmon fishing, but the best shot at river-run kings is during the spring. Depending on run conditions that can prompt closures of this fishery, April and May provide fair to good catches of spring chinooks in and around the mouth of the White Salmon. Trolling spinners or large plugs wrapped with sardine strips account for most of the spring kings.

36. LITTLE WHITE SALMON RIVER/ DRANO LAKE

Reference: **Joins the Columbia east of Cook; map B3, grid j0.**

How to get there: Take State Route 14 east from Carson or west from White Salmon to the tiny berg of Cook. Drano Lake and the mouth of the Little White Salmon are right along the highway about a mile east of Cook. To reach upriver areas, turn north at Cook and bear north on Cook-Underwood Road, then Willard Road, and finally Oklahoma Road (Forest Road 18), which runs almost to the head of the river.

Facilities: A boat ramp is located at Drano Lake, on the north side of State Route 14. Moss Creek and Oklahoma campgrounds (U.S. Forest Service) have both tent and trailer sites. Big Cedar County Park has tent sites only. Food, gas, tackle, and lodging are available in Carson and White Salmon.

Contact: Gifford Pinchot National Forest, Mount Adams Ranger District, (509) 395-2501.

Species available: Summer steelhead, chinook salmon, rainbow and brook trout.

Fishing the Little White Salmon River and Drano Lake: Much of the "river fishing" here occurs not in the river but in the big backwater at the river's mouth known as Drano Lake, and it has a long reputation for its outstanding steelhead and salmon fishing. One of the best fisheries here over the years has been the spring chinook action during April and May, when anglers have been known to catch hundreds of 10- to 30-pound springers per month. But measures to protect spring chinook runs throughout the Columbia River system prompted a closure of Drano Lake's productive springer fishery in 1995. With luck, anglers will again have an opportunity to troll big, sardine-wrapped Kwikfish and Flatfish, large spinners, and other offerings around the Highway 14 bridge to intercept large spring chinooks at the mouth of the Little White Salmon.

In the meantime, the fall chinook season remains open, and anglers trolling plugs or spinners and bouncing metal jigs or roe clusters along the bottom stand to pick off a few dozen fall salmon every year. The fishery starts in August, but September is by far the best month to try your luck.

August and September are also prime months to fish for steelhead in the Little White Salmon and Drano Lake. In fact, this is one of Washington's most productive summer steelie spots, giving up 2,000 to 3,000 fish a year.

In 1992 anglers caught nearly 5,000 steelhead during the summer season. Fishing both day and night, anglers use everything from Hot Shots and other diving plugs to fresh ghost shrimp for their fish. The largest concentrations of anglers and the biggest catches come from the lake, but fishing the moving water of the river itself can also be productive.

If you're into smaller game, try the upper reaches of the Little White Salmon during the summer season. Hatchery brook trout provide much of the action, but a few rainbows are also scattered throughout the river.

37. NORTHWESTERN LAKE (RESERVOIR)

Reference: **An impoundment on the White Salmon River, northwest of White Salmon; map B3, grid j1.**

How to get there: Take State Route 14 to the town of White Salmon and turn north on State Route 141. About 3.5 miles north of town, turn west (left) onto Lakeview Road and follow it around the north end and down the west side of the lake.

Facilities: There's a public access area with a paved boat ramp near the north end of the lake and a gravel boat ramp near the dam. Other amenities are available in the town of White Salmon.

Contact: Miller's Sports, (509) 493-2233; Inn of the White Salmon, (509) 493-2335.

Species available: Rainbow trout.

Fishing Northwestern Lake: Like many of the lakes and reservoirs in this south-central part of the state, Northwestern is stocked before the April opener with hatchery rainbows ranging from under 10 inches to over 10 pounds. If there's a moral to that story, it's that anglers should be ready for almost anything. All the usual baits and lures are used successfully on this 97-acre White Salmon River impoundment.

If you're looking for a lake to try your hand at trout fishing during the winter, when many of the state's lakes are closed to fishing, Northwestern is a good bet. After opening along with many of Washington's lakes at the end of April, it remains open to fishing through the end of February. You may, of course, freeze your butt off if you decide to go wet a line in this part of the state during the short days of January, but suit yourself.

38. ROWLAND LAKE(S)

Reference: **East of Bingen, Klickitat County; map B3, grid j2.**

How to get there: Drive east from White Salmon and Bingen on State Route 14. The highway bisects the lake about four miles east of Bingen. Turn north (left) at the western edge of the lake to follow the gravel road around the north side.

Facilities: There's a boat ramp on the lake and several spots where a small boat or canoe can be launched from the beach. Food, gas, lodging, and other amenities are available in White Salmon and Bingen.

Contact: Miller's Sports, (509) 493-2233; Inn of the White Salmon, (509) 493-2335.

Species available: Rainbow and brook trout, largemouth and smallmouth bass, crappies, yellow perch, bluegills, brown bullhead catfish.

Fishing Rowland Lakes: Most people cruise right over Rowland Lakes at about 60 miles per hour without realizing the wide variety of angling potential available there. The highway runs right through the middle of this Columbia River backwater, dividing it into northern and southern halves and giving rise to the absolutely meaningless argument: Is it one lake or two? Both lakes (or both halves, if you're in that camp) are stocked with lots of hatchery rainbows each spring, including some whopper brood-stock trout weighing several pounds each. As the lake warms and the trout fishing slows, bass anglers begin to make respectable catches of both largemouths and smallmouths, with bass fishing holding up pretty well through the summer. Panfish anglers casting bobber-and-jig rigs around the edges of the lake find perch, bluegills, and some hand-sized crappies. Night-fishing can be fairly good for brown bullheads that run about a pound apiece. Like Northwestern Lake a few miles away (see page 458), the Rowland Lakes remain open to fishing until the end of February, providing some fair winter trout-fishing opportunities.

---

39. COLUMBIA RIVER

Reference: From Bonneville Pool upstream to Lake Umatilla; map B3, grid j3.

How to get there: From the west, take State Route 14 east from Camas to parallel the north side of the Columbia. From the east, take Interstate 82 south from the Tri-Cities and turn west on State Route 14 to follow the Columbia downstream.

Facilities: Boat ramps are located at Drano Lake, Underwood, Bingen, Lyle, Horsethief Lake State Park, Maryhill State Park, John Day Dam, and Roosevelt, all on the Washington side of the river, and several more scattered along the Oregon side. Motels, restaurants, grocery stores, and other amenities are readily available in White Salmon or across the Columbia in Hood River and The Dalles. Horsethief Lake State Park has a dozen tent sites, plus rest rooms and showers. Maryhill State Park has more than 50 tent/RV sites with water, electric, and sewer hookups, as well as about 35 tent sites with no hookups.

Contact: Miller's Sports, (509) 493-2233; Inn of the White Salmon, (509) 493-2335; Horsethief Lake State Park, (509) 767-1159; Maryhill State Park, (509) 773-5007.

Species available: Steelhead, chinook salmon, sturgeon, shad, walleyes, largemouth and smallmouth bass.

Fishing the Columbia River between Bonneville Pool and Lake Umatilla: As you might expect, this long stretch of the Northwest's biggest river offers lots of angling opportunity. Depending on what you like to catch, you'll find good fishing all year long. Spring chinook angling may not be an option, but fall kings are still within the realm of possibility, especially around the major river mouths where cool water spilling into the big, warm Columbia acts like a magnet for upstream-bound salmon. September is a prime month to troll or jig around the mouths of the Little White Salmon, White Salmon, Klickitat, and Deschutes rivers. Those same spots are good bets for late summer steelheading as well. Trolling with Hot Shots, Wiggle Warts, and other diving plugs is the most popular fishing method for these eight- to 20-pound sea-run trout, but in spots where the water is moving a little, it's possible to anchor in the current and work spinners along the bottom to catch steelhead.

The sturgeon fishery isn't quite as big a deal here as it is farther downstream, but there are some productive holes along this stretch that produce their share of bragging-sized white sturgeon. One such spot is between John Day Dam and Maryhill State Park, where a deep run along the north side of the river offers fairly good catches for both bank and boat anglers. Regulations in 1995 (and probably from now on) make this stretch of the Columbia a catch-and-release sturgeon fishery the second half of the year, from July 1 through December 31, but there's nothing wrong with catching and releasing an eight-foot sturgeon on a warm summer's day.

Walleye fishing has been a popular pastime on this stretch of the Columbia since the early eighties and remains a decent option today. These big cousins to the yellow perch are scattered throughout the river, with some of the best fishing still found within a mile or so downstream of the dams. Walleye fishing is a year-round possibility here, with some of the really big fish— trophies of 10 pounds and over—caught by deep-trolling in the winter and early spring. Spinner-and-nightcrawler combinations and deep-diving plugs are the favorite rigs among walleye trollers, but you can also catch fish by vertical jigging over the many gravel bars, rock piles, and boulder patches with leadheads or even small metal jigs.

Bass are abundant throughout this part of the Columbia, with smallmouths more common than largemouths in most areas. Although you may find them virtually anywhere in the river, some of the ponds, backwaters, and river mouths are especially productive. If you don't know where else to start, try the mouth of Oregon's John Day River or the mouth of Rock Creek on the Washington side. Casting or trolling small crankbaits or working leadhead-and-grub rigs along the rocky shoreline are good ways to find enough smallmouths to keep your wrists in shape.

Although the Northwest's American shad fishery centers on the stretch of the Columbia below Bonneville Dam, these big cousins of the herring make their way well up the Columbia, and anglers make some good catches below The Dalles and John Day dams. Drifting small, brightly colored jigs or bare hooks adorned with a couple of small beads near the bottom will entice shad here just as anywhere else the fish are abundant. The best fishing is from early June through July, depending on what part of the river you're working. Check the newspapers for fish counts over the dams to get an idea of where the highest numbers of fish may be concentrated.

40. HORSETHIEF LAKE

Reference: **East of The Dalles Dam, along the Columbia River; map B3, grid j3.**

How to get there: Drive east from Lyle on State Route 14. The lake is on the south side of the highway, about three miles east of the intersection with U.S. 197.

Facilities: Horsethief Lake State Park offers a boat ramp and lots of shore access, as well as limited camping facilities. The nearest food, gas, tackle, and lodging are in Dalles, about seven miles to the southwest.

Contact: Horsethief Lake State Park, (509) 767-1159.

Species available: Rainbow trout, largemouth and smallmouth bass, crappies, brown bullhead catfish, a few walleyes.

Fishing Horsethief Lake: Like many of the other "lakes" along this stretch of the Columbia River, Horsethief is really a Columbia backwater. Stocked with hatchery rainbows ranging from pan-sized to lunker-sized, it offers good trolling and stillfishing throughout the spring. By June the smallmouth fishery comes on and provides some good catches, including an occasional trophy-class smally of four pounds or bigger. Panfish also offer lots of action through the spring and summer months. Although there certainly are walleyes here, there aren't a lot of them, and most are caught by accident rather than by design.

MAP B4

WASHINGTON MAP .... see page 5
Adjoining Maps
NORTH (map A4) .... see page 256
EAST (map B5) .... see page 482
SOUTH .... no map
WEST (map B3) .... see page 432

20 Listings
PAGES 462-481

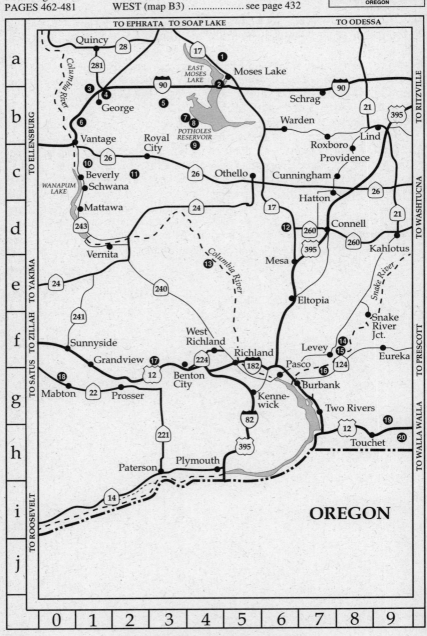

Map Section B4 features:

1. ROCKY FORD CREEK

Reference: **Flows into the north end of Moses Lake; map B4, grid a4.**

How to get there: Take Interstate 90 to Moses Lake and turn north on State Route 17. The highway crosses Rocky Ford Creek about 15 miles after you leave the interstate, and trails leading upstream and downstream provide access to the west side of the creek. To reach upper portions of the creek, turn right off State Route 17 on C Road NE and follow Department of Fish and Wildlife signs to public land along the creek on the west (left) side of the road.

Facilities: There isn't much here except pit toilets at the upper end, room to park, and a trail along the creek. Food, gas, lodging, and other amenities are available to the south in Moses Lake and to the west in Ephrata.

Contact: Tri-State Outfitters, (509) 765-9338; Department of Fish and Wildlife, Ephrata Office, (509) 754-4624.

Species available: Rainbow trout.

Fishing Rocky Ford Creek: This tiny stream that flows out of the ground east of Ephrata and into the upper end of Moses Lake (see page 464) offers anglers the very real possibility of hooking trout to 24 inches and larger. But besides being one of Washington's best quality trout waters, Rocky Ford is also one of its most challenging. The clear, cool waters are open to fly-fishing only, and you have to know what you're doing to fool one of its rainbows, most of which would have to be described as sophisticated. Adding to the challenge is the fact that you can't wade in the stream; you have to stay on the bank at all times to help protect the fragile stream bottom and lush vegetation.

Rocky Ford is only about six miles long, and fishing is confined to the Department of Fish and Wildlife lands on the upper and lower ends. The middle three miles or so are on private property and public access is prohibited. But three miles of prime stream fishing is enough for most anglers who visit Rocky Ford. You may go away fishless, but you go happy in the knowledge that you've spent a few hours in the company of some of the Northwest's largest rainbows.

Be sure to check the current fishing regulations pamphlet for details if you're thinking about fishing Rocky Ford for the first time. Besides its fly-fishing-only rules, this is the only stream in Washington where it's illegal to wade as you fish. The fragile aquatic vegetation is one of the keys to this stream's fantastic trout production, and it's protected by stay-on-the-bank regulations.

2. MOSES LAKE

Reference: **Immediately west of the town of Moses Lake; map B4, grid a4.**

How to get there: Take Interstate 90 to Moses Lake. Exit on Wapato Drive or Broadway (between the two freeway bridges) to reach the south end of the lake or follow the signs to the state park just west of the first bridge. To reach upper portions of the lake, exit north on State Route 17 and follow it three miles up the east side of the lake.

Facilities: A Department of Fish and Wildlife boat ramp is located on Pelican Horn, near the south end of the lake, with another at Moses Lake State Park (day use only), which is just north of the freeway on the lake's west side. Cascade Valley County Park, just off Valley Road near the county fairgrounds, is a decent mid-lake launch, and another can be found about two-thirds of the way up the east side, at a place the locals call Airmen's Beach. There are lots of decent restaurants and motels for all budgets in Moses Lake, as well as several campground and resort facilities.

Contact: Tri-State Outfitters, (509) 765-9338; Cascade Park Campground, (509) 766-9240; Suncrest Resort, (509) 225-3510; Lakeshore Resort, (509) 765-9201; Hallmark Inn & Resort, (509) 765-9211.

Species available: Rainbow trout, largemouth and smallmouth bass, walleyes, bluegills, yellow perch, brown bullhead catfish, lake whitefish.

Fishing Moses Lake: The personality of 6,800-acre Moses Lake has changed a lot over the years. It has been a prime rainbow trout producer, one of the state's top panfish lakes, a place where hefty largemouth bass provided top-notch action, and a place anglers could go to have a crack at a bragging-sized smallmouth bass if they did things right. Now it's perhaps best known for its fine-eating walleyes, even though you still have a chance to catch all the previously mentioned species and more.

Walleye fishing has really come on here since the late-eighties, and many anglers agree that Moses is now a better walleye lake than either Potholes Reservoir (see page 467) to the south or Banks Lake (see page 288) to the north, both of which have long been recognized as eastern Washington's best walleye producers. Trolling with spinner-and-nightcrawler rigs accounts for lots of fish at Moses, but don't hesitate to work small leadheads with tube skirts or three-inch grubs around the submerged rock piles and boulder patches. You shouldn't have to go too heavy with those sinkers or jigs, since the lake has few spots where the water is much more than 15 feet deep. Early spring provides some of the lake's best walleye action.

While walleyes reproduce on their own in Moses Lake, most of the rainbows come from Department of Fish and Wildlife hatcheries. The department typically stocks 150,000 to 180,000 small rainbows every year, and they provide pretty good fishing in the spring and fall. Anglers who troll and stillfish share in the action, and they tend to spend more time around the south end of the lake than in the northern portion.

There was a time when anglers from all over the state came to Moses to catch panfish, especially crappies and bluegills. They enjoyed fantastic fishing, and some were pigs about it. Reports of anglers catching 150, 200, even 300 crappies or more in a weekend, then taking the catch home to Seattle and illegally selling them, prompted limit reductions here several years ago, but panfish populations continued to drop. Although there are still some big bluegills and panfish, five-fish daily limits are now in effect to help spread the catch around. Minimum size limits of eight inches for bluegills and 10 inches for crappies also apply here. The best way to catch bluegills is to work a small BeetleSpin lure, half a worm, a Berkley Power Wiggler, or other small bait in and around heavy brush cover. A small bobber with a red-and-white Mini Jig suspended three or four feet below it is good medicine for crappies. Panfish action warms up in April and continues right through summer and fall.

Bass fishing is now on the tough side at Moses, and you'll have to work for every fish you hook unless you fish the lake regularly enough to keep abreast of where the fish are located and what they're hitting. I like to work spinnerbaits around the rock piles and submerged reefs in the northern half of the lake, but decent numbers of bass are also caught around the islands and shoreline structure at the south end of the lake. Spring fishing here is the best for bass.

Like many lakes in the Columbia River Basin, Moses has large populations of lake whitefish, and, just as on those other lakes, the fish are largely overlooked by anglers. They range from a pound and a half to four pounds, fight reasonably well, and will readily take a small spoon or spinner when they move into the shallows to spawn in the early spring.

---

3. QUINCY WILDLIFE AREA LAKES

Reference: **Northwest of George; map B4, grid b1.**

How to get there: Take Interstate 90 to George and then State Route 281 north to Road 5 NW and turn west (left). Drive to White Trail Road and turn left again. Stan Coffin Lake is the first lake on the left, followed by Quincy, then Burke, then Evergreen. Closed roads (hike-in only, about 1.5 miles) to the west lead to Ancient and Dusty lakes.

Facilities: Stan Coffin, Quincy, Burke, and Evergreen lakes all have rather rough boat ramps. The nearest food, gas, tackle, and lodging are in George and to the north in Quincy.

Contact: Trinidad Trading Post, (509) 787-3083; Village Inn Motel & RV Park, (509) 787-3515; Shady Tree RV Park, (509) 785-2851.

Species available: Rainbow trout, yellow perch, crappies, bluegills.

Fishing Quincy Wildlife Area Lakes: Some of these lakes are open to year-round fishing, and at least one is a popular ice-fishing lake, while the others are among the Columbia Basin's early-opening trout lakes, where the spring season kicks off March 1 and runs through July.

Burke, Quincy, and Dusty lakes open in March, and all three offer excellent fishing for rainbows ranging from 10 to 16 inches. But don't be surprised if you hook a trout or two that's even bigger. These lakes have been known to give up rainbows over five pounds, and I know of a 10-pound, 13-ouncer that was caught from Quincy Lake several years ago. Easy access and roadside boat ramps at Burke and Quincy make them especially popular with early spring anglers, but the hike-in trout fishing at Dusty Lake is well worth the effort if you don't mind a little warm-up exercise before you start casting. Stillfishing with red salmon eggs is popular at all three lakes; you can either suspend an egg or two beneath a bobber or float it up from the bottom with a little help from a mini marshmallow. After the lakes warm up a few degrees in April, fly-fishing around the edges with a variety of wet fly and nymph patterns becomes popular.

If you can't wait until March to do your fishing, visit the area in January, when a firm layer of ice covers Ancient, Stan Coffin, and Evergreen lakes. The best bet of the three is Evergreen, where some large strings of yellow perch are caught through the ice. A Swedish Pimple or just about any other small spoon or metal jig, tipped with a perch eye on the hook for flavor, is the ticket for wintertime perch here.

---

4. GEORGE AND MARTHA LAKES

Reference: **Northeast of George; map B4, grid b2.**
How to get there: Take Interstate 90 to George, turn off the freeway, and follow frontage roads along the south side of the freeway to Martha Lake or along the north side to George Lake, each about a mile east out of town.
Facilities: Food, gas, tackle, and lodging are available in George.
Contact: Shady Tree RV Park, (509) 785-2851.
Species available: Rainbow trout.
Fishing George and Martha Lakes: Two more of the small Columbia Basin seep lakes that open to fishing March 1, George and Martha tend to provide fast fishing for a week or two and then taper off rather quickly for the rest of the season. Neither lake has a developed boat ramp, so bank anglers do most of the catching, but both George and Martha can be fished very thoroughly by anglers who pack their float tubes or small boats to the edges of the lakes.

---

5. WINCHESTER WASTEWAY

Reference: **Flows into the west side of Potholes Reservoir; map B4, grid b3.**
How to get there: To reach the fishing north of Interstate 90, take Interstate 90 to the Dodson Road exit and leave the freeway to the north. Immediately turn west on the northern frontage road and follow it three miles to the west side of the wasteway. To reach southern parts of Winchester Wasteway, turn south off Interstate 90 on Dodson Road and follow it 3.5 miles to the water. The wasteway is also accessible by boat from the northwest corner of Potholes Reservoir (see page 467).
Facilities: It's possible to put a small boat in the water from places both north and south of the freeway. Food, gas, tackle, and lodging are available in

George. Potholes State Park is a few miles to the southeast, as is MarDon Resort. Both are on the west side of Potholes Reservoir.

Contact: Potholes State Park, (509) 765-7271; MarDon Resort, (509) 346-2651.

Species available: Largemouth bass, yellow perch, crappies, walleyes, rainbow trout.

Fishing Winchester Wasteway: How can something called a "wasteway" provide decent fishing? The term is a little misleading, since the "waste" refers to water that has already been "used" for irrigation in the Columbia Basin fields and is flowing back into the vast irrigation system at Potholes Reservoir. High in nutrients, the water produces a lot of fish food, and both bass and panfish grow quickly in it.

The areas just above Interstate 90 and around Potholes get fairly heavy fishing pressure at times during the spring and fall, but there are lots of places east of Dodson Road that other anglers seldom explore where you can find good fish cover. The mouth of the wasteway often provides good spring and summer walleye fishing, while the best fall action in the lower part of the wasteway is provided by schooling crappies.

6. CALICHE LAKES

Reference: **Southwest of George; map B4, grid b1.**

How to get there: Take exit 143 to the south off Interstate 90 between Vantage and George, drive a quarter-mile to the "T," and turn east (left). Drive about a mile to the lakes.

Facilities: The lakes have no facilities, but food, gas, tackle, and lodging are available in Vantage and George.

Contact: Vantage KOA, (509) 856-2230; Shady Tree RV Park, (509) 785-2851.

Species available: Rainbow trout.

Fishing the Caliche Lakes: These two little lakes along the south side of Interstate 90 are loaded with more than 10,000 rainbow trout every spring, providing good fishing opportunity for several weeks after the start of the season on March 1. Most anglers cast bait from the bank, but you can catch trout on hardware or artificial flies if you want to use them. Just ignore the looks you'll get from all the egg-dunking, marshmallow-soaking locals.

7. POTHOLES RESERVOIR

Reference: **Southwest of Moses Lake; map B4, grid b4.**

How to get there: From the southwest, take State Route 26 east from Vantage and turn north on State Route 262, following it to the southwest corner of the reservoir. From the southeast, take State Route 26 to Othello, turn north on State Route 17, then west on State Route 262 to the reservoir. From the north, take Interstate 90 to Moses Lake and turn south on State Route 17. Drive just two miles to M Road SE and turn south (right). Follow M Road to State Route 262 and turn west (right) to the south end of Potholes.

Facilities: Several boat ramps are located along the south side of Potholes Reservoir and adjoining Lind Coulee Wasteway. Fishing guides are available for Potholes and some of the surrounding lakes. MarDon Resort is a full-service facility with a cafe, a bar, a grocery and tackle store, a huge fishing dock, a boat ramp, RV and tent sites, cabins, car and boat gas, and other amenities. Potholes State Park, two miles north of the resort, has about a dozen tent sites and more than 60 RV sites with hookups, rest rooms, showers, and a boat ramp. Food, gas, and lodging are also available to the south in Othello and to the north in Moses Lake.

Contact: Potholes State Park, (509) 765-7271; MarDon Resort, (509) 346-2651; Stump-Jumper Guide Service, (509) 349-8004.

Species available: Largemouth and smallmouth bass, rainbow trout, kokanee, walleyes, crappies, yellow perch, bluegills.

Fishing Potholes Reservoir: Part of the vast Columbia Basin Irrigation Project, Potholes was formed by the construction of O'Sullivan Dam across a canal known as Crab Creek. Ranging in size from 10,000 acres in the fall to 30,000 acres in the spring, this impoundment provides fishing opportunities virtually year-round.

The north end of the reservoir is a maze of sand islands separated by winding, narrow waterways, and is commonly referred to as the "Dunes." It's an exciting place to fish, but pay attention to where you are and remember the route you took in so that you can get back out again. Besides offering excellent largemouth bass fishing, the Dunes also provide good spring fishing for walleyes, crappies, and perch. Many bass anglers cast plastic worms or grubs to shoreline cover for their fish. Spinnerbaits are also effective. A typical summertime largemouth from the Dunes is a fish of a half-pound to two pounds, but the area also produces some dandies in the four- to six-pound range.

Potholes has a reputation for good catches of large crappies, many of them taken on small spinner-and-grub combinations or leadheads fished below a bobber. The "hot" color may change many times during the season, but take along a few lures in red-and-white, yellow, and black-and-yellow and you'll probably have what you need. Fall is often best for crappies, and good places to look for them include the lower portions of Winchester and Frenchman Hills wasteways.

Perch fishing can be good any time of year at Potholes, including the hottest part of the summer. Find a school and you may catch dozens of plump eight- to 12-inchers. There are times, however, when all you can find are perch in the six-inch range, and if that happens don't hesitate to move on. Leadhead-and-worm combinations or just plain worms will take all the perch you want once you locate a school.

The shallow channels that wind throughout the Dunes warm quickly in the summer and are favorite haunts of swimmers and other non-anglers. Many families boat out to the Dunes, pick a small island that suits their fancy, pitch a tent, and call their little island home for several days. Just remember to bring plenty of drinking water.

The south end of Potholes, especially around Goose Island and along the rocky face of the dam, is another favorite spot of bass anglers, and they find good populations of both largemouth and smallmouth. Early in the summer, cast around the islands and submerged rocks with crawfish-colored crankbaits (diving plugs) or leadhead jigs fitted with curl-tail grubs in brown, gray, or green shades. By July some excellent top-water bassing can be had, especially during the first hour or two of daylight and again during the last few minutes of dusk.

Walleye fishing can be as good here as the bass action, and Potholes does produce some trophy-sized walleyes every year. Again, the south end of the reservoir, especially around Goose Island, is one of the favorite places to look for them, but walleyes are scattered throughout much of the reservoir, including the entrances to the wasteways that enter from the southwest, north, and southeast, and throughout the dunes during the spring, where they move to feed after spawning. Fish a chartreuse, red-and-white, or yellow plastic grub on a leadhead jig, being careful to tip the hook with a live nightcrawler, and you could be in business with a walleye in the 10-pound range. Trolling diving plugs or spinner-and-worm combinations are also popular walleye-fishing methods at Potholes. Some of the best news about the Potholes walleye fishery is that the reservoir seems to be producing good numbers of young fish, which bodes well for the future.

Most anglers from other parts of the Northwest come to Potholes Reservoir for the bass, walleyes, and other warm-water fish, but a high percentage of the locals come here to catch trout, and some of the rainbows they haul out are trophy-class specimens. Twelve-inchers might be average, but 'bows of five to 10 pounds and larger are caught more commonly than some people might suspect. Trolling Needlefish, Dick Nites, and other small wobbling spoons is effective, but many of the bigger trout fall to the Power Bait, marshmallows, salmon eggs, and other baits offered up by anglers stillfishing from the bank. The popular "Medicare Beach" area on the east side of the reservoir produces many big trout, as does the fishing dock at MarDon Resort near the southwest corner of Potholes.

8. LIND COULEE WASTEWAY

Reference: **Enters the southeast corner of Potholes Reservoir; map B4, grid b4.**

How to get there: From the southwest, take State Route 26 east from Vantage and turn north on State Route 262, following it past the southwest corner of Potholes Reservoir to Lind Coulee. From the southeast, take State Route 26 to Othello, turn north on State Route 17, then west on State Route 262. From the north, take Interstate 90 to Moses Lake and turn south on State Route 17. Drive two miles to M Road SE and turn south (right). Follow M Road, which parallels the west side of Lind Coulee's upper end before intersecting State Route 262. Turn west (right) on State Route 262 to reach the confluence of Lind Coulee with the southeast corner of Potholes Reservoir.

Facilities: Boat ramps are located at the west end of Lind Coulee and at the bridge where M Road crosses over the coulee. MarDon Resort is a full-service facility with a cafe, a bar, a grocery and tackle store, a huge fishing dock, a boat ramp, RV and tent sites, cabins, car and boat gas, and other amenities. Potholes State Park, two miles north of the resort, has about a dozen tent sites and more than 60 RV sites with hookups, rest rooms, showers, and a boat ramp. Food, gas, and lodging are also available to the south in Othello and to the north in Moses Lake.

Contact: Potholes State Park, (509) 765-7271; MarDon Resort, (509) 346-2651.

Species available: Largemouth and smallmouth bass, yellow perch, crappies, walleyes, rainbow trout.

Fishing Lind Coulee Wasteway: It would have been easy to lump Lind Coulee in with Potholes Reservoir, since the two offer much of the same kind of fishing for many of the same species. Lind Coulee Wasteway, in fact, is really a long, narrow extension off the southeast corner of the reservoir. The Wasteway is also different from Potholes in some ways, and the fishing is sometimes good enough to merit special recognition.

The difference is most obvious in winter, when Lind Coulee often freezes over with a thick lid of ice that supports a thriving ice fishery. While Potholes may freeze, the ice lid isn't as thick and usually isn't safe for fishing. Lind Coulee really comes into its own during this season, providing some of the best perch fishing you'll find anywhere in the Columbia Basin. Exactly where the best action may take place can vary from year to year, but you can almost always expect to find good perch action if you look around a little and go to where other anglers are congregated. The only question may be the size of the fish; they're big and fat some years, almost too small to mess with other years. Whatever their size, they'll take a small Triple Teazer, Crippled Herring, or Swedish Pimple with a perch eye or small strip of perch meat on the hook.

Winter also produces some fairly good through-the-ice catches of rainbow trout and, sometimes, large crappies. Again, the best fishing may be here today and somewhere else tomorrow, but a good place to start looking is around the end of the coulee, along M Road. The overhanging willows at the upper end of the coulee also attract crappies and bluegills at other times of the year, especially in spring and early summer.

Lind Coulee can also be a very good place to fish for bass, both largemouths and smallmouths. It offers a variety of rocky structure, shoreline cover, and warm, shallow bays that attract bass like magnets, providing productive fishing from spring until late fall.

9. POTHOLES AREA SEEP LAKES

Reference: **Southeast of Potholes Reservoir; map B4, grid b4.**

How to get there: From the north, take State Route 26 from Vantage or State Route 17 from Moses Lake to State Route 262 and take any of several gravel or dirt roads to the south from the south end of Potholes Reservoir to reach various lakes in the chain. From the south, take State Route 26 to Othello and turn north on McManaman Road. Stay on McManaman to reach a few of the lakes along the south end of the chain. To reach most of the others, turn right onto Lava Lake Road or Morgan Lake Road.

Facilities: Boat ramps are located on many of the Potholes-area seep lakes, and on others it's fairly easy to drag a boat to the edge of the lake for launching. MarDon Resort is a full-service facility with a cafe, a bar, a grocery and tackle store, a huge fishing dock, a boat ramp, RV and tent sites, cabins, car and boat gas, and other amenities. Potholes State Park, two miles north of the resort, has about a dozen tent sites and more than 60 RV sites with hook-ups, rest rooms, showers, and a boat ramp. Food, gas, and lodging are also available to the south in Othello.

Contact: Potholes State Park, (509) 765-7271; MarDon Resort, (509) 346-2651; Columbia National Wildlife Refuge, (509) 488-2668; Stump-Jumper Guide Service, (509) 349-8004.

Species available: Rainbow, brown, and Lahontan cutthroat trout; largemouth and smallmouth bass; walleyes; yellow perch; crappies; bluegills; lake whitefish.

Fishing the Potholes Area Seep Lakes: Yes, I know a good argument could be made for devoting a section to each of the more than four dozen lakes scattered around the scablands in and around the Columbia National Wildlife Refuge, but I lumped them all together for two reasons. First, by giving the driving directions and listing the facilities only once, I reduced the size of this book by enough pages to save two or three large trees. Nearly as important, I think anglers should visit this place with an open mind and no set ideas about where they want to fish or what they want to catch. If you arrive for a weekend of fishing the seeps and stubbornly spend all your time at one lake because you liked what you read about it here, you might miss out on some fantastic fishing just over the hill or just down the road. I couldn't sleep at night with that on my conscience. Some of these lakes offer excellent spring trout fishing, others are hot spots for walleyes, perch, crappies, bass, even whitefish, and you owe it to yourself to explore several of them every time you visit this fish-rich part of the state.

One of your first stops should be Soda Lake, the second-largest of the bunch at more than 180 acres. It offers perhaps the best perch fishing of any lake in the chain, and is also a good bet for walleyes. Open year-round, Soda gives up good numbers of both much of the time. If you hit the lake in March, don't be too surprised to find yourself casting small spoons, spinners, and plugs for lake whitefish, which go on a striking rampage for a couple of weeks every spring. Soda also has rainbow trout and largemouth and smallmouth bass.

Another big lake near the top end of the chain is Upper Goose, which covers more than 110 acres and which, like 50-acre Lower Goose immediately to the south, is open to year-round fishing. Both have boat ramps and provide good fishing for bass, perch, crappies, and other warm-water species.

Besides Soda and the Goose Lakes, another 30 or so of the seep lakes are open to year-round fishing. Some, like Blythe, Corral, Canal, South Teal, and the Windmill lakes, are heavily stocked with hatchery rainbows and provide good trout fishing throughout much of the year. Winter ice fishing for trout often pays big dividends on these lakes. Many of the other year-round lakes are also stocked with trout, but perhaps not as many as those I've mentioned. Of these, Quail Lake is particularly popular with one segment of the angling fraternity, the fly fish-casters. Quail is the only one of the seep lakes that's open to fly-fishing only throughout the year.

About a dozen of the seep lakes below Potholes are among the Columbia Basin lakes that open March 1 and stay open to fishing through July 31. The list includes Warden Lake, which, at 186 acres, is the largest of the entire group. It's also the most heavily stocked with rainbow trout and almost always the best early season bet in the chain when March 1 rolls around. Not only are the rainbows here abundant, but they carryover fairly well, so there's always the chance you'll hook a husky rainbow of 14, 16, even 18 inches or longer. Other seep lakes falling under the March 1 to July 31 season plan are Cascade, Deadman, Hutchinson, Shiner, Cattail, Pillar, Shoveler, Widgeon, Upper and Lower Hampton, Para (juvenile-only fishing for kids 14 and under), and South Warden Lakes.

10. LENICE, NUNNALLY, AND MERRY LAKES

Reference: **Northeast of Beverly, Grant County; map B4, grid c1.**

How to get there: Take Interstate 90 to the east side of the Columbia River (across from Vantage) and turn south onto State Route 26. When State Route 26 turns up the hill away from the river, continue south on State Route 243, following it about seven miles to the Beverly/Crab Creek Road. Turn east (left) and watch for the gravel roads to the north (left) that lead to the parking areas of the three lakes. The road to the Nunnally Lake parking area is two miles up Beverly/Crab Creek Road; the road into Merry Lake is just over four miles; the Lenice Lake turn is at the five-mile mark. A trail leads from each parking area to the south side of the lake.

Facilities: Except for pit toilets, you're pretty much on your own here. There's a small cafe in Beverly and food, gas, tackle, and lodging in Vantage.

Contact: Vantage KOA, (509) 856-2230.

Species available: Rainbow and brown trout.

Fishing Lenice, Nunnally, and Merry Lakes: Some serious fly-fish anglers may want to have me burned at the stake for lumping these three exceptional trout lakes together under a single heading, but the fact is that if you learn how to fish one, you've pretty much figured it out for all three. Selective fishery regulations (no bait, barbless, single hooks only) keep the harvest small and allow the planted rainbows and browns to reach impressive size. What's more, they're some of the toughest, strongest, most stubborn fish you'll find anywhere. I'll never forget the first Lenice Lake rainbow I ever caught, more than 20 years ago, because it was the first rainbow trout that ever took me 20 or 30 feet into the backing line on my fly reel in its first powerful run. All the trout I had caught on flies before that were little dinks that couldn't take 20 feet of line if you tied your leader around 50 of them and dropped them off a building.

You might catch a large trout from all three of these lakes at any time during their April-through-October season, but the prime time is in the early summer, when hatches of damselflies and other aquatic insects may spawn piscatorial pig-outs like you've never seen. Spoon and spinner anglers may not hit it big during one of these gorge-a-thons, but fly-casters equipped with the right patterns to match what's hatching will be in for an hour or two of fantastic fishing.

I've been known to pack, drag, push, roll, and carry small boats to these lakes, but smarter people carry float tubes to get around in once they reach the water. The trails to each of these lakes are at least a quarter of a mile—some longer—so smaller, lighter craft are certainly the best way to go.

And a word of caution is in order: This is one of those places where you may find yourself getting up close and personal with a rattlesnake that isn't all that happy to see you. Be on your toes, especially if you try to fish any of these lakes from the bank. Veteran anglers use a float tube not only to avoid the shoreline reeds that make for tough fishing, but also to get that much farther away from the rattlers.

11. LOWER CRAB CREEK

Reference: **Flows into the Columbia River south of Beverly, Grant County; map B4, grid c2.**

How to get there: Take Interstate 90 to the east side of the Columbia River near Vantage and turn south onto State Route 26. Turn off State Route 26 as it cuts left, away from the river, bear right onto State Route 243, and continue down the Columbia. Turn east (left) on Beverly/Crab Creek Road and take side roads to the north (left) for 10 miles to reach the creek.

Facilities: The nearest food, gas, tackle, and lodging are in Vantage.

Contact: Vantage KOA, (509) 856-2230.

Species available: Rainbow and brown trout.

Fishing Lower Crab Creek: The fishing isn't as good at the bottom end of this stream system as it is at the upper end, but there are a few rainbows that make their way out of the lakes above and grow to worthwhile size in the lightly fished stretches of Crab Creek between Potholes Reservoir and the stream's final destination in the Columbia. I wouldn't drive half-way across the state just to fish lower Crab Creek, but if you have a few hours on your hands after a day of fishing at Lenice Lake or on your way home from the Potholes area, do some exploring here.

12. SCOOTENEY RESERVOIR

Reference: **Southeast of Othello; map B4, grid d6.**

How to get there: Take State Route 26 to Othello and turn south on State Route 17. Turn south (right) on Schoolaney Road and east (left) on Horseshoe Road to reach the west side of the reservoir. Continue past Schoolaney Road about three miles and take either of the next two right-hand turns off the highway to reach the reservoir's east side.

Facilities: Boat ramps are located on both sides of the reservoir, and a campground with RV sites, rest rooms and showers is on the west side. The closest food, gas, tackle, and lodging are in Othello, 12 miles north.

Contact: Paul's Desert Tackle, (509) 269-4456.

Species available: Largemouth and smallmouth bass, walleyes, yellow perch, black crappies, bluegills.

Fishing Scooteney Reservoir: Although it's open year-round, many anglers save Scooteney for their winter fishing adventures, since it offers very good ice fishing, especially for yellow perch. The perch are abundant and they tend to run large, a perfect combination for anyone in search of the makings of a whole-hog fish-fry. Ice anglers also catch some nice-sized crappies and an occasional walleye, usually by accident but sometimes by design. Standard fare for winter perch is a Swedish Pimple, Triple Teazer, or Crippled Herring with a single perch eye or small strip of perch skin on the hook.

In the spring and summer, anglers find fair numbers of bass around the edges of the reservoir, and areas with ample cover may turn up some good catches of bluegills and crappies. The perch fishing also remains good in spring and early summer.

13. COLUMBIA RIVER

Reference: **From Wenatchee downstream to John Day Dam; map B4, grid e4.**

How to get there: State Route 28 between Wenatchee and Quincy provides access to the east side of the river between Wenatchee and Crescent Bar. To reach the east side of the river downstream from Vantage, turn south off Interstate 90 on State Route 243. Turn south on State Route 24 at Vernita to reach the popular stretch of river around the Vernita Bridge. Turn south off State Route 24 onto Seagull Road and then west on Road 170 to reach the popular steelhead-fishing stretch of river at Ringold. Roads out of Richland and Pasco provide access to the stretch of the Columbia between Ringold and the Tri-Cities. The best access here is via the South Columbia River Road, which runs up the east side of the river from Pasco. Access on the east side of the Columbia from the Tri-Cities to Wallula is via U.S. 12. To reach the stretch of river between McNary Dam and John Day Dam, take State Route 14 east from Wishram or west from U.S. 395.

Facilities: Wenatchee has boat ramps as well as a wide variety of options for food and lodging. Crescent Bar Resort, west of Quincy off State Route 28, has tent and RV sites along with many other facilities. The most easily accessible boat ramp on Wanapum Reservoir is the public launch at Vantage, on the north side of Interstate 90. Other nearby facilities include a KOA Campground, motels, restaurants, and gas stations. The best boat ramp for Priest Rapids Lake is near Desert Aire, off State Route 243 on the east side of the river. A boat ramp, but no other facilities, is located at the base of the Vernita Bridge, near the intersection of State Route 243 and State Route 24, and a rough boat ramp can be found on the east side of the river near the Ringold Fish Hatchery. There are several boat ramps in the Tri-Cities, including those at Island View and Columbia city parks and Sacajawea State Park. There's a boat ramp just above McNary Dam on the Washington side of the river and a host of facilities for boaters/anglers on the Oregon side of the Columbia at Umatilla Park, which is just downstream from the dam. Besides a boat ramp, Crow Butte State Park near the Benton-Klickitat county line has 50 RV sites, rest rooms with showers, and other facilities. Boat ramps can also be found at Roosevelt, Rock Creek, John Day Dam, and Maryhill State Park. The Maryhill ramp is one of the best on the river, and the park also has tent and RV sites, showers, and lots of green grass and shade trees.

Contact: Crescent Bar Resort, (509) 787-1511; Vantage KOA, (509) 856-2230; Desert Aire Motel, (509) 932-4300; Maryhill State Park, (509) 773-5007; Columbia Park Campground, (509) 783-7311; Sacajawea State Park (no overnight camping), (509) 545-2361; Crow Butte State Park, (509) 875-2644.

Species available: Steelhead, chinook salmon, sturgeon, smallmouth bass, walleyes, mountain whitefish.

Fishing the Columbia River between Wenatchee and John Day Dam: Before planning any fishing trip to this long and varied portion of the Columbia, remember that it's every bit as much a series of reservoirs as it is a river. This stretch does include the last free-flowing section of the river, but it also includes dead-water impoundments behind Rock Island, Wanapum, Priest Rapids, McNary, and John Day dams. There's so much water to fish—and so much angling variety and opportunity—that this portion of the Columbia is probably worthy of a book in its own right. On the other hand, you'll also find miles of water that's either not really worth fishing or that has been so lightly fished that little is known about it. I'll try to hit the high points—the places and species that provide the most angling opportunity and are worth driving to from anyplace in the Evergreen State.

Steelheading is a big deal here, and some of the hottest steelhead fishing on the entire Columbia River system takes place between Priest Rapids Dam and McNary Dam. Thousands of these sea-run rainbow trout swarm into this middle stretch of the river in the fall, providing excellent fishing from September to December. Steelheaders on Lake Wallula, the impoundment behind McNary Dam, like to troll Hot Shots, Power Dive Minnows, Hot Lips Express, Wiggle Warts, and other diving plugs for their fish, not only during the daylight hours, but well into the autumn darkness. Luckily, you don't need great visibility to tell when a fish comes along, because they usually pound those plugs with all the subtlety of a runaway truck. If you'd rather stand on the bank and drift-fish for your fall steelies, you might want to visit the free-flowing stretch of river at Ringold, several miles upstream from the Tri-Cities. A long gravel bar here provides room for plenty of anglers, and the fish often pass near enough to the east shore to be within easy casting range. Fresh roe clusters, Blue Fox, or Super Vibrax spinners are among the favorite strike-getters. Boaters also fish this area for steelhead, and they hook fish both with drift tackle and by pulling the same kinds of plugs that work farther downriver.

The moving water above Ringold is the scene of some productive fall salmon fishing. This so-called Hanford Reach part of the river still has a good population of naturally spawning fall chinooks, some of them monster fish of 40 pounds and larger. Trolling large spinners and big diving plugs is one way to get them. Another is to position a boat over holding fish in some of the deeper pools and work a metal jig in front of their noses until they can't take it any more and pounce savagely on the dancing slab of shiny metal. If fishing the free-flowing stretch of this big river from a boat sounds like fun, please be advised that this is big, merciless water, and a boating mistake could cost you more than a cold dunking. Don't tackle the river unless you know what you're doing.

While the middle, free-flowing part of the Columbia is lightly explored by walleye anglers, the pools at the upper and lower ends of this stretch do have walleyes in catchable numbers. The portion immediately below McNary Dam is especially interesting, since it's here that both the Oregon and Washington state-record walleyes were caught. Both of these were monster fish of more than 18 pounds. Spring provides the best shot at a trophy-class walleye of 14 pounds or bigger, but this stretch of river provides good walleye fishing virtually throughout the year. Trolling Power Dive Minnow plugs along the bottom is one of the more popular walleye-fishing techniques here, but anglers also catch them on trolled spinner-and-worm rigs or leadheads with plastic grubs bounced along the rocky bottom.

Lake Umatilla, the big impoundment behind John Day Dam, is a great place to explore for smallmouth bass. Besides having large numbers of these scrappy bronzebacks, this part of the river is home to some of the river's trophy smallmouths. Bass of four pounds and over, true lunkers of the smallmouth world, are caught with amazing regularity here. Some go for deep-diving crankbaits worked over and around submerged rock piles and underwater ledges, while others are taken on leadheads adorned with small plastic grubs. This is a good place to fish an eighth-ounce leadhead jig with a three-inch Berkley Power Grub in the productive pumpkinseed color. Columbia River smallmouths just can't seem to resist this little brown grub that seems to look an awful lot like a crawdad when twitched and hopped along the rocks and gravel.

The fishing can get a little tough along the Columbia when the cold eastern Washington winter sets in, but wintertime is prime if you happen to be a whitefish angler. If there's such a thing as an overlooked fishery on this big river, it has to be the vast whitefish population that congregates in preparation for spawning during the late fall and winter of every year. The upper end of the Hanford Reach is especially popular with whitefish anglers, and many of them catch quick 15-fish limits here throughout the winter. Small, sparsely tied flies tipped with maggots, goldenrod grubs, Power Wigglers, or stonefly larvae account for most of the fish.

White sturgeon are the monsters of the Columbia, and this stretch of the river has its share of them. The best sturgeon fishing is below McNary and John Day dams, and both of these areas have good numbers of oversized fish that provide great angling memories between the time they're hooked and the time they're carefully released back into the river to fight again. One September morning a few years ago, I caught an impressive 8½-footer below McNary. I bragged a little about my lunker-catching skills to my fishing companions, and then stood by as they caught and released sturgeon of 10½, 11, and 13 feet. There's no justice when an 8½-foot fish turns out to be the smallest of the day. Anchoring smelt, shrimp, even shad baits to the bottom is the surest way of hooking a big sturgeon below the two dams. Boat-fishing is productive below McNary, but don't try it unless you know what you're doing and understand the power and potential danger of anchoring in heavy river currents. A productive bank-fishing spot is located about a mile downstream from John Day Dam, just above Maryhill State Park.

14. EMMA LAKE

Reference: **Along the lower Snake River, northeast of Pasco; map B4, grid f8.**

How to get there: Take Pasco-Kahlotus Road northeast out of Pasco for 16 miles and turn east (right) on Murphy Road. Drive three miles and bear to the right at the "Y" to reach the north end of the lake.

Facilities: There's nothing here but the lake itself. Food, gas, tackle, and lodging are available in the Tri-Cities.

Contact: Al's Bait and Tackle, (509) 547-3090.

Species available: Yellow perch, crappies, channel catfish, brown bullhead catfish.

Fishing Emma Lake: Open year-round, Emma provides pretty good panfish action throughout much of the year. Spring and fall are excellent times to catch perch and crappies, and both can also be caught through the winter ice. Use small jigs in white combinations or all-white for crappies, and whatever you like for perch. In summer some folks fish Emma all night, catching some fairly large catfish for their efforts.

15. DALTON LAKE

Reference: **Northeast of Pasco, map B4, grid f8.**

How to get there: Take the Pasco-Kahlotus Road northeast from Pasco about 14 miles to Herman Road and turn east (right). The lake is about a mile off the highway, at the end of Herman Road.

Facilities: There's a boat ramp at the west end of the lake, and enough room to park RVs, which some people do if staying the night. Food, gas, tackle, and lodging are available in the Tri-Cities.

Contact: Al's Bait and Tackle, (509) 547-3090.

Species available: Rainbow trout, largemouth and smallmouth bass, channel catfish, yellow perch, crappies.

Fishing Dalton Lake: Not very well-known throughout the state, Dalton is a 30-acre lake that has a lot to offer. Although stocked with hatchery rainbows every year, it's the warm-water fish that really steal the show. Whether you like fat bluegills, feisty crappies, or tasty perch, you'll find lots of them here. Bass anglers working around the edge of the lake catch both large-mouths and smallmouths in fairly good numbers, and there are some big channel catfish for the benefit of anglers who like to fish at night. The lake is open year-round and is a good winter ice-fishing spot.

16. LOWER SNAKE RIVER

Reference: **Joins the Columbia River southeast of Pasco; map B4, grid g7.**

How to get there: Drive east from the Tri-Cities on State Route 124 to reach the lower end of the river. Upstream sections of the river are accessible from the town of Kahlotus by driving south for seven miles on State Route 260 or for ten miles on State Route 261.

Facilities: Besides Sacajawea State Park at the mouth of the river, there are several access areas and boat ramps on the lower end of the Snake, including

Charbonneau Park and Fishhook Park on Lake Sacajawea. Windust Park at the upper end of Lake Sacajawea also has a boat ramp, and there's another about three miles upstream, just above Lower Monumental Dam. Food, gas, tackle, and lodging are available in the Tri-Cities.

Contact: Sacajawea State Park, (509) 545-2361; Al's Bait and Tackle Shop, (509) 547-3090.

Species available: Steelhead, smallmouth bass, largemouth bass, channel catfish, white sturgeon.

Fishing the Lower Snake River: The steelheading and the smallmouth fishing are the two main draws on this part of the Columbia River's biggest tributary, and one takes off just about the time that the other begins to slow. Smallmouths come to life here as the water warms in early spring, and by June the lower end of the Snake is just about as good a place as any to cast crankbaits or bounce leadheads along the bottom for smallies in the half-pound to five-pound class. As the water cools and the bassing drops off around the end of September, the steelhead start showing up in waves, and by October steelhead fever has made just about everyone forget about bass for a while. Steelhead catches on the Snake below Lower Monumental Dam have ranged from about 1,300 to 2,000 fish a year, with the months of October, November, and December providing a bulk of the action. As in other big-water steelhead fisheries throughout the Columbia/Snake system, trolling various diving plugs is a popular and productive fishing method.

17. LOWER YAKIMA RIVER

Reference: **Flows into the Columbia south of Richland; map B4, grid f3.**

How to get there: Drive east from Yakima to Granger on Interstate 82, paralleling the river most of the 24 miles. Take Granger-Emerald Road east from Granger to parallel several miles of the river downstream of Granger. Continuing downstream, the stretch of river between Sunnyside and Prosser can be reached by driving south off Interstate 82 on State Route 241 about seven miles to the river or south from Grandview on Euclid Road. Interstate 82 parallels the river again along the 14 miles between Prosser and Benton City. Drive north from Benton City on State Route 225 for 10 miles to fish some of the lowest stretches of the Yakima.

Facilities: Several boat ramps are located along the lower Yakima, including those at Granger, the Sunnyside Wildlife Area, Horn Rapids, and the mouth of the river at Kennewick. Food, gas, tackle, and lodging are available in Yakima, Granger, Sunnyside, Grandview, Prosser, and the Tri-Cities.

Contact: Cascade Toys and Sports, (509) 965-4423; Chinook Sporting Goods, (509) 452-8205; Sunnyside Wildlife Area, (509) 837-7644.

Species available: Smallmouth and largemouth bass, channel catfish.

Fishing the Lower Yakima River: Unlike the blue-ribbon trout waters upstream from Yakima, this lower stretch of the river meanders slowly through the flat river valley, warming fairly fast in the spring and summer and offering a haven for warm-water species. Clean rock and gravel comprise much of the river bottom throughout this stretch, providing perfect habitat for smallmouth bass, and they thrive in these waters. Although it doesn't get much fishing pressure, those who do fish this part of the Yakima tell lots of stories about the huge smallmouths that live here. The extreme lower end of the Yakima also has largemouths, but this river doesn't offer a whole lot of prime largemouth bass cover. It does, however, suit channel catfish very well, and anglers have made some good catfish catches here over the years. Casting from the bank with chicken livers, nightcrawlers, and foul-smelling stinkbaits produces some channel cats of 10 pounds and over, with the best fishing usually occurring in June and July.

18. GIFFEN LAKE

Reference: **Southwest of Sunnyside; map B4, grid g0.**
How to get there: Take Interstate 82 to Sunnyside and turn south on Midvale Road, following it for four miles to the Sunnyside Wildlife Area. The lake is on the west (right) side of the road, near the end.
Facilities: There's ample bank-fishing access and room to launch a small boat here, but little else. The nearest food, gas, tackle, and lodging are in Sunnyside.
Contact: Sunnyside Wildlife Area, (509) 837-7644; Cascade Toys and Sports, (509) 965-4423.
Species available: Rainbow trout, largemouth bass, crappies, brown bullhead catfish.
Fishing Giffen Lake: Legal-sized rainbows, stocked in the spring by the Department of Fish and Wildlife, provide a few weeks of decent spring fishing here before the supply dwindles and interest wanes. That's about the time bass anglers begin hitting the lake regularly, and they hook some impressive largemouths from this 100-acre lake near the banks of the Yakima River. Crappie fishing is also fairly good in the spring, but by summer the weed growth gets out of hand, and rather than wading in with machetes blazing, most anglers give it up for the season.

19. TOUCHET RIVER

Reference: **Joins the Walla Walla River at the town of Touchet; map B4, grid g9.**
How to get there: Take U.S. 12 to Touchet and turn north on Touchet Road to reach the lower 12 miles of the river. The middle stretch of the Touchet, between Harsha and Waitsburg, is paralleled by State Route 124. To reach the upper part of the main Touchet, take U.S. 12 east from Waitsburg or west from Dayton. To reach the river's north and south forks, drive southeast out of Dayton on North Fork Touchet Road or South Fork Touchet Road.
Facilities: Food, gas, tackle, and lodging are available in Waitsburg and Dayton. Lewis and Clark Trail State Park is right along the river between Waitsburg and Dayton, and it has a limited number of campsites, rest rooms, and showers.
Contact: Lewis and Clark Trail State Park, (509) 337-6457.
Species available: Rainbow and brown trout, steelhead.

Fishing the Touchet River: The trout fishery downstream from Dayton is primarily a put-and-take effort for hatchery rainbows and browns, but it provides a lot of fun for spring and early summer anglers. Things change dramatically above Dayton, where selective fishery regulations and a two-fish limit protect a largely native rainbow trout population.

The Touchet also has a fall/winter steelhead season downstream from the Wolf Fork Bridge near Dayton. Although they can keep only marked hatchery steelies, anglers here manage to catch anywhere from 200 to 400 fish a year during this winter fishery. Depending on weather and water conditions, the catch may be spread out pretty well from December through March. But when winter conditions are nasty, the best fishing is later, in March and April, after the ice has melted and the water has warmed a little.

20. WALLA WALLA RIVER

Reference: **Joins the Columbia River south of Wallula; map B4, grid h9.**
How to get there: Take U.S. 12 east from the Tri-Cities for 14 miles or west from Walla Walla for five miles to parallel much of the river's north side.
Facilities: Food, gas, motels, RV parks, and other amenities are available in Walla Walla.
Contact: Al's Bait and Tackle, (509) 547-3090.
Species available: Steelhead, channel catfish.
Fishing the Walla Walla River: The mouth and lower reaches of the Walla Walla produce some of Washington's biggest catfish every summer, with the best fishing usually occurring in June and July. This area, in fact, has produced some whopping channel cats over the years, including at least a couple of former state-record fish. Night-fishing with chicken livers, nightcrawlers, stinkbait, and other nasty little snacks accounts for the biggest fish and the best catches.

West-siders who think they have a stranglehold on the state's best steelhead fishing might be surprised to learn that the Walla Walla is also a fine steelhead stream, giving up as many as 1,000 steelies a year. The runs come on strong in October and provide surprisingly consistent action through the winter and into March. Techniques that work for drift-anglers in western Washington will also do the trick here.

All sturgeon over six feet long must be released, but just the thought of hooking a seven- or eight-footer keeps most anglers plenty interested.

MAP B5

WASHINGTON MAP .... see page 5
Adjoining Maps
NORTH (map A5) .... see page 300
EAST .... no map
SOUTH .... no map
WEST (map B4) .... see page 462

10 Listings
PAGES 482-489

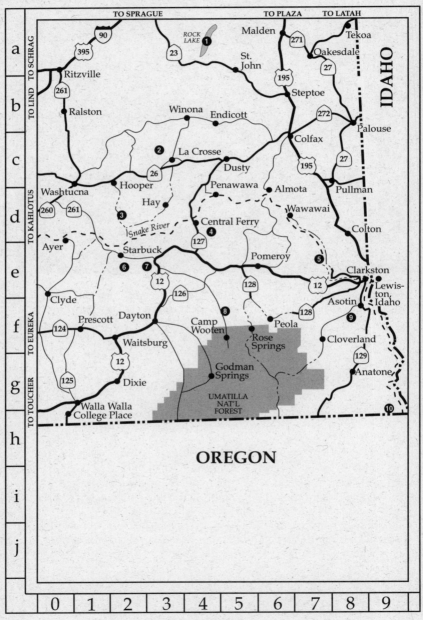

Map Section B5 features:

1. Rock Lake
2. Union Flat Creek
3. Palouse River
4. Deadman Creek
5. Upper Snake River

6. Tucannon River
7. Pataha Creek
8. Tucannon River Lakes
9. Asotin Creek
10. Grande Ronde River

1. ROCK LAKE

Reference: **Northwest of St. John; map B5, grid a4.**

How to get there: Take State Route 23 south from Sprague or west from St. John to Ewan and turn north on Rock Lake Road, which leads about three miles to the lake.

Facilities: A boat ramp is located at the south end of the lake. Food and gas are available in St. John, and tackle and lodging can be found in Cheney or Sprague.

Contact: Four Seasons Campground, (509) 257-2332; Purple Sage Motel, (509) 257-2507; Sprague Lake Resort, (509) 257-2864.

Species available: Rainbow and brown trout, largemouth bass, crappies, yellow perch, brown bullhead catfish.

Fishing Rock Lake: This narrow, seven-mile-long lake is a long way from any of eastern Washington's major population centers, so it's a good place for getting away from the crowds. Unfortunately, you can also get away from the fish at Rock Lake, depending on your timing. The best fishing is when the lake is at its clearest early in the spring season and again in the fall. During the summer, when irrigation runoff is heavy, much of the dirty water ends up in Rock Lake, lowering visibility and just plain taking some of the fun out of visiting this place.

The lake is stocked with rainbows and browns, some of which grow to impressive size, but better places can be found a few miles north if you want fast trout action. (Fishtrap, Amber, and Williams lakes come to mind. See pages 305 and 333). Anglers occasionally pick off a big brown or mature rainbow in the fall or early winter near the upper end of the lake. These trout are presumably moving up into Rock Creek to attempt spawning. At other times of year, they can be caught by casting all the usual baits from the bank or by deep-trolling with downriggers and leaded line. Gang trolls with bait are popular, as are Carey Special flies and some of the smaller Rapalas.

Bass fishing is a good bet, especially in the bays along the east side or on the shallow flats where largemouths congregate to gorge on crawdads. Anything in a crayfish finish should work well in these spots.

Although much of the lake is very deep, be careful about buzzing around parts of the lake with which you aren't familiar. There are some shallow spots where you might not expect them, and you can really do a job on the prop or the lower unit of your outboard motor if you don't pay attention.

For a lake that doesn't get all that much attention from anglers or anyone else, Rock seems to have a lot of myths and legends surrounding it. Depending on who you talk to, you might hear that the lake is haunted by the ghosts of Indians who used to camp near its south end. Others may tell you that a train once derailed and plunged to the bottom of the deep lake, and that sometimes you can still hear the sound of the moaning engine or the wail of its steam whistle rising from the depths. Still another story is that the lake has some kind of resident monster that occasionally picks off an unwitting swimmer or farm animal. I hope that last one's true, and that we might be able to communicate with the thing and train it to go for a few of the bozos on personal water-craft who like to give anglers a hard time.

2. UNION FLAT CREEK

Reference: **Joins the Palouse River west of LaCrosse, Whitman County; map B5, grid c3.**

How to get there: Drive west from Colfax on State Route 26 and turn north (right) on Union Flat Creek Road to parallel about 20 miles of the creek. Driving south out of Colfax on Almota Road and turning east (left) on Union Flat Creek Road will get you to several miles of the upper creek between State Route 26 and the town of Colton.

Facilities: Food, gas, tackle, and lodging are available in Colfax and Pullman.

Contact: Tiffany's River Inn, (509) 397-3208.

Species available: Rainbow trout.

Fishing Union Flat Creek: Planted rainbows provide fair spring and early summer fishing on this long creek that enters Washington near the small town of Uniontown and flows into the Palouse River west of LaCrosse. It doesn't have any special regulations, so feel free to fish it with bait, hardware, or flies. You'll need landowner permission to fish some of the creek, but roads paralleling its banks make for easy access in most places.

3. PALOUSE RIVER

Reference: **Joins the Snake River at Lyons Ferry, Columbia-Walla Walla county line; map B5, grid d2.**

How to get there: Take State Route 260 east from Connell for 21 miles and turn south on State Route 261 to reach the lower Palouse and Palouse Falls. The best access to upper portions of the river is provided by the Endicott Road, which is reached by driving west from Colfax about four miles on State Route 26 and turning north on Endicott Road.

Facilities: Lyons Ferry State Park and Palouse Falls State Park both have several dozen tent sites, plus rest rooms, showers, picnic areas, and other amenities. Food, gas, tackle, and lodging are available in Colfax.

Contact: Lyons Ferry State Park (509) 646-3252; Palouse Falls State Park, (509) 549-3551; Tiffany's River Inn, (509) 397-3208.

Species available: Channel catfish, smallmouth bass.

Fishing the Palouse River: Although the main Palouse and its north and south forks wind through more than 125 miles of eastern Washington's rolling countryside, making it one of the state's longest rivers, much of that length has little to offer serious anglers. The river is downright beautiful in places, especially around Palouse Falls, just a few miles upstream from the river's confluence with the Snake at Lyons Ferry. But even though the Palouse is open to year-round fishing, there isn't much angling activity. Night-fishing around the mouth of the river produces a few channel catfish, some of them of fairly respectable size, and there are some smallmouth bass to be caught in the lower river, but it seems as if the other 122 miles of river are more for looking at than for fishing.

4. DEADMAN CREEK

Reference: **Flows into the Snake River near Central Ferry; see map B5, grid d4.**

How to get there: Take State Route 127 to Central Ferry and turn east onto Lower Deadman Road, which parallels the creek for more than 10 miles.

Facilities: Central Ferry State Park has tent sites, rest rooms, showers, picnic tables, and other facilities. The nearest food, gas, tackle, and lodging are in Pullman, more than 20 miles to the east.

Contact: Central Ferry State Park, (509) 549-3551.

Species available: Rainbow trout.

Fishing Deadman Creek: Spring plants of hatchery rainbows provide most of the action here. Although the creek is open to year-round fishing, your best shot at catching trout is in May and June. Many local anglers use bait and hardware here, but it's a decent place to work a small wet fly or nymph pattern along the bottom.

5. UPPER SNAKE RIVER

Reference: **From Lower Granite Dam to the Oregon border; map B5, grid e7.**

How to get there: Drive west from Pullman on State Route 194 to Almota and the part of the river immediately downstream from Lower Granite Dam. The most accessible part of the Snake in Washington is the section from Clarkston downstream to Wawawai, where the Wawawai River Road parallels the east side of the river for more than 20 miles. Take the Snake River Road south out of Clarkston to drive along the Snake's west bank all the way to the mouth of the Grande Ronde.

Facilities: Lyons Ferry State Park, at the confluence of the Palouse and Snake rivers, has a boat ramp as well as campsites, rest rooms, showers, and other amenities. Central Ferry State Park, just off State Route 127, also has a boat ramp, plus tent and RV sites. Wawawai River Road provides access to several boat ramps on the east side of the river between Clarkston and Wawawai. Chief Timothy State Park, off U.S. 12 west of Clarkston, has a boat ramp, campsites, rest rooms, and showers. There's a boat ramp at Looking Glass Park, south of Clarkston at the mouth of Asotin Creek, and another below the mouth of the Grande Ronde River. The nearest food, gas, tackle, and lodging are in Pullman and Clarkston.

Contact: Lyons Ferry State Park, (509) 646-3252; Central Ferry State Park, (509) 549-3551; Chief Timothy State Park, (509) 758-9580; Lyons Ferry Marina, (509) 399-2001.

Species available: Steelhead, smallmouth bass, white sturgeon, channel and blue catfish, crappies, yellow perch.

Fishing the Upper Snake River: You get a little bit of everything if you spend some time investigating this section of the Snake. A lot of the Upper Snake is more like one big, continuous lake than a river, thanks to Lower Monumental, Little Goose, and Lower Granite dams, which back up much of the river between Clarkston and Kahlotus. South of Clarkston, however, the river gains speed as you move upstream toward world-famous Hells Canyon, and there's no doubt at all that you're on one of the Northwest's biggest and most inviting rivers.

Lake Herbert West, Lake Bryan, and Lower Granite Lake, the reservoirs behind the three dams on this stretch, offer very good lake smallmouth bass fishing. The fishing is best after the water warms to at least 60 degrees in the late spring, and from then on it's possible to enjoy fast action with small grubs, crawdad-finish crankbaits, and other standard smallmouth lures. Work them around the base of rock cliffs and over submerged rock piles, scattered boulders, and points of land jutting into the water.

Trolling for steelhead is also productive in the reservoirs, and the fishing is at least as good during the night as it is in daylight hours. October, November, and December provide the best catches, so be sure to bundle up if you plan a night of steelheading in this part of the state. Land a 15-pound steelhead, of course, and it will probably keep you warm and charge your batteries for another several hours. Hot Shots, Wiggle Warts, Hot Lips Express, and Hog Boss plugs are among the consistent strike-getters.

Blue catfish aren't found just anywhere in Washington, but anglers get 'em here, and some of them are bragging-sized fish of 15 pounds or more. Like the (usually) smaller channel cats, they can be caught at night on chicken livers, strips cut from sucker bellies, nightcrawlers, Berkley's Catfish Power Bait, and various stinkbaits. The upper ends of the reservoirs, where there's some moving water, often produce some of the best catfish action.

Modified versions of the catfish technique also work for sturgeon, the real monsters of the Snake. Be sure to change the bait since sturgeon prefer herring, smelt, and pieces of eel. Some of the better sturgeon holes are located immediately downstream of Clarkston, but remember, this is catch-and-release only. If you want to keep sturgeon, you'll have to fish below Lower Granite Dam.

Panfish action in the Snake River reservoirs is outstanding. Find a school of active crappies and it's not unusual to go away with 50 of the mild-flavored little fish for a day's efforts. Small leadheads adorned with red-and-white plastic skirts or tube bodies are most effective, but other color combinations also work. If you know there are panfish around but you're not getting them to hit, do some experimenting with color until you find the right one.

Most of the same species that provide action for reservoir anglers can also be found in the moving water upstream from Clarkston. Back-trolling with diving plugs is still one of the best ways to catch fall steelhead in the river, and the same crankbaits or jigs you might use for smallmouths in the reservoirs will work in moving water. The same goes for catfish and sturgeon; a good bait anchored to the bottom is the best bet for both. One difference is that summertime trout fishing is better in the river than in the reservoirs downstream. There are some husky rainbows from Hells Canyon downstream to Clarkston, including fish of 17 inches and larger, and they'll hit small spinners and wobbling spoons with great enthusiasm.

6. TUCANNON RIVER

Reference: Joins the Snake River northwest of Starbuck; map B5, grid e2.

How to get there: Take State Route 26 to Washtucna and turn south on State Route 260, following it six miles to State Route 261. Turn east and follow State Route 261 to the mouth of the Tucannon and upstream to U.S. 12. Turn south on U.S. 12 and then east on Tucannon Road to reach upstream portions of the river.

Facilities: There's a U.S. Forest Service Campground on the upper Tucannon and a good deal of public access on state and federal land. Camp Wooten State Park, located near the Forest Service facility, is an Environmental Learning Center and has no drop-in camping facilities. The nearest food, gas, tackle, and lodging are in Dayton.

Contact: Umatilla National Forest, (509) 522-6290; W. T. Wooten Wildlife Area, (509) 843-1530.

Species available: Steelhead, rainbow trout, Dolly Varden, mountain whitefish.

Fishing the Tucannon River: You'd be nuts to even think about fishing the Tucannon without first spending about two hours reading all the details listed in the current fishing regulations pamphlet. Phew! If you can get through it and still feel like going fishing, you're a serious angler.

Steelheading is the big draw, and it takes off in September and runs through the winter until March. Anglers catch 300 to 400 steelies here during a good year, most of them on the same kinds of drift-fishing gear used on western Washington steelhead streams. The stretch of river from the mouth up to the Tucannon Hatchery remains open to fishing during the winter to provide anglers with a good shot at steelheading, and it's also okay to fish for whitefish during this period. Whitefish action can be quite good, although it's enjoyed by only a few local anglers. During the spring and early summer, parts of the Tucannon are stocked with hatchery rainbows, always providing a few weeks of decent trout fishing immediately after the fish are released.

7. PATAHA CREEK

Reference: Joins the Tucannon River near Delaney, Columbia County; map B5, grid e3.

How to get there: Take U.S. 12 west from Pomeroy to parallel the south side of the creek for several miles.

Facilities: Central Ferry State Park, with tent and RV sites, is located on the Snake River, a few miles north of the creek. Food, gas, tackle, and lodging are available in Pomeroy.

Contact: Central Ferry State Park, (509) 549-3551.

Species available: Rainbow trout.

Fishing Pataha Creek: Stocked with hatchery trout, this little Tucannon River tributary provides fair fishing every spring and early summer. From its mouth to Pomeroy, Pataha Creek is open all year to all anglers, but inside the Pomeroy city limits, it's open only to juvenile anglers and only from late April through October. Upstream of Pomeroy the season runs from June 1 through October 31 for all anglers, but selective fishery regulations are in effect.

8. TUCANNON RIVER LAKES

Reference: **East of Dayton, eastern Columbia County; map B5, grid f5.**

How to get there: Take State Route 26 to Washtucna and turn south on State Route 260, following it six miles to State Route 261. Turn east and follow State Route 261 to the mouth of the Tucannon River and upstream to U.S. 12. Turn south on U.S. 12 and then east on Tucannon Road to reach upstream portions of the river and the small lakes that border it.

Facilities: There's a U.S. Forest Service Campground on the upper Tucannon, and a good deal of public access on state and federal land. Camp Wooten State Park, located near the Forest Service facility, is an Environmental Learning Center and has no drop-in camping facilities. The nearest food, gas, tackle, and lodging are in Dayton.

Contact: Umatilla National Forest, (509) 522-6290; W. T. Wooten Wildlife Area, (509) 843-1530.

Species available: Rainbow trout.

Fishing the Tucannon River Lakes: These little lakes scattered along the banks of the Tucannon River from the W. T. Wooten Wildlife Area to the Tucannon Campground cover no more than 10 acres apiece, yet they're heavily stocked with hatchery rainbows to provide good fishing throughout the spring and summer. Spring, Rainbow, Deer, Watson, and Beaver lakes have a March 1 through July 31 season, but they may not be stocked in time for the opener if the lakes are still covered with ice. Big Four Lake also opens March 1, but it has special fly-fishing-only regulations. Because Curl Lake is also used as a holding pond for steelhead smolts from the nearby Tucannon Hatchery, it doesn't open to fishing until June. Boats and float tubes are prohibited on all these little lakes, so you have to do your fishing from the bank. That's not a problem, though, since you can nearly cast from one bank to the other on most of these lakes.

Except on the fly-fishing-only waters of Big Four Lake, standard trout-getters are worms, salmon eggs, and a variety of small spoons and spinners. One favorite is the Rooster Tail spinner, and many anglers prefer various shades of green or fluorescent color schemes.

9. ASOTIN CREEK

Reference: **Flows into the Snake River south of Clarkston; map B5, grid f8.**

How to get there: Take State Route 128 to Clarkston and turn south on State Route 129 and drive six miles to the mouth of Asotin Creek. Turn west on Asotin Creek Road to follow the creek upstream.

Facilities: The Asotin Motel is located near the mouth of the creek, in the town of Asotin. Food, gas, tackle, and lodging are also available in Clarkston.

Contact: Asotin Motel, (509) 243-4888; Jay's Gone Fishing, (509) 758-8070.

Species available: Rainbow trout.

Fishing Asotin Creek: Once a fairly good little summer steelhead stream, Asotin Creek is now closed to steelheading in order to protect wild steelies that spawn here. Except for the mouth of the creek, which is open to year-round trout fishing, the season on Asotin Creek runs from June through October, and during that time it's planted with hatchery rainbows. There's a liberal eight-fish trout limit, and limit catches are common during the summer.

10. GRANDE RONDE RIVER

Reference: **Joins the Snake River near the southeastern corner of the state; map B5, grid h9.**

How to get there: Take State Route 129 south from Clarkston. The highway crosses the river about three miles from the Oregon border, and Grande Ronde Road parallels the north side of the river for several miles west of the bridge. To reach the lower few miles of the river, drive south out of Clarkston on State Route 129 to Asotin, then follow the Snake River Road along the Snake to the mouth of the Grande Ronde.

Facilities: Fields Spring State Park, located a few miles north of the river on State Route 129, has a limited number of tent sites. Food, gas, tackle, and lodging can be found in Clarkston.

Contact: Fields Spring State Park, (509) 256-3332; Jay's Gone Fishing, (509) 758-8070.

Species available: Steelhead, smallmouth bass, channel catfish.

Fishing the Grande Ronde River: While the lower end of the Grande Ronde offers some decent bass and catfish action, most anglers come here for one thing: steelheading. The steelhead action turns on around the end of September and goes strong through the winter to the end of the season in mid-April. During that time, anglers use spoons, spinners, diving plugs, and artificial flies to take as many as 400 to 500 fish a month from the deep pools and inviting runs along this beautiful river. Although roads provide access to the river mouth and to several miles of river upstream from the bridge on State Route 129, many anglers prefer to float the Grande Ronde. There's a good put-in/take-out spot at the State Route 129 bridge.

WASHINGTON FISHING RECORDS

FRESHWATER

Atlantic salmon, resident	8.96	Gregory Lepping	Goat Lake	1992
Atlantic salmon, sea-run	9.59	John Dahl	Puyallup River	1995
Black bullhead	1.16	Sean Averill	I-82 Pond #1	1994
Black crappie	4-8	John Smart	Lake Washington	1956
Blue catfish	17-12	Rangle Hawthorne	Columbia River	1975
Bluegill sunfish	2-5	Ron Hinote	Tampico Park Pond	1984
Brook trout	9-0	George Weekes	Wobbly Lake	1988
Brown bullhead	3.87	Wayne Daniels	Sprague Lake	1993
Brown trout	22-O	R. L. Henry	Sullivan Lake	1965
Burbot	17.01	Patrick Bloomer	Palmer Lake	1993
Bull trout	22-8	Louis Schott	Tieton River	1961
Channel catfish	32-8	Tom Peterman	Aspen Lake	1987
Chinook salmon	68-4	Mark Salmon	Elochoman River	1992
Chum salmon	25-10	Laura Phillips	Satsop River	1988
Coho salmon	23-8	David Bailey	Satsop River	1986
Cutthroat trout, Lahontan	18.04	Dan Beardslee	Omak Lake	1993
Cutthroat trout, resident	12-0	W. Welsh	Crescent Lake	1961
Cutthroat trout, sea-run	6-0	Bud Johnson	Carr Inlet	1943
Dolly Varden, sea-run	10-0	Forest Goodwin	Skykomish River	1982
Flathead catfish	22-8	C. L. McCary	Snake River	1981
Golden trout	3.81	Mark Morris	Okanogan County	1991
Kokanee	5.47	Don Growt	Lake Roosevelt	1993
Lake trout (Mackinaw)	30-4	Ken Janke	Loon Lake	1966
Lake whitefish	6.01	James Rose	Lind Coulee Wasteway	1990
Largemouth bass	11-9	Carl Pruitt	Banks Lake	1977
Mountain whitefish	5-2	Steven Becken	Columbia River	1983
Northern pike	32.2	Fred Ruetsch	Long Lake (Spokane Co.)	1995
Northern squawfish	6.66	Steven White	Snake River	1995
Rainbow trout	22-8	Bill Dittner	Waitts Lake	1957
Rainbow trout, Beardslee	16-5	Richard Bates	Lake Crescent	1989
Rock bass	1-6	Dion Roueche	Snake River	1995
Smallmouth bass	8-12	Ray Wonacott	Columbia River	1966
Sockeye salmon	10-10	Gary Krasselt	Lake Washington	1982

Steelhead, summer-run	35-1	Gilbert Pierson	Snake River	1973
Steelhead, winter-run	32-12	Gene Maygra	East Lewis River	1980
Tiger musky	28.25	Ronald Jutte	Mayfield Lake	1995
Walleye	18.76	Mike Jones	Columbia River	1990
White crappie	2-8	Don Benson	Columbia River	1988
Yellow bullhead	1.63	Mike Schlueter	Banks Lake	1994
Yellow perch	2-12	Larry Benthien	Snelson's Slough	1969

SALTWATER

Albacore	40-2	Tom Coss	Westport	1995
Big skate	130-0	Dan Cartwright	Double Bluff	1986
Black rockfish	10-4	Joseph Eberling	Tacoma Narrows	1980
Bocaccio	23-10	Carson Kendall	Swiftsure Bank	1987
Cabezon	23-0	Wesley Hunter	Dungeness Spit	1990
Canary rockfish	10-9	Ben Phillips	Neah Bay	1986
China rockfish	4-3	Steven Ripley	Duncan Rock	1989
Chinook salmon	70-8	Chet Gausta	Sekiu	1964
Coho salmon	19.67	Shirley Buckner	Sekiu	1995
Copper rockfish	10-0	David Northington	Point Roberts	1989
Great sculpin	4-6	Valier Stoican	Protection Island	1992
Greenstripe rockfish	1-10	David Wedeking	Possession Bar	1985
Kelp greenling	3-8	Diana Kottkey	San Juan Islands	1986
Lingcod	61-0	Tom Nelson	San Juan Islands	1986
Pacific cod	19-10	Ralph Bay	Ediz Hook	1984
Pacific halibut	288-0	Vic Stevens	Swiftsure Bank	1989
Petrale sole	7-9	John Stone	Jefferson Head	1980
Pile perch	3-9	Steve Urban	Quartermaster Harbor	1981
Quillback rockfish	7-3	Bror Hultgren	Middle Bank	1987
Ratfish	2-10	Jay Fotland	Mukilteo	1990
Red Irish lord	3-3	Ryan Dicks	Mid-channel Bank	1985
Rock sole	4-3	Alan Schram	Hein Bank	1989
Sablefish	30-0	Jeff Rudolph	Westport	1994
Sixgill shark	220-0	Jim Haines	Gedney Island	1991
Spiny dogfish	17-4	Chris Urban	Quartermaster Harbor	1984
Starry flounder	7-15	Glenn Colley	Green Point	1990
Striped seaperch	2-1	Chris Urban	Quartermaster Harbor	1980
Tiger rockfish	7-8	James Wenban	Middle Bank	1989
Yelloweye rockfish	27-12	Jan Tavis	Dallas Bank	1989
Yellowtail rockfish	7-6	Ken Culver	Westport	1992

Index

D

S

ACKNOWLEDGMENTS

Many people provided valuable assistance as I researched and wrote this book. Especially helpful were Mike O'Malley, Jim Byrd, Mark Kimball, Bob Pfeifer, Larry Peck, Jack Tipping, Bill Freymond, Bill Jordan, and Carol Turcotte of the Washington Department of Fish and Wildlife. Special thanks also to Tom Pollock, Joe Wallman, Warren Cowell, Al Long, and Kelly Hawley. To Sandy, Adam, and Max, thanks for your support and patience.

CREDITS

Publishing Manager	Rebecca Poole Forée
Senior Editor	Jean Linsteadt
Production Manager	Michele Thomas
Editorial Assistant	Aimee Larsen
Production Assistant	Alexander Lyon
Proofreader	Carole Quandt
Acquisitions Editor	Judith Pynn
Cover Design	Michele Thomas
Cover Photo	George Schwartz
Interior Photos	Terry Rudnick

ABOUT THE AUTHOR

A life-long Washingtonian, **Terry Rudnick** has fished the lakes, streams, and marine areas of the Evergreen State for as long as he can remember, and has been writing about Northwest fishing since he sold his first magazine article in 1971. An award-winning freelance writer and photographer, his feature articles and columns have appeared in more than 30 newspapers and regional and national magazines. His angling seminars and slide shows are also in demand, and he has been a featured speaker at more than three-dozen sports and boating trade shows throughout the West. His efforts on behalf of fish, fishing, and the aquatic environment earned him the 1990 National Conservationist of the Year communications award from Trout Unlimited.

Washington Fishing is the first of Rudnick's two books, both published in the spring of 1996. The other, *How to Catch a Trophy Halibut,* was coauthored with Christopher Batin and published by Alaska Angler Publications.

Leave No Trace

Leave No Trace, Inc., is a program dedicated to maintaining the integrity of outdoor recreation areas through education and public awareness. Foghorn Press is a proud supporter of this program and its ethics.

Here's how you can Leave No Trace:

Plan Ahead and Prepare
- Learn about the regulations and special concerns of the area you are visiting.
- Visit the backcountry in small groups.
- Avoid popular areas during peak-use periods.
- Choose equipment and clothing in subdued colors.
- Pack food in reusable containers.

Travel and Camp with Care
On the trail:
- Stay on designated trails. Walk single file in the middle of the path.
- Do not take shortcuts on switchbacks.
- When traveling cross-country where there are no trails, follow animal trails or spread out your group so no new routes are created. Walk along the most durable surfaces available, such as rock, gravel, dry grasses, or snow.
- Use a map and compass to eliminate the need for rock cairns, tree scars, or ribbons.
- If you encounter pack animals, step to the downhill side of the trail and speak softly to avoid startling them.

At camp:
- Choose an established, legal site that will not be damaged by your stay.
- Restrict activities to areas where vegetation is compacted or absent.
- Keep pollutants out of the water by camping at least 200 feet (about 70 adult steps) from lakes and streams.
- Control pets at all times, or leave them at home with a sitter. Remove dog feces.

Pack It In and Pack It Out
- Take everything you bring into the wild back out with you.
- Protect wildlife and your food by storing rations securely. Pick up all spilled foods.

- Use toilet paper or wipes sparingly; pack them out.
- Inspect your campsite for trash and any evidence of your stay. Pack out all trash—even if it's not yours!

Properly Dispose of What You Can't Pack Out
- If no refuse facility is available, deposit human waste in catholes dug six to eight inches deep at least 200 feet from water, camps, or trails. Cover and disguise the catholes when you're finished.
- To wash yourself or your dishes, carry the water 200 feet from streams or lakes and use small amounts of biodegradable soap. Scatter the strained dishwater.

Keep the Wilderness Wild
- Treat our natural heritage with respect. Leave plants, rocks, and historical artifacts as you found them.
- Good campsites are found, not made. Do not alter a campsite.
- Let nature's sounds prevail; keep loud voices and noises to a minimum.
- Do not build structures or furniture or dig trenches.

Minimize Use and Impact of Fires
- Campfires can have a lasting impact on the backcountry. Always carry a light-weight stove for cooking, and use a candle lantern instead of building a fire whenever possible.
- Where fires are permitted, use established fire rings only.
- Do not scar the natural setting by snapping the branches off live, dead, or downed trees.
- Completely extinguish your campfire and make sure it is cold before departing. Remove all unburned trash from the fire ring and scatter the cold ashes over a large area well away from any camp.

For more information, call 1-800-332-4100.

FOGHORN PRESS

Founded in 1985, Foghorn Press has quickly become one of the country's premier publishers of outdoor recreation guidebooks. Through its unique Books Building Community program, Foghorn Press supports community environmental issues, such as park, trail, and water ecosystem preservation. Foghorn Press is also committed to printing its books on recycled paper.

Foghorn Press books are sold throughout the United States. Call 1-800-FOGHORN (8:30-5:30 PST) for the location of a bookstore near you that carries Foghorn Press titles. If you prefer, you may place an order directly with Foghorn Press using your Visa or MasterCard. All of the titles listed below are now available, unless otherwise noted.

The Complete Guide Series

The Complete Guides are the books that have given Foghorn Press its reputation for excellence. Each book is a comprehensive resource for its subject, from *every* golf course in California to *every* fishing spot in the state of Washington. With extensive cross-references and detailed maps, the Complete Guides offer readers a quick and easy way to get the best recreational information available.

California titles include:
- *California Beaches* (704 pp) $19.95, available 5/96
- *California Boating and Water Sports* (608 pp) $19.95, available 6/96
- *California Camping* (848 pp) $19.95
- *California Fishing* (832 pp) $19.95
- *California Golf* (896 pp) $19.95
- *California Hiking* (856 pp) $18.95
- *California In-Line Skating* (496 pp) $19.95, available 5/96
- *Tahoe* (704 pp) $18.95

Other regional titles include:
- *Alaska Fishing* (640 pp) $19.95
- *Baja Camping* (294 pp) $12.95
- *Pacific Northwest Camping* (720 pp) $19.95
- *Pacific Northwest Hiking* (808 pp) $18.95
- *Rocky Mountain Camping* (576 pp) $14.95
- *Washington Fishing* (528 pp) $19.95

The Easy Series

The Easy books are perfect for families, seniors, or anyone looking for easy, fun weekend adventures. No special effort or advance planning is necessary—just head outdoors, relax, and enjoy. Look for Easy guides to Southern California and other favorite destinations in the winter of 1996.

- *Easy Biking in Northern California* (224 pp) $12.95
- *Easy Camping in Northern California* (240 pp) $12.95
- *Easy Hiking in Northern California* (240 pp) $12.95

WASHINGTON FISHING
REFERENCE MAP

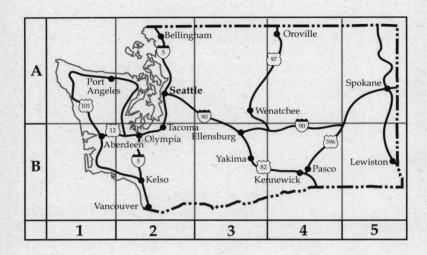